Reading Media Theory

Visit the Reading Media Theory, second edition Companion Website at **www.routledge.com/9781408285251** to find valuable **student** learning material including:

Chapters from the previous edition of the book available to download:

- Chicago School Reading: Park, R. E. (1967) *The Natural History of the Newspaper*
- Marxism Reading: Miliband, R. (1973) *The State in Capitalist Society: The Analysis of the Western System of Power*

Reading Media Theory

Thinkers, Approaches and Contexts

Second Edition

Brett Mills
University of East Anglia

David M. Barlow
University of Glamorgan

Routledge
Taylor & Francis Group

LONDON AND NEW YORK

First published 2009 by Pearson Education Limited
Second edition published 2012

Published 2013 by Routledge
2 Park Square, Milton Park, Abingdon, Oxon OX14 4RN
711 Third Avenue, New York, NY 10017, USA

Routledge is an imprint of the Taylor & Francis Group, an informa business

ISBN : 978-1-4082-8525-1 (pbk)

British Library Cataloguing-in-Publication Data
A catalogue record for this book is available from the British Library

Library of Congress Cataloging-in-Publication Data
A catalog record for this book is available from the Library of Congress
Mills, Brett.
   Reading media theory : thinkers, approaches and contexts / Brett Mills,
David M. Barlow. – 2nd ed.
      p. cm.
   Includes bibliographical references and index.
   Previous ed.: 2009.
   ISBN 978-1-4082-8525-1 (pbk.)
   1. Mass media–Philosophy.   2. Mass media–Study and teaching.   I. Barlow, David M.
(David Maxwell), 1949–   II. Title.
   P91.B34 2012
   302.2301–dc23
                                                              2012008732

Typeset in 10/12.5pt Minion by 35

CONTENTS

Timeline   viii
How to use this book   xviii
Publisher's acknowledgements   xx
About the authors   xxii

1   Introduction   1

Part I   Reading theory

2   What is theory?   7

3   What is reading?   22

Part II   Key thinkers and schools of thought

4   Liberal press theory   39

Reading: Mill, J.S. (1997 [1859]) 'Of the liberty of thought and discussion', in Bromley, M. and O'Malley, T. (eds) *A Journalism Reader*, London: Routledge, pp. 22–6.

5   F.R. Leavis   59

Reading: Leavis, F.R. (1930) *Mass Civilisation and Minority Culture*, Cambridge: Minority Press.

6   The Frankfurt school   84

Reading: Horkheimer, M. and Adorno, T.W. (2002 [1944]) *Dialectic of Enlightenment: Philosophical fragments*, translated by Jephcott, E., Stanford, California: Stanford University Press. Excerpt from Chapter 4, 'The culture industry: enlightenment as mass deception', pp. 94–8.

7   Harold D. Lasswell   103

Reading: Lasswell, H.D. (1948) 'The structure and function of communication in society', in Bryson, L. (ed.) *The Communication of Ideas*, New York: Harper and Brothers

8   The Columbia school   132

Reading: Lazarsfeld, P.F. and Merton, R.K. (1948) 'Mass communication,
popular taste and organized social action', in Bryson, L. (ed.) *The
Communication of Ideas*, New York: Harper and Brothers, pp. 95–118.

9   C. Wright Mills: Mass society theory   172

Reading: Mills, C.W. (1956) 'The mass society', in Mills, C.W. (ed.)
The Power Elite, London: Oxford University Press, pp. 298–324.

10   The Toronto school   198

Reading: Innis, H.A. (1951) 'The bias of communication', in Innis, H.A.,
The Bias of Communication, Toronto: University of Toronto Press, pp. 33–60.

11   The Centre for Contemporary Cultural Studies   225

Reading: Hall, S. (1980c) 'Encoding/Decoding', in *Culture, Media, Language:
Working papers in cultural studies, 1972–9*, Hall, S., Hobson, D., Lowe, A.
and Willis, P. (eds), London: Hutchinson, pp. 128–38.

Part III   Approaches to media theory

12   Political economy   263

Reading: Herman, E.S. (1995a) 'Media in the US political economy', in
Downing, J., Mohammadi, A. and Sreberny-Mohammadi, A. (eds) *Questioning
the Media: A critical introduction*, 2nd edition, London: Sage, pp. 77–93.

13   Public sphere   296

Reading: Habermas, J. (1974 [1964]) 'The public sphere: an encyclopedia
article', *New German Critique* 3 (1): 49–55.

14   Media effects   322

Reading: Gauntlett, D. (2005) 'Ten things wrong with the media "effects" model',
Theory.org.uk: the Media Theory Site, www.theory.org.uk/tenthings.html.

15   Structuralism   352

Reading: Todorov, T. (1990 [1978]) *Genres in Discourse*, translated by
Porter, C., Cambridge: Cambridge University Press, pp. 27–38.

16   Feminist media theory   384

Reading: van Zoonen, L. (1994) *Feminist Media Studies*, London: Sage,
pp. 11–18, 21–8.

17   Cultural theory   426

Reading: Williams, R. (1961) *The Long Revolution*, Orchard Park:
Broadview Press, pp. 57–70.

18   New Media   460

Reading: Jenkins, H. (2006) *Convergence Culture: Where old and new media
collide*, New York and London: New York University Press, pp. 1–10.

19 Postmodernism   488

Reading: Baudrillard, J. (1994 [1981]) 'The implosion of meaning in the media', in *Simulacra and Simulation*, translated by Glaser, S.F., Ann Arbor: University of Michigan Press, pp. 79–86.

20 The information society   512

Reading: Webster, F. (2002) *Theories of the Information Society*, 2nd edition, London: Routledge, pp. 8–21.

Part IV   Media theory in context

21 Production   551

Reading: Hesmondhalgh, D. (2007) *The Cultural Industries*, 2nd edition, London: Sage, pp. 3–8.

22 Texts   574

Reading: Barthes, R. (1977 [1967]) 'The death of the author', in *Image Music Text*, translated by Heath, S., London: Fontana, pp. 142–8.

23 Audiences   600

Reading: Ang, I. (1991) 'Audience-as-market and audience-as-public', in *Desperately Seeking the Audience*, London: Routledge, pp. 26–32.

24 Audiences as producers   624

Reading: Shirky, C. (2008) *Here Comes Everybody: How change happens when people come together*, London: Penguin, pp. 55–66.

Bibliography   652
Index   670

Supporting resources

Visit **www.routledge.com/9781408285251** to find valuable online resources

Chapters from the previous edition of the book available to download:

- Chicago school Reading: Park, R. E. (1967) *The Natural History of the Newspaper*
- Marxism Reading: Miliband, R. (1973) *The State in Capitalist Society: The Analysis of the Western System of Power*

Timeline

Year/s	Event	Person born (date of death in brackets)	Publication
1600s	1662–95 Licensing of the Press Act (UK)		1644 William Walwyn, *The Compassionate Samaritane* 1644 John Milton, *Areopagitica* 1689 John Locke, *Epistola de Tolerantia ad Clarissimum Virum*
1700s	1775–83 American Revolutionary War/War of Independence 1785 *The Times* (then called *The Daily Universal Register*) first published 1789 French Revolution	1770 Georg Hegel (1831)	1704 Mathew Tindal, *Reasons against Restraining the Press* 1712 John Asgill, *An Essay for the Press* 1791–92 Tom Paine, *Rights of Man* 1792 Mary Wollstonecraft, *Vindication of the Rights of Woman* 1798 William Goodwin, *Enquiry Concerning Political Justice* 1798 William Wordsworth and Samuel Taylor Coleridge, *Lyrical Ballads*
1800–50		1805 Alexis de Tocqueville (1859) 1806 John Stuart Mill (1873)	
		1818 Karl Marx (1883)	1811 James Mill, *Liberty of the Press*
		1820 Friedrich Engels (1895) 1822 Matthew Arnold (1888)	1820–21 Jeremy Bentham, *On the Liberty of the Press and Public Discussion*
		1839 Charles S. Peirce (1914)	1835–40 Alexis de Tocqueville, *Democracy in America*
		1844 Friedrich Nietzsche (1900) 1847 Carl Bücher (1930)	1845 Friedrich Engels, *The Condition of the Working Class in 1844* 1848 John Stuart Mill, *The Principles of Political Economy* 1848 Karl Marx and Friedrich Engels, *The Communist Manifesto*

Year/s	Event	Person born (date of death in brackets)	Publication
1850–99		1855 Ferdinand Tönnies (1936) 1856 Sigmund Freud (1939) 1857 Ferdinand de Saussure (1913) Thorstein Veblen (1929) 1858 Émile Durkheim (1917)	1859 John Stuart Mill, *On Liberty* 1859 Karl Marx, *A Contribution to the Critique of Political Economy*
		1864 Charles Horton Cooley (1929) Robert E. Park (1944) Max Weber (1920) 1865 Lord Northcliffe (1922)	1863 John Stuart Mill, *Utilitarianism* 1867 Karl Marx, *Das Kapital* 1869 Matthew Arnold, *Culture and Anarchy*
	1888 First Kodak camera goes on sale	1885 György Lukács [1971] 1887 Marcel Duchamp [1968] 1888 John Crowe Ransom [1974] 1889 Walter Lippmann [1974]	
	1890 University of Chicago founded		
	1891 Edison's kinetoscope built	1891 Antonio Gramsci (1937)	
	1894 First kinetoscope screenings	1894 Aldous Huxley (1963) Harold Innis (1952) Friedrich Pollock (1970)	
	1895 Lumière brothers' first film screenings	1895 Vladimin Propp [1970] Max Horkheimer [1973] F.R. Leavis [1978]	

Timeline

Year/s	Event	Person born (date of death in brackets)	Publication
1896		1896 André Breton (1966) Roman Jakobson (1982) Jean Piaget (1980)	
	1897 Guglielmo Marconi sends first wireless communication over water		
1898		1898 Bertolt Brecht (1956) Herbert Marcuse (1979)	
1899			Sigmund Freud, *The Interpretation of Dreams* Thorstein Veblen, *The Theory of the Leisure Class*
1900–19	1901 Guglielmo Marconi sends first transatlantic wireless signal	1901 Paul Lazarsfeld (1976) Jacques Lacan (1981)	
		1902 Harold Lasswell (1978)	
		1903 Theodor Adorno (1969)	
		1905 Robert Penn Warren (1989)	
		1906 Cleanth Brooks (1994)	
		1908 Claude Lévi-Strauss	
		1910 Robert Merton (2003)	
		1911 Marshall McLuhan (1980)	
	1912 British Board of Film Censors founded		
1913			Walter Lippmann, *A Preface to Politics*

Year/s	Event	Person born (date of death in brackets)	Publication
	1914		Walter Lippmann and Herbert Croly (founders), *The New Republic*
		1915 Roland Barthes (1980)	
	1916	C. Wright Mills (1962) A.J. Greimas (1992)	Ferdinand de Saussure, *Course in General Linguistics*
	1917 Russian Revolution Marcel Duchamp's 'Fountain'		
	1918	Louis Althusser (1990) George Grant (1988) Richard Hoggart	W.I. Thomas, *The Polish Peasant in Europe and America*
		1919 Daniel Bell (2011) George Gerbner (2005) Herb Schiller (2000)	
1920–45	1921	Ben Bagdikian Betty Friedan (2006) Raymond Williams (1988)	Robert E. Park and E.W. Burgess, *Introduction to the Science of Sociology*
	1922 British Broadcasting Company (BBC) founded	Erving Goffman (1982)	C.S. Johnson, *The Negro in Chicago* Robert E. Park, *The Immigrant Press and its Control* Walter Lippmann, *Public Opinion*
	1923 *Radio Times* launched		N. Anderson, *The Hobo*
	1924	Jay Blumler Jean-François Lyotard (1998) Ralph Miliband (1994)	André Breton, *The Surrealist Manifesto*
	1925	Albert Bandura Zygmunt Bauman	Robert E. Park, E.W. Burgess and R.D. McKenzie (eds), *The City*
	1926 John Logie Baird demonstrates first transmission of moving images	Michel Foucault (1984) Harold Perkin (2004)	
	1927 British Broadcasting Company becomes British Broadcasting Corporation (BBC)	Herbert Gans	Harold Lasswell, *Propaganda Techniques in the World War* E.R. Mowrer, *Family Disorganization*

First World War

Year/s	Event	Person born (date of death in brackets)	Publication
1928		Noam Chomsky Edward S. Herman Alvin Toffler	Vladimir Propp, *The Morphology of the Folktale* L. Wirth, *The Ghetto*
1929	First Oscar ceremony	Jean Baudrillard (2007) Jürgen Habermas	H.W. Zorbaugh, *The Gold Coast and the Slum* Lynd and Lynd, *Middletown*
1930	Hays code inaugurated	Pierre Bourdieu (2002)	Sigmund Freud, *Civilization and its Discontents* Harold Lasswell, *Psychopathology and Politics* F.R. Leavis, *Mass Civilization and Minority Culture*
1931		Rupert Murdoch	
1932	*Scrutiny* first published	Umberto Eco Stuart Hall	F.R. Leavis, *New Bearings in English Poetry*
1933	Adolf Hitler becomes Chancellor of Germany		
1934	Federal Communications Commission founded	Fredric Jameson	Arnold Toynbee, *A Study of History*, first volume
1936	BBC television begins		Walter Benjamin, *The Work of Art in the Age of Mechanical Reproduction*
1938		Anthony Giddens	
1939	Columbia Broadcasting System (CBS) begins broadcasting television	George Gilder Germaine Greer Tzvetan Todorov	
1940	Lazarsfeld-Stanton Program Analyzer first used at CBS		
1941		Laura Mulvey	
1942		Manuel Castells	
1943		Todd Gitlin Nichola Negroponte	
1944			Max Horkheimer and Theodor Adorno, *Dialectic of Enlightenment*
1945		John Howkins	

(Rows 1939–1945 are marked "Second World War" along the left side.)

Year/s	Event	Person born (date of death in brackets)	Publication
1946–69	1946	Clare Short John Urry	Harold Lasswell, *The Structure and Function of Communication in Society*
	1947		Walter Lippmann, *The Cold War*
	1948 National Health Service established in Britain		Lyman Bryson, *The Communication of Ideas* F.R. Leavis, *The Great Tradition*
	1949		Robert Merton, *Social Theory and Social Structure* Wilbur Schramm (ed), *Mass Communications*
	1950 European Broadcasting Union created	Richard Branson Frank Webster	Harold Innis, *Empire and Communications*
	1951	Angela McRobbie	C. Wright Mills, *White Collar* Harold Innis, *The Bias of Communication* Marshall McLuhan, *The Mechanical Bride*
	1952	Doug Henwood	
	1953 *Scrutiny* ceases publication		Jacques Lacan, *Écrits*
	1954 Comics Code Authority founded		Frederic Wertham, *Seduction of the Innocent*
	1955 ITV begins broadcasting		Alain Robbe-Grillet, *The Voyeurs*
	1956 First transatlantic television cable	Judith Butler Pierre Lévy	C. Wright Mills, *The Power Elite*
	1957 Sputnik 1 launched	Richard Florida	Roland Barthes, *Mythologies*
	1958		Hannah Arendt, *The Human Condition* Richard Hoggart, *The Uses of Literacy* Aldous Huxley, *Brave New World Revisited* Claude Lévi-Strauss, *Structural Anthropology* Raymond Williams, *Culture and Society*

Year/s	Event	Person born (date of death in brackets)	Publication
1959			Erving Goffman, *The Presentation of Self in Everyday Life* C. Wright Mills, *The Sociological Imagination*
1960			Joseph Klapper, *The Effects of Mass Communication* Raymond Williams, *Border Country*
1961	Albert Bandura's bobo doll experiments Berlin Wall erected	Diane Coyle	Raymond Williams, *The Long Revolution*
1962			Jürgen Habermas, *The Structural Transformation of the Public Sphere* Thomas Kuhn, *The Structure of Scientific Revolutions* Marshall McLuhan, *The Gutenberg Galaxy*
1963			Betty Friedan, *The Feminine Mystique*
1964	*The Sun* first published Centre for Contemporary Cultural Studies (CCCS) founded at Birmingham University	Clay Shirky	Jürgen Habermas, *The Public Sphere: An Encyclopedia Article* Claude Lévi-Straus, *The Raw and the Cooked* Marshall McLuhan, *Understanding Media* Ralph Miliband and John Saville (founders), *Socialist Register*
1966			Michel Foucault, *The Order of Things*
1967	BBC2 begins broadcasting Radio Leicester is first BBC local radio station		Roland Barthes, *The Death of the Author* Frank Kermode, *The Sense of an Ending* Marshall McLuhan, *The Medium is the Message*
1968	Student riots and general strike in Paris		
1969	First moon landing seen by 500 million television viewers worldwide First page three girl in *The Sun* Open University established PBS founded in the United States		

Year/s	Event	Person born (date of death in brackets)	Publication
1970–99	1970		Germaine Greer, *The Female Eunuch*
	1971 Ray Tomlinson sends first inter-computer email	David Gauntlett	Tzvetan Todorov, *The Poetics of Prose*
	1972		English translation of Max Horkheimer and Theodor Adorno's *Dialectic of Enlightenment* published
	1973 Martin Cooper makes the first non-vehicle mobile phone call Modern fibre optics invented Independent local radio launched in UK		Daniel Bell, *The Coming of the Post-Industrial Society* Umberto Eco, *Travels in Hyperreality* Ralph Miliband, *The State in Capitalist Society*
	1975		Umberto Eco, *A Theory of Semiotics* Michel Foucault, *Discipline and Punish* F.R. Leavis, *The Living Principle* Laura Mulvey, *Visual Pleasure and Narrative Cinema*
	1976 VHS launched		Raymond Williams, *Keywords*
	1977		Roland Barthes, *Image Music Text* Paul Willis, *Learning to Labour*
	1978		Angela McRobbie, *Jackie* Charlotte Brunsdon and David Morley, *Everyday Television* Tzvetan Todorov, *Genres of Discourse*
	1979		Umberto Eco, *The Role of the Reader* Dick Hebdige, *Subculture* Jean-François Lyotard, *The Postmodern Condition*
	1980 CNN launched		Stuart Hall, *Encoding/Decoding* Alvin Toffler, *The Third Wave*
	1981 MTV begins in the United States		Jean Baudrillard, *Simulacra and Simulation* Edward S. Herman, *Corporate Control, Corporate Power*
	1982 Channel 4 and S4C begin broadcasting First CD released		Dorothy Hobson, *Crossroads*

Year/s	Event	Person born (date of death in brackets)	Publication
1983			Todd Gitlin, *Inside Prime Time*
1984			Pierre Bourdieu, *Distinction* Stuart Hall, *The Idea of the Modern State*
1985 Live Aid concert for famine relief in Ethiopia seen by 1.5 billion television viewers worldwide			Ien Ang, *Watching Dallas* Joshua Meyrowitz, *No Sense of Place* Neil Postman, *Amusing Ourselves to Death*
1986			David Harvey, *The Condition of Postmodernity*
1988 First digital camera goes on sale			Edward S. Herman and Noam Chomsky, *Manufacturing Consent*
1989 Sky television starts broadcasting in the UK Fall of the Berlin Wall			Jürgen Habermas, *The Structural Transformation of the Public Sphere*, English translation
Gulf War	1990 BSB starts broadcasting Merger of BSB and Sky creates BSkyB		Judith Butler, *Gender Trouble* Anthony Giddens, *The Consequences of Modernity*
	1991		Ien Ang, *Desperately Seeking the Audience* Jean Baudrillard, *The Gulf War Did Not Take Place* Noam Chomsky, *Deterring Democracy* Fredric Jameson, *Postmodernism, or the Cultural Logic of Late Capitalism*
1992 First commercial SMS/text message sent			Ben Bagdikian, *The Media Monopoly*
1993 Jamie Bulger murdered European Union established			
1994			David Lyon, *The Electronic Eye* Liesbet van Zoonen, *Feminist Media Studies*
1995			Edward S. Herman, *Triumph of the Market* Frank Webster, *Theories of the Information Society* (first edition)

Year/s	Event	Person born (date of death in brackets)	Publication
	1996 Google founded Fox News launched		Ien Ang, *Living Room Wars* Manuel Castells, *The Rise of the Network Society*
	1997 *Titanic* becomes first film to gross $1 billion		Stuart Hall (ed.), *Representation*
	1999 Columbine High School shootings		Germaine Greer, *The Whole Woman*
2000+	2001 9/11 terrorist attacks in USA Wikipedia launched Apple's iPod launched		
	2002 Centre for Contemporary Cultural Studies (CCCS) closed		Noam Chomsky, *On Nature and Language* David Hesmondhalgh, *The Cultural Industries* (1st edition)
	2003 Operation Iraqi Freedom Ofcom founded MySpace launched		
	2004 Facebook launched Web 2.0 conference		
	2005 YouTube launched MySpace bought by Rupert Murdoch's News Corporation		David Gauntlett, *Ten Things Wrong with the Effects Model*
	2006 Twitter launched		
	2007 Amazon's Kindle		Anthony Giddens, *Europe in the Global Age* David Hesmondhalgh, *The Cultural Industries* (2nd edition)
	2008 Barack Obama elected – the first internet election? Sachsgate		Clay Shirky, *Here Comes Everybody*
	2009 Kodak stops producing camera film		
	2010 *Avatar* becomes the first film to gross $2 billion Apple's iPad launched		Clay Shirky, *Cognitive Surplus*
	20011 *News of the World* ceases publication		David Gauntlett, *Making is Connecting*

HOW TO USE THIS BOOK

This reader is supported by a range of features designed to help you engage with the material.

According to Mulhern, who produced a substantial historical and critical analysis of *Scrutiny*, the troubled economic and political circumstances in Britain in the decade following the First World War (1914–18) warranted such a journal (1981: 7, 47). Moreover, the space opened up by *Scrutiny* for the critical analysis of cultural institutions and practices was later occupied with great effect by the Centre for Contemporary Cultural Studies (Mulhern 1981: 329).

During the 1930s when Leavis was formulating his critique of British society, similar concerns about societal developments were being raised in Germany and America. But as Scannell (2007: 100) points out, in both the latter instances the critique occurred through the emerging discipline of sociology, whereas in Britain – where sociology had not yet emerged – the critique was launched through the newly emerging discipline of English studies.

For Leavis, 'literature was life affirming', while 'mass-civilization was life-denying', sentiments that, he argued, were evident in British literary texts which demonstrated 'serious, critical engagement with societal modernization and at the same time a redemptive resistance to it' (Scannell 2007: 100). While Leavis's elitist views about culture are now pretty unfashionable, they nevertheless remain influential.

INTRODUCTION TO THE READING

This reading is an abridged version of a pamphlet, *Mass Civilisation and Minority Culture* (from hereon *Mass Civilisation*), that was first published in 1930. The same pamphlet, but substantially developed and refined, provided the basis for *Culture and Environment: The training of critical awareness* (1933) which was co-authored with Denys Thompson, an avid supporter of Leavis and also one of his ex-students. Of interest is that Leavis's biographer, McKillop (1995), has suggested that Queenie Leavis also contributed to this publication, but was not listed as one of the authors (Scannell 2007: 101). Furthermore, the same publication apparently inspired the idea for Marshall McLuhan's (1951b) *The Mechanical Bride: Folklore of industrial man* (Stamps 1995: 110).

Mass Civilisation was, in effect, the blueprint for the journal *Scrutiny*, providing both its rationale and its editorial direction (Mulhern 1981: 34). While Scannell (2007: 100) is less than complimentary about *Mass Civilisation*, describing it as 'hastily put together', Raymond Williams acknowledges that it includes a 'body of detailed judgements' and 'an outline of history' (1958: 246). The purpose of *Mass Civilisation* was 'to argue that the traditional relationship between "civilisation" (the totality of social relations) and "culture" (the values on which "fine living" depended) had been strained to the point of rupture by the advance of "the machine"' (Mulhern 1981: 35). As you will see from the reading, 'the machine' – which might be suggested as a euphemism for technological innovations – is at the heart of Leavis's concerns.

As we noted in the introduction to this chapter, Leavis was inspired by the earlier work of Mathew Arnold. This is evident from the very start of the reading, which is launched with a quotation from Arnold's *Culture and Anarchy* (1869). You will also observe that shortly into the reading Leavis mentions a publication, *Middletown* (Lynd and Lynd 1929), which he then tends to rely on for much of the evidence that underpins his central

61

REFLECTING ON THE READING

Even in this abridged version of the reading it is possible to see why *Mass Civilisation* can be interpreted as a 'call to arms'. It has the essence of a rallying call from Leavis to colleagues, acolytes and others of like mind, the aim being to seek their support in taking a stand against the degradation of culture.

While the message in *Mass Civilisation* may have been powerful, there were doubts about its quality. Scannell, for instance, describes it as 'neither well written nor well thought out', and giving the impression of a 'hastily assembled patchwork of quotations strung together from a variety of sources' (2007: 101). However, the ideas set out in *Mass Civilisation* were further developed and refined in subsequent publications by Leavis and his colleagues, and the original was later reprinted in 1933 along with a collection of other essays in *For Continuity* (Leavis 1933; see Mulhern 1981: 63).

Mass Civilisation was Leavis's opening salvo on 'mass culture', and helped establish his reputation in the period between the First (1914–18) and Second World War (1939–45) as the most influential British critic of popular culture (Williams 2003: 27). The pamphlet both reflected and maintained a tradition that continues today (Williams 1998: 1). This tradition has two strands. The first involves a critique of popular media and entertainment forms which has at various moments in time focused on music halls, film, radio, comic books, television and, more recently, computer games.

The second strand involves what sometimes amounts to a withering critique of American cultural goods and services – even 'a revulsion against American culture' (Seaton 1997: 265). What is noteworthy – and concerning – about Leavis's warnings about American influence on English culture is that he drew most of his 'evidence' from just one source. That source, *Middletown*, was a case study of a small American town in the state of Illinois.

While Leavis's analysis in *Mass Civilisation* reflects a mass society thesis, his approach was both similar and different to others adopting a similar theoretical perspective (Bennett 1995: 348; Garnham 1990: 60; Seaton 1997: 265; Williams 2003: 27). While C. Wright Mills was primarily concerned about political questions in a mass society context and was of a Left political persuasion (see Chapter 9), Leavis's major interest was in culture, and he was on the political Right.

Similarly, while Theodor Adorno and Max Horkheimer (see Chapter 6) had views not dissimilar to Leavis about the need to defend 'high', or 'minority', culture, and on the negative influence of America, and were also critical of the cultural products being produced for the masses by the cultural industries, these two authors were on the political Left (Bennett 1995: 348).

Essentially, the 'minority' that Leavis was defending was a literary minority, whose role was to keep 'alive the literary tradition and the finest capacities of the language' (Williams 1958: 248). When Leavis spoke of the 'mass', one reasonable inference is that he actually meant the mob, the characteristics of such a group being 'gullibility, fickleness, herd-prejudice, lowness of taste and habit' (Williams 1958: 288). Williams is, of course, renowned for his observation that there are 'no masses; there are only ways of seeing people as masses' (1961: 289).

While recognising and accepting that Leavis was a key influence on his own thinking and on his own work, Raymond Williams registered his disagreement with the latter's views in (at least) two areas:

82

Introduction to the Reading

Sets each text and its author in context and shows the relevance of the reading to contemporary culture. You'll want to read this before the main reading.

Reflecting on the Reading

summarises each reading's key points and suggests further areas to explore and think about.

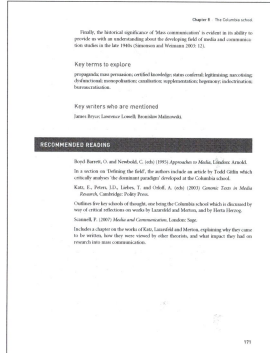

Annotations

Four types of annotation help you engage with the reading – context, content, structure, and writing style. You should refer to each as you tackle the reading. You'll find helpful background information, tips, explanations, guidance and questions to consider. Using these will make you a much more informed, critical and successful reader.

Key terms, writers, and Recommended Reading

Provide further avenues to investigate relating to the reading and its context.

PUBLISHER'S ACKNOWLEDGEMENTS

The publishers would like to thank David Barlow and Brett Mills for their skill, enthusiasm and invention in putting together this new kind of text – they've been a pleasure to work with.

The publishers and authors would also like to thank the following for their incisive and helpful comments on the draft manuscript, all of which have helped make this a better book:

Andrew Willis, University of Salford
Sharif Mowlabocus, University of Sussex
Luke Tredinnick, London Metropolitan University

We are grateful to the following for permission to reproduce copyright material:

Text

Extract 4. from *A Journalism Reader*, Routledge (M. Bromley and T. O'Malley 1997) 22–26, Reproduced by permission of Taylor and Francis Books UK; Extract 6. from *Dialectic of Enlightenment: Philosophical fragments*, Stanford University Press (M. Horkheimer and T.W. Adorno 2002) 94–98, translated by E. Jephcott, Copyright © 1944 by Social Studies Association, NY. New edition: © S. Fisher Verlag GmbH, Frankfurt am Main, 1969; English trans. © 2002 Board of Trustees of Leland Stanford Jr. University; Extract 9. from *The Power Elite*, Oxford University Press (C. Wright Mills 1956) pp. 298–324, By permission of Oxford University Press; Extract 10. from *The Bias of Communication*, University of Toronto Press (H.A. Innis 1951) 33–60, Reprinted with permission of the publisher; Extract 11. from *Culture, Media, Language: Working papers in cultural studies 1972–79 by S. Hall*, Hutchinson (S. Hall, D. Hobson, A. Lowe and P. Willis (eds) 1980), Reproduced by permission of Taylor and Francis Books, UK; Extract 12. from *Questioning the Media: A critical introduction*, Sage Publishers (J. Downing, A. Mohammadi and A. Sreberny-Mohammadi 1995), Reprinted by permission of SAGE Publications, Inc.; permission conveyed through Copyright Clearance Center Inc; Extract 13. from The public sphere: An encyclopedia article, *New German Critique*, 3 (1), 49–55 (J. Habermas 1974), Reprinted by permission of the publisher, Duke University Press, www.dukepress.edu; Extract 14. from Theory.org.uk: the Media Theory Site, www.theory.org.uk/tenthings.html, Reproduced with permission of Professor David Gauntlett; Extract 15. from *Genres in*

Discourse, Cambridge University Press (T. Todorov 1990) 27–38, translated by C. Porter, © Cambridge University Press, 1990, reprinted with permission; Extract 16. from *Feminist Media Studies*, Sage Publishers (L. van Zoonen 1994) 11–18, 21–8, Reproduced by permission of SAGE Publications, London, Los Angeles, New Delhi and Singapore; Extract 17. from *The Long Revolution*, Broadview Press (R. Williams 1961) 55–70, Reproduced by permission of The Estate of Raymond Williams; Extract 18. from *Convergence Culture: Where old and new media collide*, New York University Press (H. Jenkins 2006) 2–10, Reproduced by permission of New York University Press; Extract 19. from *Simulacra and Simulation*, University of Michigan Press (J. Baudrillard 1994) 79–86, translated by S.F. Glaser, Reprinted with permission of the University of Michigan Press; Extract 20. from *Theories of the Information Society*, 2nd, Routledge (F. Webster 2002) 8–21, Reproduced by permission of Taylor and Francis Books UK; Extract 21. from *The Cultural Industries*, 2nd Ed., Sage publishers (D. Hesmondhalgh 2007), Reproduced by permission of SAGE Publications, London, Los Angeles, New Delhi and Singapore; Extract 22. from *Image Music Texts*, Fontana (R. Barthes 1977) 142–8, translated by S. Heath; Extract 23. from *Desperately Seeking the Audience*, Routledge (I. Ang 1991) 26–32, Reproduced by permission of Taylor and Francis Books UK; Extract 24. from *Here Comes Everybody: How change happens when people come together*, Allen Lane (C. Shirky 2008) 55–66; Extract A. from *The City*, University of Chicago Press (R.E. Park, E.W. Burgess and R.D. McKenzie 1967); Extract B. from *The State in Capitalist Society: The analysis of the western system of power*, Quartet Books (R. Miliband 1973).

In some instances we have been unable to trace the owners of copyright material, and we would appreciate any information that would enable us to do so.

ABOUT THE AUTHORS

Brett Mills is Head of the School of Film and Television Studies, University of East Anglia. He is the author of *Television Sitcom* (BFI, 2005) and *The Sitcom* (Edinburgh, 2009). He is the principal investigator on the 3-year AHRC-funded research project, *Make Me Laugh: Creativity in the British Television Comedy Industry*.

Dr David Barlow was a Lecturer in Media, Culture and Communication in the Cardiff School of Creative and Cultural Industries and Director of the Centre for the Study of Media and Culture in Small Nations at the University of Glamorgan. He is a co-author (with Philip Mitchell and Tom O'Malley) of *The Media in Wales: Voices of a Small Nation* (University of Wales Press, 2005), and co-editor (with Vian Bakir) of *Communication in the Age of Suspicion: Trust and the Media* (Palgrave Macmillan, 2007).

CHAPTER 1

Introduction

This book has been produced to assist you if you are undertaking a degree in media studies or its related areas. Its primary purpose is to provide the opportunity for you to develop the knowledge and skills that are required to become a *critical reader* of media theory texts. In so doing, the book is also expected to fulfil two other related, but essentially secondary, purposes. The first is to develop your awareness and understanding of the origins, development and application of theory in the area of media studies. The second is to encourage you to use these newly acquired, or refined, abilities as a *critical reader* in ways that will enhance your written and oral communication skills. So, while the content of the book is about media theory, it is pedagogy – teaching and learning – that has driven the design.

The book was prompted by our own experience over a number of years of teaching undergraduate modules that incorporate elements of media theory. Whilst there is a surfeit of textbooks and readers that address media theory, a number of which we have used, we gradually formed the view that it would be helpful for our students – and for us – if this same subject matter could be approached and organised in a different way. The outcome is this book, which we believe is innovative because of its hybridity. This is because it combines elements of both the traditional textbook and reader collections and, thereby, avoids specific concerns that are voiced about each of these forms.

By including a wide variety of texts – or readings – on media theory, we overcome the common complaint that textbooks do not encourage students to read original texts, and even discourage them from doing so. Also, we have a different approach to that of the traditional reader collection. This is because we prepare students for the readings, intervene and comment during the readings using selected pedagogical devices, and then provide a post-reading reflection. As a result, this should help you engage with what are often difficult texts to read and understand, in ways that are designed to empower you as a *critical reader*.

The book is organised into four parts. Part One includes two chapters which, in combination, provide a rationale for the book and contextualise the first part of its title, *Reading Media Theory*. The first chapter, 'What is theory?', explains the nature of theory, what its purpose is, how it works, and why theory is integral to media studies. The second chapter, 'What is reading?', explains the purpose of reading at university, how to overcome problems with reading, what we understand by critical reading, and generally how to approach the reading of theory and higher level media analysis. Parts Two, Three and Four explain the second half of the book's title, *Thinkers, Approaches and Contexts*.

Part Two, 'Key thinkers and schools of thought', comprises eight chapters, each of which is constructed around a text that is associated with a particular school of thought or *thinker*. For example, there are chapters on the Birmingham Centre for Contemporary Cultural Studies, C. Wright Mills, F.R. Leavis and the Frankfurt school. Lack of space precludes us from including all relevant schools of thought and thinkers. Therefore, our aim has been to include those whose contribution to theory and theoretical development is generally acknowledged as significant, even controversial, by scholars in media, communication and cultural studies. Moreover, our primary interest is in pedagogy rather than covering the 'canon'.

Part Three, 'Approaches to media theory', includes nine chapters, each of which is built around a text that reflects a particular *approach* to media theory. Examples include the effects on tradition, political economy, feminist media theory, cultural theory and postmodernism. As in Part One, decisions have been required about which approaches and which texts to include. Overall, we have opted for what appear to be the most widely used approaches, and endeavoured to construct each chapter around what are generally regarded as original, key or defining texts. We are aware that some of these approaches – and some of the authors of the selected texts – have moved in and out of fashion over the years.

Part Four, 'Media theory in context', comprises four chapters, each of which is based on a reading that relates to a particular *context*. The first three contexts encompass production (or institutions), texts (or content) and audiences (or reception). They have been described by one author as the traditional media studies 'trinity' (Devereux 2007: 3). The aim here is to illustrate how theoretical ideas have been utilised to inform the ways in which production, texts and audiences can be analysed, interpreted and portrayed. The final chapter in this section explores audiences as producers, and therefore problematises this 'trinity' somewhat; this is deliberate as many have argued that newer forms of media break down the conventional way of thinking about production, texts and audiences. In this and earlier parts of the book we cross-reference to other chapters where links emerge between thinkers, approaches and contexts.

All the chapters in Parts Two, Three and Four of the book are organised and structured similarly, in that they each comprise four main sections. The first provides an introduction to the school of thought, thinker, approach or context. The second sets out an introduction to the selected reading and its author(s). The third section is where we intervene in order to encourage close engagement with the selected text. We do this through the use of a pedagogic structure that enables us to comment on the reading, dissect the arguments, explain key ideas and terminology, make reference to other relevant material, and pose questions that emerge from the text. The fourth section comprises a reflection on the reading which, where appropriate, points to its legacy or relevance in our contemporary media culture. Recommendations for further reading are provided at the end of each chapter in the form of three annotated references.

Whatever your level of study, this book will assist you in developing close-reading and analytic skills which you can then draw on for other areas of your course. It will also increase your ability to outline key theories and debates, assess different case studies critically, link theoretical approaches to a particular historical context, and to structure and present an argument – all of which are characteristics of a *critical reader*.

PART I

Reading theory

CHAPTER 2

What is theory?

DEFINING THEORY

Every week on *Match of the Day* (BBC2/1, 1964–) football pundits such as Gary Lineker and Alan Hansen pore over footage of that day's games and criticise and examine the ways in which the teams played. They argue over particular players and team formations; they look at slow-motion footage, and offer suggestions for how the team could have played better. In the end, the pundits rarely agree, even though they draw on their experience and knowledge to give evidence for their assertions. And, as the programme is weekly, they can refer back to arguments they have had previously, and, as viewers, over time we get a sense of what each particular pundit thinks is important, and what they are likely to argue.

The same is true for all sports commentators and pundits, and much television coverage of sport is taken up with such debate, analysis, supposition and prediction. In suggesting ways in which sportspeople could improve their game, such experts usually offer ideas which can never be proven or disproven; the game cannot be replayed in exactly the same way, to see if a different formation or set of tactics would have made a difference. Indeed, we spend much of our lives proposing suggestions, ideas and arguments which can never truly be tested. For example, our romantic relationships with other people are, at the outset, often predicated on guesswork. If there is someone you like, and you get to have a conversation with them, you might discuss in minute detail with your friends afterwards what was said, and what it might mean; from this, you might put together a plan for your next 'move'. A programme like *Sex and the City* (HBO, 1998–2004) is all about people discussing and debating the meanings and motives of other people, and it is rare that any arguments put forward by any participant can ever be shown to be completely true or valid. In that sense, we spend much of our lives trying to make sense of the world around us and the motivations of other people, coming to conclusions based on evidence, guesswork, experience and the advice of others.

In other words, we spend much of our time *theorising* the world around us. 'Theory' might be a word which we associate with universities and academia, and complicated writing which we find hard to make sense of, but the *processes* which produce theory are ones which are very everyday, normal and mundane. Theory can be thought of as nothing more than *a way of thinking about the world*. In media theory this process has quite specific purposes and ways of working, but this is only an extension of the kind of theorising which everyone engages in every day of their lives. In reading media theory, then, you should think of the material you encounter as a particular version of the process you go through whenever you discuss or debate anything with friends or colleagues, no matter what the subject is.

This idea that theory is a *process* is an important one. So far in your education much of the material you have encountered is likely to be pretty concrete; that is, it is *factual*, and you are required to *learn* it. It is less likely that you have encountered debates about the validity or appropriateness of what you have learned, and you are likely to have been assessed primarily on your ability to know certain things. At university level, however, it is likely that you are no longer dealing purely with factual information. Instead, universities are usually interested in introducing you to ideas and concepts over which there is much debate, and, in doing so, they encourage you to *join in that debate*. That is, you can become part of the *process* of discussion and deliberation, offering your own insights and responding to those of others. When engaging with theory, then, your role is not to read it in order to find out the 'answer'; instead, your job is to make sense of what the author has argued, and respond to that argument. One of the reasons universities often structure their teaching around seminars and discussions is precisely so you can engage in that *process* with others, putting forward ideas and responses of your own and responding to those in the reading and those put forward by your peers.

Because theory is part of a process, it is often written differently from material you may have come across in your learning before. That is, as the intention of theory is to encourage debate, discussion, and analysis, it is often deliberately provocative, aiming to elicit responses in those who read it. Many people who write theory want others to look at the world differently from how it is currently seen, and, in order to do that, they have to question and critique the 'normal' ways of thinking about things. In that sense, theory often has quite a deliberate *purpose*, forcing readers to look at the world anew, and inviting responses which are engaged, informed, and help further the *process* of theory.

This definition might still seem quite vague, and this is appropriate. Indeed, if every discussion, debate, and analysis of everything in the world is theory, it is hard to see what *does not* count as theory. We can perhaps distinguish between theory as a *process*, and the results of that process. That is, encyclopaedias and dictionaries contain *facts*, which are generally accepted to be valid and true; they therefore rarely encourage discussion and debate, and the material they contain is the end result of research and discussion amongst experts. Theory, on the other hand, can be seen as the process which results in that information. Theory asks questions, and offers suggestions, and disagrees with proposals already put forward, in order to encourage movement towards agreed, accepted conclusions. Theorising about the world is the *starting point* in making sense of it, and one of the reasons why theory might be seen as 'hard' is because it has yet to come to conclusions, and so everything is up for discussion.

In order to make sense of what theory is, Williams (2003: 16) suggests there are three types:

1. academic;
2. practitioner;
3. common sense.

Of these, it is the first which you are most likely to encounter at university; academic theory is that proposed and discussed within universities and the wider academic community, and has a purpose of investigation and criticism in order to make sense of the world.

The second and third types are usually not categorised as 'theory', though Williams demonstrates that the *process* behind each is similar to that within academic theorising. So, practitioners (such as film directors, advertising executives, television scriptwriters, actors and musicians) spend much of their time discussing and debating their own working practices, in order to make better, more successful, more interesting, innovative texts, and they consistently reflect on their own processes and look at those of others. In doing so, such practitioners *theorise* the activities they engage in as media professionals, and, over a career, any individual is likely to engage in an ongoing process of reflection and analysis.

'Common sense' theory is the kind of theorising we all engage in every day, such as the example of discussing conversations with friends cited above. Williams argues that because this is such an everyday process we rarely think of it as theorising, even though the critical reflection and analysis we engage in when doing it is identical to that required to engage in 'academic' theory. As this helpfully shows, reading media theory requires skills which are, in fact, very ordinary and everyday, and which we consistently employ as we go about our lives. Therefore, we should not think of 'media theory' as something distinct and detached from our everyday lives, but instead merely a particular application of processes which are mundane, ordinary, and necessary.

Summary

- theory is a *process*;
- theory often has a *purpose*;
- your role is to *engage* in that process;
- there are *different types* of theory.

WHAT IS THEORY FOR?

It is hoped that by now you will be getting a sense of the uses to which theory can be put, and its role not only within academia, but also within the world more generally. Because theory questions what is often accepted as fact, or common sense, it helps people develop ideas and ways of working which can lead to new insights and breakthroughs. In science, scientists often construct theoretical *models*, which are suppositions about a particular phenomenon or aspect of the physical world. The model is theoretical, but scientists then carry out experiments to see if it has any validity, or sheds any insights on existing knowledge. Often models have to be modified in response to those experiments, but without the model in the first place those experiments would not have been carried out, and the knowledge which arises would have remained unknown. In media theory the same occurs; Chapter 11 of this book covers Stuart Hall's (1980a) 'Encoding/Decoding model', where Hall proposes an idea which explains how media communication works. While he offers some evidence to support his assertion, and shows how his model responds to existing knowledge and theory, it is still primarily theoretical. Subsequent academics have questioned, critiqued and tested the model, with some seeing it as having some validity, and others arguing it needs major revision if it is to be of any use. What is important here is that without Hall's model, a wealth of research which offers insights into the ways in which communication works is unlikely to have been carried out. So one of theory's purposes is to give the impetus for newer kinds of research, which can open up a range of debates, and further knowledge to a great degree.

The rationale behind offering models can be various, and the purposes to which theory may be put can differ too. The purpose of much theory is to help explain the world, by offering ways of thinking about it, and proposing methods and approaches which might gain new insights. This type of theory, which helps explain the world, is called *normative*. However, some theory – and this is quite common in media studies – is instead far more critical, showing how the world is unfairly organised, and offering alternative, more appropriate systems. Such approaches are often less about explaining the world, and more about showing problems within the world and presenting solutions. Such theory is called *critical*, because it is critical of how things are. You will come across lots of critical theory in this book, because a lot of media studies assumes that the media helps uphold unfair inequalities in society, and so criticises this system and, quite often, proposes alternative ones. For example, the members of the Frankfurt school (see Chapter 6) certainly felt that media could be used for propaganda purposes, which led to inequality and violence within society. For the Frankfurt school, normative theory was irrelevant, because it was obvious to them how the world worked; instead, their theory is primarily critical, because it criticises the roles media play in society, and offers alternative solutions.

One of the things that can be difficult about first engaging with media theory is that it is very often critical in this way. Much media theory assumes you are interested in the relationships between media and society, and explores media as a significant factor within politics, the public and governments. In that sense, much media theory can often appear quite negative about media, which can be off-putting if you are studying the subject because you like and enjoy film, television, music and other media. It can begin to feel you are only allowed to say negative things about media, and that to discuss enjoyment and pleasure, or to be interested in theory that is purely normative, is not the way to go. Yet critical theory is also normative, because it attempts to explain how things work. Also, just because there is a history of media theory which is critical, this does not mean you have to continue this trend. More recently, people such as David Gauntlett (see Chapter 14) and Henry Jenkins (see Chapter 18) have explored the pleasures associated with media, and the ways in which people use it to make sense of themselves and their own lives. That is, there is quite a lot of normative theory out there, even if it might, at first, feel as if the majority of material you are reading is critical.

As noted earlier, one of theory's main purposes is encouraging and inspiring dialogue, criticism, debate and analysis. It is often deliberately contentious, giving you something to argue against or for. It responds to existing theory and promotes future theory. Theory attempts to ensure there is an *ongoing* conversation about key ideas, responding to existing arguments as well as to changes within media and society. In that sense, theory's aim is to ensure we take nothing for granted, or assume things are simple, straightforward or easily explicable. By consistently and rigorously questioning *everything*, theory ensures we continually interrogate the world around us, and see the media as important within society. In insisting that these are important questions, media theory plays an important role in how we think about ourselves, our society and the world at large.

Summary

- theory encourages and inspires *discussion* and *debate*;
- theory can be *normative* and/or *critical*;
- theoretical debates are *ongoing*, and encourage more theorising.

WHERE DOES THEORY COME FROM?

Thinking about where theory comes from is important for a number of reasons. In this book we have selected a range of readings that we see as important and helpful, and which together represent the field of media studies as broadly and thoroughly as possible. But where have those readings come from? Why have they been chosen? Is it because of the content, or the author? The readings come from a range of places around the world, and from different time periods; does this matter? Why is it that when some people write theory, it gets published and is then taught in universities, whereas the same does not occur for the majority of people? If *you* wrote a theoretical article, would it get published, or taught? If not, why not? What is important to recognise is that there are *processes* which theory goes through in order to end up being taught and/or read, and these might have significant implications for what constitutes 'media theory'.

For a start, in order to be read theory has to be *published*. This may sound obvious, but the processes which a piece of writing must go through in order to be published are long and complicated. For a book to be published, then, a publisher has to agree to publish it; again, this might seem obvious, but why might a publisher agree to publish one book, but not another? First, there are economic factors; while profit and loss are certainly not the overriding factor in academic publishing, it is unlikely a publisher will agree to produce a book if there is not an audience who might buy it. Secondly, different publishers have differing specialisms; many of the books you will come across in your studies are likely to have been published by companies such as Routledge, Sage, Arnold, the British Film Institute, and so on. If you were studying a different subject at university, the publishers you would come across might be quite different. And publishers change their key interests, depending on the market, or the way the subject is changing, and so on. Thirdly, the majority of publishers send book proposals to other academics, who write reports recommending whether it should be published or not; the same is true for journal articles, which are normally 'peer-reviewed' by at least two experts in the field. While there are positive aspects to this process (it means new work is judged by accepted experts), it can have drawbacks of limiting innovative work which might question or undermine the approaches taken by those experts. This means that in order to get published, established academics must approve your work, which might have implications for novelty and innovation.

What all of this amounts to is that there are a number of processes which any piece of written work must go through in order to reach readers. Indeed, academics trying to get their work published might spend quite some time trying to get their proposal accepted by a number of publishers, and while this might say something about the quality of the proposal, it could also be a result of market factors which are completely beyond the control of the author. This means that a lot of theory might be inaccessible to others, simply because it is unpublished. Indeed, if *you* had a great theory you had formulated, would you know how to go about getting it out to readers? The internet has changed people's ability to reach wider publics to an extent (see Chapter 24), but much of academia is very wary of internet publishing, unless it has gone through the same peer-review process which has been at the heart of the process for decades. Overall, then, while this is not an attempt to suggest that there is an unfair or corrupt system which limits the development of theory, it has to be acknowledged that theory only really matters once it has been read, and it can only be read once it has been published; acknowledging the specifics of the publishing system, then, is essential if you are to understand where theory comes from, and the procedures it goes through in order to reach an audience.

The consequences of these processes can be seen by the kinds of people whose theory this book covers. For a start, the vast majority of authors are male; only two readings (those on feminist media theory and audiences) are written by women. All but one of the authors (Stuart Hall) is white. All of the readings come from western countries in the northern hemisphere, spread across Canada, the United States, the United Kingdom, France and Germany. This imbalance can be seen as representative of the work usually seen to dominate the field. Because of language differences, British academics are far more likely to encounter material from English-speaking countries; those foreign-language readings which are included here often took years, if not decades, to have an impact in Britain because English-language translations were not previously available. These issues of gender, race and ethnicity can be seen as symbolic of the unrepresentative nature not only of media theory, but also of academic insitutions in general. It is likely there is also a class bias in the authors of the readings, but this is difficult to demonstrate. What all of this shows is how the producers of theory are, on the whole, not a group of people representative of society more generally, either within particular nations or more globally. Concerns about this have been raised by many scholars (Curran and Park 2000; Stratton and Ang 1996; Thornham 2007), especially as media studies is a subject with a keen interest in issues of equality and representativeness.

Theory also comes out of a *context*. That is, people who write theory do so in response to what is going on around them, and therefore it is often useful to be aware of the context which may have influenced their thinking and concerns. In Britain, for example, television has a public service broadcasting tradition (as it does in much of Europe), which means that television and radio are usually viewed as some sort of public good which can play a useful social role. In America, though, broadcasting has predominantly been seen as a product, which should be distributed via a market. Academics in America, then, work within a different context from those in Britain, which is likely to result in differing priorities, approaches and ideas.

Such contexts can often encourage a number of theorists to work in similar ways on comparable approaches and questions. Throughout this book you will come across various 'schools' made up of a number of academics, who are often categorised as a group because they worked in the same place at the same time, on analogous projects. Examples include the Frankfurt school (which includes people such as Theodor Adorno, Walter Benjamin, Jürgen Habermas, Max Horkheimer and Herbert Marcuse) and the Birmingham Centre for Contemporary Cultural Studies (including Charlotte Brunsdon, Stuart Hall, Richard Hoggart, Angela McRobbie and David Morley). The main concerns of many of these schools quite clearly respond to specific social, political and historical contexts. For example, the Birmingham Centre for Contemporary Cultural Studies was prominent in the 1960s and 1970s, at a time when great social change was occurring in Britain, with the class system evolving and an expansion in education; it should be no surprise, then, that the Centre's work focused on issues of class, equality and social structures.

What this shows is that theory is a *necessary* product of society and social change; as the world alters, it is vital that new models and ideas are proposed which attempt to make sense of what is going on. Therefore, theory does not just arise because academics want to think about the world around them; it is an inevitable product of that society, and we should take such contexts into account when reading theory. The fact that theory is a product of its context means we can attempt to categorise theories in particular ways. Over time, particular ideas or approaches come to the forefront, are explored by many people, and then often retreat into the background as newer techniques and models are offered. Defining each of these approaches is difficult, and categorising them can be problematic. In this book we explore structuralism (Chapter 15) and post-structuralism; while the one came after the other, deciding where one began and the other ended is virtually impossible. Similarly, most people agree that postmodernism (Chapter 19) is related to modernism, but whether postmodernism is a continuation of, or a rejection of, modernism is up for much debate. Again, this shows how theory is a *process*, in which ideas constantly evolve, develop and mutate.

Storey (2006: xv) argues that we can begin to define particular fields of enquiry by using three criteria:

1. the object of study;
2. the method of analysis;
3. the history of the field.

That is, what distinguishes one field of media theory from another can first be thought about in terms of what it examines. So, feminist approaches to media (Chapter 16) are different from other approaches because their primary aim is to examine issues of gender difference and inequality (this may be covered by other theories too, but it may not be their main aim). Secondly, the method can help distinguish approaches; for example, structuralist work primarily examines the text, whereas post-structuralist theory is much more interested in the audiences and consumers of texts. Finally, particular fields develop their own history, with key works or writings which many people work from (this is called a 'canon'). For film studies, for example, Laura Mulvey's (2000 [1975]) 'Visual pleasure and narrative cinema' is a key work, referred to by many of the books you will come across. It is hoped that by using these three criteria, you will be able to distinguish between different theoretical approaches to media and they are a useful tool for you to base your thinking on. Throughout this book we have used these approaches to think about the readings explored.

In conclusion, you can see that there are lots of factors which affect where theory comes from, who writes it and how it reaches you. These are all things that are useful to take into account when reading and exploring theory. Perhaps most important is that this shows that theory is merely the result of a person, or people, trying to make sense of the world around them, which is presumably what you are also interested in doing within your studies. This means that, rather than seeing theory as something which is 'difficult' and must be 'learned', you should see it as something to have a dialogue with, written by people with the same kinds of interests and enthusiasms as you.

Summary

- theory must be *published*;
- theory comes out of a *context*;
- theory is often *categorised* by schools or fields.

WHY IS THEORY SEEN AS DIFFICULT?

There is little doubt that many people find theory difficult. Indeed, the very word 'theory' often induces fear and panic in many people, who assume that they will be forced to encounter impenetrable and complex writing which they find hard to relate to their own experiences. In a sense, there is no denying that theory is 'hard', but it is important you get to grips with *why* it is hard; or, to be more accurate, that you understand that what you might find difficult is instead the inevitable product of what much theory is trying to do.

For a start, theory usually questions *everything*. Indeed, one of its main aims is to question things that seem obvious, normal and common sense. Much theory argues that what seems 'normal' in this way is in fact highly constructed and a consequence of centuries of social developments. For example, it is unlikely you think much about the language you speak, because it seems straightforward and simple to you; yet the English language is the result of centuries of development, and is, in fact, a highly complex system that is completely unnatural, to the point that it takes years to learn it (and for those people in the United Kingdom whose first language is not English, it may not seem normal at all). Media theory sees the 'language' of media in the same way, and insists that the ways in which television, film, advertising, music, newspapers and the internet communicate to us are highly complex systems, even if those systems appear simple and straightforward to us because they are all around us. In questioning everything, media theory can seem difficult because it removes all the assumptions you require in order to live an 'ordinary' life. So, one of the difficulties of media theory is that it forces you to think about things you might think not worth thinking about, and refuses to let you rely on easy, 'obvious' answers in order to come to conclusions. This can seem very frustrating, and often leads to complaints that theorists are 'reading too much into things'. This destabilising effect can be quite scary if you're used to education which gives you solid answers on which further analysis can rest. In order to deal with this difficulty, then, you have to accept media theory's insistence on questioning everything, and be prepared to engage in analysis and critique of *yourself* as well as the media.

Secondly, theory can be difficult because it often refers to, and responds to, other theory. Because the development of theory is a process, and because people want to place their work within the context of other writers, and also encourage other writers to respond to their work, it can be hard to find a way into all this interconnected information if you are new to it. Writers will normally use references to show what their work relates to, and sometimes theorists summarise key ideas, but this is certainly not always the case. Because theory is usually written to be read by other theorists, writers will often assume a certain level of knowledge and understanding, which is unlikely to be the case for most students. Textbooks like this one, plus the classes you attend at university, aim to help you find your way into this material, but there is no doubting that you are likely to come across ideas and arguments which are glossed over in particular readings, but which you could do with being given more information about in order to follow the argument. The best thing to do is to just accept this, and be aware that it never goes away; it is unlikely your teachers know every book and every idea that is ever referred to in every reading they use. Indeed, you will often find that you can work out what is being referred to by the content of the rest of the reading. And if you cannot, but the reading still makes sense, it is likely it is not essential to grasp that material in order to interpret the reading at hand. It is because of these difficulties that going back and rereading material is encouraged; as your knowledge and understanding grows, it is probable that readings that made little sense to you some time ago will be much more comprehensible once you encounter other material.

As has already been noted, theory is often interested in presenting models, which can be tested, discussed, analysed and developed. Because models, in their initial stage, are often proposals which haven't been fully tested, they often do not 'work'; that is, they cannot fully explain what it is they are a model of. In that sense, theory can seem difficult if it does not 'work'. Yet the idea that theory is only useful if it works is problematic, not least because it is very difficult to prove that a theory does work. For example, while there is plenty of evidence supporting the theory of evolution, and it is commonly accepted amongst most scientists, it is very difficult to 'prove' that evolution actually happens. Indeed, this problem of proof is one of the reasons why, in certain parts of the world, other theories explaining how humankind came to be (such as creationism and/or intelligent design) are taught alongside evolution. Proving something to be unquestionaby true is very difficult, especially when people disagree about what constitutes 'proof'. However, this should be something which should worry you less when engaging with theory. As theory's aim is to encourage debate, reflection and analysis, it is not always interested in whether it is true; instead, theory should be judged on its usefulness for sparking dialogue, discussion and new ways of thinking. You may find some of the theories you come across in this book in no way explain how you feel the world works; however, in arguing why such a theory is of no use you are still *engaging* with it, and exploring the ideas and arguments which it presents. So, theory can be difficult because it is sometimes hard to see its worth if it doesn't tell the 'truth'; you can overcome this problem by remembering that this is rarely the aim of such theory. Instead, judge the usefulness of any particular theory based on the ways in which it forces you to think and examine the world around you.

One of the reasons why you may find it difficult to relate theory to your own experiences is because of the specific contexts it arises out of, as noted above. The examples used in much theory are likely to be ones which you have little experience of, especially if it was written some time ago, or in another country. Furthermore, as the social and political contexts of much theory inform the arguments which are presented, you might find it difficult to relate to the approaches being offered. The critical theory produced by the Frankfurt school (see Chapter 6), for example, arises out of turbulent times in Germany between the two world wars, when media was being used for very specific propaganda purposes. The concerns raised by members of the Frankfurt school might seem excessive to a contemporary British reader, because the media play a significantly different role in society today. Differences in context, however, should not be used as reasons to dismiss theory. Instead, such differences help highlight the specifics of the contemporary; that is, if the worries of the Frankfurt school do seem so alien, what does that tell you about contemporary relationships between media and society? So, by seeing such theory as documents which relate to specific contexts, you can begin to pinpoint what is particular about the times and places which you are trying to make sense of. This shows how such alien theory can remain useful, even if it seems distanced and difficult.

What this shows is that theory often requires you to think *hypothetically*. In order to make sense of how the world is, you need to be able to imagine how else the world might be. What if Britain was the major global film-producing nation, and not America? What if the BBC had never existed, and instead all broadcasting in the United Kingdom was commercial? What if newspapers were public service, and paid for by a licence fee as broadcasting is? Seeing the specifics of the here and now can be hard, unless you can imagine how things could be *different*. Much theory requires this ability, for it presumes that what seems normal and obvious is, instead, socially constructed and particular. You might be used to thinking about how things *are*; thinking about how things *might be* can be hard if you have not done it before, especially if you find it difficult to see the point of such an exercise. Sometimes the intention behind this process might simply be to make sense of the world (normative research), while sometimes the unpicking of what seems normal may have the specific aim of questioning its validity and offering alternative solutions (critical research). What this shows is that in order to be comfortable with media theory, you need to understand its *purposes*, and the role it requires you, as a reader, to play.

In repeatedly questioning what seems 'normal', media theory also shows that it is interested in more than just the media. That is, media studies is not just about examining television programmes, films, adverts and newspapers. Instead, media studies places these phenomena in social, historical and political contexts, and sees them as representative of, and often upholding, much bigger systems. As a subject, media studies is a complex amalgam of film studies, literature studies, cultural studies, sociology, anthropology, politics, history, and lots of other subjects. Its remit is wide, and many theorists are interested in media precisely because they see it as having an important and influential role in contemporary society. Media theory can be difficult, then, because it asks *big* questions, and requires you to see the link between the small, mundane everydayness of media, and much bigger debates about power, equality, history and society. Depending on what you have previously studied, you might find you are dealing with topics and approaches that you have not come across before, and which you did not assume were part of media studies. For much theory it is only this bigger context that matters; for many theorists, analysing media detached from these larger processes is pointless and reductive. While this can again induce people to insist that media theory 'reads too much into things', many writers would argue that it is not reading *enough* into things which is often the problem. The scale of media studies, and media theory, is, then, truly vast, and the sheer size of the questions it asks can appear daunting. Once you accept this scale, media theory often becomes much more manageable; in many ways, it becomes much more valuable and interesting too.

The magnitude of these questions can be seen by some of the key ideas which recur within media theory. One of these is 'power', a term you are likely to encounter repeatedly, which can be a difficult idea to get hold of. This is partly because, as with many terms, different people use it in slightly different ways, so you need to be attuned to how it is being employed in particular readings. Gibson outlines a 'history of the concept of power' (2007: ix), showing how it has been employed by theorists in different ways at different times. Debates about power are commonly interested in issues of social relations; that is, the relationships, structures and systems which hold societies together, and which require members of that society to behave in particular ways in order for it to function. Examples of such social relations are the law, education, government, democracy, and so on. So, if we do not behave as society expects in relation to the law (as shown in the riots across England in the summer of 2011), we are punished; we are sent to prison. If we do not adequately succeed in education, then jobs and opportunities are limited to us. What this means is that in order for each individual to function within the society they belong to, they are bound by social structures which are probably not of their making. In these ways such structures have power *over* us: in opposition, democracy may be seen as a way in which we have power over (some aspects) of the system through voting.

Media studies' interest in power comes from an assumption that these power relationships are unequal; that is, the power exerted over the majority of people is greater than that which they are able to exert back (Braham and Janes 2002; Westwood 2002). So, feminists might argue that social structures give men more power than women, just as cultural theory often argues that a ruling elite has power over most 'ordinary' people. And because the media can be seen as a way in which power is maintained and distributed, media studies is interested in it as a central concept. Because power is a complex term, whose very existence is difficult to definitively prove, media studies has often engaged in debates about the best ways to explore, expose and measure power. Many of the theories and approaches covered in this book are attempts to answer this question, and so you may find that, while not all the readings will explicitly mention power, it is likely to be a key concern motivating much of the work you encounter.

A final problem with media theory is that it is often written in what seems to be confusing and complex language, with lots of long, complicated words. The reasons why this might be is covered in our 'What is reading?' chapter, which also suggest ways in which you might deal with language you find difficult.

In summary, there are many reasons why you might find reading media theory difficult. Some suggestions as to why these difficulties arise, and how you might deal with them, have been outlined here. In the next chapter, which deals with reading as a process, further advice will be given on this. A final point though: it is hoped that you will see such difficulties as one of the processes of learning. That is, if all of this was easy, it is likely you would not be learning anything. This means that what you need to work on are strategies for dealing with such difficulties, and to see difficulty not as a barrier to learning, but instead as a motivation for it.

Summary

- theory can be hard because it *questions everything* – including yourself;
- theory can be hard because it places media in bigger *social/political contexts*;
- theory can be hard because it refers to other theory;
- theory can be hard because it requires *hypothetical thinking*;
- theory can be hard because it doesn't always 'work';
- theory can be hard because it uses 'complex' language.

WHY IS THEORY TAUGHT?

It is likely that media theory is a compulsory part of your studies, and it is often placed as a central component of undergraduate learning in the subject. This shows how universities see media theory as a vital part of your learning, and something which must be tackled in order for you to complete your degree. Yet, it can often be hard to see why you are required to engage with material that is, first, difficult, and, secondly, sometimes seems so detached from your everyday experiences.

One of the main reasons you are taught media theory is that it is the core of the subject of media studies, and to ignore it is to do a disservice to the field. The history of media studies is one of working through different theoretical approaches to the subject, often taking such theory from other fields and adapting it to suit the needs of the analysis of media. Importantly, theory informs everything in the subject, even if there are topics or approaches which you might think have nothing to do with such abstract thinking.

For example, it is likely that, in much of your studies at both undergraduate level and before that, you engaged in quite a lot of textual analysis, taking a television programme, or film, or advert, and examining it in detail to see how it works and what it tells us about the time and place in which it was produced. This approach is also used in literature studies, where you examine a specific book or poem in detail, as well as in other humanities subjects such as history, where you might explore a historical artefact in detail, in order to ascertain what it tells us about a particular age. Because textual analysis is such a common approach, and one which you are repeatedly required to use throughout your schooling, it can end up feeling like a 'normal' way of doing things, and there is often an assumption that no theory underpins it. Yet textual analysis does have a theoretical basis, and there are debates about the best ways to carry it out, and the extent to which it is possible to produce the 'correct' or most appropriate reading of a text. Indeed, the movement from structuralism (see Chapter 15) – which is primarily a way of carrying out textual analysis – to poststructuralism – which places quite a bit of interest in the activities of specific, individual readers – is one motivated by theoretical arguments about the value of textual analysis. In that sense, *all* of your studying is related to theory, even if there might seem to be times when this is not the case. The fact that you might be doing a unit or module which explicitly calls itself 'theory' is merely demonstrating that this unit deliberately and consciously engages in such debates, when other aspects of your studies might not. One of the reasons why you are studying theory, then, is because it informs all your education, and in laying this bare, it is hoped you'll be more critical and thoughtful about what it is you are studying, and how you are studying it.

Another reason why theory is taught is because of the skills it offers you. By encouraging a critical, thoughtful engagement with material, your skills in discussion and debate are fostered, which are often seen as vital at undergraduate level. And because the material you are working with is so open for debate, you are required to construct arguments and engage with both your teacher and the other students in your class in a manner which encourages communication skills and the ability to discuss and debate with others. Considering the vast majority of jobs in the creative industries are ones where working with others, and communicating clearly and efficiently, are key, media theory offers a useful site for practising such abilities. In addition, one of the key skills which employers in the creative industries look out for is a critical and engaged mind, which shows creativity and an ability to initiate and develop ideas. Debating media theory certainly encourages such creativity, as it promotes thinking about things in new ways, developing ideas with colleagues, and going beyond what is assumed to be 'normal' and 'obvious'. So, the intellectual processes which are fostered by engaging with media theory are key ones for anyone interested in working in film, television, journalism, music, and any of the other creative industries, or any other field where thoughtful communication is required.

In addition, many of the key ideas and concepts covered by media theory are highly valuable for working in the creative industries. For example, the structuralist debates about narrative are valuable for people interested in storytelling, and scriptwriters often draw on these approaches when working. Similarly, debates about the public sphere (see Chapter 13) and the social role of broadcasting are ongoing in television and radio, especially within public service broadcasters like the BBC in the United Kingdom, PBS in America, ABC in Australia and CBC in Canada. Executives at these institutions spend much of their time discussing how they can most effectively fulfil the social roles their remits require of them, and an ability to show a working knowledge of how such topics can be thought about and discussed is helpful when working for them. So, while it has been noted that a lot of theory was written in quite different contexts from those you might live in now, it is clear that the underlying questions and debates are ongoing. Those who work in the creative industries are highly critical, thoughtful and discursive people, who spend a lot of time discussing and debating their own creative processes, and the role of culture in society; considering these are the key questions of media theory, it is clear to see that while the practice of engaging with theory gives you transferable skills which are highly useful, the specific knowledge, approaches, and topics of media theory are also invaluable for working within such industries.

Finally, media theory is taught because it is hoped that in giving you the skills to question, discuss and debate, you will be encouraged to become more thoughtful about the world around you and your position within it. One of the key aims of education, at whatever level, is to encourage you to become an engaged and thoughtful citizen who is active in your dealings with the world, and wants to know more about it. Because media theory questions everything, it shows you how things can always be different, and there might always be new ways in which things can be thought about. As a member of the public who is part of a society, living within a nation, thoughtfully, critically and actively engaging with the world around you can only be a good thing.

Summary

- theory is the *core* of studying media studies;
- theory offers useful *transferable* skills;
- theory explores debates central to the *media and creative industries*;
- theory helps develop you as a *citizen* and an *individual*.

WHAT SHOULD I DO WITH THEORY?

In the next chapter, we'll deal in more detail with the specifics of reading media theory. Of course, reading such material is probably the main interaction you'll have with theory, and working out strategies which work best for you in doing this is invaluable. Yet you should not think of theory as something only to be read, especially as reading can often feel like quite a passive activity. One of the key things you can do is ensure you are taking an *active* approach to media theory and its associated readings, as this will not only help you get more out of the material, but also aid you in relating it to your everyday experiences.

What does taking an active approach mean? First, it means you should not see theory merely as something you are required to learn, and that that is the only reason you are engaging with it. While it is important you *understand* what a particular reading is saying, this is not the same as learning it. *Learning* is about acquiring knowledge that can then be retrieved when necessary; *understanding* is about having a more interactive relationship with knowledge, and encouraging discussion, debate and analysis. You are being introduced to theory because it can help you make sense of a whole range of phenomena, and so you should be constantly thinking *why* particular readings have been chosen, and *what* you can do with them. In discussions and seminars in class you will be encouraged to think about, and discuss with others, the usefulness and appropriateness of particular bits of theory; in order to do so you need to understand it, but that is not the same as saying you have to necessarily accept it. Indeed, it is likely you will be encouraged in your assessments to take a critical view of theory, and to offer balanced arguments which show the benefits and drawbacks of a whole range of approaches. As is shown in the next chapter, being active in your engagement with theory is not only about questioning it, but also about *applying* it; how does it relate to contemporary examples, or your own experiences of the world of media? Such application might require you to develop or alter such theory; yet this is not a problem, as this is a process which thinkers have been doing for millennia. In encouraging you to adopt an active relationship to theory, then, you are only being asked to do what people have been doing for thousands of years, and will continue to do in the future.

RECOMMENDED READING

Barry, P. (2009) *Beginning Theory: An introduction to literary and cultural theory*, 3rd edition, Manchester: Manchester University Press.

By drawing on literary theory, this book helps to show the origins of media theory; contains useful 'stop and think' points offering helpful areas of discussion for each theory.

Boyd-Barrett, O. and Newbold, C. (eds) (1995) *Approaches to Media: A reader*, London: Arnold.

Thorough collection of major articles on a wide range of topics, supplemented with helpful introductions from the authors.

Williams, K. (2003) *Understanding Media Theory*, London: Arnold.

Divided into sections on the history and future of theory, production, texts and audiences, this is a useful summary of the major ideas and key thinkers.

CHAPTER 3

What is reading?

One of the first things you will notice in higher education is that everyone starts talking about books, journals, references and the library. The library building is likely to be placed centrally at your university or college, and is probably larger (and more confusing) than local libraries you might be used to. As part of your induction to your studies, you might have been taken on a library tour, and shown the many kinds of resources on offer to you. In your classes, it is likely that your teachers repeatedly refer to books and authors, and you have probably been required to buy many books or reading packs as part of your studies. This is likely to be quite different from your experiences studying at school, A-level, BTEC or any other pre-university qualification. What all of this shows is that at the core of your time at university is the assumption that you will undertake a lot of *reading*. People who work in universities often forget how this can be a massive change for many students, who might be overwhelmed by all the resources available, and be confused by many of the words employed when talking about reading.

The importance of reading – and your own engagement with that reading – is likely to be shown by your timetable. It is probable that you spend a lot less time in the classroom than was the case at school. Indeed, undergraduates are often shocked and outraged at the amount of time they are left to their own devices. This freedom is given with the deliberate intention of encouraging you to structure your own time, and to demonstrate that a key component of undergraduate study is the reading and thinking you do on your own; higher education foregrounds *independent study*. That is, it is no longer the case that you are merely required to listen to the ideas of your teachers; instead, teachers will point you in the direction of key points and ideas, but you should be developing your own ideas, your own responses, and your own ways of thinking. Reading is a key component of this, and it is why universities give you lots of time and resources to engage as closely and thoughtfully as possible with the material relevant to your studies.

This means you should think carefully about reading. It might seem absurd to spend time thinking about a skill you learnt many years ago, and which now seems obvious. However, there are lots of different ways of reading, and there are lots of different uses reading can be put to; in order to get the best out of the reading you do at university, it is therefore important for you to be aware *why* you're reading what you're reading, and what you're trying to *get out of it*.

For example, think of the various ways in which you do reading every day. Much of our reading is done in order to ascertain *facts*; looking at timetables so you can see when the next bus to university is arriving, or reading the signs on campus which direct you to the correct room, or looking at a listings guide so you can what is on television that night, are all examples of this. You might also read so that you can *communicate* with someone; reading texts, and then replying to them, or interacting with friends on social networking sites such as Facebook, are examples of this. In essence, both of these kinds of reading require the same basic skills, for you are looking at words and deciphering their meaning. Yet note that the *purpose* of reading in these cases is different, for in the former you are engaged in *gathering* information, while in the latter the intention is to more actively *engage* with the material, so you can respond to it. Also note how bus timetables and signs are written for a *general audience* in mind, while texts and e-mails are instead usually addressed to *specific people*, often only one person. This notion that different things are written with different audiences in mind is important, and worth remembering when you read as part of your studies.

Most people spend the majority of their time reading in order to gather information, as shown by the social importance attached to newspapers, and the massive growth of websites like Wikipedia. Reading is, therefore, one of the main ways in which we find out about the world around us, and its importance in offering us the ability to make sense of what is going on is why it is one of the first things taught at school. Reading at university is similarly a process in which you are encouraged to gather information about particular subject areas; however, it also has other roles and purposes, which means you are likely to need to develop new skills to extend your reading capabilities.

Summary

- Reading is something you do *every day*, so it is not something you should be wary of;
- Reading is *central* to studying at university;
- You are likely to be required to do *much more* reading at university than you have been used to in your studies before;
- Reading can fulfil a *variety* of purposes;
- University requires a *different kind of reading*, and it is important for you to work out what is required of you, and how you can best achieve this.

AT UNIVERSITY, WHAT IS READING FOR?

Of course, the main reason you're at university is to *learn*. Reading is one of the best ways you can learn, so it is obvious that universities will place reading at the heart of their activities. Indeed, as noted above, the amount of time you spend in the classroom is reduced at university, while the amount of time available to you for reading is expanded; this shows how universities believe that lecturers *teaching* you may not be the best way for you to learn, and you should instead be given as much space as possible to engage in learning through your own research, reading and thinking.

This is because in many subjects at university – especially arts and humanities ones such as media studies – the main focus moves away from facts and answers, and towards *ideas* and *arguments*. At school you might have been encouraged to learn specific facts, and your knowledge was probably assessed through your ability to know things. At university, you are instead more likely to be assessed through your ability to *discuss, think, engage* and *debate*. While certain kinds of information are unarguable, and will be covered in your classes, you are instead more likely to spend much of your time engaging with debates and arguments about which there is no accepted answer, but which you are required to show your understanding of, and ability to engage with. Here, then, reading becomes much less about gathering up a series of facts which can be regurgitated when necessary. Instead, universities are interested in your ability to deal with the complexities, contradictions and debates related to many ideas, and reading is therefore a process in which you are actively encouraged to explore, discuss, criticise and applaud the ideas which you may come across. Reading is not the end of the process; instead, it is the *start*, and what is important is what you can do with the material that you have read. ﹅

This is what is usually referred to as reading *critically*. This is an important word, which you are likely to come across often, so it is important you understand what is meant by it. To read something critically is not the same as to 'criticise' it. Critical reading is about not expecting a reading to give you final, definitive answers, but instead for it to be a tool for you to develop your own thinking. It requires you to question a reading's content, methods, assumptions and conclusions; but, again, questioning something is not the same as completely dismissing or rejecting it. A critical reading might have problems with, say, the examples an author chooses, but still find the argument which those examples are intended to illustrate a valid one. A critical approach might acknowledge that because an author is from a different country, or was writing many years ago, some of the arguments might be outdated; but at the same time, critical reading will search for those aspects which are still applicable, or think through what can be learned from those differences. It is likely that your teachers are not interested in whether the readings they have set you are right or wrong (indeed, it is likely they would say that this is a fruitless task), but instead want to use those readings as material which will help inform a debate, discussion or idea. Adopting a critical approach means that you can often find material of value in readings you utterly disagree with; in terms of maintaining motivation, this can be extremely useful.

It is hoped that you will quickly come to realise this during your studies. You are likely to be encouraged to read as much as possible, and your preparation for class is likely to be reading. Your handbooks for your classes might have lengthy book lists, with recommended and required books, as well as supplementary material. Most universities judge assignments – especially essays – through a range of criteria, one of which usually requires your work to demonstrate your research and reading. Virtually all of the key names you are taught about, and will come across in this book, have disseminated their ideas primarily through what they have written, and you will be required to have a working knowledge of who wrote what, and what those writings are about.

Very often, new students find the amount of reading required of them quite daunting. It is normally far more than has been required at school or for other qualifications, and it is often expected to be completed outside of class, rather than something done together as a group. Other factors compound these problems. For example, what you are required to read is likely to contain ideas and arguments which are new to you, and can be difficult to grasp. This is often not helped by the way in which some of it is written, with new and difficult words, abstract concepts and examples which may mean very little to you.

This means you need to develop strategies in order to overcome these problems. The most useful one is to get a sense of what reading is *for*, and why you are being required to do it. This can help you make links between your interest in the subject and the material you are required to read. If you have no idea *why* you're reading something, it can be extremely difficult to summon up the energy and interest required to complete the process. Therefore, before carrying out any reading, think about *why* you are reading it. Often, the answer to this question will be, 'because I've been told to', which isn't very helpful. But why has your teacher insisted that you read this material? What debates and ideas have you covered in class so far, and how might this reading relate to it? What are the *aims* of the course you are on, and how might this reading fit into them? You might be set questions, or things to think about, in relation to a reading; what do these tell you about what your teacher thinks are its important ideas? The ability to distinguish why and how a reading is useful and important not only can help give you the motivation to work through it, but is also a useful skill when you are carrying out your own research in the library, and have to decide which books and journals are relevant to the task you have to complete. This shows that reading does not just involve sitting down with a book and working through it; there are useful processes to complete *prior* to reading, just as there are helpful *reflective* processes which can be done *after* reading. Reading is, therefore, an *ongoing* process, in which everything you read is part of your learning, and each time you carry out reading you can reflect on what worked for you and what was less successful, so that, it is hoped, you can be more and more successful in your reading as you progress through your studies.

Summary

- Reading is for *learning*;
- Rather than reading for facts, at university, reading is about *engaging, discussing, debating* and *thinking* from an informed position;
- Reading *critically* is vital;
- Thinking about the *aims* of your reading is a useful way to set goals and priorities.

READING AND THE SELF

One of the most important things to grasp is that there is no one right way of reading that works for everyone, which is guaranteed to eradicate all the problems and difficulties associated with it. Reading is a *personal* activity, and you need to find out what is the best way of doing it for *you*.

This involves thinking about lots of questions. First, what are your motivations and interests for your course? Getting a good sense of what interests you will help you select the aspects of a particular reading which matter to you, which can help you engage with the reading as a whole. This book examines media theory, and it is likely that you have not encountered much of this material before. Your interest in media is likely to come from your enjoyment of particular kinds of media, or your admiration for a particular genre, or writer, or director. That is, very often people's motivation for the topic is about media artefacts. Media theory, on the other hand, often deals with bigger questions than this, and looks at the *social* role of media, or its political and historical implications, often with little regard for specific texts or practitioners. This may make equating *your* interest with the interests of those who write media theory a little difficult. However, you can overcome this through *application* of the material you read.

Secondly, you need to think about what you find difficult in reading. Some people find it hard knowing where to start (which might be more complex than you think). Some people find it difficult to select the *key ideas*, and summarise what a reading is *about*. Some people worry about how to take notes, and whether to write on the reading itself; in essence, this is a worry about what to do when actually carrying out the reading. And some people worry about what to do *after* reading, especially if you have difficulty remembering what a reading was about. You may have concerns which are quite different to these, for everyone responds to readings in their own, personal way. The important thing, then, is for you to get an understanding of what those problems are for *you*; it is only once you have done this that you can work out ways of dealing with these problems. And while it is useful to discuss such problems with your friends or people in your classes, you should not worry if what you find difficult is not the same as everyone else. Indeed, you might discover that other students have problems which you do not, which can be a useful demonstration of the particular skills you have.

In fact, this is very important; knowing what your skills in reading are, or the things you enjoy about reading, can help you when the process becomes difficult. If you find a particular reading difficult, it can become all too easy to convince yourself that you are not 'good enough' to deal with it, and that you will never make sense of it. Knowing what you are capable of can, therefore, not only help you work out a solution to a problem such as this, but also remind you that you certainly have the capabilities of making sense of all this stuff. This means not only that students often fail to take advantage of their particular skills, but that it can also be highly demoralising as they begin to feel that they're wasting their time.

Thirdly, you need to think about *when* and *where* is best for you to read. Some people read better at home, some in the library, some elsewhere. The authors of this book often employ different reading strategies: David often reads at home or when travelling, whereas Brett likes to find a quiet spot in the library and be surrounded by piles of books. Different times of day may affect your ability to make sense of readings, especially depending on other things you have done that day. Both David and Brett like to read in the morning, before other distractions have ruined concentration, but this is not always possible, depending on other commitments. For many people absolute silence is a must, but you need to experiment and find what is best for you. Because you are likely to be required to carry out reading quite regularly as part of your studies, it is worth trying to timetable specific reading times each week, regarding them as regular in the same way as your classes are.

To do this, you need a sense of *how long* any particular reading will take you. This can only be found out through practice. It is likely that the readings you have to do for your studies are roughly the same each week, so they should take about the same amount of time. However, this is not always the case, and a reading may come along which you have big difficulties with, and which takes more time than usual to work through. If this is the case, rather than worrying, you should think about *why* some readings take more time for you than others. This will not only give you a useful way into thinking about the reading generally; it will also help you plan in the future when similar readings come along.

Finally, you need to find out what are the most helpful things for you to do while you are reading. For example, some people mark the text and take notes as they are going through it for the first time; some people read the text as a whole first, and then go back and add notes, underlining and comments. Again, there are differences in the ways in which this book's authors read. David quite often reads material in full before going back to make notes, whereas Brett usually scribbles all over most readings the first time he reads them, summarising concepts in the margin, putting question marks next to things that he finds hard to make sense of, and underlining quotable passages or key words (of course, this is *not* done on library books). Remember that your comments on a reading are intended *only for you*, so use whatever format and language is the most useful for you. It is often advisable not to get too carried away with notes, comments and underlining, as you can end up with a reading that is confusing to look at and seems to have as many words written all over it as there are within it. Such comments should be a way of you *filtering* the information in the reading, and so should therefore pick out significant parts rather than select everything in the text.

This may make it sound like there is a lot to do when reading, and this is the case. However, what is extremely important is that you can only answer the questions outlined above if you think about *how* you read *after* you have done some reading. That is, reading must always be a *reflective* process. While it is tempting when you have finished a reading to put it to one side and go and do something else, it is worth going back to such material afterwards and think about *what* you did when reading, and how such techniques could be *improved* in the future to try to make your process more successful. For example, when Brett first started reading at university, he never wrote anything on the page, presumably out of some kind of 'respect' for the material. But he got so angry with one reading he was set that he started scribbling notes and comments all over the page. He realised afterwards this had made him have a much clearer understanding of the reading's content, and his responses to it. Since then, Brett has scribbled personal responses all over readings, which not only aids understanding, but also means that when he goes back to that reading after some time he can immediately see which bits interested him, or intrigued him, or annoyed him, or confused him. Trying out new techniques when reading can be a fruitful process, and so you must always try to make sense of the process you are going through, and adapt it in response to what works for you and what does not.

The process of reading is outlined in a number of books which suggest possible ways of going about it. For example, Maker and Lenier (1996: 2–3) suggest an Active Critical Thinking (ACT) process, which they see as encompassing six steps which should be followed whenever reading something:

1. preread;
2. read;
3. analyse what you read;
4. remember what's important;
5. make use of what you read;
6. evaluate your critical thinking skills.

Prereading involves trying to get a rough overview of what the reading is about, and the problems and successes you may have with it, before reading, so you can prepare your method of reading accordingly. Things like the title of the reading, whether it has an index, titles of subsections, names you might know in the references, how it fits into what you are studying and why your teacher has suggested you read it, are all ways of pre-reading. Very often, people start reading something without briefly looking over the whole first, which means they are not in any way prepared for what is to come. For books, it is always useful to spend a minute or so looking at the contents page, the blurb on the back, the index, and flicking through the book as a whole to see if it contains pictures or dia-grams, and get a sense of it overall. The same process can be carried out for articles and shorter pieces. Carrying out prereading can be one way of bringing to the forefront of your mind relevant information you already know about the topic before you start reading properly. This is, therefore, a very useful step.

Reading in this system involves reading the article fully without making any kinds of notes, or worrying about words or phrases you do not understand. Maker and Lenier sug-gest you go on to the third stage, *analysing what you read*, which involves you working through the reading again, this time making notes, identifying key arguments, thinking about evidence, raising questions, and so on. If this is done thoroughly, then you should be able to move on to the next stage – *remembering what's important* – fairly easily, because your notes and comments will clearly signal the key ideas and debates, and help to focus your response to the reading down to the main points.

Making use of what you read is the next stage, and involves you discussing, debating, and applying the reading's ideas. This may happen in class, where your teacher will invite you as a group to think about the material covered by the reading. However, it is worth-while carrying out this activity elsewhere. Thinking of your own examples, which either support or question the reading's arguments, is one way of linking the reading to your own knowledge, and therefore anchoring the material within a framework that makes sense to you. It is likely that any reading you are carrying out for your studies has also been set for other students that you know, so it is also worthwhile discussing and debating the material with them. It can sometimes feel easier to do this outside of the classroom, if you are worried about misunderstanding the article or making it known to your teacher that you are having difficulties (having said that, teachers usually really want to know which bits of reading the class finds difficult so they can be discussed together, so you should not worry about admitting this). The notion that reading should be used outside of class is an important one, and so you should take every opportunity you can to relate conversations or experiences to material you're covering.

The final stage is to *evaluate your critical thinking skills*. This can take a number of forms. As outlined earlier, it can involve thinking about the difficulties you encountered with the reading, and wondering whether there are other ways you could have tackled it which would have helped you. Discussions with others, whether inside the classroom or not, might also help you think about your understanding of the material (though be wary of assuming you have understood less than everyone else – this is often a result of bravado on the part of those who insist they understand *everything*). A more formal way in which you can evaluate your skills is by looking at the kinds of feedback you get from your assignments, and what they suggest about your ability to engage with, and understand, what you have read. Feedback on assignments is intended to suggest how you might improve your work, and so you should respond to it practically, rather than just seeing it as criticism. If assignment feedback suggests you have problems in this area, speak to your tutor, who will likely have suggestions about how you might go about improving your skills, drawing on your existing abilities. The notion that you should think repeatedly about how you read and how you can improve this activity should be a continual process; to be sure, it is one which your teachers and tutors engage in, and they have probably been reading this kind of material for years.

While Maker and Lenier's ACT structure is a useful one, remember that none of this is set in stone, and you should work out which process is best for you. For example, it is common to conflate points 2 and 3, writing comments on a reading when it is first read. You can also often flick back to earlier parts in a reading if something later on alters your perception of it. Although you need to be careful with such a technique, as the *progression* of an argument is important, and reading things out of order might mean you get quite a different meaning from it. Discussion and debate with colleagues and students about readings is a vital part of the process, and helps you discover the various ways in which a reading can be made sense of. In that sense, you might want to try Maker and Lenier's scheme for yourself, and it is certainly a very good place to start; however, if you end up tweaking it a little because doing that helps you with your reading, then that is no problem. As has been stated repeatedly, you need to ascertain what works for *you*.

Summary

- There is not a single right way to read, and you need to find out what reading strategy works best for *you*;
- To do this, it is a good idea to find out what you find difficult about reading, and what you're *good* at;
- Working out *how long* reading takes you means you can prepare and plan for each reading you are required to do;
- Thinking about what to do *before and after* reading, as well as during, is recommended;
- Reading must always be a *reflective* process.

PROBLEMS WHEN READING

While you may have worked out the approach to reading which best works for you, it is still likely that you will encounter problems and difficulties with many readings. There may be concepts you find difficult to grasp, examples which mean nothing to you, sentences which you read again and again and cannot make sense of, or words which you have never come across before. Working out strategies to deal with these problems is important, to ensure that these difficulties do not persuade you to give up on the reading altogether or, more importantly, make you think you are not capable of making sense of the reading at all.

As with all approaches to reading, while advice on how to deal with these problems can be given, the particular approach that best works for you will depend on your own learning style, which can be gleaned from trying a range of approaches until you find the most effective one. Perhaps the most important bit of advice is not to give up. Many readings are difficult, and it is rare you will come across one which makes perfect sense to you the first time you read it. Indeed, considering the aim of reading is for you to *learn something new*, a reading which fails to throw up problems and confusion is one that you are likely to be getting little out of. Reading can be difficult precisely because its role is to make you think differently, or think about things you are not used to pondering, so its difficulty is merely a sign that you are encountering something new. If you think about when you start to learn anything – such as a musical instrument, or the rules of a sport, or how a machine works – the relevant language and ideas are often difficult to grasp, precisely because of the novelty. In such examples as these we usually accept there will be difficulty, and work our way through it. Perhaps it is so frustrating when reading is difficult because reading, once learned, is meant to be pretty easy, and it feels odd and embarrassing not to be able to make sense of something someone has written. But there is a difference between the *technical* skill of reading, and the *cognitive* process of making meaning, and while you spend much time at school learning the former, at university it is likely that it is the latter which is difficult.

Here's a confession: the authors of this book often find reading difficult. Indeed, while they may not admit it, all your teachers and lecturers often find reading difficult. As noted above, such readings *are* difficult, because their difficulty is a consequence of their novelty and originality. The question becomes *what you do* about this difficulty. The first thing is to revel in the difficulty, precisely because it proves you are being presented with something new, which is surely one of the things you want to happen at university. Easy readings are boring, because they do not tell you anything new, or challenge your thinking. Working through the process of making sense of complicated writing is one of the pleasures of academic thinking. The fact that academics get together at conferences and discuss what certain readings mean, and write books trying to make sense of them, and put together lectures hoping to explain them to you, shows that they are also engaged in this complex interpretive process, which you should be trying to do too.

So what should you do when you get stuck with a reading? For example, what if you come across a word or term you do not understand? A recurring term in many of the readings in this book is the 'public sphere' (see Chapter 13), and it is pretty hard to guess what is meant by it if you have not come across it before. First of all, you need to work out if you really need to know what the term means in order to carry on with the reading. If the term is a key one, on which the argument rests, it is best to get a sense of it, otherwise continuing is rather pointless. However, quite often, individual words are not necessary for an understanding of the whole, so it is often best to ignore the word and move on. That is not to say that you forget about it forever, but it is to say that if you stop at every word you do not understand, it is likely that getting through the reading will take days if not weeks. So, it is common practice when bewildered by a word to carry on reading for a few sentences, probably until the end of the paragraph and maybe the start of the next one, to see if you can make sense of what is being said without knowing the precise meaning of the word. Indeed, it is sometimes possible to work out what a word means by seeing what comes *after* it in the reading. Most of the time, it is the general thrust of the main argument which is key to understanding a reading, and this can be gleaned without an understanding of every single word. Therefore, if it is possible to make sense of the reading without knowing a particular word, ignore it and carry on, maybe coming back to it later. What is helpful about this process is that it means you are continuing to make progress in the reading, rather than being stuck at one word. This can (hopefully) be a very positive experience; it means you've *learned* something.

What if you feel understanding a word you do not know is vital to the reading? If you cannot work it out from its context, you need to find a meaning from somewhere else. The most obvious place is a dictionary, and such a book is often useful to have by your side during your studies. However, you need to be careful with dictionaries, especially general usage ones such as those produced by Oxford or Collins. As these dictionaries are made for a general audience, they often do not contain words from specific subject areas. In addition, if they do contain those words, they might have quite general definitions which could be quite different to the particular ways in which certain authors use them. For example, Roland Barthes's use of the word 'myth' (see Chapter 22) is not the same as the general use of the word (though it has some connections), and it is important that you have an understanding of how it is meant to be understood by this particular author. Much better, then, is a subject specific dictionary, such as *A Dictionary of Communication and Media Studies* (Watson and Hill 2000), *The Penguin Dictionary of Media Studies* (Abercrombie and Longhurst 2007) or *A Dictionary of Media and Communication* (Chandler and Munday 2011), where it is likely terms will be outlined with reference to specific authors, and the debates and arguments concerning them will be explored.

The same process can be used for sentences or paragraphs you find difficult. First, simply move on, and then see if the meaning is clearer once you have finished the reading and come back to the difficult section. In larger blocks of text like this, it is useful to think about what in particular you are finding difficult. Is it that there are specific words you do not know? Is it that it relates to examples you are unfamiliar with? Is it that you know the examples, but do not understand how they relate to what is being argued? Do you not understand the argument? Is the whole thing written in a complex style, where it is just difficult to follow what is being said at all? Working out exactly what the problem is not only means you can pinpoint what needs to be resolved, but should also help you realise what you *can* make sense of. Figuring out what you *do* understand can be useful as this information can serve as the basis from which you try to figure out the bits you are having problems with. It will also likely make you realise the problem is much smaller than you might have first thought, as it is probably one specific bit of a sentence or paragraph which is confusing you, rather than the whole.

If, after all of this, you still have some difficulties, do not worry. If the reading was simple and straightforward, it is unlikely it would have been set for you to cover. The next step should be to talk to someone, perhaps your tutor, or perhaps someone else who is studying the same reading, and may be having the same problems, or may be able to explain what you are finding difficult. Most importantly, you should not give up; this stuff is meant to be hard as it is introducing you to ways of thinking you are not used to. And this material is likely to be covered in class – where you are given time and space to discuss it – and so you should use this time as an opportunity to engage in discussion and debate about it.

Summary

- You're likely to come across things in readings which you find difficult, but this is *intentional* as such reading is intended to introduce you to ideas and arguments you are unfamiliar with;
- You need to work out what *strategy* for dealing with such problems works for you; pinpointing the precise problem often helps;
- Remember to *ask for help*: by discussing it with other students, seeing your tutor or debating it in class.

ACADEMIC LANGUAGE

One of the complaints made repeatedly about reading theory is that it is overly complex, with many long words, complicated sentences, and examples which mean little to those reading it. Also, so many writers write in many different ways that while you may have read lots of stuff which you have found you have been able to make sense of, there might suddenly be a reading which completely baffles you. Furthermore, many of the readings may have been written quite some time ago, or in different countries, and it is difficult to see how they apply to your studies or your interests. For many students, media theory is quite unlike anything they have ever read before, and it is very surprising to discover that it is something you are required to engage with in order to pass your degree. And if you cannot see *why* you have to read something, it is difficult to summon up the energy or persistence to carry on when difficulties arise.

These problems arise for a number of reasons. The first one is that, quite often, there's a disparity between what universities see 'media studies' as, and what the world outside universities see it as. Media studies often gets criticised in the press as an easy subject, which involves watching television all day. However, the field of media studies as an academic subject has a long tradition of being socially and politically motivated, for it assumes that the media have a significant role to play in the relationships between the public, the state and society. This means that media theory is often about issues of power, society, politics and the individual, and so covers a large range of ideas and topics. Also, media studies has repeatedly drawn on a range of approaches and methods, which means it is a complex field of study, which is constantly changing and has a convoluted history. The *range* of work done by media studies is, then, very wide, and this can be startling for someone who has particular expectations of what it involves.

This means the subject area has never fully coalesced into one concrete whole, whose terms and approaches can be neatly summarised. The sheer range of terms, concepts, and ideas you will encounter is probably quite bewildering. That these ideas are used to examine something often seen as quite straightforward – the media – can often make people feel things are being overcomplicated, and results in the common complaint that authors are 'reading too much into things'. However, the very point being made by authors is that things that appear to be simple, are, in fact, extremely complex, and it is the ways in which they are made to appear simple which needs to be explored. The subject, therefore, is very often about making the simple complex; or, more accurately, it is about making transparent those things whose complexity is repeatedly denied.

Much theoretical writing uses complex words and terms you have probably not come across before. While this may seem strange, it is worth bearing in mind that all subjects – whether studied at university or not – have their own language. If you were studying medicine, for example, you would be required to learn all the terms for parts of the body, just as computing students come across a wealth of words related to the technologies of computers. In all sports similar subject-specific terms abound, with, for example, manoeuvres in activities like ice-skating or surfing given names which are likely to be incomprehensible to anyone who is not a keen follower. In having a wealth of complex and specific terms media studies is merely following the example of all other subjects, where words are required to express ideas which are specific to it but are not normally encountered in everyday conversation. You should see 'new' words, then, not as deliberately difficult and intended to obscure meaning; quite the opposite, they are coined and employed by writers precisely because they encapsulate ideas they wish to convey.

One of the reasons theory might seem difficult is that most of it was not written with students in mind. That is, much theory is written for other academics, and responds to existing bits of theory which someone else has written. It therefore often assumes that readers know a whole range of necessary terms and ideas, and so does not see the need to bother defining or explaining them. Indeed, if every bit of writing explained all the words it used, it would never get on to saying anything new or interesting. As the 'What is theory?' chapter showed, much theory is a complex dialogue between various thinkers, and so your job as a student is to try to make sense of this conversation. It is the job of your teacher, and textbooks like this, to try to help you make sense of this material, giving you the resources to enter into the conversation.

Yet, there is another reason why language in media studies is often complex. As the subject is about communication, it is often interested in the ways in which languages function. For example, structuralists (see Chapter 15) argue that there are underlying 'structures' to media, which we must understand in order to make sense of it. For many people language is a powerful system, which has massive effects on society, even though it is often seen as 'natural' and 'objective'. People who see language in this way have, therefore, often deliberately played around with language, precisely because they want to show how it works and demonstrate the problems at the heart of all communication. For many feminists, for example, language helps uphold male dominance over women; at its simplest level, this has led to debates over whether words such as 'chairman' and 'mankind' should be replaced with 'chairperson' and 'humankind'. What all of this demonstrates is that, for a lot of media studies, language is a site of contention, and not simply a tool whose communicative power is straightforward and unproblematic. Complex writing is, therefore, sometimes a deliberate attempt to force the reader to adopt a detached, thoughtful stance, questioning everything they are presented with, showing how language is a powerful phenomenon within our culture. Of course, this can make reading such material difficult; but, in these cases, difficulty can sometimes be the intention, as writers want to question the idea that language, and media, are uncomplicated and straightforward.

Overall, then, it is unlikely that you will never get confused by words or terms when carrying out your reading. But, as with all reading, you should develop strategies for dealing with these problems. Key to this approach is thinking about *why* something is difficult, and accepting that such difficulty may be deliberate, in order to make you think. Difficulty is, therefore, not a stumbling block, but instead an opportunity to engage with a new idea which should help you develop your thinking.

Summary

- Media theory is probably very *different* from what you have read before, and it can sometimes be hard to see how it relates to your interests;
- Complex words and terms are encountered in *all* subjects, and media studies is no exception;
- Much media theory is written for an *audience* who is assumed to understand these terms; it is often not written with students in mind;
- Some writers deliberately *play around* with language, to demonstrate the complexities of communication.

AFTER READING

As noted above, reading is not a process which occurs only when you are reading set material; it is something which draws on your studies overall, and other experiences outside of your studies. While the things you cover in education might sometimes feel detached from your everyday life, you are likely to find it easier to remember what you have read, and find it useful, if you can find ways to relate it to things outside of the classroom. For media theory this should be fairly easy, as such theory should resonate every time you watch television, or go to the cinema, or encounter any other kind of media. This is not to say all your experiences will prove that everything you have read is 'correct'; quite the opposite, your experiences might help you adopt a critical approach to the material. The most important thing is that you should consistently have what you have read in mind, *using* theory to make sense of the world around you, and simultaneously using the world around you to think about theory. Doing this means you are likely to build up lots of responses, ideas and examples, which can then be drawn on when you have to write essays or do other assessments.

The relationship between your own written work and the material you read is an important one. It is all too easy to end up seeing reading as something you do with things written by other people, and writing as something you do in response to it. But you should also be reading *your own work*. Developing critical reading skills is useful because you can bring these abilities to bear on your own work, critiquing your essays and assessments in the same way that you analyse course material. Reading essays before you submit them, and rereading them when they are returned to you, in the light of the comments and feedback you are given on them, is a vital way of seeing how you can improve your own work.

So, do not think of reading as something which is only done with things you are given to read by your tutors; and do not think of reading skills as ones which are only of value when encountering that kind of material. Reading skills are, instead, a vital building block in your studies overall, helping you to engage with a range of material, and giving you a vital tool which can help you improve your own work. The fact that such reading skills can be used in this variety of ways, and help support a whole range of critical and analytical skills which will be useful not only in your studies, but also in whatever route you take when you leave education, is why your course places such importance on reading as a whole.

RECOMMENDED READING

Fairbairn, G.J. and Fairbairn, S.A. (2001) *Reading at University: A guide for students*, Buckingham and Philadelphia: Open University Press.

Explores all aspects of the process of reading, with useful tips on how to develop your own skills.

Maker, J. and Lenier, M. (1996) *Academic Reading with Active Critical Thinking*, Belmont CA: Wadsworth.

Outlines an Active Critical Thinking (ACT) approach towards reading, which you might find a useful model to adopt.

PART II

Key thinkers and schools of thought

CHAPTER 4

Liberal press theory

Mill, J.S. (1997 [1859]) 'Of the liberty of thought and discussion', in Bromley, M. and O'Malley, T. (eds) *A Journalism Reader*, London: Routledge, pp. 22–6.

INTRODUCTION TO LIBERAL PRESS THEORY

In democratic societies, the notion of a 'free press' has come to be seen as an 'unchallenge-able dogma' (Lichtenberg 2002: 173). Despite this, members of the media and other social commentators still feel it necessary, from time to time, to remind the populace about the need to protect 'freedom of speech' and 'freedom of the press' – which is generally taken to include the media as a whole. More often than not, these reminders about the importance of press freedom tend to occur when journalists and their employers are being accused of unnecessary intrusion into the private lives of people in the public eye, and also in cases where media organisations are seeking to take credit for exposing the failings of governments, public sector institutions or big business.

The 'run' on the Northern Rock bank in late 2007 is one recent example where the press, and the mass media generally, demonstrated their 'watchdog' role. In doing so, they reminded the wider public that a 'free' media was essential in order to report on matters that were judged to be in the 'public interest'. However, this might be contrasted with the occasion in the early months of 2008 when most of the British media set aside their watchdog role and conformed to the government's request not to report Prince Harry's term of soldiering in Afghanistan.

There have also been numerous instances of press intrusion that have been judged to be inappropriate, the most obvious example being at the time of writing, of the ongoing investigations into alleged phone hacking at the newspaper publisher, News International. Indeed, this story is an interesting one for debates about the freedom of the press, for while the allegations suggest that newspapers cannot function without some form of regulation and control, the events only came to light *because* of the freedom of the press, whereby one journalist – Nick Davies of *The Guardian* – pursued the story for many years.

This story was reported globally, and has informed debates the world over concerning the roles the media play in social life, and the extent to which such activities are a force for good or ill. Whether or not the behaviour of media owners, editors and journalists in such an instance is thought to be reasonable, these examples underline the need to think critically about what we understand by 'public interest', 'freedom of speech' and 'freedom of the press'.

Given that the idea of a free press appears to be ingrained in our consciousness, it is not surprising that the concept is very rarely subjected to critical appraisal. As a result, its history remains hidden and the theory which it spawned, and which continues to underpin it, is seldom challenged or subjected to debate either in public discussion forums or in the mainstream media.

John Keane argues that 'press freedom' is 'a distinctive organising principle of the modern European and North American worlds' (1991: 7–8), which began in Britain before spreading first to America and then to other parts of Europe. There is a further commonality in respect of both continents. That is, the first demands for press freedom arose in the context of political turmoil (Briggs and Burke 2002: 96–102). In England it was the English Revolution (1640) – more commonly known as the English Civil War – and in America, the American Revolution (1776), and similarly in France, the French Revolution (1789).

In addition to oral communication in the form of speeches, sermons and plays, the print media also played a key role in these conflicts through the release of pamphlets, newspapers and books. In England, a wide range of publications that were critical of state censorship and which defended press freedom were produced by small-scale printers. Two of the more famous publications in this vein are William Walwyn's *The Compassionate Samaritane* (1644) and John Milton's *Areopagitica* in 1644 (Briggs and Burke 2002: 89; Keane 1991: 8–9).

In France, prior to and during the French Revolution, a number of publications emerged supporting calls for a free press. They included an adaptation of Milton's *Areopagitica*, published in France in 1788. The titles of other publications, such as Marie-Joseph Chénier's *Denunciation of the Inquisitors of Thought* (1789), and Jacques-Pierre Brissot's *Memoir on the Need to Free the Press* (1789), also capably conveyed their intentions (Briggs and Burke 2002: 98–9). In America, it was only after violent popular opposition to the imposition of a stamp tax on pamphlets, newspapers and advertising that this financial penalty was removed in 1766.

Following the American Revolution, the notion of a free press was embedded in the First Amendment of the Bill of Rights passed by the American Congress in 1791: 'Congress shall make no law respecting an establishment of religion, or prohibiting the free exercise thereof; or abridging the freedom of speech or of the press' (cited in Briggs and Burke 2002: 193). However, a lack of clarity about the meaning of this statement has prompted much public discussion since. It has also led to intervention by the courts, who have been asked to adjudicate on matters of free expression.

Some argue that the First Amendment has not produced a better media system. Moreover, that it has further advantaged already privileged individuals and commercial corporations rather than 'ordinary' working people. For example, Curran (1997a: 367) asserts that the First Amendment 'has enabled publishers to resist state laws giving victims of press attacks the right of reply, and . . . has been invoked against residual public service obligations on the grounds that these infringe the free speech rights of TV station owners'.

In Britain, it is generally understood that the press achieved their freedom in the mid-nineteenth century. The key events are seen to be the lapsing of the 1695 Licensing Act, the lifting of stamp duties – known as the 'taxes on knowledge' – in 1855, and the ending in 1861 of excise duties on paper (Briggs and Burke 2002: 51; Curran 1997b: 7). There is, though, a contrary view about this particular interpretation of press freedom. Amongst others, Curran (1997b: 7–9) takes issue with this version, arguing that it was the introduction of advertising and the flowering of market forces that ultimately proved to be a more effective means of censorship rather than the earlier legalistic measures imposed by the state. The same forces also resulted in the demise of a previously active and widely read radical press in Britain.

It was as a result of this supposed freedom of the press in the mid-nineteenth century that the notion of a 'Fourth Estate' emerged, the other three estates being the church, judiciary and the commons (Allan 1999: 195). Underpinning the idea of a Fourth Estate was an acknowledgement of the independence and political importance of the press, and a belief that journalists acted as a voice for the public and were accountable to that public. With the introduction of broadcasting in the twentieth century, there was a brief but unsuccessful attempt to describe this new media sector as the Fifth Estate (Briggs and Burke 2002: 192).

Concepts such as 'freedom of the press', 'freedom of speech' and the 'Fourth Estate' have informed – and continue to underpin – what is variously referred to as the liberal theory of the press, or liberal press theory. This theory holds that 'the freedom of the press is rooted in the freedom to publish in the free market' (Curran 1997c: 287). Liberal theory argues that the press – and mass media in general – serve democracy in three ways: they play a key role in informing the electorate; they provide a means of overseeing and 'checking' on government – the watchdog role; they articulate public opinion (Curran 1997c: 287).

While a liberal theory of the press still holds considerable sway amongst the wider populace, as indicated above, it has also been subjected to withering criticism (see, for example, Curran and Seaton 1997; Curran 2005). Such critiques tend to be underpinned by a political economy perspective (see Chapter 12 in this book), which is informed by the work of Karl Marx. Essentially, a Marxist perspective holds that as mass media organisations are owned and operated by ruling, or elite groups, in society, the individuals running them will ensure that these institutions reinforce the dominant ideology in a way that appears to be 'common sense', thus helping maintain class inequalities (Allan 1999: 51).

What, then, were the arguments that fuelled and reinforced the ideas of free speech and a free press, and which eventually led to the articulation of a liberal theory of the press that is still used to defend media systems in democracies around the world? Keane (1991: 10–20) identifies four distinguishable but overlapping arguments. Each one can be viewed as constituting a defence of the liberty of the press. The first is described as a *theological* defence. This line of argument is discernible in a number of published sources, but particularly so in Milton's *Areopagitica* (see above), where he 'pleaded for a free press in order to let the love of God and the "free and knowing spirit" flourish' (p. 11).

Essentially, Milton believed that it was not only unworkable and inefficient to impose comprehensive restrictions on the press, but it was also 'repugnant because it stifles the exercise of individual's freedom to think, to exercise discretion and to opt for a Christian life' (p. 12). Milton was, though, against absolute freedom of the press, believing that 'popish' books should be banned, and that the law should be used to deal with abuses and licentiousness.

The second argument about press freedom is not informed by religious beliefs but is based on the idea of the *rights of individuals*. Its philosophical basis is traceable in publications by John Locke (*Epistola de tolerantia ad clarissimum virum*, 1689), Mathew Tindal (*Reasons Against Restraining the Press*, 1704) and John Asgill (*An Essay for the Press*, 1712). This type of argument became more popular after the American and French Revolutions with the wide availability of controversial publications by writers such as Tom Paine (*Rights of Man*, 1791–92) and Mary Wollstonecraft (*Vindication of the Rights of Woman*, 1792). In effect, this argument holds that individuals not only have the right to decide for themselves on matters of politics or religion, but also have the right to express their views freely, whether or not such views accord with those of government (Keane 1991: 13).

The third argument rests on the theory of *utilitarianism* (Keane 1991: 15). The basis of this philosophical standpoint was evident in publications by William Goodwin (*Enquiry Concerning Political Justice*, 1798), James Mill (*Liberty of the Press*, 1811) and in most detail by Jeremy Bentham (*On the Liberty of the Press and Public Discussion*, 1820–21). Bentham is renowned for coining the slogan, 'the greatest happiness for the greatest number', which is thought to epitomise utilitarianism (Marshall 1998: 685).

When used in defence of the liberty of the press, a utilitarianism perspective considers state censorship unjustified because it maintains the power of despotic governments, it nullifies public opinion which, in turn, reduces the happiness of the populace. A free press is considered an 'ally of happiness' because it acts as a counterweight to government, helping to ensure that laws are only be introduced if they are considered to be of benefit to the majority, and also help prevent corruption in the bureaucracy (Keane 1991: 16).

Keane identifies the fourth defence of press freedom as resting on the *attainment of truth*. This argument assumes that truth can only emerge as a result of unrestricted discussion amongst citizens. Early authors hinting at this defence of press freedom include Leonard Busher (*Religion's Peace: Or, a plea for Liberty of Conscience*, 1614) and Joseph Priestly (*An Essay on the First Principles of Government; and on the Nature of Political, Civil and Religious Liberty*, 1768), but the most substantial and influential publication was John Stuart Mill's *On Liberty* in 1859. It is from this text that the reading for this chapter has been drawn.

INTRODUCTION TO THE READING

The selected reading, 'Of the liberty of thought and discussion', is an abridged version of the second chapter of J.S. Mill's *On Liberty*. Published in 1859, *On Liberty* comprised five chapters. The abridged extract used for this reading first appeared in *A Journalism Reader* (1997), edited by Michael Bromley and Tom O'Malley. J.S. Mill's article is located immediately after one by his father, James Mill, entitled 'Liberty of the Press'. Bromley and O'Malley (1997: 1) include both these works in order to provide an insight into the historical development of journalism and the ideas that informed and underpinned its practice.

Bromley and O'Malley (1997) set out a further reason for including the work of both these authors. That is, the ideas of Mill senior and Mill junior are thought to represent the 'high minded, high Liberal theory' that was indicative of 'nineteenth century philosophising about the relationship between press, government, liberty and truth' (Bromley and O'Malley 1997: 2). Somewhat ironically, while J.S. Mill had numerous articles published in the press, he was rather disdainful about the practice of journalism as this extract suggests:

> In France the best thinkers and writers of the nation write in the journals and direct public opinion; but our daily and weekly writers are the lowest hacks of literature which, when it is a trade, is the vilest and most degrading of all trades because more of affectation and hypocrisy and more subservience to the baser feelings of others are necessary for carrying it on, than for any other trade, from that of the brothel-keeper up.
>
> *(Elliott, cited in Allan 1999: 21; see also Briggs and Burke 2002: 203)*

Born in London in 1806, John Stuart Mill, or J.S. Mill as he became known, died in France in 1873. He was educated at home by his father, James Mill, a respected philosopher and historian, with the assistance of Jeremy Bentham (see above), a close friend of the family. Although a practising journalist, J.S. Mill is best known as a philosopher and political economist, and is generally regarded as playing a major role in shaping thought and political discourse in the nineteenth century (Ryan 1969: 43). He was also a Liberal Member of Parliament for the (London) City and Westminster constituency between 1856 and 1868.

Of his many publications, J.S. Mill is best known for the following: *The Principles of Political Economy: With some of their applications to social philosophy* (1848); *On Liberty* (1859); *Utilitarianism* (1863); *The Subjection of Women* (1869); *Three Essays on Religion* (1874). Unlike many celebrities today, his autobiography, *Autobiography of John Stuart Mill* (1873), was not published until the year of his death.

The selected extract from 'Of the Liberty of Thought and Discussion' requires close and repeated reading and, if possible, you are encouraged to read the text in full at some point. As Bromley and O'Malley (1997: 2) point out, when J.S. Mill published *On Liberty* he was writing for middle and upper-class readers who were used to coping with 'tightly reasoned, allusive argument'. Aside from the depth and density of argument, the style of writing adds another hurdle for the reader, as it is indicative of the period in which it was written. Nonetheless, this work by J.S. Mill is considered to be the 'most influential and secular' defence of the liberty of the press in the nineteenth century (Keane 1991: 17).

1

J.S. Mill

Of the liberty of thought and discussion

The time, it is hoped, is gone by when any defence would be necessary of the 'liberty of the press' as one of the securities against corrupt or tyrannical government.[1] No argument, we may suppose, can now be needed against permitting a legislature or an executive, not identified in interest with the people, to prescribe opinions to them and determine what doctrines or what arguments they shall be allowed to hear . . . Let us suppose, therefore, that the government is entirely at one with the people, and never thinks of exerting any power of coercion unless in agreement with what it conceives to be their voice. But I deny the right of the people to exercise such coercion, either by themselves or by their government. The power itself is illegitimate. The best government has no more title to it than the worst. It is as noxious, or more noxious, when exerted in accordance with public opinion than when in opposition to it. If all mankind minus one were of one opinion, mankind would be no more justified in silencing that one person than he, if he had the power, would be justified in silencing mankind. Were an opinion a personal possession of no value except to the owner, if to be obstructed in the enjoyment of it were simply a private injury, it would make some difference whether the injury was inflicted only on a few persons or on many. But the peculiar evil of silencing the expression of an opinion is that it is robbing the human race, posterity as well as the existing generation – those who dissent from the opinion, still more than those who hold it. If the opinion is right, they are deprived of the opportunity of exchanging error for truth; if wrong, they lose, what is almost as great a benefit, the clearer perception and livelier impression of truth produced by its collision with error . . .

1. This extract is from the *Essay On Liberty*, which was published in 1859 and which has subsequently been widely regarded, particularly in the United States of America, as a founding statement of the liberal journalism ethos with its foregrounding of the rights to individual freedom, especially the freedom of speech. Mill was generally disdainful of journalism, yet he wrote hundreds of newspaper articles.

NOTES

 1

Context

Although Mill refers to the 'liberty of the press' in this opening sentence, the discussion that follows is not in any way concerned with industrial aspects of the press. Rather, it concentrates on making a case for valuing expressions of opinion in order that truth can emerge.

In the first chapter of *On Liberty*, Mill explains that what he means by liberty of thought is the liberty to speak and write. He also acknowledges that while these liberties exist in many countries, it is not always the case that the philosophical and practical grounds on which they rest are clearly understood by opinion leaders or the wider populace.

Content

The opening sentence expresses one of the key elements of liberal press theory: that is, the role of the press, or media, as a watchdog which keeps a check on the state. However, Mill's key point in this opening section rests on a view that to silence the opinion of just one person is unacceptable and unhealthy, because it deprives individuals and the wider society – now and into the future – in two ways. First, because the opinion may in fact be true. Secondly, because even if the opinion proves to be false it enables a 'stronger' truth to emerge, because of what he neatly describes as a 'collision with error'.

Structure

You may already have noticed how Mill's structuring of sentences differs from other readings in this book. Particularly noticeable are the number of phrases, or clauses, that make up some sentences. While this allows the author constantly to qualify, or justify, his arguments, it can be disruptive for the reader.

Writing Style

Note how Mill writes in the first person in this opening section. This reflects his intention to influence debate on matters about which he had very strong feelings.

READING

2

We can never be sure that the opinion we are endeavouring to stifle is a false opinion; and if we were sure, stifling it would be an evil still.

First, the opinion which it is attempted to suppress by authority may possibly be true. Those who desire to suppress it, of course, deny its truth; but they are not infallible. They have no authority to decide the question for all mankind and exclude every other person from the means of judging. To refuse a hearing to an opinion because they are sure that it is false is to assume that their certainty is the same thing as absolute certainty. All silencing of discussion is an assumption of infallibility. Its condemnation may be allowed to rest on this common argument, not the worse for being common.

Unfortunately for the good sense of mankind, the fact of their fallibility is far from carrying the weight in their practical judgment which is always allowed to it in theory; for while everyone well knows himself to be fallible, few think it necessary to take any precautions against their own fallibility, or admit the supposition that any opinion of which they feel very certain may be one of the examples of the error to which they acknowledge themselves to be liable . . . Nor is his faith in this collective authority at all shaken by his being aware that other ages, countries, sects, churches, classes, and parties have thought, and even now think, the exact reverse. He devolves upon his own world the responsibility of being in the right against the dissentient worlds of other people; and it never troubles him that mere accident has decided which of these numerous worlds is the object of his reliance, and the same causes which make him a churchman in London would have made him a Buddhist or Confucian in Peking. Yet it is as evident in itself, as any amount of argument can make it, that ages are no more infallible than individuals – every age having held many opinions which subsequent ages have deemed not only false but absurd; and it is as certain that many opinions, now general, will be rejected by future ages, as it is that many, once general, are rejected by the present . . .

If even the Newtonian philosophy were not permitted to be questioned, mankind could not feel as complete assurance of its truth as they do now. The beliefs which we have most warrant for have no safeguard to rest on but a standing invitation to the whole world to prove them unfounded. If the challenge is not accepted, or is accepted and the attempt fails, we are far enough from certainty still, but we have done the best that the existing state of human reason admits of . . .

Strange it is that men should admit the validity of the arguments for free discussion, but object to their being 'pushed to an extreme', not seeing that unless the reasons are good for an extreme case, they are not good for any case. Strange they should imagine that they are not assuming infallibility when they acknowledge that there should be free discussion on all subjects which can possibly be doubtful, but think that some particular principle or doctrine should be forbidden to be questioned because it is so certain, that is, because they are certain that it is certain. To call any proposition certain, while there is anyone who would deny its certainty if permitted, but who is not permitted, is to assume that we ourselves, and those who agree with us, are the judges of certainty, and judges without hearing the other side . . .

2 Content

Mill opens this section by arguing that it is not easy to know whether an opinion is false, but even if it is, there are good reasons why it should not be stifled. He then offers three reasons to support this assertion before bringing the argument to a close. First, those who deny the truth of an opinion are, by implication, asserting their own infallibility, but their own certainty does not equate with 'absolute certainty'. Also, those denying the validity of an opinion cannot speak for all. As a result, the opinion should not be stifled. What does he mean by the final sentence in the second paragraph which relates to the silencing of discussion: 'Its condemnation may be allowed to rest on this common argument, not the worse for being common'?

To help support his second reason for not stifling opinion, Mill engages the distinction between theory and practice. While people know that they can be fallible, they still find it difficult to accept the possibility that one of their own strongly held opinions may be wrong. As Mill points out, this is still the case even when people realise that over time and across continents, there is ample evidence of previously held opinions later turning out to be misinformed.

Mill's third reason for arguing that we should be prepared to confront beliefs that we hold not to be true is because our view only becomes stronger once it has been subjected to scrutiny and critical appraisal by others. Even then, according to Mill, we can never be certain that such an opinion is the truth, but we can argue that everything possible has been done to test its validity.

Mill closes the argument by recapping on men's lack of awareness about their own fallibility on the matter of free discussion. To paraphrase, Mill asserts that while the idea of free discussion is accepted, it comes with conditions. That is, free discussion is not possible when it comes to opinions being expressed that are contrary to the pre-existing certainties held by men on such matters. Essentially, Mill is questioning how we can argue that something is certain unless we hear and understand opposing views.

Writing Style

Note how Mill only refers to men and, as was evident in the introduction to this reading, most of the leading commentators on press freedom were men, except for Mary Wollstonecraft. However, in this instance, 'men' can be understood to mean the population as a whole.

Context

Having just raised the issue of gender, it should be noted that Mill is acknowledged as someone who wrote on the role of women and the family. His main text on these matters was *The Subjection of Women* (1869), which is considered an important work in the history of feminism. Also, during his time as a Liberal Member of Parliament, Mill fought hard to obtain the vote for women, but this did not occur until 1918 (Ryan 1969: 44).

READING

3

Let us now pass to the second division of the argument, and dismissing the supposition that any of the received opinions may be false, let us assume them to be true and examine into the worth of the manner in which they are likely to be held when their truth is not freely and openly canvassed. However unwillingly a person who has a strong opinion may admit the possibility that his opinion may be false, he ought to be moved by the consideration that, however true it may be, if it is not fully, frequently, and fearlessly discussed, it will be held as a dead dogma, not a living truth.

There is a class of persons (happily not quite so numerous as formerly) who think it enough if a person assents undoubtingly to what they think true, though he has no knowledge whatever of the grounds of the opinion and could not make a tenable defence of it against the most superficial objections . . . This is not knowing the truth. Truth, thus held, is but one supersitition the more, accidentally clinging to the words which enunciate a truth . . .

Whatever people believe, on subjects on which it is of the first importance to believe rightly, they ought to be able to defend against at least the common objections . . . On every subject on which difference of opinion is possible, the truth depends on a balance to be struck between two sets of conflicting reasons. Even in natural philosophy, there is always some other explanation possible of the same facts; some geocentric theory instead of heliocentric, some phlogiston instead of oxygen; and it has to be shown why that other theory cannot be the true one; and until this is shown, and until we know how it is shown, we do not understand the grounds of our opinion. But when we turn to subjects infinitely more complicated, to morals, religion, politics, social relations, and the business of life, three-fourths of the arguments for every disputed opinion consist in dispelling the appearances which favour some opinion different from it . . . He who knows only his own side of the case knows little of that. His reasons may be good, and no one may have been able to refute them. But if he is equally unable to refute the reasons on the opposite side, if he does not so much as know what they are, he has no ground for preferring either opinion . . . Nor is it enough that he should hear the arguments of adversaries from his own teachers, presented as they state them, and accompanied by what they offer as refutations. This is not the way to do justice to the arguments or bring them into real contact with his own mind. He must be able to hear them from persons who actually believe them, who defend them in earnest and do their very utmost for them. He must know them in their most plausible and persuasive form; he must feel the whole force of the difficulty which the true view of the subject has to encounter and dispose of, else he will never really possess himself of the portion of truth which meets and removes that difficulty. Ninety-nine in a hundred of what are called educated men are in this condition even of those who can argue fluently for their opinions. Their conclusion may be true, but it might be false for anything they know; they have never thrown themselves into the mental position of those who think differently from them, and considered what such persons may have to say; and, consequently, they do not, in any proper sense of the word, know the doctrine which they themselves profess . . . So essential is this discipline to a real understanding of moral and human subjects that, if opponents of all-important truths do not exist, it is indispensable to imagine them and supply them with the strongest arguments which the most skilful devil's advocate can conjure up . . . If the teachers of mankind are to be cognisant of all that they ought to know, everything must be free to be written and published without restraint.

3 Content

Having established that all opinions should be aired, including 'wrong' ones, Mill outlines here why it is in the interests of those who believe their opinions to be infallible to hear and understand contrary views. He encapsulates this nicely by saying that if people do not involve themselves in such a process their views might best be described as 'dead dogma' rather than 'living truth'. He defends this argument by stating that it is necessary to know why we believe something to be true, and also to be able to mount an informed defence in the face of opposing views. This requires knowing and understanding the 'common objections' that might be put forward. In Mill's view, 'truth depends on a balance to be struck between two sets of conflicting reasons', and he recognises that the methods used to ascertain truth are different in the sciences and humanities.

For example, in the area of politics and social relations, as opposed to natural philosophy, Mill argues that establishing truth is as much about dismantling opposing views as being able to marshal and present one's own argument. His 'clincher' is that if opposing views are not known, where is the basis for preferring one 'truth' over others? He goes on to argue that it is not enough just to hear opposing views filtered through a teacher, for example, but in order to fully understand and feel the intensity of any contrary opinion, it is essential to hear it from a genuine advocate or protagonist. Mill asserts that virtually all 'educated men' have not had this experience and do not, therefore, have the 'portion of truth' that comes from such encounters. This leads him to conclude that these 'educated men' cannot 'in any proper sense of the word, know the doctrine which they themselves profess'.

At least four questions arise from the argument that Mill sets out here. First, who is he referring to when he uses the term 'educated men'? Secondly, as Mill chooses not to define some of the key words that are essential to his argument, how do you think Mill understands the idea of 'truth'? How might he define it? Thirdly, how do you respond to the view that in order to get as close to the truth as possible, it is essential to hear the full force of opposing views from those who hold them? Fourthly, to what extent does this latter argument have any currency when considered in relation to the organisation of contemporary mass media and the practices of journalists and news reporters?

Structure

Note again how Mill begins with an initial proposition, or assertion, and then proceeds to explore, explain and illustrate, sometimes by the use of examples. You will also have become aware of the way in which Mill constructs his closely argued sentences. Furthermore, note how Mill rarely uses additional sources to support his argument. Obviously one reason for this is that Mill was one of a small number of writers who had begun to think critically about such matters and to disseminate their views in published form.

Writing Style

We need to remember that this text was published in 1859. Hence, Mill can talk without hesitation about a singular notion of truth (and untruth), certainty (and uncertainty), fallibility (and infallibility) in a way that would be quickly challenged today.

READING

4

If, however, this mischievous operation of the absence of free discussion, when the received opinions are true, were confined to leaving men ignorant of the grounds of those opinions, it might be thought that this, if an intellectual, is no moral evil and does not affect the worth of the opinions, regarded in their influence on the character. The fact, however, is that not only the grounds of the opinion are forgotten in the absence of discussion, but too often the meaning of the opinion itself. The words which convey it cease to suggest ideas, or suggest only a small portion of those they were originally employed to communicate. Instead of a vivid conception and a living belief, there remain only a few phrases retained by rote; or, if any part, the shell and husk only of the meaning is retained, the finer essence being lost . . .

5

It still remains to speak of one of the principal causes which make diversity of opinion advantageous, and will continue to do so until mankind shall have entered a stage of intellectual advancement which at present seems at an incalculable distance. We have hitherto considered only two possibilities: that the received opinion may be false, and some other opinion, consequently, true; or that, the received opinion being true, a conflict with the opposite error is essential to a clear apprehension and deep feeling of its truth. But there is a commoner case than either of these: when the conflicting doctrines, instead of one being true and the other false, share the truth between them, and the nonconforming opinion is needed to supply the remainder of the truth of which the received doctrine embodies only a part. Popular opinions, on subjects not palpable to sense, are often true, but seldom or never the whole truth. They are a part of the truth, sometimes a greater, sometimes a smaller part, but exaggerated, distorted, and disjointed from the truths by which they ought to be accompanied and limited. Heretical opinions, on the other hand, are generally some of these suppressed and neglected truths, bursting the bonds which kept them down, and either seeking reconciliation with the truth contained in the common opinion, or fronting it as enemies, and setting themselves up, with similar exclusiveness, as the whole truth . . . Even progress, which ought to superadd, for the most part only substitutes one partial and incomplete truth for another; improvement consisting chiefly in this, that the new fragment of truth is more wanted, more adapted to the needs of the time than that which it displaces. Such being the partial character of prevailing opinions, even when resting on a true foundation, every opinion which embodies somewhat of the portion of truth which the common opinion omits ought to be considered precious, with whatever amount of error and confusion that truth may be blended . . .

4 Content

Here, Mill argues that the knowledge of 'teachers of mankind' is dependent on there being no restraint on free expression, and he then recalls the earlier notion of opinion as either 'dead dogma' or 'living truth'. Without discussion which involves engaging with differing views, Mill believes that both the grounds that helped form an opinion and its meaning may be lost. What does Mill mean here by the 'mischievous operation of the absence of free discussion'?

Writing Style

As this type of philosophical writing requires constant qualifications, it is helpful if the author avoids lengthy and complex sentences. So, you are advised to avoid constructing a sentence like the one here that begins, 'If, however . . .'.

Yet, Mill should be applauded for his insightful use of analogy and cogent expression: for example, where he describes the remaining remnants of meaning as 'shell and husk', and earlier when he uses the phrase 'exchanging error for truth' as a means of conveying the process taking place.

5 Content

The main point being made here is about the reality of part truths. Mill argues that it may often be the case that rather than there being an opinion that is wholly true or wholly false, both may be part truths. For Mill, diversity of opinion only results from the exposure of every 'portion of truth' that is not currently considered to be part of 'common opinion'.

To what extent is the 'common opinion' described here similar, or different, to the notion of public opinion?

Context

Here, Mill introduces a key factor that is still used in discussions about the contemporary press and wider mass media. He was certainly correct in thinking that 'diversity of opinion' would continue to be an important issue well after his own lifetime.

Writing Style

In this section Mill provides all readers and writers with an example of a useful tactical ploy. That is, the way in which a quick rehearsal, or reminder, of previous ideas or issues can also be used as a mechanism to move the argument on to the next stage. He does this in the sentence beginning, 'We have hitherto considered . . .'. Is this a strategy that you use, or could use?

READING

6

Unless opinions favourable to democracy and to aristocracy, to property and to equality, to co-operation and to competition, to luxury and to abstinence, to sociality and to individuality, to liberty and discipline, and all the other standing antagonisms of practical life, are expressed with equal freedom and enforced and defended with equal talent and energy, there is no chance of both elements obtaining their due; one scale is sure to go up, and the other down. Truth, in the great practical concerns of life, is so much a question of the reconciling and combining of opposites that very few have minds sufficiently capacious and impartial to make the adjustment with an approach to correctness, and it has to be made by the rough process of a struggle between combatants fighting under hostile banners . . . Only through diversity of opinion is there, in the existing state of human intellect, a chance of fair play to all sides of truth. When there are persons to be found who form an exception to the apparent unanimity of the world on any subject, even if the world is in the right, it is always probable that dissentients have something worth hearing to say for themselves, and that truth would lose something by their silence . . .

The exclusive pretention made by a part of the truth to be the whole must and ought to be protested against; and if a reactionary impulse should make the protestors unjust in their turn, this one-sidedness, like the other, may be lamented but must be tolerated . . .

I do not pretend that the most unlimited use of the freedom of enunciating all possible opinions would put an end to the evils of religious or philosophical sectarianism . . . I acknowledge that the tendency of all opinions to become sectarian is not cured by the freest discussion, but is often heightened and exacerbated thereby; the truth which ought to have been, but was not, seen, being rejected all the more violently because proclaimed by persons regarded as opponents. But it is not on the impassioned partisan, it is on the calmer and more disinterested bystander, that this collision of opinions works its salutary effect. Not the violent conflict between parts of the truth, but the quiet suppression of half of it, is the formidable evil; there is always hope when people are forced to listen to both sides; it is when they attend only to one that errors harden into prejudices, and truth itself ceases to have the effect of truth by being exaggerated into falsehood . . .

6   Content

Mill sets out here what he sees as 'the great practical concerns of life', asserting that debates on such matters need to air all sides of an argument and to do so vigorously. It is, he argues, as a result of such combative debate that truth emerges. In the course of such debates, and in keeping with his central thesis, Mill stresses the need to pay attention at all times to those views that are thought to be in the minority. This is because those that dissent from the majority may also have something to contribute, or as Mill would put it, a certain portion of the truth to offer.

The latter point offers an important insight which retains currency today. This is because debates about resources and/or policy which involve people from a variety of ethnic groups can often become heated, and attract wide coverage in the mass media. Mill accepts that while free expression is unlikely to change the position of warring parties and may even exacerbate and heighten the claims being made by opposing factions, the immediate beneficiary of such 'collision of opinions' is the 'disinterested bystander'. Mill contends that 'the formidable evil' is not the airing of what may be two partial truths, but the possibility that one side's opinion may be suppressed.

First of all, what is your response to Mill's view that truth comes about 'by the rough process of a struggle between combatants fighting under hostile banners'? Secondly, and thinking particularly about the idea of press freedom, explain why this argument is, or is not, relevant in contemporary society.

Context

Writing in the nineteenth century, Mill favoured free expression and, in doing so, recognised the possibility that it could amplify the voices of religious and other sectarian groups. Whereas John Milton (see above) adopted a different position in the seventeenth century, arguing against absolute freedom of the press and recognising the need for regulation in certain instances.

READING

7

We have now recognised the necessity to the mental well-being of mankind (on which all their other well-being depends) of freedom of opinion, and freedom of the expression of opinion, on four distinct grounds, which we will now briefly recapitulate:

First, if any opinion is compelled to silence, that opinion may, for aught we can certainly know, be true. To deny this is to assume our own infallibility.

Secondly, though the silenced opinion be an error, it may, and very commonly does, contain a portion of the truth; and since the general or prevailing opinion on any subject is rarely or never the whole truth, it is only by the collision of adverse opinions that the remainder of the truth has any chance of being supplied.

Thirdly, even if the received opinion be not only true, but the whole truth; unless it is suffered to be, and actually is, vigorously and earnestly contested, it will, by most of those who receive it, be held in the manner of a prejudice, with little comprehension or feeling of its rational grounds. And not only this, but fourthly, the meaning of the doctrine itself will be in danger of being lost or enfeebled, and deprived of its vital effect on the character and conduct: the dogma becoming a mere formal profession, inefficacious for good, but cumbering the ground and preventing the growth of any real and heartfelt conviction from reason or personal experience.

7   Content

Mill ends, as you can see, by recapping on the four distinct grounds that he has provided in support of the argument for freedom of opinion and the freedom to express an opinion.

REFLECTING ON THE READING

In reflecting on the reading, three issues emerge that warrant attention. The first requires consideration of how J.S. Mill understands the notion of 'truth'. The second necessitates a review of the limitations, or 'blindspots', of liberal press theory. The third demands that we consider why the language associated with a theory developed in the eighteenth century has recently re-emerged in public debates about media policy.

When J.S. Mill was writing about 'freedom of speech' and 'freedom of the press' he didn't appear to consider the possibility that the discovery of truth would *not* be at the heart of all individual expression, whether spoken or written. For example, Keane (1991: 19) notes how 'instances of artistic, ethical and political expression' may be intended to 'entertain, shock, praise, condemn or inspire' rather than be employed to search out, or ascertain, truth.

To some extent we still experience debates concerning such matters, and particularly so in terms of the claims and counter-claims about whether media 'entertainment' genres contribute to, or assist with, truth-seeking. The following observation by James Curran addresses a similar theme, but focuses on a media system rather than a specific genre. Curran (2005: 136) asserts that it is the 'market-driven, entertainment-centred' American media system that is responsible for leaving 'large numbers of its citizens politically ignorant' (see also Wayne 2003: 94).

Concern about the pursuit of truth by public service or commercial media operators, whether by way of 'serious' or 'playful' content, brings to attention another criticism that has been levelled against J.S. Mill. That is, he believed there was one truth, whereas the predominant view today would be more likely to argue for 'a plurality of immeasurable truths' (Keane 1991: 20–21).

The idea of truth, or truths, is taken up by Stevenson (2002). He draws on the work of John Fiske (1989a, 1989b) to argue against those who demand that news bulletins need to be 'more accurate and objective', because these sorts of requests simply act to reinforce the views of those in positions of power. Instead, he suggests, 'a more democratic form of journalism would seek to ironise truth claims by seeking to reveal the ways in which they are socially and historically produced' (Stevenson 2002: 93).

In contemporary society we are further reminded about the existence of different forms of 'truth' by the interventions of a vast army of public relations professionals and 'spin doctors'. Their role is to persuade others about the veracity of a particular 'truth' in the course of pursuing identified political and/or economic goals (see, for example, Bakir and Barlow 2007; Franklin 2004).

On the limitations of liberal press theory, Keane refers to a gap in the nineteenth century between the utopian ideal and the reality of a 'limited-circulation, harassed and deeply corrupted press' (1991: 35). Five 'internal blindspots' of the theory are identified, which its advocates either overlooked or failed to recognise. First, there was a preoccupation with the possibility of external censorship – by the state – but little recognition that the structure and nature of the industry could result in self-censorship, both by organisations and individuals (p. 35). Secondly, there was a naivety in the view that communications media could replicate the intimacy and directness of the face-to-face interaction that was possible in the Greek *polis* (p. 38). Thirdly, the matter of representation was not fully considered, in the sense that in large-scale societies it is inevitable that at some point someone will speak on behalf of others, and all opinions just cannot be fully re-presented in the public domain (p. 43).

The fourth 'blindspot' relates to the view that private ownership of the means of communication was essential for freedom of communication, and that the market was envisaged as an unbiased arena in which public opinions circulated freely (Keane 1991: 45). In reality, the liberty of the press was curtailed as a result of market competition, which resulted in the emergence of a small number of 'media barons' in the first half of the twentieth century, and the later creation of a few transnational media conglomerates which had achieved a global reach by the early years of the twenty-first century (see, for example, Curran and Seaton 1997; Thussu 2006). A fifth 'blindspot' is suggested because these avid 'defenders of a free press' proclaimed their right to subject all other views and opinions to critical scrutiny, but were most reluctant to be questioned themselves, simply assuming 'their ability to know everything, to refute their opponents and concretely to resolve all differences' (p. 50).

Finally, to what extent does the work of J.S. Mill and early modern liberal press theory have any relevance in the first decade of the twenty-first century? Curran (2005: 122) deplores and regrets our continuing reliance on classical liberal theory for an understanding of the press and wider mass media in contemporary society, and rigorously dismantles the popular arguments that are trotted out to defend the theory. Yet, his analysis confirms the re-emergence of much of the language that was associated with the development of liberal press theory three centuries ago. Today, market liberals speak of the need for 'freedom' and 'choice', whether this relates to the purchase of food, clothes, leisure activities or media products.

Moreover, we are constantly reminded that an era of 'scarcity' and 'regulation' has ended, and that this has resulted from the introduction of new information and communication technologies which have been enabled by digitisation. These new technologies now provide 'pull', as well as 'push', audio-visual options, and enable access to a myriad of education, information and entertainment resources. However, this requires that people have the disposable income necessary to maintain and replace the associated hardware and software, and have the cultural resources to maximise the opportunities enabled by these new technologies (see, for example, Murdock and Golding 2005).

The language of 'freedom of speech' and 'freedom to publish' now takes place in the context of the internet, with assertions from those in power that as we can all be publishers and broadcasters (see Chapter 24), there is no need to fear the power and reach of large transnational media conglomerates. However, the number of channels is wrongly imagined as equating with an equivalent plurality of views, and diversity of ownership decreases as a result of the mergers and takeovers that occur not just in nation-states but increasingly across the globe.

In such a climate, state-sponsored, or state-protected, public service broadcasters are subjected to wide-ranging attacks by market liberals because, in a variety of ways, these media institutions are thought to stifle individual choice and restrict the opportunities for the expansion of commercially funded media. The same critics argue that market competition is the only way to eliminate state interference and to ensure press and broadcasting freedom. In this sense, parallels can be drawn between the era of J.S. Mill and the contemporary period.

In the former period, state regulation and censorship of the press – and, therefore, free speech – were seen to be liberated once the 'taxes of knowledge' were removed. In the current era, advocates of liberal press theory argue that it is only when state-supported public service media monopolies are abolished that we will 'enter an age of full "liberty of the press"' (Keane 1991: 62).

Key terms to explore

Liberty of the press; tyrannical government; diversity of opinion; received doctrine; heretical opinion; sectarian; capacious; dogma.

Key writers who are mentioned

Isaac Newton.

RECOMMENDED READING

Curran, J. and Seaton, J. (2009) *Power Without Responsibility: The press and broadcasting in Britain*, 7th edition. London: Routledge.

First section provides a detailed account of press history in the United Kingdom, including discussions about press freedom, industrialisation, press barons, regulation, and consolidation of ownership.

Curran, J. (2005) 'Mediations of democracy', in Curran, J. and Gurevitch, M. (eds) *Mass Media and Society*, 4th edition. London: Arnold.

This account offers a stinging critique of liberal press theory. Three key democratic functions of the mass media are identified and then subjected to close and critical analysis.

Keane, J. (1991) *The Media and Democracy*, Cambridge: Polity Press.

Examines the relationship between the media and democracy and challenges conventional assumptions of journalists, policymakers and academics.

CHAPTER 5

F.R. Leavis

Leavis, F.R. (1930) *Mass Civilisation and Minority Culture*, Cambridge: Minority Press.

INTRODUCTION TO F.R. LEAVIS

Frank Raymond Leavis, or F.R. Leavis as he is more commonly known, is renowned for his outspoken views on popular media and entertainment forms in the 1930s, and is identified with a form of literary criticism that gradually evolved into what we now know as cultural studies (Scannell 2007: 99; Turner 1996: 12).

The emergence of this new field of study occurred shortly after the Second World War (1939–45) through the work of Raymond Williams's *Culture and Society 1780–1950* (1958) and *The Long Revolution* (1961; see Chapter 17 in *this* book), and Richard Hoggart's *The Uses of Literacy* (1958). Moreover, it flourished when the Centre for Contemporary Cultural Studies was established at Birmingham University in 1964, with Richard Hoggart as the founding director (see Chapter 11). While Hoggart and Williams were protégés of Leavis, their backgrounds, interests and analytic approaches to the study of culture were quite different from those of their mentor (Scannell 2007: 103).

Leavis's primary interest was in literary texts and modern literature in particular. Essentially, his aim was to identify 'a canon of rich and rewarding texts' which could be returned to 'as privileged objects' (Turner 1996: 22). In this respect, the approach adopted by Hoggart and Williams differed markedly. They adapted Leavis's literary analysis into a form of textual analysis which could be used to 'read' other cultural texts, such as popular fiction and popular music (Turner 1996: 12).

Having been appropriated from literary studies, 'text' – previously restricted to a medium on which something was written – was now being used to describe the 'object or site of one's analysis', whether this was a film, television programme or a photograph (Turner 1996: 22). As the meaning of 'text' changed, so did the intentions of those doing the analysis. The newly adapted form of textual analysis involved 'examining the formal internal features and contextual location of a text to ascertain what readings or meanings' could be gained from it (Hartley 2002b: 227).

Leavis's views on culture have their origins in the work of Mathew Arnold. Arnold's major work, *Culture and Anarchy* (1869), argued that the rapid process of industrialism in the late eighteenth and nineteenth centuries had undermined traditional communities, and had resulted in an 'aesthetic barrenness of the culture' which had the potential for social unrest and from which 'social anarchy would ensue' (Scannell 2007: 97; Turner 1996: 39).

Leavis formed the view that it was the duty of an educated minority to decide on what constituted '"great" literature, "fine" art and "serious" music' and to preserve it for 'the masses' (Hartley 2002b: 52). Essentially, Leavis was suggesting that this group of intellectuals had to take a leading role in resisting 'the forces of the new mass civilisation' (Higgins 2001: 90).

The targets of Leavis's ire were the relatively newly established institutions of the popular press, advertising, film, broadcasting, and the emergence of popular fiction. For Leavis, these developments represented a dominant cultural trend which epitomised vulgarity, simplicity and commercialism, and which could be contrasted with the traditional, or 'organic', culture of earlier eras (Critcher 1979: 38; Turner 1996: 40; Williams 1958: 256–7). These changes in society challenged the way of life and the values that Leavis, his wife Queenie (1900–82) and other like-minded colleagues who comprised this intellectual minority held dear (Williams 1961: 250).

In seeking to defend these values in the face of an emerging popular culture, Leavis was invoking the earlier sentiments expressed by Mathew Arnold. In other words, Leavis was defending '"culture" against "anarchy"' (Hebdige 1982: 198). The extent of Leavis's influence is demonstrated by terms such as 'Leavism' and 'Leavisite' which soon entered the discourse.

Known primarily as a British literary critic and probably the most powerful influence on English studies since the 1930s (Bullock and Stallybrass 1977: 342), Leavis was born in Cambridge, England, and after postgraduate study took up a position in the English Faculty at Cambridge University where he spent most of his working life.

The titles of his many publications give an indication of the focus and scope of his work. They include: *Mass Civilization and Minority Culture* (1930) (from which the reading in this chapter is drawn); *New Bearings in English Poetry: A study of the contemporary situation* (1932b); *How to Teach Reading: A primer for Ezra Pound* (1932a); *Culture and Environment: The training of critical awareness* (with Denys Thompson) (1933); *The Great Tradition: George Eliot, Henry James, Joseph Conrad* (1948); *The Living Principle: 'English' as a discipline of thought* (1975).

Leavis also wrote with his wife Queenie who was also a published author in her own right. Both F.R. and Queenie Leavis had focused on aspects of 'mass culture' in the course of their doctoral studies. Leavis's PhD thesis was entitled 'Journalism and literature: a historical study of the relations between them in England', while Queenie's was, 'Fiction and the reading public', her focus being the popular novel (Scannell 2007: 200).

Along with Queenie and other colleagues, Leavis maintained his rage against 'mass culture' through the publication *Scrutiny* (1932–53), an English literary critical journal produced on a quarterly basis. The aim of the journal was to 'undertake an investigation of the contemporary world', going beyond literary criticism to engage 'with the movement of modern civilization', and F.R. Leavis was its chief editor for most of the journal's 20-year existence (Mulhern 1981: 47).

According to Mulhern, who produced a substantial historical and critical analysis of *Scrutiny*, the troubled economic and political circumstances in Britain in the decade following the First World War (1914–18) warranted such a journal (1981: 7, 47). Moreover, the space opened up by *Scrutiny* for the critical analysis of cultural institutions and practices was later occupied with great effect by the Centre for Contemporary Cultural Studies (Mulhern 1981: 329).

During the 1930s when Leavis was formulating his critique of British society, similar concerns about societal developments were being raised in Germany and America. But as Scannell (2007: 100) points out, in both the latter instances the critique occurred through the emerging discipline of sociology, whereas in Britain – where sociology had not yet emerged – the critique was launched through the newly emerging discipline of English studies.

For Leavis, 'literature was life affirming', while 'mass-civilization was life-denying', sentiments that, he argued, were evident in British literary texts which demonstrated 'serious, critical engagement with societal modernization and at the same time a redemptive resistance to it' (Scannell 2007: 100). While Leavis's elitist views about culture are now pretty unfashionable, they nevertheless remain influential.

INTRODUCTION TO THE READING

This reading is an abridged version of a pamphlet, *Mass Civilisation and Minority Culture* (from hereon *Mass Civilisation*), that was first published in 1930. The same pamphlet, but substantially developed and refined, provided the basis for *Culture and Environment: The training of critical awareness* (1933) which was co-authored with Denys Thompson, an avid supporter of Leavis and also one of his ex-students. Of interest is that Leavis's biographer, McKillop (1995), has suggested that Queenie Leavis also contributed to this publication, but was not listed as one of the authors (Scannell 2007: 101). Furthermore, the same publication apparently inspired the idea for Marshall McLuhan's (1951b) *The Mechanical Bride: Folklore of industrial man* (Stamps 1995: 110).

Mass Civilisation was, in effect, the blueprint for the journal *Scrutiny*, providing both its rationale and its editorial direction (Mulhern 1981: 34). While Scannell (2007: 100) is less than complimentary about *Mass Civilisation*, describing it as 'hastily put together', Raymond Williams acknowledges that it includes a 'body of detailed judgements' and 'an outline of history' (1958: 246). The purpose of *Mass Civilisation* was 'to argue that the traditional relationship between "civilisation" (the totality of social relations) and "culture" (the values on which "fine living" depended) had been strained to the point of rupture by the advance of "the machine"' (Mulhern 1981: 35). As you will see from the reading, 'the machine' – which might be suggested as a euphemism for technological innovations – is at the heart of Leavis's concerns.

As we noted in the introduction to this chapter, Leavis was inspired by the earlier work of Mathew Arnold. This is evident from the very start of the reading, which is launched with a quotation from Arnold's *Culture and Anarchy* (1869). You will also observe that shortly into the reading Leavis mentions a publication, *Middletown* (Lynd and Lynd 1929), which he then tends to rely on for much of the evidence that underpins his central thesis. 'Middletown' is a pseudonym for Muncie, a mid-western town in the American state of Illinois.

Essentially, *Middletown* illuminates the effects of industrialism in all the aspects of life of this small American community. Described as a 'classic study of social and cultural change' (Scannell 2007: 101), *Middletown* is also depicted as 'frightening', because much of its media – in particular advertisements and newspapers – are described as 'cheap and nasty' (Williams 1958: 253). For Seaton, *Middletown* captured a sense of the 'increasing isolation of individuals, social fragmentation, and the pervasiveness of the profit motive in a typical American town' (1997: 265).

While Mathew Arnold's concerns about culture resulted from the perceived impact of industrialism in the mid-nineteenth century, Leavis' anxieties centred on the emergence of various forms of mass media and the ways in which these powerful institutions posed a threat to society and culture in the first half of the twentieth century. Both Arnold's and Leavis's fears offer a useful reminder of the need to recognise both change and continuity when considering the introduction of new information and communication technologies.

Today, of course, it is the internet that attracts the doomsayers, and the current mantra is typified by references to 'dumbing down', which is either applied in blanket form to culture more generally, or is used derogatively to describe specific cultural texts and practices. Also, as notions of 'high culture' and 'low – or mass – culture' still abound, Leavis's basic premise in *Mass Civilisation* is still prescient, and the debate continues.

READING

1

"And all wise and experienced persons know, that bad and mean writings, of particular tendencies, will secure tenfold the number of readers of good and high productions. Popular authors cannot bear to admit or hear this. But how can it be otherwise? Will the uncultivated mind admire what delights the cultivated? Will the rude and coarse enjoy what is refined? Do the low endure the reasonings which justify subordination? Will the butterflies of fashion encourage any marks of distinction but their own gay colours?"

The Autobiography, Times, Opinions and
Contemporaries of Sir Egerton Brydges.

"All things are a flowing
Sage Heracleitus says;
But a tawdry cheapness
Shall outlast our days.

Even the Christian beauty
Defeats—after Samothrace;
We see τὸ καλόν
Decreed in the market place
       *   *   *   *   *

O bright Apollo
τίν ἀνδρα, τίν ἦρωα, τίνα, θεὸν,
What god, man or hero
Shall I place a tin wreath upon!"
   Hugh Selwyn Mauberley. *Ezra Pound.*

F.R. Leavis

Mass Civilisation and Minority Culture

"And this function is particularly important in our modern world, of which the whole civilisation is, to a much greater degree than the civilisation of Greece and Rome, mechanical and external, and tends constantly to become more so."

Culture and Anarchy. 1869.

Writing Style

As indicated in our introduction to the reading, Leavis begins with a quotation from Mathew Arnold's *Culture and Anarchy* (1869). The practice of beginning a piece of writing in this way is not unusual. What are the advantages and disadvantages of this approach?

READING

1

(continued)

FOR Matthew Arnold it was in some ways less difficult. I am not thinking of the so much more desperate plight of culture to-day,[1] but (it is not, at bottom, an unrelated consideration) of the freedom with which he could use such phrases as "the will of God" and "our true selves." To-day one must face problems of definition and formulation where Arnold could pass lightly on. When, for example, having started by saying that culture has always been in minority keeping, I am asked what I mean by "culture," I might (and do) refer the reader to *Culture and Anarchy*; but I know that something more is required.

2

In any period it is upon a very small minority that the discerning appreciation of art and literature depends: it is (apart from cases of the simple and familiar) only a few who are capable of unprompted, first-hand judgment. They are still a small minority, though a larger one, who are capable of endorsing such first-hand judgment by genuine personal response. The accepted valuations are a kind of paper currency based upon a very small proportion of gold. To the state of such a currency the possibilities of fine living at any time bear a close relation. There is no need to elaborate the metaphor: the nature of the relation is suggested well enough by this passage from Mr. I.A. Richards, which should by now be a *locus classicus*:

> "But it is not true that criticism is a luxury trade. The rearguard of Society cannot be extricated until the vanguard has gone further. Goodwill and intelligence are still too little available. The critic, we have said, is as much concerned with the health of the mind as any doctor with the health of the body. To set up as a critic is to set up as a judge of values. . . . For the arts are inevitably and quite apart from any intentions of the artist an appraisal of existence. Matthew Arnold, when he said that poetry is a criticism of life, was saying something so obvious that it is constantly overlooked. The artist is concerned with the record and perpetuation of the experiences which seem to him most worth having. For reasons which we shall consider . . . he is also the man who is most likely to have experiences of value to record. He is the point at which the growth of the mind shows itself."[2]

1. "The word, again, which we children of God speak, the voice which most hits our collective thought, the newspaper with the largest circulation in England, nay with the largest circulation in the whole world, is the *Daily Telegraph*!"—*Culture and Anarchy*.
2. *The Principles of Literary Criticism*, p. 61.

NOTES

 ## Content

The two quotations that precede the reading – and particularly the first one – offer an indication about Leavis's views on culture and the cultivated. Similarly, in asserting that 'culture has always been in minority keeping', Leavis provides a further clue as to his thinking on such matters.

Context

Would the third sentence still retain meaning today if we substituted Arnold's name for Leavis? Also, what is Leavis suggesting when he juxtaposes the *Daily Telegraph* and the *News of the World* in the footnote?

Content

Having established his basic premise that culture is the preserve of a minority, Leavis begins to imply what he means by 'minority'. Who do you think is included in this minority? What qualifications and/or characteristics are needed to become a member of this exclusive group?

Context

To support his argument, Leavis draws on the work of I.A. Richards, referring to it as a '*locus classicus*'. What does this mean and why is it in italics?

Richards was a significant figure in literary criticism whose publications, *Principles of Literary Criticism* (1924) and *Science and Poetry* (1926) evoked a sense of culture which was 'essentially a renewed definition of the importance of art to civilisation' (Williams 1958: 239). This is conveyed to some extent in the quotation from Richards that Leavis includes here. Richards, a literary critic, was a leading academic in the English Faculty at Cambridge University and a major influence on Leavis. For some while, Leavis also acted as a freelance for Richards, meaning that he did some teaching for him. 'Freelancer' was a term used to describe a lower level academic whose income was derived from fees paid by students who attended their classes (Mulhern 1981: 22).

The following quotation, taken from Richard's *Principles of Literary Criticism* (1924), confirms the considerable influence that he had on Leavis:

> With the increase of population the problem presented by the gulf between what is preferred by the majority and what is accepted as excellent by the most qualified opinion has become infinitely more serious and appears likely to become threatening in the near future. For many reasons standards are much more in need of defence than they used to be.

(*Richards 1924: 36, cited in Williams 1961: 240*)

Writing Style

Note the gendered text, which is also a feature of earlier eras and which remained a tendency through much of the twentieth century. Apropos this point, we already observed in the introduction to this chapter that Queenie Leavis, wife of F.R. Leavis, was a regular contributor to published pieces but not always acknowledged as one of the authors.

READING

3

This last sentence gives the hint for another metaphor. The minority capable not only of appreciating Dante, Shakespeare, Donne, Baudelaire, Hardy (to take major instances) but of recognising their latest successors constitute the consciousness of the race (or of a branch of it) at a given time. For such capacity does not belong merely to an isolated aesthetic realm: it implies responsiveness to theory as well as to art, to science and philosophy in so far as these may affect the sense of the human situation and of the nature of life. Upon this minority depends our power of profiting by the finest human experience of the past; they keep alive the subtlest and most perishable parts of tradition. Upon them depend the implicit standards that order the finer living of an age, the sense that this is worth more than that, this rather than that is the direction in which to go, that the centre[3] is here rather than there. In their keeping, to use a metaphor that is metonymy also and will bear a good deal of pondering, is the language, the changing idiom, upon which fine living depends, and without which distinction of spirit is thwarted and incoherent. By "culture" I mean the use of such a language. I do not suppose myself to have produced a tight definition, but the account, I think, will be recognised as adequate by anyone who is likely to read this pamphlet.

4

It is a commonplace to-day that culture is at a crisis. It is a commonplace more widely accepted than understood: at any rate, realisation of what the crisis portends does not seem to be common. I am, for instance, sometimes answered that it has all happened before, during the Alexandrian period, or under the Roman Empire. Even if this were true it would hardly be reassuring, and I note the contention mainly in order to record my suspicion that it comes from Spengler,[4] where, of course, authority may also be found for an attitude of proud philosophic indifference. For Spengler, the inexorable cycle moves once more to its inevitable end. But the common absence of concern for what is happening is not to be explained by erudition or philosophy. It is itself a symptom, and a phrase for it comes aptly to hand in Mr. H. G. Wells' new book, *The Autocracy of Mr. Parham*: "Essentially it was a vast and increasing inattention."

It seems, then, not unnecessary to restate the obvious. In support of the belief that the modern phase of human history is unprecedented it is enough to point to the machine. The machine, in the first place, has brought about change in habit and the circumstances of life at a rate for which we have no parallel. The effects of such change may be studied in *Middletown*, a remarkable work of anthropology, dealing (I am afraid it is not superfluous to say) with a typical community of the Middle West. There we see in detail how the automobile (to take

---

3. ". . . the mass of the public is without any suspicion that the value of these organs is relative to their being nearer a certain ideal centre of correct information, taste and intelligence, or farther away from it."—*Culture and Anarchy*.
4. A good account of some aspects of the modern phase may be found in *The Decline of the West*, Vol. II, C. IV.

NOTES

3   Content

Here, Leavis sets out what he sees as the special attributes and abilities of the minority. It is they, he argues, that know and set standards; it is they who know the value of things, and they who know the direction that society should be taking. Note, again, how Mathew Arnold's thinking about the limitations of a mass public inform Leavis's thinking.

When Leavis equates 'culture' with the use of language, he is drawing again on the work of I.A. Richards. In doing so, Leavis is implying that as other carriers of culture, such as the family and the community, are dissolving, it is only through language that culture can be protected and maintained (Mulhern 1981: 36).

Writing Style

Note how up to this point in the reading, Leavis has on a number of occasions used, or made mention of, metaphors. How useful do you think this technique has been in conveying his key ideas?

4   Content

What is the main point that Leavis is making in this first paragraph? Are there any parallels to be drawn with our contemporary era?

Although this is the first time that *Middletown* is mentioned, Leavis fails to make explicit that this is a pseudonym for a small town in the American state of Illinois. To what extent is it defensible to use the experience of one allegedly typical town in America to generalise more broadly – even to a different continent? What reasons could be given in defence of this approach?

When Leavis refers to 'a breach in continuity' in the final sentence of the second paragraph, what does he mean?

Writing Style

Three points, none of which are related, can be made here. First, Leavis cites Oswald Spengler, but fails to empower the reader by listing the full citation details. Secondly, how would you rewrite the opening sentence of the second paragraph to make it more transparent? Thirdly, note how Leavis's style regularly involves the use of brackets for asides or qualifications. You might want to compare this approach with that of J.S. Mill, who in an earlier century used commas instead of brackets for similar purposes (see Chapter 4 on liberal press theory).

READING

4

(continued)

one instance) has, in a few years, radically affected religion,[5] broken up the family, and revolutionised social custom. Change has been so catastrophic that the generations find it hard to adjust themselves to each other, and parents are helpless to deal with their children. It seems unlikely that the conditions of life can be transformed in this way without some injury to the standard of living (to wrest the phrase from the economist): improvisation can hardly replace the delicate traditional adjustments, the mature, inherited codes of habit and valuation, without severe loss, and loss that may be more than temporary. It is a breach in continuity that threatens: what has been inadvertently dropped may be irrecoverable or forgotten.

5

To this someone will reply that Middletown is America and not England. And it is true that in America change has been more rapid, and its effects have been intensified by the fusion of peoples. But the same processes are at work in England and the western world generally, and at an acceleration. It is a commonplace that we are being Americanised, but again a commonplace that seems, as a rule, to carry little understanding with it. Americanisation is often spoken of as if it were something of which the United States are guilty. But it is something from which Lord Melchett, our "British-speaking"[6] champion, will not save us even if he succeeds in rallying us to meet that American enterprise which he fears, "may cause us to lose a great structure of self-governing brotherhoods whose common existence is of infinite importance to the future continuance of the Anglo-Saxon race, and of the gravest import to the development of all that seems best in our modern civilisation."[7] For those who are most defiant of America do not propose to reverse the processes consequent upon the machine. We are to have greater efficiency, better salesmanship, and more mass-production and standardisation. Now, if the worst effects of mass-production and standardisation were represented by Woolworth's there would be no need to despair. But there are effects that touch the life of the community more seriously. When we consider, for instance, the processes of mass-production and standardisation in the form represented by the Press, it becomes obviously of sinister significance that they should be accompanied by a process of levelling-down.

5. "One gains a distinct impression that the religious basis of all education was more taken for granted if less talked about thirty-five years ago, when high school 'chapel' was a religio-inspirational service with a 'choir' instead of the 'pep session' which it tends to become to-day." *Middletown*, by R. S. and H. M. Lynd, p. 204. This kind of change, of course, is not due to the automobile alone.

6. "That would be one of the greatest disasters to the British-speaking people, and one of the greatest disasters to civilisation."—Lord Melchett, *Industry and Politics*, p. 278.

7. *Ibid.*, 281.

5 Content

Here, Leavis mounts a defence of his earlier generalisation of societal changes in America to England. In comparing the two societies, what do you understand by his reference to 'the fusion of peoples' in America? What, if anything, might be inferred here about England – which we have to presume does also include the other nations that make up the United Kingdom?

Having made mention of 'the machine' on a number of occasions, Leavis is now moving on to consider how the machine has influenced mass-production and standardisation, first in relation to the press, and later in respect of film, broadcasting, popular fiction and advertising.

Context

Here is yet another opportunity to emphasise the importance of thinking about continuity while considering the nature and impact of change. For example, Leavis refers to fears about becoming 'Americanised'. This proved to be a continuous theme throughout the twentieth century, evidenced by terms such as 'Cocacolaisation' and 'McDonaldisation'. Moreover, America's relationship with – and influence on – Britain remains a point of consternation in the early years of this current century. Why is it now less likely that England, or Britain, would be referred to as an 'Anglo-Saxon race'?

READING

6

Of Lord Northcliffe, Mr. Hamilton Fyfe, his admiring biographer, tells us (*Northcliffe: An Intimate Biography*, p. 270):

"He knew what the mass of newspaper-readers wanted, and he gave it to them. He broke down the dignified idea that the conductors of newspapers should appeal to the intelligent few. He frankly appealed to the unintelligent many. Not in a cynical spirit, not with any feeling of contempt for their tastes; but because on the whole he had more sympathy with them than with the others, and because they were as the sands of the sea in numbers. He did not aim at making opinion less stable, emotion more superficial. He did this, without knowing he did it, because it increased circulation."

Two pages later we are told:

"The Best People did read the *Daily Mail*. It was now seen in first-class railway compartments as much as in third-class. It had made its way from the kitchen and the butler's pantry of the big country house up to the hall table."

"Giving the public what it wants," is, clearly, a modest way of putting it. Lord Northcliffe showed people what they wanted, and showed the Best People that they wanted the same as the rest. It is enough by way of commentary on the phrase to refer to the history of the newspaper press during the last half-century: a history of which the last notable event is the surrender of the *Daily Herald* to the operation of that "psychological Gresham Law" which Mr. Norman Angell notes:

". . . the operation of a psychological Gresham Law; just as in commerce debased coin, if there be enough of it, must drive out the sterling, so in the contest of motives, action which corresponds to the more primitive feelings and impulses, to first thoughts and established prejudices, can be stimulated by the modern newspaper far more easily than that prompted by rationalised second thought."[8]

"Let us face the truth," says Mr. Norman Angell further on; "the conditions of the modern Press cause the Bottomleys more and more and the Russells and Dickinsons less and less to form the national character. The forces under review are not merely concerned with the mechanical control of ideas. They transform the national temperament."[9]

---

8. *The Press and the Organisation of Society*, p. 33.
9. *Ibid.*, p. 43.
   V. also p. 35: "When Swift wrote certain of his pamphlets, he presented a point of view contrary to the accepted one, and profoundly affected his country's opinion and policy. Yet at most he circulated a few thousand copies. One of the most important was printed at his own expense. Any printer in a back street could have furnished all the material capital necessary for reaching effectively the whole reading public of the nation. To-day, for an unfamiliar opinion to gain headway against accepted opinion, the mere mechanical equipment of propaganda would be beyond the resources of any ordinary individual."

6 Content

Leavis uses the term 'levelling-down' to convey the impact of the press, while today we would be more likely to see, or hear, references to 'dumbing-down', which essentially has the same meaning. Again, Leavis's 'evidence' is more or less based on a single example, that of Lord Northcliffe's press empire (see *Context* below). What is Leavis implying by his reference to Northcliffe's 'admiring biographer', and what evidence would Leavis cite in support of his carefully chosen description?

In the final sentence of the quotation from Norman Angell, what is it that the press do to 'transform the national temperament'? How would you counter such an argument?

Context

The point that Leavis makes in the second footnote on this page is one that was taken up with some gusto in the latter decades of the twentieth century by political economists such as, amongst others, Murdock and Golding (2005). That is, once the press became industrialised the ability of ordinary people to start a newspaper was seriously constrained by the high costs involved, resulting in a deleterious impact on the plurality of opinion circulating in the public sphere (see Chapter 12 on political economy and Chapter 13 on the public sphere).

Leavis's reference to Northcliffe invokes the perceived power of the so-called press barons who emerged in the early decades of the twentieth century on both sides of the Atlantic. In Britain, the oft-cited examples include Northcliffe, Rothermere and Beaverbrook – all of whom eventually became Lords – and in America, Hearst and Pulitzer (Allan 1999: 2). Northcliffe, founder of the *Daily Mail*, was renowned for his motto 'Get me a murder a day' (Williams 1998).

The quotation from Norman Angell refers to Gresham's Law, which Leavis then uses as a means of assessing other popular media and entertainment forms. In its application to culture, Gresham's Law suggests that '[j]ust as bad money will drive out good, so bad culture will drive out good' (Williams 2001: 20).

If we follow the argument being set out in this reading, Leavis clearly gives this law some credence. However, in *Culture is Ordinary*, Raymond Williams suggests that the analogy in Gresham's Law is defective, arguing that in whatever field that we might examine, be it literature, music or newspapers, there has not been a 'shrinking consumption of things we can all agree to be good' (Williams 2001: 20).

READING

7

All this, again, is commonplace, but commonplace, again, on which it seems necessary to insist. For the same "psychological Gresham Law" has a much wider application than the newspaper press. It applies even more disastrously to the films: more disastrously, because the films have a so much more potent influence.[10] They provide now the main form of recreation in the civilised world; and they involve surrender, under conditions of hypnotic receptivity, to the cheapest emotional appeals, appeals the more insidious because they are associated with a compellingly vivid illusion of actual life. It would be difficult to dispute that the result must be serious damage to the "standard of living" (to use the phrase as before). All this seems so obvious that one is diffident about insisting on it. And yet people will reply by adducing the attempts that have been made to use the film as a serious medium of art. Just as, when broadcasting is in question, they will point out that they have heard good music broadcasted and intelligent lectures. The standardising influence of broadcasting hardly admits of doubt, but since there is here no Hollywood engaged in purely commercial exploitation the levelling-down is not so obvious. But perhaps it will not be disputed that broadcasting, like the films, is in practice mainly a means of passive diversion, and that it tends to make active recreation, especially active use of the mind, more difficult.[11] And such agencies are only a beginning. The near future holds rapid developments in store.

10. "The motion picture, by virtue of its intrinsic nature, is a species of amusing and informational Esperanto, and, potentially at least, a species of aesthetic Esperanto of all the arts; if it may be classified as one, the motion picture has in it, perhaps more than any other, the resources of universality. . . . The motion picture tells its stories directly, simply, quickly and elementally, not in words but in pictorial pantomime. To see is not only to believe; it is also in a measure to understand. In theatrical drama, seeing is closely allied with hearing, and hearing, in turn, with mental effort. In the motion picture, seeing is all—or at least nine-tenths of all."—*Encyclopædia Britannica*, 14th Ed.—"Motion Pictures: A Universal Language."

The *Encyclopædia Britannica*, fourteenth edition, is itself evidence of what is happening: "humanised, modernised, pictorialised," as the editors announce.

11. Mr. Edgar Rice Burroughs (creator of Tarzan) in a letter that I have been privileged to see, writes: "It has been discovered through repeated experiments that pictures that require thought for appreciation have invariably been box-office failures. The general public does not wish to think. This fact, probably more than any other, accounts for the success of my stories, for without this specific idea in mind I have, nevertheless, endeavoured to make all of my descriptions so clear that each situation could be visualised readily by any reader precisely as I saw it. My reason for doing this was not based upon a low estimate of general intelligence, but upon the realisation that in improbable situations, such as abound in my work, the greatest pains must be taken to make them appear plausible. I have evolved, therefore, a type of fiction that may be read with the minimum of mental effort." The significance of this for my argument does not need comment. Mr. Burroughs adds that his books sell at over a million copies a year. There is not room here to make the comparisons suggested by such documents as the *Life of James Lackington* (1791).

7   Content

Having dealt with the press, Leavis now turns his attention to film, which, he argues, poses a greater threat to society because it has a 'more potent influence' than newspapers. Film is virtually dismissed as a 'serious medium of art', and, like broadcasting, is seen as providing only 'passive diversion' rather than active stimulation for the mind. Although Leavis does not make specific mention of readers, listeners or viewers, what is he implying about the role and agency of audiences?

As previously, Leavis supports his arguments with only limited 'evidence'. In this case, the *Encyclopaedia Britannica* is used as a way to illustrate the particular powers of film as a medium – even though the 'modernisation' of this very publication is seen by Leavis as yet another example of levelling-down. He also bolsters his views about film being a medium of passive diversion by including an extract from the creator of *Tarzan*. To what extent and in what ways is this particular piece of 'evidence' persuasive?

READING

8

Contemplating that deliberate exploitation of the cheap response which characterises our civilisation we may say that a new factor in history is an unprecedented use of applied psychology. This might be thought to flatter Hollywood, but, even so, there can be no room for doubt when we consider advertising, and the progress it has made in two or three decades. (And "advertising" may be taken to cover a great deal more than comes formally under that head.) "It ought to be plain even to the inexperienced," writes an authority, Mr. Gilbert Russell (in *Advertisement Writing*), "that successful copywriting depends upon insight into people's minds: not into individual minds, mark, but into the way average people think and act, and the way they react to suggestions of various kinds." And again: "Advertising is becoming increasingly exact every day. Where instinct used to be enough, it is being replaced by inquiry. Advertising men nowadays don't say, 'The public will buy this article from such and such a motive': they employ what is called market research to find out the buying motives, as exactly as time and money and opportunity permit, from the public itself."

So, as another authority, Mr. Harold Herd, Principal of the Regent Institute, says (*Bigger Results from Advertising*): "Now that advertising is more and more recruiting the best brains of the country we may look forward to increasingly scientific direction of this great public force."

Mr. Gilbert Russell, who includes in his list of books for "A Copy Writer's Bookshelf" the works of Shakespeare, the Bible, *The Forsyte Saga, The Oxford Book of English Verse, Fiery Particles* by C.E. Montague and Sir Arthur Quiller-Couch's *The Art of Writing*, tells us that:

"Competent copy cannot be written except by men who have read lovingly, who have a sense of the romance of words, and of the picturesque and the dramatic phrase; who have versatility enough and judgment enough to know how to write plainly and pungently, or with a certain affectation. Briefly, competent copy is a matter not only of literary skill of a rather high order, but also skill of a particular specialised kind."

8 Content

Having warned that the prospects for culture are likely to get worse, Leavis now focuses his attention on the negative impact of advertising. He notes an emerging practice, market research, which we now take for granted, but which has become much more sophisticated and pervasive since the 1930s when Leavis was writing.

Leavis also observes the beginning of another trend, that is, the use of academic research – in this case applied psychology – for the purpose of developing, refining and targeting communication in pursuit of commercial gain or for propaganda campaigns. To what extent does Leavis make a convincing case about the impact of advertising on society and culture? If you were to counter Leavis's views, what arguments would you mount?

On this occasion Leavis supports his arguments with quotations from, and references to, three sources. The first being *Advertising Writing*, the second *Bigger Results from Advertising*, while the third source is *The Art of Writing*, which implies that the ideas, images and vocabulary necessary for the production of good advertising copy are dependent on the copywriter's prior reading of 'classic' texts, which might include those of Shakespeare and even the Bible.

Structure

You may have already noticed a pattern in the way that Leavis constructs this reading. He relies heavily on some fairly long quotations – and particularly so in the section that deals with Lord Northcliffe – and uses a number of substantial footnotes which go beyond simply listing citation details. To what extent does this combination of quotations and footnotes help in conveying his arguments or make them more difficult to follow?

READING

9

The influence of such skill is to be seen in contemporary fiction. For if, as Mr. Thomas Russell (author of "What did you do in the Great War, daddy?"), tells us, "English is the best language in the world for advertising," advertising is doing a great deal for English. It is carrying on the work begun by Mr. Rudyard Kipling, and, where certain important parts of the vocabulary are concerned, making things more difficult for the fastidious. For what is taking place is not something that affects only the environment of culture, stops short, as it were, at the periphery. This should be obvious, but it does not appear to be so to many who would recognise the account I have given above as matter of commonplace. Even those who would agree that there has been an overthrow of standards, that authority has disappeared, and that the currency has been debased and inflated, do not often seem to realise what the catastrophe portends.

10

The prospects of culture, then, are very dark. There is the less room for hope in that a standardised civilisation is rapidly enveloping the whole world. The glimpse of Russia that is permitted us does not afford the comfort that we are sometimes invited to find there. Anyone who has seen Eisenstein's film, *The General Line*, will appreciate the comment made by a writer in the *New Republic* (June 4, 1930), comparing it with an American film:

"One fancies, thinking about these things, that America might well send *The Silent Enemy* to Russia and say, 'This is what living too long with too much machinery does to people. Think twice, before you commit yourselves irrevocably to the same course.'"

But it is vain to resist the triumph of the machine. It is equally vain to console us with the promise of a "mass culture" that shall be utterly new. It would, no doubt, be possible to argue that such a "mass culture" might be better than the culture we are losing, but it would be futile: the "utterly new" surrenders everything that can interest us.[12]

What hope, then, is there left to offer? The vague hope that recovery *must* come, somehow, in spite of all? Mr. I. A. Richards, whose opinion is worth more than most people's, seems to

12. "... indeed, this gentleman, taking the bull by the horns, proposes that we should for the future call industrialism culture, and then of course there can be no longer any misapprehension of their true character; and besides the pleasure of being wealthy and comfortable, they will have authentic recognition as vessels of sweetness and light."—*Culture and Anarchy*.

9   Content

Leavis contends that the knowledge and skills being used to develop advertising copy are now being used to produce contemporary fiction, a trend which he obviously deplores. Why is it that he sees developments such as this – and similarly in the case of the press, film and broadcasting – as the stepping stones to catastrophe? What is happening? What is being lost? Who loses? Does anyone gain?

Context

Again, the borrowing from, and merging of, media forms, genres and texts that Leavis alludes to – and which he is so concerned about – is now a feature of our contemporary society. Moreover, academic journals have been established to study some of these trends. Two such journals, *Adaptation* (Oxford Journals) and the *Journal of Adaptation in Film and Performance* (Intellect), have been created specifically to address the boom in adaptations that continue to be profitable for the creative industries sector.

Leavis's insights into contemporary fiction may have been assisted by Queenie's earlier PhD, which focused on the popular novel.

10   Content

In this final section of the reading Leavis summarises his concerns about culture, as he perceives it, and the threat posed by its emerging foe, 'mass culture'. Yet again, he relies on three of the key sources that have informed the reading: Mathew Arnold; I.A. Richards and Oswald Spengler. Leavis's overall mood is one of pessimism, although he does suggest a hint of optimism when he raises the possibility 'that the machine will yet be made a tool'. What do you think he means by this?

Context

Leavis's suggestion about the prospects of a 'standardised civilisation . . . enveloping the whole world' continue to resonate. However, today, concerns about standardisation are reframed as debates about homogeneity, which is seen to result from globalisation. Contrary views have also been formulated, which, in casting doubt on the global–local logic, have resulted in the creation of concepts such as 'glocal' and 'lobal'.

Rather surprisingly, Leavis cites Henry Ford, founder in America of the Ford motor company. Today, Ford's views about the future would probably be seized upon as epitomising the lack of forward planning by so-called 'captains' of industry that has led to current concerns about global warming.

READING

10
(continued)

authorise hope: he speaks of "reasons for thinking that this century is in a cultural trough rather than upon a crest"; and says that "the situation is likely to get worse before it is better."[13] "Once the basic level has been reached," he suggests, "a slow climb back may be possible. That at least is a hope that may be reasonably entertained."[14] But it is a hope that looks very desperate in face of the downward acceleration described above, and it does not seem to point to any factor that might be counted upon to reverse the process.

Are we then to listen to Spengler's[15] (and Mr. Henry Ford's[16]) admonition to cease bothering about the inevitable future? That is impossible. Ridiculous, priggish and presumptuous as it may be, if we care at all about the issues we cannot help believing that, for the immediate future, at any rate, we have some responsibility. We cannot help clinging to some such hope as Mr. Richards offers; to the belief (unwarranted, possibly) that what we value most matters too much to the race to be finally abandoned, and that the machine will yet be made a tool.

It is for us to be as aware as possible of what is happening, and, if we can, to "keep open our communications with the future."

13. *Practical Criticism*, p. 320.

14. *Ibid.*, p. 249.

15. "Up to now everyone has been at liberty to hope what he pleased about the future. Where there are no facts, sentiment rules. But henceforward it will be every man's business to inform himself of what *can* happen and therefore of what with the unalterable necessity of destiny and irrespective of personal ideals, hopes or desires, *will* happen."—*The Decline of the West*, Vol. I, p. 39.

16. "But what of the future? Shall we not have over-production? Shall we not some day reach a point where the machine becomes all powerful, and the man of no consequence?

No man can say anything of the future. We need not bother about it. The future has always cared for itself in spite of our well-meant efforts to hamper it. If to-day we do the task we can best do, then we are doing all that we can do.

Perhaps we may over-produce, but that is impossible until the whole world has all its desires. And if that should happen, then surely we ought to be content."—*To-day and To-morrow.* HENRY FORD, pp. 272–273.

REFLECTING ON THE READING

Even in this abridged version of the reading it is possible to see why *Mass Civilisation* can be interpreted as a 'call to arms'. It has the essence of a rallying call from Leavis to colleagues, acolytes and others of like mind, the aim being to seek their support in taking a stand against the degradation of culture.

While the message in *Mass Civilisation* may have been powerful, there were doubts about its quality. Scannell, for instance, describes it as 'neither well written nor well thought out', and giving the impression of a 'hastily assembled patchwork of quotations strung together from a variety of sources' (2007: 101). However, the ideas set out in *Mass Civilisation* were further developed and refined in subsequent publications by Leavis and his colleagues, and the original was later reprinted in 1933 along with a collection of other essays in *For Continuity* (Leavis 1933; see Mulhern 1981: 63).

Mass Civilisation was Leavis's opening salvo on 'mass culture', and helped establish his reputation in the period between the First (1914–18) and Second World War (1939–45) as the most influential British critic of popular culture (Williams 2003: 27). The pamphlet both reflected and maintained a tradition that continues today (Williams 1998: 1). This tradition has two strands. The first involves a critique of popular media and entertainment forms which has at various moments in time focused on music halls, film, radio, comic books, television and, more recently, computer games.

The second strand involves what sometimes amounts to a withering critique of American cultural goods and services – even 'a revulsion against American culture' (Seaton 1997: 265). What is noteworthy – and concerning – about Leavis's warnings about American influence on English culture is that he drew most of his 'evidence' from just one source. That source, *Middletown*, was a case study of a small American town in the state of Illinois.

While Leavis's analysis in *Mass Civilisation* reflects a mass society thesis, his approach was both similar and different to others adopting a similar theoretical perspective (Bennett 1995: 348; Garnham 1990: 60; Seaton 1997: 265; Willliams 2003: 27). While C. Wright Mills was primarily concerned about political questions in a mass society context and was of a Left political persuasion (see Chapter 9), Leavis's major interest was in culture, and he was on the political Right.

Similarly, while Theodor Adorno and Max Horkheimer (see Chapter 6) had views not dissimilar to Leavis about the need to defend 'high', or 'minority', culture, and on the negative influence of America, and were also critical of the cultural products being produced for the masses by the cultural industries, these two authors were on the political Left (Bennett 1995: 348).

Essentially, the 'minority' that Leavis was defending was a literary minority, whose role was to keep 'alive the literary tradition and the finest capacities of the language' (Williams 1958: 248). When Leavis spoke of the 'mass', one reasonable inference is that he actually meant the mob, the characteristics of such a group being 'gullibility, fickleness, herd-prejudice, lowness of taste and habit' (Williams 1958: 288). Williams is, of course, renowned for his observation that there are 'no masses; there are only ways of seeing people as masses' (1961: 289).

While recognising and accepting that Leavis was a key influence on his own thinking and on his own work, Raymond Williams registered his disagreement with the latter's views in (at least) two areas:

The concept of a cultivated minority, set over against a 'decreated' mass, tends, in its assertion, to a damaging arrogance and scepticism. The concept of a wholly organic and satisfying past, to be set against a disintegrated and dissatisfying present, tends in its neglect of history to a denial of real social experience.

(Williams 1958: 255)

Although Williams acknowledged that Leavis's views on culture became 'widely influential' (1961: 246), some years later he argued that the Leavisite defence of 'high culture', while still present, had lost ground and was now 'clearly residual' (1983[1976]: 183). However, notions of 'high' and 'low' culture, and of the 'cultivated' and 'uncultivated', still abound, even though they may not always be made explicit. Similarly, so do recollections of a more satisfactory traditional, or organic, culture of earlier eras, mistaken as these accounts may be.

Moreover, advocates of the Leavisite view of culture set out in *Mass Civilisation* have, even in the contemporary period, continued to be influential. For example, Hartley asserts that certain groups and organisations have offered versions of this ideology to 'highly placed elites in government, administrative, intellectual and even broadcasting circles' in order to represent their own '*sectional* interests . . . as *general* interests' (2002b: 52).

Key terms to explore

minority civilisation; mass culture; the machine; breach in continuity; Americanisation; standardisation; Gresham's Law; levelling-down; passive diversion; standardised civilisation.

Key writers who are mentioned

Mathew Arnold; I.A. Richards; Oswald Spengler; H.G. Wells; Rudyard Kipling.

RECOMMENDED READING

Mulhern, F. (1981) *The Moment of 'Scrutiny'*, London: Verso.

Documents the history and impact of *Scrutiny* (1932–53), the English literary journal that was inspired by the work of Leavis and edited by him.

Scannell, P. (2007) *Media and Communication*, London: Sage.

The fourth chapter provides an overview of the lives, works and impact of F.R. Leavis, Richard Hoggart and Raymond Williams.

Wyatt, J. (1990) *Commitment to Higher Education*, Buckingham: Society for Research into Higher Education and Open University Press.

Examines the views of seven thinkers on higher education and includes chapters – based around key texts – on F.R. Leavis.

CHAPTER 6

The Frankfurt school

Horkheimer, M. and Adorno, T.W. (2002 [1944]) *Dialectic of Enlightenment: Philosophical fragments*, translated by Jephcott, E., Stanford, California: Stanford University Press. Excerpt from Chapter 4, 'The culture industry: enlightenment as mass deception', pp. 94–8.

INTRODUCTION TO THE FRANKFURT SCHOOL

Amidst all the 'thinkers' and 'schools' included in this section of the book, the Frankfurt school is perhaps unique. This is not simply due to the contribution to theory made by its members and, in particular, their work on the commercialisation of culture in mass society, but because the emergence and interests of the Frankfurt school in the early 1920s are indelibly linked to a troubled period in European affairs.

While it is not within the brief of this chapter to rehearse the relevant history, scholars such as Held (1980) and Wiggershaus (1994) provide detailed accounts, noting the impact of the First World War (1914–18); the Russian Revolution; the 'Stalinisation' of Russia; the subjugation by Moscow of Communist Parties in other parts of Europe; the emergence of Nazism and Fascism during the 1920s and 1930s – epitomised by Hitler's emergence in Germany, Mussolini's in Italy and Franco's in Spain; the weakening of Germany's Communist Party, and clampdowns on other political organisations seen as hostile to the state.

While the major work of the Frankfurt school was confined to a period before and after the Second World War (1939–45), its impact still reverberates. This becomes apparent in most textbooks that address theory relating to media, culture and communication, where the names of Max Horkheimer and Theodor Adorno, two key members of the Frankfurt school, are likely to appear. Moreover, in order to understand fully the context of recent developments which have seen governments hailing the 'creative industries' as a new industrial sector (see Chapter 21), universities establishing faculties with the same name, and increasing numbers of jobs for 'creative professionals', knowledge of the Frankfurt school's theorisation of the 'culture industry' is helpful.

Variously referred to as the 'Frankfurt School of Critical Theory' (Hesmondhalgh 2002: 15), the 'Frankfurt school' (note the lower case 's'; Katz et al. 2003: 56), and the 'Frankfurt School of Social Research' (Marshall 1998: 130), its formal title was the Institution of Social Research (the Institute). What prompted its creation, according to Stamps, was a crisis on the left of politics following the First World War which resulted in 'the failure and fragmentation of socialism in Germany, the quiescence of workers in response to the Weimar republic's reformism, and the growth of anti-semitism' (1995: 23). It was only in the 1960s, well after its most productive period, that the Institute attracted the label, 'Frankfurt School' (Hartley 2002b: 90). Note that by simply exposing its original title, we have gained at least some idea about the role of the Institute.

However, the Institute and the Frankfurt school should not be thought of as one and the same, and neither should it be assumed that those associated with both bodies had similar academic backgrounds and interests. For example, although also members of the Institute, Max Horkheimer (philosopher, sociologist, social psychologist), Theodor Adorno (philosopher, sociologist, musicologist), Herbert Marcuse (philosopher), Leo Löwenthal (student of popular culture and literature) and Friedrich Pollock (economist and specialist on problems of national planning) constituted the Frankfurt school (Held, 1980: 15). However, others such as Eric Fromm (psychoanalyst, social psychologist), Franz Neumann (political scientist, with expertise in law), Otto Kirchheimer (political scientist, with expertise in law), Henryk Grossman (political economist), Arkadij Gurland (economist, sociologist), and Walter Benjamin (essayist and literary critic) were simply members of the Institute (Held 1980: 14).

It is also not uncommon to find references made to a first and second generation of the Frankfurt school. Hence, Jürgen Habermas (see Chapter 13) is suggested as one of the most renowned members of the 'second generation' of the Frankfurt school (Lechte 1994: 186). For Held (1980: 38) the retirements and, later, deaths of Adorno (1969), Pollock (1970) and Horkheimer (1973) spelled the end of the Frankfurt school, although the Institute continued to exist.

What constitutes a 'school' in this context is often contentious, hence the use of apostrophes. However, Wiggershaus argues that the Frankfurt school did constitute a 'school', but more so at certain periods than at others. This was because it had the following characteristics: an institutional framework (the Institute of Social Research); a charismatic intellectual personality (Max Horkheimer); a manifesto, in the form of Horkheimer's inaugural lecture to the Institute in 1931; a new paradigm which was described – but not consistently – as 'critical theory'; and a journal to publish scholarly work (Wiggershaus 1994: 2).

Why the Frankfurt school was seen not to constitute a 'school' throughout its life is explained by the peculiar circumstances of the era. For example, shortly after Hitler's appointment as Chancellor in January 1933, the Institute was raided by police and closed. It received the following message from the Gestapo (the Secret State Police):

> In accordance with clauses 1 and 3 of the Act of 26 May 1933 (RGBI I, p. 293) confiscating communist property, the Institute of Social Research in Frankfurt am Main is hereby seized and confiscated in favour of the Free State of Prussia, as the aforementioned Institute has encouraged activities hostile to the state. Signed: pp Dr Richter-Brohm [July, 1933].

> (*Wiggershaus 1994: 128*)

While the Institute's programme was inspired by Marxist thinking, it had no party affiliations, and it welcomed scholars of differing political persuasions (Held 1980: 29). Nevertheless, the events described above forced the Institute to move from Frankfurt to Geneva in 1933, to New York in 1935 and to Los Angeles in 1941, although it remained under the 'umbrella' of the University of Columbia between 1934 and 1946 (Wiggershaus 1994: 144–5, 402).

It was not until the early 1950s that the Institute returned to Frankfurt in Germany. Clearly, these moves disrupted the lives of its members and changed the research agenda. Both Held (1980) and Wiggershaus (1994) make reference to the personal dislocation and disorientation felt by these German scholars in adapting to an alien culture, their situation exacerbated by concerns about the loss of relatives and friends as well as financial difficulties. The move to America also disrupted their research. Moreover, the difficulties involved in writing in German for German audiences, whilst also attempting to engage with a new community of scholars – with a different intellectual tradition – in America, was also problematic.

There are suggestions that the research and publication work undertaken in America was far less radical in its orientation. Two reasons are provided for this. The first was because of concerns about attracting unwarranted political attention, as these scholars came from a country – Germany – with whom America was at war. Related to this, there was also the possibility of deportation, remembering that the Second World War spanned 1939 to 1945 (see, for example, Wiggershaus 1994: 255–6). Secondly, these scholars were dependent on the types of projects that potential sponsors required, or that they were prepared to support (Jay 1973, cited in Held 1980: 35). As a result, this period in the 'New World' has been described as one of 'productive decay' (Wiggershaus 1994: 261).

Felix Weil, the son of a millionaire, provided the initial funding for the Institute. In keeping with his wishes, Marxism provided the 'inspiration and theoretical basis' of the Institute's programme of work which, under its first Director, Carl Grunberg, employed scholars from a variety of disciplinary backgrounds (Held 1980: 31). Hence, it is not surprising to find the Institute described as a 'centre for socialist research' (Marshall 1998: 131). Similarly, Stamps (1995: 23) refers to the organisation as the first school of German neo-Marxists – even 'renegade Marxists' – because of their departure from elements of Marxian thinking. Following Grundberg's retirement in 1929, Max Horkheimer was appointed Director in 1930, and in his inaugural lecture in January 1931 set out his vision for the Institute (Wiggershaus 1994: 38).

Having made clear that any study of social phenomena could not be studied in isolation from the economy, Horkheimer argued for a programme of interdisciplinary study. He emphasised the value of drawing on both qualitative and quantitative techniques, but insisted that empirical work should not be seen as a substitute for theoretical analysis, because 'concepts like society, culture and class, indispensable to all enquiry, cannot be simply transcribed into empirical terms' (Held 1980: 33–4).

For Horkheimer, the central question for members of the Institute involved 'the interconnection between the economic life of society, the psychic development of the individual and transformations in the realm of culture' (Held 1980: 33; see also Wiggershaus 1994: 38). Horkheimer's intentions for the Institute shaped the research questions that directed its early work, some of which are included below. As you may already be aware, the last of these questions has a direct relationship to the selected reading in this chapter.

Nazism and fascism rose to dominate central and southern Europe. How was this possible? How did these movements attain large-scale support?

Given the fate of Marxism in Russia and Western Europe, was Marxism itself nothing other than a stale orthodoxy? Was there a social agent capable of progressive change? What possibilities were there for effective socialist practice?

Social relationships, for example those created by the family, appeared open to manipulation. Was a new type of ideology being formed? If so, how was this affecting everyday life?

Areas of culture appeared open to direct manipulation. Was a new type of ideology being formed? If so, how was this affecting everyday life?

(Held 1980: 35)

Critical theory is famously associated with the Frankfurt school, but in particular with Adorno, Horkheimer, Marcuse and Habermas, who are seen as its 'four central figures' (Held 1980: 15). However, the task of defining critical theory is less straightforward. In fact, it might be suggested that it is perhaps easier to state what it is *not*, rather than what it *is*! (Held 1980: 24).

Influenced by the earlier writing of Lukacs and Hegel, amongst others, the Frankfurt school's critical theorists rejected 'both the economic determinism of Soviet Marxism and the American tradition of mass communications research' (Curran et al. 1977: 312). Their 'departure from Marxism' was due to a belief that capitalism had found ways of overcoming its contradictions and developed strategies which had enabled the working class to become 'incorporated into the system' (Hartley 2002b: 90; Marshall 1998: 131). It is of note that Briggs and Burke (2002: 248–9) argue that members of the Frankfurt school 'abandoned' critical theory on their return to Germany after the Second World War.

There is, though, an acknowledgement that the descriptor, critical theory, did not represent the wide range of disciplines and personnel represented at the Institute, and that it actually disguised major differences between Horkheimer, Adorno and Marcuse, and also between Adorno and Benjamin (Held 1980: 34: Stevenson 2002: 54–5). Similarly, the definition and use of critical theory is further complicated as the so-called first and second generations of the Frankfurt school interpreted it differently.

For example, the latter period of the Frankfurt school is associated with Habermas, whose work is judged as rather more optimistic that the pessimism of the earlier period. Katz et al. (2003: 57) ably capture the contrasting positions, describing Habermas as someone who 'caught a glimpse of the functional, rather than dysfunctional, potential of the media as an agent of the "public sphere"'.

However, what the critical theorists of the Frankfurt school had in common was a belief that, 'through an examination of contemporary social and political issues they could contribute to a critique of ideology and to the development of a non-authoritarian and non-bureaucratic politics' (Held 1980: 16). Moreover, they eschewed specific political solutions, arguing that the 'process of liberation' involved '*self*-emancipation and *self*-creation' (Held 1980: 25–6).

It was as a result of a gradual shift in their work from an emphasis on family and socialisation, to a concentrated critique of mass culture (Curran et al. 1977: 312), that the Frankfurt school – and Horkheimer and Adorno in particular – became known to activists, academics and policymakers. The reading selected for this chapter is primarily responsible for this attention, and it continues to attract barbs and bouquets.

INTRODUCTION TO THE READING

The reading is an abridged extract from a chapter which is almost legendary in the field of media, culture and communication studies. The chapter in question, and the book from where it is drawn, prompted the following accolade: 'For sheer intelligence, fascination, audacity, and stimulation, I know no text in the wobbly canon of media theory that can match the "The Culture Industry" and *Dialectic of Enlightenment*' (Peters 2003: 71).

The book first appeared in German, released in limited numbers as a hectographic typescript from the Institute for Social Research, in 1944. The aim of the authors was to publish it on the fiftieth birthday of their close friend and colleague, Friedrich Pollock (Noerr 2002: 217). In 1947, *Dialektik der Aufklarung* (*Dialectic of Enlightenment*) was published in Amsterdam, and after the circulation of a number of pirated versions, it was republished in Germany in 1969 (Peters 2003: 60). It was not until 1972 that the book was translated into English, and this followed the translation of other works by members of the Frankfurt school during the 1960s (Newbold 1995a: 328).

Like most of the members of the Frankfurt school, Horkheimer and Adorno were German-Jewish intellectuals (Stamps 1995: 23). Although christened Theodor Wiesengrund Adorno, his middle name was dropped because it sounded Jewish when he moved to New York in 1938 to rejoin the relocated Institute (Lechte 1994: 177). Adorno was born in Frankfurt am Main in September 1903. His father had a wholesale wine business and his mother had been a successful singer before her marriage. Having studied philosophy, sociology, psychology and music, Adorno was primarily interested in the latter, publishing articles on music and at one point sought employment as a music critic for the *Berliner Zeitung* (Lechte 1994: 177; Wiggershaus 1994: 82). Adorno first joined the Institute in 1931, shortly after Horkenheimer's appointment as Director (Wiggershaus 1994: 93–4).

Like Adorno, Max Horkheimer also came from a relatively wealthy background. Born in Stuttgart in February 1895, his father was a successful businessman who owned several textile factories. Horkheimer was expected to follow his father into the family business, but after a period of illness which saw him conscripted into the army and then released because of poor health, he went on to study psychology, philosophy and economics at university in Munich before transferring to Frankfurt (Wiggershaus 1994: 42–5).

There is some conjecture about the authorship of the 'Culture industry' chapter and *Dialectic of Enlightenment*. Where the book, or chapter, has been referenced by other authors (see, for example, Curran et al. 1977), Adorno is sometimes listed as the first author. However, as Peters notes, the authors' own choice is 'Horkheimer and Adorno' (2003: 63–4). Noerr, the editor, also makes mention of such matters, indicating that both authors 'repeatedly stressed their joint responsibility for the entire work' (2002: 219–220).

The 'Culture industry' chapter first appeared in a British media studies text in 1977 (in an abridged format) within a section entitled, 'The mediation of cultural meanings' (Curran et al. 1977: 349–83). In their introduction to this section, Curran et al. refer to Horkheimer and Adorno's cultural pessimism (1977: 313), and there is a sense that this particular chapter epitomises the major thrust of the book as a whole. That is, it illustrates how mass culture has 'become an organ of soft domination', the aim of the book being to 'explain how the dream of enlightenment backfired' (Peters 2003: 63).

We must, though, remember that both Horkheimer and Adorno had a particular view about what constituted 'culture', and what role or purpose it played in wider society.

Essentially, for both authors, 'culture' was equated with art, and a belief that it should – ideally – 'act as a form of critique of the rest of life, and could provide a utopian vision of how a better life might be possible' (Hesmondhalgh 2002: 15; see Chapter 5 on F.R. Leavis in *this* book for more on this kind of discussion).

The era in which this book was written helps explain its pessimism and suspicion about the culture industry. It was produced during the Second World War while its two authors were in America as a result of being exiled from Nazi Germany. Given the nature of this era and the personal and professional situation of both authors, it is apposite that Horkheimer and Adorno have been described as 'men in dark times' (Arendt 1958, cited in Peters 2003: 65). It was also an era when one sector of cultural production was particularly heavily concentrated. Peters (2003: 66) notes that in the 1940s, Hollywood produced 95 per cent of all films on general exhibition in America.

Although life in the capitalist democracy of America was a far cry from Nazi Germany, Horkheimer and Adorno did nevertheless find similarities between the two contexts. The experience of American cinema and commercial radio confirmed Horkheimer and Adorno's view that '"enlightenment" had turned into "mass deception" through the machinations of "the culture industry"' (McGuigan 1996: 76).

We will return to the notion of 'culture industry' in our reflections on the reading, but at this point it is helpful to understand how and why Horkheimer and Adorno adopted this concept. Initially, the two authors had begun with the descriptor of 'mass culture' to capture what they were observing. However, they were concerned that the use of 'mass culture' could be interpreted as culture emanating from the people – implying an active role in the process – whereas what they wanted to get across to their readers was that culture had actually been commodified; it was something that was bought and sold (Hesmondhalgh 2002: 15; McGuigan 1996: 76).

As a result, they ditched 'mass culture', inserting in its place 'culture industry'. The rationale for linking 'culture' with 'industry' was that it was considered to be 'more unambiguously damning' (McGuigan 1996: 76). Hesmondhalgh, amongst others, has little time for Horkheimer and Adorno's analysis and conclusions, although he acknowledges that the two authors 'provide the fullest and most intelligent version of the extreme pessimistic view of the industrialisation of culture' (2002: 16–17).

While the selected reading is only a short and abridged extract from the 'Culture industry' chapter, there are a number of reasons why it is not an easy read. Aside from the disciplinary, professional and cultural backgrounds of the two authors, the era in which it was written and its translation from German into English, there are other challenges awaiting the reader. Some are flagged by the book's editor, who acknowledges that its five chapters are 'highly uncoordinated' and, thereby, hardly qualify the book to be considered a unified piece of writing (Noerr 2002: 217). Additionally, there is a recognition that it is difficult to read because of 'the peculiarly dense, allusive and demanding nature of the text' (Noerr 2002: 218–19).

Such concerns are echoed by Peters (2003). He suggests that there are two 'barriers to understanding': one being the structure and composition of the text, and the other being cross-cultural, meaning that the authors presume a thorough knowledge – on the part of the reader – of European history and intellectual thought (Peters 2003: 61).

Peters offers the following advice. Take the chapter (and book) 'as something to think with or against, not as a final vision of the world', on the basis that the 'first principle of critical theory is that thought is always historical and therefore provisional' (2003: 61).

READING

1

M. Horkheimer and T.W. Adorno

The Culture Industry: Enlightenment as Mass Deception

The sociological view that the loss of support from objective religion and the disintegration of the last precapitalist residues, in conjunction with technical and social differentiation and specialization, have given rise to cultural chaos is refuted by daily experience. Culture today is infecting everything with sameness. Film, radio, and magazines form a system. Each branch of culture is unanimous within itself and all are unanimous together. Even the aesthetic manifestations of political opposites proclaim the same inflexible rhythm. The decorative administrative and exhibition buildings of industry differ little between authoritarian and other countries. The bright monumental structures shooting up on all sides show off the systematic ingenuity of the state-spanning combines, toward which the unfettered entrepreneurial system, whose monuments are the dismal residential and commercial blocks in the surrounding areas of desolate cities, was already swiftly advancing. The older buildings around the concrete centers already look like slums, and the new bungalows on the outskirts, like the flimsy structures at international trade fairs, sing the praises of technical progress while inviting their users to throw them away after short use like tin cans. But the town-planning projects, which are supposed to perpetuate individuals as autonomous units in hygienic small apartments, subjugate them only more completely to their adversary, the total power of capital. Just as the occupants of city centers are uniformly summoned there for purposes of work and leisure, as producers and consumers, so the living cells crystallize into homogenous, well-organized complexes. The conspicuous unity of macrocosm and microcosm confronts human beings with a model of their culture: the false identity of universal and particular. All mass culture under monopoly is identical, and the contours of its skeleton, the conceptual armature fabricated by monopoly, are beginning to stand out. Those in charge no longer take much trouble to conceal the structure, the power of which increases the more bluntly its existence is admitted. Films and radio no longer need to present themselves as art. The truth that they are nothing but business is used as an ideology to legitimize the trash they intentionally produce. They call themselves industries, and the published figures for their directors' incomes quell any doubts about the social necessity of their finished products.

NOTES

 ### Writing Style

This opening paragraph is indicative of the reading as a whole in terms of the style of writing, the type of language being used and the withering critique. It reflects the disciplinary background and occupation of Horkheimer and Adorno and who they envisage as their primary audience. In this instance, it is likely to be their peers in the university community and intellectuals outside the academy.

Their use of vocabulary and, in particular, what one might describe as key 'influencing' words is worth noting. For example, their description of culture as 'infecting everything with sameness' is both powerful and provocative.

Content

It will be interesting when – or if – you become conscious of the pessimism that is so closely associated with the writings of the Frankfurt school, and what examples you feel able to point to in this reading that justifies such a label.

What you are also likely to be noticing, even in this first paragraph, is that while Horkheimer and Adorno are using general examples to back up and illustrate their arguments, they are not citing the work of other authors. There will, though, be moments where you find yourself asking, 'Where is the evidence for that assertion, or what evidence could they provide?'

The major focus, as you will have noted already, is on the macro context rather than that of the micro. This is evident in the number of references to industry, business and mass culture.

While we might now take for granted that film, radio and magazines are part of an industry or separate industrial sectors, why do Horkheimer and Adorno label them as such here?

To what extent do we still hear assertions similar to those made by the authors in the final few sentences of this – rather long – paragraph?

There are a number of references to 'power' in this paragraph. In what ways do Horkheimer and Adorno use this concept, and where – or with whom – do they suggest the power lies? (See our Chapter 2, What is theory?)

Context

As always, we need to remind ourselves of the era in which the reading was produced and, in this case, where it was written. We know from earlier in the chapter that Horkheimer and Adorno moved from Germany to America in the 1930s, and that this reading was initially written during the Second World War while they were in the United States, and where one of them, Horkheimer, spent some time in Los Angeles.

So, when the authors refer in this paragraph to the similarity between industry buildings in 'authoritarian and other countries', our initial hypothesis would rightly be that they are referring to fascist Germany and, amongst other countries, the 'free market' democracy of the United States. We might, therefore, wonder about the extent to which their theorising could be relevant beyond these contexts: what do you think?

READING

2

Interested parties like to explain the culture industry in technological terms. Its millions of participants, they argue, demand reproduction processes which inevitably lead to the use of standard products to meet the same needs at countless locations. The technical antithesis between few production centers and widely dispersed reception necessitates organization and planning by those in control. The standardized forms, it is claimed, were originally derived from the needs of the consumers: that is why they are accepted with so little resistance. In reality, a cycle of manipulation and retroactive need is unifying the system ever more tightly. What is not mentioned is that the basis on which technology is gaining power over society is the power of those whose economic position in society is strongest. Technical rationality today is the rationality of domination. It is the compulsive character of a society alienated from itself. Automobiles, bombs, and films hold the totality together until their leveling element demonstrates its power against the very system of injustice it served. For the present the technology of the culture industry confines itself to standardization and mass production and sacrifices what once distinguished the logic of the work from that of society. These adverse effects, however, should not be attributed to the internal laws of technology itself but to its function within the economy today. Any need which might escape the central control is repressed by that of individual consciousness. The step from telephone to radio has clearly distinguished the roles. The former liberally permitted the participant to play the role of subject. The latter democratically makes everyone equally into listeners, in order to expose them in authoritarian fashion to the same programs put out by different stations. No mechanism of reply has been developed, and private transmissions are condemned to unfreedom. They confine themselves to the apocryphal sphere of "amateurs," who, in any case, are organized

↓

NOTES

1

(continued)

Another observation about the context – and which relates to the latter point above – concerns the range of media forms which are at the centre of this analysis. With television yet to become a mass medium, Horkheimer and Adorno concentrate on radio, film and magazines. However, while Hollywood was obviously the centre for film production, the dominant model of radio in America was the commercial form, whereas in Britain the emphasis was on 'public service' as defined by the BBC. Later in the reading, but not included in the extract published here, the authors do also make reference to the use of radio by the Nazi leadership in Germany.

How do you think Horkheimer and Adorno would have viewed the BBC as an organisation, and how might they have judged its output on radio and television?

Structure

Note how the thrust of the chapter becomes apparent in the first sentence and is confirmed in the second. It is almost as if the first two sentences encapsulate a hypothesis, antithesis and thesis. After the sentence in which Horkheimer and Adorno refer to the 'sameness' of culture, note how in the next few sentences a series of contrasting examples are used to support and underpin the notion of 'sameness'.

2

Content

It is evident in the opening sentence that this paragraph is focusing on the relationship between technology and the culture industry. While the discussion concentrates on the industry, there are also references to consumers, listeners and, although not named as such, media texts.

With technology at the heart of this discussion, yet again there are references to 'power'. Who is it that Horkheimer and Adorno believe to have power, why do they have it, and how do they use it? Also, who doesn't have power?

Having begun the paragraph by indicating why and how those in the culture industry frame debates about the use of technology, Horkheimer and Adorno end by outlining what they consider to be a more honest explanation. What are the key points made by the authors in this paragraph?

Context

Three observations might be made here. First, the cultural industry's reproductive capacity and its distribution networks are considered here in a national or transnational sense, whereas today we would refer to an international, or even, global market for such goods. Unlike in the 1940s, technological developments now allow many of these cultural products to be produced in digital format and sold and distributed electronically.

Secondly, the discussion here about the role and use of technology – and the extent to which all relevant perspectives are considered publicly – continues to be relevant. We still hear arguments from those in, and representing, the industry about how new technological developments will help in maximising consumer choice and provide better quality products. Equally, counter-arguments

READING

2

(continued)

from above. Any trace of spontaneity in the audience of the official radio is steered and absorbed into a selection of specializations by talent-spotters, performance competitions, and sponsored events of every kind. The talents belong to the operation long before they are put on show; otherwise they would not conform so eagerly. The mentality of the public, which allegedly and actually favors the system of the culture industry, is a part of the system, not an excuse for it. If a branch of art follows the same recipe as one far removed from it in terms of its medium and subject matter; if the dramatic denouement in radio "soap operas" is used as an instructive example of how to solve technical difficulties—which are mastered no less in "jam sessions" than at the highest levels of jazz—or if a movement from Beethoven is loosely "adapted" in the same way as a Tolstoy novel is adapted for film, the pretext of meeting the public's spontaneous wishes is mere hot air. An explanation in terms of the specific interests of the technical apparatus and its personnel would be closer to the truth, provided that apparatus were understood in all its details as a part of the economic mechanism of selection. Added to this is the agreement, or at least the common determination, of the executive powers to produce or let pass nothing which does not conform to their tables, to their concept of the consumer, or, above all, to themselves.

3

If the objective social tendency of this age is incarnated in the obscure subjective intentions of board chairmen, this is primarily the case in the most powerful sectors of industry: steel, petroleum, electricity, chemicals. Compared to them the culture monopolies are weak and dependent. They have to keep in with the true wielders of power, to ensure that their sphere of mass society, the specific product of which still has too much of cozy liberalism and Jewish intellectualism about it, is not subjected to a series of purges. The dependence of the most powerful broadcasting company on the electrical industry, or of film on the banks, characterizes the whole sphere, the individual sectors of which are themselves economically intertwined. Everything is so tightly clustered that the concentration of intellect reaches a level

NOTES

2

(continued)

suggest that the wider public are often marginalised – even intentionally – in debates about the introduction of new technologies.

The transition to digital television in the United Kingdom is a recent example of such debates. Two contrasting perspectives – technological determinism and cultural determinism – provide a means of conceptualising, understanding and influencing such developments (see, for example, Winston 1995).

Thirdly, one other matter raised in this paragraph also resonates today, and it arises in relation to the discussion about radio in which the notion of 'active' and 'passive' listeners is suggested. Today's interactivity – enabled by technological developments – has provided the means for a 'mechanism of reply', and a preponderance of alternative radio services, legal and illegal, have emerged to challenge the hegemony of the predominant forms of radio, commercial and public service.

Writing Style

The authors begin this paragraph by referring to 'interested parties', but don't name them. Should they give examples, or is it right to assume that we will know what is meant by this term? In this context, who might these interested parties be? What are their interests?

In the following sentences, phrases such as 'they argue' and 'it is claimed' occur. Is there a need for 'evidence' to be provided here in order to substantiate these claims? If so, what might that 'evidence' consist of?

Structure

Note how Horkheimer and Adorno first set out, or set up, the position of the industry in the first few sentences of this paragraph. Once done, they then begin their critique with the sentence, 'In reality, a cycle of manipulation and retroactive need is unifying the system ever more tightly.' The remainder of the paragraph is used by Horkheimer and Adorno to 'unpack' this statement. If they have done so successfully, you should understand what they mean by it. What, exactly, are the key points that the authors are trying to get across here?

3

Content

Here, Horkheimer and Adorno begin a closer scrutiny of the culture industry. This necessitates consideration of the relationship between the culture industry and other industrial sectors, and recognition that this type of analysis cannot occur without taking account of the wider capitalist economic system.

While the culture industry is considered to be less powerful than a selected number of other industries, its dependency on other sectors is made clear, with particular references made to electronics and finance. There is also mention of the relatively limited power of the culture industry and its need to stay onside with 'the true wielders of power'. In relation to this assertion, what do you

READING

(continued)

where it overflows the demarcations between company names and technical sectors. The relentless unity of the culture industry bears witness to the emergent unity of politics. Sharp distinctions like those between A and B films, or between short stories published in magazines in different price segments, do not so much reflect real differences as assist in the classification, organization, and identification of consumers. Something is provided for everyone so that no one can escape; differences are hammered home and propagated. The hierarchy of serial qualities purveyed to the public serves only to quantify it more completely. Everyone is supposed to behave spontaneously according to a "level" determined by indices and to select the category of mass product manufactured for their type. On the charts of research organizations, indistinguishable from those of political propaganda, consumers are divided up as statistical material into red, green, and blue areas according to income group.

3
(continued)

think the authors mean when they say that the product of the cultural industry 'still has too much of cozy liberalism and Jewish intellectualism about it'? Also, what sort of purges could they mean, and who might instigate them?

A number of the issues and concerns raised here about the culture industry in the 1940s are relevant today and, to a certain degree, prefigure current debates (see *Context* below). Note also the reference here to 'mass society', a further confirmation of a theoretical perspective favoured by the authors and which clearly influences their analysis.

Having established the power and interdependency of the industrial sectors, including the culture industry, the authors turn their attention in the second half of the paragraph to the areas of consumption and consumers. As the aim, or logic, of the industry is to maximise consumption, this requires the identification, classification and organisation of consumers in order to ensure that they can be effectively targeted. Here, again, we see the authors suggesting an all-powerful industry which manipulates a weak, malleable – yet apparently accepting – consumer. In what ways does this 'fit' with the pessimism that is generally associated with the Frankfurt school?

Context

Although this account of the culture industry was first published over sixty years ago, it identifies trends that have become ever more pronounced in the intervening period, and highlights issues that continue to exercise concern in some quarters.

First, the research on consumers and their behaviour has become much more sophisticated, and technological advances have enabled easier and more accurate targeting of consumers by advertisers through mobile phones and 'narrow-niching' digital radio services.

Secondly, the culture industry, or industries – a development we will return to in reflecting on this reading – have been re-branded by some governments as the 'creative industries' and become a key sector of contemporary economies.

Thirdly, the potential for this sector of the economy to be subject to purges remains a key concern. You may be able to think of recent examples and how and why they have occurred.

Fourthly, the power – as well as the huge salaries and other perks – of those who chair and make up the boards of organisations in all sectors of industry, now often with global rather than local (national) interests, generates widespread media coverage.

Fifthly, it is now generally acknowledged that politicians and political messages are 'sold' via the culture industry in a similar manner to cultural goods (see, for example, Franklin 2004).

Sixthly, the interdependency and close relationship between industry sectors, which is highlighted by the authors, predates the situation today, where these relationships – sometimes conceived of as horizontal and vertical integration – now span the globe.

READING

4

The schematic nature of this procedure is evident from the fact that the mechanically differentiated products are ultimately all the same. That the difference between the models of Chrysler and General Motors is fundamentally illusory is known by any child, who is fascinated by that very difference. The advantages and disadvantages debated by enthusiasts serve only to perpetuate the appearance of competition and choice. It is no different with the offerings of Warner Brothers and Metro Goldwyn Mayer. But the differences, even between the more expensive and cheaper products from the same firm, are shrinking—in cars to the different number of cylinders, engine capacity, and details of the gadgets, and in films to the different number of stars, the expense lavished on technology, labor and costumes, or the use of the latest psychological formulae. The unified standard of value consists in the level of conspicuous production, the amount of investment put on show. The budgeted differences of value in the culture industry have nothing to do with actual differences, with the meaning of the product itself. The technical media, too, are being engulfed by an insatiable uniformity. Television aims at a synthesis of radio and film, delayed only for as long as the interested parties cannot agree. Such a synthesis, with its unlimited possibilities, promises to intensify the impoverishment of the aesthetic material so radically that the identity of all industrial cultural products, still scantily disguised today, will triumph openly tomorrow in a mocking fulfillment of Wagner's dream of the total art work. The accord between word, image, and music is achieved so much more perfectly than in *Tristan* because the sensuous elements, which compliantly document only the surface of social reality, are produced in principle within the same technical work process, the unity of which they express as their true content. This work process integrates all the elements of production, from the original concept of the novel, shaped by its sidelong glance at film, to the last sound effect. It is the triumph of invested capital. To impress the omnipotence of capital on the hearts of expropriated job candidates as the power of their true master is the purpose of all films, regardless of the plot selected by the production directors.

NOTES

4   Content

The focus of attention here is on the goods produced by the culture industry, and trends detected in what Horkheimer and Adorno describe as the 'technical media', such as radio, film and television. The themes that dominate this paragraph are those of illusion and uniformity, and, by implication, the naivety and powerlessness of the consumer.

Keen to reinforce the similarities between the culture industry and other industries, Horkheimer and Adorno use goods produced by the motor industry to illustrate how expert commentators, reviewers and analysts 'talk up' the advantages and disadvantages of one product over another when they are essentially the same. The imperative of the industry is to emphasise that consumers benefit from competition and choice.

Having established the point, the authors suggest that the same illusory behaviour takes place in the film industry, and cite as examples productions by the two (then) biggest film studios in America, Warner Brothers and Metro Goldwyn Mayer. However, the authors suggest that the gap between the most expensive and cheapest versions – of cars and films – is now decreasing, arguing that it is the 'conspicuous production', or level of cash investment, that has now become the 'unified standard of value'. What do they mean by this statement?

Turning to the 'technical media', the authors reference a classic artist and his work – invoking notions of high culture and low culture – to predict that once there is a synthesis between images, words and music, television will act as a catalyst for a further reduction in the range and diversity of materials being produced. This, they suggest is an inevitability of the industrial process, and – rather gloomily – the 'triumph of invested capital'.

Explain what Horkheimer and Adorno mean by the final sentence of this paragraph: 'To impress the omnipotence of capital on the hearts of expropriated job candidates as the power of their true master is the purpose of all films, regardless of the plot selected by the production directors.'

Context

As in note 3 above, there are parallels between the era described by the two authors and that of today. For example, 'choice' and 'competition' are part of the mantra spouted by industry profes-sionals and those politicians and policymakers who are persuaded that the 'market place', rather than public service, is a better way of deciding upon and dispensing services. The extent to which this enhances, or diminishes, diversity and plurality is a current debate which is keenly fought.

Similarly, it is argued that this shift in sentiment and policy is having a detrimental effect on publicly funded public service broadcasters, such as the BBC in Britain and the ABC in Australia, and on the television sector more generally. Somewhat ironically, many in the music industry have also contested the notion of choice through the medium of their own cultural products, two examples being Queen's 'Radio Ga Ga', and Bruce Springsteen's '57 Channels (And Nothin' On)'.

With a nod to Horkheimer and Adorno's referencing of illusion and uniformity, there are also arguments that the industrial logic which leads to endless reissues or adaptations of earlier cultural products can result in lesser investment in new ideas, artists and formats. What are your views about this?

REFLECTING ON THE READING

In full, the chapter from which the reading is drawn, 'The culture industry: enlightenment as mass deception', stretches to over fifty pages. However, while we hope you will eventually read it in full, our abridged extract does portray the essence of Horkheimer and Adorno's perspective on the culture industry, a term that is now indelibly linked to the Frankfurt school.

Even with a regular dictionary and a specialist subject dictionary to hand, the complex and technical language make it a difficult text to read, interrogate and, ultimately, understand. Yet even then, interpretations and judgements are likely to vary. Peters notes that since its first release during the Second World War this particular chapter has been 'hailed, vilified and misunderstood' (2003: 58), and that for many it 'evokes a monochrome image of zombified images presided over by an unholy alliance of Hitler and Hollywood' (2003: 59).

Before moving on to consider the extent to which this reading has influenced the development of media theory, and whether Horkheimer and Adorno's work still has relevance today, there is some value in reflecting on the second phrase of the chapter's title, 'Enlightenment as mass deception'. Horkheimer and Adorno provide their own definition of enlightenment:

> Enlightenment, understood in the widest sense as the advance of thought, has always aimed at liberating human beings from fear and installing them as masters. Yet the wholly enlightened earth is radiant with triumphant calamity.

> *(Horkheimer and Adorno 2002: 1)*

How does 'enlightenment' become 'mass deception', and what in this context is meant by 'mass deception'? The answers can vary. For example, Katz et al. (2003: 56) summarise Horkheimer and Adorno's position as 'conceiving of American culture as an industry with an assembly line for the manufacture of messages of false consciousness'. However, Stevenson (2002: 53) argues that the 'effectiveness of the culture industry was not secured through a deceptive ideology, but by the removal from the consciousness of the masses of any alternative to capitalism'.

A further dimension of 'mass deception' is provided by Peters, who describes mass culture as 'an organ of soft domination' in which people 'are active agents in their own duping' (2003: 63, 64). This assertion flows from Horkheimer and Adorno's insightful, but rather damning, assessment of advertising, which occurs towards the end of 'The culture industry' chapter:

> The most intimate actions of human beings have become so entirely reified, even to themselves, that the idea of anything peculiar to them survives only in extreme abstraction: personality means hardly more than dazzling white teeth and freedom from body odor and emotions. That is the triumph of advertising in the culture industry: the compulsive imitation by consumers of cultural commodities which, at the same time, they recognize as false.

> *(Horkheimer and Adorno 2002: 136)*

Horkheimer and Adorno's work, and that of the early Frankfurt school, have since been consigned to the first phase of media research and theory, one in which the media was suggested as an all-powerful and generally unmediated force that impacted negatively on mass culture (Turner 1996: 184). The second phase of media research is associated with the emergence of mass communication research in America during the 1960s, when the media was seen as reflecting the plurality of society, hence the assertion that pluralism 'made redundant' the Frankfurt school's earlier 'warnings about the manipulative potential of mass culture' (Turner 1996: 185).

However, while the Frankfurt school's all-embracing analysis of the culture industry is now generally acknowledged as being overly pessimistic, there are some elements of their work that remain relevant today. Three such elements are identified by Peters (2003: 66). First, the trend towards 'massive concentration' within the industry; secondly, what he describes as 'the packaging of resistance', and thirdly, the practice of incorporating 'audience preferences into the products themselves'.

For McGuigan, it is Horkheimer and Adorno's ability to illuminate the gap between rhetoric and reality – or the 'promotional ideology and the evidence of actual conditions' (1996: 78) – that attracts acclaim. The example he provides is one to which we are all likely to relate. This is the '[e]ndless propaganda concerning individualism and choice' which, it is argued, 'vastly exaggerates the power that "consumers" exercise over their daily lives' (p. 78). Peters has one more observation on Horkheimer and Adorno's 'culture industry'. Essentially, he believes that their analysis predates contested debates about the 'false, and now tired, dichotomy of either audience resistance or industrial manipulation' (Peters 2003: 59). In his view, Horkheimer and Adorno would simply have said, 'Both'!

A final point can be made on the relationship between Horkheimer and Adorno's notion of the 'culture industry' and that of the 'creative industries'. The latter term has been adopted by some governments in Europe and beyond to describe and support – through policy – what has become a significant and growing generator of gross domestic product (Hesmondhalgh 2002: 14).

Horkheimer and Adorno's original concept of the culture industry attracted renewed attention from academics, policymakers and activists in the late 1970s and during the 1980s (Garnham 1990: 165). This resulted in a preference for the plural, 'cultural industries', rather than its singular form. This change in emphasis was further underpinned by work undertaken by Miege (1979, 1987, 1989), a French sociologist, who is credited with exposing flaws in Horkheimer and Adorno's original theorisation of 'culture industry' (McGuigan 1996: 80).

Amongst other observations, Miege argued that the term 'cultural industries' better reflected the reality of what was a complex sector of the economy, pointing out that broadcasting, the press and the recording industry all operated in quite different ways (Hesmondhalgh 2002: 15–16; McGuigan 1996: 80).

In the 1980s, theory began to inform practice, as the cultural industries were seen as a vehicle to assist with the urban regeneration of a number of British cities (McGuigan 1996: 81–7). These developments were sparked by a policy proposal first developed in 1983 for the Labour Party administered Greater London Council (GLC) by Nicholas Garnham (1990: 154–68). Essentially, Garnham's analysis in London found that the cultural industries dominated the city's economy, and that there was a tendency for public funding to 'subsidize the existing tastes and habits of the better off' (1990: 164).

On coming to government in 1997, Tony Blair's 'New' Labour administration seized on the cultural industries as a tool for economic growth and community regeneration, but renamed the sector the 'creative industries'. In addition to music, film, television, radio and publishing, the sector would now comprise 'fashion, art, theatre, architecture, crafts, graphics, advertising, software, and journalism' (Smith 1998: 15).

The irony of this development is worth illuminating: that is, encouragement for investment in the cultural industries by those on the political Left, when Horkheimer and Adorno's original theorisation, 'culture industry', was actually 'hostile to the industrialisation of culture' (McGuigan 1996: 75).

Finally, it is worth noting that when 'New' Labour's first Secretary of State for Culture, Media and Sport, Chris Smith, published his vision for the creative industries, *Creative Britain* (1998), no mention was made of the Frankfurt school, nor of the original formulation 'culture industry'.

Key terms to explore

culture industry; enlightenment as deception; technical rationality; individual consciousness; culture monopolies; insatiable uniformity; omnipotence of capital.

Key writers who are mentioned

Tolstoy.

RECOMMENDED READING

Bottomore, T. (1984) *The Frankfurt School*, Chichester: Ellis Horwood Limited; London: Tavistock Publications.

Examines the rise, decline and significance of the Frankfurt school, focusing on the body of ideas developed and their dissemination.

Held, D. (1980) *Introduction to Critical Theory: Horkheimer to Habermas*, Cambridge: Polity Press.

Provides a detailed analysis of the Frankfurt school and its key players, and an in-depth introduction to, and evaluation of, critical theory.

Katz, E., Peter, J.D., Liebes, T., and Orloff, A. (eds) (2003) *Canonic Texts in Media Research*, Cambridge: Polity Press.

Outlines five key schools of thought, one being the Frankfurt school, which is discussed by way of critical reflections on works by Horkheimer and Adorno, and by Walter Benjamin.

CHAPTER 7

Harold D. Lasswell

Lasswell, H.D. (1948) 'The structure and function of communication in society', in Bryson, L. (ed.) *The Communication of Ideas*, New York: Institute for Religious and Social Studies, pp. 37–51.

INTRODUCTION TO HAROLD LASSWELL

Harold Dwight Lasswell was born in Illinois in the United States. Variously described as a political scientist and communications theorist, he spent most of his working life at the University of Chicago and then at Yale University (Dennis and Wartella 1996: 188).

Lasswell's first published works of substance focused on propaganda. His interest in this topic reflected the era in which he grew up and in which he began work. This was a period which saw innovations in propaganda by the British in the First World War (1914–18), claims by the advertising and public relations industries in the 1920s about their ability to 'engineer consent', and the use of propaganda by fascists in Europe and communists in the Soviet Union during the 1930s (Williams 2003: 30).

Not surprisingly, Lasswell's interests led to his first book, *Propaganda Techniques in the World War* (1927). This was followed by further publications dealing with related issues such as *Psychopathology and Politics* (1930), and, with Smith and Casey, *Propaganda and Promotional Activities: An annotated bibliography* (1935), and *Propaganda, Communication, and Public Opinion: A comprehensive reference guide* (1946).

Lasswell's work on propaganda was ground-breaking because it illustrated how, why and under what conditions propagandists could be successful and, in doing so, indicated when and why audiences were most likely to be susceptible to the 'message' being communicated (see, for example, Curran and Seaton 1997: 129, 268). As a result, Lasswell's work exposed the simplicity and limitations of the (then) prevailing 'magic bullet' or 'hypodermic needle' model of communication (Williams 2003: 30).

However, Lasswell is best known for his seminal work on communication, 'The structure and function of communication in society', which is the selected reading for this chapter. He is also listed as one of 'the "founding fathers" of communication research in the United States' (Schramm 1963, cited in Hardt 1995: 10). This accolade is due, at least in part, to the fact that Lasswell was one of a small number of researchers who began to distance themselves from the 'cultural/historical interpretation of communication' exemplified by thinkers such as those of the Chicago school.

Lasswell's preference was for quantitative approaches to analysis and investigation, a shift that helped establish communication research as a legitimate discipline, or field of study, in the United States (Hardt 1995: 11). This shift in direction was not without controversy. Critics argued that a preoccupation with methodological matters diverted attention from the significant social and political problems facing a post-war society, the latter deemed to be more worthy of research endeavour (Hardt 1995: 11).

Lasswell's 'The structure and function of communication in society' has received a great deal of attention and is often cited in texts about media and communication. For example, Williams refers to it as the 'most quoted description of the communication process' (2003: 6), while Briggs and Burke describe it as 'a simple but deservedly famous classic formula' (2002: 5). Similarly, Boyd-Barrett argues that this work by Lasswell 'helped to define the principal questions of communication studies' (1995b: 72), and Laughey describes it as a 'pioneering theoretical model of media effects' (2007: 8).

Lasswell's influence became evident in textbooks on communication research that were published during the 1950s and 1960s. However, and perhaps not surprisingly, given Lasswell's methodological preferences, these texts were seen to typify 'empiricist investigation and analysis', an approach that would later attract substantial criticism once it became less fashionable (Curran et al. 1977: 2).

INTRODUCTION TO THE READING

'The structure and function of communication in society' was first published in Lyman Bryson's edited collection, *The Communication of Ideas* (1948). This volume, which included a wide range of contributors all of whom were based in America, illuminated a diversity of theoretical and methodological approaches. It was one of a number of books published around this time that began to mark out an emerging field of communication research.

While Bryson's role as editor might not appear to be an obvious choice, given that he was employed at Columbia's Teachers College and specialised in adult education, his involvement in the project resulted from earlier membership of the Rockefeller Communications Group. This group, funded by the Rockefeller Foundation, carried out research in the areas of media and communication and came to be dominated by social scientists specialising in quantitative methods (Simonson and Weimann, 2003: 16). Hence, it is not surprising to find that Bryson's volume also includes a contribution from Paul Lazarsfeld (whom you can read more about in Chapter 8 of *this* book).

The chapters in Bryson's book had their origins in a series of lectures delivered to a graduate school in New York organised by the Institute for Religious and Social Studies between November 1946 and February 1947. The theme set for the graduate school was

'The problems of the communication of ideas'. This theme is the subject of Bryson's opening chapter, in which he makes two key points after providing a critical reflection on the fifteen contributions that make up the volume.

His first point is that 'there is no systematic outline of a theory of communication'. His second, that 'every thoughtful student of human behaviour today, no matter what he calls his field, is likely to find something which he will have to call "communication" obtrudes itself in the complex' (Bryson 1948: 1–2). The gendered nature of Bryson's language is not unusual in this period, even though the volume includes two chapters by Margaret Mead, the famous anthropologist.

When this reading is referred to in other texts on media, culture and communication, more often than not, it is Lasswell's dissection of the communication process that is the object of attention. As you will see, Lasswell opens the reading by defining the act of communication in the form of a series of questions:

Who, Says What, In Which Channel, To Whom, With What Effect?

(Lasswell 1948: 37)

Lewis and Slade describe this as a 'transmission model of communication' because it charts 'the pathways that communication takes', and it assumes that 'information, understanding and thoughts travel along these paths as if they were objects' (1994: 8; see also Carey 1989: 15–16). One benefit of this conceptualisation was that it illuminated three distinct elements of the communication process, those of production, content and reception, thereby providing the opportunity for specialisation in one or other area by researchers (Williams 2003: 46).

However, Lasswell's model is also categorised as an example of functionalism (Marshall 1998: 241), as it demonstrates a functional analysis of mass communication. It does so because it considers the functions, or effects, of communicative acts. In the case of mass communication, functionalism 'centres on the role of the media in the maintenance of social order and social structure, and examines how they perform or do not perform certain tasks necessary for the maintenance of equilibrium in society' (Williams 2003: 48).

As you will see in the reading, Lasswell makes the case for the media performing three social functions. The first function is *surveillance*, where the media provide information for individuals and society at large about the world which they inhabit. The second function, *correlation*, is the process by which the media explain and interpret events and, in doing so, provide a means of 'connecting' the different elements in society. The third function, *transmission*, is where the media act as an agency of socialisation, disseminating a society's social and cultural heritage to the next generation.

In order to explain his model of communication and to illustrate its functional characteristics, Lasswell follows the sociologist Emile Durkheim in using a biological, or organic, analogy (see, for example, Marshall 1998: 467). While the use of this analogy may be off-putting in the first instance, its value becomes evident as the reading progresses. Although biological analogy was a popular way of analysing the role of communication in society from the nineteenth century onwards, it has been superseded more recently by mechanical and cybernetic metaphors (Boyd-Barrett 1995b: 72).

While Lasswell's 'The structure and function of communication in society' has been lauded by media academics for the reasons noted above, it does have its limitations. As you read it, try and identify what these limitations might be.

READING

1

Harold D. Lassewell

The structure and function of communication in society

The Act of Communication

A convenient way to describe an act of communication is to answer the following questions:

> Who
> Says What
> In Which Channel
> To Whom
> With What Effect?

The scientific study of the process of communication tends to concentrate upon one or another of these questions. Scholars who study the "who," the communicator, look into the factors that initiate and guide the act of communication. We call this subdivision of the field of research *control analysis*. Specialists who focus upon the "says what" engage in *content analysis*. Those who look primarily at the radio, press, film and other channels of communication are doing *media analysis*. When the principal concern is with the persons reached by the media, we speak of *audience analysis*. If the question is the impact upon audiences, the problem is *effect analysis*.[1]

Whether such distinctions are useful depends entirely upon the degree of refinement which is regarded as appropriate to a given scientific and managerial objective. Often it is simpler to combine audience and effect analysis, for instance, than to keep them apart. On the other hand, we may want to concentrate on the analysis of content, and for this purpose subdivide the field into the study of purport and style, the first referring to the message, and the second to the arrangement of the elements of which the message is composed.

Structure and Function

Enticing as it is to work out these categories in more detail, the present discussion has a different scope. We are less interested in dividing up the act of communication than in viewing the act as a whole in relation to the entire social process. Any process can be examined in two frames of reference, namely, structure and function; and our analysis of communication will deal with the specializations that carry on certain functions, of which the following may be clearly distinguished: (1) The surveillance of the environment; (2) the correlation of the parts of society in responding to the environment; (3) the transmission of the social heritage from one generation to the next.

1. For more detail, consult the introductory matter in Bruce L. Smith, Harold D. Lasswell and Ralph D. Casey, *Propaganda, Communication, and Public Opinion: A Comprehensive Reference Guide*, Princeton University Press, Princeton, 1946.

NOTES

1 Structure

In all, the reading comprises thirteen subsections. While the final subsection provides a summary, the opening one does not constitute an introduction in the traditional sense. In other words, it doesn't set out how the author intends to tackle the subject matter. It is only after reading the second subsection, 'Structure and function', that the focus and purpose of the reading becomes clear.

Would the reading have benefited from the inclusion of a brief introductory section? If the reading had begun with a separate introduction, would this have undermined what could be described as a rather dramatic opening to the reading where Lasswell lists the component parts of an act of communication?

Context

As indicated above, the reading was produced in 1947 by Lasswell in response to a theme ('The problems of the communication of ideas') identified for a graduate school. By this time, Lasswell had already established a reputation as an expert in communication, particularly relating to propaganda.

Note how Lasswell makes clear, very early in the reading, that he is writing about the 'scientific study' of communication, remembering that it was during this period in the United States that efforts were being made to establish mass communication as a legitimate field of study, or discipline. Why did Lasswell need to make this point about his scientific approach?

Content

It seems somewhat ironic that Lasswell is probably best known for this opening paragraph, yet he doesn't return to discuss or reflect on it in the remainder of the reading.

In essence, Lasswell's formulation simply provides a mechanism for him to indicate – in the second subsection – that he intends not to dissect the communication act, but to analyse it 'as a whole', and to do so 'in relation to the entire social process'.

What do you think he means by 'entire social process'? If you were asked to describe an act of communication by way of a series of questions, would your response differ from that of Lasswell's? If so, how and why?

Lasswell's key intentions in this reading – and his functionalist analytic framework – become apparent in the second half of this subsection, where he identifies three social functions of communication: *surveillance*, *correlation* and *transmission*. It is not until much later in the reading that Lasswell returns to each of these social functions.

Writing Style

Note how Lasswell uses 'we' here and throughout the reading. What does he mean by 'we' when he uses it in the first subsection? What are the advantages and disadvantages of adopting this style?

READING

2

Biological Equivalencies

At the risk of calling up false analogies, we can gain perspective on human societies when we note the degree to which communication is a feature of life at every level. A vital entity, whether relatively isolated or in association, has specialized ways of receiving stimuli from the environment. The single-celled organism or the many-membered group tends to maintain an internal equilibrium and to respond to changes in the environment in a way that maintains this equilibrium. The responding process calls for specialized ways of bringing the parts of the whole into harmonious action. Multi-celled animals specialize cells to the function of external contact and internal correlation. Thus, among the primates, specialization is exemplified by organs such as the ear and eye, and the nervous system itself. When the stimuli receiving and disseminating patterns operate smoothly, the several parts of the animal act in concert in reference to the environment ("feeding," "fleeing," "attacking").[2]

In some animal societies certain members perform specialized roles, and survey the environment. Individuals act as "sentinels," standing apart from the herd or flock and creating a disturbance whenever an alarming change occurs in the surroundings. The trumpeting, cackling or shrilling of the sentinel is enough to set the herd in motion. Among the activities engaged in by specialized "leaders" is the internal stimulation of "followers" to adapt in an orderly manner to the circumstances heralded by the sentinels.[3]

Within a single, highly differentiated organism, incoming nervous impulses and outgoing impulses are transmitted along fibers that make synaptic junction with other fibers. The critical points in the process occur at the relay stations, where the arriving impulse may be too weak to reach the threshold which stirs the next link into action. At the higher centers, separate currents modify one another, producing results that differ in many ways from the outcome when each is allowed to continue a separate path. At any relay station there is no conductance, total conductance or intermediate conductance. The same categories apply to what goes on among members of an animal society. The sly fox may approach the barnyard in a way that supplies too meager stimuli for the sentinel to sound the alarm. Or the attacking animal may eliminate the sentinel before he makes more than a feeble outcry. Obviously there is every gradation possible between total conductance and no conductance.

Attention in World Society

When we examine the process of communication of any state in the world community, we note three categories of specialists. One group surveys the political environment of the state as a whole, another correlates the response of the whole state to the environment, and the third transmits certain patterns of response from the old to the young. Diplomats, attachés, and foreign correspondents are representative of those who specialize on the environment.

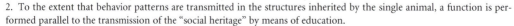

2. To the extent that behavior patterns are transmitted in the structures inherited by the single animal, a function is performed parallel to the transmission of the "social heritage" by means of education.
3. On animal sociology see: Warder C. Allee, *Animal Aggregations*, University of Chicago Press, Chicago, 1931; *The Social Life of Animals*, Norton, New York, 1935.

NOTES

2 Structure

After outlining three social functions of communication, one way to structure the next part of this reading would have been to use *surveillance*, *correlation* and *transmission* as subheadings, and then, under each one, explain how and why they constituted social functions. Instead, commencing in the subsection 'Biological equivalencies', Lasswell draws on biological analogies – or 'equivalencies' – to build, develop and substantiate his arguments throughout the remainder of the reading.

Content

Lasswell first teases out the characteristics of single-celled and multi-celled organisms, focusing on the relationship between an organism and its environment, with a particular interest in how equilibrium is maintained. He goes on to point out the importance of *specialist* communicative roles in some animal societies, and then draws attention to the notion of *conductance* – with gradations from none to total – to illustrate the relationship between effective communication and survival.

With a particular interest in communication and using a biological analogy, Lasswell has thus demonstrated the major interests of functionalism, that is, a 'focus on system-wide properties and on issues of system survival, adaptation and change' (Boyd-Barrett 1995b: 72). This analysis 'sets up' the framework which Lasswell uses in the remaining subsections.

For example, in the next subsection, 'Attention to world society', Lasswell focuses his gaze on the process of communication in a singular state or in a world community, suggesting that three groups of communication specialists can be identified: one whose prime role is surveillance, another whose responsibility is correlation, and a third who are involved in the process of transmission. He then goes on to suggest the types of professionals who would be involved in each of these specialist – and functional – activities.

Using concepts such as *conductance*, *relay points* and *attention frames*, Lasswell then focuses on the process by which communications originating from outside a state, reach, or don't reach, a wider audience. Here, he recognises the power and functions of certain specialists, the varied speed of communication, and the centrality of major metropolitan and political centres as communication hubs in developed countries. The contrast is then made with the distant centres in peripheral – or what we might now term 'developing' – countries.

To what extent do Lasswell's concepts of *conductance*, *relay points* and *attention frames* have any use or value today? While Lasswell makes mention of audiences, what role does he accord to them in these acts of communication, and what, if any, power does he imagine them having?

Context

While the means of communication have changed substantially since this article was published in 1948, the 'gap' between the resources available to developed and developing countries, implied here by Lasswell, remains substantial. Can you provide examples illustrating this rich–poor divide?

READING

(continued)

Editors, journalists, and speakers are correlators of the internal response. Educators in family and school transmit the social inheritance.

Communications which originate abroad pass through sequences in which various senders and receivers are linked with one another. Subject to modification at each relay point in the chain, messages originating with a diplomat or foreign correspondent may pass through editorial desks and eventually reach large audiences.

If we think of the world attention process as a series of *attention frames*, it is possible to describe the rate at which comparable content is brought to the notice of individuals and groups. We can inquire into the point at which "conductance" no longer occurs; and we can look into the range between "total conductance" and "minimum conductance." The metropolitan and political centers of the world have much in common with the interdependence, differentiation, and activity of the cortical or subcortical centers of an individual organism. Hence the attention frames found in these spots are the most variable, refined, and interactive of all frames in the world community.

At the other extreme are the attention frames of primitive inhabitants of isolated areas. Not that folk cultures are wholly untouched by industrial civilization. Whether we parachute into the interior of New Guinea, or land on the slopes of the Himalayas, we find no tribe wholly out of contact with the world. The long threads of trade, of missionary zeal, of adventurous exploration and scientific field study, and of global war, reach the far distant places. No one is entirely out of this world.

Among primitives the final shape taken by communication is the ballad or tale. Remote happenings in the great world of affairs, happenings that come to the notice of metropolitan audiences, are reflected, however dimly, in the thematic material of ballad singers and reciters. In these creations far away political leaders may be shown supplying land to the peasants or restoring an abundance of game to the hills.[4]

When we push upstream of the flow of communication, we note that the immediate relay function for nomadic and remote tribesmen is sometimes performed by the inhabitants of settled villages with whom they come in occasional contact. The relayer can be the school teacher, doctor, judge, tax collector, policeman, soldier, peddler, salesman, missionary, student; in any case he is an assembly point of news and comment.

4. Excellent examples are given in Robert Redfield's account of *Tepoztlan, A Mexican Village: A Study of Folk Life*, University of Chicago Press, Chicago, 1930.

NOTES

(continued)

A further point might be made about what we now refer to as globalisation. Although Lasswell doesn't mention the term, his recognition that varying forms of communication – through missionaries, trade and war – enabled an interconnected world, acts as a reminder that globalisation should be seen as a process and not as a sudden event.

A further point might be made here about Lasswell's use of a biological analogy and his focus on 'top down', rather than 'bottom up', communication. As a sociologist, Lasswell would have been aware of the work of Emile Durkheim, a French sociologist and one of the 'founding fathers' of the discipline, who pointed to the value of using an organic analogy to understand society (Marshall 1998: 175, 467).

Also, with a background in psychology, Lasswell would be aware of the biological bases of behaviour, hence his use of equivalencies in the physical organism and other animal species. Similarly, the focus on 'top down' communication has its origins in Lasswell's earlier research, which examined the ways in which propaganda had been developed and used by states during periods of war, and also in response to internal conflicts.

Writing Style

Two points can be made about style. The first might be more about technique than writing style, but Lasswell's use of analogy prompts four questions. First, what do you think he means by 'false analogy'? Secondly, to what extent is his selected analogy useful in this reading and, if so, why? Thirdly, what other analogies can you think of that have been used in discussions about mass communication? Fourthly, what are the pros and cons of using analogy as a means of analysis and explanation?

You may have already observed that Lasswell – perhaps conforming to the style required by the editor of this publication – uses footnotes for additional material and citations. Also, note that he cites a number of his own publications in these footnotes.

READING

3

More Detailed Equivalencies

The communication processes of human society, when examined in detail, reveal many equivalencies to the specializations found in the physical organism, and in the lower animal societies. The diplomats, for instance, of a single state are stationed all over the world and send messages to a few focal points. Obviously, these incoming reports move from the many to the few, where they interact upon one another. Later on, the sequence spreads fanwise according to a few to many pattern, as when a foreign secretary gives a speech in public, an article is put out in the press, or a news film is distributed to the theaters. The lines leading from the outer environment of the state are functionally equivalent to the afferent channels that convey incoming nervous impulses to the central nervous system of a single animal, and to the means by which alarm is spread among a flock. Outgoing, or efferent impulses, display corresponding parallels.

The central nervous system of the body is only partly involved in the entire flow of afferent-efferent impulses. There are automatic systems that can act on one another without involving the "higher" centers at all. The stability of the internal environment is maintained principally through the mediation of the vegetive or autonomic specializations of the nervous system. Similarly, most of the messages within any state do not involve the central channels of communication. They take place within families, neighborhoods, shops, field gangs, and other local contexts. Most of the educational process is carried on the same way.

A further set of significant equivalencies is related to the circuits of communication, which are predominantly one-way or two-way, depending upon the degree of reciprocity between communicators and audience. Or, to express it differently, two-way communication occurs when the sending and receiving functions are performed with equal frequency by two or more persons. A conversation is usually assumed to be a pattern of two-way communication (although monologues are hardly unknown). The modern instruments of mass communication give an enormous advantage to the controllers of printing plants, broadcasting equipment, and other forms of fixed and specialized capital. But it should be noted that audiences do "talk back," after some delay; and many controllers of mass media use scientific methods of sampling in order to expedite this closing of the circuit.

Circuits of two-way contact are particularly in evidence among the great metropolitan, political and cultural centers in the world. New York, Moscow, London and Paris, for example, are in intense two-way contact, even when the flow is severely curtailed in volume (as between Moscow and New York). Even insignificant sites become world centers when they are transformed into capital cities (Canberra in Australia, Ankara in Turkey, the District of Columbia, U.S.A.). A cultural center like Vatican City is in intense two-way relationship with the dominant centers throughout the world. Even specialized production centers like Hollywood, despite their preponderance of outgoing material, receive an enormous volume of messages.

A further distinction can be made between message controlling and message handling centers and social formations. The message center in the vast Pentagon Building of the War Department in Washington, D.C., transmits with no more than accidental change incoming messages to addressees. This is the role of the printers and distributors of books; of dispatchers,

NOTES

3 Content

Here the biological analogy is continued by identifying equivalencies between the specialisations integral to physical organisms, and those evident in the communication processes of human society. Three equivalencies are suggested.

First, beginning with the example of the diplomatic service, Lasswell suggests that the incoming and outgoing communication channels of a single state have a similar function to the afferent and efferent channels that convey impulses to and from the central nervous system of a single animal. This is because in each case these processes provide information that will enable both of these entities – or systems – to act in ways which are intended to aid survival, and also to ensure equilibrium in the context of their respective environments.

Lasswell's second equivalence flows from a recognition that living organisms, in addition to having a central nervous system, rely on a number of automatic systems to help maintain internal equilibrium. States, he argues, are similar to the extent that they have ongoing communication channels and processes that don't actively involve central, or higher level, channels of communication. He gives examples of these channels, one being families, suggesting that they and other local institutions help the state maintain internal equilibrium acting, as they do, as part of the 'education process'.

Lasswell's third equivalence is what he refers to as 'circuits of communication'. This concept is used for two purposes: first, to distinguish between what might be considered as predominantly one-way, or two-way, circuits of communication; secondly, to provide examples of two-way circuits in the form of major world political and cultural centres.

In the case of the former, a distinction is made between a conversation – suggested as a two-way circuit of communication – and the 'one-way' communication effected by the 'modern instruments of mass communication'. Here Lasswell recognises the power and interests of those that control mass media, but he also makes reference to audiences. What do you think Lasswell means by audience 'talk back'? Is he suggesting that this constitutes a two-way circuit of communication?

In recalling the year when this reading was published, Lasswell's list of major world centres is probably predictable. Here, New York, Moscow, London and Paris are all suggested as 'intense' two-way circuits of communication. However, and thinking particularly about the historical epoch in which Lasswell was writing, why would there be a reduced flow in the volume of communication between Moscow and New York?

Lasswell's final observation in this subsection relates to the roles of those involved in maintaining the circuits of communication, recalling his earlier use of concepts such as *conductance* and *relay stations* or *relay points*. Here, he makes the distinction between the message manipulators and the message handlers, or 'symbol specialists', a category in which he includes editors, censors and propagandists, to which we might add 'spin doctors' and public relations professionals in contemporary times.

To what extent is the concept, *circuits of communication*, relevant in the current era of globalisation?

READING

3

(continued)

linemen, and messengers connected with telegraphic communication; of radio engineers, and other technicians associated with broadcasting. Such message handlers may be contrasted with those who affect the content of what is said, which is the function of editors, censors, and propagandists. Speaking of the symbol specialists as a whole, therefore, we separate them into the manipulators (controllers) and the handlers; the first group typically modifies content, while the second does not.

4

Needs and Values

Though we have noted a number of functional and structural equivalencies between communication in human societies and other living entities, it is not implied that we can most fruitfully investigate the process of communication in America or the world by the methods most appropriate to research on the lower animals or on single physical organisms. In comparative psychology when we describe some part of the surroundings of a rat, cat, or monkey as a stimulus (that is, as part of the environment reaching the attention of the animal), we cannot ask the rat; we use other means of inferring perception. When human beings are our objects of investigation, we can interview the great "talking animal." (This is not that we take everything at face value. Sometimes we forecast the opposite of what the person says he intends to do. In this case, we depend on other indications, both verbal and non-verbal.)

In the study of living forms, it is rewarding, as we have said, to look at them as modifiers of the environment in the process of gratifying needs, and hence of maintaining a steady state of internal equilibrium. Food, sex, and other activities which involve the environment can be examined on a comparative basis. Since human beings exhibit speech reactions, we can investigate many more relationships than in the non-human species.[5] Allowing for the data furnished by speech (and other communicative acts), we can investigate human society in terms of values; that is, in reference to categories of relationships that are recognized objects

---

5. Properly handled, the speech event can be described with as much reliability and validity as many non-speech events which are more conventionally used as data in scientific investigations.

Context

(continued)

While Lasswell's recognition that some previously 'insignificant sites' could become major world centres is obviously correct, his analysis nevertheless suggests a centre–periphery perspective which plots all other places in relation to a centre which is the United States. Therefore, we might want to consider the view that simply describing these relationships as two-way circuits of communication disguises, or diverts attentions from, questions about the respective power and influence of the communicators.

Keeping in mind the content of communication and the biological analogy, provide examples that illustrate how two-way communication flows between the Vatican and other dominant centres, and Hollywood and its dominant centres, function to assist each organisation, or system, in maintaining internal and external equilibrium.

Structure/writing style

In approaching the half-way point of the reading you will have noted how Lasswell's style involves structuring the text by the use of shortish paragraphs, all roughly the same length. Do you think that this makes the material easier to engage with?

Writing Style

Note how Lasswell uses the first part of this opening sentence to both recap and remind readers that the reading to date has been organised around the 'functional and structural equivalencies between human societies and other living entities'.

Structure

You may need to have a sociological dictionary handy when reading this next section. It illustrates that the original research paper and the subsequently published reading were aimed at a specialist audience. Here, Lasswell introduces a number of key concepts, such as institutions, ideology and social structure (see *Context* below). However, the point to note is how these and other core concepts are used to construct the framework that enables the analysis, which in turn leads to explanation.

Content

Staying with his biological analogy, Lasswell uses the first two paragraphs for three purposes. First, and using comparative psychology as a reference point, he points out the additional methodological opportunities that are available to researchers who are investigating the 'talking animal'.

Secondly, he notes that a further opportunity for researchers interested in human, rather than non-human, species is that they can go beyond enquiries into *needs* to explore *values*. Although Lasswell provides a definition of the latter, you might want to make your own enquiry for a more nuanced understanding. Also, while he suggests it is relatively simple to identify at least two *values* associated with the United States, he doesn't indicate how this might be done, and neither does

READING

(continued)

of gratification. In America, for example, it requires no elaborate technique of study to discern that power and respect are values. We can demonstrate this by listening to testimony, and by watching what is done when opportunity is afforded.

It is possible to establish a list of values current in any group chosen for investigation. Further than this, we can discover the rank order in which these values are sought. We can rank the members of the group according to their position in relation to the values. So far as industrial civilization is concerned, we have no hesitation in saying that power, wealth, respect, well being, and enlightenment are among the values. If we stop with this list, which is not exhaustive, we can describe on the basis of available knowledge (fragmentary though it may often be), the social structure of most of the world. Since values are not equally distributed, the social structure reveals more or less concentration of relatively abundant shares of power, wealth and other values in a few hands. In some places this concentration is passed on from generation to generation, forming castes rather than a mobile society.

In every society the values are shaped and distributed according to more or less distinctive patterns (*institutions*). The institutions include communications which are invoked in support of the network as a whole. Such communications are the ideology; and in relation to power we can differentiate the political *doctrine*, the political *formula* and the *miranda*.[6] These are illustrated in the United States by the doctrine of individualism, the paragraphs of the Constitution, which are the formula, and the ceremonies and legends of public life, which comprise the miranda. The ideology is communicated to the rising generation through such specialized agencies as the home and school.

Ideology is only part of the myths of any given society. There may be counter ideologies directed against the dominant doctrine, formula, and miranda. Today the power structure of world politics is deeply affected by ideological conflict, and by the role of two giant powers, the United States and Russia.[7] The ruling elites view one another as potential enemies, not only in the sense that interstate differences may be settled by war, but in the more urgent sense that the ideology of the other may appeal to disaffected elements at home and weaken the internal power position of each ruling class.

6. These distinctions are derived and adapted from the writings of Charles E. Merriam, Gaetano Mosca, Karl Mannheim, and others. For a systematic exposition see the forthcoming volume by Harold D. Lasswell and Abraham Kaplan.

7. See William T.R. Fox, *The Super-Powers*, Harcourt, Brace, New York, 1944, and Harold D. Lasswell, *World Politics Faces Economics*, McGraw-Hill, New York, 1945.

NOTES

(continued)

he acknowledge that the examples provided, *power* and *respect*, might be interpreted in quite different ways within that country, depending on issues such as ethnicity, gender, social class and geographic location.

Thirdly, and more by inference than explicit statement, he reminds that research into the process of communication in human societies is a scientific endeavour, even if using other than quantitative methods. Apropos this point, note how Lasswell makes reference to *reliability* and *validity* in the footnote. What do you understand by these two terms, and why does he use them?

In the third paragraph of this subsection, Lasswell makes three further claims about values.

First, he claims that it is possible to identify the values of any given group, list them in order of desirability, and then position members of the group in relation to the values as ranked. Secondly, but without citing evidence, he lists the core values of 'industrialised civilization' which, it is argued, provide a means of predicting the 'social structure of most of the world'. Thirdly, after recognising that power and wealth tend to be concentrated 'in a few hands', he concludes that 'values are not equally distributed'.

The wording used here acts as a reminder that the concept, *values*, can be understood in quite different ways. For example, while individuals might hold the same values, the extent to which they can practise, uphold or achieve them will obviously vary according to a variety of circumstances, some of which are noted above. Also, other observers might note that the author, Lasswell, being a white, (then) middle-aged, middle-class, American citizen, would approach a discussion about values from a particular, and privileged, position (this recurring problem in media theory is explored in Chapter 1 of *this* book).

Lasswell now moves to the nub of his argument in this subsection: that is, to consider the way in which communications, disseminated through various institutions, shape and maintain values in human society. Here, communications are seen as 'the ideology' which is passed on to future generations via the home and school. Described as 'specialised agencies' by Lasswell, these institutions are involved in the 'transmission of the social heritage from one generation to the next'.

In the final paragraph, Lasswell goes on to recognise the scope for counter-ideology to be developed which threatens the dominant power structure, explained here as comprising the political doctrine, political formula and political miranda. Such opposition may emerge within a society, or be apparent in the behaviour of external forces such as other states. The role of communication in dealing with actual and potential conflicts is taken up by Lasswell in the next subsection.

Context

Two points might be made here. One is about Lasswell's educational background, and the other is about contemporary similarities with the period in which the reading was published.

This subsection, in particular, illuminates Lasswell's academic background. Here, within the space of five paragraphs, he makes reference to concepts such as values, institutions, social structure, power, ideology, ruling elites and myths, all of which are analytic tools likely to be used by sociologists and political scientists, and in the case of myths, anthropologists. However, given that the reading was

READING

5

Social Conflict and Communication

Under the circumstances, one ruling element is especially alert to the other, and relies upon communication as a means of preserving power. One function of communication, therefore, is to provide intelligence about what the other elite is doing, and about its strength. Fearful that intelligence channels will be controlled by the other, in order to withhold and distort, there is a tendency to resort to secret surveillance. Hence international espionage is intensified above its usual level in peacetime. Moreover, efforts are made to "black out" the self in order to counteract the scrutiny of the potential enemy. In addition, communication is employed affirmatively for the purpose of establishing contact with audiences within the frontiers of the other power.

These varied activities are manifested in the use of open and secret agents to scrutinize the other, in counter intelligence work, in censorship and travel restriction, in broadcasting and other informational activities across frontiers.

Ruling elites are also sensitized to potential threats in the internal environment. Besides using open sources of information, secret measures are also adopted. Precautions are taken to impose "security" upon as many policy matters as possible. At the same time, the ideology of the elite is reaffirmed, and counter ideologies are suppressed.

The processes here sketched run parallel to phenomena to be observed throughout the animal kingdom. Specialized agencies are used to keep aware of threats and opportunities in the external environment. The parallels include the surveillance exercised over the internal environment, since among the lower animals some herd leaders sometimes give evidence of fearing attack on two fronts, internal and external; they keep an uneasy eye on both environments. As a means of preventing surveillance by an enemy, well known devices are at the disposal of certain species, *e.g.*, the squid's use of a liquid fog screen, the protective coloration of the chameleon. However, there appears to be no correlate of the distinction between the "secret" and "open" channels of human society.

Inside a physical organism the closest parallel to social revolution would be the growth of new nervous connections with parts of the body that rival, and can take the place of, the existing structures of central integration. Can this be said to occur as the embryo develops in the mother's body? Or, if we take a destructive, as distinct from a reconstructive, process, can we properly say that internal surveillance occurs in regard to cancer, since cancers compete for the food supplies of the body?

NOTES

4

(continued)

published in 1948, you might find it helpful to look up these concepts in more recently published sociological dictionaries, as well as those concerned with key concepts in communication, cultural and media studies (see, for example, Hartley 2002b; Marshall 1998).

The second point relates to Lasswell's reference to ideological conflict between nation-states, his example being the United States and Russia in the late 1940s. At that time the conflict centred on the struggle for dominance of capitalism or communism. What are the current ideological conflicts that dominate world politics, and which states are involved and why?

5

Content

Having sketched out how and why ideological conflicts emerge within and between states, Lasswell uses this subsection to outline how ruling elites use communication not only to maintain their own power but also to undermine that of their rivals.

First, he considers external threats, suggesting that the function of communication is to provide intelligence about the activities, intentions and strength of rivals, and also to establish contacts with individuals and groups within the boundaries of the other power.

Similarly, particular forms of communication are used to identify, assess and counter threats within the internal environment. Lasswell's reference to the introduction of particular policy measures, the use of covert operations, and the use of strategic communication both to support the dominant ideology and to undermine counter-ideology have a resonance today, particularly in respect of the so-called 'war on terror'.

Structure

Note the neat, logical – even symmetrical – way in which Lasswell organises his argument in this subsection. He first deals with human society, both in terms of the internal as well as external environment, and then uses the same approach to illustrate patterns in the animal kingdom. Also, in the case of both, he refers to the 'specialised agencies' that are involved in monitoring, and responding to, emergent threats and opportunities.

READING

6

Efficient Communication

The analysis up to the present implies certain criteria of efficiency or inefficiency in communication. In human societies the process is efficient to the degree that rational judgments are facilitated. A rational judgment implements value-goals. In animal societies communication is efficient when it aids survival, or some other specified need of the aggregate. The same criteria can be applied to the single organism.

One task of a rationally organized society is to discover and control any factors that interfere with efficient communication. Some limiting factors are psychotechnical. Destructive radiation, for instance, may be present in the environment, yet remain undetected owing to the limited range of the unaided organism.

But even technical insufficiencies can be overcome by knowledge. In recent years short-wave broadcasting has been interfered with by disturbances which will either be surmounted, or will eventually lead to the abandonment of this mode of broadcasting. During the past few years advances have been made toward providing satisfactory substitutes for defective hearing and seeing. A less dramatic, though no less important, development has been the discovery of how inadequate reading habits can be corrected.

There are, of course, deliberate obstacles put in the way of communication, like censorship and drastic curtailment of travel. To some extent obstacles can be surmounted by skillful evasion, but in the long run it will doubtless be more efficient to get rid of them by consent or coercion.

Sheer ignorance is a pervasive factor whose consequences have never been adequately assessed. Ignorance here means the absence, at a given point in the process of communication, of knowledge which is available elsewhere in society. Lacking proper training, the personnel engaged in gathering and disseminating intelligence is continually misconstruing or overlooking the facts, if we define the facts as what the objective, trained observer could find.

In accounting for inefficiency we must not overlook the low evaluations put upon skill in relevant communication. Too often irrelevant, or positively distorting, performances command prestige. In the interest of a "scoop," the reporter gives a sensational twist to a mild international conference, and contributes to the popular image of international politics as chronic, intense conflict, and little else. Specialists in communication often fail to keep up with the expansion of knowledge about the process; note the reluctance with which many visual devices have been adopted. And despite research on vocabulary, many mass communicators select words that fail. This happens, for instance, when a foreign correspondent allows himself to become absorbed in the foreign scene and forgets that his home audience has no direct equivalents in experience for "left," "center," and other factional terms.

Besides skill factors, the level of efficiency is sometimes adversely influenced by personality structure. An optimistic, outgoing person may hunt "birds of a feather" and gain an uncorrected and hence exaggeratedly optimistic view of events. On the contrary, when pessimistic, brooding personalities mix, they choose quite different birds, who confirm their gloom. There are also important differences among people which spring from contrasts in intelligence and energy.

↓

NOTES

 ## Content

Lasswell's biological analogy is used here to consider the equivalencies in human societies and animal societies in respect of the purpose of efficient communication. For human societies, he argues, efficient communication is achieved if 'rational judgments are facilitated', and for the animal world, 'when it aids survival'. Lasswell then goes on to identify six reasons why communication could be deemed inefficient.

First, the limiting nature of certain technologies. Secondly, obstacles intentionally set in place to impede communication, such as censorship. Thirdly, the ignorance or lack of knowledge on the part of individual communicators. Fourthly, the lack of skills demonstrated by individual communicators or their unwillingness, or inability, to update or develop new skills. Fifthly, 'defects', or 'flaws', in the personality structure of communicators. Sixthly, and in relation to the wider society, where certain values, such as power, are intentionally distorted.

The implication to be drawn from this analysis is that if such inefficiencies could be overcome, then communication would become more efficient, thereby helping to facilitate a society's 'rational judgements'.

Writing Style

Two points are worthy of note. Once again we see instances of how Lasswell introduces a concept, or term, and in the same sentence, or the one that follows, he provides a brief definition or explanation. Some of the examples in this subsection are 'efficient communication', 'rational judgement', 'ignorance' and 'facts'.

Similarly, to help illustrate, clarify or substantiate his arguments, Lasswell makes regular use of examples. In this subsection, he does so by providing instances of poor skills, failings in vocabulary, personality flaws and distorted values. He returns to this notion of distorted values later in the reading.

Context

The era in which this reading was published becomes evident in the third paragraph, when Lasswell makes reference to some of the limitations of broadcast technology and the resultant impact on the efficiency of communication. He would probably be astounded by the developments that have occurred since 1948 and the resulting efficiencies in communication. However, along with change there is also continuity.

For example, while the introduction of e-mail has brought about efficiencies, it has also introduced challenges that, if not handled correctly, can result in previously unimagined inefficiencies. Moreover, if one was to undertake a functional audit of communication today in the way that Lasswell does, the likelihood is that the inefficiencies would be similar.

At least two questions might usefully be posed about Lasswell's material in terms of its relevance to contemporary society, one quite specific and the other more general. First, to what extent is the concept of *social class* still helpful when asking questions about communication? Secondly, to what degree is it useful to consider the idea of *efficient* and *inefficient* communication in terms of the wider society today?

READING

6

(continued)

> Some of the most serious threats to efficient communication for the community as a whole relate to the values of power, wealth and respect. Perhaps the most striking examples of power distortion occur when the content of communication is deliberately adjusted to fit an ideology or counter ideology. Distortions related to wealth not only arise from attempts to influence the market, for instance, but from rigid conceptions of economic interest. A typical instance of inefficiencies connected with respect (social class) occurs when an upper class person mixes only with persons of his own stratum and forgets to correct his perspective by being exposed to members of other classes.

7

> *Research on Communication*
>
> The foregoing reminders of some factors that interfere with efficient communication point to the kinds of research which can usefully be conducted on representative links in the chain of communication. Each agent is a vortex of interacting environmental and predispositional factors. Whoever performs a relay function can be examined in relation to input and output. What statements are brought to the attention of the relay link? What does he pass on verbatim? What does he drop out? What does he rework? What does he add? How do differences in input and output correlate with culture and personality? By answering such questions it is possible to weigh the various factors in conductance, no conductance and modified conductance.
>
> Besides the relay link, we must consider the primary link in a communication sequence. In studying the focus of attention of the primary observer, we emphasize two sets of influences: Statements to which he is exposed; other features of his environment. An attaché or foreign correspondent exposes himself to mass media and private talk; also, he can count soldiers, measure gun emplacements, note hours of work in a factory, see butter and fat on the table.
>
> Actually it is useful to consider the attention frame of the relay as well as the primary link in terms of media and non-media exposures. The role of non-media factors is very slight in the case of many relay operators, while it is certain to be significant in accounting for the primary observer.

7 Content

For Lasswell, one advantage of analysing inefficiencies in the chain of communication is that it points both to where research can be directed, and to the sorts of questions that might be asked (some of which he lists).

If we were to employ these questions and analyse the results, we would need to be clear about the meanings of concepts introduced earlier in the reading, such as 'relay function', 'conductance' and 'attention frame', to which Lasswell now adds 'relay link' and 'primary link' or 'primary observer'.

Bearing in mind Lasswell's discussion in the previous subsection about the factors that impede efficient communication, what does he mean by the following statement: '[e]ach agent is a vortex of interacting environmental and predispositional factors'? Also, what sort of information is Lasswell looking for in response to the following question? 'How do differences in input and output correlate with culture and personality?'

Writing Style

You will have noted the gendered nature of the text which tends to be the norm for material published in this era.

READING

8

Attention Aggregates and Publics

It should be pointed out that everyone is not a member of the world public, even though he belongs to some extent to the world attention aggregate. To belong to an attention aggregate it is only necessary to have common symbols of reference. Everyone who has a symbol of reference for New York, North America, the Western Hemisphere or the globe is a member respectively of the attention aggregate of New York, North America, the Western Hemisphere, the globe. To be a member of the New York public, however, it is essential to make demands for public action in New York, or expressly affecting New York.

The public of the United States, for instance, is not confined to residents or citizens, since non-citizens who live beyond the frontier may try to influence American politics. Conversely, everyone who lives in the United States is not a member of the American public, since something more than passive attention is necessary. An individual passes from an attention aggregate to the public when he begins to expect that what he wants can affect public policy.

Sentiment Groups and Publics

A further limitation must be taken into account before we can correctly classify a specific person or group as part of a public. The demands made regarding public policy must be debatable. The world public is relatively weak and undeveloped, partly because it is typically kept subordinate to sentiment areas in which no debate is permitted on policy matters. During a war or war crisis, for instance, the inhabitants of a region are overwhelmingly committed to impose certain policies on others. Since the outcome of the conflict depends on violence, and not debate, there is no public under such conditions. There is a network of sentiment groups that act as crowds, hence tolerate no dissent.[8]

From the foregoing analysis it is clear that there are attention, public and sentiment areas of many degrees of inclusiveness in world politics. These areas are interrelated with the structural and functional features of world society, and especially of world power. It is evident, for instance, that *the strongest powers tend to be included in the same attention area*, since their ruling elites focus on one another as the source of great potential threat. The strongest powers usually pay proportionately less attention to the weaker powers than the weaker powers pay to them, since stronger powers are typically more important sources of threat, or of protection, for weaker powers than the weaker powers are for the stronger.[9]

The attention structure within a state is a valuable index of the degree of state integration. When the ruling classes fear the masses, the rulers do not share their picture of reality with

---

8. The distinction between the "crowd" and the "public" was worked out in the Italian, French and German literature of criticism that grew up around Le Bon's over-generalized use of the crowd concept. For a summary of this literature by a scholar who later became one of the most productive social scientists in this field, see Robert E. Park, *Masse und Publikum; Eine methodologische und soziologische Untersuchung*, Lack and Grunau, Bern, 1904. (Heidelberg dissertation.)

9. The propositions in this paragraph are hypotheses capable of being subsumed under the general theory of power, referred to in footnote 6. See also Harold D. Lasswell and Joseph M. Goldsen, "Public Attention, Opinion and Action," *The International Journal of Opinion and Attitude Research*, Mexico City, I, 1947, pp. 3–11.

8   Content

In this and the following subsection, Lasswell uses examples of particular localities (New York), regions (North America), states (the United States) and the world as a whole (the globe). He also distinguishes between 'publics', 'attention aggregates' and 'sentiment groups'.

Publics, he argues, can only be construed as such if they are actively involved, through debate, in shaping public policy, but may in certain circumstances be barred from doing so by ruling elites.

Lasswell then proposes that the notion of publics, attention aggregates and sentiment groups provides a useful way of understanding the varying degrees of inclusiveness that exist in 'world politics'. He concludes that all three groups are 'interrelated with the structural and functional features of world society and especially of world power'.

With a focus on the external environment of states, he then illustrates the latter point by contrasting the 'attention area' of stronger powers with those of weaker powers. The concept, 'attention area', is similar to that of 'attention frame', which is discussed on page 110.

The latter two paragraphs of this second subsection, 'Sentiment groups and publics', focuses on the internal environment of a state, with Lasswell suggesting the concept of 'attention structure' (which is used again in the following subsection) as an indicator of 'state integration'. Here – reflecting Lasswell's interest in state propaganda – the focus is on how ruling elites manipulate the communication channels in order to ensure internal equilibrium.

The final paragraph begs at least three questions. First, what do you understand by the meaning of 'truth' in this context? Secondly, how could channels of communication be organised in the way suggested by Lasswell? Thirdly, can you think of actual examples where, at least to some degree, this manipulation or distortion of communication has occurred in recent times?

Context

Attention might be drawn to Lasswell's use of 'world public', and his contention that this particular public is 'relatively weak and underdeveloped'. This idea resonates with Jürgen Habermas's notion of the public sphere (see Chapter 13). However, Lasswell's thinking is more akin to the idea of a global public sphere, rather than the local – as in nation-state – public sphere imagined by Habermas.

Structure

Your immediate reaction to this subsection may be that its relevance and relationship to the reading to date is not clear. If so, this is understandable, as the subject matter does not obviously follow that discussed in the preceding subsection.

When this occurs, one obvious strategy for you to adopt is to continue reading in the hope that connections and relevance subsequently become apparent. If this advice is followed, you will see that Lasswell uses these two subsections, 'Attention aggregates' and 'Sentiment groups and publics', to provide a backdrop for a discussion in the penultimate subsection about public opinion and enlightenment.

READING

8

(continued)

the rank and file. When the reality picture of kings, presidents and cabinets is not permitted to circulate through the state as a whole, the degree of discrepancy shows the extent to which the ruling groups assume that their power depends on distortion.

Or, to express the matter another way: If the "truth" is not shared, the ruling elements expect internal conflict, rather than harmonious adjustment to the external environment of the state. Hence the channels of communication are controlled in the hope of organizing the attention of the community at large in such a way that only responses will be forthcoming which are deemed favorable to the power position of the ruling classes.

9

The Principle of Equivalent Enlightenment

It is often said in democratic theory that rational public opinion depends upon enlightenment. There is, however, much ambiguity about the nature of enlightenment, and the term is often made equivalent to perfect knowledge. A more modest and immediate conception is not perfect but equivalent enlightenment. The attention structure of the full time specialist on a given policy will be more elaborate and refined than that of the layman. That this difference will always exist, we must take for granted. Nevertheless, it is quite possible for the specialist and the layman to agree on the broad outlines of reality. A workable goal of democratic society is equivalent enlightenment as between expert, leader and layman.

Expert, leader and layman can have the same gross estimate of major population trends of the world. They can share the same general view of the likelihood of war. It is by no means fantastic to imagine that the controllers of mass media of communication will take the lead in bringing about a high degree of equivalence throughout society between the layman's picture of significant relationships, and the picture of the expert and the leader.

9 Content

Within the space of the first two sentences, Lasswell introduces two concepts that have not previously appeared in the reading and which assume a certain level of understanding on the part of the reader.

The first is 'rational public opinion', which is not defined, but which flows from the discussion in the preceding subsections about what constitutes a 'public'. The second is enlightenment, which is also not defined, but is recognised by the author as an ambiguous term (see, for example, Marshall 1998: 194).

Lasswell 'needs' both of these concepts to set up the argument being made in this subsection. That is, as rational public opinion is dependent on enlightenment, or perfect knowledge, which is unrealistic, the goal for democratic society should be 'equivalent enlightenment'. He then proceeds to explain, using examples, the meaning of this term, and the implications for experts, leaders and laymen.

As Lasswell's explanation is somewhat abbreviated, at least three questions emerge. First, can 'equivalent enlightenment' enable 'rational public opinion'? Secondly, how do you respond to the assertion that so-called experts will always have a better understanding of policy than the layman (sic)? Thirdly, what do you understand by Lasswell's prediction about the mass media of communication in the final sentence?

Structure

You may have noted the technique that Lasswell uses to launch his argument. First, referring to democratic theory, he 'sets up' the idea that rational public opinion is dependent on enlightenment. Having done so, he then proceeds to destabilise this perspective by using one (of many potential) meanings of enlightenment to justify his proposition of equivalent enlightenment.

READING

10

Summary

The communication process in society performs three functions: (a) *surveillance* of the environment, disclosing threats and opportunities affecting the value position of the community and of the component parts within it; (b) *correlation* of the components of society in making a response to the environment; (c) *transmission* of the social inheritance. In general, biological equivalents can be found in human and animal associations, and within the economy of a single organism.

In society, the communication process reveals special characteristics when the ruling element is afraid of the internal as well as the external environment. In gauging the efficiency of communication in any given context, it is necessary to take into account the values at stake, and the identity of the group whose position is being examined. In democratic societies, rational choices depend on enlightenment, which in turn depends upon communication; and especially upon the equivalence of attention among leaders, experts and rank and file.

NOTES

Writing Style

(continued)

Apropos the point made above, also note how Lasswell fails to cite any sources that support his use of, '[i]t is often said', in the first sentence, and similarly 'the term is often made equivalent to' in the second sentence. If this was your work that had been submitted for assessment, the person marking would be likely to ask, 'By whom?'

Context

Lasswell's use and interpretation of 'public opinion' might usefully be contrasted with that of Jürgen Habermas.

10 Content

As stated in the second subsection of the reading, Lasswell's intention was not to divide up and analyse each stage of an act of communication, but to examine 'the act as a whole in relation to the entire social process'. Moreover, his aim was to elucidate three specialised functions of communication: those of surveillance, correlation and transmission.

In what is termed a 'Summary', rather than a conclusion, Lasswell rehearses his biological analogy to remind that equivalent specialised systems perform similar functions in animal species and single-cell organisms. He closes the reading with three sentences, each of which provides a succinct summary of what he sees as its key findings.

Does this summary reflect your understanding of the reading? To what extent do Lasswell's findings on the three specialised functions of communication have any relevance today? After critically reflecting on the methods used by Lasswell, the evidence cited in support of the arguments, and the conclusions that are drawn, what do you think are the strengths and limitations of his work?

REFLECTING ON THE READING

As indicated in the introduction to this chapter, the selected reading has received wide attention, not primarily because it sets out three functions of communication, but for the reason that Lasswell separates out the key components of 'an act of communication' in the form of five questions.

His reason for setting out the five questions in this way was that he felt it provided a clear and helpful way of identifying the type of research being undertaken by communication scholars at that time. In doing so, he also noted that researchers were tending to concentrate their research activity on one, or other, of the following areas: control analysis, content analysis, media analysis, audience analysis and effects analysis.

Williams (2003: 6) applauds Lasswell's framework because it provides a convenient and helpful way of illustrating the points at which media researchers and teachers have invested their attention. Similarly inspired, Manoff and Schudson (1986) assert that all newspaper reporters should use at least some of Lasswell's questions to formulate their opening paragraphs (cited in Briggs and Burke 2002: 251).

Likewise, Boyd-Barrett (1995d: 270) suggests that Lasswell's 'Who, Says What, To Whom' helped drive interest in studying media occupations and media professionals, and the 'To whom' component prompted a further question, 'How many', which was thought to be extremely relevant 'as the masses emerged in the nineteenth century' (Briggs and Burke 2002: 5).

However, this reading by Lasswell has also been the subject of some criticism. For example, Boyd-Barrett suggests the following as major limitations of Lasswell's analysis: it doesn't take sufficient account of the immediate, historical, social or institutional contexts of communication; it presumes that the media act upon society and are not themselves acted on; and, it tends to be overly positive about the media in the sense that insufficient account is accorded to issues of ownership, motivation, profit and the potential for 'sleaze' (Boyd-Barrett 1995b: 72–3).

More generally, there are differing views on the extent to which a functional perspective on communication – as demonstrated in this reading by Lasswell – is relevant and useful in contemporary times. For example, McQuail argues that 'the underlying vague assumptions that in many ways the mass media contribute (by their "effects") to this or that "positive" (functional) or "negative" (dysfunctional) outcome for "society"' is still evident in mass media research (2002: 7).

On the other hand, Carey (1989) has a very different view, arguing that there has been a marked shift away from functional approaches following the '"interpretive turn" in media sociology' (Stevenson 2002: 77); you can explore this interpretive turn in this book, if you look at the sections on the Centre for Contemporary Cultural Studies (Chapter 11) and cultural theory (Chapter 17).

Key terms to explore

attention frames; conductance; equivalencies; afferent channels; efferent channels; circuits of communication; message handlers; message manipulators; ideology; counter-ideology; ruling elites; internal and external equilibrium; efficient communication; rational judgements;

attention aggregates; publics; sentiment groups; structural and functional features of world society; democratic theory; rational public opinion; enlightenment; equivalent enlightenment.

Key writers who are mentioned

Bruce L. Smith; Ralph D. Casey; Warder C. Allee; Robert Redfield; Charles E. Merriam; Gaetano Mosca; Karl Mannheim; Abraham Kaplan; William T.R. Fox; Joseph M. Goldsen; and other publications by the author himself.

RECOMMENDED READING

Boyd-Barrett, O. and Newbold, C. (eds) (1995) *Approaches to Media: A reader*, London: Arnold.

Has a section on early theories in media research of which one is functionalism, and includes a brief extract from the reading by Lasswell that we have used in this chapter.

Lasswell, H.D. (1927) *Propaganda Techniques in the World War*, New York: Peter Smith.

Classic text on propaganda techniques and the materials used, which is based on American, British, French and German experience in the First World War.

Willliams, K. (2003) *Understanding Media Theory*, London: Arnold.

Sets out to unravel and explain a number of schools of thought and different approaches to media theory, and includes a useful section on functionalism.

CHAPTER 8

The Columbia school

Lazarsfeld, P.F. and Merton, R.K. (1948) 'Mass communication, popular taste and organized social action', in Bryson, L. (ed.) *The Communication of Ideas*, New York: Harper and Brothers, pp. 95–118.

INTRODUCTION TO THE COLUMBIA SCHOOL

The Columbia school is known for its pioneering work in studying the *effects* of mass communication. As a result, what came to be known as 'communications research' in America is indelibly associated with the Columbia school (Katz et al. 2003: 10).

However, not everyone has been enthralled with its work. In particular, criticism has centred on the research questions being asked, the methods that were employed and the theoretical developments that emerged. Hence, members of the Columbia school have been lauded by their supporters, but vilified by their critics (Simonson and Weimann 2003: 14).

For example, one such critic has asserted that the Columbia school was responsible for introducing and establishing a 'dominant paradigm' of media research, which

> drained attention from the power of the media to define normal and abnormal social and political activity, to say what is politically real and legitimate and what is not; to justify the two-party political structure; to establish certain political agendas for social attention and to contain, channel and exclude others; and to shape the images of opposition movements.

(Gitlin 1995: 21)

Other critics have included members of the Frankfurt school (see Chapter 6), who while collaborating on a research project with colleagues at Columbia in 1941 (Hardt 1995: 15), considered them to be servile to the culture industry (Katz et al. 2003: 56). Nevertheless, the work undertaken at Columbia continues to have resonance today, and it is unlikely that any contemporary textbook on media theory will fail to cite the work of this school or its director and founder, Paul Lazarsfeld.

Lazarsfeld, a psychologist and mathematician, had come to the United States from Austria in 1933 on a Rockefeller fellowship. Owing to the political situation in Austria in the mid-1930s, Lazarsfeld decided to stay in the United States and, in 1937, was appointed Director of the Princeton Radio Project, at Princeton University, which was also funded by the Rockefeller Foundation. Here, Lazarsfeld began research on the psychological effects of radio by studying radio audiences and using laboratory experiments to do so (Sills 1996: 107).

Much of the research data he collected came from commercial radio stations owned and operated by the Columbia Broadcasting System (CBS), which by 1965 was being described as 'the largest advertising and communications medium in the world' (Dennis and Wartella 1996: 190). Within a few years the Radio Project had been renamed as the Office of Radio Research and, in 1940, it was relocated to Columbia University in New York. By 1944 it had come under the auspice of the Bureau of Applied Social Research (the Bureau), with Lazarsfeld as the director (Sills 1996: 108).

Even though CBS had its own research department, at one point employing up to 100 people, it continued to work closely with the Bureau, providing Lazarsfeld and his co-researchers with both finance and access to the company's radio stations (Sills, 1996: 106). Being so close to the industry and also reliant on it for funding, the Columbia school was vulnerable to accusations of compromise. Lazarsfeld recognised this in a later reflection on the era, making clear that his dilemma was to 'keep the Bureau [of Applied Social Research] manoeuvring between the intellectual and political purist and an industry from which I wanted cooperation without having to "sell out"' (cited in Hardt 1995: 14).

Between 1939 and 1949 Lazarsfeld, as sole author or co-author, published extensively on the effects of radio in special issues of the *Journal of Applied Psychology* and in other volumes of essays, as well as publishing analyses of two nationwide surveys of radio listeners throughout America (Sills 1996: 108). Some of this work was co-authored with Frank Stanton, his long-standing colleague at CBS, who established its research department before being appointed as president of the company, a position he held until 1971 (Sills 1996: 106).

The Columbia school can be seen as a 'staging post' in the development of media theory. This is because the growth of mass communication research in America during the 1940s, 1950s and 1960s has been deemed the second phase of media research (McQuail 1977: 72; Turner 1996: 184). The Columbia school's 'personal influence' or 'limited effects' paradigm, which led to theoretical developments such as the 'two-step model' and 'uses and gratifications' (see Chapter 14 for further detail on 'media effects' discussions), epitomised this second phase of media research (Williams 2003: 174–9).

The 'two-step model', or 'two-step flow' idea, emerged from a 1940 study which focused on how people made decisions about voting, the aim being to examine the role of the media in decision-making (Katz 1996: 61–2). The findings of this study were later published in *The People's Choice: How the voter makes up his mind in a presidential campaign* (Lazarsfeld et al. 1944). It is worth noting how this and other later studies, 'Patterns of influence: a study of interpersonal influence and communications behaviour in a local community' (Merton 1949a), *Voting: A study of opinion formation in a presidential campaign* (Berelson et al. 1954), and *Personal Influence: The part played by people in the flow of mass communication* (Lazarsfeld and Katz 1955), are also described as 'diffusion research' (Katz 1996: 61).

The research developments pioneered at the Columbia school were aimed at dethroning the theoretical ideas that dominated the first phase of media research which spanned the early decades of the twentieth century. Research during this time is variously labelled as the 'hypodermic-needle model' (coined originally by Harold Lasswell; see Chapter 7), the 'bullet model', the 'model of unlimited effects', and 'transmission belt' theory (Carey 1996: 22; Williams 2003: 171). It was an era in which society was envisaged as 'mass society' (see Chapter 9), and mass communications were understood to be injecting 'ideas, attitudes, and dispositions towards behaviour into passive, atomized, extremely vulnerable individuals' (Gitlin 2002: 29).

Essentially, and this is what infuriated critics of the Columbia school, this second phase of media research theorised that the mass media had very limited influence, and that rather than being the subject of manipulation, people – or audiences – were themselves manipulators of the media (Curran et al. 1995: 103).

In reflecting on these first two eras of mass communication research, Carey (1989) characterises them as distinct in two particular ways. The first model envisaged communication 'as a mode of domination' in which people were 'motivated to pursue power', while the second – and, in particular, 'uses and gratifications' – imagined communication 'as a form of therapy' which enabled people 'to flee anxiety' (Carey 1989: 147).

A further differentiation between the first and second phases of media research was the way in which researchers viewed theory. Although somewhat of a generalisation, researchers in the former era could be characterised as 'theorists', while those in the second phase were primarily seen as 'methodologists' (Williams 2003: 44). For example, rather than beginning with a theoretical framework to study the media, researchers at Columbia and other American universities undertaking research on the media and mass communication during this period, emphasised the need to be more scientific. For them, this meant the use of empirical research from which theory would be generated (Williams 2003: 44–5). This approach was famously criticised by C. Wright Mills, who described it as 'abstracted empiricism' (Halloran 1995: 35; Williams 2003: 14).

Nevertheless, members of the Columbia school are credited with a number of methodological initiatives. These include: the 'Lazarsfeld–Stanton Program Analyser' which was used to test audience reactions to radio programmes; the development and refinement of 'content analysis' as a tool for research work; the use of 'snowball sampling' as a way of selecting survey respondents; and the pioneering of 'deviant case analysis', which provided a means of assessing the attributes of respondents considered to fall outside normal patterns of behaviour (Sills 1996: 109–110).

The Columbia approach to the study of mass communication soon became the academic orthodoxy, leading to many other studies that replicated the approaches and methods pioneered at Columbia (Gitlin 2002: 28). It also defined mass communication research in America for some years (Boyd-Barrett and Newbold 1995: 5; Hardt 1995: 16). It was not until the late 1960s and 1970s that Columbia's dominance – hence the idea of a 'dominant paradigm' – was seriously challenged. This occurred from two different directions.

One challenge came from scholars working in the empirical tradition within a liberal framework, who questioned some of the findings of Columbia scholars and also the way in which their studies were reported. The other challenge came from scholars operating within a Marxist and neo-Marxist critical tradition, who argued that as the media 'were ideological agencies that played a central role in maintaining class domination', any 'research studies that denied media influence were so disabled in their theoretical approach' that they were hardly worth reading (Curran et al. 1995: 103).

Columbia's work on media effects, usefully described as 'mut[ing] the power of the media' (Katz 1996: 62), was first encapsulated in a 1949 dissertation by Joseph Klapper. It was later revised and published as a book, *The Effects of Mass Communication* (1960), by the same author (Sills 1996: 108).

The grouping of researchers into two different camps prompts recall of one further controversy that has its origins in an ideological debate between the Frankfurt school (see Chapter 6) and the Columbia school (Katz et al. 2003: 7). While Curran et al. (1995) draw a distinction between researchers operating within a liberal tradition and those working from a critical tradition, the debate between the Columbia and Frankfurt schools was about the difference between 'administrative research' and 'critical research'.

Although this dualism has little potency today, it is mentioned here because it does have a relationship with the development of media theory. The term 'administrative research' was first coined by Lazarsfeld (Williams 2003: 14)), who defined it as research which 'is carried through in the service of some kind of administrative agency of public or private character' (Hardt 1995: 15). This is evident in the account below, which also usefully juxtaposes administrative research with critical research:

> Administrative research (within western industrialized societies) tended to pose questions appearing to take for granted the innate rationality and social justice of the existing social order, whereas critical theory problematizes and relativizes social order as one which, to varying degrees of stability or instability, has been constructed in favour of certain interests over others.
>
> (*Boyd-Barrett 1995b: 73–4*)

Even in the mid-1990s, Newbold (1995b: 118) argued that most research on mass communication in America had been administrative in the sense described here, and had been funded by government or industry. Again, this requires attention to the historical period, and a reminder that Columbia's dominance spanned the Second World War and the later and lengthy Cold War era (Hardt 1995: 14; Robinson 1996: 161; Simonson and Weimann 2003: 16; Williams 2003: 45).

While Lazarsfeld may have defended his closeness to the industry by saying that the research helped broadcasters improve the service that they were offering to the public (Katz 2003: 56), critics argue that 'administrative research' has primarily served the interests of governments, market research agencies, media organisations and commerce in general (Gitlin 2002: 26; Hardt 1995: 16).

Moreover, it is also claimed that the preoccupation with empiricism that is most closely associated with Columbia, but which was also practised at other American universities, avoided or inhibited conceptual and theory development, and mitigated against the possibility of social change (Halloran 1995: 34–5; Williams 2003: 45).

INTRODUCTION TO THE READING

Lazarsfeld and Merton's 'Mass communication, popular taste and organized social action' (from hereon 'Mass communication') was first published in Lyman Bryson's edited collection, *The Communication of Ideas* (1948). This volume, which included a wide range of contributors – albeit all working and living in America – and which illuminated a diversity of theoretical and methodological approaches, was one of a number published around this time. It began to mark out an emerging field of communications research.

While Bryson taught at Columbia's Teachers College, specialising in adult education, his involvement in the book stemmed from his earlier membership of the Rockefeller Communications Group. This body was funded by the Rockefeller Foundation to undertake research in the areas of media and communication, but it came to be dominated by social scientists specialising in quantitative methods, in particular Harold Lasswell and Paul Lazarsfeld (Simonson and Weimann 2003: 16). Hence, it is not surprising that Bryson includes contributions from both researchers in this edited collection.

Bryson's volume was based on a series of lectures delivered to a graduate school organised by the Institute for Religious and Social Studies between November 1946 and February 1947 which took as its theme, 'The problems of the communication of ideas'. This is the subject of the first chapter, written by Bryman, in which he makes two key points after reflecting on the wide-ranging contributions to the volume. First, 'there is no systematic outline of a theory of communication'. Secondly, 'every thoughtful student of human behaviour today, no matter what he calls his field, is likely to find something which he will have to call "communication" obtrudes itself in the complex' (Bryson 1948: 1–2).

The only chapter in the volume specifically addressing mass communication, Lazarsfeld and Merton's 'Mass communication', was introduced to a wider audience shortly afterwards when it was reprinted in Wilbur Schramm's edited volume *Mass Communications* (1949), another text that confirmed the emergence of a new area of study.

While we have the benefit of reading the final draft of Lazarsfeld and Merton's 'Mass communication', it is useful to know something about how it was produced, and the process by which it came to be published. To do so, some context is necessary. After studying at Harvard University and Tulane University in New Orleans, Robert Merton joined Columbia University at the same time as Lazarsfeld and was then appointed Associate Director of the Bureau of Applied Social Research in 1942, holding the post until 1971 (Simonson and Weimann 2003: 19). Not surprisingly, with a background in sociology, an interest in social theory and recognised for his expertise on Marx, Merton was regarded as the theorist, and Lazarsfeld the methodologist (Simonson and Weimann 2003: 18).

While Lazarsfeld wrote and delivered the original lecture at the graduate school, he acknowledged that it was not publishable in its (then) current form, handing it over to Merton for polishing and completion (Simonson and Weimann 2003: 17, 21). Merton added a complete new section, 'Some social functions of the mass media', within which he listed three functions, 'The status conferral function', 'The enforcement of social norms' and 'The narcotizing dysfunction'. Merton also reworked the final section of the reading by introducing three new theoretical labels, 'Monopolization', 'Canalization' and 'Supplementation' (Simonson and Weimann 2003: 25).

In addition to this reading, Merton published one other work on mass communication with Lazarsfeld, 'Studies in Radio and Film Propaganda' (1943). It was a study of propaganda in wartime. Merton also produced a book, *Mass Persuasion: The social psychology of a war bond drive* (1946), which used interviews with listeners to find out why they had pledged to buy war bonds after hearing a radio programme that had been specifically designed for that purpose (Sills 1996: 113). However, Merton is most renowned for his theoretical contributions to sociology, which appear in *Social Theory and Social Structure* (1949b), a book that has been reprinted many times.

You may or may not agree, but Simonson and Weimann (2003: 21) argue that, in tandem, Lazarsfeld and Merton produced a 'beautifully written, conceptually elegant, and historically informed overview of the mass media's roles and social effects in the mid-twentieth century' (2003: 21). It is, also, they suggest, a 'classic because it is still good to think with' (p. 13).

1

Paul F. Lazarsfeld and Robert K. Merton

Mass communication, popular taste and organized social action

Problems engaging the attention of men change, and they change not at random but largely in accord with the altering demands of society and economy. If a group such as those who have written the chapters of this book had been brought together a generation or so ago, the subject for discussion would in all probability have been altogether different. Child labor, woman suffrage or old age pensions might have occupied the attention of a group such as this, but certainly not problems of the media of mass communication. As a host of recent conferences, books and articles indicate, the role of radio, print and film in society has become a problem of interest to many and a source of concern to some. This shift in public interest appears to be the product of several social trends.

Social Concern with the Mass Media

Many are alarmed by the ubiquity and potential power of the mass media. A participant in this symposium has written, for example, that "the power of radio can be compared only with the power of the atomic bomb." It is widely felt that the mass media comprise a powerful instrument which may be used for good or for ill and that, in the absence of adequate controls, the latter possibility is on the whole more likely. For these are the media of propaganda and Americans stand in peculiar dread of the power of propaganda. As the British observer, William Empson, recently remarked of us: "They believe in machinery more passionately than we do; and modern propaganda is a scientific machine; so it seems to them obvious that a mere reasoning man can't stand up against it. All this produces a curiously girlish attitude toward anyone who might be doing propaganda. 'Don't let that man come near. Don't let him tempt me, because if he does I'm sure to fall.'"

The ubiquity of the mass media promptly leads many to an almost magical belief in their enormous power. But there is another and, probably, a more realistic basis for widespread concern with the social role of the mass media; a basis which has to do with the changing types of social control exercised by powerful interest groups in society. Increasingly, the chief power groups, among which organized business occupies the most spectacular place, have come to adopt techniques for manipulating mass publics through propaganda in place of more direct means of control. Industrial organizations no longer compel eight year old children to attend the machine for fourteen hours a day; they engage in elaborate programs of "public relations." They place large and impressive advertisements in the newspapers of the nation; they sponsor numerous radio programs; on the advice of public relations counsellors they organize prize contests, establish welfare foundations, and support worthy causes. Economic power seems to have reduced direct exploitation and turned to a subtler type of psychological exploitation, achieved largely by disseminating propaganda through the mass media of communication.

NOTES

 ## Structure

Perhaps because the reading was first delivered as a lecture, the first paragraph doesn't provide the reader with an outline of its overall purpose or a brief summary of its integral parts.

Essentially, it is the first section, 'Social concern with the mass media', that provides an introduction to the reading. This leaves the second – and rather wordily entitled – section, 'The social role of the machinery of mass media', to set the scene for consideration of three substantive areas, each of which are suggested as 'social roles' of the mass media.

The first addresses social functions of the mass media. The second examines the relationship between structures and constraints on mass media. The third considers the extent to which the mass media might be used to achieve 'designated social objectives'.

In this first section, 'Social concern with the mass media', note how Lazarsfeld and Merton first outline the perceived concerns of the public, then summarise them, before finally moving on to reflect critically on their standing and worth. The thorny issue of how to define and measure 'effects' is left to the final paragraph of this first section.

Context

Three points might be made about context. The first is that the reading was originally planned and delivered as a lecture at a graduate school on the theme of problems associated with communication. Hence, the reading begins with an outline of perceived problems associated with mass media.

The second point concerns the era which the paper is addressing and the timing of its delivery. With a focus on the (then) contemporary period and delivered shortly after the end of the Second World War, it is not surprising to find reference to the atomic bomb, the use of propaganda and, on occasions, Nazi Germany.

The third point to be made on the context relates to the focus of analysis. The geographic focus is America, although there is a recognition here, and later in the reading, that the structure and ownership of mass media in America is different from that of other countries.

Content

Lazarsfeld and Merton first make clear that any considerations about social concerns must be seen in the context of the wider society and economy. Without citing any particular sources as 'evidence', they go on to suggest three reasons why the mass media have 'become a problem of interest to many and a source of concern to some'.

The first involves the 'ubiquity and potential power of the mass media', which they later suggest, at least in part, is due to people's irrational fears and general insecurity. You will recall from the first section of this chapter that Paul Lazarsfeld's academic background was in psychology. The second reason for concern is that the mass media are involved in stifling people's critical faculties, which leads to 'unthinking conformism'. The third reason is that the growth and prevalence of mass media is leading to a lowering of 'aesthetic tastes and popular cultural standards'.

READING

(continued)

This change in the structure of social control merits thorough examination. Complex societies are subject to many different forms of organized control. Hitler, for example, seized upon the most visible and direct of these: organized violence and mass coercion. In this country, direct coercion has become minimized. If people do not adopt the beliefs and attitudes advocated by some power group—say, the National Association of Manufacturers—they can neither be liquidated nor placed in concentration camps. Those who would control the opinions and beliefs of our society resort less to physical force and more to mass persuasion. The radio program and the institutional advertisement serve in place of intimidation and coercion. The manifest concern over the functions of the mass media is in part based upon the valid observation that these media have taken on the job of rendering mass publics conformative to the social and economic *status quo*.

A third source of widespread concern with the social role of mass media is found in their assumed effects upon popular culture and the esthetic tastes of their audiences. In the measure that the size of these audiences has increased, it is argued, the level of esthetic taste has deteriorated. And it is feared that the mass media deliberately cater to these vulgarized tastes, thus contributing to further deterioration.

It seems probable that these constitute the three organically related elements of our great concern with the mass media of communication. Many are, first of all, fearful of the ubiquity and potential power of these media. We have suggested that this is something of an indiscriminate fear of an abstract bogey stemming from insecurity of social position and tenuously held values. Propaganda seems threatening.

There is, secondly, concern with the present effects of the mass media upon their enormous audiences, particularly the possibility that the continuing assault of these media may lead to the unconditional surrender of critical faculties and an unthinking conformism.

Finally, there is the danger that these technically advanced instruments of mass communication constitute a major avenue for the deterioration of esthetic tastes and popular cultural standards. And we have suggested that there is substantial ground for concern over these immediate social effects of the mass media of communication.

A review of the current state of actual knowledge concerning the social role of the mass media of communication and their effects upon the contemporary American community is an ungrateful task, for certified knowledge of this kind is impressively slight. Little more can be done than to explore the nature of the problems by methods which, in the course of many decades, will ultimately provide the knowledge we seek. Although this is anything but an encouraging preamble, it provides a necessary context for assessing the research and tentative conclusions of those of us professionally concerned with the study of mass media. A reconnaissance will suggest what we know, what we need to know, and will locate the strategic points requiring further inquiry.

To search out "the effects" of mass media upon society is to set upon an ill defined problem. It is helpful to distinguish three facets of the problem and to consider each in turn. Let us, then, first inquire into what we know about the effects of the existence of these media in our society. Secondly, we must look into the effects of the particular structure of ownership

NOTES

(continued)

Remembering that this reading was produced over fifty years ago, a survey today might easily identify these same concerns about contemporary mass media. Certainly, the third and final reason for concern brings to mind notions of 'high' and 'low' culture, leading to one critic, Sills describing this reading as 'an analysis of what today might be called "culture wars"' (1996: 113). (See Chapter 5 for a background on these ideas.)

In the second and third paragraphs of this first section Lazarsfeld and Merton mention powerful interest groups. They then go on to point out that while some societies have been 'controlled' by direct means of intimidation and coercion, American society is subject to more subtle forms of control through the mass media of communication. This analysis suggests similarities with Herman and Chomsky's (1994 [1988]) later developed and published 'propaganda model'. (See Chapter 12.)

However, when it comes to reflecting on the collective efficacy of all three concerns, a number of doubts are raised. These are primarily about the lack of evidence or, in the authors' words, 'certified knowledge' that is currently available to support such concerns, the lack of appropriate methods to acquire such evidence – remembering Lazarsfeld's acknowledged expertise in methodology, and a recognition that to discover '"the effects" of mass media upon society' is 'an ill-defined problem'.

Nevertheless, the authors end by suggesting three lines of enquiry which, by implication, make the study of 'effects' a more clearly delineated problem which can be tackled. The remainder of the reading responds, more or less, to these three lines of enquiry.

Writing Style

As we pointed out earlier in this chapter, much of the academic writing in this era tended not to be gender inclusive and this is evident throughout the reading. This aside, the writing is clear, accessible and generally free of jargon.

However, Lazarsfeld and Merton choose not to provide details on William Empson, who is cited on the first page, which would help in assessing the worth of his observation on America's faith in propaganda. Note also that while the authors generally make their arguments with some authority, they also appear to recognise areas of uncertainty. This becomes apparent when they say, 'It seems probable that . . .', and also where they acknowledge their conclusions as 'tentative'.

READING

1

(continued)

and operation of the mass media in this country, a structure which differs appreciably from that found elsewhere. And, finally, we must consider that aspect of the problem which bears most directly upon policies and tactics governing the use of these media for definite social ends: our knowledge concerning the effects of the particular contents disseminated through the mass media.

2

The Social Role of the Machinery of Mass Media

What role can be assigned to the mass media by virtue of the fact that they exist? What are the implications of a Hollywood, a Radio City, and a Time-Life-Fortune enterprise for our society? These questions can of course be discussed only in grossly speculative terms, since no experimentation or rigorous comparative study is possible. Comparisons with other societies lacking these mass media would be too crude to yield decisive results and comparisons with an earlier day in American society would still involve gross assertions rather than precise demonstrations. In such an instance, brevity is clearly indicated. And opinions should be leavened with caution. It is our tentative judgment that the social role played by the very existence of the mass media has been commonly overestimated. What are the grounds for this judgment?

It is clear that the mass media reach enormous audiences. Approximately seventy million Americans attend the movies every week; our daily newspaper circulation is about forty-six million, and some thirty-four million American homes are equipped with radio, and in these homes the average American listens to the radio for about three hours a day. These are formidable figures. But they are merely supply and consumption figures, not figures registering the effect of mass media. They bear only upon what people do, not upon the social and psychological impact of the media. To know the number of hours people keep the radio turned on gives no indication of the effect upon them of what they hear. Knowledge of consumption data in the field of mass media remains far from a demonstration of their net effect upon behavior and attitude and outlook.

As was indicated a moment ago, we cannot resort to experiment by comparing contemporary American society with and without mass media. But, however tentatively, we can compare their social effect with, say, that of the automobile. It is not unlikely that the invention of the automobile and its development into a mass owned commodity has had a significantly greater effect upon society than the invention of the radio and its development into a medium of mass communication. Consider the social complexes into which the automobile has entered. Its sheer existence has exerted pressure for vastly improved roads and with these, mobility has increased enormously. The shape of metropolitan agglomerations has been significantly affected by the automobile. And, it may be submitted, the inventions which enlarge the radius of movement and action exert a greater influence upon social outlook and daily routines than inventions which provide avenues for ideas—ideas which can be avoided by withdrawal, deflected by resistance and transformed by assimilation.

NOTES

2 Structure

As we have seen in other chapters of this book, the 'technique' used to set up this second section of the reading is not uncommon. In this instance, the first paragraph begins with questions and ends with a 'tentative judgement'. This then allows Lazarsfeld and Merton to use the remainder of this section to establish the reasons for their earlier judgement, and then to reiterate it in the final sentence. How useful is this technique and is it one that you do, or could, employ?

Content

Yet again, Lazarsfeld and Merton remind us about the need to see findings as 'tentative', but feel able to conclude that the social role of the mass media has been 'overestimated'. Three reasons are provided to support this view.

First, the plethora of data accumulated by media organisations and researchers on press circulation, cinema attendance, the number of radio sets purchased and the average number of hours people listen to radio on a daily basis, say nothing about the impact on people – 'the effect of mass media'. Secondly, the mass media and particularly radio – Lazarsfeld's particular area of expertise – have had a far lesser effect on society than the introduction of the automobile. The third reason has a psychological basis and its origins lie in an earlier socio-historical period.

Essentially, the argument is that people feel duped, given that society has reached a stage where 'progress' has enabled a greater availability of leisure time, and yet elements of the population choose to use this time consuming what would now be referred to as popular cultural products.

Again, this references the dualism of 'high' and 'low' culture, which the authors capture nicely by suggesting popular preference for the music and light entertainment provided by the Columbia Broadcasting System, as opposed to the rather more sophisticated offerings available at Columbia University! You will no doubt have heard, or seen, similar analogies used, but with different and more contemporary reference points.

How useful do you think this comparison is between the impact of radio as a means of mass communication and that of the automobile? To what extent do readers, listeners and audiences feature in this account? How do Lazarsfeld and Merton explain, and allocate, power in their assessment of the mass media? What arguments could you mount to dispute the conclusions reached by the authors at the end of this section?

READING

2

(continued)

Granted, for a moment, that the mass media play a comparatively minor role in shaping our society, why are they the object of so much popular concern and criticism? Why do so many become exercised by the "problems" of the radio and film and press and so few by the problems of, say, the automobile and the airplane? In addition to the sources of this concern which we have noted previously, there is an unwitting psychological basis for concern which derives from a socio-historical context.

Many make the mass media targets for hostile criticism because they feel themselves duped by the turn of events.

The social changes ascribable to "reform movements" may be slow and slight, but they do cumulate. The surface facts are familiar enough. The sixty hour week has given way to the forty hour week. Child labor has been progressively curtailed. With all its deficiencies, free universal education has become progressively institutionalized. These and other gains register a series of reform victories. And now, people have more leisure time. They have, ostensibly, greater access to the cultural heritage. And what use do they make of this unmortgaged time so painfully acquired for them? They listen to the radio and go to the movies. These mass media seem somehow to have cheated reformers of the fruits of their victories. The struggle for freedom for leisure and popular education and social security was carried on in the hope that, once freed of cramping shackles, people would avail themselves of major cultural products of our society, Shakespeare or Beethoven or perhaps Kant. Instead, they turn to Faith Baldwin or Johnny Mercer or Edgar Guest.

Many feel cheated of their prize. It is not unlike a young man's first experience in the difficult realm of puppy love. Deeply smitten with the charms of his lady love, he saves his allowance for weeks on end and finally manages to give her a beautiful bracelet. She finds it "simply divine." So much so, that then and there she makes a date with another boy in order to display her new trinket. Our social struggles have met with a similar denouement. For generations, men fought to give people more leisure time and now they spend it with the Columbia Broadcasting System rather than with Columbia University.

However little this sense of betrayal may account for prevailing attitudes toward the mass media, it may again be noted that the sheer presence of these media may not affect our society so profoundly as is widely supposed.

3

Some Social Functions of the Mass Media

In continuing our examination of the social role which can be ascribed to the mass media by virtue of their "sheer existence," we temporarily abstract from the social structure in which the media find their place. We do not, for example, consider the diverse effects of the mass media under varying systems of ownership and control, an important structural factor which will be discussed subsequently.

NOTES

| 2 | Context |

(continued)

It is of some interest that Lazarsfeld and Merton note public concern about the mass media, but not about air travel and automobiles. Today, the likelihood is that public concerns would encompass all three. It would probably be the internet and its association with paedophiles, gambling and identity fraud that would replace the concerns that were being aired about radio in the 1940s.

Writing Style

How helpful, or appropriate, is the authors' use of 'puppy love'? While it would not have been deemed sexist at the time, one still wonders how it was received by the original audience. Whatever your own response, its use here provides a reminder for all writers. The point being the need to consider the usefulness – now, and in the future – of the examples that we use when trying to establish or illustrate a particular point.

| 3 | Structure |

You will recall that this section was not part of Lazarsfeld's original lecture, but was developed and added by Merton for the published version that appeared in Bryson's edited collection.

In reading this section, you might want to consider how each of these 'social functions' might have been dealt with differently if the authors had not decided to 'temporarily abstract from the social structure in which the media find their place'.

READING

3

(continued)

The mass media undoubtedly serve many social functions which might well become the object of sustained research. Of these functions, we have occasion to notice only three.

THE STATUS CONFERRAL FUNCTION. The mass media *confer* status on public issues, persons, organizations and social movements.

Common experience as well as research testifies that the social standing of persons or social policies is raised when these command favorable attention in the mass media. In many quarters, for example, the support of a political candidate or a public policy by *The Times* is taken as significant, and this support is regarded as a distinct asset for the candidate or the policy. Why?

For some, the editorial views of *The Times* represent the considered judgment of a group of experts, thus calling for the respect of laymen. But this is only one element in the status conferral function of the mass media, for enhanced status accrues to those who merely receive attention in the media, quite apart from any editorial support.

The mass media bestow prestige and enhance the authority of individuals and groups by *legitimizing their status*. Recognition by the press or radio or magazines or newsreels testifies that one has arrived, that one is important enough to have been singled out from the large anonymous masses, that one's behavior and opinions are significant enough to require public notice. The operation of this status conferral function may be witnessed most vividly in the advertising pattern of testimonials to a product by "prominent people." Within wide circles of the population (though not within certain selected social strata), such testimonials not only enhance the prestige of the product but also reflect prestige on the person who provides the testimonials. They give public notice that the large and powerful world of commerce regards him as possessing sufficiently high status for his opinion to count with many people. In a word, his testimonial is a testimonial to his own status.

The ideal, if homely, embodiment of this circular prestige-pattern is to be found in the Lord Calvert series of advertisements centered on "Men of Distinction." The commercial firm and the commercialized witness to the merit of the product engage in an unending series of reciprocal pats on the back. In effect, a distinguished man congratulates a distinguished whisky which, through the manufacturer, congratulates the man of distinction on his being so distinguished as to be sought out for a testimonial to the distinction of the product. The workings of this mutual admiration society may be as non-logical as they are effective. The audiences of mass media apparently subscribe to the circular belief: "If you really matter, you will be at the focus of mass attention and, if you *are* at the focus of mass attention, then surely you must really matter."

This status conferral function thus enters into organized social action by legitimizing selected policies, persons and groups which receive the support of mass media. We shall have occasion to note the detailed operation of this function in connection with the conditions making for the maximal utilization of mass media for designated social ends. At the moment, having considered the "status conferral" function, we shall consider a second: the enforced application of social norms through the mass media.

NOTES

3

(continued)

Apropos this last point, you will note that the authors of certain selected readings in other chapters of this book take the view that the mass media cannot be appropriately studied if abstracted from the social structure in which they are situated. What is your view on this matter?

Context

While we might find the three 'social functions' of the mass media rather obvious today, these ideas were clearly at the 'cutting edge' of media theorisation in the late 1940s.

It is also necessary to remind ourselves that television was yet to appear, so the mass media being considered here are the press, film and radio broadcasting.

Writing Style

Given that we know this section was written by a different hand, can you see any changes in the style of writing? Certainly this is the first part of the reading that sets out to theorise mass media by conceptualising some particular social functions. You might also notice a more regular use of *italics* for the purpose of emphasis, aside, that is, from the titles of newspapers which are expected to be italicised.

Content

Although a number of social functions of the media are inferred, only three are included here. In the view of Lazarsfeld and Merton, the first, 'status conferral', can be taken for granted, although no references are cited to enable the reader to explore this phenomenon in more detail should they wish to do so.

Status conferral occurs when mass media proffer support for selected policies, people or groups. Such support is believed to legitimise the status of the said policy, person or group. However, what is not considered is what happens when mass media choose not to favour or offer such support, or when reporting or coverage is distinctly unfavourable, and more importantly, who makes such decisions and for what reasons.

Lazarsfeld and Merton also suggest that status conferral in the area of public policy and political candidature is likely to be assisted by the perceived status of the mass media source. In this case *The Times* is mentioned, being a publication of stature and status in that era. It is hardly likely that this same newspaper would be selected for this reason today. Moreover, it is unlikely that Lazarsfeld and Merton would have considered the possibility that *The Times* would now be part of a transnational media conglomeration News Corporation that has recently incorporated the *Wall Street Journal* into its stable of media outlets.

It is also noticeable that most of this first subsection is devoted to how status conferral operates in relation to advertising. If a similar explanation were to be provided today on status conferral and advertising/sponsorship, there is no doubt that mention would be made of 'brands' and 'celebrities'.

Setting aside the 60 or so years since this conception of the mass media appeared, to what extent does this social function of status conferral have any value today and, it if does, would it be theorised differently? In a similar vein, would you bracket off a 'certain selected social strata' – as the authors do – when considering the status conferral function today?

READING

4

THE ENFORCEMENT OF SOCIAL NORMS. Such catch phrases as "the power of the press" (and other mass media) or "the bright glare of publicity" presumably refer to this function. The mass media may initiate organized social action by "exposing" conditions which are at variance with public moralities. But it need not be prematurely assumed that this pattern consists *simply* in making these deviations widely known. We have something to learn in this connection from Malinowski's observations among his beloved Trobriand Islanders. There, he reports, no organized social action is taken with respect to behavior deviant from a social norm unless there is *public* announcement of the deviation. This is not merely a matter of acquainting the individuals in the group with the facts of the case. Many may have known privately of these deviations—*e.g.*, incest among the Trobri-anders, as with political or business corruption, prostitution, gambling among ourselves—but they will not have pressed for public action. But once the behavioral deviations are made simultaneously public for all, this sets in train tensions between the "privately tolerable" and the "publicly acknowledgeable."

The mechanism of public exposure would seem to operate somewhat as follows. Many social norms prove inconvenient for individuals in the society. They militate against the gratification of wants and impulses. Since many find the norms burdensome, there is some measure of leniency in applying them, both to oneself and to others. Hence, the emergence of deviant behavior and private toleration of these deviations. But this can continue only so long as one is not in a situation where one must take a public stand for or against the norms. Publicity, the enforced acknowledgment by members of the group that these deviations have occurred, requires each individual to take such a stand. He must either range himself with the non-conformists, thus proclaiming his repudiation of the group norms, and thus asserting that he, too, is outside the moral framework or, regardless of his private predilections, he must fall into line by supporting the norm. *Publicity closes the gap between "private attitudes" and "public morality."* Publicity exerts pressure for a single rather than a dual morality by preventing continued evasion of the issue. It calls forth public reaffirmation and (however sporadic) application of the social norm.

In a mass society, this function of public exposure is institutionalized in the mass media of communication. Press, radio and journals expose fairly well known deviations to public view, and as a rule, this exposure forces some degree of public action against what has been privately tolerated. The mass media may, for example, introduce severe strains upon "polite ethnic discrimination" by calling public attention to these practices which are at odds with the norms of non-discrimination. At times, the media may organize exposure activities into a "crusade."

The study of crusades by mass media would go far toward answering basic questions about the relation of mass media to organized social action. It is essential to know, for example, the extent to which the crusade provides an organizational center for otherwise unorganized individuals. The crusade may operate diversely among the several sectors of the population. In some instances, its major effect may not be so much to arouse an indifferent citizenry as to alarm the culprits, leading them to extreme measures which in turn alienate the electorate. Publicity may so embarrass the malefactor as to send him into flight as was the case, for

NOTES

Context

In this second subsection, it is not surprising to find that the press are the primary mass media being considered, and the area to which Lazarsfeld and Merton look for examples to support their second identified social function.

This is because of the rich press history available to them and a recognition that while radio journalism did exist, America's commercial radio system, still only in its third decade of operation, did not enjoy the same campaigning reputation as the press.

Hence, the authors refer to the 'power of the press' and 'the bright glare of publicity' – to which Lazarsfeld and Merton could also have added the 'free' press, or the press as 'watchdog'. Ideas such as these have become embedded in everyday parlance over a century or more (see Chapter 4 on liberal press theory).

Again, we are reminded that it is the American context that is under scrutiny, with examples drawn from the *The New York Times* and *Harper's Weekly*. Similarly, Lazarsfeld and Merton's only cited source, James Bryce, limits the focus of his work to America.

Writing Style

Note, again, that Lazarsfeld and Merton choose not to empower the reader by providing citation details on two other sources used, Bronislaw Malinowski, the anthropologist, and Lawrence Lowell. In particular, the latter reference means very little unless we know more about the source, such as his role and when and why he made the observation that is attributed to him.

Content

According to Lazarsfeld and Merton, a second social function is enabled when the mass media use public exposure to apply or enforce social norms. This is where the mass media respond to, or initiate, organised social action. While this may relate to the behaviour of a particular individual, the authors provide two more general examples, one being an attempt to restrain 'polite ethnic discrimination', while the other is about drawing attention to corruption in public bodies and private business.

The authors go on to suggest that such actions by mass media might be defined as a crusade, hence the familiar notion of crusading or campaigning journalists. The purpose of such crusades was one, or all, of the following: to embarrass, spotlight, or prompt the 'offender(s)' into more extreme behaviour which will, in turn, spark public interest; to rouse public interest and if this is to be effective, public issues must be defined in simple 'black and white' terms; and, to serve the self-interest of the mass media organisation. However, the authors restrict self-interest to advances in 'power and prestige', rather than recognising the financial interest that is wholly, or partly, instrumental in many such media campaigns.

In this subsection we see the obvious influence of Merton's sociological background, with reference to 'social norms', 'social action', 'deviant behaviour' and deliberations about the distinctions that

READING

4

(continued)

example, with some of the chief henchmen of the Tweed Ring following exposure by *The New York Times*. Or the directors of corruption may fear the crusade only because of the effect they anticipate it will have upon the electorate. Thus, with a startlingly realistic appraisal of the communications behavior of his constituency, Boss Tweed peevishly remarked of the biting cartoons of Thomas Nast in *Harper's Weekly*: "I don't care a straw for your newspaper articles: my constituents don't know how to read, but they can't help seeing them damned pictures."[1]

The crusade may affect the public directly. It may focus the attention of a hitherto lethargic citizenry, grown indifferent through familiarity to prevailing corruption, upon a few, dramatically simplified, issues. As Lawrence Lowell once observed in this general connection, complexities generally inhibit mass action. Public issues must be defined in simple alternatives, in terms of black and white, to permit of organized public action. And the presentation of simple alternatives is one of the chief functions of the crusade. The crusade may involve still other mechanisms. If a municipal government is not altogether pure of heart, it is seldom wholly corrupt. Some scrupulous members of the administration and judiciary are generally intermingled with their unprincipled colleagues. The crusade may strengthen the hand of the upright elements in the government, force the hand of the indifferent and weaken the hand of the corrupt. Finally, it may well be that a successful crusade exemplifies a circular, self-sustaining process, in which the concern of the mass medium with the public interest coincides with its self-interest. The triumphant crusade may enhance the power and prestige of the mass medium, thus making it, in turn, more formidable in later crusades, which, if successful, may further advance its power and prestige.

Whatever the answer to these questions, mass media clearly serve to reaffirm social norms by exposing deviations from these norms to public view. Study of the particular range of norms thus reaffirmed would provide a clear index of the extent to which these media deal with peripheral or central problems of the structure of our society.

5

THE NARCOTIZING DYSFUNCTION. The functions of status conferral and of reaffirmation of social norms are evidently well recognized by the operators of mass media. Like other social and psychological mechanisms, these functions lend themselves to diverse forms of application. Knowledge of these functions is power, and power may be used for special interests or for the general interest.

A third social consequence of the mass media has gone largely unnoticed. At least, it has received little explicit comment and, apparently, has not been systematically put to use for furthering planned objectives. This may be called the narcotizing dysfunction of the mass media. It is termed *dys*functional rather than functional on the assumption that it is not in the

1. James Bryce, *The American Commonwealth*, Volume 2. Copyright 1898 by Macmillan and Company; 1910, 1914 by The Macmillan Company; 1920 by The Right Honorable Viscount Bryce.

NOTES

4

(continued)

can be made between 'public' and 'private'. This brief discussion about public and private and the way in which 'publicity' is being defined might usefully be contrasted with Habermas's use of the same terminology in outlining his notion of the public sphere (see Chapter 13). Meantime, how do you respond to the assertion here that 'Publicity closes the gap between "private attitudes" and "public morality"'?

Presumably, it was also Merton's decision to include a contrast between the personal interactions of a traditional society and the mediated communication of a mass society. However, what we don't learn about is who makes the decision in the traditional society to move towards a public announcement about the deviation from social norms and why such a decision is made.

An additional point might also be made about the decisions by mass media to engage in the 'enforcement of social norms'. What is missing from this discussion is consideration about who decides on which social norms are to be enforced and which are to be ignored, and why such decisions are made.

Also, when and why campaigns, or crusades, are to be initiated or responded to and when they are not. These decisions require consideration about issue of power, but this is not discussed – although such matters are perhaps alluded to in the final sentence of the subsection. Of course, the authors' earlier decision in this section to abstract the media from the wider social and economic structure in which they operate may be the reason for such omissions.

Finally, if this theory – of the mass media enforcing social norms – is useful to 'think with', as was suggested by one author in our introduction to this reading, consider the following questions. What recent mass media campaigns or crusades come to mind? What social norms were enforced? Who were the chief beneficiaries?

5

Structure

Given our concluding comments above, it is somewhat strange to find this subject matter, on power and special interests, located in a paragraph that opens – but seemingly has little to do with – the social function discussed in this final subsection. It is only in the second paragraph that Lazarsfeld and Merton turn their attention to the third social function of the mass media, which is described as *dysfunctional*. Why do they describe it as such?

Writing Style

You may already have noticed the tendency towards the use of dualisms in this subsection. For example: knowing and doing; active and passive; function and dysfunction. What are the pros and cons of using this technique? Note, again, how Lazarsfeld and Merton refer to 'scattered studies', but fail to cite any examples.

READING

5

(continued)

interest of modern complex society to have large masses of the population politically apathetic and inert. How does this unplanned mechanism operate?

Scattered studies have shown that an increasing proportion of the time of Americans is devoted to the products of the mass media. With distinct variations in different regions and among different social strata, the outpourings of the media presumably enable the twentieth century American to "keep abreast of the world." Yet, it is suggested, this vast supply of communications may elicit only a superficial concern with the problems of society, and this superficiality often cloaks mass apathy.

Exposure to this flood of information may serve to narcotize rather than to energize the average reader or listener. As an increasing meed of time is devoted to reading and listening, a decreasing share is available for organized action. The individual reads accounts of issues and problems and may even discuss alternative lines of action. But this rather intellectualized, rather remote connection with organized social action is not activated. The interested and informed citizen can congratulate himself on his lofty state of interest and information and neglect to see that he has abstained from decision and action. In short, he takes his secondary contact with the world of political reality, his reading and listening and thinking, as a vicarious performance. He comes to mistake *knowing* about problems of the day for *doing* something about them. His social conscience remains spotlessly clean. He *is* concerned. He *is* informed. And he has all sorts of ideas as to what should be done. But, after he has gotten through his dinner and after he has listened to his favored radio programs and after he has read his second newspaper of the day, it is really time for bed.

In this peculiar respect, mass communications may be included among the most respectable and efficient of social narcotics. They may be so fully effective as to keep the addict from recognizing his own malady.

That the mass media have lifted the level of information of large populations is evident. Yet, quite apart from intent, increasing dosages of mass communications may be inadvertently transforming the energies of men from active participation into passive knowledge.

The occurrence of this narcotizing dysfunction can scarcely be doubted, but the extent to which it operates has yet to be determined. Research on this problem remains one of the many tasks still confronting the student of mass communications.

6

The Structure of Ownership and Operation

To this point we have considered the mass media quite apart from their incorporation within a particular social and economic structure. But clearly, the social effects of the media will vary as the system of ownership and control varies. Thus to consider the social effects of American mass media is to deal only with the effects of these media as privately owned enterprises under profit oriented management. It is general knowledge that this circumstance is not inherent in the technological nature of the mass media. In England, for example, to say nothing of Russia, the radio is to all intents and purposes owned, controlled and operated by government.

NOTES

5

(continued)

Content

Essentially, the argument here exposes what Lazarsfeld and Merton see as a paradox. That is, as the mass media provide more and more information, the public – or certain sections of it – are less likely, rather than more likely, to become energised and engaged in organised social action. What do you understand by social action?

Lazarsfeld and Merton's assertions are, though, qualified to some degree in the final paragraph of the subsection. Here, while they have no doubt about the existence of the 'narcotizing dysfunction', they do acknowledge the need for more research to be conducted in order to determine its actual impact. This, they say, is 'one of the many tasks confronting the student of mass communication'. How this would be conducted and whether it would be worth the effort is open to conjecture.

One option for the student of mass communication would be to turn to the work of the Frankfurt school. While Horkheimer and Adorno start from a different theoretical premise and end up with a different conclusion, their notion of mass deception which is perpetrated by the culture industry resonates with the passivity and distraction of the citizenry suggested here. However, while Lazarsfeld and Merton make no mention of consumers, they do make reference to citizens, but only those who are 'interested and informed'. These citizens, it is suggested, having gorged themselves on all available information, err away from taking direct social action, but achieve it vicariously through the knowing rather than doing.

Not only do Lazarsfeld and Merton not tell us about the 'unknowing' and 'uninformed' citizens, but they also fail to acknowledge that those citizens who have the resources to allow for two daily newspapers, regular evening dinners and time to listen to the radio, probably do not need to involve themselves in any organised social action, as the system caters adequately for their needs. Moreover, no mention is made of the relationship between media diversity and plurality.

In the second paragraph, Lazarsfeld and Merton suggest the narcotising dysfunction as an 'unplanned mechanism', which has not apparently 'been systematically put to use for furthering planned objectives'. What do they mean by this? For what, or why, would this mechanism be used? How and under what circumstances would or could it be used? Finally, what use or value does this theory on 'narcotising dysfunction' have today?

6

Structure

Although these next three sections appear by their presentation to be separate and autonomous, the intention of the authors appears to be that the first, 'The structure of ownership and operation', provides the framework within which the following two, 'Social conformism' and 'Impact on popular taste', are to be considered.

Content

At last, some might say, Lazarsfeld and Merton appear to recognise the need to consider the mass media as part of a wider social and economic structure. Additionally, they also point out that the

READING

The structure of control is altogether different in this country. Its salient characteristic stems from the fact that except for movies and books, it is not the magazine reader nor the radio listener nor, in large part, the reader of newspapers who supports the enterprise, but the advertiser. Big business finances the production and distribution of mass media. And, all intent aside, he who pays the piper generally calls the tune.

Social Conformism

Since the mass media are supported by great business concerns geared into the current social and economic system, the media contribute to the maintenance of that system. This contribution is not found merely in the effective advertisement of the sponsor's product. It arises, rather, from the typical presence in magazine stories, radio programs and newspaper columns of some element of confirmation, some element of approval of the present structure of society. And this continuing reaffirmation underscores the duty to accept.

To the extent that the media of mass communication have had an influence upon their audiences, it has stemmed not only from what is said, but more significantly from what is not said. For these media not only continue to affirm the *status quo* but, in the same measure, they fail to raise essential questions about the structure of society. Hence by leading toward conformism and by providing little basis for a critical appraisal of society, the commercially sponsored mass media indirectly but effectively restrain the cogent development of a genuinely critical outlook.

This is not to ignore the occasionally critical journal article or radio program. But these exceptions are so few that they are lost in the overwhelming flood of conformist materials. The editor of this volume, for example, has been broadcasting a weekly program in which he critically and rationally appraises social problems in general and the institution of radio in particular. But these fifteen minutes in which Mr. Bryson addresses himself to such questions over one network constitute an infinitesimally small drop in the weekly flood of materials from four major networks, from five hundred and seventy or so unaffiliated stations, from hundreds of magazines and from Hollywood.

Since our commercially sponsored mass media promote a largely unthinking allegiance to our social structure, they cannot be relied upon to work for changes, even minor changes, in that structure. It is possible to list some developments to the contrary, but upon close inspection they prove illusory. A community group, such as the PTA, may request the producer of a radio serial to inject the theme of tolerant race attitudes into the program. Should the producer feel that this theme is safe, that it will not antagonize any substantial part of his audience, he may agree, but at the first indication that it is a dangerous theme which may alienate potential consumers, he will refuse, or will soon abandon the experiment. Social objectives are consistently surrendered by commercialized media when they clash with economic gains. Minor tokens of "progressive" views are of slight importance since they are included only by grace of the sponsors and only on the condition that they be sufficiently acceptable as not to alienate any appreciable part of the audience. Economic pressure makes for conformism by omission of sensitive issues.

NOTES

(continued)

overarching structure, whatever that might be, will shape the mass media, noting that technology is also thus shaped.

They then move on to distinguish between America's predominantly privately owned and profit-oriented mass media system, and those systems that are state owned or controlled. In the latter, the authors include England and Russia (see *Context* below), but choose not to enlarge on the relationship between the media and the state in each of these two countries.

They then outline how America's mass media are predominantly reliant on advertising revenue, indicating how big business controls its financing, production and distribution. This sets the scene for the section on 'Social conformism'. In this section, which to some extent must have been inspired by Merton's acknowledged interest and expertise in Marxian theory, the authors 'pull no punches'.

They spell out in detail how the ownership and organisation of the mass media ensure and secure conformism and, in so doing, they also take the opportunity to undermine often-heard counter-arguments. For example, they make clear that it is as much about what is not included – or what is *not* said – as about what *is* said. Also, they acknowledge that while some critical articles, programmes or news items do enter the public domain, the very few that do are lost in the avalanche of material that can be regarded as 'conformist'.

While this analysis was based on America's mass media system and completed some sixty years ago, what value does this theory of the media as a force of social conformism have today?

Context

As this reading was published in the late 1940s, the reference to England's state-controlled media occurs before the introduction of commercial television and radio in the United Kingdom. At this time, apart from incursions from mainland Europe by Radio Luxembourg, the BBC had a monopoly on radio broadcasting in the United Kingdom.

The reason for using the example of Russia, rather than other countries, is likely to be due to its military might, its communist political system and what would prove to be a lengthy Cold War between the two nations.

The other contextual matter of note relates to Lazarsfeld and Merton's outlining of the scale of America's broadcasting system. What has changed dramatically in the intervening period is the pattern of ownership, so today the two authors would find that most of these then unaffiliated radio stations in the USA would now be owned by a small number of large media groups such as ClearChannel.

READING

7

Impact Upon Popular Taste

Since the largest part of our radio, movies, magazines and a considerable part of our books and newspapers are devoted to "entertainment," this clearly requires us to consider the impact of the mass media upon popular taste.

Were we to ask the average American with some pretension to literary or esthetic cultivation if mass communications have had any effect upon popular taste, he would doubtlessly answer with a resounding affirmative. And more, citing abundant instances, he would insist that esthetic and intellectual tastes have been depraved by the flow of trivial formula products from printing presses, radio stations and movie studios. The columns of criticism abound with these complaints.

In one sense, this requires no further discussion. There can be no doubt that the women who are daily entranced for three or four hours by some twelve consecutive "soap operas," all cut to the same dismal pattern, exhibit an appalling lack of esthetic judgment. Nor is this impression altered by the contents of pulp and slick magazines, or by the depressing abundance of formula motion pictures replete with hero, heroine and villain moving through a contrived atmosphere of sex, sin and success.

Yet unless we locate these patterns in historical and sociological terms, we may find ourselves confusedly engaged in condemning without understanding, in criticism which is sound but largely irrelevant. What is the historical status of this notoriously low level of popular taste? Is it the poor remains of standards which were once significantly higher, a relatively new birth in the world of values, largely unrelated to the higher standards from which it has allegedly fallen, or a poor substitute blocking the way to the development of superior standards and the expression of high esthetic purpose?

If esthetic tastes are to be considered in their social setting, we must recognize that the effective audience for the arts has become historically transformed. Some centuries back, this audience was largely confined to a selected aristocratic elite. Relatively few were literate. And very few possessed the means to buy books, attend theaters and travel to the urban centers of the arts. Not more than a slight fraction, possibly not more than one or two per cent, of the population composed the effective audience for the arts. These happy few cultivated their esthetic tastes, and their selective demand left its mark in the form of relatively high artistic standards.

With the widesweeping spread of popular education and with the emergence of the new technologies of mass communication, there developed an enormously enlarged market for the arts. Some forms of music, drama and literature now reach virtually everyone in our society. This is why, of course, we speak of *mass* media and of *mass* art. And the great audiences for the mass media, though in the main literate, are not highly cultivated. About half the population, in fact, have halted their formal education upon leaving grammar school.

With the rise of popular education, there has occurred a seeming decline of popular taste. Large numbers of people have acquired what might be termed "formal literacy," that is to say, a capacity to read, to grasp crude and superficial meanings, and a correlative incapacity for

7 Content

Essentially, this section takes as its theme the following question. What are the effects of the mass media on popular taste (see also *Context* below)? You might want to ponder on why this question is selected for enquiry, and why Lazarsfeld and Merton's response appears to command more page space that that allowed for virtually all other sections of this reading. Moreover, it is particularly interesting to reflect on how the authors suggest their initial question could be researched. We come back to this below.

The section opens with Lazarsfeld and Merton's first explicit mention of entertainment. There is, though, no acknowledgement that such content can also be educative and informative and, likewise, no suggestion that content on news and related material could also be considered entertaining.

This introduction then moves into a damning indictment of standards and tastes in the late 1940s, referring to what we would now call 'popular culture'. Here, we see inferences about 'high' and 'low' culture in a discussion which plots the deterioration of aesthetic standards and popular tastes.

Lazarsfeld and Merton note the necessity of setting such a discussion in a social and historical context, and do so by suggesting that the rise in literacy, popular education and the emergence of new technologies of mass communication have made the arts and popular culture accessible to a wider audience.

Obviously the authors are only providing an overview. However, they make no mention of how 'elite' arts have enjoyed funding from the taxpayer, but have not been accessible to most of the population.

Lazarsfeld and Merton now return to their original concern, acknowledging that their discussion up to this point has provided some background but not answered the question they posed. It is a question 'as complex as it is unexplored', and one that can only be successfully tackled by 'disciplined research'. But what do you make of their proposed lines of enquiry?

Essentially, three core questions are suggested. First, '[Has] mass media . . . robbed the intellectual and artistic elite of the arts forms which might otherwise have been accessible to them'? Secondly, '[Has] the electrification of the arts supplie[d] power for a significantly greater proportion of dim literary lights'? Thirdly, '[A]re the operators of commercialised mass media caught up in a situation in which they cannot, whatever their private preferences, radically raise the esthetic standards of their products?'

It is the third of the three questions that occupies Lazarsfeld and Merton in most of the remainder of this section. Today, we might find some of their responses somewhat naive, and their tendency to 'blame' audiences for the failings of the broadcasters rather misguided. Lazarsfeld did, though, attract much of the funding for his research from the radio industry.

It is also somewhat surprising to find that the authors don't themselves reflect on earlier sections in the reading where they touch on the need for broadcasters to maximise audiences in order to ensure advertising revenue.

READING

full understanding of what they read.[2] There has developed, in short, a marked gap between literacy and comprehension. People read more but understand less. More people read but proportionately fewer critically assimilate what they read.

Our formulation of the problem should now be plain. It is misleading to speak simply of the decline of esthetic tastes. Mass audiences probably include a larger number of persons with cultivated esthetic standards, but these are swallowed up by the large masses who constitute the new and untutored audience for the arts. Whereas yesterday the elite constituted virtually the whole of the audience, they are today a minute fraction of the whole. In consequence, the average level of esthetic standards and tastes of audiences has been depressed, although the tastes of some sectors of the population have undoubtedly been raised and the total number of people exposed to communication contents has been vastly increased.

But this analysis does not directly answer the question of the effects of the mass media upon public taste, a question which is as complex as it is unexplored. The answer can come only from disciplined research. One would want to know, for example, whether mass media have robbed the intellectual and artistic elite of the art forms which might otherwise have been accessible to them. And this involves inquiry into the pressure exerted by the mass audience upon creative individuals to cater to mass tastes. Literary hacks have existed in every age. But it would be important to learn if the electrification of the arts supplies power for a significantly greater proportion of dim literary lights. And, above all, it would be essential to determine if mass media and mass tastes are necessarily linked in a vicious circle of deteriorating standards or if appropriate action on the part of the directors of mass media could initiate a virtuous circle of cumulatively improving tastes among their audiences. More concretely, are the operators of commercialized mass media caught up in a situation in which they cannot, whatever their private preferences, radically raise the esthetic standards of their products?

In passing, it should be noted that much remains to be learned concerning standards appropriate for mass art. It is possible that standards for art forms produced by a small band of creative talents for a small and selective audience are not applicable to art forms produced by a gigantic industry for the population at large. The beginnings of investigation on this problem are sufficiently suggestive to warrant further study.[3]

2. *Ibid.*, Part IV, Chapter LXXX, James Bryce perceived this with characteristic clarity: "That the education of the masses is nevertheless a superficial education goes without saying. It is sufficient to enable them to think they know something about the great problems of politics: insufficient to show them how little they know. The public elementary school gives everybody the key to knowledge in making reading and writing familiar, but it has not time to teach him how to use the key, whose use is in fact, by the pressure of daily work, almost confined to the newspaper and the magazine. So we may say that if the political education of the average American voter be compared with that of the average voter in Europe, it stands high; but if it be compared with the functions which the theory of the American government lays on him, which its spirit implies, which the methods of its party organization assume, its inadequacy is manifest." *Mutatis mutandis*, the same may be said of the gap between the theory of "superior" cultural content in the mass media and the current levels of popular education.
3. *Cf.* Chapter XVI.

NOTES

7

(continued)

Would Lazarsfeld and Merton – as they speculate – have found 'positive achievements' had been made in improving aesthetic tastes if they could have re-examined this matter in 1976?

What we *can* say is that research in recent decades has enabled those of our generation to have a much more sophisticated understanding of audiences and media consumption (see Chapter 23 on audiences).

Context

The second paragraph prompts recall of an old adage: 'The more things change the more they stay the same.' This is because if a similar question were put to the 'average' person today, the likely response would be similar. However, the examples and media forms would be different.

For example, while Lazarsfeld and Merton focus on film, radio and magazines, today's respondents would be more likely to cite television, computer games and the internet as the main 'culprits', and the notion of 'dumbing-down' would no doubt also be mentioned.

The second point to be made here relates to the authors' judgement about soap operas and the women that listened to them – and we should remember that soaps began on radio. Clearly, feminist media studies and research into media consumption has enabled other more informed perspectives about such matters (see Chapter 16 on feminist media theory).

The final point is about the national context. The authors bemoan the poor standard of content in a variety of media forms and reflect on how that might be changed. However, while canvassing some options, what they don't do is reflect on the structure and organisation of mass media in America and how it is organised elsewhere.

Previously they had seemingly sneered at the state control of broadcasting in the United Kingdom, but what they could have mentioned was the rationale and philosophy that shaped the BBC, with its commitment to educate, inform and entertain and, in doing so, its claim to cater for all the population at least for some of the time.

Writing Style

Given that both Lazarsfeld and Merton, together and separately, had conducted studies that included work on audiences, it is surprising that no data are included or cited from such work.

Structure

The final paragraph of this section sits rather oddly with what comes before and what follows. While it is sometimes helpful to provide a summary of the material covered in a particular section, or of a whole document, this seems peculiarly placed, given that it is not a technique that is employed consistently by the authors in this reading. Of course, it may be that it was used as a way of helping integrate Merton's new and reworked material into the original lecture delivered by Lazarsfeld.

READING

Sporadic and consequently inconclusive experiments in the raising of standards have met with profound resistance from mass audiences. On occasion, radio stations and networks have attempted to supplant a soap opera with a program of classical music, or formula comedy skits with discussions of public issues. In general, the people supposed to benefit by this reformation of program have simply refused to be benefited. They cease listening. The audience dwindles. Researches have shown, for example, that radio programs of classical music tend to preserve rather than to create interest in classical music and that newly emerging interests are typically superficial. Most listeners to these programs have previously acquired an interest in classical music; the few whose interest is initiated by the programs are caught up by melodic compositions and come to think of classical music exclusively in terms of Tschaikowsky or Rimsky-Korsakow or Dvorak.

Proposed solutions to these problems are more likely to be born of faith than knowledge. The improvement of mass tastes through the improvement of mass art products is not as simple a matter as we should like to believe. It is possible, of course, that a conclusive effort has not been made. By a triumph of imagination over the current organization of mass media, one can conceive a rigorous censorship over all media, such that nothing was allowed in print or on the air or in the films save "the best that has been thought and said in the world." Whether a radical change in the supply of mass art would in due course reshape the tastes of mass audiences must remain a matter of speculation. Decades of experimentation and research are needed. At present, we know conspicuously little about the methods of improving esthetic tastes and we know that some of the suggested methods are ineffectual. We have a rich knowledge of failures. Should this discussion be reopened in 1976, we may, perhaps, report with equal confidence our knowledge of positive achievements.

At this point, we may pause to glance at the road we have traveled. By way of introduction, we considered the seeming sources of widespread concern with the place of mass media in our society. Thereafter, we first examined the social role ascribable to the sheer existence of the mass media and concluded that this may have been exaggerated. In this connection, however, we noted several consequences of the existence of mass media: their status conferral function, their function in inducing the application of social norms and their narcotizing dysfunction. Secondly, we indicated the constraints placed by a structure of commercialized ownership and control upon the mass media as agencies of social criticism and as carriers of high esthetic standards.

We turn now to the third and last aspect of the social role of the mass media: the possibilities of utilizing them for moving toward designated types of social objectives.

8

Propaganda for Social Objectives

This final question is perhaps of more direct interest to you than the other questions we have discussed. It represents something of a challenge to us since it provides the means of resolving the apparent paradox to which we referred previously: the seeming paradox arising from the assertion that the significance of the sheer existence of the mass media has been exaggerated and the multiple indications that the media do exert influences upon their audiences.

What are the conditions for the effective use of mass media for what might be called "propaganda for social objectives"—the promotion, let us say, of non-discriminatory race relations, or of educational reforms, or of positive attitudes toward organized labor? Research indicates that, at least, one or more of three conditions must be satisfied if this propaganda is to prove effective. These conditions may be briefly designated as (1) monopolization (2) canalization rather than change of basic values and (3) supplementary face to face contact. Each of these conditions merits some discussion.

Monopolization

This situation obtains when there is little or no opposition in the mass media to the diffusion of values, policies or public images. That is to say, monopolization of the mass media occurs in the absence of counter propaganda.

In this restricted sense, monopolization of the mass media is found in diverse circumstances. It is, of course, indigenous to the political structure of authoritarian society, where access to the media of communication is wholly closed to those who oppose the official ideology. The evidence suggests that this monopoly played some part in enabling the Nazis to maintain their control of the German people.

But this same situation is approximated in other social systems. During the war, for example, our government utilized the radio, with some success, to promote and to maintain identification with the war effort. The effectiveness of these morale building efforts was in large measure due to the virtually complete absence of counter propaganda.

Similar situations arise in the world of commercialized propaganda. The mass media create popular idols. The public images of the radio performer, Kate Smith, for example, picture her as a woman with unparalleled understanding of other American women, deeply sympathetic with ordinary men and women, a spiritual guide and mentor, a patriot whose views on public affairs should be taken seriously. Linked with the cardinal American virtues, the public images of Kate Smith are at no point subject to a counter propaganda. Not that she has no competitors in the market of radio advertising. But there are none who set themselves systematically to question what she has said. In consequence, an unmarried radio entertainer with an annual income in six figures may be visualized by millions of American women as a hard working mother who knows the recipe for managing life on fifteen hundred a year.

This image of a popular idol would have far less currency were it subjected to counter propaganda. Such neutralization occurs, for example, as a result of preelection campaigns by Republicans and Democrats. By and large, as a recent study has shown, the propaganda issued

8 Content

Essentially, the aim of Lazarsfeld and Merton in this final section of the reading is to illuminate the 'conditions' that enable the effective use of mass media for 'propaganda for social objectives'.

Propaganda, in this instance, is not related to wartime activities, but what we might now describe as 'progressive' social objectives, of which the authors provide examples. Note that all the examples relate to possible changes *within* the existing social and economic structure, rather than being directed at that structure.

In order that the mass media are effective in such propaganda exercises, the authors suggest that one or more 'conditions' have to be satisfied. These conditions are represented by three concepts: 'monopolization', 'canalization' and 'supplementation'. However, we are not informed about when, how and why these were devised, but we do know that they were added by Merton to Lazarsfeld's original lecture (Simonson and Weimann 2003: 25).

After defining 'monopolization', Lazarsfeld and Merton first turn to authoritarian regimes, such as Nazi Germany and, later, the Soviet Union, where they suggest such practices are 'indigenous to the political structure' of societies such as these.

However, they also recognise that 'monopolization' can occur in other social systems, citing the Second World War as an example, and that it can also be achieved by way of 'commercialized propaganda'. The example that Lazarsfeld and Merton use in this instance is drawn from a study, 'Mass persuasion', conducted by Merton, which we refer to in our introduction to this reading.

You will no doubt be able to think of other personalities – or celebrities – who have been similarly successful at 'selling' a message or brand. Also, you may be able to recall examples where the equivalent of 'counter propaganda' has been mounted which has 'neutralized', or undermined, the potential for 'monopolization'. Although no actual evidence is cited, Lazarsfeld and Merton conclude that 'virtual monopolization of the media . . . will produce discernible effects on audiences'.

Lazarsfeld and Merton move to the second 'condition', distinguishing between the effectiveness of 'canalization' in delivering results relating to advertising, and its lack of success in delivering results in the case of propaganda. Examples are given for both situations, but no details or reasons are provided that help explain the apparent failings of the propaganda campaigns targeted at reducing prejudice.

As Lazarsfeld and Merton don't begin this paragraph with a definition of 'canalization', can you provide one in the space of a single sentence? On a related note, could we say today that advertising does not set out to change attitudes and behaviour?

The final subsection opens by explaining the condition of 'supplementation' and providing an example of how it has been operationalised in America – although the substance of Father Coughlin's message is not provided. Other examples, of Nazi Germany and the Soviet Union, are used to illustrate how mass media sources – used for purposes of indoctrination – have been reinforced at local and regional levels by a variety of means.

(continued)

by each of these parties neutralizes the effect of the other's propaganda. Were both parties to forego their campaigning through the mass media entirely, it is altogether likely that the net effect would be to reproduce the present distribution of votes.

This general pattern has been described by Kenneth Burke in his *Attitudes Toward History* ". . . businessmen compete with one another by trying to *praise their own commodity* more persuasively than their rivals, whereas politicians compete by slandering the *opposition*. When you add it all up, you get a grand total of absolute praise for business and grand total of absolute slander for politics."

To the extent that opposing political propaganda in the mass media are balanced, the net effect is negligible. The virtual monopolization of the media for given social objectives, however, will produce discernible effects upon audiences.

Canalization

Prevailing beliefs in the enormous power of mass communications appear to stem from successful cases of monopolistic propaganda or from advertising. But the leap from the efficacy of advertising to the assumed efficacy of propaganda aimed at deeprooted attitudes and ego involved behavior is as unwarranted as it is dangerous. Advertising is typically directed toward the canalizing of preexisting behavior patterns or attitudes. It seldom seeks to instil new attitudes or to create significantly new behavior patterns. "Advertising pays" because it generally deals with a simple psychological situation. For Americans who have been socialized in the use of a toothbrush, it makes relatively little difference which brand of toothbrush they use. Once the gross pattern of behavior or the generic attitude has been established, it can be canalized in one direction or another. Resistance is slight. But mass propaganda typically meets a more complex situation. It may seek objectives which are at odds with deeplying attitudes. It may seek to reshape rather than to canalize current systems of values. And the successes of advertising may only highlight the failures of propaganda. Much of the current propaganda which is aimed at abolishing deep-seated ethnic and racial prejudices, for example, seems to have had little effectiveness.

Media of mass communication, then, have been effectively used to canalize basic attitudes but there is little evidence of their having served to change these attitudes.

Supplementation

Mass propaganda which is neither monopolistic nor canalizing in character may, nonetheless, prove effective if it meets a third condition: supplementation through face to face contacts.

A case in point will illustrate the interplay between mass media and face to face influences. The seeming propagandistic success achieved some years ago by Father Coughlin does not appear, upon inspection, to have resulted primarily from the propaganda content of his radio talks. It was, rather, the product of these centralized propaganda talks *and* widespread local organizations which arranged for their members to listen to him, followed by discussions among themselves concerning the social views he had expressed. This combination of a

NOTES

8

(continued)

The authors then highlight three particular benefits of this combination. First, local discussions reinforce the centrally disseminated media message. Secondly, the central media message reduces the need for 'persuasive' work by local organisers. Thirdly, national media coverage legitimates a popular movement, confers status on local organisers and organisations, and provides a local platform for nationally known speakers.

In brief, here is the rub! The authors argue that these conditions – 'monopolization', 'canalization' and 'supplementation' – rarely operate in combination, and they provide reasons for this.

As a result, this allows them to conclude that the mass media are not engaged in mass propaganda and 'do not exhibit the degree of social power commonly attributed to them'. Hence, the current social and economic structure of society – or the status quo – is maintained, with the mass media playing a key role.

After finishing this reading, and particularly the final section, you may find it interesting to compare and contrast the analysis and conclusions arrived at by Lazarsfeld and Merton with those of Herman and Chomsky (see Chapter 12 on political economy) and, to a lesser degree, C. Wright Mills (see Chapter 9), as they too 'charge' the mass media with 'manufacturing consent'.

Again, thinking specifically about the final section, what is Lazarsfeld and Merton's conception of 'audience(s)'? More specifically, what does their analysis and conclusion suggest about the power and role of the audience? To what extent does this discussion about the role of the mass media in delivering propaganda have any value today, and how useful are the three 'conditions' when thinking about media in the twenty-first century?

Structure

You may have noted that the authors provide no overall conclusion to the reading. The last few paragraphs simply provide a summary to the final section. Would some sort of conclusion, including a critical reflection on the theoretical ideas outlined, have been useful to you as a reader?

Writing Style

We, the readers, are addressed as 'you' in the first paragraph for the first time in the reading. This is probably how Lazarsfeld delivered the original lecture and it was overlooked by the editor, or not seen as a problem, in this published version.

There are a number of instances where the two authors are presumably referencing their own work, but none is actually cited. In one instance you may have noted the phrase 'research indicates . . .', but no citations are provided as examples. Would this type of additional information have been helpful?

READING

(continued)

central supply of propaganda (Coughlin's addresses on a nationwide network), the coordinated distribution of newspapers and pamphlets and locally organized face to face discussions among relatively small groups—this complex of reciprocal reinforcement by mass media and personal relations proved spectacularly successful.

Students of mass movements have come to repudiate the view that mass propaganda in and of itself creates or maintains the movement. Nazism did not attain its brief moment of hegemony by capturing the mass media of communication. The media played an ancillary role, supplementing the use of organized violence, organized distribution of rewards for conformity and organized centers of local indoctrination. The Soviet Union has also made large and impressive use of mass media for indoctrinating enormous populations with appropriate ideologies. But the organizers of indoctrination saw to it that the mass media did not operate alone. "Red corners," "reading huts" and "listening stations" comprised meeting places in which groups of citizens were exposed to the mass media in common. The fifty-five thousand reading rooms and clubs which had come into being by 1933 enabled the local ideological elite to talk over with rank and file readers the content of what they read. The relative scarcity of radios in private homes again made for group listening and group discussions of what had been heard.

In these instances, the machinery of mass persuasion included face to face contact in local organizations as an adjunct to the mass media. The privatized individual response to the materials presented through the channels of mass communication was considered inadequate for transforming exposure to propaganda into effectiveness of propaganda. In a society such as our own, where the pattern of bureaucratization has not yet become so pervasive or, at least, not so clearly crystallized, it has likewise been found that mass media prove most effective in conjunction with local centers of organized face to face contact.

Several factors contribute to the enhanced effectiveness of this joining of mass media and direct personal contact. Most clearly, the local discussions serve to reinforce the content of mass propaganda. Such mutual confirmation produces a "clinching effect." Secondly, the central media lessen the task of the local organizer, and the personnel requirements for such subalterns need not be as rigorous in a popular movement. The subalterns need not set forth the propaganda content for themselves, but need only pilot potential converts to the radio where the doctrine is being expounded. Thirdly, the appearance of a representative of the movement on a nationwide network, or his mention in the national press, serves to symbolize the legitimacy and significance of the movement. It is no powerless, inconsequential enterprise. The mass media, as we have seen, confer status. And the status of the national movement reflects back on the status of the local cells, thus consolidating the tentative decisions of its members. In this interlocking arrangement, the local organizer ensures an audience for the national speaker and the national speaker validates the status of the local organizer.

This brief summary of the situations in which the mass media achieve their maximum propaganda effect may resolve the seeming contradiction which arose at the outset of our discussion. The mass media prove most effective when they operate in a situation of virtual "psychological monopoly," or when the objective is one of canalizing rather than modifying basic attitudes or when they operate in conjunction with face to face contacts.

READING

8
(continued)

But these three conditions are rarely satisfied conjointly in propaganda for social objectives. To the degree that monopolization of attention is rare, opposing propagandas have free play in a democracy. And, by and large, basic social issues involve more than a mere canalizing of preexistent basic attitudes; they call, rather, for substantial changes in attitude and behavior. Finally, for the most obvious of reasons, the close collaboration of mass media and locally organized centers for face to face contact has seldom been achieved by groups striving for planned social change. Such programs are expensive. And it is precisely these groups which seldom have the large resources needed for these expensive programs. The forward looking groups at the edges of the power structure do not ordinarily have the large financial means of the contented groups at the center.

As a result of this threefold situation, the present role of mass media is largely confined to peripheral social concerns and the media do not exhibit the degree of social power commonly attributed to them.

By the same token, and in view of the present organization of business ownership and control of the mass media, they have served to cement the structure of our society. Organized business does approach a virtual "psychological monopoly" of the mass media. Radio commercials and newspaper advertisements are, of course, premised on a system which has been termed free enterprise. Moreover, the world of commerce is primarily concerned with canalizing rather than radically changing basic attitudes; it seeks only to create preferences for one rather than another brand of product. Face to face contacts with those who have been socialized in our culture serve primarily to reinforce the prevailing culture patterns.

Thus, the very conditions which make for the maximum effectiveness of the mass media of communication operate toward the maintenance of the going social and cultural structure rather than toward its change.

REFLECTING ON THE READING

We are yet again reminded about the need to understand something about the era in which a paper or article is written and published, and also about the background and interests of the author(s).

'Mass communication, popular taste, and organized social action' ('Mass communication') was published in 1948, shortly after the end of the Second World War (1939–45). Prior to, and during this, period the two authors, Lazarsfeld and Merton, had worked closely with – and been funded by – government and industry bodies.

Each author brought a particular perspective to the study of media and communication but, in collaborating, their different academic backgrounds, interests and skills proved complementary. Lazarsfeld, a psychologist, was seen as the 'methodologist', while Merton, a sociologist, was regarded as the 'theorist'.

We also have the benefit of knowing that the published reading was developed over a period of time, with Merton adding significant theoretical sections to the original version that was first delivered as a lecture by Lazarsfeld to a graduate school. While the introduction and merging of Merton's contributions initially appear to be seamless, further 'close' reading illuminates some instances of repetition, and questions about whether the organisation and sequencing of material could have been improved.

Simonson and Weimann (2003: 26) claim that the 'power of a theoretical essay can be measured by the ongoing vitality of its ideas', with 'Mass communication' being seen as an 'exemplary case' (2003: 26). Similarly, Katz et al. refer to this reading as 'revolutionary and relevant' (2003: 26). Perhaps not surprisingly, it is a reading that is regularly cited in texts that deal with theory relating to media and communication.

'Mass communication' can also be 'read' in different ways. For example, while it has been seen as a classic example of the 'limited effects of media research', others argue that it does *not* exemplify the 'dominant paradigm', it does *not* suggest the media as insignificant social forces, and it *cannot* be categorised as 'administrative research' (Simonson and Weimann 2003: 12). Clearly, statements such as these aim to rebut the regular, and sometimes virulent, criticism that has been directed at Lazarsfeld and other members of the Columbia school (see, for example, Gitlin 1995; 2002).

It is argued that 'Mass communication' remains theoretically significant because it includes insights that continue to have currency today. For example, the three listed social functions – The status conferral function, The enforcement of social norms, The narcotizing dysfunction – are suggested as 'pre-cursors' to later developed theories such as 'agenda-setting research, the third-person effect, the ritual view of communication, and theories of media and hegemony' (Simonson and Weimann 2003: 27–9).

Moreover, in the contemporary world of multinational media conglomerates where deregulation has become the dominant idea, where ownership has become increasingly consolidated, where commercial media are displacing, or undermining, publicly funded media, and where jobs in public relations and marketing have multiplied, Lazarsfeld and Merton's three conditions – 'monopolization', 'canalization' and 'supplementation' – remain powerful ideas 'to think with'.

Finally, the historical significance of 'Mass communication' is evident in its ability to provide us with an understanding about the developing field of media and communication studies in the late 1940s (Simonson and Weimann 2003: 12).

Key terms to explore

propaganda; mass persuasion; certified knowledge; status conferral; legitimising; narcotising; dysfunctional; monopolisation; canalisation; supplementation; hegemony; indoctrination; bureaucratisation.

Key writers who are mentioned

James Bryce; Lawrence Lowell; Bronislaw Malinowski.

RECOMMENDED READING

Boyd-Barrett, O. and Newbold, C. (eds) (1995) *Approaches to Media*, London: Arnold.

In a section on 'Defining the field', the authors include an article by Todd Gitlin which critically analyses 'the dominant paradigm' developed at the Columbia school.

Katz, E., Peters, J.D., Liebes, T. and Orloff, A. (eds) (2003) *Canonic Texts in Media Research*, Cambridge: Polity Press.

Outlines five key schools of thought, one being the Columbia school which is discussed by way of critical reflections on works by Lazarsfeld and Merton, and by Herta Herzog.

Scannell, P. (2007) *Media and Communication*, London: Sage.

Includes a chapter on the works of Katz, Lazarsfeld and Merton, explaining why they came to be written, how they were viewed by other theorists, and what impact they had on research into mass communication.

CHAPTER 9

C. Wright Mills: Mass society theory

Mills, C.W. (1956) 'The mass society', in Mills, C.W. (ed.) *The Power Elite*, London: Oxford University Press, pp. 298–324.

INTRODUCTION TO MASS SOCIETY THEORY

The obvious starting questions are: what is mass society theory, how is it related to the media, when did this theory emerge, and who developed, or is associated with, it? One way of beginning to explore these questions is to recall a spoof radio programme broadcast in America in 1938 which reported that Martians were invading the earth: *The War of the Worlds*. It led to 'a panic of national proportions' (Cantril et al. 1940, cited in Williams 2003: 42–3).

Broadcast in semi-documentary style from Los Angeles in the United States, the programme resulted in hordes of people leaving the city, apparently believing it was under attack (McCullagh 2002: 152). In a subsequent reflection on the impact of this broadcast, what became evident was the large degree of power that people attributed to the media. This broadcast provides a way of beginning to think about what is understood by mass society theory, and why and how this theory is related to the media.

Before focusing specifically on the theory itself, it is necessary to reflect briefly on issues of lineage, and particularly the *idea* of mass society and its disciplinary roots. It was the work of Alexis de Tocqueville, a French sociologist who travelled around the United States in the early 1830s, that provided the basis for subsequent debates about mass society. His major work, *Democracy in America* (1835–40), was seen as a warning against 'the "tyranny of the majority", by which "every citizen, being assimilated to all the rest, is lost in the crowd"' (cited in Marshall 1998: 669).

The work of de Tocqueville warned about imminent 'social disintegration' (Williams 2003: 24), and the concerns he raised were echoed in the work of three eminent sociologists in the nineteenth century. Emile Durkheim (1858–1917) proposed the idea of 'anomie' in this new era, Max Weber (1864–1920) introduced the notion of bureaucracy, and Ferdinand Tönnies (1855–1936) noted distinctions between the relationships in small-scale and large-scale societies, famously characterised as *gemeinschaft* (community) and *gesellschaft* (association) (see, for example, Marshall 1998).

Each of these writers responded to what they saw as profound changes occurring in western societies from the middle of the nineteenth century onwards. Essentially, these societal transformations were attributed to industrialisation, urbanisation, advances in science, colonialism, the emergence of mass democracy and mass education, and developing systems of public communication (McQuail 2005: 51; Williams 2003: 23).

These developments were seen as indicative of a shift from traditional communities, where local and social ties were strong, to a 'mass society' in which individuals were increasingly isolated from each other and, by implication, much more vulnerable to manipulation or persuasion by newly emerging mass political movements and mass media (McCullagh 2002: 152; Williams 2003: 24).

Despite such concerns being raised about mass society, these views tended to be dismissed as 'elitist nostalgia' (Marshall 1998: 399). However, the emergence of fascism and totalitarianism in Europe and the Soviet Union between 1930 and 1960 brought about a reappraisal of views about mass society, resulting in its 'naming' as a theory – mass society theory (McQuail 2005: 54).

The introduction and wide application of the word 'mass' occurred in the period between the First World War (1914–18) and Second World War (1939–45), coinciding with the noticeable expansion and availability, particularly in western societies, of radio, telephone, cinema, newspapers, novels and records. Hence, the emergence of labels such as 'mass communication', 'mass media', 'mass production', 'mass entertainment' 'mass markets', 'mass politics' and 'mass culture' (Scannell 2003: 74). When used in this way, 'mass' more often than not has negative connotations. It suggests the 'uneducated, ignorant and potentially irrational, unruly and even violent' (McQuail 2005: 54), and masses in this context are seen as comprising 'the urban, industrial working classes' (Scannell 2003: 74).

However, the mobilisation of press and film during the First World War (1914–18) by the warring states in Europe and the United States for purposes of propaganda (Redley 2007), the later co-option of mass media for ideological purposes in Nazi Germany and the Soviet Union, and the use of news and entertainment by the Allies in the Second World War again for propaganda purposes, all lent weight to the arguments made by mass society theorists that the media could be used as a potent influence on the masses (McQuail 2005: 51).

What does mass society theory suggest about audiences – listeners, viewers and readers? A simple response would be that audiences are constructed as dopes, dupes or, in recent parlance, couch potatoes. Two examples will suffice.

In a critical reflection on an article about television that was first published in 1953, reference is made to a 'television audience' being 'atomised and vulnerable – the essence of mass society' (Katz and Dayan 2003: 132). Similarly, a critical reflection on a piece of research undertaken with listeners to radio in 1941 describes the female listeners as 'com[ing] across as alienated, isolated, helpless victims of mass society, of the patriarchal system, and of the mass media, which operate as an effective tool in the service of both the society and the system' (Liebes 2003: 40).

The pessimism evident in mass society theory was reflected in the work of intellectuals both on the political Right and the political Left. Their interests focused on the social, cultural and political levels of society. For example, in the United Kingdom in the 1930s the conservative critic F.R. Leavis (see Chapter 5) railed against the importation of American cultural goods and the emergence of a mass culture driven solely by the profit motive (Boyd-Barrett 1995b: 68; Turner 1996: 39–40). Similarly, in the United States it was members of the Left-leaning Frankfurt school who provided a withering critique on the impact of mass popular culture (see Chapter 6).

With a focus primarily on the political, rather than social or cultural, level of society, C. Wright Mills is cited as a key representative of mass society theory, arguing that a 'power elite' is able to manipulate the masses, despite the existence of apparently democratic structures (Boyd-Barrett 1995b: 68).

Mass society theory is not a theory of the media. Nevertheless, the media are implicated in the theory, in that they are envisaged as one of the 'foundation stones of the mass society' and a key element in the process of social change (McQuail 2005: 94; Williams 2003: 29). Mass society theory thus gave 'a primacy to the media as a causal factor' (McQuail 2005: 94–5). This will quickly become evident in the reading.

INTRODUCTION TO THE READING

The reading selected for this chapter, 'The mass society', is drawn from chapter 13 of *The Power Elite* (1956). The book was written by Charles Wright Mills, or C. Wright Mills as he became known. It focuses on American society and comprises fifteen chapters, the titles of which give some indication about its tone and content. In addition to 'The mass society', other chapters include: 'The very rich', 'The chief executives', 'The corporate rich', 'The warlords', 'The military ascendancy', 'The political directorate' and, to demonstrate its cutting-edge credentials in the 1950s, there is a chapter entitled, 'The celebrities'.

While the jacket notes of *The Power Elite* might be expected to describe the book as fascinating, controversial, provocative and absorbing – as they do – independent commentators have since echoed similar views. For example, Peters describes Mills as 'unfurl[ing] a theory of mass society' in which the media 'do not simply shape people's voting, fashion, movies, or shopping choices, but provide ordinary people with their aspirations, identities, and even experiences' (2003: 219–20).

A similar assessment is provided by Williams, who argues that the account by Mills suggests a small powerful elite controlling American society and exercising 'control through the media and other social institutions, including the education system' (2003: 27). The book jacket also includes selected quotations from published reviews. Two of the reviewers, one from the *New York Times* and one from *Harper's Magazine*, acknowledge the book's insightful and powerful arguments, and its ability to change minds.

Mills, who was born in 1916 and died in 1962, was a professor of sociology at the University of Columbia in the United States. A leading critic of American society, Mills produced the majority of his major works during the 1950s. In addition to *The Power Elite* (1956), these included *White Collar: The American middle classes* (1951), *The Sociological Imagination* (1959) and *Sociology and Pragmatism: The higher learning in America* (1967). Described as a 'public intellectual', Mills aimed his writing at a 'general and educated audience' (Docherty et al. 1993, cited in Williams 2003: 15).

Mills believed that the object of research and publication was 'the growth of reason and the emancipation of humanity', and that this required a critical and empirical sociological approach informed by biography and history (Peters 2003: 220). In this respect, Mills was sharply critical of approaches to research that relied on highly abstract theorising ('grand theory'), and methods that were solely dependent on quantitative research techniques ('abstracted empiricism') (see, for example, Marshall 1998).

His insistence that research should focus on the relationship between the social, personal and political dimensions of people's lives was illustrated in the *The Sociological Imagination* (1959), where he outlined a view of the world that illuminated connections between private problems and public issues. The same depth and breadth of thinking and analysis are evident when he turns his attention to the mass media in the reading that follows.

Mills sees the mass media as integral to his analysis of mass society. Thus, he takes account of the wider social, political and economic structures in America. You will quickly realise that the author ascribes great power to the media and their owners, but makes not one mention of 'media effects' (see Chapter 14). Why is this? The answer, according to Peters (2003: 220), is that Mills does not use this term because he considers the impact of the media to be so obviously pervasive and significant, rather than rare and limited.

Also, as you may have realised, the book is a critique of American society, so the examples and illustrations used by the author all pertain to that geographic context. Given that the author is writing for a general but educated audience rather than for a specific professional group, or a particular academic community, the reading is generally jargon free, logically ordered and reasonably accessible.

However, as with other readings in this book, it needs close – and sometimes repeated – reading. Having a general dictionary and, as the author is a sociologist, a dictionary of sociology to hand, would be helpful.

READING

1

C.W. Mills

The Mass Society

In the standard image of power and decision, no force is held to be as important as The Great American Public. More than merely another check and balance, this public is thought to be the seat of all legitimate power. In official life as in popular folklore, it is held to be the very balance wheel of democratic power. In the end, all liberal theorists rest their notions of the power system upon the political role of this public; all official decisions, as well as private decisions of consequence, are justified as in the public's welfare; all formal proclamations are in its name.

2

In a *public*, as we may understand the term, (1) virtually as many people express opinions as receive them. (2) Public communications are so organized that there is a chance immediately and effectively to answer back any opinion expressed in public. Opinion formed by such discussion (3) readily finds an outlet in effective action, even against—if necessary—the prevailing system of authority. And (4) authoritative institutions do not penetrate the public, which is thus more or less autonomous in its operations. When these conditions prevail, we have the working model of a community of publics, and this model fits closely the several assumptions of classic democratic theory.

At the opposite extreme, in a *mass*, (1) far fewer people express opinions than receive them; for the community of publics becomes an abstract collection of individuals who receive impressions from the mass media. (2) The communications that prevail are so organized that it is difficult or impossible for the individual to answer back immediately or with any effect. (3) The realization of opinion in action is controlled by authorities who organize and control the channels of such action. (4) The mass has no autonomy from institutions; on the

NOTES

1 Structure

The first thing to note is the technique being used by Mills to 'set up' the reading: that is, he outlines a commonly held belief, or assumption, with the intention of subjecting it to a close and critical analysis.

Content

Apropos the point above, a close reading of this first paragraph should indicate that the opening assumption is not one shared by the author. Rather, one gets the sense that he can barely wait to begin the interrogation.

Why does Mills make the distinction between 'official life' and 'popular folklore', and what do you understand by his reference to 'liberal theorists'? Also, can you recall recent instances of politicians and business leaders invoking 'the public' when arguing for, or justifying, certain policy directions or decisions?

Context

While the geographic context being studied is America, the role and power attributed to the public are similar in any so-called liberal democracy. The ideas outlined here are not dissimilar to Habermas's notion of the public sphere, where stress is laid on the 'political role' of the public (see Chapter 13 on the public sphere).

Writing Style

Why does Mills refer to the 'The Great American Public', rather than, say, the American people, and why is it presented in upper-case?

2 Writing Style

First, note that Mills does not illuminate or substantiate his arguments by citing any references or using specific examples. What is also evident here, and again on occasions later in the reading, is that Mills delineates key points with numbers, a technique that is unlikely to be encouraged by your tutors. We must presume that the author adopts this technique to aid our understanding. Does this style influence how you read this section, and does it help or hinder your understanding of the issues being considered?

Structure

Note how the author uses these three paragraphs. While communications is the key thread, the purpose of the first and second paragraphs is to differentiate between 'public' and 'mass', while the third is used to synthesise the argument being presented. Is this an approach that you do, or could, employ at appropriate points in your own writing?

READING

(continued)

contrary, agents of authorized institutions penetrate this mass, reducing any autonomy it may have in the formation of opinion by discussion.

The public and the mass may be most readily distinguished by their dominant modes of communication: in a community of publics, discussion is the ascendant means of communication, and the mass media, if they exist, simply enlarge and animate discussion, linking one *primary public* with the discussions of another. In a mass society, the dominant type of communication is the formal media, and the publics become mere *media markets*: all those exposed to the contents of given mass media.

3

The institutional trends that make for a society of masses are to a considerable extent a matter of impersonal drift, but the remnants of the public are also exposed to more 'personal' and intentional forces. With the broadening of the base of politics within the context of a folk-lore of democratic decision-making, and with the increased means of mass persuasion that are available, the public of public opinion has become the object of intensive efforts to control, manage, manipulate, and increasingly intimidate.

In political, military, economic realms, power becomes, in varying degrees, uneasy before the suspected opinions of masses, and, accordingly, opinion-making becomes an accepted technique of power-holding and power-getting. The minority electorate of the propertied and the educated is replaced by the total suffrage—and intensive campaigns for the vote. The small eighteenth-century professional army is replaced by the mass army of conscripts—and by the problems of nationalist morale. The small shop is replaced by the mass-production industry—and the national advertisement.

NOTES

2

(continued)

In this section we can see Mills begin to theorise. As a result, we are encouraged to think about the nature of communications in two different kinds of societies, one being a community of publics, or primary publics – which is not dissimilar to the idea of a series of public spheres – and the other a mass society. Neither one is 'real', but is constructed by the author in order to explicate his central argument: that is, a 'power elite' controls American society.

However, as we now know, the concepts and ideas that emerge as a result of such theorising often have explanatory power and retain some currency well beyond the period when they first enter the public domain. For example, here we are introduced to the idea of a mass society controlled, at least in part, by a power elite, and a mass media which relegates publics to 'mere *media markets*'.

While the power of these arguments has waned, they are still used by advocates of community media who emphasise their interest in publics, not markets, and lay emphasis on the interests of citizens rather than consumers (see, for example, Jankowski and Prehn 2002).

Three questions emerge here. First, in what ways is the distinction between 'mass' and 'public', as outlined here, useful? Secondly, to what extent does this particular interpretation of 'public' fit with the idea of public service broadcasting? Responding to this question will help you consider why some broadcasters have sought to claim, and retain, this mantle. Thirdly, what does Mills mean when he states that 'agents of authorised institutions penetrate this mass, reducing any autonomy it may have in the formation of opinion by discussion'?

3 ## Content

In these two paragraphs Mills focuses on the increasing importance of means of mass persuasion, or opinion-management, in the transition to a 'society of masses'. Three key points are made.

First, the introduction of universal suffrage, which succeeded the earlier 'minority electorate of the propertied and the educated', is suggested as a major challenge to those in positions of political, economic and military power. As a result, the power elite are required to find ways of managing or manipulating public opinion.

Secondly, the author provides a sense of the societal transformations taking place, noting the displacement of small with large and more centralised institutions. Specific examples are provided to indicate the reasons why 'means of mass persuasion' are required.

Thirdly, what underpins this analysis is the view that 'opinion-making becomes an accepted technique for power-holding and power-getting'.

What do you think the author means when he refers to the 'remnants of the public'? To what extent is 'opinion-making' a means of getting and obtaining power? Can you provide examples?

READING

4

As the scale of institutions has become larger and more centralized, so has the range and intensity of the opinion-makers' efforts. The means of opinion-making, in fact, have paralleled in range and efficiency the other institutions of greater scale that cradle the modern society of masses. Accordingly, in addition to their enlarged and centralized means of administration, exploitation, and violence, the modern elite have had placed within their grasp historically unique instruments of psychic management and manipulation, which include universal compulsory education as well as the media of mass communication.

5

Early observers believed that the increase in the range and volume of the formal means of communication would enlarge and animate the primary public. In such optimistic views—written before radio and television and movies—the formal media are understood as simply multiplying the scope and pace of personal discussion. Modern conditions, Charles Cooley wrote, 'enlarge indefinitely the competition of ideas, and whatever has owed its persistence merely to lack of comparison is likely to go, for that which is really congenial to the choosing mind will be all the more cherished and increased.'[1] Still excited by the break-up of the conventional consensus of the local community, he saw the new means of communication as furthering the conversational dynamic of classic democracy, and with it the growth of rational and free individuality.

1. Charles Horton Cooley, *Social Organization* (New York: Scribner's, 1909), p. 93. Cf. also Chapter IX.

NOTES

4   Content

Here, the author juxtaposes a pessimistic and an optimistic view of the mass media, reinforcing the former and undermining the latter. Three points are made in the first paragraph.

First, the growth and centralisation of institutions was matched by a parallel expansion and intensity of opinion-making. Secondly, the elite of the modern era were fortunate to have at their disposal means of opinion-making that were not available to their forbears. Thirdly, two such means, the media of mass communication and universal compulsory education, are now seen as 'instruments of psychic management and manipulation'. Note that there is no debate about any of the assertions made here.

What do you understand by 'psychic management and manipulation'? Also, following the argument developed by the author, why would the 'modern elite' need to use the media in this way?

Context

One point here is worth noting about change and continuity. Mills identifies two parallel trends – the growth and centralisation of institutions, and parallel developments in opinion-making – that occur in a national context. If we were to engage with these issues today, it would also require us to think in a global context.

5   Content

Mills chooses to draw on the words of Charles Cooley, whose more optimistic views about the media were published well before the widespread availability of film, radio and television. Cooley's views about the role and potential of the media of communication are closely allied with a liberal perspective, unlike the view held by Mills. Why can it be said that Cooley's views fit with a liberal perspective on the media?

Context

This paragraph draws attention to why, how and when an author uses a particular reference. In this case, Cooley's apparent – and, in the view of the author, misguided – optimism about the media of communication suits Mills's purposes. However, as Cooley is writing in the early 1900s, Mills – writing in the 1950s – has the benefit of a further forty years or so to inform his own perspective on the media, a period which spanned two world wars.

Optimistic views, or forecasts, like that of Cooley's are not unusual. All significant developments in new media and communication technologies tend to be accompanied by a profusion of statements about how life-changing they will be and how they will enhance democracy. The reality, though, may be somewhat different.

READING

6

No one really knows all the functions of the mass media, for in their entirety these functions are probably so pervasive and so subtle that they cannot be caught by the means of social research now available. But we do now have reason to believe that these media have helped less to enlarge and animate the discussions of primary publics than to transform them into a set of media markets in mass-like society. I do not refer merely to the higher ratio of deliverers of opinion to receivers and to the decreased chance to answer back; nor do I refer merely to the violent banalization and stereotyping of our very sense organs in terms of which these media now compete for 'attention.' I have in mind a sort of psychological illiteracy that is facilitated by the media, and that is expressed in several ways:

7

1. Very little of what we think we know of the social realities of the world have we found out first-hand. Most of 'the pictures in our heads' we have gained from these media—even to the point where we often do not really believe what we see before us until we read about it in the paper or hear about it on the radio.[2] The media not only give us information; they guide our very experiences. Our standards of credulity, our standards of reality, tend to be set by these media rather than by our own fragmentary experience.

Accordingly, even if the individual has direct, personal experience of events, it is not really direct and primary: it is organized in stereotypes. It takes long and skillful training to so uproot such stereotypes that an individual sees things freshly, in an unstereotyped manner. One might suppose, for example, that if all the people went through a depression they would all 'experience it,' and in terms of this experience, that they would all debunk or reject or at least refract what the media say about it. But experience of such a *structural* shift has to be organized and interpreted if it is to count in the making of opinion.

2. See Walter Lippmann, *Public Opinion* (New York: Macmillan, 1992), which is still the best account of this aspect of the media. Cf. especially pp. 1–25 and 59–121.

NOTES

6 Context

In reflecting on the first sentence, we need to remember that this work was published in 1956. Could such a statement be made today? Identify the grounds that could be provided in support of, and against, such an assertion.

Content

Having identified the limitations of prevailing research methods, the author then goes on to assert – without identifying any supporting references – that the mass media have transformed 'primary publics' into 'media-markets in mass-like society'. Note, how, in using the next sentence as a bridge to the final one, the author takes the opportunity – virtually in passing – to further denigrate the media.

Having argued that the media facilitate 'a sort of psychological illiteracy', the author then proceeds to identify four ways in which this occurs and proceeds to deal with each one in turn.

What is meant by 'violent banalization and stereotyping', and why has Mills placed apostrophes around 'attention'?

7 Writing Style

While Mills has provided few additional references or specific examples to illustrate or substantiate his lines of argument, a great deal of detail is provided in the course of outlining four ways in which the media 'facilitate psychological illiteracy'. You might want to look briefly at each of these four points first and then go back to read each one in detail. This will give you a sense of the direction of travel.

Content

As you will see – and are probably expecting – Mills attributes great power to the media and little, if any, to audiences (see Chapters 23 and 24). This becomes clear immediately, when it is suggested that we are almost totally dependent on the media for an understanding of the world around us and how we should act upon that world.

In these first two paragraphs, Mills argues that individual and direct experience is in itself not sufficient to challenge the way we might think about a particular event. This is because, in essence, we have been conditioned by the media to think in stereotypes. Therefore, following this logic, the author argues that even if we all suffered a bout of depression, our understanding of this illness would be informed more by media stereotypes of the condition than by our own experience.

What does Mills mean by a *structural* shift, and how is it related to public opinion?

Context

In the first paragraph, Mills is citing the work of Walter Lippmann on public opinion to support the arguments being made. This citing, together with the concepts and insights used, betrays Mills's academic background, which is in sociology.

READING

8

The kind of experience, in short, that might serve as a basis for resistance to mass media is not an experience of raw events, but the experience of meanings. The fleck of interpretation must be there in the experience if we are to use the word experience seriously. And the capacity for such experience is socially implanted. The individual does not trust his own experience, as I have said, until it is confirmed by others or by the media. Usually such direct exposure is not accepted if it disturbs loyalties and beliefs that the individual already holds. To be accepted, it must relieve or justify the feelings that often lie in the back of his mind as key features of his ideological loyalties.

9

Stereotypes of loyalty underlie beliefs and feelings about given symbols and emblems; they are the very ways in which men see the social world and in terms of which men make up their specific opinions and views of events. They are the results of previous experience, which affect present and future experience. It goes without saying that men are often unaware of these loyalties, that often they could not formulate them explicitly. Yet such general stereotypes make for the acceptance or the rejection of specific opinions not so much by the force of logical consistency as by their emotional affinity and by the way in which they relieve anxieties. To accept opinions in their terms is to gain the good solid feeling of being correct without having to think. When ideological stereotypes and specific opinions are linked in this way, there is a lowering of the kind of anxiety which arises when loyalty and belief are not in accord. Such ideologies lead to a willingness to accept a given line of belief; then there is no need, emotionally or rationally, to overcome resistance to given items in that line; cumulative selections of specific opinions and feelings become the pre-organized attitudes and emotions that shape the opinion-life of the person.

8

Content

If you think the author's line of argument to date has been difficult to penetrate, it now becomes slightly more dense! Having established that the experience of 'raw events' alone is not enough to resist the stereotypes imposed by mass media, what is required, according to the author, is 'the experience of meanings'.

What this suggests is that experience has to be accompanied by some degree of reflection or, as the author puts it, a 'fleck of interpretation', if an experience is to become meaningful and, thereby, enable the required 'structural shift'.

However, what obstructs such a shift taking place is that individuals don't trust their own experience, unless it is 'confirmed by others or by the media'. So, following this line of argument, an individual is unlikely to accept or respond to new experiences if the resultant insights or viewpoints do not 'fit' with their already established 'ideological loyalties'.

What do you understand by the term 'ideological loyalties'? Can you identify your own ideological loyalties? Also, what does Mills mean when he says that 'experience is socially implanted'? What role is implied for the mass media in this statement?

Writing Style

Note that the text is gender specific. It is always 'his'. Why is this?

9

Structure

If you read this paragraph a few times you will see how Mills 'builds' his argument (see *Content* below).

Content

Here, Mills 'fleshes out' some of the key ideas introduced previously. Again, 'stereotypes' underpin much of the analysis, with Mills referring to 'stereotypes of loyalty', 'general stereotypes' and 'ideological stereotypes'.

Mills suggests that men have a view of the world that relies on beliefs and feelings which are underpinned by 'stereotypes of loyalty' about which they may not even be aware. These loyalties have a continuity, in the sense that they been formed through past experience and will affect current and future experience. They also provide emotional comfort when individuals are being challenged with new and different viewpoints and opinions. In other words, it is easier and more comfortable for an individual to stick with already established beliefs – or loyalties – than to deal with the anxieties that might arise when faced with new and challenging opinions. Reliance on such stereotypes reaffirms already established beliefs, reduces openness to new ideas and, in Mills's view, leads to a situation where 'pre-organized attitudes and emotions . . . shape the opinion-life of the person'.

READING

10

These deeper beliefs and feelings are a sort of lens through which men experience their worlds, they strongly condition acceptance or rejection of specific opinions, and they set men's orientation toward prevailing authorities. Three decades ago, Walter Lippmann saw such prior convictions as biases: they kept men from defining reality in an adequate way. They are still biases. But today they can often be seen as 'good biases'; inadequate and misleading as they often are, they are less so than the crackpot realism of the higher authorities and opinion-makers. They are the lower common sense and as such a factor of resistance. But we must recognize, especially when the pace of change is so deep and fast, that common sense is more often common than sense. And, above all, we must recognize that 'the common sense' of our children is going to be less the result of any firm social tradition than of the stereotypes carried by the mass media to which they are now so fully exposed. They are the first generation to be so exposed.

11

11. So long as the media are not entirely monopolized, the individual can play one medium off against another; he can compare them, and hence resist what any one of them puts out. The more genuine competition there is among the media, the more resistance the individual might be able to command. But how much is this now the case? *Do* people compare reports on public events or policies, playing one medium's content off against another's?

The answer is: generally no, very few do: (I) We know that people tend strongly to select those media which carry contents with which they already agree. There is a kind of selection of new opinions on the basis of prior opinions. No one seems to search out such counter-statements as may be found in alternative media offerings. Given radio programs and magazines and newspapers often get a rather consistent public, and thus reinforce their messages

NOTES

(continued)

Writing Style

Note again how the writing is obviously gendered, except for the final sentence where 'person' appears. Could it be that the author is using 'men' generically, suggesting humans and thereby including women – although 'man' would tend to be used if this was the intention – or is he highlighting a specific characteristic of the male psyche?

Whatever your view, you will also be aware that the analysis is general, in the sense that there is no attempt to distinguish men in terms of social class, age, education, ethnicity or occupation. Can we criticise the author for a generalisation of this kind, or is it appropriate in the context of this reading? How persuasive is the concluding sentence?

10 Content

In the last of these five paragraphs that are used to illustrate why and how the mass media can be seen to facilitate 'psychological illiteracy', Mills uses a metaphor to underpin the key argument. That is, the 'pre-organized' attitudes, values and beliefs held by men can be likened to that of a lens, which shapes how they view the world and, most importantly, induces an acceptance of the status quo – an 'orientation toward prevailing authorities'.

Here, Mills draws again on Walter Lippmann, introducing the notion of 'bias' to distinguish between 'ordinary' men and the 'opinion-makers' and 'higher authorities'. Mills also adds a note of urgency to the discussion, using the phrase 'we must recognize' in successive sentences. The reason for this becomes clear in the final sentence, where Mills warns about the dangers for the (then) current generation of children, implying that their view of the world would be conditioned by the 'stereotypes carried by the mass media', rather than by any 'firm social tradition'.

There are two key phrases that need close reading before moving on. The first is where the author refers to 'prior convictions' stopping men 'defining reality in an adequate way'. What is meant by this? Secondly, what do you understand by the idea of 'lower common sense' as a 'factor of resistance'? Finally, even though this reading was published in the 1950s, does the 'message' in the last two sentences have any currency today?

11 Content

The second argument in support of the idea that the mass media facilitate 'psychological illiteracy' relates to the monopolisation, or consolidation, of the media and related issues of diversity and plurality. These are matters that are discussed at a number of points in this volume and from a variety of perspectives.

Essentially, Mills is looking to contest the view that the more media, or channels, there are, the more likely it is that individuals are in a position to choose between such media and, in doing so, 'resist' a particular line of opinion. Mills uses a question to move from the 'theory' to the 'reality', thus allowing him to set out two reasons why individuals are unlikely to be able to 'play off' the content of one medium against others.

READING

11

(continued)

in the minds of that public. (2) This idea of playing one medium off against another assumes that the media really have varying contents. It assumes genuine competition, which is not widely true. The media display an apparent variety and competition, but on closer view they seem to compete more in terms of variations on a few standardized themes than of clashing issues. The freedom to raise issues effectively seems more and more to be confined to those few interests that have ready and continual access to these media.

12

III. The media have not only filtered into our experience of external realities, they have also entered into our very experience of our own selves. They have provided us with new identities and new aspirations of what we should like to be, and what we should like to appear to be. They have provided in the models of conduct they hold out to us a new and larger and more flexible set of appraisals of our very selves. In terms of the modern theory of the self,[3] we may say that the media bring the reader, listener, viewer into the sight of larger, higher reference groups—groups, real or imagined, up-close or vicarious, personally known or distractedly glimpsed—which are looking glasses for his self-image. They have multiplied the groups to which we look for confirmation of our self-image.

More than that: (1) the media tell the man in the mass who he is—they give him identity; (2) they tell him what he wants to be—they give him aspirations; (3) they tell him how to get that way—they give him technique; and (4) they tell him how to feel that he is that way even when he is not—they give him escape. The gaps between the identity and aspiration lead to technique and/or to escape. That is probably the basic psychological formula of the mass media today. But, as a formula, it is not attuned to the development of the human being. It is the formula of a pseudo-world which the media invent and sustain.

3. Cf. Gerth and Mills, *Character and Social Structure* (New York: Harcourt, Brace, 1953), pp. 84 ff.

NOTES

11

(continued)

The arguments being put will not be unknown to you. First, in summary, people choose to access media with which they feel comfortable and, as a result, the 'messages' of the broadcasters are consistently reinforced. Secondly, in brief, the assumption that the content of different media varies substantially is, according to the author, flawed. While there might be an 'apparent variety', this is more likely to relate to style and emphasis around a 'few standardized themes', rather than sharp differences in the type of issues or topics covered and the ways in which they are addressed.

Again, these sorts of arguments retain currency some sixty years after the publication of this reading (see, for example, Allan 1999). Moreover, the sentiment in the final sentence has since been echoed by John Keane (1995: 263), who argued that both public service and commercial media 'distribute entitlements to speak and to be heard and seen unevenly'.

Writing Style

As previously, Mills remains consistent, in the sense that he rarely cites references or provides examples to substantiate the arguments being made. Although each point is clearly made and carefully argued, this is a 'closed', rather than 'open', reading. Also, in parts, as intimated above, the author takes on a campaigning position. This bears similarity to the interest in values that Golding and Murdock (2000: 72) cite as a key plank of critical political economy (see Chapter 12).

12 Content

As with previous sections of this reading, it may be useful to peruse these two paragraphs first before reading them again more closely.

What becomes apparent, almost immediately, is the degree of power being attributed to the mass media. In this instance, which is the third example of the way in which the mass media are responsible for encouraging 'psychological illiteracy', the focus is on identity and aspiration. Simply put, the argument is that the mass media provide us with identities and aspirations as well as the techniques to achieve them, or to believe that they have been so achieved.

To what extent do you hear these, or similar, arguments made today? Who would be likely to use such arguments and why would they make them? How would the arguments made here by the author be countered today, and what perspectives/theories would be used to support a counter-view?

Writing Style/Structure

What we also see here is a recognisable technique used by Mills. The first paragraph in this section is used to set out his ideas about identities and aspirations; the second provides the 'evidence' but, as is often the case, without additional references or concrete illustrations, and he ends with a concluding sentence or two.

So, the author lists four key points, each set out clearly and concisely, which it is argued represent a 'basic psychological formula of the mass media' and lead to the creation of a 'pseudo-world' that the said media seek to maintain.

READING

13

IV. As they now generally prevail, the mass media, especially television, often encroach upon the small-scale discussion, and destroy the chance for the reasonable and leisurely and human interchange of opinion. They are an important cause of the destruction of privacy in its full human meaning. That is an important reason why they not only fail as an educational force, but are a malign force: they do not articulate for the viewer or listener the broader sources of his private tensions and anxieties, his inarticulate resentments and half-formed hopes. They neither enable the individual to transcend his narrow milieu nor clarify its private meaning.

The media provide much information and news about what is happening in the world, but they do not often enable the listener or the viewer truly to connect his daily life with these larger realities. They do not connect the information they provide on public issues with the troubles felt by the individual. They do not increase rational insight into tensions, either those in the individual or those of the society which are reflected in the individual. On the contrary, they distract him and obscure his chance to understand himself or his world, by fastening his attention upon artificial frenzies that are resolved within the program framework, usually by violent action or by what is called humor. In short, for the viewer they are not really resolved at all. The chief distracting tension of the media is between the wanting and the not having of commodities or of women held to be good looking. There is almost always the general tone of animated distraction, of suspended agitation, but it is going nowhere and it has nowhere to go.

14

But the media, as now organized and operated, are even more than a major cause of the transformation of America into a mass society. They are also among the most important of those increased means of power now at the disposal of elites of wealth and power; morever, some of the higher agents of these media are themselves either among the elites or very important among their servants.

NOTES

12   Context

(continued)

You have probably also noticed that rather than refer to 'audiences' – as in later academic studies of the media – the author opts for readers, listeners and viewers who, by implication, are seen as powerless in the face of mass media.

13   Content

Now we come to the fourth and final example of why the author believes that the mass media are responsible for bringing about a form of 'psychological illiteracy'. While the third example charged the media with intruding into the experience of self by shaping identities and aspirations, this one continues the theme of intrusion but in respect of 'privacy', with television identified as the main culprit.

The mass media are seen as a 'malign force'. This is because they are thought not to be successful in helping individuals to understand and make sense of their own social milieu and in transcending that milieu. In other words, the mass media fail to illuminate the connection between public issues and personal troubles.

Rather, Mills argues, the mass media find ways of diverting attention away from such connections through the use of programming frameworks and by way of particular techniques of distraction, one being the creation of a tension 'between the wanting and the not having of commodities'. So much so that the mass media are seen as maintaining an ongoing 'general tone of animated discussion [and] suspended agitation'.

Why is it that the author focuses his criticism particularly on television? What do you understand by Mills's reference to the 'destruction of privacy in its full human meaning'? What is Mills getting at when he links 'artificial frenzies' – via programmes – to violence and humour?

Before reading the final few paragraphs of this reading, you might want to recall and reflect on the four reasons provided by the author to support his claims that the mass media facilitate psychological illiteracy.

14   Content

Here, in wrapping up the arguments set out so far in the reading, Mills makes three assertions about the relationship between media and power.

First, the media – as they are organised and operated – have been instrumental in transforming America 'into a mass society'. Secondly, the media are, in effect, 'tools', that are available for use by the 'elites' in American society. Thirdly, the owners or operators of media organisations are themselves members – or servants – of those same power elites. Here, we see ideas that re-emerge in the later work of Herman and Chomsky (1944 [1988]).

Note that no names of media moguls are provided and neither are any members of the so-called 'power elite' identified. In terms of the assertions being made, in what ways might it have been helpful if Mills had provided examples?

READING

15

Alongside or just below the elite, there is the propagandist, the publicity expert, the public-relations man, who would control the very formation of public opinion in order to be able to include it as one more pacified item in calculations of effective power, increased prestige, more secure wealth. Over the last quarter of a century, the attitudes of these manipulators toward their task have gone through a sort of dialectic:

16

In the beginning, there is great faith in what the mass media can do. Words win wars or sell soap; they move people, they restrain people. 'Only cost,' the advertising man of the 'twenties proclaims, 'limits the delivery of public opinion in any direction on any topic.'[4] The opinion-maker's belief in the media as mass persuaders almost amounts to magic—but he can believe mass communications omnipotent only so long as the public is trustful. It does not remain trustful. The mass media say so very many and such competitively exaggerated things; they banalize their message and they cancel one another out. The 'propaganda phobia,' in reaction to wartime lies and postwar disenchantment, does not help matters, even though memory is both short and subject to official distortion. This distrust of the magic of media is translated into a slogan among the opinion managers. Across their banners they write: 'Mass Persuasion Is Not Enough.'

4. J. Truslow Adams, *The Epic of America* (Boston: Little, Brown, 1931), p. 360.

NOTES

15 Content

Having established links between elites and mass media, the author turns his attention to what we would now describe as the public relations industry.

According to Mills, the approach to public relations work has undergone a process of transformation, which he likens to 'a sort of dialectic'. As this dialectic is to be explored in the following paragraph, note how the author signals the continuity by use of a colon.

Context

Mills suggests that the changing attitudes of public relations workers – or 'manipulators' – occurred over the course of a quarter of a century. This is another reminder that we always need to be aware about when items are published. Given that this reading was published in the late 1950s, what significant events had occurred in the first half of the twentieth century?

If you are not already sure about the meaning of dialectic, by reading the next two paragraphs its meaning should become clear.

Writing Style

Again the gender emphasis is obvious, as is the author's apparent disdain for an industry whose goal, he suggests, is the manipulation of public opinion in the interests of power, prestige and wealth.

16 Content

Here, Mills summarises the changing positions of the public relations industry, starting with a biblical inflection – 'in the beginning'.

Initially, according to the author, the industry believed that if there was sufficient funding available, the preferred 'public opinion' could be delivered. Hence, the idea of mass media, or mass communications, as 'mass persuaders' – an idea that became pervasive after publication of *The Hidden Persuaders* by Vance Packard (1957). However, as public trust dissipates because of exaggeration, propaganda and lies propagated by the mass media, reliance on persuasion alone to deliver public opinion is no longer adequate.

Context

Here, virtually for the first time, we see recognition that listeners, readers and viewers are able to exert at least some degree of power by withdrawing their trust in the face of flaws in the mass media.

Are you now clear about why the author thought that 'dialectic' was a useful way of conceptualising the changing attitudes of the public relations industry?

READING

17

Frustrated, they reason; and reasoning, they come to accept the principle of social context. To change opinion and activity, they say to one another, we must pay close attention to the full context and lives of the people to be managed. Along with mass persuasion, we must somehow use personal influence; we must reach people in their life context and *through* other people, their daily associates, those whom they trust: we must get at them by some kind of 'personal' persuasion. We must not show our hand directly; rather than merely advise or command, we must manipulate.

18

Now this live and immediate social context in which people live and which exerts a steady expectation upon them is of course what we have called the primary public. Anyone who has seen the inside of an advertising agency or public-relations office knows that the primary public is still the great unsolved problem of the opinion-makers. Negatively, their recognition of the influence of social context upon opinion and public activity implies that the articulate public resists and refracts the communications of the mass media. Positively, this recognition implies that the public is not composed of isolated individuals, but rather of persons who not only have prior opinions that must be reckoned with, but who continually influence each other in complex and intimate, in direct and continual ways.

17 Content

So, with 'mass persuasion' seen to be somewhat limited in its ability to deliver public opinion, the public relations industry recognises the need to look more closely at the social context in which people live their lives in order to find ways of exerting personal influence more directly, or through 'those whom they trust'. Hence the author's view that manipulation rather than persuasion becomes the primary tool of the 'opinion managers'.

18 Content

Mills sets out how these industries perceive both the difficulties and the opportunities of engaging with, and influencing, the 'primary public'. In terms of difficulties, it is the public's refraction of, and resistance to, mass media messages, or at least those that comprise the 'articulate public'. In terms of opportunities, resistance demonstrates that people have existing views about the world (which may be open to change), and people live their lives through a variety of social and other networks (through which they may be influenced).

Who, or what, is the 'articulate public'?

Context

Although writing in the 1950s, Mills's view that it is the *primary public* that preoccupies 'opinion managers' and 'opinion-makers' in advertising and public relations, appears still to be the case today.

Note how in this paragraph Mills returns to his earlier key distinction between *public* – a community of publics, or primary publics – and *mass* – a mass society. His thesis on the role of the mass media is also evident: that is, rather than encouraging and animating discussion in *primary publics* and linking one with another, in a mass society the media are the dominant form of communication with the result that such publics simply become 'media markets'.

REFLECTING ON THE READING

Having studied the reading, you will still probably be reflecting on its central thrust and the ways in which Mills constructs and supports his arguments. It is also impossible to avoid noticing the contrasting power that Mills attributes to the mass media and to audiences. There are a number of other issues that are worth considering in response to the reading.

First, there is some value in reflecting on the standing of the reading and the status of the author among his peers. Secondly, it is useful to recall the era of publication and also to consider the motives, or ambitions, of the author. Thirdly, while mass society theory is no longer fashionable, its basic premise is apparent in contemporary references to the media. Fourthly, and related to the previous point, it is important to note that that there are advocates of mass society theory who argue that it continues to have explanatory power.

The reading and the book from which it is drawn are widely cited in texts that address mass media and mass communication. Moreover, McQuail describes *The Power Elite* as a 'seminal study of the discontents of modern life', drawing, as it does, 'on a long radical critique of industrialism and capitalism' (2002: 71). For McQuail, the strengths of Mills's analysis are his ability to illustrate the extent to which people are dependent on the cultural industries, in this case news and advertising, for a view of the world (p. 71).

While McQuail implies that a similar observation might appropriately be made about the cultural industries in contemporary times, he also highlights one key limitation of Mills's analysis: that is, the explicit assumptions made about the controlling ability of the media and the malleability of listeners, readers and viewers (2002: 71).

Only with the benefit of hindsight is it possible to consider the work of C. Wright Mills alongside that of other authors of the same era and suggest a similarity of mission. Peters (2003: 221) does just this, bracketing Mills's *The Power Elite* (1956), Raymond Williams's *Culture and Society* (1958), Hannah Arendt's *The Human Condition* (1958), Aldous Huxley's *Brave New World Revisited* (1958), Raymond Williams's *Long Revolution* (1961) and Jürgen Habermas's *Structural Transformation of the Public Sphere* (1962), suggesting that they all had something in common.

The similarity is that each of these writers envisage 'communication as cure and disease of modern life', and all 'deal with the threat of mass society, of lonely crowds, and seek ways to rebuild a more vital democracy' (Peters 2003: 221). The mass media are obviously central in respect of these concerns.

While mass society theory is now no longer in vogue, due to its undervaluing of the social contexts of media consumption, its influence is still apparent. This is evident in a number of ways (McQuail 2002: 18; 2005: 94–5). For example, the decline in political participation, and voting in particular, is often explained by cynical politicians manipulating the mass media.

Also, there are still regular instances where elements of the mass media are accused of sexualising young girls, grooming children as consumers and, more recently, being seen at least partly responsible for bringing about an increase in obesity in adults and children.

Moreover, allegations of 'dumbing-down' are also levelled at the mass media, and an increase in commercial channels is sometimes cited as evidence of a 'corrupted' public sphere. Finally, while many enjoy the material benefits of contemporary society, the apparent isolation, unhappiness and dislocation of others prompts nostalgia for the close-knit communities of earlier eras, and resonates with those who identify with the anomie of mass society theory.

However, while mass society theory may these days be confined to the opening chapters of texts books on the media (Rothenbuhler 2003: 110), some argue that it remains a very helpful way of explaining events over the past few decades.

For example, Boyd-Barrett cites as a key moment the resurgence of free-market capitalism in the United Kingdom and United States in 1979/80 after Conservative and Republican victories respectively, and notes the following tendencies in 'advanced' countries over a number of years: moves to undermine traditional loyalties to political parties; attacks on the support for trade-unions; weakening of the nuclear family; decreasing security for white and blue-collar employment; increases in violent and non-violent crime; national power elites colluding with international business. As a result of these tendencies, it is argued that the state and the economic interests that drive the state's policies are much better placed to manipulate individuals (Boyd-Barrett 1995b: 70).

These reflections lend weight to the notion that 'traditions [or theories] do not die, but are transformed or, lying dormant for periods of time, are rediscovered and adapted' (Boyd-Barrett 1995b: 69).

Key terms to explore

liberal theorists; universal suffrage; primary publics; psychological illiteracy; stereotypes; ideological loyalties; status quo; pseudo-world; power elite; dialectic; mass persuasion; opinion-managers.

Key writers who are mentioned

Charles Cooley; Walter Lippmann.

RECOMMENDED READING

Eldridge, J. (1983) *C. Wright Mills*, Chichester: Ellis Horwood; London: Tavistock Publications.

Provides a review of the life and work of C. Wright Mills, and devotes one section to a critical analysis of *The Power Elite*.

McQuail, D. (ed.) (2002) *McQuail's Reader in Mass Communication Theory*, London: Sage.

Has a section on 'Mass media and society' which includes four readings, one being an extract from C. Wright Mills's *The Power Elite*.

Scannell, P. (2007) *Media and Communication*, London: Sage.

As a wider context to the work of C. Wright Mills, part one of this book, 'The masses', includes chapters on 'Mass communication', 'Mass culture' and 'The end of the masses'.

CHAPTER 10

The Toronto school

Innis, H.A. (1951) 'The bias of communication', in Innis, H.A., *The Bias of Communication*, Toronto: University of Toronto Press, pp. 33–60.

INTRODUCTION TO THE TORONTO SCHOOL

Here again is a reminder about the role of cities in the development of media theory (see, for example, Chapter 6 on the Frankfurt school and Chapter 11 on the Birmingham Centre for Contemporary Cultural Studies). However, as you may be aware from your own reading, the Toronto school does not have the same cachet as those noted above. Neither is it referred to as often as other schools of thought. The reasons for this are outlined below.

Interest in particular theories and theoreticians does wax and wane over time. This is certainly the case with Herbert Marshall McLuhan, one of the Toronto school's most celebrated members, while the work of his eminent colleague, Harold Adams Innis, remains less well known (Scannell 2007: 129). Similarly, Eric Havelock, who was also at the university of Toronto for some time, rarely receives a mention in this context (see, for example, Briggs and Burke 2002: Stamps 1995: 129).

Two reasons have been suggested for the relative marginalisation of the Toronto school. One is related to the type of research carried out by Innis and McLuhan and how it has been perceived and reported, and the other is attributed to what has been described as the 'geopolitical marginality' of Canada (Theall 1975: 1).

Stevenson associates the Toronto school with the origins of 'Canadian social theory' (2002: 119), while Carey describes it as the home of 'Canadian communication theory' (1975: 27). For Katz et al. the Toronto school is best known as the 'centre for the social effects of media technologies', its work being generally categorised as 'technological determinism' (2003: 6, 154). This perspective represents the view that technology 'shapes society and can be a cause of social change' (Burton 2005: 201).

However, Stamps takes issue with this description of the Toronto school, arguing that the work published by the school during the period between 1930 and 1975 would be better described as 'critical theories of modernity' (1995: xiv). Her reason being that Innis and McLuhan 'studied Western consciousness by shining a shaft of light along a forgotten aspect of its history – namely, the development of communications systems, or media' (p. 3). Similarly, Scannell (2007: 142) acknowledges the fresh and novel approach pioneered by the Toronto school in shifting the focus of research away from a preoccupation with media *content* to that of media *forms*.

Nevertheless, it is reasonable to suggest that the work of both Innis and McLuhan has not attracted the attention that it warrants. In part, at least, this is explained by their Canadian roots and the fact that their research interests were sparked by the geopolitical history of Canada. To illustrate this point, Stamps argues that a 'Eurocentric bias' favours the work of western thinkers, such as, for example, Foucault, Freud, Habermas and Marx, and 'robs us' of the insights provided by Innis and McLuhan (1995: 3–4). Moreover, Stamps suggests that in some circles 'technological determinism' is suggested as 'uniquely Canadian' and, therefore, 'uniquely crude' (p. xiv)!

Similarly, Carey (1975: 27–8) refers to a resistance in America to Canadian scholarship on communication theory, and notes how in the 1970s Innis's work was barely acknowledged. While this marginalisation is partly explained by Innis's Canadian citizenship, his popularity was not helped because of his stated belief that 'Canadian scholars should correct the bias of British and American scholarship and to blunt its penetration into spheres where it had no explanatory significance' (p. 29).

The Toronto school is, more or less, solely associated with Harold Innis and Marshall McLuhan, both of whom are described as entering the field of media studies 'through a side-door' (Katz et al. 2003: 154). In other words, Innis originally trained as an economist and McLuhan in English literature. Innis was born in Canada and tends to be referred to as either a political economist or an economic historian (Kroker 1984: 16; Thussu 2006: 58). He served overseas in the First World War (1914–18) after completing an undergraduate degree at McMaster University in Toronto, and returned to undertake doctoral studies at the University of Chicago (Dennis and Wartella 1996: 187).

Innis later joined the Department of Political Economy at the University of Toronto, where he spent the rest of his working life (Stamps 1995: 41). His major publications include the following: *A History of the Canadian Pacific Railway* (1971 [1923]); *The Fur Trade in Canada: An introduction to Canadian economic history* (1984 [1930]); *The Cod Fisheries: The history of an international economy* (1978 [1940]); *Political Economy in the Modern State* (1946); *The Bias of Communication* (1964 [1951]); and *Empire and Communications* (1972 [1950]).

Also born in Canada, McLuhan completed his doctoral studies at Cambridge in the United Kingdom in 1943. He taught at St Louis University in Missouri and later moved to St Michael's College at the University of Toronto, where he spent the remainder of his career, taking charge of the Centre for Culture and Technology from 1963 to 1980 (Dennis and Wartella 1996: 189; Stamps 1995: 146). Although McLuhan's best-known works are *The Gutenberg Galaxy: The making of typographic man* (1962) and its sequel *Understanding Media: The extensions of man* (1964), his other publications include: *The Mechanical Bride: Folklore of industrial man* (1951b); *The Medium is the Massage: An inventory of effects* (with Quentin Fiore) (1967); *Culture is our Business* (1970a); and *From Cliché to Archetype* (1970b).

McLuhan was certainly influenced by the work of Innis (Meyrowitz 2002: 103; Stamps 1995: 122). Although their working lives overlapped, Innis's career was ending at the time when McLuhan's was taking shape. While Innis tended to focus almost exclusively on oral and written communication, McLuhan focused on the (then) new medium of television, presenting himself as 'the interpreter of a new age of communication' (Scannell 2007: 130). Following the publication of *Understanding Media: The extension of man* in 1964, McLuhan achieved what would be described today as celebrity status. His popularity then waned, but it was revived in the 1990s (Meyrowitz 2003: 200–8).

Probably best known for aphorisms such as 'the global village', 'hot' and 'cool' media, and 'the medium is the message', not all of which were correctly understood and interpreted, McLuhan was lauded by some of his peers but strongly criticised by others (Meyrowitz 2003: 208–10; Scannell 2007: 129–38). While McLuhan has attracted a substantial audience around the world within and beyond the academy, Innis has been judged a 'far more important theoretician' (Godfrey 1986: vii).

Writing from a Canadian perspective, Stamps argues that it was due to the work of Innis and McLuhan that the study of media became accepted as a 'valuable contribution to understanding contemporary society' (1995: 3). Likewise, Stevenson (2002: 119) acknowledges the contribution of the Toronto school to the social theory of mass communication. Essentially, this is because their work aimed to illuminate how the technological apparatus of the mass media shaped social relations in the contemporary world.

As a result of emphasising the *constitutive* rather than *incidental* role of technology, Meyrowitz (2002: 102–6) – himself influenced by Innis and McLuhan (Robinson 1996: 165) – classified this type of scholarly work as 'medium theory'. This was because it focused on the individual characteristics of a particular medium.

The work carried out by Innis, McLuhan, and George Grant, another Canadian scholar, prompted Kroker to argue that 'Canada's principal contribution to North American thought consists of a highly original, comprehensive, and eloquent discourse on technology' (1984: 7).

INTRODUCTION TO THE READING

Outside Canada, Innis's two most well-known books are *Empire and Communications* and *The Bias of Communication*. It is from the latter, a collection of essays which with some variations summarise the former, that this reading is drawn. The reading has the same title, *The Bias of Communication*, as the book in which it appears. The origins of the reading lie in an academic paper presented by Innis at the University of Michigan in 1949. The book, which includes an introduction by Marshall McLuhan, was published only shortly before Innis's death in 1952.

In the preface, Innis provides some background information about the collection of essays that make up the book, and what prompted its publication. According to Innis, the key question to which he is responding is, 'Why do we attend to the things to which we attend?' While making it clear that he does not provide a definitive answer to this question, Innis argues that the essays in the book 'emphasize the importance of communication in determining "things to which we attend" and suggest also that changes in communication will follow changes in "the things to which we attend"' (1951: xvii). This gives some indication that Innis may not be an easy read!

This reading, *The Bias of Communication* (*The Bias*), is often referred to in standard textbooks on media and communication, and almost always when the discussion turns towards the matter of technological developments and consideration of time–space issues. While Innis, like most theorists, has his critics, he is also praised in equal part. For instance, Blondheim (2003) argues that *The Bias* is an important, even canonic, text for four reasons.

First, Innis's work emerges from a historical analysis which has two dimensions: one deals with the 'study of communication in history' and the other addresses 'the history of communication' (Blondheim 2003: 165). Secondly, Innis focused on the actual medium or technological artefact in order to examine 'processes of communication and their social significance' (Blondheim 2003: 165). As we noted above, it was as a result of this approach that Innis (and McLuhan) attracted the label 'technological determinist'. Thirdly, Innis's training as an economist enabled him to adapt the theory of monopoly to the study of communication (Innis 1951: xvi). This resulted in Innis creating the term 'monopoly of knowledge', which when applied to communications included the monopoly of knowledge, artefacts and skills, and remains a key concern in the current era:

> When certain media or knowledge products dominate society's communication environment, the peculiar dynamics of oligopoly make for amplification and perpetuating the hold of those media or bodies of knowledge, block the emergence of alternatives, and ultimately enhance the effects of the monopolistic media and skills on society and on its political, social and cultural profile.
>
> (*Blondheim 2003: 166*)

Fourthly, and finally, Innis's *The Bias* is lauded because it introduces the idea of a 'time–space divide', a mechanism that is used both to plot and analyse the emergence of communication media throughout history, and also to illustrate how these media have impacted on communication systems, societies and their respective cultures (Blondheim 2003: 166).

Innis's notion of a time–space divide arose as a result of his earlier work on the staples that were so essential to the Canadian economy, evidenced particularly in *The Fur Trade in Canada: An introduction to Canadian economic history* (Carey, 1989). Innis was intent on understanding what in particular had enabled the flows of European migrants to the 'new World' of North America, and concluded that while 'inventions in shipbuilding, navigation and warfare' were crucial, developments in communications such as 'high speed sailing craft, reliable instruments and, most important, printing' were also central to migration (Carey 1989: 158). It was this realisation that prompted Innis to chart the history of earlier oral and literate cultures and, in doing so, conjure terms such as 'space-binding' and 'time-binding' cultures, and 'space-biased' and 'time-biased' media.

Carey explains that differences between space-binding and time-binding cultures can be ascertained by examining three areas: structures of interests (the things that were thought about), the symbols that were used (the things that they thought with) and how a particular community was envisaged. For example, the interests of space-binding cultures centred primarily on space, meaning 'land as real estate, voyage, discovery, movement, expansion, empire, control' (1989: 160). Symbols, in this instance, included such things as the arts of navigation, civil engineering, the price system and bureaucracies. Community was envisaged not as a particular place, but 'communities in space', being 'mobile, connected over vast distances by appropriate symbols, forms, and interests' (p. 160).

Time-binding cultures, on the other hand, were preoccupied with time, which meant history, continuity and permanence; their symbols were fiduciary, turning on trust and relying on the oral, mythopoetic, religious and ritualistic, while their sense of community was 'rooted in place', demonstrating 'intimate ties and a shared historical culture' (Carey 1989: 166).

Preferring to use 'biased' rather than 'binding', Stamps (1995: 74–6) explains why the media of communication in time-biased cultures would never become mass media. This was because the preferred media of communication in such cultures, for example chiselling hieroglyphics on stone, was heavy, both in terms of weight but also in terms of culture, because of the time, skills and knowledge invested in creating each form of communication. In contrast, the preferred media of communication in space-biased cultures, for example the use of writing on papyrus, parchment or paper, was much easier to adapt as a form of mass media.

Hence, Innis's title, *The Bias*, means, in effect, that the use of different combinations of media and materials would enable quite different degrees of control over space and time (Scannell 2007: 127). Time-binding media would be more capable of delivering knowledge over periods of time and into the future and reinforcing collective memory, whereas space-binding media would be much more effective in enabling knowledge transfer across geographical space (Blondheim 2003: 166). The development and maintenance of empires is explained by Innis as resulting from the development and gradual improvements in space-biased media.

Given the nature of Innis's historical analysis and the epochs to which he paid special attention, it is not surprising that his elucidation of a time–space divide in relation to communication is recognised as significant by other scholars. Scannell, for example, asserts that Innis's 'most basic historical distinction in terms of communication is between oral and literate cultures' (2007: 127). Blondheim concludes similarly, '[t]he divergence of orality and literacy serves as the fundamental model, as well as the historical origin, of the time-media/space-media polarity' (2003: 166).

While you may already be of the view that Innis's ideas require close attention and some considered reflection in order to understand them, there is yet another hurdle to be overcome once you begin the reading. This is due to what has been described as Innis's 'textual problems' (Blondheim 2003: 160). There is a widely held view that Innis's works are not reader 'friendly', being variously described as 'elliptical', 'knotted', 'cryptic', 'compressed', 'opaque', and 'maddeningly obscure' (cited in Stamps 1995: 91).

Also, readers of *The Bias* remark on lapses, inconsistencies and contradictions. This includes McLuhan (1951a: x, xi, xii) in his introduction to the book. Blondheim is also critical of Innis's style, noting that *The Bias* seems to consist of a 'recurring parade of historical facts and experiences' which are ordered chronologically (2003: 159). Stamps likens some of Innis's work to 'patchwork' (1995: 91), in the sense that there are sometimes sudden shifts in direction or emphasis, and because quotations inserted by Innis are not always adequately linked to the preceding or following text.

While Innis's leap from the study of Canadian economic history to the history of media and communication might not seem an obvious transition, McLuhan believed it to be completely logical: 'Media are major resources like economic staples. In fact, without railways, the staples of wheat and lumber can scarcely be said to exist. Without the press and the magazine, wood pulp could not exist as a staple either' (1951a: xv). However, Innis's change of focus did transform his research methods, as he began to rely almost exclusively on secondary sources for the first time (Scannell, 2007: 126; Stamps, 1995: 67). As Blondheim points out, this resulted in a double 'filtering' (2003: 159) of material, first by the secondary sources that Innis consulted, and then through his own interpretation of that material.

It is, however, accepted that Innis's sources were numerous and extremely diverse. For example, his historical references included volumes on western thought (including knowledge, politics, language, religion and mythology), material histories of media (including stone to paper and histories of the alphabet) and cultural histories (including material on music, literature, architecture and art) (Stamps 1995: 68). Carey (1989: 189) describes Innis as truly interdisciplinary, operating simultaneously as a geographer, historian, economist and political scientist.

While Innis is likely to be difficult to read, the work required by the reader is judged to be effort well spent. Stamps notes how McLuhan likened the task facing the reader as something akin to a 'do-it-yourself kit', while her preferred analogy is the 'archaeological dig' (1995: 96), because unless the reader does some digging the potential rewards will remain hidden. Owing to the substantial length of the selected reading, what appears here is a significantly abridged version. You are, though, encouraged to seek out the full text and to read it all.

1

H.A. Innis

The Bias of communication[1]

The appearance of a wide range of cultural phenomena at different periods in the history of Western civilization has been described by Professor A.L. Kroeber in *Configurations of Cultural Growth* (Berkeley, 1944). He makes suggestive comments at various points to explain the relative strength or weakness of cultural elements but refrains from extended discussion. I do not propose to do more than add a footnote to these comments and in this to discuss the possible significance of communication to the rise and decline of cultural traits. A medium of communication has an important influence on the dissemination of knowledge over space and over time and it becomes necessary to study its characteristics in order to appraise its influence in its cultural setting. According to its characteristics it may be better suited to the dissemination of knowledge over time than over space, particularly if the medium is heavy and durable and not suited to transportation, or to the dissemination of knowledge over space than over time, particularly if the medium is light and easily transported. The relative emphasis on time or space will imply a bias of significance to the culture in which it is imbedded.

Immediately we venture on this inquiry we are compelled to recognize the bias of the period in which we work. An interest in the bias of other civilizations may in itself suggest a bias of our own. Our knowledge of other civilizations depends in large part on the character of the media used by each civilization in so far as it is capable of being preserved or of being made accessible by discovery as in the case of the results of archaeological expeditions.[2] Writing on clay and on stone has been preserved more effectively than that on papyrus. Since durable commodities emphasize time and continuity, studies of civilization such as Toynbee's tend to have a bias toward religion and to show a neglect of problems of space, notably administration and law. The bias of modern civilization incidental to the newspaper and the radio will presume a perspective in consideration of civilizations dominated by other media. We can do little more than urge that we must be continually alert to the implications of this bias and perhaps hope that consideration of the implications of other media to various civilizations may enable us to see more clearly the bias of our own. In any case we may become a little more humble as to the characteristics of our civilization. We can perhaps assume that the use of a medium of communication over a long period will to some extent determine the character of knowledge to be communicated and suggest that its pervasive influence will eventually create a civilization in which life and flexibility will become exceedingly difficult to maintain and that the advantages of a new medium will become such as to lead to the emergence of a new civilization.

1. A paper presented at the University of Michigan on April 18, 1949.
2. See the complaint that archaeologists have been unduly concerned with objects of art. S. Clarke and R. Engelbach, *Ancient Egyptian Masonry, the Building Craft* (London, 1930), p. vi.

NOTES

1 Content

Over the course of the final three sentences of the introductory paragraph, Innis sets out his thesis. In beginning with the statement, 'A medium of communication has an important influence on . . .', it is evident that Innis's first priority is with the characteristics of a medium rather than with matters of content or audience. Similarly, in the second paragraph, Innis suggests that a particular medium of communication 'will to some extent determine the character of knowledge to be communicated' and, over time, could lead to the emergence of 'new' media on the margins of that civilisation, resulting in its eventual demise.

In making statements such as these, Innis attracts the label of technological determinist. However, and bearing in mind the definition of technological determinism that we provided above, you might want to consider whether this label is correctly applied as you progress through the reading.

Innis uses the second paragraph to provide a brief explanation on what he means by 'bias', and makes it clear that his historical analysis is going to address very early forms of media and communication, such as writing on clay and on papyrus. However, in referring to 'new' media such as radio and bearing in mind that the reading was published in 1951, it quickly becomes apparent that television will not be considered.

Context

The first point to make about context is that Innis immediately cites the author (Kroeber, 1944) who has inspired this reading. Like Kroeber, Innis takes as his unit of analysis 'civilizations' (Blondheim 2003: 173). Similarly, Innis cites the work of Arnold Toynbee, renowned for his multi-volume *A Study of History* (1934–61), which dealt with the emergence and decline of civilisations and religion. Innis's reading of such material led him to the view that authors such as Toynbee had not adequately taken account of the role of communication, an omission he set out to correct.

Structure

Note how Innis uses the first paragraph to very obviously introduce the reading, setting out what he is intending to do and why the matters he is about to discuss are worthy of consideration. To what extent is this a good example of how to introduce a piece of work?

Writing Style

You will note after these first two paragraphs where Innis writes in the first person, singular and plural, that he reverts to a third-person address in the remainder of the reading. In suggesting that he is about to add a 'footnote' to the work of A.L. Kroeber, Innis rather understates both the complexity of his ideas and the length of this contribution which, in total, runs to twenty-seven pages.

Note also how he weaves a key word from the title of the reading within the final sentence of this introductory paragraph. As you will see, Innis's preferred method for listing sources and noting other relevant material is by way of footnotes.

READING

2

Egyptian civilization appears to have been powerfully influenced by the character of the Nile. Utilization of its periodic floods depended on the unified control of an absolute authority. It has been claimed that the discovery of the sidereal year as early as 4241 B.C. made it possible to work out a calendar avoiding the difficulties of a year dependent on the moon. The discovery and the adoption of a calendar with the certainty of dates for religious festivals facilitated the establishment of an absolute monarchy and the imposition of the authority of Osiris and Ra, the Nile and the Sun, on upper Egypt. Success of the monarchy in acquiring control over Egypt in terms of space necessitated a concern with problems of continuity or time. The idea of immortality strengthened the position of the monarch. Mummification and construction of the pyramids as devices for emphasizing control over time were accompanied by the development of the art of pictorial representation as part of the funerary ritual and by the emergence of writing. The spoken word, by which the orders of the monarch were given, in itself possessed creative efficiency which in turn was perpetuated in the written word in the tomb. Pictorial decorations became hieroglyphic script. Writing gradually developed toward phoneticism and by the time of Menes (about 3315 B.C.) many picture signs had a purely phonetic value and were regularly spelled out. Autocratic monarchy developed by divine right culminated in the pyramids of about 2850 B.C. Private property disappeared and all arable land became the king's domain.

The monopoly of knowledge centring around stone and hieroglyphics was exposed to competition from papyrus as a new and more efficient medium. Royal authority began to decline after about 2540 B.C. and its decline was possibly coincident with the discovery of the solar year by the priestly class as a device to overcome the deficiencies of the sidereal year in which a day was gained each year.

The increasing use of papyrus and the brush was accompanied by the development of the hieratic character and the emergence of the profession of scribes. Writing and thought were secularized. Administration was extended following the spread of writing and reading. The social revolution involved in a shift from the use of stone to the use of papyrus and the increased importance of the priestly class imposed enormous strains on Egyptian civilization and left it exposed to the inroads of invaders equipped with effective weapons of attack. The Hyksos or Shepherd Kings captured and held Egypt from 1660 to 1580 B.C. The strength of Egyptian cultural elements facilitated reorganization, and mobilization of resources was directed to expulsion of the invaders. The introduction of the horse and light four-spoked chariots enabled Egyptian rulers not only to expel the Hyksos but also to conquer vast new territories and to build an empire.

An extension of political organization to include peoples of different races and religions reflecting a temporary solution of problems of space in government compelled the king to attempt a solution of problems of continuity. Worship of the solar disc was designed to provide an imperial religion which would overrule distinctions between Egyptians and foreigners. Failure to overcome the hostility of the entrenched priestly class in Egypt was followed by imperial decline and eventually by the subjugation of Egypt by the Assyrians and the Persians. A monopoly of knowledge supported by a difficult script resisted demands for

↓

NOTES

2 ## Writing Style

These paragraphs are representative of the remainder of the reading, in that they are very detailed, generally accessible – if read closely and patiently – but do rely to some extent on the reader having some understanding of the civilisations that are discussed. Having a dictionary or encyclopaedia to hand will be helpful.

The interdisciplinary approach undertaken by Innis is also perfectly evident, with obvious links to geography, politics, architecture, religion and mythology. Although, for the most part, Innis does not cite any of the sources from where he has gained access to this material, we know from above that they are almost all secondary sources.

Content

What Innis is trying to do here is demonstrate how different types of media impacted on the nature of communication and the communicative process which, over time, changed the nature of the civilisation. This section witnesses the introduction of one of Innis's key concepts – 'monopoly of knowledge'.

Innis points out how mummification, the building of pyramids, pictorial decorations, hieroglyphic scripts and the emergence of writing, all helped to emphasise continuity and control over time within this civilisation. However, eventually the dominant role of stone and hieroglyphics brought about what Innis refers to as a *monopoly of knowledge*, which was challenged by the introduction of a new and more efficient medium, that of papyrus.

Innis goes on to illustrate how the introduction of this new medium impacted on the Egyptian civilisation, bringing about a 'social revolution'. In summary, these changes resulted in, first, a change in the internal power structure of the civilisation; secondly, the occupation by an invading force and, thirdly, once repelled, the conquering of other lands and an attempt to find ways of managing and communicating across a new and expansive empire. Ultimate failure to do so, according to Innis, was because 'a monopoly of knowledge supported by a difficult script resisted demands for change', leading eventually to the end of the Egyptian empire.

Context

What you see here in terms of the way that Innis deals with the Egyptians is an approach that he undertakes in relation to all the civilisations and epochs that are addressed in this reading. In other words, references to media and communication occur in the context of an account that always incorporates other dimensions, be they economic, cultural, political or social.

Structure

Innis doesn't work by providing a brief summary of key points or ideas and then developing or explaining them. Rather, the narrative style might be likened to a story which builds slowly towards a conclusion, forcing the reader to wait for the salient points on media and communication technologies.

READING

2

(continued)

change and brought the Egyptian Empire to an end. With abundant supplies of papyrus and the conservative influence of religion on writing, pictographic writing was maintained and the emergence of consonantal signs was largely a result of the introduction of foreign names and words. The spoken word tended to drift away from the written word in spite of the efforts of Ikhnaton to bring them into closer accord.

3

With the advantage of new instruments of war such as the long bow and the long pike and of an improved alphabet, the Persians rapidly built up an empire to take the place of the empire of the Assyrians. As a result of support from the priests Cyrus became king of Babylon in 536 B.C. Cambyses added Egypt to the Empire in 525 B.C. The problems of the Assyrians in dominating two divergent religious centres were inherited by the Persians. They were solved in part by a policy of toleration in which subject peoples were allowed to keep their gods and their religions. The Jews were released from captivity in Babylonia in 539 B.C. and Judah became the centre of an effective religious organization. The Persians developed an elaborate administration based on a system of roads and the use of horses to maintain communication by post with the capital. Satrapies were created and three officials, a satrap, a military governor, and a secretary of state, each acting independently of the other and directly responsible to the capital, were appointed. But centralization of power in the hands of the king quickly brought to the fore the problem of administrative capacity and of continuity or the problem of time. Difficulties increased with the tenacious religious centres of Babylonia, Egypt, and Jerusalem and with peoples such as the Greeks located on the fringe of the Empire. The introduction of new tactics of warfare enabled Alexander to overthrow the Empire in the decisive battles of 333 B.C. and 331 B.C. Oriental empires succeeded in organizing vast areas and in solving territorial problems but failed to find a solution to problems of continuity and of time. The empires of Assyria and Persia emphasized control over space but were unable to solve the problems of time in the face of the monopolies of religion in Babylonia and Egypt.

NOTES

2

(continued)

As you may have already noted and as some of his critics observe, Innis does have a tendency to build his narrative through a lengthy parade of facts and experiences.

3 Content

As previously, Innis's analysis tends to prioritise the role of transport, weaponry and communication in the development of civilisations and empires. Here, he considers the rise and fall of the Persian empire, noting how they experienced problems similar to those of the previous Assyrians. The Persians, like the Assyrians, were able to master and manage large spaces – the former, through communication that relied on an improved alphabet and a postal service enabled by an efficient system of roads and the use of horses.

However, both empires were unable to deal effectively with problems about time and continuity, because of pre-existing religious monopolies of knowledge which were centred in parts of the conquered territory. As Scannell reminds us, while space-biased media 'underpin political power, time-biased media help entrench religious power' (2007: 128).

The other point to note here, which is a constant theme throughout *The Bias*, is where threats to the survival of empires or civilisations emerge. Again, as in the case of the Egyptians, Innis locates these threats on the fringes or margins, socially or geographically, of the existing civilisation (see, for example, Stamps 1995: 79).

In this instance it is the 'tenacious religious centres' within the Persian empire and the Greeks on the fringe that pose the threats. The implication being that a civilisation is increasingly at risk if it fails to achieve equilibrium between time-biased media and space-biased media.

Writing Style

Again, it is not clear from which sources Innis is drawing this material. In not listing these sources Innis deprives the reader of the opportunity to access them out of interest, or to check his interpretation of that material.

Context

Note how Innis moves between discussions about civilisations and empires. As we noted above, Innis's other most well-known book on communication is *Empire and Communications* which was first published in 1950, shortly before *The Bias*. Interestingly, *Empire and Communications* is not listed as a source; why might this be?

READING

4

The Phoenician Semitic consonantal alphabet was taken over by the Greeks on the north shore of the Mediterranean. Unlike the peoples of Aryan speech in Asia Minor the Greeks escaped the full effect of contact with the civilizations of Egypt and Babylonia. The necessity of crossing water enabled the Greeks to select cultural traits of significance to themselves and to reject others. Without a script they had built up a strong oral tradition centring about the courts of conquering people from the north. The Homeric poems were the work of generations of reciters and minstrels and reflected the demands of generations of audiences to whom they were recited. This powerful oral tradition bent the consonantal alphabet to its demands and used five of the twenty-four letters as vowels. As vowels were equal in value to consonants they were used in each written word. The written language was made into an instrument responsive to the demands of the oral tradition. Introduction of the alphabet meant a concern with sound rather than with sight or with the ear rather than the eye. Empires had been built up on communication based on sight in contrast with Greek political organization which emphasized oral discussion. Greece escaped the problem of worship of the written word which had embarrassed oriental empires. The delay in the introduction of writing until possibly as late as the beginning of the seventh century, the difficulties of securing large and regular supplies of papyrus from Egypt, and the limitations of stone as a medium combined to protect the oral tradition. No energy was lost in learning a second language and monopolies of knowledge could not be built around a complex script.

5

The effectiveness of the oral tradition in the development of the state became evident in the success with which the Greeks checked the expansion of the Persian Empire and in the cultural flowering of Athens in the fifth century. A powerful stimulus was given to philosophical speculation by the arrival of Ionian refugees from Miletus. The Dionysiac ritual and the choral lyric as perfected by Pindar provided the background for the development of the drama[3] under Aeschylus, Sophocles, and Euripides. In the second half of the fifth century writing began to make its encroachments on the oral tradition. Nietzsche has pointed to the significance of music, in which the joy of annihilation of the individual was understood, to tragedy. Disappearance of the spirit of music was followed by the decline of tragedy.[4] An increase in laws reflected an interest in prose. Literature in prose increased rapidly after the beginning of the Peloponnesian War. Plays were widely read in the time of Euripides. By the end of the fifth century the *boustrophedon* style had been abandoned and changed to writing from left to right. The Ionic alphabet was adopted in Athens with the codification and republication of the laws in 403–2 B.C.[5]

3. J.E. Harrison, *Prolegomena to the Study of Greek Religion* (Cambridge, 1908), p. 568.
4. F. Nietzsche, *The Birth of Tragedy from the Spirit of Music* (Edinburgh, 1923), pp. 120–7.
5. W.S. Ferguson, *The Treasures of Athena* (Cambridge, Mass., 1923), p. 178.

4   Content

Innis's analysis suggests that Greece, by way of its geographical location and its careful selection and absorption of relevant and useful cultural traits of others, was able to maintain a 'strong oral tradition'. This oral tradition was transmitted by way of 'generations of reciters and minstrels' and was for an extended period of time the dominant medium of communication, resisting subservience to a written language.

In this respect, Innis suggests that Greece differed sharply from earlier civilisations. This was because its dominant means of communication had been based on sound, emphasising oral discussion, and not on sight, through a written language. The longevity of this oral culture was also assisted as a result of papyrus not being readily available and stone not being the most suitable medium to safeguard an oral tradition. Given Innis's earlier references to monopolies of knowledge, what do you understand by the final sentence in this paragraph?

Writing Style

You may already be thinking about whether it would be useful to have a very early map of the world handy! While it is not essential to do so, some level of awareness about the size and proximity of the locales to which Innis refers would provide a greater understanding of the challenges facing those charged with developing, implementing and maintaining systems of effective communication across such spaces.

5   Content

The main thrust of this section of the reading is the decline of the oral tradition in Greece, its undermining occurring as the culture becomes increasingly permeated by writing. The apparently divisive nature of writing is seen as the catalyst for internal unrest, which ends in war and the defeat of Athens.

Although not included in this abridged version, a subsequent quotation by Nietzsche is used to convey Innis's views about written culture: 'Everyone being allowed to read ruineth in the long run not only writing but also thinking' (cited in Innis 1951: 44). Innis is acknowledged as an avid fan of oral culture, believing it to be powerful and vital.

An additional observation about the specific characteristics of the situation pertaining to Greece is also helpful in respect of Innis's time–space divide. Scannell (2007: 127–8) offers two points. First, the 'simplicity and flexibility' of the Greek alphabet enabled both the preservation and dissemination of knowledge, and also mitigated against the emergence of monopolies of knowledge controlled by certain classes or groups in that society.

READING

5

(continued)

An increase in writing in Athens created divergences in the Greek community and accentuated differences particularly with Sparta. The Athenian Empire proved unable to meet the strains imposed by diverging cultures. Athenian courts were unable to escape charges of favouritism to democratic states. Interstate co-operation imposed demands which could not be met. The end came with the outbreak of war and the defeat of Athens.

6

The bureaucratic development of the Roman Empire and success in solving problems of administration over vast areas were dependent on supplies of papyrus. The bias of this medium became apparent in the monopoly of bureaucracy and its inability to find a satisfactory solution to the problems of the third dimension of empires, namely time. A new medium emerged to meet the limitations of papyrus. The handicaps of the fragile papyrus roll were offset by the durable parchment codex. With the latter the Christians were able to make effective use of the large Hebrew scriptures and to build up a corpus of Christian writings. The contributions of Alexandrian scholars in translating the Hebrew scriptures into Greek and the development of a Christian centre of learning at Caesarea after 231 A.D. checked the influence of a Babylonian priesthood, which had been encouraged by the Seleucids to check the influence of Persian religion, and which had been reconciled with Persian religion after the fall of Babylon in 125 A.D. Support of these religions for the Sassanid dynasty after 228 A.D. hindered the spread of the Roman Empire and compelled Constantine to select a new capital in Constantinople in 330 whence he could command the interest of a Christian population. The problem of the Roman Empire in relation to time was solved by the support of religion in the Christian church. The cumulative bias of papyrus in relation to bureaucratic administration was offset by an appeal to parchment as a medium for a powerful religious organization. Recognition of Christianity was followed by the drastic suppression of competing pagan cults.

NOTES

5

(continued)

Secondly, while the power and persistence of oral culture was preserved by open debate and philosophical discussion in the Athenian agora, it was only possible through the 'small-scale political geography' of a city-state such as Athens. Scannell (2007: 128) makes the contrast with Rome, which was originally a city-state before the expansion of an empire dictated the need for a sophisticated infrastructure that included the use of papyrus, parchment and writing to maintain its reach and power.

Writing Style

Even in this abridged version of *The Bias* you may have already seen evidence of repetition by Innis. We should, of course, remember that he was restricted to writing by hand and/or using a typewriter. Without a word processor he was also deprived of features that include 'cut and paste' and 'find and replace'.

Here again Innis presumes a substantial degree of knowledge on the part of the reader. While some sources are listed in the footnotes, there are instances here where he refers to specific events, ideas and styles of performance that are unlikely to be known to most readers.

6

Content

The main point here relates to the bias, over time or space, of different media. As established above, writing on papyrus was the media of communication used by the Romans to develop and maintain their empire. As a space-biased, or space-binding, medium, papyrus served the purpose of communicating knowledge across the geographical space of the empire. However, its fragility as a material meant that it was not efficient in dealing with time and continuity, in the sense understood by Innis: that is, the capacity of a medium to aid collective memory by communicating knowledge from the past to the present, and from the present into the future.

In this instance parchment emerges as a new and more durable medium and, according to Innis, helps solve resistance within certain parts of the empire. In essence, this occurs because the Romans are able to garner support from the Christian Church which, with the availability of a new medium, can now record existing scriptures and build up a collection of writing. At another point in this reading, but not included in this abridged version, Innis argues that '[p]archment became the medium through which a monopoly of knowledge was built up by religion' (1951: 49).

Writing Style

There are two points that we as writers might want to bear in mind. First, given that this material is very detailed, the use of very lengthy sentences such as the one in the middle of this paragraph (beginning 'The contributions of . . .') are better avoided.

Questions also arise about whether there would have been other ways of organising and presenting this material. Is all the detail required? Could the huge number of historical facts have been dealt with differently while still ensuring the integrity of the work? Would some of this material have been more appropriately placed in an appendix?

READING

7

This monopoly of knowledge invited the competition of a new medium, namely paper from China. Discovery of the technique of making paper from textiles provided a medium with which the Chinese, by adaptation of the brush for painting to writing, were able to work out an elaborate system of pictographs. A system of four to five thousand characters was used for ordinary needs "enabling those who speak mutually unintelligible idioms to converse together, using the pencil instead of the tongue."[6] Its effectiveness for this purpose meant the abandonment of an attempt to develop an alphabet system.

An elaborate development of writing supported the position of the scholarly class in administration of the empire. In turn a wide gap between a limited governing class and the mass of the people led to the spread of Buddhism from India. The monopoly of knowledge of the Brahmins in India based on the oral tradition and the limitations of communication had led to the spread of Buddhism with its emphasis on writing and its appeal to the lower classes. After Alexander, Buddhism had been encouraged but decline of Macedonian power brought a revival of the power of the Brahmins and migration of Buddhism to China. Access to supplies of paper in China enabled Buddhists to develop block printing on a large scale. Confucianism gained by the influence of the state and the reproduction of the classics. A script which provided a basis for administration in China and emphasized the organization of an empire in terms of space proved inadequate to meet the demands of time and China was exposed to dynastic problems and to the domination of the Mongols from 1280 to 1368.

8

The spread of Mohammedanism to the east was followed by introduction to the technique of paper production. After establishment of a capital at Baghdad by the Abbasids paper manufacturing expanded and became the basis for an intense interest in learning. The Nestorians excommunicated from the church had established schools in which Greek and Latin works were translated into Syriac. Closing of the schools in Athens by Justinian in 529 A.D. had been followed by the migration of scholars to Persia. From this background of learning Baghdad became a centre for translators of Greek, Syriac, and Persian works into Arabic.

Paper production spread from Baghdad to the West. After the capture of Baghdad by the Mongols in 1258, manufacturing was confined to western centres. With its development in Italy in the latter part of the thirteenth century new processes were introduced and a much better quality of paper produced. The art of paper making spread to France in the fourteenth

6. Edward Clodd, *The Story of the Alphabet* (New York, 1913), p. 182.

214

7 Content

Here, the focus moves to China where a new medium and a new writing technology are developed. Paper is the new medium, and 'an elaborate system of pictographs' is the new written technology. This new form of writing has the advantage of overcoming differences in spoken language and, thereby, provides a means of communicating and administrating across distances or space. However, as Innis goes on to illustrate, in the process of transition from an oral tradition to a literary culture there is the risk that divisions will occur and consequences will follow.

In the example being considered here, divisions emerge between the elite and the lower levels of society, which in turn leads to the flowering of Buddhism and, ultimately, the demise of the empire. In part, at least, this is because a new medium and elaborate form of communication that deals adequately with space is not as efficient in addressing the demands of time.

Essentially, the logic of Innis's argument is that by considering the characteristics of a medium of communication, in this case both parchment and papyrus, it is possible to deduce how and in what ways the introduction of such a medium impacts on, or influences, the culture in which it appears.

What does Innis mean in the opening sentence of this section when he says, 'This monopoly of knowledge invited the competition of a new medium . . .'?

Context

The potential for such divisions is a constant. As Scannell reminds, writing has always been linked with political, economic and religious power, and inevitably leads to distinctions between 'the lettered and unlettered, the educated and the uneducated', as 'reading and writing is a passport to individual self-advancement'. As ever, 'literacy gives rise to educated elites . . . that gravitate to the centres of power' (Scannell 2007: 127).

8 Content

This section opens with Innis noting the emergence of Baghdad as a centre of learning as it becomes a base for paper production. However, the art of papermaking gradually moved to western countries, such as France and Italy. Logically, with major cities being the main consumers of paper the centres of production needed to be nearby. According to Innis, this shift in the sites of production to 'commercial cities', increasingly with universities and cathedrals, and the escalating manufacture and use of paper, eventually undermined the power – and monopolies of knowledge – of the rural monasteries.

Why would there have been religious prejudice against a product of Arabic origin and how might these views have been 'broken down'? Also, note in the final paragraph how Innis refers to the 'effects of the introduction of paper'. In this instance, what does he judge to be the effects?

READING

8

(continued)

century. Since linen rags were the chief raw material and the large cities provided the chief market for paper, production was determined to an important extent by proximity to cities with access to supplies of water and power. The commercial revolution beginning about 1275 paralleled increasing production of paper. The activity of the commercial cities of Italy weakened the Byzantine Empire. Religious prejudice against a product of Arabic origin was broken down and the monopoly of knowledge held by the monasteries of rural districts was weakened by the growth of cities, cathedrals, and universities.

The effects of the introduction of paper suggested by the rise of Baghdad were evident also in the concern with learning among the Mohammedans in Sicily and Spain. Large libraries were collected in Spain and following the recapture of Moorish cities by the Spaniards their contents in philosophy, mathematics, and medicine were made available to Europe.

9

Monopolies of knowledge controlled by monasteries were followed by monopolies of knowledge controlled by copyist guilds in the large cities. The high price for large books led to attempts to develop a system of reproduction by machine and to the invention of printing in Germany which was on the margin of the area dominated by copyists. The centralized control of France was less adapted to evasion than the numerous political divisions of Germany. The coarse brown parchment of Germany led to an interest in the use of paper. The beauty of Gothic script in manuscript[7] and its adaptability to printing were other factors emphasizing an interest in the invention with its numerous problems of ink, production of uniform type on a large scale, and a press capable of quick operation. Abundance of paper in Italy and political division similar to that of Germany led to the migration of printers to Italian cities and to the development of Roman and italic types. Printing in Paris was delayed until 1469 and in England until even later.

Manuscripts which had accumulated over centuries were reproduced and by the end of the fifteenth century printers became concerned with the possibilities of new markets. Commercialism of the publisher began to displace the craft of the printer. The vernacular offered new authors and new readers. The small book and the pamphlet began to replace the large folios. In England, Caxton avoided the competition of Latin books produced on the Continent and attempted to widen his own market. He wrote in the Prologue to the *Eneydos*: "And that comyn englysshe that is spoken in one shyre varyeth from another. . . . I haue reduced and translated this sayd booke in to our englysshe, not ouer rude ne curyous, but in suche termes as shall be vnderstanden. . . ."[8]

7. A.W. Pollard, *Early Illustrated Books* (New York, 1927), pp. 7–8.
8. Cited G.M. Trevelyan, *English Social History* (New York, 1942), p. 82.

Writing Style

(continued)

Having grumbled above about the endless detail, here is an instance where it would have been helpful to have more. For example, we could have been told which cities in Italy were regarded as the 'commercial cities', and which cities in France were major production centres for paper.

Context

Apart from the value of knowing something about the history of Baghdad as a centre for paper production and knowledge production, mention here of this part of the world is a reminder of how current references to this city rarely make connections with its historical past.

Content

If there is a pattern in Innis's analysis, it is the emergence and later decline of monopolies of knowledge that was due, at least in part, to the introduction of newly emerging media technologies and forms of communication.

In this instance, religious monopolies of knowledge controlled by monasteries are followed by copyist guilds, a medieval association of craftsmen. Driven by commercial imperatives, they seek out a new form of technology – the printing press – which is the catalyst for a substantial growth in printed matter.

As Innis explains, for various reasons, it was Germany rather than France that joined Italy in this venture, with German printers flooding there for work.

Yet again, this account by Innis stresses the role of a medium of communication in the process of change, and how the introduction of such technologies impact on the wider culture.

For example, in this second paragraph, Innis sets out the consequences that flow from the development of the printing press and the printing techniques that use more elaborate typefaces, such as Gothic, Roman and italics: a commercial press emerges with implications for both publishers and printers; smaller and 'popular' books and pamphlets are published; and books are translated from one language to another if there is a market for them.

However, Innis always considers the arrival of these technological and communicative innovations in a wider and comparative context, making clear the geographic, historical, religious, economic and political factors that facilitate, or militate against, their introduction and absorption into culture.

Context

As Innis notes above, German printers moved to Italy for work during a period in which printing boomed. Similarly, Briggs and Burke attribute the emergence of printing presses in over 250 locations in Europe by the year 1500 to a 'diaspora of German printers' (2002: 15).

READING

10

In England the absolutism of the Tudors involved suppression of printing but encouragement of the Renaissance and of the Reformation. Abolition of the monasteries and disappearance of clerical celibacy were followed by sweeping educational reforms. The printing press became "a battering-ram to bring abbeys and castles crashing to the ground."[9] Freedom from the Salic law made it possible for women to ascend the throne and to encourage the literature of the court. Restrictions on printing facilitated an interest in the drama and the flowering of the oral tradition in the plays of Shakespeare.

Suppression of printing limited the attention to language which characterized France. Dictionaries were gradually developed but the English language was not adequate to the precision of the law codes of the Continent. Printing and improved communication strengthened a representative system in parliament. Suppression was met by newsletters and the rise of coffee-houses. The absolute power of parliament emerged to offset the absolute power of monarchy and annihilated the claims of common law which persisted in the colonies. It became the basis of public credit. The revolution of 1689 was followed by establishment of the Bank of England in 1694. Again, the revolution brought an end to the Licensing Act in 1694. Immediately large numbers of papers were printed and the first daily appeared in 1701. In the Augustan age, Addison and Steele reconciled "wit and virtue, after a long and disastrous separation, during which wit had been led astray by profligacy and virtue by fanaticism." Limitations of the hand press led to a political war of pamphlets and to the imposition of a stamp tax in 1712. The excessive burden of a tax on a commodity selling at a very low price compelled printers to undertake compendious works such as weeklies and monthlies and Ephraim Chambers's *Universal Dictionary of Arts and Sciences* which appeared in 1728. Restrictions on political writing hastened the development of other types of literature such as the novel and children's books and the establishment of circulating libraries.

11

An emphasis on literature in England in the first half of the nineteenth century incidental to the monopoly of the newspaper protected by taxes on knowledge and absence of copyright legislation in the United States compelled American writers to rely on journalism.[10] Publishers in New York such as Harper after the introduction of the steamship line drew on the vast stores of English literature and made them available to the enormous reading public of the United States.[11] Publishers and paper dealers such as Cyrus W. Field and Company opposed proposals for international copyright in 1852.[12] The emphasis on news which consequently

9. Trevelyan, *English Social History*, p. 58.
10. E.L. Bradsher, *Mathew Carey, Editor, Author and Publisher: A Study in American Literary Development* (New York, 1912), p. 79; and L.F. Tooker, *The Joys and Tribulations of an Editor* (New York, 1924), pp. 3–10.
11. J.H. Harper, *The House of Harper* (New York, 1912), p. 89.
12. *Ibid.*, p. 108.

10 Content

Here Innis reminds about the need to recognise the important interrelationship between economics and communication. First, the imposition of taxes on newspapers, known as 'taxes on knowledge' (see Chapter 4 on liberal press theory), led to the introduction of other forms of publication. Secondly, the growth of these publications, in particular periodicals and cheap editions of novels, resulted in the advent of literary agents. In combination, these developments eventually undermined the monopoly of the circulating libraries.

Innis also highlights how contextual constraints on communication lead to unexpected and sometimes paradoxical outcomes. For example, he illustrates how the suppression of printing led to a revival of the oral tradition, not only through the staging of plays, but also in the coffee houses, where debate emerged as a way of keeping power in check (see Chapter 13 on the public sphere). This indicates that conditions of suppression, or censorship, can generate alternative forms of communication.

Writing Style

Turning his attention to England, Innis's interdisciplinary approach is again apparent, as are the oftnoted characteristics of his style of writing. As Carey describes it, and it is particularly evident in this section of the reading: 'Facts of history are paraded chronologically, one by one, and Innis, the philosopher in the grandstand, contributes comments on them as they relate to his philosophical focus: the dynamics of communication and culture' (1996: 175). The quotation included in this section of the reading is an example of Innis's idiosyncratic style.

Context

Yet again, Innis assumes much on the part of his readers. For example, a number of the events (revolution), periods (Augustan age) and laws (Salic) are unlikely to be known about or fully understood by some readers. While this might be overcome by having various dictionaries to hand, it can make for a slow read.

11 Content

In this section, Innis demonstrates how developments in technologies, including transport, both facilitated and undermined the monopolies enjoyed by political centres, political power and particular forms of media in England and America.

For example, London's monopoly was strengthened by being a central railway hub, but the development of the telegraph provided the scope for competition from other provincial centres. The interrelationship between transport and communication is also emphasised in the example of a new steamship service being introduced between the two continents, which resulted in English literature being exported and disseminated throughout the United States.

Innis also suggests a relationship between American political culture, the monopoly of knowledge enjoyed by the press, and the development of new technological innovations in printing. Controversially, Innis believed that the First Amendment of the American Constitution 'did not so

READING

11

(continued)

characterized American journalism protected by the Bill of Rights supported the development of technological inventions in the fast press, the stereotype, the linotype, and the substitution of wood for rags. As in England the telegraph destroyed the monopoly of political centres and contributed, in destroying political power, to the outbreak of the Civil War. Technological development had its effects in the new journalism in England and on the Continent. The varying effects of technological change spreading from the United States destroyed the unity of Europe and contributed to the outbreak of the First World War.

12

The monopoly of knowledge centring around the printing press brought to an end the obsession with space and the neglect of problems of continuity and time. The newspaper with a monopoly over time was limited in its power over space because of its regional character. Its monopoly was characterized by instability and crises. The radio introduced a new phase in the history of Western civilization by emphasizing centralization and the necessity of a concern with continuity. The bias of communication in paper and the printing industry was destined to be offset by the bias of the radio. Democracy which in the words of Guizot sacrificed the past and the future to the present was destined to be offset by planning and bureaucracy.

NOTES

(continued)

much grant freedom of speech and press as gave constitutional protection to technology and in this sense restricted rather than expanded freedom' (Carey 1989: 163).

Extending his analysis of Innis's views on this matter, Carey argues that the free press clause strengthened the newspaper's monopoly of knowledge, resulting in this medium 'spreading values of commercialism and industrialism and furthering the spatial bias of print' (1989: 163). What does Carey mean here? What is the basis of his argument?

Writing Style

In an introduction to the book in which this reading appears, Marshall McLuhan (1951a: ix) reflects on Innis's style of writing, remarking that '[e]ach sentence is a compressed monograph'.

While this may be seen as an exaggeration, the final two sentences in this abridged section are good examples of the point made by McLuhan. The first is the assertion about the effects of technological developments on 'new journalism', and the second, the assertion that the effects of technological change were a factor in the outbreak of the First World War.

Content

In this final paragraph, Innis reflects on the longer term bias of the newspaper, arguing that its monopoly over space was undermined by an inability to cope adequately with regional, or local, characteristics, and that, ultimately, its monopoly was over time and continuity.

Radio becomes the new medium, a technology that according to Innis introduces, or brings about, a 'new phase in the history of Western civilisation'. However, Innis's description of the characteristics of this new medium, particularly its emphasis on centralisation, is disputed by McLuhan, who accuses him of 'technological blindness' (1951a: xii).

McLuhan, instead, suggests that '[e]lectric light and power, like all electronic media, are profoundly decentralising and separatist in their psychic and social consequences' (1951a: xii). This comment by McLuhan signals the scope and direction of his own research interests.

Structure

Although not identified as a conclusion or summary, this final section displays a continuation of three themes that permeate the entire reading.

First, by studying the characteristics of a medium of communication, an appraisal can be made of its influence within a particular cultural setting.

Secondly, such study will reveal whether the medium of communication is better suited to deliver knowledge over time or over space.

Thirdly, whether time-biased (or time-binding) or space-biased (or space-binding), this will be significant to the cultural setting in which it operates.

REFLECTING ON THE READING

As this abridged version of *The Bias* demonstrates, an Innis text can be hard work for the reader. According to Melody, a reasonable level of understanding will be achieved only if the reader applies her/his own 'knowledge, experience and interpretive abilities' to the 'detailed descriptive analysis and analytical insights' (1981: 7–8) provided by Innis. Like a number of the readings in this book, this one requires repeated and close scrutiny to get the maximum benefit.

In reflecting on *The Bias* and Innis's overall contribution to scholarship, there are three aspects of his work that are worthy of note. The first involves consideration of the extent to which Innis was influenced by the Chicago school (Harvey 1987). The second reflects on the claims that Innis was an innovator, in the sense not only of the focus and scope of his work on communication, but also of his methodological approach. The third attends to questions about the enduring aspects of Innis's work and relevance of *The Bias* in the current era.

While it may be the case that the Chicago school was a significant factor in influencing Innis's intellectual interests, to argue that he 'should be considered as the most eminent of the Chicago group', as McLuhan (1951a: xvi) does, is judged to be 'absurd' (Carey 1989: 143). Innis did, however, undertake his doctoral studies at the University of Chicago.

One suggestion is that Innis was inspired by work on communication undertaken by Charles Horton Cooley, a core member of the Chicago school (Blondheim 2003: 177). However, it is generally accepted that Innis rejected Chicago's perspective on communication that understood it as a positive and cohesive source for societal betterment; a view also rejected by Blondheim who describes it as a 'Whig interpretation' (2003: 181), and by Carey who suggests that it simply perpetuates a long line of argument which typifies the 'rhetoric of the technological sublime' (1989: 44).

When Innis began his research into communication systems and the longer-term implications of technological change in those systems, he adopted a holistic and inter-disciplinary approach. This approach was against the grain of much social science research at that time when disciplinary borders were sacrosanct, and specialisations within those – albeit artificial – boundaries was the norm. It was a result of such an approach, described as 'historical, empirical, interpretive and critical', that Innis created 'a historically grounded theory of communications' (Carey 1989: 145).

It was only later that holistic and systematic approaches to research became more fashionable amongst researchers (Blondheim 2003: 179; Melody 1981: 10). In this respect, Innis was ahead of this time, as he also was in marking out the particular aspect of communication research for which he made his name. In doing so, Innis has been described as 'revolutionary', because he 'isolated communication as an aspect of history and culture, and further posit[ed] its development as a key to unlocking the vicissitudes of mind, matter, and their interface' (Blondheim 2003: 173).

It may be difficult for those of us who have come to accept descriptions of our world as a 'communications society' or 'information society' (see Chapter 20) to get excited about Innis's history of communication and theoretical insights that were generated nearly sixty years ago. We do, though, need to recognise that Innis's work was taking place before communication was fully recognised as a worthy focus of study in its own right, and before most universities had established departments or faculties with a specific brief to study media, culture and communication (Blondheim 2003: 173).

Moreover, Innis was seen as a leader amongst his peers because he was one of the first to recognise the importance of the 'interrelationship and interdependence between economics and communication' (Melody 1981: 11). In particular, Innis noted three aspects: first, 'communication patterns and information flows are central to economic development'; secondly, 'communication technologies are the building blocks for most other technologies in the economic system'; thirdly, in any analysis of communication and development, it is essential to recognise that 'economic incentives and market forces have powerful influences on communication patterns and information flows' (Melody 1981: 11).

There are three areas where Innis's work and that of the Toronto school are seen as enduring, one being an early insight into media imperialism, a second being the application of the concept 'monopoly of knowledge' to communication, and the third being the insights generated about time and space.

Innis is credited with illuminating the process of 'media imperialism', although he did not name it. This insight came about as a result of his work on the economic history of Canada, where he traced the routes of trade and the routes of culture. This brought about a recognition that America imported goods such as paper and pulp from Canada – under the doctrine of 'free trade' – and then exported them back in the form of newspapers, magazines, books and, most importantly, advertising – under the doctrine of 'freedom of information' (Carey 1989: 150, 159). It was by way of exporting commodities such as these to Canada, and other parts of the world, that America was able to exert a 'cultural hegemony . . . through the global circulation of its cultural goods' (Scannell 2007: 125).

With a background in economics, Innis took the theory of economic monopoly – the control of supply by a single source – and applied it to a study focusing on communication and culture (Carey 1989: 39). Essentially, Innis's concern about communication was that a move from an oral tradition to a reliance on writing and printing produced a distinction between producer and consumer, and a tendency for 'knowledge' to be determined by certain classes and institutions, with the resulting possibility of monopolies being created (Carey 1989: 39). The reality of monopolies, or oligopolies, is certainly a contemporary issue, with the emergence of transnational media conglomerates controlling multimedia interests which include broadcasting, newspapers, magazines and, more recently, social-networking sites and search engines.

The work of Innis and McLuhan on linking communication and media to issues of time and space is acknowledged as innovative. The insights, theories and perspectives generated by both men have prompted other theorists to undertake research into contemporary issues relating to time and space. Examples include Joshua Meyrowitz's (*No Sense of Place: The impact of electronic media on social behaviour*, 1985), David Harvey's (*The Condition of Postmodernity*, 1986) and Anthony Giddens's (*The Consequences of Modernity* (1990)).

Moreover, Innis's earlier insights remain germane in an era where technological innovations have fuelled a spatial bias into contemporary communications, enabling a phenomenon that is widely referred to as 'globalisation', but also bringing closer the ambitions of those who seek to extend our current civilisation to other planets in the solar system.

In closing, it seems appropriate to return to the idea of Innis as a technological determinist. Blondheim argues that '*communication* determinist' (2003: 172) is a more apt description. This is because Innis's emphasis lay not primarily on technology as the key determinant, but rather the 'processes of communication' and associated institutions that affected 'the nature of societies' and 'the course of their history' (p. 172).

Key terms to explore

monopoly of knowledge; social revolution; political organisation; problems of space/ problems of continuity; subjugation; priestly organisation; monopolies of religion; vernacular; taxes on knowledge; telegraph; new journalism; bias of communication.

Key writers who are mentioned

A.L. Kroeber; Freidrich Nietzsche; Arnold Toynbee.

RECOMMENDED READING

Katz, E., Peters, J.D., Liebes, T. and Orloff, A. (eds) (2003) *Canonic Texts in Media Research*, Cambridge: Polity Press.

Outlines five key schools of thought; one being the Toronto school which is discussed by way of critical reflections on work by Harold Innis and by Marshall McLuhan.

Scannell, P. (2007) *Media and Communication*, London: Sage.

Includes a chapter which reflects on and contextualises the work of Harold Innis and Marshall McLuhan at the University of Toronto.

Stamps, J. (1995) *Unthinking Modernity: Innis, McLuhan, and the Frankfurt School*, Montreal: McGill-Queen's University Press.

Compares the work of two of Canada's best-known theorists, Harold Innis and Marshall McLuhan, with those of two theorists associated with the Frankfurt school, Theodor Adorno and Walter Benjamin.

CHAPTER 11

The Centre for Contemporary Cultural Studies

Hall, S. (1980c) 'Encoding/Decoding', in *Culture, Media, Language: Working papers in cultural studies, 1972–9*, Hall, S., Hobson, D., Lowe, A. and Willis, P. (eds), London: Hutchinson, pp. 128–38.

INTRODUCTION TO THE CENTRE FOR CONTEMPORARY CULTURAL STUDIES

The Centre for Contemporary Cultural Studies (usually abbreviated to 'CCCS', and sometimes known as 'the Birmingham Centre') was an influential research centre at the University of Birmingham, from 1964 to 2002. It pretty much defined and led what is now often referred to as 'British cultural studies' – which has some distinctions from cultural studies in other countries and at other institutions – and 'has exerted an influence far beyond what anyone could have expected' (Turner 2003: 65). While not strictly a Centre whose focus was media, much of its work centred on the roles media plays within society, and many of its studies have been influential in the development of analysis of the media. Indeed, the Centre often took an interdisciplinary approach, which has been a hallmark of much cultural studies. It drew on methodological approaches from sociology and anthropology; it incorporated a range of theories, such as post-structuralism and feminism; and it was interested in a variety of activities and aspects of culture, such as subcultures, popular culture and the media. For many academics – especially those from sociology – this interdisciplinarity constituted an irreverent disregard for the accepted way of doing things, as Hall himself notes (1980b: 21). Much of the work had radical aspects to it, questioning the social structures which produce contemporary culture, and exploring how that culture affects society. In doing so, it adopted a predominantly left-wing, Marxist approach, which questioned the assumptions often attached to the capitalist structures which drive most contemporary societies. Indeed, the Centre can be seen as being led by a succession of 'intellectual misfits' (Rojek 2003: 64) whose work repeatedly demonstrates unease with the accepted practices of higher education.

A key part of the Centre's work was exploring class. It is often argued that Britain is a nation with a history of class divisions (Reid 1998), even though many people now suggest that we live in a 'classless society' (Adonis and Pollard 1997); indeed, it has been argued that the Centre's focus on class reveals its inherent 'Englishness' (Gibson 2007: 85). 'Class' is a difficult term, as it is hard to come up with a system for definitively working out whether someone is working-class, middle-class, upper-class, or something else. Should class be measured in terms of wealth, or education, or upbringing, or culture, or a combination of factors? Added to this is that, in contemporary Britain, 'class' is often seen as an outdated word, which suggests social movement is impossible. It is rare for people to easily identify themselves as belonging to a certain class, even though, a hundred or so years ago, this might have been something many people would have probably stated with pride. You might feel that class has no value to you, and that you should instead be judged as an individual and on your own actions, rather than a 'group' you might belong to. While cultural studies agrees that 'class' is a complex term, it is determined to argue that it is still a useful one. We still live in a society where there is a link between, for example, the area you come from and your likelihood to go to university (Duke and Layer 2005); politicians and civil servants are more likely to come from certain backgrounds than others (Marsh et al. 2001); and there is a link between wages and class (Naylor et al. 2002). It might be useful to think of 'class' as all those things which affect people's access to a range of things (education, work, power), and which limit their expectations in life. Think about what class means to you; how would you define your class position? Do you think there are differences between you and people from other backgrounds (perhaps this is most evident when you leave home to study at university)? While you may find it a problematic concept, it is important you have a working idea of what is meant by it, as it is a recurring idea in media theory.

The founder of the Centre was Richard Hoggart, who is probably best known for his influential book, *The Uses of Literacy* (1958). In that book Hoggart adopted some of the approaches that came to define the work of CCCS; in particular, the assumption that everyday, common-sense cultural activities can be read as representative of broader social structures, especially those concerned with social power. It is an autobiographical book, in which Hoggart explores his own background and upbringing, showing how, amongst other things, class has left an indelible mark on his life.

Stuart Hall became the Director of the Centre after Hoggart, in 1968, and while the general ethos remained the same, Hall encouraged work which examined the ways in which texts work, and the Centre developed work on 'other' audiences, such as subcultures and women. In doing so, Hall encouraged a wider notion of class, acknowledging that other factors – such as gender, race and social groupings – also inform the ways in which culture is related to social power. This interest in the workings of texts, and the insistence on exploring the relationship between production (what media-makers do) and consumption (what audiences do), can be seen in the 'Encoding/Decoding model'.

Key works to have come out of the Centre include Paul Willis's *Learning to Labour* (1977), Charlotte Brunsdon and David Morley's *Everyday Television* (1978), Angela McRobbie's *Jackie* (1982 [1978]), Dick Hebdige's *Subculture* (1979) and Dorothy Hobson's *Crossroads* (1982). Of these, Hobson, McRobbie, and Brunsdon and Morley examine texts that are usually seen as very normal, and everyday: the 'Jackie' in McRobbie's title was a highly popular magazine for teenagers; the 'Crossroads' in Hobson's title was a weekday soap opera broadcast on ITV; Brunsdon and Morley's work looked at the daily BBC1 magazine programme *Nationwide* (1969–83). In exploring such topics, these writers were demonstrating that not only were previously unexamined texts rich and complex, but also that, in investigating how audiences used them, the interaction between consumers and products was a ripe site for social and political analysis. The methods used in these studies were also innovative, with interviews and focus groups with 'ordinary' people to see what they made of these cultural forms. With this approach, researchers were not only attempting to give 'ordinary' people a voice, but also to explore how everyday life and media consumption interact. The same can be seen in Hebdige's book, which explores various groups such as punks and teddy boys to see the relationships between class, race, music and social identity. Willis's book is perhaps the most 'straightforwardly' political, as it deals with the ways in which males from working-class backgrounds 'learn' their place in society, eventually taking up the kinds of jobs which offer them little social power. Again, these studies involved interacting with real people, and it may be these methodological interventions which the Centre made – placing 'ordinary' people at the core of analysis – which can be seen as one of its most radical and significant statements.

The Centre was closed in 2002, in a shock decision which resulted in criticism from around the world. The reasons for this were various, some of which were financial and some political; indeed, because of the nature of universities it is impossible to know definitively the causes. Suffice to say, the closure can be seen as a significant moment in the progress of British cultural studies, which, while many of its approaches have been adopted across a wealth of humanities and social sciences subjects, could be seen as having its glory days in the past. Indeed, the fact that the reading included here – in a book on media studies – is one from a Centre for *Cultural* Studies, shows how the Centre's work has influenced research and thinking beyond its immediate remit.

INTRODUCTION TO THE READING

Stuart Hall was director of CCCS from 1968 to 1979. He was born in Kingston, Jamaica in 1932, and moved to Britain in the 1950s before studying at Oxford University. He has written and edited a great number of books and influential articles, such as *The Idea of the Modern State* (1984), *Questions of Cultural Identity* (1996, with Paul du Gay) and *Representation* (1997). His recurring themes are issues of power in society. Much of this centres on the ways in which communication relates to power, whether this is through spoken and/or written language or, more commonly, through media and cultural texts. This idea of the power structures in communication is a key one in much media and cultural analysis, yet Hall has repeatedly questioned the notion that texts 'contain' meanings which then lead to the reproduction of power structures. Instead, he is among many theorists who see the audience as having some power, and that the meanings of texts only arise once they are read by people; this can also be seen in Barthes's 'The death of the author' reading from *Image Music Text* (1977 [1967]) in Chapter 22 in *this* book. This is not to suggest that audiences are equally powerful; but it is to say that debates about the social role of media must take into account what audiences do with texts, as much as it must explore media production and the techniques of the texts themselves. In this way, Hall's theorising can be seen to influence audience research directly, particularly those ethnographic studies which explore what it is that audiences do. Indeed, Morley's *The 'Nationwide' Audience* (1980) is a direct response to Hall's work, where he carries out fieldwork which tests and develops some of Hall's hypotheses.

It is because of this recent development in analysis of the audience that the reading here has become so influential. In 'Encoding/Decoding' Hall argues that there are two processes which result in media communication: first, there is the process which involves media producers creating texts; secondly, there is the process whereby audiences read and make sense of those texts. While researchers had looked at audiences before, Hall's work is interesting because it places these two processes in balance, seeing each of them as equally important. While this theory could be seen as demonstrating the 'active' nature of media audiences, it is important not to overstate this. Instead, Hall argues that the ways in which the two processes are carried out are limited by, and affected by, a set of social and communication conventions which means that power might instead exist somewhere else: that is, 'communication is *systematically* distorted' (Procter 2004: 57). This is to say that, while media producers could produce anything they want, they rarely do, as they are bound by codes of professionalism, audience expectations, and, importantly, the norms which govern how the media communicates. For example, there's no real reason why a male newsreader wears a shirt and tie, for the news is still the news if he is wearing a t-shirt and baseball cap; yet, news conventions means that this never happens. Similarly, while audiences could read programmes in a range of ways, readings are likely to be broadly similar because they are as aware of those conventions as the producers are; therefore, even though we might know it doesn't matter whether a newsreader wears a tie or not, we would still probably be surprised if he didn't. For Hall the question therefore becomes the relationship between these two processes, whereby production exists within a particular context, and reading exists within a similar context; there is no law stating newsreaders must wear ties, yet there's a balance between audience expectations and production conventions.

It is important that you are aware that Hall is presenting a theoretical model here: that is, while he does offer a few examples to support his argument, his primary aim is not to deliver unarguable proof. Instead, a model is an attempt to suggest how things might work, which can then be tested, if necessary, by empirical research. This might seem odd, considering many of the key books the Centre produced, cited above, are very much empirical research, with researchers interacting with real people in great detail. Yet lying behind such research are theoretical assumptions about the ways in which the world works, and appropriate ways to investigate it. Indeed, the Centre produced a lot of theoretical work, and one of its most obvious strengths was in the interplay between its theory and practice, with members developing research methods to interrogate and develop the studies and theorising of others.

Because of the lack of evidence in this reading, you might work through it thinking, 'But how does Hall know this?'; the point is that he doesn't, but the model offers a useful way of presenting novel ways of thinking about things, which might never be explored if only empirical research was carried out. In that sense, this is very much media *theory*, exploring and presenting debates and ideas, and more interested in thinking and analysis than research and conclusions. You should think of theory as part of a *process* of thinking things through, rather than a statement of fact; indeed, Hall's work has adopted a range of approaches and shifted its emphases through his career, showing that he 'has been on quite a theoretical journey' himself (Turner 2003: 59).

READING

1

Stuart Hall

Encoding/decoding[1]

Traditionally, mass-communications research has conceptualized the process of communication in terms of a circulation circuit or loop. This model has been criticized for its linearity – sender/message/receiver – for its concentration on the level of message exchange and for the absence of a structured conception of the different moments as a complex structure of relations. But it is also possible (and useful) to think of this process in terms of a structure produced and sustained through the articulation of linked but distinctive moments – production, circulation, distribution/consumption, reproduction. This would be to think of the process as a 'complex structure in dominance', sustained through the articulation of connected practices, each of which, however, retains its distinctiveness and has its own specific modality, its own forms and conditions of existence. This second approach, homologous to that which forms the skeleton of commodity production offered in Marx's *Grundrisse* and in *Capital*, has the added advantage of bringing out more sharply how a continuous circuit – production–distribution–production – can be sustained through a 'passage of forms'.[2] It also highlights the specificity of the forms in which the product of the process 'appears' in each moment, and thus what distinguishes discursive 'production' from other types of production in our society and in modern media systems.

2

The 'object' of these practices is meanings and messages in the form of sign-vehicles of a specific kind organized, like any form of communication or language, through the operation of codes within the syntagmatic chain of a discourse. The apparatuses, relations and practices of production thus issue, at a certain moment (the moment of 'production/circulation') in the form of symbolic vehicles constituted within the rules of 'language'. It is in this discursive form that the circulation of the 'product' takes place. The process thus requires, at the production end, its material instruments – its 'means' – as well as its own sets of social (production) relations – the organization and combination of practices within media apparatuses. But it is in the *discursive* form that the circulation of the product takes place, as well as its distribution to different audiences. Once accomplished, the discourse must then be translated

---

1. This article is an edited extract from 'Encoding and Decoding in Television Discourse', CCCS Stencilled Paper no. 7.
2. For an explication and commentary on the methodological implications of Marx's argument, see S. Hall, 'A reading of Marx's 1857 *Introduction to the Grundrisse*', in *WPCS* 6 (1974).

NOTES

1 Structure

Hall begins by making assumptions about the ways in which relevant research has usually been carried out. Note that he offers no evidence for this – something you might get criticised for if you did it in an essay. This is because this article is written for a specific audience in mind, and it is one that would hold the same assumptions as Hall and therefore the evidence does not need to be spelled out. Similarly, he notes that the approach has been criticised, but does not say by whom.

Context

This approach is placed within the context of Marx's work. Marx is someone you'll come across a lot in media studies, and was certainly a key thinker for many members of CCCS.

Writing Style

Note how much of the writing so far – and that in the rest of the reading – doesn't include many specific examples. Instead, Hall writes more generally, taking a much wider approach than detailed examination of smaller elements might allow. This is one of the ways in which theory often works, especially when it attempts to theorise much larger, social processes. You might find this difficult to deal with at first; indeed, one of the ways in which you could work on understanding the reading is to see if you can relate it to specific media examples you can think of.

Content

Here Hall places media communication as a 'process'; other authors in this book have said the same kind of thing. This is important, because it is the ways in which this process works that Hall wants to investigate.

2 Content

Hall discusses 'discourse' here. This is an important idea, which says that there are particular ways in which societies talk about things, and if you don't use those ways it is difficult for people to know what you are trying to say. Hall is arguing that when communication is produced it must use these discourses; but it must also adopt the institutional frameworks and industrial practices within media industries. This can be seen as suggesting there are only particular ways of saying things, and only certain things that can be said. Hall argues that those discourses are then used by people to make sense of the media messages which have been created. If we do not know those discourses we cannot make sense of the media; which is why sometimes media from a different place, or a different time, can be quite confusing. Importantly, Hall discusses 'social practices'; that is, he insists that when we read a media message, we don't just make sense of it, it also helps inform the ways in which we, and the society we live in, act. In this way, he is placing his analysis within a social context, which is often important to the work of CCCS, and cultural studies as a whole.

READING

2

(continued)

– transformed, again – into social practices if the circuit is to be both completed and effective. If no 'meaning' is taken, there can be no 'consumption'. If the meaning is not articulated in practice, it has no effect. The value of this approach is that while each of the moments, in articulation, is necessary to the circuit as a whole, no one moment can fully guarantee the next moment with which it is articulated. Since each has its specific modality and conditions of existence, each can constitute its own break or interruption of the 'passage of forms' on whose continuity the flow of effective production (that is, 'reproduction') depends.

3

Thus while in no way wanting to limit research to 'following only those leads which emerge from content analysis',[3] we must recognize that the discursive form of the message has a privileged position in the communicative exchange (from the viewpoint of circulation), and that the moments of 'encoding' and 'decoding', though only 'relatively autonomous' in relation to the communicative process as a whole, are *determinate* moments. A 'raw' historical event cannot, *in that form*, be transmitted by, say, a television newscast. Events can only be signified within the aural-visual forms of the televisual discourse. In the moment when a historical event passes under the sign of discourse, it is subject to all the complex formal 'rules' by which language signifies. To put it paradoxically, the event must become a 'story' before it can become a *communicative event*. In that moment the formal sub-rules of discourse are 'in dominance', without, of course, subordinating out of existence the historical event so signified, the social relations in which the rules are set to work or the social and political consequences of the event having been signified in this way. The 'message form' is the necessary 'form of appearance' of the event in its passage from source to receiver. Thus the transposition into and out of the 'message form' (or the mode of symbolic exchange) is not a random 'moment', which we can take up or ignore at our convenience. The 'message form' is a determinate moment; though, at another level, it comprises the surface movements of the communications system only and requires, at another stage, to be integrated into the social relations of the communication process as a whole, of which it forms only a part.

3. J.D. Halloran, 'Understanding television', Paper for the Council of Europe Colloquy on 'Understanding Television' (University of Leicester 1973).

NOTES

Writing Style

Note the many words in inverted commas in this paragraph; why is this? In particular, why is 'language' in inverted commas? What kinds of 'social practices' is Hall referring to? What is the difference between 'production' and 'reproduction' here, and why does Hall prefer the latter?

3	## Structure

Here we come across Hall's first use of the words 'encoding' and 'decoding' which make up the reading's title. Ensuring you understand what he means by them is, therefore, vital.

Context

The historical events which Hall discusses here (again, without specific examples) would be things like the fall of the Berlin Wall (1989), or the funeral of the Princess of Wales (1997), or Live 8 (2005). These events have to be turned into stories – which employ certain discourses – in order to be made into television. What is the difference between an 'event' and a 'story' here, and why does it matter?

Content

In looking at the processes which lead to media texts, Hall is arguing that we should not be examining the texts themselves, but instead how those texts come into being. In this way, he is arguing against a simplistic textual analysis approach (an approach which, generally speaking, has consistently dominated the analysis of cultural forms).

READING

4

From this general perspective, we may crudely characterize the television communicative process as follows. The institutional structures of broadcasting, with their practices and networks of production, their organized relations and technical infrastructures, are required to produce a programme. Using the analogy of *Capital*, this is the 'labour process' in the discursive mode. Production, here, constructs the message. In one sense, then, the circuit begins here. Of course, the production process is not without its 'discursive' aspect: it, too, is framed throughout by meanings and ideas: knowledge-in-use concerning the routines of production, historically defined technical skills, professional ideologies, institutional knowledge, definitions and assumptions, assumptions about the audience and so on frame the constitution of the programme through this production structure.

5

Further, though the production structures of television originate the television discourse, they do not constitute a closed system. They draw topics, treatments, agendas, events, personnel, images of the audience, 'definitions of the situation' from other sources and other discursive formations within the wider socio-cultural and political structure of which they are a differentiated part. Philip Elliott has expressed this point succinctly, within a more traditional framework, in his discussion of the way in which the audience is both the 'source' and the 'receiver' of the television message. Thus – to borrow Marx's terms – circulation and reception are, indeed, 'moments' of the production process in television and are reincorporated, via a number of skewed and structured 'feedbacks', into the production process itself. The consumption or reception of the television message is thus also itself a 'moment' of the production process in its larger sense, though the latter is 'predominant' because it is the 'point of departure for the realization' of the message. Production and reception of the television message are not, therefore, identical, but they are related: they are differentiated moments within the totality formed by the social relations of the communicative process as a whole.

Writing Style

'Crudely'? Isn't there a problem here? Isn't Hall acknowledging his model lacks subtlety and detail?

Structure

Now Hall has outlined his theory in general, he moves here into discussing how it works in practice, and breaks the process up into its constituent parts.

Content

Importantly, Hall sees a range of factors as affecting the production process. This is not to suggest that individuals have no creativity or individualism at all; but it is to say that such creativity and individualism is filtered through, and tempered by, a whole range of social expectations. Note how he remarks that the production process is affected by things outside of it; media producers are not independent creatures completely cut off from social and political concerns.

Content

What is meant by a 'closed system'? In what ways might it be 'open'? While it seems obvious that the audience is a 'receiver', how is an audience a 'source' of a message?

Writing Style

While this is complicated abstract writing, the key point is at the end of the paragraph: that is, the distinction between production and reception as two separate (but connected) moments within the communication process.

READING

6

At a certain point, however, the broadcasting structures must yield encoded messages in the form of a meaningful discourse. The institution-societal relations of production must pass under the discursive rules of language for its product to be 'realized'. This initiates a further differentiated moment, in which the formal rules of discourse and language are in dominance. Before this message can have an 'effect' (however defined), satisfy a 'need' or be put to a 'use', it must first be appropriated as a meaningful discourse and be meaningfully decoded. It is this set of decoded meanings which 'have an effect', influence, entertain, instruct or persuade, with very complex perceptual, cognitive, emotional, ideological or behavioural consequences. In a 'determinate' moment the structure employs a code and yields a 'message': at another determinate moment the 'message', via its decodings, issues into the structure of social practices. We are now fully aware that this re-entry into the practices of audience reception and 'use' cannot be understood in simple behavioural terms. The typical processes identified in positivistic research on isolated elements – effects, uses, 'gratifications' – are themselves framed by structures of understanding, as well as being produced by social and economic relations, which shape their 'realization' at the reception end of the chain and which permit the meanings signified in the discourse to be transposed into practice or consciousness (to acquire social use value or political effectivity).

7

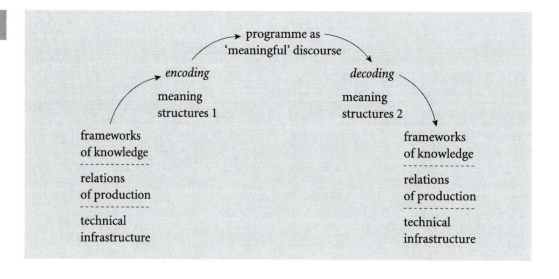

6 | Writing Style

Note how careful Hall is with the word 'effect', putting it in inverted commas and adding a caveat afterwards. Here Hall is placing his work in relation to all those effects studies which have been central to media analysis (see Chapter 14).

Context

What kinds of 'structures of understanding' affect how research sees the consequences of media?

7 | Content

This diagram neatly sums up Hall's ideas, and is referred to a lot in subsequent studies.

READING

8

Clearly, what we have labelled in the diagram 'meaning structures 1' and 'meaning structures 2' may not be the same. They do not constitute an 'immediate identity'. The codes of encoding and decoding may not be perfectly symmetrical. The degrees of symmetry – that is, the degrees of 'understanding' and 'misunderstanding' in the communicative exchange – depend on the degrees of symmetry/asymmetry (relations of equivalence) established between the positions of the 'personifications', encoder-producer and decoder-receiver. But this in turn depends on the degrees of identity/non-identity between the codes which perfectly or imperfectly transmit, interrupt or systematically distort what has been transmitted. The lack of fit between the codes has a great deal to do with the structural differences of relation and position between broadcasters and audiences, but it also has something to do with the asymmetry between the codes of 'source' and 'receiver' at the moment of transformation into and out of the discursive form. What are called 'distortions' or 'misunderstandings' arise precisely from the *lack of equivalence* between the two sides in the communicative exchange. Once again, this defines the 'relative autonomy', but 'determinateness', of the entry and exit of the message in its discursive moments.

9

The application of this rudimentary paradigm has already begun to transform our understanding of the older term, television 'content'. We are just beginning to see how it might also transform our understanding of audience reception, 'reading' and response as well. Beginnings and endings have been announced in communications research before, so we must be cautious. But there seems some ground for thinking that a new and exciting phase in so-called audience research, of a quite new kind, may be opening up. At either end of the communicative chain the use of the semiotic paradigm promises to dispel the lingering behaviourism which has dogged mass-media research for so long, especially in its approach to content. Though we know the television programme is not a behavioural input, like a tap on the knee cap, it seems to have been almost impossible for traditional researchers to conceptualize the communicative process without lapsing into one or other variant of low-flying behaviourism. We know, as Gerbner has remarked, that representations of violence on the TV screen 'are not violence but messages about violence':[4] but we have continued to research the question of violence, for example, as if we were unable to comprehend this epistemological distinction.

4. G. Gerbner *et al.*, *Violence in TV Drama: A Study of Trends and Symbolic Functions* (The Annenberg School, University of Pennsylvania 1970).

8 · Writing Style

What is meant by an 'immediate identity', and why is Hall keen to argue that it is not applicable to his model?

Content

As already noted, Hall is keen to distinguish the different moments in the process outlined in his diagram. At the end of this paragraph he notes how sometimes communication fails, or audiences get different meanings than were intended by producers. This is because there might sometimes be a disparity between the tools used by audiences to decode a text and those used by producers to encode it. Importantly, Hall doesn't say either of these is more important: that is, it's not as if the producers are 'right' and the audience got it 'wrong', for neither side of the process is prioritised.

9 · Context

Following on from the previous paragraph, Hall sees his approach as having significant consequences for the ways we understand the audience. As he notes, media research has always ended up making assumptions about the effects media content has on those who view it, to varying degrees. However, by placing audience activity as equal to the processes of production, Hall hopes this will open up new areas of research which don't simplify audience activity as merely the end result of the communication process.

Writing Style

Notice Hall's repeated use of 'we' here; who is he talking about? In this way, do *you* feel you're part of the audience this reading is directed towards?

READING

10

The televisual sign is a complex one. It is itself constituted by the combination of two types of discourse, visual and aural. Moreover, it is an iconic sign, in Peirce's terminology, because 'it possesses some of the properties of the thing represented'.[5] This is a point which has led to a great deal of confusion and has provided the site of intense controversy in the study of visual language. Since the visual discourse translates a three-dimensional world into two-dimensional planes, it cannot, of course, *be* the referent or concept it signifies. The dog in the film can bark but it cannot bite! Reality exists outside language, but it is constantly mediated by and through language: and what we can know and say has to be produced in and through discourse. Discursive 'knowledge' is the product not of the transparent representation of the 'real' in language but of the articulation of language on real relations and conditions. Thus there is no intelligible discourse without the operation of a code. Iconic signs are therefore coded signs too – even if the codes here work differently from those of other signs. There is no degree zero in language. Naturalism and 'realism' – the apparent fidelity of the representation to the thing or concept represented – is the result, the effect, of a certain specific articulation of language on the 'real'. It is the result of a discursive practice.

11

Certain codes may, of course, be so widely distributed in a specific language community or culture, and be learned at so early an age, that they appear not to be constructed – the effect of an articulation between sign and referent – but to be 'naturally' given. Simple visual signs appear to have achieved a 'near-universality' in this sense: though evidence remains that even apparently 'natural' visual codes are culture-specific. However, this does not mean that no codes have intervened; rather, that the codes have been profoundly *naturalized*. The operation of naturalized codes reveals not the transparency and 'naturalness' of language but the depth, the habituation and the near-universality of the codes in use. They produce apparently 'natural' recognitions. This has the (ideological) effect of concealing the practices of coding which are present. But we must not be fooled by appearances. Actually, what naturalized codes demonstrate is the degree of habituation produced when there is a fundamental alignment and reciprocity – an achieved equivalence – between the encoding and decoding sides of an exchange of meanings. The functioning of the codes on the decoding side will frequently assume the status of naturalized perceptions. This leads us to think that the visual sign for 'cow' actually *is* (rather than *represents*) the animal, cow. But if we think of the visual representation of a cow in a manual on animal husbandry – and, even more, of the linguistic sign 'cow' – we can see that both, in different degrees, are *arbitrary* with respect to the concept of the animal they represent. The articulation of an arbitrary sign – whether visual or verbal – with the concept of a referent is the product not of nature but of convention, and the conventionalism of discourses requires the intervention, the support, of codes. Thus Eco has argued

5. Charles Peirce, *Speculative Grammar*, in *Collected Papers* (Cambridge, Mass.: Harvard University Press 1931–58).

10 ### Context

Hall mentions semiotics, and then refers to Charles S. Peirce (1839–1914), who is a key figure in the development of that approach; see *The Writings of Charles S. Peirce* (1982). Indeed, this article was written at a 'high point' for semiotics, where it was busily influencing much of the work on media and culture. Again, Hall doesn't go into detail about semiotics, as he assumes the readers will have some kind of working knowledge of it.

Content

While it might seem obvious that a dog on television is not the same as one in 'real life', the fact is that we often see some relationship between media representations and the 'real world'. It is this relationship which realism relies upon, and helps foster. Hall does not get into lengthy discussions about realism here, as that is not his focus; instead, he is interested in noting that there are relationships between media content and the 'real world' outside of it. You might want to look at some books on realism to see what these debates are about (Armstrong 2005; King 2005).

11 ### Context

Much of cultural studies argues that many of the things it analyses are difficult to spot because of this 'naturalizing' process Hall mentions. Certainly language *feels* natural, as we rarely question why a particular word is used to represent a particular thing. Where can you see such 'naturalizing' processes in action in media? Think about genre and conventions for things like horror films, where we often bring unquestioned assumptions to texts, hoping that they will fulfil them.

Content

Semiotics says there are different kinds of signs. Hall refers to 'iconic' ones here: that is, signs which have a visual similarity to the thing they represent, with the most obvious example being a photograph of an object. However, cultural studies argues that there are still processes which lead to us reading signs in this way, even if they seem natural to us, and therefore these processes need to be investigated.

READING

11

(continued)

that iconic signs 'look like objects in the real world because they reproduce the conditions (that is, the codes) of perception in the viewer'.[6] These 'conditions of perception' are, however, the result of a highly coded, even if virtually unconscious, set of operations – decodings. This is as true of the photographic or televisual image as it is of any other sign. Iconic signs are, however, particularly vulnerable to being 'read' as natural because visual codes of perception are very widely distributed and because this type of sign is less arbitrary than a linguistic sign: the linguistic sign, 'cow' possesses *none* of the properties of the thing represented, whereas the visual sign appears to possess *some* of those properties.

12

This may help us to clarify a confusion in current linguistic theory and to define precisely how some key terms are being used in this article. Linguistic theory frequently employs the distinction 'denotation' and 'connotation'. The term 'denotation' is widely equated with the literal meaning of a sign: because this literal meaning is almost universally recognized, especially when visual discourse is being employed, 'denotation' has often been confused with a literal transcription of 'reality' in language – and thus with a 'natural sign', one produced without the intervention of a code. 'Connotation', on the other hand, is employed simply to refer to less fixed and therefore more conventionalized and changeable, associative meanings, which clearly vary from instance to instance and therefore must depend on the intervention of codes.

13

We do *not* use the distinction – denotation/connotation – in this way. From our point of view, the distinction is an *analytic* one only. It is useful, in analysis, to be able to apply a rough rule of thumb which distinguishes those aspects of a sign which appear to be taken, in any language community at any point in time, as its 'literal' meaning (denotation) from the more associative meanings for the sign which it is possible to generate (connotation). But analytic distinctions must not be confused with distinctions in the real world. There will be very few instances in which signs organized in a discourse signify *only* their 'literal' (that is, near-universally consensualized) meaning. In actual discourse most signs will combine both the denotative and the connotative *aspects* (as redefined above). It may, then, be asked why we retain the distinction at all. It is largely a matter of analytic value. It is because signs appear to acquire their full ideological value – appear to be open to articulation with wider ideological discourses and meanings – at the level of their 'associative' meanings (that is, at the connotative

6. Umberto Eco, 'Articulations of the cinematic code', in *Cinemantics*, no. 1.

NOTES

12   Context

The distinctions between 'denotation' and 'connotation' are indeed key ones in semiotic analysis. Note again that Hall doesn't tell us which thinkers or writings he's referring to.

13   Structure

Following on from the previous paragraph, Hall refutes the 'denotation/connotation' distinction. You might wonder, then, why he mentions it, or if you need to understand the concept fully if you are to make sense of Hall's argument. Indeed, Hall suggests the distinction only matters in terms of analysing media, and doesn't really matter in the 'real world'. He is placing his argument within academic debates, and showing how he disagrees with other work. In that sense, you do not need to understand the distinction fully to make sense of the article; but you do to make sense of the article within the academic context and debate of which it is a part.

READING

13

(continued)

level) – for here 'meanings' are *not* apparently fixed in natural perception (that is, they are not fully naturalized), and their fluidity of meaning and association can be more fully exploited and transformed.[7] So it is at the connotative *level* of the sign that situational ideologies alter and transform signification. At this level we can see more clearly the active intervention of ideologies in and on discourse: here, the sign is open to new accentuations and, in Vološinov's terms, enters fully into the struggle over meanings – the class struggle in language.[8] This does not mean that the denotative or 'literal' meaning is outside ideology. Indeed, we could say that its ideological value is strongly *fixed* – because it has become so fully universal and 'natural'. The terms 'denotation' and 'connotation', then, are merely useful analytic tools for distinguishing, in particular contexts, between not the presence/absence of ideology in language but the different levels at which ideologies and discourses intersect.[9]

14

The level of connotation of the visual sign, of its contextual reference and positioning in different discursive fields of meaning and association, is the point where *already coded* signs intersect with the deep semantic codes of a culture and take on additional, more active ideological dimensions. We might take an example from advertising discourse. Here, too, there is no 'purely denotative', and certainly no 'natural', representation. Every visual sign in advertising connotes a quality, situation, value or inference, which is present as an implication or implied meaning, depending on the connotational positioning. In Barthes's example, the sweater always signifies a 'warm garment' (denotation) and thus the activity/value of 'keeping warm'. But it is also possible, at its more connotative levels, to signify 'the coming of winter' or 'a cold day'. And, in the specialized sub-codes of fashion, sweater may also connote a fashionable style of *haute couture* or, alternatively, an informal style of dress. But set against the right visual background and positioned by the romantic sub-code, it may connote 'long autumn walk in the woods'.[10] Codes of this order clearly contract relations for the sign with the wider universe of ideologies in a society.

7. See the argument in S. Hall, 'Determinations of news photographs', in *WPCS* 3 (1972).
8. Vološinov, *Marxism And The Philosophy of Language* (The Seminar Press 1973).
9. For a similar clarification, see Marina Camargo Heck, 'Ideological dimensions of media messages', pages 122–7.
10. Roland Barthes, 'Rhetoric of the image', in *WPCS* 1 (1971).

13 Context

(continued)

Hall mentions class here. This might seem unrelated to the rest of the article. But remember that Hall adopted a Marxist approach early on, and class is central to Marx's thinking (Lebowitz 1992). Also, cultural studies has always been interested in class; or, more accurately, in the power disparities which result from class structures (Munt 2000). Hall does not go into class in detail because it is assumed that you will see this as relevant. It also helps place what may seem like an abstract, detached piece of theorising within socio-political debates, which may help you see some relevance to the discussion as a whole.

14 Writing Style

Here there is analysis of a more specific example, as Hall discusses advertising, which may help you ground the abstract theorising in something more everyday. Advertising is a useful example because it is media communication which has a specific purpose, which is to sell you things. Therefore, advertising wants audiences to have particular responses to the communication it creates. Hall draws on Barthes to show that advertising often uses connotations of objects for its appeal; a reading from Barthes is in Chapter 22 in *this* book, but for the discussion Hall covers here, Barthes's *Mythologies* (1973 [1957]) is more relevant. The discussion of clothing is useful, because we often don't think of clothes in terms of their practical purposes – to cover us, and keep us warm – but instead categorise them in a whole set of other ways, including trends and fashions, and what clothing says about us.

Content

Is this really what a sweater means? Does it really have all these possible meanings? Isn't a sweater sometimes just a sweater?

READING

15

These codes are the means by which power and ideology are made to signify in particular discourses. They refer signs to the 'maps of meaning' into which any culture is classified; and those 'maps of social reality' have the whole range of social meanings, practices, and usages, power and interest 'written in' to them. The connotative levels of signifiers, Barthes remarked, 'have a close communication with culture, knowledge, history, and it is through them, so to speak, that the environmental world invades the linguistic and semantic system. They are, if you like, the fragments of ideology'.[11]

16

The so-called denotative *level* of the televisual sign is fixed by certain, very complex (but limited or 'closed') codes. But its connotative *level*, though also bounded, is more open, subject to more active *transformations*, which exploit its polysemic values. Any such already constituted sign is potentially transformable into more than one connotative configuration. Polysemy must not, however, be confused with pluralism. Connotative codes are *not* equal among themselves. Any society/culture tends, with varying degrees of closure, to impose its classifications of the social and cultural and political world. These constitute a *dominant cultural order*, though it is neither univocal nor uncontested. This question of the 'structure of discourses in dominance' is a crucial point. The different areas of social life appear to be mapped out into discursive domains, hierarchically organized into *dominant or preferred meanings*. New, problematic or troubling events, which breach our expectancies and run counter to our 'common-sense constructs', to our 'taken-for-granted' knowledge of social structures, must be assigned to their discursive domains before they can be said to 'make sense'. The most common way of 'mapping' them is to assign the new to some domain or other of the existing 'maps of problematic social reality'. We say *dominant*, not 'determined', because it is always possible to order, classify, assign and decode an event within more than one 'mapping'.

11. Roland Barthes, *Elements of Semiology* (Cape 1967).

15 Writing Style

What are the 'maps of meaning' and 'maps of social reality' Hall refers to here?

Content

For Hall, and other semioticians, these connotations have social power, because they draw on ways in which societies tell us we should think about things. Like much cultural studies, Hall here discusses what might seem like a simple, everyday topic – clothes – and sees within it massive ideas about social structures and power. This is discussed in books such as Barthes (2006 [1967]) and Guy et al. (2001).

16 Content

Earlier, Hall noted that the decoding aspect of his model needs to be seen to be as significant as the encoding part. This means that audiences are capable of reading texts in a variety of ways: what's called 'polysemy'. Yet here Hall adds a note of caution, for he does not want us to think he is arguing that there are an infinite number of possible readings, nor that, more importantly, all of the various possible readings are of equal likelihood. That is, because there is a 'dominant cultural order', certain readings are more likely, and these are a consequence of social norms and expectations. These he calls 'dominant or preferred readings'. Later in the article he discusses other possible readings. This idea of 'preferred readings' has been hugely influential, and it's a phrase you might come across in a range of media studies readings.

Writing Style

What are the 'maps of meaning' and 'maps of social reality' referred to here? And what's the difference between 'polysemy' and 'pluralism'?

READING

17

But we say 'dominant' because there exists a pattern of 'preferred readings'; and these both have the institutional/political/ideological order imprinted in them and have themselves become institutionalized.[12] The domains of 'preferred meanings' have the whole social order embedded in them as a set of meanings, practices and beliefs: the everyday knowledge of social structures, of 'how things work for all practical purposes in this culture', the rank order of power and interest and the structure of legitimations, limits and sanctions. Thus to clarify a 'misunderstanding' at the connotative level, we must refer, *through* the codes, to the orders of social life, of economic and political power and of ideology. Further, since these mappings are 'structured in dominance' but not closed, the communicative process consists not in the unproblematic assignment of every visual item to its given position within a set of pre-arranged codes, but of *performative rules* – rules of competence and use, of logics-in-use – which seek actively to *enforce* or *pre-fer* one semantic domain over another and rule items into and out of their appropriate meaning-sets. Formal semiology has too often neglected this practice of *interpretative work*, though this constitutes, in fact, the real relations of broadcast practices in television.

18

In speaking of *dominant meanings*, then, we are not talking about a one-sided process which governs how all events will be signified. It consists of the 'work' required to enforce, win plausibility for and command as legitimate a *decoding* of the event within the limit of dominant definitions in which it has been connotatively signified. Terni has remarked:

> By the word *reading* we mean not only the capacity to identify and decode a certain number of signs, but also the subjective capacity to put them into a creative relation between themselves and with other signs: a capacity which is, by itself, the condition for a complete awareness of one's total environment.[13]

19

Our quarrel here is with the notion of 'subjective capacity', as if the referent of a televisional discourse were an objective fact but the interpretative level were an individualized and private matter. Quite the opposite seems to be the case. The televisual practice takes 'objective' (that is, systemic) responsibility precisely for the relations which disparate signs contract with one another in any discursive instance, and thus continually rearranges, delimits and prescribes into what 'awareness of one's total environment' these items are arranged.

12. For an extended critique of 'preferred reading', see Alan O'Shea, 'Preferred reading' (unpublished paper, CCCS, University of Birmingham).
13. P. Terni, 'Memorandum', Council of Europe Colloquy on 'Understanding Television' (University of Leicester 1973).

17

Content

Again, Hall suggests a link between the 'preferred readings' and the social conventions and norms we use to govern our lives. However, this is not to suggest that the former is merely a result of the latter. Instead, media communication helps support those social conventions by relying on them and reproducing them. Therefore, the media, by this argument, helps uphold the social system it relies on to make sense. This is not to say that media producers actively do this in a contrived way because they want the social order to remain stable; instead it is to say it is an unavoidable by-product of the desire to produce texts which make sense to audiences. The idea that the media helps reproduce social structures – whether deliberately or not – is central to cultural studies debates, and can be connected to discussions about media and power which run throughout this book, in, for example, the readings on political economy (Chapter 12) and the public sphere (Chapter 13).

18

Content

Note the word 'work' here. Hall has kept referring to his model as looking at a 'process'. This is to signal that everything he is discussing is neither inevitable nor natural, but that work has to be carried out in order for the social structures he maligns to be maintained. This is not something that has just happened; it is something that is happening, and we are part of the process. This is important because it means the process can be challenged and dismantled, and cultural studies often calls for such alterations to the social order.

19

Context

Here, Hall places his argument within the context of existing writing on the topic. He quotes Terni so that you don't have to seek that material out to follow his argument. As noted before, much academic work responds to that of others, and this is a common way of putting together an argument.

READING

20

This brings us to the question of misunderstandings. Television producers who find their message 'failing to get across' are frequently concerned to straighten out the kinks in the communication chain, thus facilitating the 'effectiveness' of their communication. Much research which claims the objectivity of 'policy-oriented analysis' reproduces this administrative goal by attempting to discover how much of a message the audience recalls and to improve the extent of understanding. No doubt misunderstandings of a literal kind do exist. The viewer does not know the terms employed, cannot follow the complex logic of argument or exposition, is unfamiliar with the language, finds the concepts too alien or difficult or is foxed by the expository narrative. But more often broadcasters are concerned that the audience has failed to take the meaning as they – the broadcasters – intended. What they really mean to say is that viewers are not operating within the 'dominant' or 'preferred' code. Their ideal is 'perfectly transparent communication'. Instead, what they have to confront is 'systematically distorted communication'.[14]

In recent years discrepancies of this kind have usually been explained by reference to 'selective perception'. This is the door via which a residual pluralism evades the compulsions of a highly structured, asymmetrical and non-equivalent process. Of course, there will always be private, individual, variant readings. But 'selective perception' is almost never as selective, random or privatized as the concept suggests. The patterns exhibit, across individual variants, significant clusterings. Any new approach to audience studies will therefore have to begin with a critique of 'selective perception' theory.

21

It was argued earlier that since there is no necessary correspondence between encoding and decoding, the former can attempt to 'pre-fer' but cannot prescribe or guarantee the latter, which has its own conditions of existence. Unless they are wildly aberrant, encoding will have the effect of constructing some of the limits and parameters within which decodings will operate. If there were no limits, audiences could simply read whatever they liked into any message. No doubt some total misunderstandings of this kind do exist. But the vast range must contain *some* degree of reciprocity between encoding and decoding moments, otherwise we could not speak of an effective communicative exchange at all. Nevertheless, this 'correspondence' is not given but constructed. It is not 'natural' but the product of an articulation between two distinct moments. And the former cannot determine or guarantee, in a simple sense, which decoding codes will be employed. Otherwise communication would be a perfectly equivalent circuit, and every message would be an instance of 'perfectly transparent communication'. We must think, then, of the variant articulations in which encoding/decoding can be combined. To elaborate on this, we offer a hypothetical analysis of some possible decoding positions, in order to reinforce the point of 'no necessary correspondence'.[15]

14. The phrase is Habermas's, in 'Systematically distorted communications', in P. Dretzel (ed.), *Recent Sociology 2* (Collier-Macmillan 1970). It is used here, however, in a different way.
15. For a sociological formulation which is close, in some ways, to the positions outlined here but which does not parallel the argument about the theory of discourse, see Frank Parkin, *Class Inequality and Political Order* (Macgibbon and Kee 1971).

20 ## Writing Style

Note here how Hall mentions 'much research', but doesn't cite any. In the next paragraph, note how Hall states that the problem he mentions has 'been explained' in a particular way, but offers no evidence for this.

Content

Do you agree with the reasons Hall gives here for why audience members sometimes take different meanings from texts than producers intended?

21 ## Writing Style

Hall draws on many assumptions here, all of which are unsupported. This is not to suggest they are 'wrong'; however, it is to note that this is the way theory often works, and its validity does not necessarily have to be measured against quantitative research, particularly as most people are likely to agree with Hall's assertions.

READING

22

We identify *three* hypothetical positions from which decodings of a televisual discourse may be constructed. These need to be empirically tested and refined. But the argument that decodings do not follow inevitably from encodings, that they are not identical, reinforces the argument of 'no necessary correspondence'. It also helps to deconstruct the common-sense meaning of 'misunderstanding' in terms of a theory of 'systematically distorted communication'.

23

The first hypothetical position is that of the *dominant-hegemonic position*. When the viewer takes the connoted meaning from, say, a television newscast or current affairs programme full and straight, and decodes the message in terms of the reference code in which it has been encoded, we might say that the viewer *is operating inside the dominant code*. This is the ideal-typical case of 'perfectly transparent communication' – or as close as we are likely to come to it 'for all practical purposes'. Within this we can distinguish the positions produced by the *professional code*. This is the position (produced by what we perhaps ought to identify as the operation of a 'metacode') which the professional broadcasters assume when encoding a message which has *already* been signified in a hegemonic manner. The professional code is 'relatively independent' of the dominant code, in that it applies criteria and transformational operations of its own, especially those of a technico-practical nature. The professional code, however, operates *within* the 'hegemony' of the dominant code. Indeed, it serves to reproduce the dominant definitions precisely by bracketing their hegemonic quality and operating instead with displaced professional codings which foreground such apparently neutral-technical questions as visual quality, news and presentational values, televisual quality, 'professionalism' and so on. The hegemonic interpretations of, say, the politics of Northern Ireland, or the Chilean *coup* or the Industrial Relations Bill are principally generated by political and military elites: the particular choice of presentational occasions and formats, the selection of personnel, the choice of images, the staging of debates are selected and combined through the operation of the professional code. How the broadcasting professionals are able *both* to operate with 'relatively autonomous' codes of their own *and* to act in such a way as to reproduce (not without contradiction) the hegemonic signification of events is a complex matter which cannot be further spelled out here. It must suffice to say that the professionals are linked with the defining elites not only by the institutional position of broadcasting itself as an 'ideological apparatus',[16] but also by the structure of *access* (that is, the systematic 'over-accessing' of selective elite personnel and their 'definition of the situation' in television). It may even be

16. See Louis Althusser, 'Ideology and ideological state apparatuses', in *Lenin and Philosophy and Other Essays* (New Left Books 1971).

22 Content

In order to demonstrate that his theory isn't drawing on empirical analysis, Hall notes here that he is offering 'hypothetical' positions which require such research. In that sense, he's offering a theoretical model, which future research could validate, disprove, or modify. This idea of proffering a model, which future work can test, is a common one in a number of academic subjects, and you may come across other such models in your reading. The value of models is that they allow you to think beyond existing research, and may open up areas of enquiry which would not have been reached if only empirical approaches are used. What does this tell you about the processes theory goes through?

23 Content

Importantly, Hall distinguishes between the work of media practitioners and the social norms which inform their work. That is, the meaning of a programme cannot be defined by examining the makers' intentions, for they themselves draw upon the normalised way of making media in order to produce their text successfully. In this way, producers are as trapped within hegemonic positions as audiences are. This is significant because it says we should not focus research on practitioners, but instead go beyond that to the factors and social conventions within which practitioners work. But how are 'professionals . . . linked with the defining elites'? Are there places where this link is not concrete? And does such a link completely define media professionals' activity?

READING

23

(continued)

said that the professional codes serve to reproduce hegemonic definitions specifically by *not overtly* biasing their operations in a dominant direction: ideological reproduction therefore takes place here inadvertently, unconsciously, 'behind men's backs'.[17] Of course, conflicts, contradictions and even misunderstandings regularly arise between the dominant and the professional significations and their signifying agencies.

24

The second position we would identify is that of the *negotiated code* or position. Majority audiences probably understand quite adequately what has been dominantly defined and professionally signified. The dominant definitions, however, are hegemonic precisely because they represent definitions of situations and events which are 'in dominance' (*global*). Dominant definitions connect events, implicitly or explicitly, to grand totalizations, to the great syntagmatic views-of-the-world: they take 'large views' of issues: they relate events to the 'national interest' or to the level of geo-politics, even if they make these connections in truncated, inverted or mystified ways. The definition of a hegemonic viewpoint is (a) that it defines within its terms the mental horizon, the universe, of possible meanings, of a whole sector of relations in a society or culture; and (b) that it carries with it the stamp of legitimacy – it appears coterminous with what is 'natural', 'inevitable', 'taken for granted' about the social order. Decoding within the *negotiated version* contains a mixture of adaptive and oppositional elements: it acknowledges the legitimacy of the hegemonic definitions to make the grand significations (abstract), while, at a more restricted, situational (situated) level, it makes its own ground rules – it operates with exceptions to the rule. It accords the privileged position to the dominant definitions of events while reserving the right to make a more negotiated application to 'local conditions', to its own more *corporate* positions. This negotiated version of the dominant ideology is thus shot through with contradictions, though these are only on certain occasions brought to full visibility. Negotiated codes operate through what we might call particular or situated logics: and these logics are sustained by their differential and unequal relation to the discourses and logics of power. The simplest example of a negotiated code is that which governs the response of a worker to the notion of an Industrial Relations Bill limiting the right to strike or to arguments for a wages freeze. At the level of the 'national interest' economic debate the decoder may adopt the hegemonic definition, agreeing that 'we must all pay ourselves less in order to combat inflation'. This, however, may have little or no relation to his/her willingness to go on strike for better pay and conditions or to oppose the Industrial Relations Bill at the level of shop-floor or union organization. We suspect that the great majority of so-called 'misunderstandings' arise from the contradictions and disjunctures between hegemonic-dominant encodings and negotiated-corporate decodings. It is just these mismatches in the levels which most provoke defining elites and professionals to identify a 'failure in communications'.

17. For an expansion of this argument, see Stuart Hall, 'The external/internal dialectic in broadcasting', *4th Symposium on Broadcasting* (University of Manchester 1972), and 'Broadcasting and the state: the independence/impartiality couplet', AMCR Symposium, University of Leicester 1976 (CCCS unpublished paper).

24 Context

Hall's 'negotiated code' is one in which audiences, while aware of the intended, dominant meaning of a text, instead respond to it differently, or place it within different contexts. By stating that audiences are capable of actively reinterpreting messages while being aware of their intention, Hall allies himself with those who see audiences as active, critical readers, rather than 'couch potatoes' simplistically absorbing the content of media. Much work at this time was exploring the active nature of audiences, and a lot of the research carried out at the Centre for Contemporary Cultural Studies (CCCS) placed audiences and individuals as the focus, rather than texts and producers. This work of Hall occupies an important position in the development of the subject, then, because it gives a theoretical model which can be drawn on by those wanting to study audience activity.

Content

Do you agree with Hall's assertion about 'Majority audiences'? If the majority of the audience does take the 'dominant-hegemonic position', what proportion do you think takes the 'negotiated position', and what factors would encourage this?

Writing Style

Because of his Left position, it is unsurprising that Hall draws on a worker-legislation example to demonstrate his point.

READING

25

Finally, it is possible for a viewer perfectly to understand both the literal and the connotative inflection given by a discourse but to decode the message in a *globally* contrary way. He/she detotalizes the message in the preferred code in order to retotalize the message within some alternative framework of reference. This is the case of the viewer who listens to a debate on the need to limit wages but 'reads' every mention of the 'national interest' as 'class interest'. He/she is operating with what we must call an *oppositional code*. One of the most significant political moments (they also coincide with crisis points within the broadcasting organizations themselves, for obvious reasons) is the point when events which are normally signified and decoded in a negotiated way begin to be given an oppositional reading. Here the 'politics of signification' – the struggle in discourse – is joined.

25 Writing Style

The 'oppositional code' is outlined much more briefly than the other two. Is this because Hall sees it as less convincing, or because he feels its meaning is obvious?

Content

Following on from the previous paragraph, what proportion do you think adopts the 'oppositional' position, and what factors would encourage this?

Structure

You might also notice there is not really a conclusion to this paper. At least, Hall does not summarise his argument in the way you might expect, or point towards future research. Different writers will, at different times, conclude their writing in a variety of ways, and it is worth noting to what use conclusions are put. Here it might be that as this is a theoretical model in a Working Papers series, the conventions which are adopted in other areas are seen not to apply.

REFLECTING ON THE READING

Perhaps the most fruitful way to reflect initially on the reading is to think to what extent you find Hall's argument convincing. Do you agree that the activity of 'decoding' is as important as 'encoding'? Do you see that both of these activities take place within institutional and social structures which help define, and limit them? In that sense, how convinced are you by Hall's – and cultural studies' – assertion that all moments of communication can be examined for their political implications, especially related to social power? As noted in the introduction, this work supports the wealth of audience studies which followed it, and helped move cultural studies and media studies away from the approach that traditionally dominated film studies and literature studies, which sees the practitioner and the text as the most important aspects of intellectual enquiry and which in film studies has been called 'auteur theory' (Grant 2008). You might, then, want to relate this reading to that on 'Audiences' in this book (Chapter 23), as well as to other readings on that subject that you might have carried out in your studies.

Perhaps the most fruitful way to do this is to think about the times you have disagreed with someone else over the meaning of a film, or television programme, or some other media text. Perhaps you saw a murder mystery drama but couldn't work out what had happened at the end; perhaps you watched a horror film and one of you was scared but the other wasn't; perhaps you saw a comedy which included jokes that one of you found offensive but the other didn't. Hall would argue that these examples show that you each decoded the film in a slightly different way, and this demonstrates the validity in examining audience responses to texts. But you might also want to think *to what extent* your readings were different. Presumably readings are not so different for films: when what one of you thought was a horror film, the other thought was a comedy, for example. This might demonstrate the aspect of encoding. In all, thinking about differences in readings is a good way to think about applying this model; but be careful not to overstate such differences, because exploring similarities is meaningful too.

You could also reflect on the ways in which Hall constructs his argument, especially considering the defiantly theoretical approach he adopts. As has been noted throughout, very little evidence is offered for many of Hall's assertions, but this is an acceptable method of working within such theorising. His arguments may seem unfounded when we're used to constantly being asked for, and being presented with, evidence. What kind of study would you suggest might be the best way of testing this model? As the Centre was so interested in exploring 'ordinary' people, how would you go about doing this? What popular media texts do you think should be researched, and why? And what might thinking about those texts tell us about issues of power within society?

Finally, it is hoped you can see a value in presenting a model as Hall does here, especially as it led on to a wealth of empirical studies which applied, tested, and developed his arguments. In doing so, it is hoped you have developed a confidence and ease with which to make sense of such models, and to feel comfortable with theory as theory.

Key terms to explore

discourse; syntagmatic chain; polysemic; hegemony.

Key writers who are mentioned

Karl Marx; Philip Elliott; George Gerbner; Charles S. Peirce; Umberto Eco; Valentin Vološinov; Roland Barthes; P. Terni.

RECOMMENDED READING

Hall, S., Hobson, D., Lowe, A., and Willis, P. (eds) (1980) *Culture, Media, Language: Working papers in cultural studies, 1972–9*, London: Hutchinson.

Highly influential collection of major papers written at CCCS; not the easiest of reads, but clearly demonstrates the Centre's key objectives and interests.

Morley, David (1980) *The 'Nationwide' Audience*, London: British Film Institute.

Classic study of television audiences, with approaches and method influenced by Hall's encoding/decoding model; fascinating findings.

Turner, Graeme (2003) *British Cultural Studies*, 3rd edition, London and New York: Routledge.

Overview of the history and development of British cultural studies, showing how CCCS responded to previous theories and influenced subsequent ones.

PART III

Approaches to media theory

CHAPTER 12

Political economy

Herman, E.S. (1995a) 'Media in the U.S. political economy', in Downing, J., Mohammadi, A. and Sreberny-Mohammadi, A. (eds) *Questioning the Media: A critical introduction*, 2nd edition. London: Sage, pp. 77–93.

INTRODUCTION TO POLITICAL ECONOMY

It may not be immediately evident what constitutes a political economic analysis, and what such an approach offers to the study of media, culture and communication. Nevertheless, the relevance and value of a political economy perspective soon becomes apparent when reflecting on a number of media-related controversies that occurred during the first few months of 2007. Two events in particular caught the attention of the mainstream media. They also generated a great deal of activity in cyberspace.

Celebrity Big Brother (Channel 4, 2007) resulted in allegations of racist bullying, attracted numerous complaints by viewers to Ofcom (the UK communications regulator), led to the withdrawal of one programme sponsor (The Carphone Warehouse), generated concerns about the high cost of voting via 'premium' phone lines, and prompted questions by politicians, policymakers and industry players about whether a public service broadcaster such as Channel 4 should be involved in such programming. However, there was much hand-rubbing and 'high fiving' by Endemol UK who made the programme, as the international publicity generated by the controversy helped launch the 'brand' into new overseas markets, such as India (see Hobson 2010: 184–5 for an overview of this event).

During the same period, there was a similar but less frenzied and more localised debate in the media about a public disagreement between Virgin Media (incorporating NTL, the cable company) and BSkyB over the latter's investment in ITV. Virgin's Richard Branson saw this as a 'threat to democracy', as News Corporation (owners of BSkyB) already had a significant share of the newspaper market in the United Kingdom.

If we are interested in trying to understand and explain why these events occurred, how they might best be resolved and why they attracted media attention, political economy theorists would argue that we need to go beyond a focus solely on audiences in their role as either consumer or citizen, beyond an isolated study of the texts in question, and also beyond the production of those texts. In other words, our enquiry would need to consider the wider political and economic context, as the above events reflect four major trends that have occurred at both national and international levels over recent years (Hamelink, cited in Boyd-Barrett 1995c: 191).

First, both events remind us about the mergers and takeovers of media companies which have led to the creation of large media conglomerations. Secondly, these events serve as a reminder that some of these organisations (for example, News Corporation) have expanded their operations throughout the world, hence the term *transnational* conglomerate. Thirdly, the above events reflect a gradual shift in society that has led to the 'market', rather than 'public service', as the preferred way of delivering goods and services – including an increasing array of 'cultural' products. This, in turn, has resulted in governments reducing rules and regulations, a process referred to as deregulation, co-regulation or re-regulation. Fourthly, the above events vividly illustrate how digitisation and interactivity have helped transform when, how, where and why we access and consume cultural products. These changes, and particularly the move towards technological convergence, have provided the rationale for a single communications regulatory body in the United Kingdom, Ofcom, which has replaced the previous sector-specific regulators.

Such an analysis draws attention to four key features of a political economic approach to the study of media, culture and communications (Golding and Murdock 2000: 72–4). The first requires that the media are studied holistically. In other words, the economy is not seen as a separate domain, but is interrelated with social, cultural and political life. The second requires a historical perspective, noting changes over a period of time in, for example, the growth of the media, the extended reach of media corporations, the increasing commodification of social and cultural life, evidenced by the ongoing costs of the hardware and software required to participate in an 'information society', and the changing role of the state (see Chapter 20 on the information society). The third involves a concern about 'the balance between capitalist enterprise and public intervention', illustrated in recent years by the privatisation of previously publicly owned and operated public services, and more recently by the pressure to restrict the growth of public service broadcasters such as the BBC. The fourth involves a commitment to moral philosophy, requiring attention to concerns about 'justice, equity and the public good'.

It is this latter concern about ethics and values that differentiates political economy from mainstream economics (Hesmondhalgh 2002: 30–1), and a further distinction can be made between *critical* and *classical* political economy (Golding and Murdock 2000: 72, 76; Williams 2003: 94). Critical political economy is concerned primarily with *power* and how it is constituted and executed, unlike classical political economy where the emphasis is on exchange, consumer choice and freedom – ideas that are echoed by those favouring market-based mechanisms. Critical political economy also aims to illuminate the constraints that shape the lives of 'ordinary' people, and to point out the implications where there is an unequal access to resources. It also recognises the limitations of the 'free' market and argues for public intervention – via government – to 'correct' the resultant deficiencies.

Critical political economy emerged in the 1960s and 1970s in response to the growth and expansion of media industries, whose research budgets were invested in a wide range of projects, which ranged from 'how to produce radio and television receivers to how to sell products to mass audiences' (Mosco 1996: 12). The turn towards critical political economy, which draws on a Marxian framework (Williams 2003: 75–8), was seen as a rejection of two of the dominant research approaches used in the 1950s. One encompassed media effects studies (see Chapter 14), which centred on individuals (Boyd-Barrett 1995c: 189). The other was the 'culturalist tradition' (see Chapters 11 and 17), which focused on texts (Garnham 1979: 119).

However, the interests of those adopting a critical political economy approach are varied. In the United Kingdom, critical political economy has tended to centre on the 'liberalization, commercialization and privatization of the communication industries', and the close relationships forged between major media players and policy bodies (Murdock and Golding 1973; Mosco 1996: 19). Critical political economy in the developing world, or 'Third World', has challenged earlier 'modernization theory' which asserted that the import of media forms and communications technologies into developing countries would bring about progressive economic, social and cultural modernisation (see, for example, Hamelink 1995; Mosco 1996: 19; Thussu 2006: 46).

In North America, critical political economy has examined the growth – and power and influence – of transnational media conglomerates, and involved researchers working actively with trade unions and citizen groups with the aim of introducing alternatives to the dominant media (Mosco 1996: 19). In *The Media Monopoly*, Bagdikian identifies a limited number of companies that dominated the American media, suggesting that they had the power to set agendas and, thereby, dictate what Americans should be thinking about (1992: xxxi).

It is from this latter tradition that the reading in this chapter is drawn. However, as you read it, bear in mind what has been suggested as the main limitation of a critical political economy approach. That is, it is criticised for 'placing too much stress on production at the expense of the consumption process and proffering an erroneous image of the viewer, reader and listener as a passive dupe' (Williams 2003: 95).

INTRODUCTION TO THE READING

The selected reading is taken from an edited volume published in 1995. The three editors, John Downing, Annabelle Sreberny-Mohammadi and Ali Mohammadi, as well as being jointly responsible for the editorial comment, each have a chapter in the volume which reflects their own academic backgrounds and research interests.

The volume includes a selection of contributions that span a diverse range of critical perspectives on media studies, hence its title, *Questioning the Media: A critical introduction*. The contributions are organised under five main subheadings, with the selected reading for this chapter appearing in a subsection headed, 'Media, power and control'. This highlights two key concerns, 'power' and 'control', that are a focus of political economic analysis.

The title of this reading, 'Media in the U.S. political economy', gives a clear indication about its geographic focus and theoretical perspective. This author, Edward Herman, is Professor Emeritus of the Annenberg School for Communication and of the Wharton School of Finance, University of Pennsylvania. He is the author of number of articles and books including, amongst others, *Corporate Control, Corporate Power* (1981), *The Real Terror Network: Terrorism in fact and propaganda* (1982), *Triumph of the Market: Essays on politics, economics and the media* (1995b). However, Herman is best known for his work on the 'propaganda model', which is the subject of the selected reading.

The origins of this reading need to be recognised. Essentially, it is a brief summary of the opening chapter of an expansive – and some would say iconic – book that was first published in 1988, and which continues to be controversial because its central thesis contends that the mass media are propagandist. Entitled, *Manufacturing Consent: The political economy of the mass media*, it was written by Edward Herman and Noam Chomsky, the latter also a respected academic and activist whose publications, amongst others, include, *Towards a New Cold War* (1982), *The Chomsky Reader* (1987), *Deterring Democracy* (1991) and *On Nature and Language* (2002), and who is Institute Professor, Department of Linguistics and Philosophy, at the Massachusetts Institute of Technology.

The reading has a clear and logical structure. There are three main sections, and a brief final section incorporates the conclusions. The first section, 'Three alternative perspectives', identifies three different ways of explaining the workings of the mass media in the USA. Essentially, the author quickly exposes the limitations of two of these perspectives and then moves on to argue that the third perspective, the propaganda model, is a far better way of illustrating the power and influence of the mass media. The second main section, 'The political-economic filters of mass media messages', outlines the five filters which, in combination, comprise the propaganda model. As the reading focuses on the news media in the USA, the data and examples used to support or illustrate the arguments relate to that country. The author uses the third section, 'Propaganda campaigns and the mass media', to illustrate the role of the political economic filters in a number of propaganda campaigns, all involving the USA. The conclusions are brief and flow from the earlier analysis.

While Herman and Chomsky are acknowledged as developing the propaganda model, they do recognise earlier work conducted on propaganda such as that by Walter Lippmann in, for example, *Public Opinion* (1965 [1922]). Sociologists use 'model' in a variety of ways, sometimes as a synonym for theory, but in most instances to aid conceptualisation, explanation and to simplify the phenomena being studied.

Having noted the titles of the author's previous publications and also those of Chomsky, you are correct in anticipating a reading that is persuasively argued and unambiguous in its meaning and intention. However, it is important that you reflect critically on the arguments being made and the evidence used to support them. Equally, while the reading focuses on mass media in the United States, you might want to consider whether the propaganda model, as outlined in this reading, could have relevance in other contexts.

READING

1

Edward Herman

Media in the U.S. Political Economy

Three Alternative Perspectives

It is widely agreed among media analysts that the mass media play an important role in the political economy of the United States, managing the flow of entertainment, news, and political opinion. But there is sharp disagreement on the nature and character of media influence and on the degree to which they are an independent force or merely reflect and transmit the views of other important power interests in the country. For example, there is a neoconservative school that points its finger at the centralization of the media in a top tier of "East Coast Establishment" newspapers and television networks, and also at the elevated status of star journalists and TV interviewers—their high salaries, their alleged power, liberal background, and bias. In this view, the very high status of the media stars and their ability to command large audiences gives the liberal culture considerable freedom of action in the mass media. Its representatives are therefore said to be able to push views hostile to business and the government's foreign policy and at odds with the majority attitudes of the working class and middle America (Lichter, Rothman, & Lichter, 1986).

2

Representatives of the liberal/"gatekeeper" and propaganda analyses (discussed below) deny both that the stars can do as they like and that the mass media have any kind of bias against the status quo. They stress three types of evidence against the neoconservative view: the checks built into the way media operate, how unlikely it is that institutions so firmly embedded in the corporate government world could display systematic antiestablishment bias, and the evidence of actual media output. Both consider the neoconservatives to be speaking for just one wing of opinion inside the national power structure, attacking representatives of the liberal wing of elite opinion as though its members were dangerous enemies of the American way of life.

The most prominent analyses in the United States of how the media came to be as they are come from liberal newsroom and "gatekeeper" studies, as exemplified by the works of Leon Sigal (1973), Edward J. Epstein (1973), Gaye Tuchman (1978), Herbert Gans (1979), and Todd Gitlin (1983). Although there are differences among them, they all focus on journalists and media organizations rather than on the system at large or government and major advertisers. These latter are brought into the picture only as sources, pressure groups, regulators, or commercial clients. "Gatekeeper" researchers interview media personnel and watch them working to see how they decide on output, with little emphasis on examining and comparing actual outputs and their results. They stress how practical organizational needs shape news media choices directly or indirectly. Let us explore this view a little further.

NOTES

1   Writing Style

Note how Herman opens with a statement about which he claims there is wide agreement and follows it with another about which he asserts there would be 'sharp disagreement'. This is a neat way of beginning the reading as it then allows Herman to go on – as he does – to unravel why there is disagreement, who is disagreeing, and on what basis.

You may also have noticed that he does not cite any references, which allow us, the readers, to know who, for example, these 'media analysts' are. Also, note how the use of 'widely agreed' in the opening sentence alludes to the possibility of disagreement without having to provide detailed explanation.

Context

If we were to insert, say, the United Kingdom, or Ireland or South Africa in place of the United States, would each of the first two sentences still make sense?

In the second part of this first paragraph we are reminded again about the societal and cultural context of the reading – and given fairly strong hints about Herman's position on certain matters by the use of particular words and phrases.

What do you understand by terms such as 'a neoconservative school', 'liberal background' and 'bias'? In what ways are these arguments and the terminology being used similar and different to what we experience in the United Kingdom?

2   Content

Having identified a neoconservative view of the mass media, Herman now begins the process of countering this perspective. He does this by setting out three arguments which would find favour with critics of the neoconservative position. Why does he describe one alternative perspective as 'liberal "gatekeeper"'? Although Herman goes on to discuss this perspective in more detail, you might want to consider what is meant by 'gatekeeper' in this instance.

Writing Style

Note how Herman refers to the use of 'evidence' as a way of establishing a case to undermine the neoconservative position. This prompts questions about what would constitute evidence, and how it could be compiled and presented. Note how Herman 'joins' with us, the readers, in the final sentence. Is this an appropriate or useful technique?

Context

In the second paragraph Herman lists a number of references, the most recent of which is from 1983, which are described as 'liberal newsroom and "gatekeeper" studies'. While he recognises that there are differences between these studies, no details are provided. Herman goes on to indicate how this research is carried out and why, in his view, it has limitations. In doing so, he

READING

3

News organizations seek sources of authoritative and credible news on a regular basis. These requirements are interconnected: If a highly placed person makes some statement, this is newsworthy in itself. The more authoritative and credible the source, the easier it is to accept statements without checking, and the less expensive is news making. Hence the paradox that even if untrue, such statements may be broadcast without commentary, as "objective" news.

The most highly placed news source is, of course, the government. An oft-cited statistic, based on Leon Sigal's (1973) examination of 2,850 stories in the *New York Times* and *Washington Post*, is that 46% of the stories originated with U.S. federal government officials or agencies and 78% with government officials in general, domestic or foreign. Second only to the government as a news source is business, which also showers the media with a vast array of press releases from individual firms, trade associations, and public relations offshoots.

It is also the case that internal media rules and professional codes help powerful board members or media owners not to have to intervene all the time in editorial decisions. For the most part, journalists reproduce the standard choices of the powerful by a process of self-censorship (see Rodríguez, Chapter 8). Those on the lower rungs of the news ladder need to be alert to the news values at the top in order to produce acceptable copy.

Newsroom gatekeeper studies have added a great deal to the understanding of media processes. Nevertheless, they focus too heavily on organizational criteria of choice, often illustrated by struggles within the media as told by media personnel. They suffer from a lack of theory and measurement of actual media output. As a result, they tend to exaggerate the potential media professionals have for dissent and "space," and to neglect how the usual news choices reinforce the status quo.

4

A third way of looking at the workings of the mass media stresses their role as part of the national power structure. This approach, which will be examined below, shares a number of features with gatekeeper analyses, but pulls the threads together into an integrated whole and gives more attention to the real interplay between the media and their sources, and to the purposes and effects of news choices and propaganda campaigns. I will call it the *propaganda* model.

2

(continued)

provides us with clues about the scope of the third – and his preferred – perspective, the propaganda model.

As a way of trying to anticipate later arguments by Herman, what do you see as the main limitations of this second perspective?

3 ## Content

In this section Herman elaborates on his critique of the liberal/'gatekeeper' perspective. Data compiled during the 1970s is used to suggest that government and business are both the main subjects and the main source of news stories. However, the point being made is that the news media's insatiable appetite for authoritative and credible stories can lead to misleading or untruthful reports.

The next matter to be considered is the oft-heard view that media owners interfere in the daily operation of their media businesses. Essentially, the argument being made is that such intervention is unnecessary because journalists self-censor. The reason given for this is that they are aware of the preferred 'news values' of senior managers and act accordingly.

First, how do you react to the view that government and business are, in effect, subsidising the media, and that they may also be acting deceitfully? Secondly, how useful is this idea of self-censorship, and what do you understand by the view that 'the usual news sources reinforce the status quo'?

Context

You may want to look at Bob Franklin's *Packaging Politics* (2004) for a more recent discussion about government spending on communications, and at Stuart Allan's *News Culture* (1999) for a discussion on news values.

Structure

Note how Herman usefully summarises his critique of the newsroom liberal/'gatekeeper' studies before introducing a third way of understanding the workings of the mass media.

4 ## Content

Having disentangled and exposed the limitations of the neoconservative and liberal/'gatekeeper' analyses, Herman uses this final paragraph to suggest the propaganda model as a more holistic way of analysing and understanding the role and power of the mass media. Before proceeding, you might want to consider what you understand by 'propaganda', the contexts in which it tends to be used, who would be most likely to use it and why?

Has Herman's analysis persuaded you of the failings of the first two perspectives? If so, how has this been achieved? If not, what else could he have done to be more persuasive?

READING

5

The Political-Economic Filters of Mass Media Messages

The basic proposition of this chapter is as follows. In a system of concentrated wealth and power, the inequality in command of resources inevitably affects access to, and the performance of, a private media system. Money and power will penetrate the media by direct control or indirect influence, and will filter out the news thought unfit for most of us to consider. We may trace out this filtering process through the following:

1. the size, concentrated ownership, owner wealth, and profit orientation of the dominant mass media firms
2. advertising as the primary income source of the mass media
3. the dependence of the media on information provided by government, business, and "experts" funded and approved by these primary sources
4. "flak" as a means of disciplining the media
5. "anticommunism" as a national secular religion and ideological control mechanism

These elements interact with and reinforce one another. They fix the boundaries of media discourse and the definition of what is newsworthy, and they explain the origins and operations of propaganda campaigns.

6

SIZE AND OWNERSHIP OF THE MASS MEDIA: THE FIRST FILTER

By 1850, improvements in technology and the drive to communicate with a mass audience that could be "sold" to advertisers had developed newspaper technology to a level that made entry into the business very difficult without substantial financial resources. Thus the first filter—the very large investment needed to own a major newspaper or other mass medium—was already in force over a century ago and has become increasingly effective since. In 1987 there were some 1,500 daily newspapers, 11,000 magazines, 10,000 radio and 1,500 TV stations, 2,400 book publishers, and 7 movie studios in the United States—some 25,000 media entities in all. But most of the news dispensers among this set were small and depended on the national media and wire services for all but very local news. Many more were part of multimedia chains.

In 1983, Ben Bagdikian reported in his book *The Media Monopoly* that by the beginning of the 1980s most U.S. mass media—newspapers, magazines, radio, television, books, and movies—were controlled by 50 corporations (pp. 4–5). Four years later, in his 1987 revision of the book, Bagdikian observed that 29 corporations now accounted for the same majority fraction as the 50 largest had controlled shortly before (p. xvi). These giants are also diversified into other fields, including insurance, banking, advertising, frozen foods, tobacco, weapons production, and nuclear energy.

↓

NOTES

5   Structure

Note how this reading relies on clearly defined sections which are delineated with bold subheadings. You might want to consider the strengths and limitations of this approach. Also, is it helpful to begin this section by summarising the reading's 'basic proposition'?

Context

You may have noticed that 'media messages', in this instance, appear to refer to news alone, and does not include other types of informational or entertainment programming.

Content

Although an explanation of each 'filter' follows, you might find it helpful at this point to ponder briefly on their scope and meaning. If there are words or ideas that you are unsure about, try the dictionary, thesaurus and/or Google. For example, it would be helpful if you had some understanding of what is meant by 'flak' before encountering its use in this context.

6   Content

In making the case for the first of these five filters, Herman demonstrates his political economy credentials. He does so by using a historical perspective to help us understand how, and why, in the contemporary period we have a number of transnational media conglomerates. 'Evidence', in the form of examples and figures, is used to support the argument, although only one reference (Bagdikian 1983) is cited. Would it have been helpful if Herman had listed all the sources that enabled him to present this barrage of figures?

You might want to undertake your own research on the size and reach of current transnational media conglomerates, in order to assess the extent to which the trends identified here have continued (see, for example, Thussu 2006).

In the fourth paragraph of this section Herman turns his attention to another concern of political economists, that of regulation, arguing that the power and profit interests of major media companies have brought about a loosening of rules and regulations. This is facilitated by media executives mixing in the same business and social circles as members of the corporate community and, inevitably, of some politicians. The author makes reference to the Federal Communications Commission (FCC), which is the US equivalent of Ofcom, the UK communications regulator.

READING

(continued)

The dominant media companies are large, profit-seeking corporations, owned and controlled by very wealthy boards and individuals. Many are run completely as moneymaking concerns, and for the others as well there are powerful pressures from stockholders, directors, and bankers to focus on the bottom line. These pressures intensified over the 1980s as media stocks became stock market favorites and actual or prospective owners of media properties were able to generate great wealth from increased audience size and advertising revenues (e.g., Rupert Murdoch, Time Warner, and many others). This encouraged the entry of speculators and takeovers, and increased the pressure and temptation to focus more intensively on profitability.

These trends accelerated when the rules were loosened limiting media monopolies, cross-ownership of media in the same area of the country, the number of TV and radio stations the networks could own, and media control by nonmedia companies (e.g., ABC, CBS, NBC). The Federal Communications Commission also abandoned many of its restrictions—which were not very strict anyway—on broadcast commercials, TV violence, and the "Fairness Doctrine" (which supported equal broadcasting time for opposing views), opening the door to purely moneymaking dictates over the use of the airwaves.

Those who control the media giants come into close relation with the corporate community through joint membership on boards of directors and business relations with commercial and investment bankers. These are their sources of credit, who help with banking services and advise both on opportunities to buy media firms and on takeover threats from other firms. Banks and similar "institutional" investors are also large owners of media stock. These holdings, individually and collectively, do not convey control on a daily basis, but if managers fail to pursue actions that favor shareholder returns, institutional investors will be inclined to sell the stock (depressing its price) or to listen sympathetically to outsiders contemplating takeovers.

These investors constitute a force that helps to integrate media companies into market strategies and away from responsibility to the democratic process. The large media companies have also diversified beyond the media field, and nonmedia companies have established a strong presence in the mass media. The most important cases of the latter are GE (General Electric), which owns the NBC network, and Westinghouse, which owns major TV broadcasting stations, a cable network, and a radio station network. GE and Westinghouse are both huge, diversified, multinational companies heavily involved in the controversial areas of weapons production and nuclear power.

NOTES

Context

(continued)

To assess the validity of the views expressed here, you may want to use the internet to check out the names and professional backgrounds of the senior executives and board members of these regulatory bodies, noting the rationale for their appointment, how they were appointed and by whom. It is also interesting to track what jobs they move on to after finishing their association with the regulatory body.

You may also want to check out the extent to which regulatory changes in one country are then taken up by others. For example, the United Kingdom had separate regulators for radio, television and telecommunications before the introduction of Ofcom in 2003. Was the FCC in the United States the model for Ofcom?

Context

These two paragraphs highlight a further trend that is now well established and which is sometimes referred to as 'horizontal integration'. This term has been coined because media (and other large businesses) have increasingly moved into other industrial sectors through mergers and takeovers. As a result, the financial interests of media and other large corporations are not always immediately evident to the viewer, reader or listener.

For example, when Rupert Murdoch's News Corporation bought MySpace in July 2005 it was perhaps not evident to the site's users who the new owner was. News Corporation sold MySpace in 2011; do you know who owns it now, and does it matter?

READING

8

Another structural relationship of importance is the media companies' dependence on and ties with government. Apart from the issues raised in Chapters 6 and 7 of this volume, the major media also depend on the government for more general policy support. All business firms are interested in taxes, interest rates, labor policies, and the level of enforcement of the antitrust (anti-business monopoly) laws.

Thus during the 1980s the systematic reduction of business taxes, weakening of labor unions, and relaxation of antitrust law enforcement benefited media corporations as well as other members of the business community. GE and Westinghouse depend on the government to subsidize their expensive research and development of nuclear power and defense. *Reader's Digest, Time, Newsweek*, and movie and TV syndication sellers also depend on diplomatic support for their rights to penetrate foreign cultures with U.S. commercial and cultural messages. The media giants, advertising agencies, and great multinational corporations have a close interest in a favorable climate of investment in the Third World, and their relationships with the government in these policies are intimate.

9

THE ADVERTISING LICENSE TO DO BUSINESS: THE SECOND FILTER

Newspapers obtain about 75% of their revenues from advertisers, general-circulation magazines about 50%, and broadcasters almost 100%. Before advertising became prominent, the price of a newspaper had to cover the costs of doing business. With the growth of advertising, papers that attracted ads could sell copies well below production costs. Papers without advertising faced a serious dilemma: to raise their prices or to have less surplus to invest in making the paper more salable (features, attractive format, promotion). An advertising-based media system will tend to drive out of existence or into marginality the media companies that depend on selling price alone. With advertising, the free market does not yield a neutral system in which the consumers decide which media will suit them best. The advertisers' choices heavily influence media prosperity—and survival (Barnouw, 1978).

8 ## Content

The final two paragraphs highlight another key area of interest in any political economic analysis: that is, the 'structural relationship' between large media corporations and governments – at home and abroad. As Herman makes clear, media companies are dependent for their success on governments creating a favourable business climate to ensure growth and profitability, and they are also reliant on governments for assistance in 'penetrat[ing] foreign cultures'.

Context

For a clear and informative account of the relationship between the US government and that country's communications industry see, for example, Herb Schiller (1998).

9 ## Writing Style

Here is another illustration of why we should always look carefully at titles and subtitles. Authors often invest a great deal of time in constructing such headings. So, before examining the content of this section, you might want to consider the meaning of this subheading, and in particular how 'license' is used.

Content

The key point being made in this first paragraph is that advertisers and advertising influence the prosperity and survival of media organisations and media forms. Note, again, that Herman uses a brief historical overview to illustrate how the introduction of advertising impacted on newspapers.

Thinking particularly about newspapers and magazines, how do you respond to the idea that it is advertisers, as much as, or rather than, consumers, that influence the success of these media?

READING

10

Since the introduction of press advertising, working-class and radical papers have constantly been at a serious disadvantage, as their readers have tended to be of modest means, a factor that has always reduced advertiser interest in media they patronized. Working-class and radical media also suffer from more overt political discrimination by advertisers, as many firms refuse to patronize media they perceive as damaging to their interests. Advertisers also select among specific broadcasts on the basis of criteria that are culturally and politically conservative. Advertisers on national television are for the most part very large corporations, such as Philip Morris, Procter & Gamble, General Motors, Sears, and RJR Nabisco. These advertisers will rarely sponsor programs that seriously criticize sensitive corporate activities, such as ecological degradation, the workings of the military-industrial complex, or corporate support of and benefits from Third World tyrannies.

As advertising spots increase in price, broadcasters lose even more money on programs if advertisers shun them. For instance, ABC Television's once-in-a-blue-moon feature on the impact of nuclear war on the United States, *The Day After* (1983), had almost all advertisers canceling their options on spots during or around the program. So as the broadcasters come under (a) more pressure to behave as profit makers and (b) less pressure from the FCC to operate a public service, there is a strong tendency for them to eliminate programming that has significant public affairs content.

10 Content

Following the argument set out in the preceding paragraph, Herman asserts that working class and radical media, primarily newspapers, have experienced substantial disadvantages since the introduction of advertising. Similar arguments are made for television. While Herman is referring to the USA, you might want to consider whether a similar case could be made in respect of the press and commercial television in the United Kingdom.

In doing so, this will prompt questions about the impact of advertising on channels with a public service broadcasting remit, and whether organisations such as the BBC provide adequate space for the 'voices' marginalised by commercial media. Also, can you identify any working-class or radical media operating in the United Kingdom today? What is it, exactly, that makes them radical?

Context

Even though this reading was published in 1995, the points raised in this final paragraph are pertinent today in the United Kingdom. For example, the term 'dumbing-down' has been used by campaigning groups to describe a situation where there appears to have been a decline in public-service type programming. Also, as with the FCC in the USA, Ofcom is similarly accused of allowing such developments in the United Kingdom. Websites such as that of the Campaign for Press and Broadcasting Freedom, and Public Voice track such developments.

It was inevitable that a more commercialised and multichannel environment would impact on public service broadcasters such as the BBC. You may wish to consider the extent to which public service broadcasters (or publicly funded content) can provide a counter to this second filter.

READING

11

SOURCING MASS MEDIA NEWS: THE THIRD FILTER

The mass media are drawn into an intimate relationship with the power structure, national and local, because of cost factors and mutual interests. Cost savings dictate that the media concentrate their reporters where significant news often occurs, where important rumors and leaks abound, and where regular press conferences are held. The White House, Pentagon, and State Department in Washington, D.C., and, on a local basis, city hall and the police department, are the subject of regular news "beats" for reporters. Business corporations and trade groups are also regular suppliers of stories deemed newsworthy. These organizations turn out a large volume of material that meets the demands of news organizations for reliable, scheduled input.

Government and corporate sources also have the credibility associated with their status. Partly to maintain the image of objectivity, but also to protect themselves from criticisms of bias and the increasingly serious threat of libel suits, the media need news that can be portrayed as accurate. Information from sources that may be presumed credible also reduces investigative expense, whereas material from sources that are not seemingly credible, or that will elicit criticism and threats, requires careful and costly checking.

Thus when President Reagan asserted in March 1986 that the Nicaraguan government was heavily involved in drug smuggling, this was immediately published without checking. (It was a false statement.) On the other hand, a steady stream of claims by imprisoned drug traders and even by U.S. intelligence and Drug Enforcement Administration personnel that the U.S.-backed Nicaraguan Contras were smuggling drugs into the United States, with official connivance (L. Cockburn, 1988), was treated much more cautiously, was held to require stringent checking, and received little media coverage (even though, in this case, the claims were true).

12

The information operations of the powerful government and corporate bureaucracies that constitute primary news sources are vast and skillful. They have special and unequal access to the media. Because they supply news, have continuous contact with the reporter on the beat, and can freeze reporters out of news stories if they are uncooperative, the powerful can use personal relationships, threats, and rewards to influence and coerce media personnel.

Perhaps more important, powerful sources regularly take advantage of reporters' routines and need for copy to "manage" the media, to manipulate them into following the agenda of one vector or another in the power structure. Part of this management process consists of showering the media with stories that serve to reinforce a particular framework by which to interpret events.

11   Writing Style

Before considering the arguments used to support this third filter, note again how Herman has selected a key – and appropriately suggestive – word, 'sourcing', for the subheading.

Content

Herman argues that sourcing occurs, or is enabled, as a result of three factors. The first, hinted at earlier, is due to 'cost factors and mutual interests'. In other words, to keep costs down, resources are directed at the people and places where scoops and stories are most likely to emerge: that is, members or representatives of government, state departments and business corporations. The second aspect here is that as stories need to be credible, for the reasons noted by Herman, and as sources such as these are expected to provide the required quality, cost savings occur as checking is deemed unnecessary. Herman then provides examples that expose the flaws in such assumptions. Can you think of other more recent examples?

How persuasive is the argument that the media are 'drawn into an intimate relationship with the power structure'?

12   Content

The second argument in support of this third filter rests on the vast array of 'information professionals', otherwise known as public relations personnel or 'spin doctors', which governments and big corporations have at their disposal (see, for example, Bakir and Barlow 2007; Franklin 2004). As a result, the power to grant, or deny, journalists access to stories is seen as a means of managing, or manipulating, the media agenda. This is further assisted by the informational power that can be used – through press releases, briefings and 'off the record' interviews – to 'push' certain agendas or influence the way in which particular events are reported. What points could be made to counter this argument?

READING

13

The relation between power and sourcing extends beyond providing continuing "news" to molding the supply of "experts." Official sources could be threatened by highly respectable alternative sources that offer dissident views with obvious knowledge. Energetic attempts are made to reduce this problem by "co-opting the experts" (that is, finding like-minded specialists, paying them as consultants, funding their research, and organizing think tanks that will hire them and help to publish their findings).

During the 1970s and early 1980s, a string of institutions were created and old ones were reactivated in order to propagandize the corporate viewpoint. Among the most important of these institutions were the Heritage Foundation, the American Enterprise Institute, and the Georgetown Center for Strategic and International Studies. Many hundreds of intellectuals were brought to these institutions, and their work was funded and disseminated to the media in a sophisticated program that can reasonably be defined as a propaganda effort.

14

FLAK AND THE ENFORCERS: THE FOURTH FILTER

Flak here refers to negative responses to media statements or programs. It may take the form of letters to the media, telegrams, phone calls, petitions, lawsuits, speeches and bills before Congress, or other modes of complaint, threat, and punitive action. It may be organized centrally or locally, or it may consist of the entirely independent actions of individuals. For example, individuals may call in or write to protest the showing of a movie they regard as sacrilegious or subversive; or the gun lobby may mobilize its members to complain about a program that points up the hazards of private gun ownership.

If flak is produced on a large scale, it can be both uncomfortable and costly to the media. Positions have to be defended within the organization and without, sometimes before legislatures and possibly even in court. Advertisers may withdraw patronage. TV advertising is mainly of consumer goods that are readily subject to organized boycott. During the McCarthy years in the early 1950s (see below as well as Downing, Chapter 14), many advertisers and

↓

NOTES

13 Content

The third and final dimension of the sourcing filter is enabled by two means, both of which involve the 'power structure' in 'moulding' – or colloquially, buying off – key sources of information. The first way in which this occurs is by funding the 'experts' in the expectation that research or consultancy findings will concur with the views of those commissioning such work. The second way in which this 'moulding' occurs is when industrial sectors, or politically aligned organisations, establish, or sponsor, research institutes, industry bodies, or policy 'think tanks' with the aim of influencing government policy.

Context

The co-opting of pliable 'experts' only ever becomes evident to the general public on those rare occasions when it emerges that a favourable report on a particular industry, for example, gambling, has been produced by a researcher who has benefited – or is likely to benefit – financially or otherwise from that industry.

Writing Style

In relation to the co-opting of experts, Herman does not provide any specific examples. He does though provide some details of institutions in the USA that were set up to support corporate viewpoints. However, no references are provided which allow us, the reader, to follow up on the examples that are provided. Neither is there any explanation on exactly how these institutions influenced – or attempted to influence – government policy. The provision of more information and examples would have been helpful.

How persuasive, overall, is the case being made for this third filter?

14 Writing Style

Yet another dramatic subheading which reminds us how the 'original' meaning of words (and phrases) can be co-opted for use in an entirely different context. In this instance, make sure that you have an idea about the formal meaning of 'flak', and 'enforcers', before reading on. Note how Herman first defines 'flak', then explains its impact on media organisations, and finally considers the relationship to power.

Content

In this context, flak is seen as adverse criticism directed at a media organisation and/or particular employees following the public airing of a programme, article, film, advertisement or statement. As Herman is writing about the USA, the examples are from that country. However, you might be able to recall recent examples of flak campaigns in the United Kingdom. He goes on to outline the potential cost – financially and in public relations terms – to the media organisation, its employees and even the programme's participants.

READING

broadcasters were coerced into silence and the blacklisting of employees by organized and determined Red hunters' threats to organize consumer boycotts. Advertisers are still concerned about possibly offending constituencies that might produce flak, and demand for "suitable" programming is a continuing feature of the media environment.

The ability to produce flak, especially costly and threatening flak, is related to power. The 1967 CBS documentary *The Selling of the Pentagon*, which focused on armed services and military contractor propaganda designed to scare the public into believing that more weapons are always needed, aroused the ire of very substantial interests, and the negative feedback was great, even including congressional hearings.

Serious flak increased in close parallel with business's increased resentment of media criticism of its activities, and the corporate offensive of the 1970s and 1980s. Along with its other political investments of those years, the corporate community sponsored the growth of institutions such as the American Legal Foundation, Capital Legal Foundation, Accuracy in Media (AIM), the Center for Media and Public Affairs, and the Media Institute. These may be regarded as institutions organized for the specific purpose of producing flak. The function of AIM, for example, is to harass the media and put pressure on them to follow the corporate agenda and a hard-line rightist foreign policy. It conditions the media to expect trouble and cost increases for violating conservative standards.

15

ANTICOMMUNISM AS A CONTROL MECHANISM: THE FIFTH FILTER

The final filter is the ideology of anticommunism. The threat of social rather than business ownership has always been the specter haunting property owners, as it threatens the very root of their class position and superior status. The Soviet (1917), Chinese (1949), and Cuban (1959) revolutions were all traumas to U.S. elites. The ongoing conflicts and well-publicized abuses of communist states contributed for decades to elevating opposition to communism to a first principle of U.S. ideology and politics.

This ideology has helped mobilize the populace against an enemy, and because the concept of "communism" is fuzzy, it can be used against anybody advocating policies threatening property interests or supportive of accommodation with communist states, or any kind of radicalism. Being labeled communist has almost always unnerved the U.S. Left and labor movement and served to slow down radical opposition movements.

Liberals, often accused of being procommunist or insufficiently anticommunist, are kept continually on the defensive in a nation where anticommunism is like a dominant unifying religion. This generally causes liberals to behave very much like conservatives. In the cases of the U.S. subversion of Guatemala (1947–1954) and the military attacks on Nicaragua (1981–1987), allegations of communist links and a communist threat caused many liberals to support CIA intervention; others lapsed into silence, paralyzed by fear of being tarred with

NOTES

14

(continued)

Herman's final point is that the ability to generate organised and targeted flak campaigns is related to power, in that it takes money and other resources to organise, prepare and disseminate such material. With that in mind, he lists a number of bodies in the USA that were established specifically for the purpose of generating flak, and also to provide advanced warnings to media organisations that violations of the status quo (or conservative standards) would attract flak.

The author makes the point that flak campaigns can be organised centrally, or locally, and can also result from the actions of individuals. How would you explain the flak targeted at Channel 4 during the 2007 edition of *Celebrity Big Brother*? What were the motivations of those generating the flak? What were the outcomes of this flak attack?

15

Structure

Herman deals with the fifth filter in four stages. The first provides a historical context for this ideology; the second illustrates how the ideology can be used to mobilise the population against perceived internal and external 'enemies'; the third considers how the ideology is used in the provision of news, while the fourth considers the currency of the ideology in the 'new world order' following the collapse of Soviet style communism.

Content

This final filter is perhaps more difficult to grasp than the earlier ones. As the subheading indicates, the ideology of anti-communism is suggested as a control mechanism on the mass media, thereby ensuring that news and information entering the public domain conforms to this ideology. Herman cites earlier communist revolutions and media coverage of 'abuses' by other communist states as the reasons why US property owners, or 'class elites', have an ever-present concern about communism (see Chapter 9 on C. Wright Mills).

Moreover, he argues that because the concept of communism is not always clearly defined or understood, it can be – and has been – used to label and, thereby, undermine the position of individuals, groups and organisations who are thought to be working against the *status quo*. The risk of being so labelled, according to the author, has spooked Liberals and those on the left of

15

(continued)

charges of disloyalty to the national religion. In the 1950s and 1960s, the FBI under J. Edgar Hoover defined support for African American civil rights as "communist," and even though this did not stop the movement, almost all felt compelled to take the charge seriously.

The anticommunist control mechanism penetrates the system to exercise a profound influence on the mass media. In normal times as well as in periods of "Red scares" (see below), issues tend to be framed in terms of a two-sided world of communist and anticommunist powers, with gains and losses allocated to one side or the other and rooting for "our side" considered entirely legitimate news practice.

It is a moot question how powerful anticommunism will be in the aftermath of the collapse of Soviet communism and disintegration of the Soviet bloc from 1989, and the retreat from communism elsewhere. It should be noted, however, that the fear of communism antedated the Russian revolution, and that inflated claims of a Red (anarchist, or communist) upheaval and "outside agitator" threat were a common characteristic of business, government, and media reactions to labor disputes in the late nineteenth century (Donner, 1990). In Latin America and in some U.S. business circles, communism has long been identified with any demands and challenges from below (Herman, 1982, pp. 33–36). The Western establishment will surely be subjected to such challenges in the "new world order," already under economic slowdown and strain, and it is possible that the traditional response will follow.

However, without a powerful and nuclear-armed Evil Empire (Reagan's term for the Soviet Union) in the wings, tying labor disputes to a foreign enemy may be more difficult, and anti-labor propaganda may have to rely more on claims of violence and the damage to the community from work stoppages. As regards foreign policy, the U.S. invasion of Panama in 1989 and the assault on Iraq in 1991 show that demonization of a noncommunist enemy and alleged threats to oil supplies and international law, and from drug dealers, with full mass media cooperation, are a highly satisfactory substitute for anticommunism for U.S. leaders (Mowlana, Gerbner & Schiller, 1992; Shalom, 1993).

NOTES

15

(continued)

United States politics, placing them on the defensive, and in some circumstances undermining their ability to be seen as credible speakers on matters of public concern.

With regard to the news media, Herman argues that they tend towards a portrayal of the world that is either communist or anti-communist, and have no hesitation in identifying whose side they are on. This is not dissimilar to the position articulated by George Bush in relation to the war in Iraq: 'You are for us or against us'. However, lest we think that the use of anti-communist ideology is only a relatively recent phenomenon, Herman reminds that it was used by business, government and the media in the late nineteenth century to undermine labour disputes.

The final paragraph directs us to consider the relevance of this fifth filter in the contemporary period. As is evident, substitutes can easily be found for anti-communism in the battle to win hearts and minds over the direction of United States foreign policy and, it is argued, with full cooperation of the mass media.

In considering the validity of this perspective, assess the view that 'the war on terror' acted as a filter in the British news media prior to and during the early stages of the second Iraq war.

READING

16

Propaganda Campaigns and the Mass Media

The five filters discussed above narrow the range of news that passes through the gates, and even more sharply limit what can become "big news," that is; sustained news campaigns rather than occasional dissident reports ("little news"). By definition, news from leading establishment sources meets one major filter requirement and is readily used by the mass media.

Dissident voices, opposition to U.S. policies from poorly funded individuals and groups, domestic and foreign, are at a disadvantage as credible sources. They do not seem "serious" in terms of the way reality is perceived by the gatekeepers or other powerful parties who influence the filtering process. The mass media and government can therefore make an event "newsworthy" merely by giving it their sustained attention. By the same token, they can make another perfectly newsworthy event a nonhappening for the bulk of the population. The government and mass media can also make a story that serves their needs into a major propaganda campaign.

Major propaganda campaigns are not spontaneous. They tend to be well timed to provide the ideological mobilization sought by important domestic power groups. The Red scare of 1919–1920 took place at a time when labor organization was very active across the country, and when big business was alarmed at the challenge to its power in the factories. Many thousands of radicals of all sorts of views were arrested, violently hauled from their homes; many were imprisoned, and a number were deported (Kennedy, 1980, pp. 278–279, 288–292). It was claimed that they were plotting to overthrow the government.

A second example of a propaganda campaign is that of Senator Joseph McCarthy and the Red scare associated with his name (McCarthyism) in the late 1940s and early 1950s (Caute, 1978). Once again, the nation was said to be under dire threat of collapse from communist subversion, including 205 supposed Soviet agents in the State Department. This campaign served well to weaken the New Deal reform coalition that had formed under the Roosevelt presidency in 1933–1945, and replaced it with a Cold War/arms race/probusiness/labor-control policy alignment.

A third example is the alleged Bulgarian/KGB involvement in the 1981 shooting of Pope John Paul II. This factually flimsy claim was transformed into a major international propaganda campaign (Herman & Brodhead, 1986). It was a period of heightened tension between the Soviet Union and the United States—and its allies, including Italy—over the placement of advanced nuclear missiles in Western Europe. Antinuclear movements were becoming extremely active in both Western Europe and the United States, and the "news" of a sinister, callous plot to assassinate the most important leader of world Christendom was a potent way to revivify the communist specter.

16   **Structure**

The reading began with a critique of the neo-conservative and liberal 'gatekeeper' perspectives. It is at this point that Herman draws on the five political economic filters of mass media messages to make the case for a third perspective, the propaganda model.

Content

Herman begins with a reminder that the mass media's requirement for 'big', rather than 'little news', and the need for a ready supply of stories from apparently credible sources can determine an event to be 'newsworthy' – whether or not this is justified – and can dismiss or marginalise other, perhaps more 'newsworthy', events. As a result, government and mass media have it in their power to transform a story into a major propaganda campaign if it serves their needs. Three examples are provided of propaganda campaigns in the United States media. Before moving on, consider the following questions.

In reflecting on the three examples provided by Herman, what role would each of the five filters have played in helping create and maintain these propaganda campaigns? What evidence could be used to (a) illustrate the role of the filters, and (b) justify the view that these were indeed propaganda campaigns? Where would you find that evidence?

READING

17

News stories in this framework are selected on a highly politicized basis. In 1984, a respected and militant supporter of Polish Solidarity, Father Popieluszko, was kidnapped in Warsaw, beaten, and murdered by a cell of the Polish secret police. This ugly event was highlighted in U.S. media: *The New York Times* ran 78 articles and 3 editorials; *Time* and *Newsweek*, combined, ran 16 articles; and CBS News broadcast 46 news items. Yet the murders, sometimes even more hideous, of 100 clergy, nuns, and other religious workers by agents of U.S. client regimes in Latin America over the period 1964–1980 attracted far less media coverage. Only 57 *New York Times* articles (no editorials), 10 *Time* and *Newsweek* articles, and 37 CBS News items were allocated to their fates, indicating that "unworthy" victims in a friendly state were valued at less than one-hundredth of "worthy" victims in a communist state, as measured by media attention.

These split standards have great ideological significance. Continued emphasis on the real and alleged misdeeds of the enemy serves to convince people to feel seriously threatened by stop-at-nothing enemies and so of the need for new weapons, even though their research and development have usually been under way for years already. The playing down and rationalization of "own side" repression in friendly client states, such as Indonesia, Zaire, and Guatemala, allow us in the United States to hold on to our self-image as citizens of a beneficent and humane government, in contrast with the image of enemy countries, whose governments assassinate leaders and repress democratic movements.

17 **Structure**

Herman uses these next two paragraphs to illustrate the power of anti-communist ideology in shaping the selective reporting by the mass media, and to reinforce an earlier point that 'rooting for "our side"' is regarded as an 'entirely legitimate news practice'.

Content

Through a content analysis of four US news outlets, Herman contrasts the reporting of violent events in two different countries. He concludes that 'worthy victims' in a communist state will receive much more coverage in the mass media than the 'unworthy victims' in states that are friends of the United States of America. Herman goes on to demonstrate the ideological importance of such reporting in respect of weapons development, a nation's self-image, and the global promotion of that image.

What are the limitations and strengths of a content analysis such as this? Also, what does Herman mean by 'worthy' and 'unworthy' victims?

The examples provided by Herman are, in one sense, timeless. For example, in the course of debates about the 'war on terror', the populace in the United States of America and the United Kingdom have been constantly reminded about the need for extra investment in security, the need to maintain leadership in weaponry, and that our values of freedom and democracy are worth fighting for.

Writing Style

Note how Herman subtly hints at his nationality when he refers to 'us'.

READING

18

The elite and the mass media, however, are not a solid monolith on all issues. Where the powerful are in disagreement with each other, the agents of power will reflect a certain diversity of tactical judgments on how to attain their shared overall aims. They will still exclude views and facts that challenge their aims.

Even when there is no internal elite dissent, there is still some slippage in the mass media, and information that tends to undermine the official line can be found, though rarely on the front page. This is one of the strengths of the U.S. system. The volume of inconvenient facts can expand, as it did during the Vietnam War in the period from 1963 to 1975, in response to the growth of a critical constituency. Even in this exceptional case, however, it was very rare for news and comment to find its way into the mass media unless it was inside the framework of established dogma (postulating benevolent U.S. aims, the United States responding to communist aggression and terror).

Apologists for U.S. policy in Southeast Asia at that time still point to "communist atrocities," periodic "pessimism" of media pundits over the war's winnability, and the debates over tactics as showing that the media were "adversarial" and even "lost" the war (Braestrup, 1977). The seeming "reasonableness" of the media process, with inconvenient facts allowed sparingly and within the official framework of assumptions, with fundamental dissent excluded altogether from "big news," and with small-scale alternative media harassed but not wiped out altogether, makes for a propaganda system far more credible and effective in putting over a patriotic agenda than one with official censorship.

19

Conclusions

The political economy of the U.S. mass media is dominated by communication gatekeepers who are not media professionals so much as large profit-making organizations with close ties to government and business. This network of the powerful provides news and entertainment filtered to meet elite demands and to avoid offending materials. The filtering process is imperfect, however. Although they agree on basic premises, the elite frequently disagree on tactics, and beyond this, normal news-making processes do not screen out all inconvenient facts and stories. It is extremely rare, however, for such dissonant items to graduate to act as a framework that questions generally accepted principles, or to be part of "big news." This presentation of dissident themes only episodically, within official frameworks, and implemented by free-market forces without state censorship, enhances the credibility of the dominant ideology and perspectives.

NOTES

18 Content

For those of you who have, up to this point, been unconvinced about the validity of the five filters, and the idea that the mass media engage in propaganda campaigns, the last three paragraphs might be persuasive.

Herman acknowledges that the power elites are not one unified mass who act in concert, but that while tactics may differ, their overall aims – although not specified – remain shared. It is as a result of these differences over strategy and tactics that there is 'slippage' in the mass media, meaning that while stories critical of the status quo will emerge, they are unlikely to be given prominence. However, if and when they do, such as in the case of the Vietnam War, Herman argues that such stories are more likely than not to be framed by 'established dogma' – an important point that we pick up in the question below.

The final paragraph gets to the nub of the reading. That is, the United States of America does not need to rely on official censorship of the media to ensure a patriotic agenda, as it is enabled by five political economic filters which ensure an effective and 'invisible' propaganda system.

Ensure that you are clear about your understanding of 'established dogma', and then consider whether news reports in the United Kingdom and United States of America about the war in Iraq have been framed in such a way.

19 Writing Style/Structure

This is a short and snappy ending that summarises Herman's key arguments. Note that he does not return explicitly to the two perspectives discussed in the first section of the reading. He does, though, highlight their limitations while reiterating the strengths of the propaganda model. This is evident in the first sentence where Herman argues that it is not solely media professionals who are the main communication gatekeepers, but 'large profit-making organizations with close ties to government and business'. Note also how he makes reference to the practice of 'news and entertainment filtered to meet elite demands'. This is the first time that entertainment is mentioned in this reading.

REFLECTING ON THE READING

As you will have observed, the reading includes barely any reflection by Herman on the limitations of the propaganda model, no insights on how it was actually constructed and little indication about how it was received. The reasons for this are more than likely due to the editorial requirements of the volume in which the reading was published, rather than an oversight by the author.

Herman has, though, subsequently published reflections on the propaganda model and, in doing so, rebutted criticism that it was conspiratorial and simplistic. In one example that was published seven years after the reading and fourteen years after *Manufacturing Consent: The political economy of the mass media* (1988), Herman points out that the model is one of 'media behaviour and performance' and not one of 'media effects' (2002: 63). However, he does highlight how and why the model could be utilised by citizens and consumers: 'the propaganda model can help activists understand where they might best deploy their efforts to influence mainstream media coverage on issues' (p. 63).

On the value of the model and the validity of the filters in contemporary times, Herman is crystal clear. It is his view that the first two filters, 'ownership' and 'advertising', have become increasingly important, that the 'professional autonomy of journalists has been reduced', and that the internet will be unlikely to serve democratic communication if 'left to the market' (Herman 2002: 65). On 'sourcing' and 'flak', the author cites the growth in public relations professionals, plus an over-reliance on public relations releases as news sources, as evidence that these two filters have 'strengthened as mechanisms of elite influence' (p. 65). While acknowledging that the fifth filter, 'anti-communist ideology', has lost much of its currency since the demise of the Soviet Union, the expansion of capitalism has enabled the substitution of the phrase, 'the miracle of the market' (p. 65). However, in the current era it may be that 'the war on terror' is being used as a fifth filter.

As we indicated in the introduction to this chapter, while a critical political economic approach shares certain assumptions and values, the way it has been utilised in work relating to the developing world, Europe and North America has varied. It is, therefore, not surprising that there are differences in interpretation and emphasis. For example, while Golding and Murdock acknowledge the veracity of the propaganda model, they also suggest a flaw, pointing out that '[o]wners, advertisers and key political personnel cannot always do as they wish' (2000: 73), because they too have to operate 'within structures that constrain as well as facilitate, imposing limits as well as offering opportunities' (p. 74). In making this statement, they are highlighting contradictions in the system, and reminding that a close analysis of these *limits* is a key task for critical political economy.

In the course of a critical reflection on the reading you will no doubt find yourself weighing up the way in which it was organised, presented, argued, and whether alternative positions and perspectives are adequately considered. For example, in outlining the model and the five filters, did the author identify and explore the contradictions raised by Golding and Murdock (2000)? Finally, you might also want to consider the relevance, or otherwise, of the propaganda model in the contemporary period.

Key terms to explore

anti-establishment; apologists; dissident voices; dominant ideology; gatekeeper(s); self-censorship; ideological mobilisation; McCarthyism; neo-conservative; propaganda; 'Red Scares'; structural relationships; 'worthy' and 'unworthy' victims.

Key writers who are mentioned

Ben Bagdikian; Herbert Gans; Todd Gitlin; Herb Schiller; Leon Sigal; Gaye Tuchman.

RECOMMENDED READING

Boyd-Barrett, O. (1995c) 'The political economy approach', in Boyd-Barrett, O., and Newbold, C. (eds), *Approaches to Media*, London: Arnold.

Includes an introductory section on the political economy tradition, and abridged readings by Herb Schiller, Graham Murdock and Peter Golding, Nicholas Garnham, and Dallas Smythe.

Golding, P. and Murdock, G. (2000) 'Culture, communications and political economy', in Curran, J., and Gurevitch, M. (eds) *Mass Media and Society*, 3rd edition. London: Arnold.

Sets out the core features of a critical political economy approach to the study of culture and communications.

Herman, E.S. and Chomsky, N. (1994 [1988]) *Manufacturing Consent: The political economy of the mass media*, London: Vintage.

Classic text which outlines the case for a 'propaganda model' of the mass media, illustrating by way of numerous examples the workings of its five news 'filters'.

CHAPTER 13

Public sphere

Habermas, J. (1974 [1964]) 'The public sphere: an encyclopedia article', *New German Critique*, 3 (1): 49–55.

INTRODUCTION TO THE PUBLIC SPHERE

It would be a challenging question in any pub quiz: 'Explain the relationship between a concept derived from the seventeenth century, the work of a twentieth century German philosopher, and twenty-first century celebrities such as Bono, Thom Yorke, Brooke Kinsella and Matt Damon'. In this introduction these connections are quickly illuminated, and a full reading of the chapter will enable an understanding of what is understood by the 'public sphere'.

Jürgen Habermas is the German philosopher who is generally credited with coining the term 'public sphere'. He was a member of the Frankfurt School of Critical Theory (see Chapter 6). While Habermas is often referred to in textbooks that deal with media theory, he only produced one major work on the media. Before we examine Habermas's work on the public sphere, it may be helpful to reflect on why, where and how we may have come across this term.

Few of us would dispute the view that much of the global news agenda in the early years of this twenty-first century has been dominated by the war in Iraq, the environment, poverty in parts of Africa, and obesity. It is in relation to debates, discussions and comment about such issues that the concept of the public sphere – while not always named as such by journalists, commentators or bloggers – is invoked. In particular, there are three ways in which this occurs and they are interrelated.

The first involves the range of 'voices' that are allowed, or invited, to participate in such debates. Traditionally, it has been politicians, policymakers, prominent journalists and academics that have tended to dominate news and current affairs, and – it is interesting to note – members of these same groups have moved rapidly to establish a web presence via the internet. However, these traditional commentators have been joined in 'new' media by 'celebrities' who have lent their voices to – and sometimes initiated – debates about contentious issues, with the intention of impacting on politics and changing government policy at local and global levels.

In this respect, we may have seen, read or heard that certain celebrities have participated in the public sphere. The obvious examples are Radiohead's Thom Yorke on the environment, U2's Bono on debt in the developing world, *East Enders* actor Brooke Kinsella on youth violence, Bob Geldof on poverty in Africa, and Matt Damon (alongside other celebrities such as Brad Pitt and Don Cheadle) on mass atrocities such as Darfur.

The second way in which the public sphere is invoked relates to what we understand by 'public opinion'. How often do we read or hear that the public thinks this, or the public thinks that? Where does this public view actually come from; who has participated – and who hasn't – in the discussions that led to what is referred to as public opinion? Is it just the traditional media voices, or this small, but increasingly vocal, group of celebrities, or the now numerous public relations professionals that are responsible for generating public opinion? Or does public opinion actually emerge as a result of wide-scale participation in contemporary debates by 'ordinary' people? To what extent does opinion polling and its almost immediate transformation into 'headlines' by the electronic and print media reflect, or influence, public opinion? Habermas's work on the public sphere provides a way of thinking about and responding to such questions.

Finally, the third way in which the concept of the public sphere is invoked arises with the increasing tendency to use the term 'dumbing-down' as a way of describing contemporary media. Here, what is being implied is that the number, quality and diversity of – generally – news and current affairs broadcasts have diminished, and that they have been replaced by 'reality' and 'make-over' programmes. In the case of the broadcast media, it is the ever-present search for increased ratings that is cited as a reason for the dumbing-down. Similarly, in the case of the press, it is the pressure to maintain sales in an increasingly competitive market place that is given as the reason for a prevalence of celebrity-led stories, particularly in the tabloids.

A further element of this dumbing-down argument is that the media – and television is generally seen as the greatest 'sinner' – has over recent years targeted, or 'constructed', readers, listeners and viewers primarily as consumers, or buyers, rather than citizens. Overall, then, dumbing-down is seen as a process which results in a less vibrant, poorly informed and only partial public sphere, where the act and process of citizenship is undermined. Of course, another way of conceptualising the process of dumbing-down would be to suggest that the public sphere has been incorporated into the capitalist system; however, you might also want to explore arguments that we are 'dumbing up', such as in Steven Johnson's *Everything Bad is Good for You* (2005).

What is so fascinating about Habermas's conception of the public sphere is that while it emerges from an analysis of British, French and German society in the seventeenth century, the concept has explanatory and visionary potential in the twenty-first century. This is because it provides a unique way of examining the relationship between the media, the state, business and ordinary people, while providing the scope to imagine or envisage how these relationships might be redrawn in the interests of a more democratic society.

Habermas's one major work on the media was *The Structural Transformation of the Public Sphere: An inquiry into a category of bourgeois society* (*STPS*). This was first published in German in 1962, but it was not until 1989 that it was translated and published in English. Why, you might ask, was it not translated earlier, and why 1989?

One of the reasons given is that Habermas's work was thought to offer a new way of thinking about the media at a time when communism was collapsing in Eastern Europe, and capitalism was thriving in the United Kingdom and United States of America because of the pro-market policies of, respectively, Prime Minister Margaret Thatcher and President Ronald Reagan (Boyd-Barrett 1995a: 231).

While we encourage you to read Habermas's *STPS* in full, the reading in this chapter provides an extremely brief synopsis of the key elements of his thesis. Hence its title, 'The public sphere: an encyclopedia article'. Like *STPS*, this reading has been translated from German into English. It was first published in 1964 but did not appear in English until 1974. The source of publication, an academic journal, gives a clear indication of the target audience. As a result, it is not an easy read. Also, in common with many translated works, some words in the original language do not have a neat equivalent in the new tongue.

We are, therefore, reliant on third parties for the translation, in this case Sara and Frank Lennox, and a further person, Peter Hohendahl, for an interpretation of some of the key words and ideas. This additional material appears in the footnotes and provides some useful contextual and factual information.

Divided into four segments, the reading has a clear, logical structure which is signalled in the latter part of its title, 'an encyclopedia article'. Essentially, after defining what is meant by the public sphere, Habermas tracks its emergence in the seventeenth century through to its decline – and eventual 'structural transformation' – which began in the mid-nineteenth century. You may, though, be best advised to think more about what might constitute the *principles* of the public sphere, rather than whether it has actually ever been realised.

Finally, it is noteworthy that Habermas describes the public sphere as a concept, whereas Garnham (1986: 29) refers to it as a theory, Hjarvard (1993: 89) as an ideal, and Boyd-Barrett (1995a: 230) as a discourse. We might, therefore, ask why there is differing terminology, and whether it matters. The choice of vocabulary is likely to reflect the disciplinary background of the writer, and it also implies a judgement about utility or worth.

Here, yet again, we are reminded about the benefits of returning to the work of the person, or persons, who are credited with developing a particular theory, and to make our own judgements, instead of relying solely on the reports and interpretations of other writers.

READING

1

Jürgen Habermas

The Public Sphere: An Encyclopedia Article (1964)[1]

1. *The Concept.* By "the public sphere" we mean first of all a realm of our social life in which something approaching public opinion can be formed. Access is guaranteed to all citizens. A portion of the public sphere comes into being in every conversation in which private individuals assemble to form a public body.[2] They then behave neither like business or professional people transacting private affairs, nor like members of a constitutional order subject to the legal constraints of a state bureaucracy. Citizens behave as a public body when they confer in an unrestricted fashion—that is, with the guarantee of freedom of assembly and association and the freedom to express and publish their opinions—about matters of general interest. In a large public body this kind of communication requires specific means for transmitting information and influencing those who receive it. Today newspapers and magazines, radio and television are the media of the public sphere.

---

1. Originally appeared in Fischer Lexicon, *Staat und Politik*, new edition (Frankfurt am Main, 1964), pp. 220–226.
2. Habermas' concept of the public sphere is not to be equated with that of "the public," i.e. of the individuals who assemble. His concept is directed instead at the institution, which to be sure only assumes concrete form through the participation of people. It cannot, however, be characterized simply as a crowd. (This and the following notes by Peter Hohendahl.)

NOTES

Writing Style

There is no gentle opening or introduction to this reading. Habermas simply begins by linking the public sphere directly with the formation of public opinion. Definitions of key terms only emerge gradually and generally only partially.

Content

Habermas asserts that an element or portion of the public sphere comes into being when (even just a few) people gather together as *citizens* to discuss matters of common interest. Habermas then moves on to clarify this statement by adding two qualifications. First, the people that come together in this way can only be considered a *public* body if they 'step out' of their private roles as business or professional people – thereby acting as citizens – when they engage in such discussions. Secondly, when Habermas refers to 'the public' or 'public body', he does not just mean a crowd of people but the 'institution', which suggests individual citizen rights and responsibilities.

When Bono, Thom Yorke, Brooke Kinsella or Matt Damon intervene in the public sphere by making comments about matters that relate in various ways to government policy, to what extent have they 'stepped out' of their private roles and away from their private interests, and can these two positions be separated? Also, when we read or hear about citizen rights and responsibilities, what does this actually mean?

Context

Here we see the first connection between the concept of the public sphere, the media and contemporary society. Essentially, Habermas argues – quite sensibly – that we cannot all be in the same space at the same time to engage in discussions of common interest. We are, therefore, reliant on radio, television and the press to act as the main media of the public sphere. Obviously, Habermas was writing before the advent of the internet (see Chapter 18).

READING

2

We speak of the political public sphere in contrast, for instance, to the literary one, when public discussion deals with objects connected to the activity of the state. Although state authority is so to speak the executor of the political public sphere, it is not a part of it.[3] To be sure, state authority is usually considered "public" authority, but it derives its task of caring for the well-being of all citizens primarily from this aspect of the public sphere. Only when the exercise of political control is effectively subordinated to the democratic demand that information be accessible to the public, does the political public sphere win an institutionalized influence over the government through the instrument of law-making bodies. The expression "public opinion" refers to the tasks of criticism and control which a public body of citizens informally—and, in periodic elections, formally as well—practices *vis-à-vis* the ruling structure organized in the form of a state. Regulations demanding that certain proceedings be public *(Publizitätsvor-schriften)*, for example those providing for open court hearings, are also related to this function of public opinion. The public sphere as a sphere which mediates between society and state, in which the public organizes itself as the bearer of public opinion, accords with the principle of the public sphere[4]—that principle of public information which once had to be fought for against the arcane policies of monarchies and which since that time has made possible the democratic control of state activities.

3. The state and the public sphere do not overlap, as one might suppose from casual language use. Rather they confront one another as opponents. Habermas designates that sphere as public which antiquity understood to be private, i.e. the sphere of non-governmental opinion making.

4. The principle of the public sphere could still be distinguished from an institution which is demonstrable in social history. Habermas thus would mean a model of norms and modes of behavior by means of which the very functioning of public opinion can be guaranteed for the first time. These norms and modes of behavior include: a) general accessibility, b) elimination of all privileges and c) discovery of general norms and rational legitimations.

NOTES

2 ## Content

In this section Habermas points to a distinction between the *political* public sphere and the *literary* public sphere. This is on the basis that it is only in the case of the former that discussion addresses issues relating to the state. No evidence is provided here to substantiate this judgement. However, the distinction being made implies a valuing of one sphere over another.

Similar judgements have been made in respect of television programmes, where it is argued that only news and current affairs address political matters, while other genres are deemed 'non-political' because they are oriented toward entertainment. Such a view is, of course, naive, as 'reality TV', 'soaps' and 'sitcoms' also address matters of common interest that pertain to government policy.

Can you give examples of the types of issues that are addressed in 'soaps' that touch on matters of wider public interest?

Habermas goes on to illuminate and underline the power and role of public opinion, reminding us, yet again, about the need to reflect on the meaning of certain words. For example, while state and local authorities are described as *public* authorities, the *public* sphere is seen as separate from the state. Here we see an intervention by Peter Hohendahl, whose interpretation in the footnotes is somewhat sharper, suggesting that the public sphere and the state are, in fact, opponents that confront each other. Habermas returns to this point later in the reading.

To what extent is Peter Hohendahl's intervention – suggesting the idea of confrontation – useful in making clear the relationship between the public sphere and the state? What are the pros and cons of using footnotes in this way?

Context

Another writer sheds some light on the distinctions being made here. Fraser describes the public sphere as 'conceptually distinct from the state; it is a site for the production and circulation of discourses that can in principle be critical of the state' (1992: 110).

It is through such discourses – which produce public opinion – that the public exercise what Habermas refers to as 'informal' control of the state. This is in addition to the more formalised control exercised periodically through voting at election times.

Can you think of any recent examples where public opinion has acted as a form of informal control?

READING

3

It is no coincidence that these concepts of the public sphere and public opinion arose for the first time only in the eighteenth century. They acquire their specific meaning from a concrete historical situation. It was at that time that the distinction of "opinion" from "opinion publique" and "public opinion" came about. Though mere opinions (cultural assumptions, normative attitudes, collective prejudices and values) seem to persist unchanged in their natural form as a kind of sediment of history, public opinion can by definition only come into existence when a reasoning public is presupposed. Public discussions about the exercise of political power which are both critical in intent and institutionally guaranteed have not always existed—they grew out of a specific phase of bourgeois society and could enter into the order of the bourgeois constitutional state only as a result of a particular constellation of interests.

4

2. *History.* There is no indication European society of the high middle ages possessed a public sphere as a unique realm distinct from the private sphere. Nevertheless, it was not coincidental that during that period symbols of sovereignty, for instance the princely seal, were deemed "public." At that time there existed a public representation of power. The status of the feudal lord, at whatever level of the feudal pyramid, was oblivious to the categories "public" and "private," but the holder of the position represented it publicly: he showed himself, presented himself as the embodiment of an ever present "higher" power. The concept of this representation has been maintained up to the most recent constitutional history. Regardless of the degree to which it has loosed itself from the old base, the authority of political power today still demands a representation at the highest level by a head of state. Such elements, however, derive from a pre-bourgeois social structure. Representation in the sense of a bourgeois public sphere,[5] for instance the representation of the nation or of particular mandates, has nothing to do with the medieval representative public sphere—a public sphere directly linked to the concrete existence of a ruler. As long as the prince and the estates of the realm still "are" the land, instead of merely functioning as deputies for it, they are able to "re-present"; they represent their power "before" the people, instead of for the people.

---

5. The expression "represent" is used in a very specific sense in the following section, namely to "present oneself." The important thing to understand is that the medieval public sphere, if it even deserves this designation, is tied to the *personal.* The feudal lord and estates create the public sphere by means of their very presence.

NOTES

3   Content

Here, we return to the key concepts and their origins. A distinction is made between 'mere opinion' and public opinion, the latter only coming about as a result of a reasoning public. Habermas asserts that concepts such as the public sphere, and its corollary public opinion, only emerged in the context of specific developments in the eighteenth century. In other words, they did not exist prior to this time and only became meaningful during a particular phase of bourgeois society, that is, the emergence of 'competitive market capitalism' (Garnham 1986: 29).

Is the distinction between 'mere opinion' and 'public opinion' useful in helping to clarify the meaning of the latter? What does Habermas mean by a reasoning public? When is a public not reasoning?

Context

The process and period of transition to which Habermas refers is encapsulated in the following summary by McGuigan: '[T]he bourgeois public sphere was the medium through which the middling classes wrested power from absolute rulers and the feudal aristocracy' (1996: 25).

4   Context

Having first defined the public sphere, Habermas now turns his attention to 'History'. However, we should note here that Habermas's historical analysis does not necessarily accord with that of other writers (see, for example, Dahlgren 1991: 5).

Content

The key issue here is the distinction that Habermas makes between the 'bourgeois public sphere' and the 'public representation of power', which he describes as 'representative publicity'.

While Habermas argues that there was no distinction between *public* and *private* in feudal times, monarchs and other branches of royalty did *re-present* their power publicly to, or in front of, the people in various ways. This occurred – and still does – through symbols, ceremonies and other regalia.

For Habermas, representative publicity can be contrasted with that of the public sphere, as the former 'is about the display of prestige, not critical discussion, spectacle not debate and appearance before the people, as on a stage, but not for them' (Peters 1993: 545).

Writing Style

As a way of trying to convey the meaning of 'representative publicity', Habermas uses the word 'represent', which we know and use regularly, but he presents it with a hyphen. Does this presentation help you to see this word and its meaning in a different light?

READING

5

The feudal authorities (church, princes and nobility), to which the representative public sphere was first linked, disintegrated during a long process of polarization. By the end of the eighteenth century they had broken apart into private elements on the one hand, and into public on the other. The position of the church changed with the reformation: the link to divine authority which the church represented, that is, religion, became a private matter. So-called religious freedom came to insure what was historically the first area of private autonomy. The church itself continued its existence as one public and legal body among others. The corresponding polarization within princely authority was visibly manifested in the separation of the public budget from the private household expenses of a ruler. The institutions of public authority, along with the bureaucracy and the military, and in part also with the legal institutions, asserted their independence from the privatized sphere of the princely court. Finally, the feudal estates were transformed as well: the nobility became the organs of public authority, parliament and the legal institutions; while those occupied in trades and professions, insofar as they had already established urban corporations and territorial organizations, developed into a sphere of bourgeois society which would stand apart from the state as a genuine area of private autonomy.

6

The representative public sphere yielded to that new sphere of "public anthority" which came into being with national and territorial states. Continuous state activity (permanent administration, standing army) now corresponded to the permanence of the relationships which with the stock exchange and the press had developed within the exchange of commodities and information. Public authority consolidated into a concrete opposition for those who were merely subject to it and who at first found only a negative definition of themselves within it. These were the "private individuals" who were excluded from public authority because they held no office. "Public" no longer referred to the "representative" court of a prince endowed with authority, but rather to an institution regulated according to competence, to an apparatus endowed with a monopoly on the legal exertion of authority. Private individuals subsumed in the state at whom public authority was directed now made up the public body.

Society, now a private realm occupying a position in opposition to the state, stood on the one hand as if in clear contrast to the state. On the other hand, that society had become a concern of public interest to the degree that the reproduction of life in the wake of the developing market economy had grown beyond the bounds of private domestic authority. *The bourgeois public sphere* could be understood as the sphere of private individuals assembled into a public body, which almost immediately laid claim to the officially regulated

↓

NOTES

5   Content

Here, the main theme is the collapse of feudal society and the displacement of representative publicity with the bourgeois public sphere. This is enabled as a result of the key players – the church, the princes (or royalty) and the nobility – experiencing a loss of power and a change to their status. Habermas doesn't define feudal society, contextualise it, nor date it; can you?

Yet again, the words *public* and *private* are important, signalling and reflecting the nature of the changes that are taking place. While the church retains a *public* role and presence, religion becomes a 'private matter'. Similarly, the *private* household expenditure of the royal court is now distinguished from the 'public budget'.

Likewise, institutions such as the military and the bureaucracy achieve greater independence as they become separated from the control of the *private* royal court; the feudal estates are dismantled to provide new roles for the nobility (in parliament and the legal institutions), and a new sphere of bourgeois society emerges comprising those in trades and professions.

Context

The bourgeoisie, according to Garnham were a 'new political class' who had 'both the time and material resources to create a network of institutions within civil society, such as newspapers, learned and debating societies, publishing enterprises, libraries, universities, polytechnics and museums, within which a new political power, public opinion, could come into existence' (1986: 29–30).

6   Content

Habermas introduces another key term, 'public authority'. It is public authority that replaces the representative public sphere, as national and territorial states emerge with the range of permanent institutions that we see in some form today. This results in a change of status for private individuals, who are now subject to public authority and not, as previously, the royal court.

What are the types of 'permanent institutions' to which Habermas is referring?

Habermas now moves to complete the 'History' jigsaw puzzle. The transformations outlined above lead to a situation where society is a private realm that is separate from the public authority of the state.

However, with a need to ensure the continuing development of an early form of market capitalism which had outgrown 'private domestic authority', private individuals begin to act as a public body in the wider public interest by 'taking on' the public authority with the aim of influencing decisions and making it accountable.

They do this through the medium of debate which leads to public opinion. For Habermas, this is the bourgeois public sphere in action, and he ends the paragraph by outlining the role played by the media, in this instance the press.

READING

6

(continued)

"intellectual newspapers" for use against the public authority itself. In those newspapers, and in moralistic and critical journals, they debated that public authority on the general rules of social intercourse in their fundamentally privatized yet publically relevant sphere of labor and commodity exchange.

7

3. *The Liberal Model of the Public Sphere.* The medium of this debate—public discussion—was unique and without historical precedent. Hitherto the estates had negotiated agreements with their princes, settling their claims to power from case to case. This development took a different course in England, where the parliament limited royal power, than it did on the continent, where the monarchies mediatized the estates. The third estate then broke with this form of power arrangement since it could no longer establish itself as a ruling group. A division of power by means of the delineation of the rights of the nobility was no longer possible within an exchange economy—private authority over capitalist property is, after all, un-political. Bourgeois individuals are private individuals. As such, they do not "rule." Their claims to power *vis-à-vis* public authority were thus directed not against the concentration of power, which was to be "shared." Instead, their ideas infiltrated the very principle on which the existing power is based. To the principle of the existing power, the bourgeois public opposed the principle of supervision—that very principle which demands that proceedings be made public *(Publizität)*. The principle of supervision is thus a means of transforming the nature of power, not merely one basis of legitimation exchanged for another.

NOTES

(continued)

What do you understand by Habermas's reference to market capitalism outgrowing 'private domestic authority'?

Context

Not surprisingly, Habermas's account of this bourgeois public sphere has been the subject of critical scrutiny by many authors. For example, Hjarvard queries 'whether this classical public sphere, which Habermas seeks to identify, was a historical reality or the ideal for which the early bourgeoisie strived' (1993: 88–9).

Context

In this third section of the reading Habermas uses a label, 'liberal', to describe the public sphere. In doing so, Habermas is suggesting a more optimistic orientation towards the media than that of his colleagues in the Frankfurt school (see Chapter 6). What also becomes evident at this stage of the reading is that Habermas is concerned not only with the emergence of the public sphere, but also its subsequent decline.

Content

Habermas argues that the idea of debate in the form of public discussion which makes 'public authority' accountable is a new phenomenon. Previously, he suggests, disputes about power and resources were sorted out privately, although arrangements for doing so varied between different countries. However, the emergence of the bourgeoisie brought about a different way of thinking about and, ultimately, transforming power.

Although not a word that we would naturally associate with major transformations, it was by way of the principle of *supervision* that members of the bourgeoisie asserted their power. Their demand was for a greater degree of openness – publicness, or publicity – on the part of the public authority. This is another reminder about the importance of certain words and their meanings. As Peters notes, while 'publicity' once 'meant openness of discussion and commerce as well as popular access to government', in the contemporary era it 'suggests public relations' (1993: 542–3).

What does Habermas mean by 'liberal' in this context? Also, Habermas mentions England here, but to which other countries on 'the continent' is he also referring?

READING

8

In the first modern constitutions the catalogues of fundamental rights were a perfect image of the liberal model of the public sphere: they guaranteed the society as a sphere of private autonomy and the restriction of public authority to a few functions. Between these two spheres, the constitutions further insured the existence of a realm of private individuals assembled into a public body who as citizens transmit the needs of bourgeois society to the state, in order, ideally, to transform political into "rational" authority within the medium of this public sphere. The general interest, which was the measure of such a rationality, was then guaranteed, according to the presuppositions of a society of free commodity exchange, when the activities of private individuals in the marketplace were freed from social compulsion and from political pressure in the public sphere.

9

At the same time, daily political newspapers assumed an important role. In the second half of the eighteenth century literary journalism created serious competition for the earlier news sheets which were mere compilations of notices. Karl Bücher characterized this great development as follows: "Newspapers changed from mere institutions for the publication of news into bearers and leaders of public opinion—weapons of party politics. This transformed the newspaper business. A new element emerged between the gathering and the publication of news: the editorial staff. But for the newspaper publisher it meant that he changed from a vendor of recent news to a dealer in public opinion." The publishers insured the newspapers a commercial basis, yet without commercializing them as such. The press remained an institution of the public itself, effective in the manner of a mediator and intensifier of public discussion, no longer a mere organ for the spreading of news but not yet the medium of a consumer culture.

8 Content

Here, Habermas more or less repeats an earlier point when he suggests that modern societies replicated the characteristics of the liberal public sphere as they comprised, on one hand, a 'sphere of private autonomy' and, on the other, a sphere of public authority that was restricted 'to a few functions'. Separate from both was the public sphere, which enabled private individuals to come together as citizens in a public body to debate matters of common interest and transmit those societal concerns to the state.

He argues that it is through debate in the public sphere that political authority is transformed into rational authority. In this context, 'rational' is concerned with the preservation of general (or public) interest: that is, freedom of association and expression, and freedom to go about one's business as a private individual in the marketplace.

How would you distinguish between political authority and rational authority? Also, why does Habermas surround the word rational with apostrophes?

Context

Fraser likens the public sphere to a 'space in which citizens deliberate about their common affairs', 'an institutionalized arena of discursive interaction', an arena 'conceptually distinct from the state', and a 'site for the production and circulation of discourses that can in principle be critical of the state' (1992: 110–11).

Try to visualise – even draw – a diagram which provides a representation of Habermas's conception of the public sphere, illustrating its relationship to the state and the private spheres of home and business.

9 Content

On only a few occasions in this reading does Habermas specifically make mention of the media. Here, he focuses on the link between the press and the bourgeois public sphere in the eighteenth century, and draws attention to the emergence of 'literary journalism' and the challenge it posed to the existing 'news sheets'.

The key point being made is that as the newspapers and magazines of the bourgeois public sphere begin to reflect and disseminate public opinion, the nature of the press itself begins to change through a division of labour, which sees the introduction of editorial staff.

Habermas's last few lines in this paragraph underline what he sees as the ideal role of the media in relation to the public sphere. That is, the media – at this time, newspapers and magazines – have moved beyond simply collecting and disseminating news to a situation where they are operating as an organ of the people, in the sense of mediating and intensifying public opinion. His next remark is particularly significant. While the media are commercially successful, they have not yet

10

This type of journalism can be observed above all during periods of revolution when newspapers of the smallest political groups and organizations spring up, for instance in Paris in 1789. Even in the Paris of 1848 every half-way eminent politician organized his club, every other his journal: 450 clubs and over 200 journals were established there between February and May alone. Until the permanent legalization of a politically functional public sphere, the appearance of a political newspaper meant joining the struggle for freedom and public opinion, and thus for the public sphere as a principle. Only with the establishment of the bourgeois constitutional state was the intellectual press relieved of the pressure of its convictions. Since then it has been able to abandon its polemical position and take advantage of the earning possibilities of a commercial undertaking. In England, France, and the United States the transformation from a journalism of conviction to one of commerce began in the 1830s at approximately the same time. In the transition from the literary journalism of private individuals to the public services of the mass media the public sphere was transformed by the influx of private interests, which received special prominence in the mass media.

(continued)

become 'the medium of consumer culture'. Here, Habermas hints at what he later interprets as a decline of the public sphere.

What is the change that Habermas is anticipating in his reference to the media as a 'medium of consumer culture'?

Context

The day-to-day operation of the public sphere is brought to life by Poole, who writes: '[t]he institutions that made this discursive space possible were the coffee houses [of which there were 3,000 in eighteenth-century London], salons, clubs, English magazines such as *The Spectator* and *The Tatler*, reading societies and lending libraries. For many commentators, it was the London coffee houses . . . that exemplified the public sphere' (1989: 14).

Writing Style

Did you notice that this is the first time Habermas has used a quotation from the work of another writer? Unfortunately, details of the reference are not provided.

Content

Continuing his theme from the last paragraph, Habermas provides exemplars of the press mediating public opinion in pre- and post-revolutionary France during the latter part of the eighteenth century and early nineteenth century. He then moves on to make what appears to be a general – rather than country specific – observation that the emergence of a 'political newspaper' was further evidence of a 'struggle for freedom and public opinion'. This leads on to the implication that even though a public sphere may not be demonstrable in history, or actually realisable, it is a worthy and desirable principle.

The final few lines of the paragraph are focused on charting the changing nature of the press and the subsequent decline of the public sphere. According to Habermas, once constitutional states come into being, the press abandon a 'journalism of conviction' for 'one of commerce', having recognised the commercial possibilities of mass circulation. As a result, a media previously concerned primarily with public interest and public opinion becomes a mass media dominated by private interests.

What evidence could be used to support, or undermine, Habermas's assertion that a journalism of commerce displaced a journalism of conviction? Do these ideas have any relevance today?

Context

A number of authors have queried the actual existence of the public sphere. For example, Verstraeten argues that the public sphere 'has never been realized . . . [a]t best there has been some "initiative"' (1996: 349). Taking a slightly different tack, Peter Hohendahl (in footnote 4

READING

11

4. *The Public Sphere in the Social Welfare State Mass Democracy.* Although the liberal model of the public sphere is still instructive today with respect to the normative claim that information be accessible to the public,[6] it cannot be applied to the actual conditions of an industrially advanced mass democracy organized in the form of the social welfare state. In part the liberal model had always included ideological components, but it is also in part true that the social pre-conditions, to which the ideological elements could at one time at least be linked, had been fundamentally transformed. The very forms in which the public sphere manifested itself, to which supporters of the liberal model could appeal for evidence, began to change with the Chartist movement in England and the February revolution in France. Because of the diffusion of press and propaganda, the public body expanded beyond the bounds of the bourgeoisie. The public body lost not only its social exclusivity; it lost in addition the coherence created by bourgeois social institutions and a relatively high standard of eduction. Conflicts hitherto restricted to the private sphere now intrude into the public sphere.

Group needs which can expect no satisfaction from a self-regulating market now tend towards a regulation by the state.

6. Here it should be understood that Habermas considers the principle behind the bourgeois public sphere as indispensable, but not its historical form.

NOTES

(continued)

on page 302) underlines the importance of the principle of the public sphere, setting out norms and modes of behaviour that would be required in order to guarantee the functioning of public opinion.

In charting the transformation of the public sphere, Poole asserts that '[t]he concerns of the major bourgeois media became not only that of profit maximisation, but also that of excluding or subordinating oppositional voices' (1989: 15–16). Similarly, Curran (1996: 82) suggests that the public are squeezed out of the public sphere as economic interests and the state begin to bargain with each other.

What value is there in teasing out the principles of an 'ideal' public sphere, even though an actual public sphere may never have existed?

11 Content

In this fourth and final section of the reading, Habermas charts the decline of the public sphere as a result of its 'structural transformation'. Essentially, Habermas argues that the bourgeois public sphere was transformed by a series of major societal changes which eventually resulted in what he describes as the emergence of the Social Welfare State Mass Democracy.

Do you recognise the term 'Social Welfare State Mass Democracy'? What does Habermas mean by this?

Social changes occurring over the course of a number of centuries are dealt with in the space of a few paragraphs. Two specific examples of significant social change are mentioned, those of the revolution in France and the Chartist movement in the United Kingdom. It was these and other major economic and social changes, such as the industrial revolution and the growth of capitalism, that resulted in an expanded public body – beyond the previous exclusivity of the bourgeoisie – and a changing public sphere.

Context

Additional perspectives on these changes are provided by other writers. For example, Dahlgren suggests that 'industrialization, urbanization, the growth of literacy and the popular press, and not least the rise of the administrative and interventionist state' (1991: 4) contributed to the decline of the public sphere.

Garnham, however, introduces a sense of irony about its decline, arguing that the public sphere 'was destroyed historically by the very forces that had brought it into existence': in other words, capitalism, but in an advanced form which is known as monopoly capitalism. This led to an 'uneven distribution of wealth', 'rising costs to enter the public sphere' and, as a result, 'unequal access and control over that sphere' (1986: 30).

READING

12

The public sphere, which must now mediate these demands, becomes a field for the competition of interests, competitions which assume the form of violent conflict. Laws which obviously have come about under the "pressure of the street" can scarcely still be understood as arising from the consensus of private individuals engaged in public discussion. They correspond in a more or less unconcealed manner to the compromise of conflicting private interests. Social organizations which deal with the state act in the political public sphere, whether through the agency of political parties or directly in connection with the public administration. With the interweaving of the public and private realm, not only do the political authorities assume certain functions in the sphere of commodity exchange and social labor, but conversely social powers now assume political functions. This leads to a kind of "refeudalization" of the public sphere. Large organizations strive for political compromises with the state and with each other, excluding the public sphere whenever possible. But at the same time the large organizations must assure themselves of at least plebiscitary support from the mass of the population through an apparent display of openness (*demonstrative Publizität*).[7]

13

The political public sphere of the social welfare state is characterized by a peculiar weakening of its critical functions. At one time the process of making proceedings public (*Publizität*) was intended to subject persons or affairs to public reason, and to make political decisions subject to appeal before the court of public opinion. But often enough today the process of making public simply serves the arcane policies of special interests; in the form of "publicity" it wins

7. One must distinguish between Habermas' concept of "making proceedings public" (*Publizität*) and the "public sphere" (*Oeffentlichkeit*). The term *Publizität* describes the degree of public effect generated by a public act. Thus a situation can arise in which the form of public opinion making is maintained, while the substance of the public sphere has long ago been undermined.

12 Content

Habermas cites two interrelated reasons for the introduction of state regulation. The first is due to the failure of a self-regulating market to meet the needs of the wider population. The second is that 'private' matters which were previously confined to the sphere of the home and business now spill out into the public sphere. In order to ram home the implications of these changes, Habermas uses the example of law-making.

Here, he contrasts the previously civil and rational debates between individuals who set their private interests aside to act in the public sphere, with a range of interest groups which now begin to operate in the public sphere primarily for their own ends, rather than for the public good. Habermas describes an 'interweaving of the public and private realm'.

Habermas doesn't elaborate on the interest groups to which he refers. Who or what might they be? To what extent does his phrase an 'interweaving of the public and private realm' have any meaning today?

The final two key points in this section are crucial. Here, Habermas introduces the idea of a '"refeudalisation" of the public sphere'. The second point suggests that the struggle between large organisations to win resources and ensure settlements by the state in their favour, leads to deceitful and manipulative behaviour. In the translation from German into English, this behaviour is described as 'an apparent display of openness'.

What evidence has Habermas provided to justify his 'refeudalisation' thesis? How might you counter such an argument?

Context

Dahlgren (1991) reflects on the changing nature of the public and private domains that Habermas describes, and summarises the resultant implications. The result, he argues, was a 'blurring of distinctions between public and private in political and economic affairs, a rationalization and shrinking of the private intimate sphere (family life) and the gradual shift from an (albeit limited) public of political and cultural debaters to a mass public of consumers' (p. 4).

13 Content

Here, Habermas highlights the apparent failings of the public sphere in a social welfare state and, in particular, its capacity to act critically. By way of example, he notes how individual opinions and policy intentions would, at one time, have been subject to public scrutiny and debate in the public sphere – described here as 'the court of public opinion' – before being accepted or enacted. This is contrasted with the contemporary situation about which Habermas makes two key points.

His first point is that matters of public interest are simply placed in the public domain on the basis that the actuality of publicity is more than adequate to achieve 'public prestige for people or affairs'. Habermas continues by pointing out that the generation of publicity – via public relations

READING

13

(continued)

public prestige for people or affairs, thus making them worthy of acclamation in a climate of non-public opinion. The very words "public relations work" *(Oeffentlichkeitsarbeit)* betray the fact that a public sphere must first be arduously constructed case by case, a public sphere which earlier grew out of the social structure. Even the central relationship of the public, the parties and the parliament is affected by this change in function.

14

Yet this trend towards the weakening of the public sphere as a principle is opposed by the extension of fundamental rights in the social welfare state. The demand that information be accessible to the public is extended from organs of the state to all organizations dealing with the state. To the degree that this is realized, a public body of organized private individuals would take the place of the now-defunct public body of private individuals who relate individually to each other. Only these organized individuals could participate effectively in the process of public communication; only they could use the channels of the public sphere which exist within parties and associations and the process of making proceedings public *(Publizität)* which was established to facilitate the dealings of organizations with the state. Political compromises would have to be legitimized through this process of public communication. The idea of the public sphere, preserved in the social welfare state mass democracy, an idea which calls for a rationalization of power through the medium of public discussion among private individuals, threatens to disintegrate with the structural transformation of the public sphere itself. It could only be realized today, on an altered basis, as a rational reorganization of social and political power under the mutual control of rival organizations committed to the public sphere in their internal structure as well as in their relations with the state and each other.

Translated by Sara Lennox and Frank Lennox

NOTES

13

(continued)

work – requires the construction of what one might describe as a phoney public sphere when, for example, there is a need to win public approval about matters of resource allocation and policy direction.

How useful is the notion of a phoney public sphere being created? Can you think of recent examples where it could be argued that this has actually occurred?

14

Content

Habermas moves towards a conclusion by elaborating on what he means by a structural transformation of the public sphere. He suggests the occurrence of a simultaneous process. That is, the public sphere is weakened as the information rights of people in the social welfare state are strengthened.

For Habermas, it is a structural transformation because as information rights are extended to all organisations that deal with the state, public communication becomes controlled by a 'public body of organized private individuals' through a variety of means, instead of a 'public body of private individuals' who, in the era of the bourgeois public sphere, knew and were known to each other.

The outcome, according to Habermas, is that this undermines the 'idea of the public sphere', that is, the 'rationalization of power through the medium of public discussion among private individuals'.

What exactly is the distinction that Habermas is making between a 'public body of private individuals', and a 'public body of organized private individuals'?

Habermas ends the reading somewhat pessimistically, recognising that the recreation of a public sphere today would require significant reorganisation and reconfiguration, and would need to focus on the role and operation of organisations, not individuals.

One final point on which to speculate is whether Habermas would have a different view about the decline of the public sphere with the advent of the internet.

Context

Interestingly, the challenge of recreating the type of public sphere as envisaged by Habermas has been taken on by some academics. For example, both Curran (2000: 142–8) and Keane (1995: 263–8) have argued for structural changes to the media in order to move closer to Habermas's ideal of the public sphere.

Moreover, Habermas has also reflected on his earlier work on the public sphere. As Curran observes, Habermas's later work 'implies greater confidence in the capacity of civil society to offset concentrations of power, greater hope that the media will facilitate meaningful debate, and greater faith in the critical independence of media audiences' (2000: 136).

REFLECTING ON THE READING

The selected reading is challenging and requires serious and considered reflection on the words, phrases, assertions and arguments used by Habermas. It also requires, or encourages, at least some understanding of the major social, political, economic and cultural shifts that occurred from the seventeenth century onwards. This is the period in which Habermas locates both the emergence, and decline, of the bourgeois public sphere.

However, as you will be aware from your wider reading, Habermas's concept of the public sphere has attracted the critical attention of other writers. To varying degrees this criticism has focused on his methodology, arguments and conclusions (see, for example, Stevenson 2002; Thompson 1994). Nevertheless, detractors and advocates alike agree that the public sphere retains relevance in contemporary society.

The most frequently cited insights associated with the public sphere relate to the principles it invokes and its potential as a model, or vision, for the role of the media in a democratic society (see, for example, Curran 1996: 82; Dahlgren 1991: 5; Garnham 1986: 31).

Likewise, Golding and Murdock suggest the public sphere as a 'yardstick' (2000: 77) against which judgements can be made about existing systems of public communications, and corrective measures suggested. This is not dissimilar to the approach taken by Sparks (2001), who explores the extent to which the internet could be envisaged as a global public sphere.

It is, therefore, not surprising that the concept of the public sphere continues to be cited in a number of different ways in discussions about 'old' and 'new' media. For example, connections are made between the media and notions of citizens and citizenship, consumers and consumerism, public opinion and public relations, and democracy. Moreover, such discussions encourage some reflection on the origins of key words, such as 'public', 'private' and 'publicity', and how their meanings have changed over time.

Key terms to explore

publicity; liberal theory; bourgeois; bourgeoisie; Chartist; consumer culture; public opinion; monopoly capitalism; feudal.

Key writers who are mentioned

Karl Bücher.

RECOMMENDED READING

Boyd-Barrett, O. (1995a) 'Conceptualising the "public sphere"', in Boyd-Barrett, O., and Newbold, C. (eds) *Approaches to Media*, London: Arnold.

Has a specific section on the public sphere which reflects on its origins, and includes abridged readings by Jürgen Habermas, Nicholas Garnham, John B. Thompson, Philip Elliott and John Keane.

Sparks, C. (2001) 'The internet and the global public sphere', in Bennett, W.L., and Entman, R.M. (eds) *Mediated Politics: Communication in the future of democracy*, Cambridge: Cambridge University Press.

A critical appraisal of Habermas's notion of the public sphere is followed by an assessment of whether the internet can be conceived as a global public sphere.

Stevenson, N. (2002) *Understanding Media Cultures*, 2nd edn, London: Sage.

Examines Habermas's notion of the public sphere, his links with the Frankfurt school, and considers how the idea of the public sphere relates to public service broadcasting and to citizenship.

CHAPTER 14

Media effects

Gauntlett, D. (2005) 'Ten things wrong with the media "effects" model', *Theory.org.uk: the Media Theory Site*, www.theory.org.uk/tenthings.html.

On 20 April 1999 two pupils of Columbine High School in Littleton, Colorado – Dylan Klebold and Eric Harris – walked into their school armed with guns, knives and bombs. They wandered the corridors shooting and killing. By the end of the day they were both dead, along with twelve students and one teacher. Almost as soon as the massacre was over debates started raging as to why they had carried it out. While investigations were carried out into the boys' backgrounds and families, their actions were quickly linked to the music of the rock star Marilyn Manson, who cancelled his scheduled performance in Columbine in respect to the dead. It was discovered that Klebold and Harris had acquired much of the information about how to construct their weapons from the internet. While many experts argue that such violence is a consequence of a multitude of factors, many aspects of the debate quickly focused on the media.

On 12 February 1993 two eleven-year-olds – Jon Venables and Robert Thompson – led the toddler James Bulger, whom they had picked up at Bootle Strand Shopping Centre, Liverpool, out onto a disused railway line where they hit him and threw bricks at him, eventually leaving him dead on the tracks. The ensuing investigation and conviction of two such young murderers led to much speculation as to the causes of the crime. Very quickly, the fact that the boys had thrown blue paint on Bulger's face was picked up as being similar to an event in the horror film, *Child's Play 3* (dir. Bender, 1991). This led to a nationwide debate about 'video nasties', children's access to them, and their effects, culminating in David Alton MP's attempt to bolster controls of such material as part of the Criminal Justice Act (1994). The incident is one still referred to repeatedly by those supporting stronger controls for media, and reignited the debate about the relationship between audiences, society and the media.

As long as there has been culture, there has been concern about its effect upon the people who consume it. Aristotle worried that poetry was degrading the populace in ancient Greece (1996 [*c*.335 BC]). The colloquial language of Wordsworth and Coleridge's *Lyrical Ballads* (1798) was seen as corrupting the purity of literature. The debates about media effects, then, are not new. What is important about reading work on media effects is to question the assumptions such work starts from – when a tragedy such as Columbine occurs why do so many people immediately look to the media for a cause? And for those who disagree with this opinion, is it really possible that the media has no effect on its users? If there are no effects, how come media make us cry, laugh, be scared or get angry? Our relationships to media are often intense, emotional and personal, so perhaps it is logical that we are in some way 'changed' by what we consume. And how does this relate to society; if such relationships are personal, how can we think about what *mass* media does to *mass* audiences? The effects debate is one about the roles media play in society; notably, they often approach this topic with negative assumptions.

One of the key concerns in media debates is the 'need to protect children' (Barker and Petley 1997: 5) from the effects of the media. Indeed, the vast majority of research carried out on media and society has looked at children's use of, and relationship with, media, especially television (van Evra 2004). Many of the most vocal voices in this debate see television as a negative influence on children. Marie Winn, for example, sees children's use of television as an 'addiction' (1985: 23–34), likening the pleasures the medium offers to the highs of drug abuse. Such concerns are often linked to worries about the passivity of media consumption, which Neil Postman (1985) sees as contributing to our disengagement from the important things in society, as we turn into nations of 'couch potatoes'. Worries about children are also raised for other media; famously, Frederic Wertham's (1954) *Seduction of the Innocent* so raised concerns in America about the depiction of violence in crime and superhero comics that the Comics Code Authority was inaugurated in 1954 in order to censor and classify content. More recently, concerns about new media, especially the internet, have given new impetus to the debate, especially as parents often worry that they have little understanding of their children's use of the technology (Löhr and Mayer 1999; Livingstone 2002). The concern about children is not the *only* debate about media effects, but it is the most public one, with news stories about, say, childhood obesity or paedophilia, inflected through debates about media, society and children (see Schrøder et al. 2003: 35–7, Levine and Harrison 2009, Walsh-Childers and Brown 2008, and Miah and Rich 2010 for overviews of these concerns).

That said, it is important to note that many authors have argued the opposite, and see children's interactions with media as socially useful events. Furthermore, many authors have argued that children's interactions with media are actually very complex, and from a young age people display sophisticated media literacy which undermines the assumption that children are passive dupes, unthinkingly accepting whatever the media throws at them. This has been shown in terms of television (Buckingham 1993; Messenger Davies 1997) and, more recently, in examination of children and the internet (Seiter 1999; Buckingham 2007).

Therefore, what is significant is how central this debate is seen to be for our understanding of the media as a whole; the vast majority of government money spent on academic research goes on examining effects, and it would be pointless having regulations and regulators like Ofcom unless it was assumed media could be a social problem. This also means that the literature on the subject is often more politicised than for many other areas of analysis, and commonly calls for particular changes and developments. Reading work on media effects, then, requires you to be constantly aware of the intentions behind any particular piece. Debates on media effects are highly volatile, and this can make sorting through the material difficult, with little space on offer for sober reflection. Helpfully, though, this shows that it is assumed this debate *matters*; that is, if you have worried that sometimes media theory has little connection to the 'real world', this is certainly not the case here. This gives added impetus to the debates, but also brings significant complications.

INTRODUCTION TO THE READING

It is quite clear in this reading that David Gauntlett does indeed have a particular motivation, and that the rationale of the article is to demonstrate systematically the problems inherent in much existing effects research. It is not as if Gauntlett is oblique about this; the title alone tells you his intention to note what is 'wrong' with other approaches. You may wonder whether such a deliberately subjective stance is acceptable, and how helpful it is in developing dialogue and debate. It is noticeable how exasperated Gauntlett is with the continuing obsession with a debate which he sees as clearly flawed. In that sense, this reading is an *intervention* in the ongoing debate about media effects, which intends to have certain outcomes and 'shake up' the academic community. This should be taken into account when reading it; exactly who is Gauntlett intending to be his audience, and what consequences does this have for the reading?

David Gauntlett is a prominent, public academic, who has spent his career engaging in research activities which have deliberately involved the public, and have crossed the traditional divide between the academic community and the outside world. He became a professor at a young age, demonstrating the impact of his work and the standing he holds within academia. His public profile is at least partly attributable to the website he runs (www.theory.org.uk) which this reading is taken from. The website is a useful research resource, with many articles and discussions on topics such as identity, gender and the relationships between media, society and the individual. The website also demonstrates a more 'fun' approach to theory and those who produce it than you might be used to, with mock-ups of 'theory trading cards' so you can play 'Top Trumps' with theorists, as well as Lego constructions of various thinkers. Gauntlett was one of the first British media academics to realise the potential of the internet as a place in which ideas and theories can be discussed in a more informal manner than is often the case. His work has also experimented with new research approaches – check out his ArtLab and Lego work (www.artlab.org.uk).

This informality can be seen in this reading. Considering article titles are often impenetrable and only make sense once you have read the whole piece, this reading makes clear from the outset what its intentions are. It also adopts a format – a list of ten things – which is quite unusual in academic work. This means the reading is made up shorter segments, which may help accessibility. Overall, you may find this an 'easier' reading than many others you have encountered. While this may help understanding, it is worth you bearing in mind if there are problems with such an approach, as well as benefits.

While much of the theory you will encounter supports its arguments through new research carried out by the writer, this is not really the case here. Instead, Gauntlett works through the work of others, showing the flaws and problems in the ways in which research is carried out, and the resulting conclusions drawn from it. Running throughout is a concern about *methods*, and the *methodologies* which they are drawn from. Quite often, the words 'method' and 'methodology' are used interchangeably, although it is important to be aware of the difference, even though the two are closely related. A 'method' is an approach used to find something out; 'methodology' is the assumptions and principles which support and justify that method. If, in a piece of research, you use a questionnaire, then that questionnaire is your method; the reasons *why* you chose that method, and the assumptions you draw on to demonstrate why questionnaires are a useful research tool, demonstrate your methodology. Gauntlett critiques the methods employed by media effects researchers; he also critiques the methodologies which are used to justify those methods. Importantly, he sees methodologies as making significant assumptions about audiences, which are political in nature. That is, there is no such thing as fully independent, objective research, because methodologies always require assumptions, and those assumptions are inevitably problematic. Much theory you read argues over *what* has been found out; here Gauntlett repeatedly tackles *how* it has been found out, which may be a different approach to theory than that you are used to.

Gauntlett states in his introductory note the various versions this article has gone through, showing how research moves on and develops. Also note that this is the version he has chosen to go on his website; why might this be? Do you bring different expectations to the piece because it was published on the internet?

It might also be worth noting your views on the topic of media effects before you start. Do you think violent media (however that is defined) can have effects upon individuals and society? Do you think the media did play a role in the shootings at Columbine, or the murder of Jamie Bulger? And if you think there is no direct, causal, inescapable link between media and social violence, do you think the media alters society in any way at all? Considering much of our media is regulated – with bodies like Ofcom overseeing television and the internet, and the British Board of Film Classification deciding at what age you are allowed to see certain films – can you see why this might be necessary? On the other hand, if you feel that the media have no effect upon society, do you think it would therefore be okay for all regulation to be done away with, and for there to be total freedom of speech? If so, do you think it is okay for hardcore porn to be broadcast on television at 3 p.m., or would this worry you? Should racist and sexist views be allowed in the media, or should there be regulation to restrict or ban it? What is your view on the media effects debate?

READING

1

David Gauntlett

Ten things wrong with the media 'effects' model

Introductory note: This article was first published as 'Ten things wrong with the "effects model"' in *Approaches to Audiences*, edited by Roger Dickinson, Ramaswani Harindranath and Olga Linne (Arnold, 1998). A different version appeared as part of the chapter 'The worrying influence of "media effects" studies', in *Ill Effects: The Media/Violence Debate (Second Edition)*, edited by Martin Barker and Julian Petley (Routledge, 2001). The version that appears here is basically a version that I produced for inclusion in *Media Studies: The Essential Resource*, edited by Philip Rayner, Peter Wall and Stephen Kruger (Routledge, 2004), and is an 'optimum mix' of both previous versions, but is mostly similar to the first one. The article, and much more material on media effects research, also appears in my book *Moving Experiences, Second Edition: Media Effects and Beyond* (John Libbey, 2005). Readers will be reassured – or perhaps appalled – to note that little has changed in the field of media effects studies since the piece was first written.

2

It has become something of a cliché to observe that despite many decades of research and hundreds of studies, the connections between people's consumption of the mass media and their subsequent behaviour have remained persistently elusive. Indeed, researchers have enjoyed an unusual degree of patience from both their scholarly and more public audiences. But a time must come when we must take a step back from this murky lack of consensus and ask – why? Why are there no clear answers on media effects?

NOTES

1   ## Context

Before his article even begins Gauntlett insists on placing it in its historical context. What is noticeable here is that this reading has gone through a number of revisions, and is available in a variety of versions. Some authors often rewrite their work, responding to comments and criticisms from other writers, or just bringing their material up to date. This is one of the reasons why referencing is so important, so that if you are working from *this* version of the article no one confuses it with other versions. Also note Gauntlett's regret that his work has not altered the debate much; this might be representative of the problems that exist in getting new ideas into a mass arena.

2   ## Content

A cliché, where? Surely it is much more common to hear people insisting there *is* a link between media and violence, and there are many studies which seem to demonstrate it. Gauntlett gives no references here, so we are none the wiser as to who is uttering this cliché.

Structure

By stating his research questions so early on, Gauntlett gives a clear structure to his writing, and ensures the reader knows what its aims are.

READING

3

There is, as I see it, a choice of two conclusions which can be drawn from any detailed analysis of the research. The first is that if, after over 60 years of a considerable amount of research effort, direct effects of media upon behaviour have not been clearly identified, then we should conclude that they are simply *not there to be found*. Since I have argued this case, broadly speaking, elsewhere (Gauntlett, 1995), I will here explore the second possibility: that the media effects research has quite consistently taken the *wrong approach* to the mass media, its audiences, and society in general. This misdirection has taken a number of forms; for the purposes of this chapter, I will impose an unwarranted coherence upon the claims of all those who argue or purport to have found that the mass media will routinely have direct and reasonably predictable effects upon the behaviour of their fellow human beings, calling this body of thought, simply, the 'effects model'. Rather than taking apart each study individually, I will consider the mountain of studies – and the associated claims about media effects made by commentators – as a whole, and outline ten fundamental flaws in their approach.

4

1. The effects model tackles social problems 'backwards'

To explain the problem of violence in society, researchers should begin with that social problem and seek to explain it with reference, quite obviously, to those who engage in it: their background, lifestyles, character profiles, and so on. The 'media effects' approach, in this sense, comes at the problem *backwards*, by starting with the media and then trying to lasso connections from there on to social beings, rather than the other way around.

3 | Writing Style

This might be more chatty writing than you are used to. What is the point in saying 'as I see it'; doesn't this reduce his argument to nothing more than his opinion?

Context

Gauntlett refers to his own work here. He shows that this article develops from his previous work, but also tells you what this article is *not* about. This places this article in a clear historical context, with reference to his other publications.

Content

If the 'coherence' he is imposing is 'unwarranted', what is the justification in doing it?

Structure

Again, notice the really clear way in which Gauntlett explains what he is doing, why he is doing it and how he is doing it. Are most of the readings you have come across written in this way?

4 | Writing Style

Gauntlett is very insistent throughout this article that 'effects' and 'media effects' are in inverted commas, even so in the title. Why has he made this choice?

READING

5

This is an important distinction. Criminologists, in their professional attempts to explain crime and violence, consistently turn for explanations not to the mass media but to social factors such as poverty, unemployment, housing, and the behaviour of family and peers. In a study which *did* start at what I would recognise as the correct end – by interviewing 78 violent teenage offenders and then tracing their behaviour back towards media usage, in comparison with a group of over 500 'ordinary' school pupils of the same age – Hagell & Newburn (1994) found only that the young offenders watched *less* television and video than their counterparts, had less access to the technology in the first place, had no unusual interest in specifically violent programmes, and either enjoyed the same material as non-offending teenagers or were simply *uninterested*. This point was demonstrated very clearly when the offenders were asked, 'If you had the chance to be someone who appears on television, who would you choose to be?':

'The offenders felt particularly uncomfortable with this question and appeared to have difficulty in understanding why one might want to be such a person . . . In several interviews, the offenders had already stated that they watched little television, could not remember their favourite programmes and, consequently, could not think of anyone to be. In these cases, their obvious failure to identify with any television characters seemed to be part of a general lack of engagement with television' (p. 30).

6

Thus we can see that studies which begin by looking at the perpetrators of actual violence, rather than at the media and its audiences, come to rather different conclusions – and there is certainly a need for more such research.

7

(Another study of the viewing preferences of young offenders was commissioned in the UK (Browne & Pennell, 1998), but this made the 'backwards' mistake of showing violent videos to the offenders – putting violent media content onto the agenda from the start – rather than discussing the offenders' everyday viewing choices. The study, which had some methodological flaws (see Gauntlett, 2001), was only able to hint that some violent individuals may enjoy watching violent material more than non-violent people do, if you actually sit the participants down, and show them the videos. Of course such a study is unable to tell us anything about 'media effects'.)

The fact that effects studies take the media as their starting point, however, should not be taken to suggest that they involve sensitive examinations of the mass media. As will be noted below, the studies have typically taken a stereotyped, almost parodic view of media content.

NOTES

5 Context

Gauntlett refers to criminologists here, many of whom spend much of their time trying to work out why people commit crime. While media studies has often employed ideas from a whole range of disciplines, it has engaged with criminology rather less, which might be surprising considering the amount of research being carried out on the relationships between media and crime. Why might criminology be a discipline which media theorists do not often refer to? It should be noted that, conversely, the ideas presented by media studies and, in particular, cultural studies *have* been taken up by some criminologists, in an attempt to explain crime as a cultural phenomenon; see Presdee (2000).

Content

Throughout this article Gauntlett refers to particular studies to demonstrate his arguments. This helps give evidence for his position. But you might ask how representative these studies are. If Williams (2003: 183) notes that over 7,000 pieces of research have been carried out on 'effects', how can one be representative of their findings overall? Indeed, one of the problems in this debate is that so much research has been carried out that anyone can find evidence for any argument they adopt. That said, is it useful for Gauntlett to refer to studies in this way?

6 Structure

Here Gauntlett summarises his findings and also states what needs to be done next. In this way he repeatedly offers useful pointers for the development of his argument.

7 Writing Style

Why is this whole paragraph in brackets?

READING

8

In more general terms, the 'backwards' approach involves the mistake of looking at individuals, rather than society, in relation to the mass media. The narrowly individualistic approach of some psychologists leads them to argue that, because of their belief that particular individuals at certain times in specific circumstances may be negatively affected by one bit of media, the removal of such media from society would be a positive step. This approach is rather like arguing that the solution to the number of road traffic accidents in Britain would be to lock away one famously poor driver from Cornwall; that is, a blinkered approach which tackles a real problem from the wrong end, involves cosmetic rather than relevant changes, and fails to look at the 'bigger picture'.

9

2. The effects model treats children as inadequate

The individualism of the psychological discipline has also had a significant impact on the way in which children are regarded in effects research. Whilst sociology in recent decades has typically regarded childhood as a social construction, demarcated by attitudes, traditions and rituals which vary between different societies and different time periods (Ariés, 1962; Jenks, 1982, 1996), the psychology of childhood – developmental psychology – has remained more tied to the idea of a universal individual who must develop through particular stages before reaching adult maturity, as established by Piaget (e.g. 1926, 1929). The developmental stages are arranged as a hierarchy, from incompetent childhood through to rational, logical adulthood, and progression through these stages is characterised by an 'achievement ethic' (Jenks, 1996, p. 24).

10

In psychology, then, children are often considered not so much in terms of what they *can* do, as what they (apparently) cannot. Negatively defined as non-adults, the research subjects are regarded as the 'other', a strange breed whose failure to match generally middle-class adult norms must be charted and discussed. Most laboratory studies of children and the media presume, for example, that their findings apply only to children, but fail to run parallel studies with adult groups to confirm this. We might speculate that this is because if adults were found to respond to laboratory pressures in the same way as children, the 'common sense' validity of the experiments would be undermined.

8 Writing Style

How useful is the driver analogy Gauntlett uses? Does it help you follow his argument? And is it the kind of writing you are used to coming across?

9 Context

As has been noted, media studies draws on the work of a range of disciplines; here Gauntlett outlines the problem with this. Different disciplines adopt different approaches, and make different assumptions about the individual within society. Much 'effects' work has been carried out by psychologists, which necessarily work from certain assumptions about the individual which, Gauntlett argues, downplays many social factors. As can be seen, the assumptions made by researchers inevitably affect the kinds of conclusions reached.

10 Context

Gauntlett questions the assumptions about the differences between children and adults; do you agree with him? Exactly what are the differences between adults and children? Are they biological, or social, or cultural? Why do we insist on distinguishing between people by age? Would it matter if these categories were got rid of?

Content

Have you come across the concept of the 'other' elsewhere? And why is class mentioned here? Do you think class plays a part in this debate?

Writing Style

Note that 'common sense' is in inverted commas. Why might this be, and how does this relate to media studies' thinking about common sense?

READING

11

In her valuable examination of the way in which academic studies have constructed and maintained a particular perspective on childhood, Christine Griffin (1993) has recorded the ways in which studies produced by psychologists, in particular, have tended to 'blame the victim', to represent social problems as the consequence of the deficiencies or inadequacies of young people, and to 'psychologize inequalities, obscuring structural relations of domination behind a focus on individual "deficient" working-class young people and/or young people of colour, their families or cultural backgrounds' (p. 199). Problems such as unemployment and the failure of education systems are thereby traced to individual psychology traits. The same kinds of approach are readily observed in media effects studies, the production of which has undoubtedly been dominated by psychologically-oriented researchers, who – whilst, one imagines, having nothing other than benevolent intentions – have carefully exposed the full range of ways in which young media users can be seen as the inept victims of products which, whilst obviously puerile and transparent to adults, can trick children into all kinds of ill-advised behaviour.

This situation is clearly exposed by research which seeks to establish what children can and do understand about and from the mass media. Such projects have shown that children can talk intelligently and indeed cynically about the mass media (Buckingham, 1993, 1996), and that children as young as seven can make thoughtful, critical and 'media literate' video productions themselves (Gauntlett, 1997, 2005).

12

3. Assumptions within the effects model are characterised by barely-concealed conservative ideology

The systematic derision of children's resistant capacities can be seen as part of a broader conservative project to position the more contemporary and challenging aspects of the mass media, rather than other social factors, as the major threat to social stability today. Effects studies from the USA, in particular, tend to assume a level of television violence which is simply not applicable in Canada, Europe or elsewhere, and which is based on content analysis methods which count all kinds of 'aggression' seen in the media and come up with a correspondingly high number. George Gerbner's view, for example, that 'We are awash in a tide of violent representations unlike any the world has ever seen . . . drenching every home with graphic scenes of expertly choreographed brutality' (1994, p. 133), both reflects his hyperbolic view of the media in the US and the extent to which findings cannot be simplistically transferred across the Atlantic. Whilst it is certainly possible that gratuitous depictions of violence might reach a level in US screen media which could be seen as unpleasant and unnecessary, it cannot always be assumed that violence is shown for 'bad' reasons or in an uncritical light.

NOTES

11 ## Writing Style

Why does Gauntlett see these studies – and not others – as 'valuable'? Note the subtle ways in which he suggests the significance of some studies over others; his stance towards such research is clearly implied, although without the blatant dismissal of work he finds lacking.

Content

Do you think Gauntlett believes psychologists *do* have 'benevolent intentions'? Note the very precise way in which this sentence is written, including the placing of this phrase within dashes.

12 ## Content

Check you know what is meant by 'conservative' here. In doing so, you might discover some clues as to Gauntlett's position, considering he appears to situate himself in opposition to such conservatism.

Context

In distinguishing between American media and that elsewhere in the world, as well as the 'effects studies' carried out there and elsewhere, Gauntlett is making an important point about the context of media research. Quite often we read research and theory from different countries (and different times) and these usually respond quite specifically to their context. Transferring such material to the here and now can be problematic, and must always be acknowledged. Many of the studies cited in 'effects' debates – whether positive or negative – are American; can these be used as evidence in debates in Britain?

READING

13

Even the most 'gratuitous' acts of violence, such as those committed by Beavis and Butt-Head in their eponymous MTV series, can be interpreted as rationally resistant reactions to an oppressive world which has little to offer them (see Gauntlett, 1997). The way in which media effects researchers talk about the *amount* of violence in the media encourages the view that it is not important to consider the *meaning* of the scenes involving violence which appear on screen.

14

Critics of screen violence, furthermore, often reveal themselves to be worried about challenges to the status quo which they feel that some movies present (even though most European film critics see most popular Hollywood films as being ridiculously status quo-friendly). For example, Michael Medved, author of the successful *Hollywood vs. America: Popular Culture and the War on Traditional Values* (1992) finds worrying and potentially influential displays of 'disrespect for authority' and 'anti-patriotic attitudes' in films like *Top Gun* – a movie which others find embarrassingly jingoistic. The opportunistic mixing of concerns about the roots of violence with political reservations about the content of screen media is a lazy form of propaganda. Media effects studies and TV violence content analyses help to sustain this approach by maintaining the notion that 'antisocial' behaviour is an objective category which can be measured, which is common to numerous programmes, and which will negatively affect those children who see it portrayed.

15

4. The effects model inadequately defines its own objects of study

The flaws numbered four to six in this list are more straightforwardly methodological, although they are connected to the previous and subsequent points. The first of these is that effects studies have generally taken for granted the definitions of media material, such as 'antisocial' and 'prosocial' programming, as well as characterisations of behaviour in the real world, such as 'antisocial' and 'prosocial' action. The point has already been made that these can be ideological value judgements; throwing down a book in disgust, sabotaging a nuclear missile, or smashing cages to set animals free, will always be interpreted in effects studies as 'antisocial', not 'prosocial'.

NOTES

13 Content

Do you agree with Gauntlett's reading of *Beavis and Butt-Head* (MTV: 1993–97, 2011–)? What about violence in other cartoons, such as *Family Guy* (Fox: 1999–02, 2005–) or *South Park* (Comedy Central: 1997–)? While this example may show the variety of ways in which media can be understood, does this necessarily undermine studies which argue 'effects' do exist?

14 Writing Style

Notice the quite forthright language being used here; 'opportunistic', 'political reservations', 'propaganda'. What does this tell us about Gauntlett's view of such approaches? While it might be quite clear what his stance is, note also, though, how he manages to maintain a critical and thoughtful relationship to the material. This shows how it is possible to demonstrate your position without necessarily being bombastic and unnecessarily dismissive.

15 Structure

Here Gauntlett helpfully summarises what is to come in the reading; in doing so, he also highlights the links between the material. Considering this reading is chopped up into ten smaller sections, it is probably sensible for him to make connections in this way to show the overall coherence of the argument.

Content

The debate about what constitutes 'violence' onscreen is a complex one. It is often used when talking about cartoons, which may contain lots of 'violence', but surely it is of a different kind to that in say, news programmes or soap operas. In distinguishing between 'antisocial' and 'prosocial' violence Gauntlett is arguing that there are times when violence might be seen as having positive social consequences, and therefore not all violence is inherently and equally 'bad'. Gauntlett offers three examples here; do you see such violent acts as 'justified'?

READING

16

Furthermore, actions such as verbal aggression or hitting an inanimate object are recorded as acts of violence, just as TV murders are, leading to terrifically (and irretrievably) murky data. It is usually impossible to discern whether very minor or extremely serious acts of 'violence' depicted in the media are being said to have led to quite severe or merely trivial acts in the real world. More significant, perhaps, is the fact that this is rarely seen as a problem: in the media effects field, dodgy 'findings' are accepted with an uncommon hospitality.

17

5. The effects model is often based on artificial elements and assumptions within studies

Since careful sociological studies of media effects require amounts of time and money which limit their abundance, they are heavily outnumbered by simpler studies which are usually characterised by elements of artificiality. Such studies typically take place in a laboratory, or in a 'natural' setting such as a classroom but where a researcher has conspicuously shown up and instigated activities, neither of which are typical environments. Instead of a full and naturally-viewed television diet, research subjects are likely to be shown selected or specially-recorded clips which lack the narrative meaning inherent in everyday TV productions. They may then be observed in simulations of real life presented to them as a game, in relation to inanimate objects such as Bandura's famous 'bobo' doll, or as they respond to questionnaires, all of which are unlike interpersonal interaction, cannot be equated with it, and are likely to be associated with the previous viewing experience in the mind of the subject, rendering the study invalid.

Such studies also rely on the idea that subjects will not alter their behaviour or stated attitudes as a response to being observed or questioned. This naive belief has been shown to be false by researchers such as Borden (1975) who have demonstrated that the presence, appearance and gender of an observer can radically affect children's behaviour.

NOTES

16 Content

These are questions of method. In questioning *how* researchers come to their conclusions, Gauntlett is investigating the methods commonly adopted in such studies. While this is common in debates about theory and research, what is noticeable is that Gauntlett also attempts to examine *why* researchers are happy to use methods which others see as questionable. In his references to class and conservatism, he is arguing there is a link between social 'norms' and expectations, and the methods adopted by researchers. That is, if these methods are faulty, this is no accident, but is instead a consequence of social structures which motivate the research in the first place.

17 Context

It is quite rare for authors to note the limitations placed upon research by time and money. This is clearly a factor in the make-up of studies. The fact that so many studies have been carried out on effects is because governments and other bodies are often willing to fund such research, and are less interested in other approaches. So while you must think about the historical and geographical context of a piece of research, this shows that you must take other practical considerations into account too.

Content

Bandura's bobo doll experiments were highly influential, and appeared to demonstrate a direct causal link between media content and social violence. Many researchers since have questioned their validity for the reasons Gauntlett states. The problem of the effect of the researcher on people is one that no academic discipline has managed to solve, and so all studies are in some way 'artificial'. Do you think this completely invalidates such research?

READING

18

6. The effects model is often based on studies with misapplied methodology

Many of the studies which do not rely on an experimental method, and so may evade the flaws mentioned in the previous point, fall down instead by applying a methodological procedure wrongly, or by drawing inappropriate conclusions from particular methods. The widely-cited longitudinal panel study by Huesmann, Eron and colleagues (Lefkowitz, Eron, Walder & Huesmann, 1972, 1977), for example, has been less famously slated for failing to keep to the procedures, such as assessing aggressivity or TV viewing with the same measures at different points in time, which are necessary for their statistical findings to have any validity (Chaffee, 1972; Kenny, 1972). (A longitudinal panel study is one in which the same group of people – the panel – are surveyed and/or observed at a number of points over a period of time.) The same researchers have also failed to adequately account for why the findings of this study and those of another of their own studies (Huesmann, Lagerspetz & Eron, 1984) absolutely contradict each other, with the former concluding that the media has a marginal effect on boys but no effect on girls, and the latter arguing the exact opposite (no effect on boys, but a small effect for girls). They also seem to ignore that fact that their own follow-up of their original set of subjects 22 years later suggested that a number of biological, developmental and environmental factors contributed to levels of aggression, whilst the mass media was not even given a mention (Huesmann, Eron, Lefkowitz & Walder, 1984). These astounding inconsistencies, unapologetically presented by perhaps the best-known researchers in this area, must be cause for considerable unease about the effects model. More careful use of similar methods, such as in the three-year panel study involving over 3,000 young people conducted by Milavsky, Kessler, Stipp & Rubens (1982a, 1982b), has only indicated that significant media effects are not to be found.

19

Perhaps the most frequent and misleading abuse of methodology occurs when studies which are simply *unable* to show that one thing causes another are treated as if they have done so. Such is the case with correlation studies, which can easily find that a particular personality type is also the kind of person who enjoys a certain kind of media – for example, that violent people like to watch 'violent films' – but are quite unable to show that the media use has *produced* that character. Nevertheless psychologists such as Van Evra (1990) and Browne (1998, 1999) have assumed that this is probably the case. There is a logical coherence to the idea that children whose behaviour is antisocial and disruptional will also have a greater interest in the more violent and noisy television programmes, whereas the idea that the behaviour is a *consequence* of these programmes lacks both this rational consistency, and the support of the studies.

18 ## Content

Gauntlett sees it as significant that the same research methods carried out by the same people resulted in different and contradictory results. Do you see this as a problem? Does this invalidate these studies, or is there a different response which could be taken? This problem of the conflicting results found by many studies is profound; but how often do you hear this mentioned when worries about media effects are discussed in the media?

Writing Style

Again, note the ways in which Gauntlett, through his use of language, clearly criticises the approaches taken.

19 ## Content

The issue being raised here is one of the relationship between *correlation* and *causation*. That is, the fact that it can be demonstrated that behaviour changes when certain stimuli are altered (in this case, that people who are violent watch more violent programming) does not prove either that there is a link between the two, or, if there is a link, the direction in which effects occur. As Gauntlett notes, being violent might be the *cause* of watching a lot of violent programming, rather than the other way around. It is noticeable that the vast majority of studies which 'prove' media effects merely demonstrate *correlation*; it is virtually impossible to prove *causation*, even though such studies usually assume that correlation demonstrates it.

20

7. The effects model is selective in its criticisms of media depictions of violence

In addition to the point that 'antisocial' acts are ideologically defined in effects studies (as noted in item three above), we can also note that the media depictions of 'violence' which the effects model typically condemns are limited to fictional productions. The acts of violence which appear on a daily basis on news and serious factual programmes are seen as somehow exempt. The point here is not that depictions of violence in the news should necessarily be condemned in just the same, blinkered way, but rather to draw attention to another philosophical inconsistency which the model cannot account for. If the antisocial acts shown in drama series and films are expected to have an effect on the behaviour of viewers, even though such acts are almost always ultimately punished or have other negative consequences for the perpetrator, there is no obvious reason why the antisocial activities which are always in the news, and which frequently do *not* have such apparent consequences for their agents, should not have similar effects.

21

8. The effects model assumes superiority to the masses

Surveys typically show that whilst a certain proportion of the public feel that the media may cause other people to engage in antisocial behaviour, almost no-one ever says that they have been affected in that way themselves. This view is taken to extremes by researchers and campaigners whose work brings them into regular contact with the supposedly corrupting material, but who are unconcerned for their own well-being as they implicitly 'know' that the effects could only be on others. Insofar as these others are defined as children or 'unstable' individuals, their approach may seem not unreasonable; it is fair enough that such questions should be explored. Nonetheless, the idea that it is unruly 'others' who will be affected – the uneducated? the working class? – remains at the heart of the effects paradigm, and is reflected in its texts (as well, presumably, as in the researchers' overenthusiastic interpretation of weak or flawed data, as discussed above).

NOTES

20   ## Content

This demonstrates the difficulty in defining what counts as 'violent' media content. As Gauntlett notes, the vast majority of fictional representations of violence are presented as 'bad', and violent people are usually condemned and punished; this is certainly the moral code that most soap operas adhere to. In that sense, while violence may occur on screen, it can be argued that, in fictional portrayals, it is quite clear that they're coded as 'wrong'. But is the same true for factual portrayals? Indeed, think about the ways in which governments justify war or military intervention; here violence is presented as justified, and with a purpose, and therefore acceptable. Overall, there are methodological considerations here, and Gauntlett suggests that merely talking of 'violence' belies a complex range of depictions which can be read in many ways.

21   ## Context

Which surveys? Where are Gauntlett's sources?

Content

This is a significant point. How come researchers and regulators can handle watching violent material, but the general public apparently cannot? Staff at the British Board of Film Classification, who spend much of their time watching a range of media and deciding which age range it is suitable for, must encounter more violent material than most; yet there is little concern for *their* welfare. While Gauntlett raises this as a methodological issue, he clearly also sees it as one about social power. The 'masses' that are the focus of this research are often working class, and there is clearly a hierarchical assumption about who can and cannot handle problematic material. This means that this preponderance of 'effects' research can be read as symptomatic of assumptions about the general public more widely, and so there is an ideological debate about the kinds of research that are carried out, and who is defined as a 'problem' to be solved.

READING

22

George Gerbner and his colleagues, for example, write about 'heavy' television viewers as if this media consumption has necessarily had the opposite effect on the weightiness of their brains. Such people are assumed to have no selectivity or critical skills, and their habits are explicitly contrasted with preferred activities: 'Most viewers watch by the clock and either do not know what they will watch when they turn on the set, or follow established routines rather than choose each program as they would choose a book, a movie or an article' (Gerbner, Gross, Morgan & Signorielli, 1986, p. 19). This view – which knowingly makes inappropriate comparisons by ignoring the serial nature of many TV programmes, and which is unable to account for the widespread use of TV guides and digital or video recorders with which audiences plan and arrange their viewing – reveals the kind of elitism and snobbishness which often seems to underpin such research. The point here is not that the content of the mass media must not be criticised, but rather that the mass audience themselves are not well served by studies which are willing to treat them as potential savages or actual fools.

23

9. The effects model makes no attempt to understand meanings of the media

A further fundamental flaw, hinted at in points three and four above, is that the effects model *necessarily* rests on a base of reductive assumptions and unjustified stereotypes regarding media content. To assert that, say, 'media violence' will bring negative consequences is not only to presume that depictions of violence in the media will always be promoting antisocial behaviour, and that such a category exists and makes sense, as noted above, but also assumes that the medium holds a singular message which will be carried unproblematically to the audience. The effects model therefore performs the double deception of presuming (a) that the media presents a singular and clear-cut 'message', and (b) that the proponents of the effects model are in a position to identify what that message is.

NOTES

| 22 | **Writing Style** |

This is quite angry writing. It is also the second time Gauntlet has directly criticised George Gerbner. He raises an interesting point about the way in which researchers select their language; talk of 'heavy' viewing clearly has negative connotations, and it also assumes a norm against which 'heavy' can be measured. This means that methodological decisions clearly have ideological assumptions within them, and perhaps Gauntlett's anger arises from his disagreement with these assumptions. Do you think this is an appropriate writing style?

| 23 | **Structure** |

Note the reference to previous ideas in the article. This helps draw together the individual ideas separated by the numerical structure Gauntlett uses.

Content

Much of the theory you have come across is likely to argue that there is a variety of ways in which media can be consumed and understood, and it does not have only *one* meaning. In structuralist terms, texts are *polysemic* (see Chapter 15 on structuralism). As Gauntlett notes, 'media effects' research must assume that there is one meaning to a text, which everyone reads in the same way, for once various readings are acknowledged, it becomes extremely difficult to argue that people are affected in a specific way. In that sense, Gauntlett is here relating the debate to a whole range of research (which he references in the next paragraph) which is commonly not part of the effects debate. Although, think about how *you* have been taught about media; to what extent does the educational system acknowledge and validate the range of readings you and your peers might carry out?

READING

24

The meanings of media content are ignored in the simple sense that assumptions are made based on the appearance of elements removed from their context (for example, woman hitting man equals violence equals bad), and in the more sophisticated sense that even *in* context the meanings may be different for different viewers (woman hitting man equals an unpleasant act of aggression, *or* appropriate self-defence, *or* a triumphant act of revenge, *or* a refreshing change, *or* is simply uninteresting, *or* any of many further alternative readings). In-depth qualitative studies have unsurprisingly given support to the view that media audiences routinely arrive at their own, often heterogeneous, interpretations of everyday media texts (e.g. Buckingham, 1993, 1996; Hill, 1997; Schlesinger, Dobash, Dobash & Weaver, 1992; Gray, 1992; Palmer, 1986). Since the effects model rides roughshod over both the meanings that actions have for characters in dramas *and* the meanings which those depicted acts may have for the audience members, it can retain little credibility with those who consider popular entertainment to be more than just a set of very basic propaganda messages flashed at the audience in the simplest possible terms.

25

10. The effects model is not grounded in theory

26

Finally, and underlying many of the points made above, is the fundamental problem that the entire argument of the 'effects model' is not substantiated with any theoretical reasoning beyond the bald assertions that particular kinds of effects will be produced by the media. The basic question of *why* the media should induce people to imitate its content has never been adequately tackled, beyond the simple idea that particular actions are 'glamorised'. (However, antisocial actions are shown really *positively* so infrequently that this is an inadequate explanation.) Similarly, the question of how merely seeing an activity in the media would be translated into an actual *motive* which would prompt an individual to behave in a particular way is just as unresolved. The lack of firm theory has led to the effects model being rooted in the set of questionable assumptions outlined above – that the mass media (rather than people) should be the unproblematic starting-point for research; that children will be unable to 'cope' with the media; that the categories of 'violence' or 'antisocial behaviour' are

24   ## Content

Do you agree that the action of a man hitting a woman can have the range of meanings Gauntlett suggests here? Is this range infinite, or is there a 'core' meaning which must be appropriate to *all* interpretations of this act? And why does Gauntlett specify '*popular* entertainment' here? Think how this relates to debates about popular and mass culture which recur throughout your reading.

25   ## Content

It might seem odd that this is the first time that 'theory' is explicitly mentioned, especially as this suggests that the rest of the reading is *not* about theory. Yet it is clear the whole piece *is* about theory; the question here is that 'media effects' debates have failed to develop theory specifically about, and responding to, its aims and findings. Throughout this section, then, Gauntlett raises a set of questions which 'media effects' studies never asks; while this can be seen as a criticism, the bigger query might be *why* it is that such questions are not asked.

26   ## Content

Can you answer any of these questions? Why might the media try to induce people to mimic its content? How might seeing violence turn into violent action? Do these questions undermine the 'media effects' assumptions in the way Gauntlett intends, or are they easily answerable?

Structure

This is a helpful summary of all the points raised in the article. It therefore shows the links between the issues, and that they are not merely a list of unrelated concerns.

READING

26

(continued)

clear and self-evident; that the model's predictions can be verified by scientific research; that screen fictions are of concern, whilst news pictures are not; that researchers have the unique capacity to observe and classify social behaviour and its meanings, but that those researchers need not attend to the various possible meanings which media content may have for the audience. Each of these very substantial problems has its roots in the failure of media effects commentators to found their model in any coherent theory.

27

So what future for research on media influences?

28

The effects model, we have seen, has remarkably little going for it as an explanation of human behaviour, or of the media's role in society. Whilst any challenging or apparently illogical theory or model reserves the right to demonstrate its validity through empirical data, the effects model has failed also in that respect. Its continued survival is indefensible and unfortunate. However, the failure of this particular *model* does not mean that the impact of the mass media can no longer be considered or investigated. Indeed, there are many fascinating questions to be explored about the influence of the media upon our perceptions, and ways of thinking and being in the world (Gauntlett, 2002), which simply get ignored whilst the research funding and attention is going to shoddy effects studies.

29

It is worrying to note the numbers of psychologists (and others) who conduct research according to traditional methodological recipes, despite the many well-known flaws with those procedures, when it is so easy to imagine alternative research methods and processes. (For example, see the website www.artlab.org.uk, and Gauntlett (2005), for information about the 'new creative audience studies' in which participants are invited to make media and artistic artefacts *themselves*, as a way of exploring their relationships with mass media.) The discourses about 'media effects' from politicians and the popular press are often laughably simplistic. Needless to say, academics shouldn't encourage them.

27   ## Structure

It is quite common for articles to end on suggestions for future research, and this is the case here. This is a fruitful way of drawing together the disparate arguments, and showing a positive outcome, rather than ending merely on a list of criticisms.

28   ## Content

Gauntlett is careful here to distinguish between his criticisms of the 'effects model', and the assumption that there is therefore no relationship between media and society. Indeed, he is a leading proponent in such studies, but he is instead interested in that relationship as a complex, reciprocal one, rather than one of cause and effect.

Context

Note the mention of research funding again. Why does money keep going to what Gauntlett calls 'shoddy' work?

29   ## Context

Gauntlett refers here to the relationship between academia, the press and politicians, which is often not mentioned by many writers. The implication is that the debate he is engaged in matters because it is one in the public agenda, and informs political decisions. This shows how debates about theory quite clearly do have 'real-world' implications, and that academics' positions on such arguments have marked consequences for the world around us. This might be a useful corrective to debates about the 'usefulness' of theory.

REFLECTING ON THE READING

Before the reading it was suggested that you thought about your own views on the media effects debate; now you have completed the reading, what do you think? Do you agree with Gauntlett, or do you find flaws with his argument? In his second section he criticises the view developmental psychologists take of children; do you see his point, or do you see a necessity for children to be protected in some way? Can you see how different kinds of violence might be difficult to categorise, and that different viewers might read them differently, or do you think violence is, instead, easy to spot? In essence, has this article changed your thinking at all; it may not have entirely persuaded you, but has it raised any doubts, or made you think you need to know more, than was the case before you read it?

Throughout the reading Gauntlett critiques the methods employed by many researchers; do you agree with his criticisms? Perhaps more importantly, what do you think of Gauntlett's method? Are there approaches, or ideas, or arguments which he doesn't take on board, or think about? If you go to Gauntlett's website and look at the research methods he has employed, can you make any similar criticisms?

What about the article's structure? As was noted in the Introduction, the 'ten things' approach breaks the article up into smaller chunks, which may make it easier to read. But are there problems with this format? Why are some of the sections longer than others? Aren't some more detailed, and give more references, than others? Indeed, why *ten* sections? Are they all necessary, or should there have been more? Is ten just a nice round number, and the arguments have been categorised in order to fit that format? Does this restrict the power of the overall argument? And think about your own work: is this an approach you could take in your essays, and, if so, when and where would it be appropriate to do so?

Finally, it has been noted that this article is one version of a series of similar articles published in various places. In the introductory note to this version, Gauntlett notes that little has changed since he wrote the first version. But what about now? If you were asked to update this article, and write a new version, what would you change? Has the media effects debate moved on at all? What are the consequences of the research methods Gauntlett (and others) employ? Are there newer studies which either support or critique Gauntlett's position? As has been said throughout this book, theory is an ongoing process, which responds to new ideas, new research, and changes in society; if you were to engage in that process here, and write an updated version, what would it contain?

Key terms to explore

audiences; children; content analysis; correlation; developmental psychology; effects; methodology; prosocial/antisocial behaviour; stereotypes; violence.

Key writers who are mentioned

Albert Bandura; David Buckingham; George Gerbner; Christine Griffin; Michael Medved; Jean Piaget.

RECOMMENDED READING

Barker, Martin, and Julian Petley (eds) (1997) *Ill Effects: The media/violence debate*, London and New York: Routledge.

Collection of essays not only examining debates about media effects, but also exploring the discourses surrounding such debates, to see why 'effects' is such a recurring topic in media studies.

Bryant, J. and Oliver, M.B. (eds) (2009) *Media Effects: Advances in theory and research*, 3rd edition, New York and London: Routledge.

Comprehensive coverage of key debates and methodological approaches, covering a wide range of media.

Livingstone, Sonia (2002) *Young People and New Media: Childhood and the changing media environment*, London: Sage.

Useful attempt to examine how young people have responded to recent changes in media technology, especially the internet; the book draws on audience research carried out by Livingstone.

CHAPTER 15

Structuralism

Todorov, T. (1990 [1978]) *Genres in Discourse*, translated by Porter, C., Cambridge: Cambridge University Press, pp. 27–38.

INTRODUCTION TO STRUCTURALISM

How do you make decisions about what films you want to see? Do you read reviews, or go on recommendations from friends? Are there certain actors you like, whose films you always go and see? Or perhaps there are particular directors whose films interest you? Do trailers make a difference to your choices? Or do you just turn up to the cinema with your friends, and decide then whatever takes your fancy? If so, how does that process work; do you go on the title, or the poster, or something else? Thinking about how we make decisions about what to consume – as well as what *not* to consume – tells us significant things about how we categorise the wealth of media options available to us. It means we think of ourselves as the kind of person who likes that kind of film, or that kind of music, or those kinds of television programmes, or that magazine. Our decisions result from a lot of factors – previous knowledge, advertising, how we are feeling that day, who we are with, and so on – but they all show that we often have certain *expectations* for a media text when we decide to consume it. If you go to see a James Bond film you assume there will be lots of action, and gadgets; if you buy *The Guardian* you would expect noticeably different content from that of, say, *The Sun*; in the first few episodes of *The X Factor* (ITV, 2004–) you perhaps hope to see very bad singers making fools of themselves. So, while media must be different and innovative in order to be interesting, it must also, in many ways, be the same, so we know what to expect and are not disappointed.

· For us to have expectations, there must be recurring characters, stories and ideas within media which we expect and recognise. These might alter subtly within different series, or across time, but remain roughly the same. Many of the characters in soap operas, for example, remain constant, and when they leave, they are often replaced by similar ones. Similarly, the stories in soap operas recur, with births, marriages and deaths central, and lots of narratives based around love, with relationships and secret affairs happening again and again. It is the idea that stories have recurring, repeatable, constant elements that is the core of structuralism.

Structuralism – as its name implies – is 'fundamentally a way of thinking about the world which is predominantly concerned with the perception and description of structures' (Hawkes 2003: 6). It works from the idea that, if you distil most stories down to their basic elements, you will find that they are, roughly, all the same. They have recurring characters, who carry out recurring actions, heading towards recurring endings. So soap opera characters fall in and out of love, again and again and again, and the stories remain the same year after year. Our interest often lies less in *what* happens, and more in *how* it happens. And it is clear from this that we know and understand the structures which stories rely upon, and use those structures to make sense of the stories. Structuralism is about examining those structures, finding common and recurring elements in stories across genres, media, cultures and throughout time. Indeed, it is often quite surprising to find that ancient literature, while often difficult to understand because of changes in language, often has the same basic storytelling elements as the most recent film or television programme.

You might ask why all this matters; so what if all stories draw on the same basic elements? Perhaps this just means that these must be the best ways of telling stories, and help aid our enjoyment? This could be true. However, it could also be argued that the preponderance of recurring structures helps limit the kinds of stories that can be told. To go back to the James Bond example; how do you tell a Bond story in which 007 is defeated by the villain? How would we enjoy it? How do you make a soap opera character interesting if they are not someone who argues with people, falls in love repeatedly, and so on? If there are certain ways of telling stories, this makes it easier for certain kinds of stories to be told: similarly, it makes it very hard to tell other kinds of stories in a way which is comprehensible. This can have significant political and ideological consequences, as it normalises certain kinds of stories and ways of storytelling, and makes other kinds quite difficult. For example, many feminists have used structuralism to show that men and women are required to act in particular ways in stories, with men usually being more central and more active (Gilbert and Gubar 1979). The same could be said to be true for issues of, say, class or race, where we expect certain characters to behave in certain ways; this is the basis of stereotypes (Pickering 2001). This means structuralism has significance for social inequalities, and so has a purpose beyond merely pointing out how stories work.

It is important to be aware of the history of structuralism. It arose out of linguistics, through the anthropological work of people like Ferdinand de Saussure and Claude Lévi-Strauss. Such theorists attempted to work out how language *worked*: that is, how we learned to make sense of it in everyday situations. Therefore, Structuralism is often related to ideas of grammar in writing, in which there are learned 'rules' about how to put together a sentence 'correctly'. This means that, like much media theory, it was created by people whose primary interest was *not* media; it has instead been *applied* to media by subsequent thinkers, who argue that the assumptions that exist for spoken or written language can be applied to the languages of a whole range of media. Structuralism is a controversial term, especially as the vast majority of people associated with it – including Lévi-Strauss and Saussure – reject it. One of the key ways in which structuralist analysis is carried out is through semiotics: see Chapter 22, on texts, in *this* book for more on this area.

This reading comes from Tzvetan Todorov's *Genres in Discourse* (1990 [1978]). Todorov is a Bulgarian philosopher, now living and working in France, who has worked on literary theory, culture and history, in books such as *The Poetics of Prose* (1977 [1971]), *The Conquest of America* (1999 [1984]), and *Hope and Memory* (2003 [2000]). The title of the book is a bit of a misnomer, as it is not all about genre, and is instead a collection of essays which explore specific texts, definitions and categorisations of literature, and, to a large extent, poetry. Throughout his writing Todorov uses lots of examples, but these are commonly from French literature, and so you might not have come across many of them before. As a reader, the sensible thing for you to do is think of your own examples which will help you make sense of the argument.

Todorov is perhaps best known for his analysis of the 'uncanny': that is, events within stories which are unexpected and surprising. Even though structuralism argues that stories have common and recurring elements, it acknowledges that differences between stories must exist in order to remain interesting. Neale calls this 'repetition and difference' (1980: 48). Similarly, 'Genres "evolve" because the act of belonging to a genre involves both adoption of and resistance to its conventions' (Duff 2000: 7–8). Todorov outlines a number of ways in which it is possible to respond to unexpected events in a story, depending on how unexpected they are, and how they relate to narrative and genre. What is interesting here is that Todorov is beginning to examine the ways in which *readers* make sense of texts, and acknowledges these might be various. Structuralism is sometimes criticised for suggesting that all readers make sense of a text in exactly the same way; indeed, it has to make this implication, otherwise it is rather pointless to note that stories have an underlying common structure. In acknowledging a range of responses, Todorov is beginning to note that these underlying structures are part of a communicative *process*, which is shaped and limited by the text, but not fully and solely defined by it. It is important to note that Todorov does not take this very far, and it was subsequent analysts that instead did so. Indeed, as you are going through this reading, note how often Todorov assumes that the reading *he* makes of examples is the one *everyone* will make.

Genres are important to structuralism, because they help demonstrate how texts use recurring forms and events. Genre is an important idea in media studies as a whole, and much analysis is generically structured. Genre is 'a matter of discrimination and taxonomy: of organising things into recognisable classes' (Frow 2006: 51). Pretty much all media forms are generically classified and promoted through genre. So, film posters for romantic comedies are usually quite different to those for, say, science fiction ones, and you can tell very quickly what type of film the poster is for. When you press the 'TV Guide' button on a Sky⁺ box it takes you to a menu where it categorises all the programmes on offer, giving you genres such as news, sport, documentary, entertainment, children's TV, and so on. Now, these categories are never fully defined; in which genre do we place a children's documentary about sport, for example: is it a children's programme, a documentary or a sports programme? But it does mean that there is a system which has evolved to help us make sense of the range of media on offer to us, and that system means that we come to texts with certain expectations (which might not be fulfilled, but probably will be). Therefore, genre analysis *is* structuralist analysis, even if it is not always referred to as such. It is therefore unsurprising that Todorov should be interested in genres.

This reading is a translation, with all the problems that implies. For example, different people might translate something in a different way, and so if you looked at another edition of this book you might find it quite different. As this work is about the structures of communication and the ways in which language 'works', this problem might be seen to be more pressing. Yet, other than becoming fluent in French, you can do nothing but rely on the rigour of the translator. This shows how communication relies on sets of processes which are social and cultural, and often beyond our immediate control.

1

T. Todorov

The Two Principles of Narrative

Since we are about to take up the question of narrative, let me begin by telling a story.

Ricciardo Minutolo is in love with Filippello's wife Catella. Despite his best efforts, however, Ricciardo's love is not returned. When he discovers that Catella is extremely jealous of her husband, Ricciardo decides to take advantage of this weakness. After making a public display of his lack of interest in Catella, he finds an occasion to convey the same impression to her directly; at the same time, he informs her of approaches Filippello has purportedly made to his own wife. Catella is furious and wants all the details. Nothing could be easier, Ricciardo replies. Filippello has made a date to meet Ricciardo's wife the next day, at a nearby bath house; Catella has only to show up there instead, and she will be convinced of her husband's treachery. So Catella goes to the bath house – where she finds Ricciardo in her husband's place. She fails to recognize him, however, as the meeting place is completely dark. Catella cooperates with the desires of the man she takes to be her husband, but then immediately begins to reproach him, explaining that she is not Ricciardo's wife, but Catella. Ricciardo reveals in turn that he himself is not Filippello. Catella is distraught, but Ricciardo convinces her that scandal would be in no one's interests, and "how much more savoury a lover's kisses are than those of a husband."[1]

So all ends well, and Boccaccio adds that this tale was praised by all who first heard it.

2

The foregoing text consists of a sequence of propositions that is easily recognized as a narrative. But what *makes* it a narrative? Let us go back to the beginning of the story. First Boccaccio describes Naples, the setting for the action; next he presents the three protagonists; after that, he speaks of Ricciardo's love for Catella. Is that a narrative? Here I think we can readily agree that the answer is "no." This judgment does not depend on the dimensions of the text; the passage in question takes only two paragraphs in Boccaccio, but we sense that it could be five times as long without making any difference. On the other hand, when Boccaccio says: "Such was his state of mind when . . ." (and in the French translation there is a change of tense here from the imperfect to the *passé simple*), the narrative takes off. The explanation seems straightforward. The beginning of the text presents the description of a state of affairs. That does not suffice for narrative, however, as narrative requires the unfolding of an action, change, difference.

1. *The Decameron of Giovanni Boccaccio*, Trans. Richard Aldington (New York: Dell Publishing Company, 1982) 207, "Third Day, Sixth Tale."

1

Structure

Todorov begins with an example, telling a story in detail. As his aim is to examine the ways in which narratives work, it seems sensible to offer an example which he can then analyse. Do you find this a useful approach? Also note what kind of narrative Todorov recounts; it comes from Boccaccio, who is a fourteenth century Italian author and poet. While it is not at all necessary for you to know this in order to understand the story and Todorov's analysis of it, what might this selection tell us about Todorov himself?

2

Content

Notice the significance attached to 'makes' by it being in italics; this demonstrates Todorov's idea that narratives are a process, and that events have to be actively turned into a narrative.

Writing Style

Note how Todorov refers to 'us' and 'we'. Here, he is acknowledging you, as a reader. This could be seen as a helpful way to involve you in the argument. However, he also suggests 'we can readily agree', assuming you respond the same as him; what if you disagree? What if Todorov's assumption is wrong?

READING

3

Every change constitutes in fact a new narrative link. Ricciardo learns of Catella's extreme jealousy – which allows him to conceive of his plan – after which he can carry it out – Catella reacts as Ricciardo had hoped – the meeting takes place – Catella reveals her true identity – Ricciardo reveals his – they discover their happiness together. Each action thus isolated follows the previous one and most of the time the two are in a causal relation. Catella's jealousy is a *condition* of the plan that is concocted; the plan has the meeting as a *consequence*; public condemnation is *implied* by adultery; and so on.

4

Description and narrative both presuppose temporality, but the temporality differs in kind. The initial description was situated in time, to be sure, but in an ongoing, continuous time frame, whereas the changes that characterize narrative slice time up into discontinuous units: duration-time as opposed to event-time. Description alone is not enough to constitute a narrative; narrative for its part does not exclude description, however. If we needed a generic term to include both narrative texts and descriptive texts (that is, texts containing only descriptions), we might choose the term *fiction* (the French cognate term is used relatively rarely). This would have two advantages: first, because fiction includes narration *and* description; second, because it evokes the transitive and referential use made of words in each case (and the texts of someone like Raymond Roussel, who bases narrative on the distance that exists between two senses of a given word, do not constitute counterexamples), as opposed to the intransitive, literal use that is made of language in poetry.

5

This way of looking at narrative as the chronological and sometimes causal linkage of discontinuous units is of course not new. Vladimir Propp's work on the Russian fairy tale, which leads to similar conclusion, is widely known today. Propp uses the term *function* for each action isolated when actions are seen from the perspective of their usefulness to the story; and he postulates that for all the Russian fairy tales there are only thirty-one types of function. "If we read through all of the functions one after another, we quickly observe that one function develops out of another with logical and artistic necessity. We see that not a single function excludes another. They all revolve on a single pivot, and not . . . on a variety of pivotal stocks."[2] Functions come in sequence and are not alike.

2. Vladimir Propp, *Morphology of the Folktale*, ed. Svatava Pirkova-Jakobson, trans. Lawrence Scott, Publication Ten of the Indiana University Research Center in Anthropology, Folklore and Linguistics (Bloomington, 1958), p. 12.

3   Writing Style

How do you respond to the recurring use of dashes to construct a sentence? Would you be allowed to do this in your writing?

Content

This is a key idea in structuralism: that narratives rely on ideas of cause and effect, which are usually presented in that order. A random set of events does not make a narrative; there must be some way in which events are linked, responding to one another. If you think about the times you have been confused by a film, because characters act strangely, or things happen which cannot be explained, you will realise that your confusion is a result of an expectation that stories should be logical, motivated by cause and effect.

4   Writing Style

The writing style changes considerably here. We move from an analysis of an example to more complex theorising of what has been demonstrated. Do you find this paragraph difficult? If so, does Todorov's analysis of the example earlier help your understanding?

Content

Todorov uses the word 'fiction' here in a way you might not agree with. As you may have realised, theorists often offer their own definitions for a word, which might be related to normal everyday use, or which might deliberately contradict general understandings of it. It is important you are aware of how different people use different words; this is why it is often also important in your own writing that you make clear what you mean by certain words, especially those used in a variety of ways by various writers.

5   Context

Todorov notes his analysis is not new, and places it in the context of Vladimir Propp's *Morphology of the Folktale* (1968 [1928]). Propp analysed hundreds of Russian fairy tales that had been handed down through generations, and found that they all had the same basic narrative structure and main characters. It can be seen that this is useful evidence for structuralists, who argue that there are underlying structures within all forms of communication. Propp's work is central to structuralism, even though it took some thirty years for it to be translated into English. His structures can be applied to the majority of mainstream texts today, such as Hollywood films, soap operas, and the ways in which news is reported. Note that, like Note 4, the word 'function' is used here in a specific way, which Todorov defines to ensure we understand what is meant by it.

READING

6

Propp analyzes one tale, "The Swan-Geese," in its entirety; we shall summarize his analysis here. This is the story of a young girl who neglects to look after her little brother. The swan-geese kidnap him, the girl goes off to find him, and succeeds, thanks to the wise counsel of a hedgehog. She takes her brother away; the swan-geese set out in pursuit, but, with the help of the river, the apple tree, and the woodstove, she manages to get him home safe and sound. In this narrative Propp singles out twenty-seven elements, of which eighteen are functions (the others are descriptions, transitions, and so forth) belonging to the canonical list of thirty-one. Each function is situated on the same level as, while being totally different from, all the others; one function is related to another only through chronological succession.

7

The validity of this analysis can be questioned, particularly as regards the possibility that Propp may have confused generic (and empirical) necessity with theoretical necessity. All the functions may be equally necessary to the Russian fairy tale; but are they all necessary for the same reasons? Let us try an experiment. When I told the Russian tale, I omitted some of the initial functions: for example, the girl's parents had forbidden her to stray from the house; the girl had chosen to go off to play; and so on. The tale is nevertheless a narrative, fundamentally unchanged. On the other hand, if I had not said that a girl and a boy were playing at home, or that the geese had kidnapped the boy, or that the girl had gone looking for him, there would have been no narrative, or a different one. We may conclude that not all functions are necessary to the narrative in the same way; a hierarchical order has to be introduced.

8

If we analyze "The Swan-Geese" this way, we shall discover that the tale includes five obligatory elements: (1) the opening situation of equilibrium; (2) the degradation of the situation through the kidnapping of the boy; (3) the state of disequilibrium observed by the little girl; (4) the search for and recovery of the boy; (5) the reestablishment of the initial equilibrium – the return home. If any one of these five actions had been omitted, the tale would have lost its identity. Of course one can imagine a tale that omits the first two elements and begins with a situation that is already deficient; or a tale might omit the last two elements and end on an unhappy note. But we sense that these would be two halves of the cycle, whereas here we have the cycle in full. Theoretical research has shown – and empirical studies have confirmed – that this cycle belongs to the very definition of narrative: one cannot imagine a narrative that fails to contain at least a part of it.

6 **Structure**

Again, we have an example here. This helps make clear Propp's analysis. However, Todorov goes on to criticise Propp's approach, so this example is being used to give Todorov material which he can apply his own analysis to.

Content

You might wonder to what extent Todorov's summary of Propp is accurate. This is not to say it is not accurate, but different people would summarise an idea in a different way. If you read Propp you might think Todorov is misrepresenting him. This is always something to bear in mind when one writer discusses another.

7 ## Content

This makes clear Todorov's argument. It shows how he sees his work as *developing* that of Propp's: that is, he wants to modify it rather than reject it. Indeed, if Propp's analysis did not exist, Todorov would not have been able to do his. This shows how theory often draws on existing theory, and that theorising is an ongoing process dependent on the interplay of various writers and thinkers.

8 ## Content

Do you agree with Todorov that, if any of those elements he says are obligatory had been omitted, the story would still have made some kind of sense, but would have felt 'deficient'? If so, it shows that you bring expectations to a story that must be fulfilled in order for it to feel complete. Structuralism argues that these expectations come from our acquaintance with, and understanding of, the conventions and functions inherent in the majority of stories.

Writing Style

Note that Todorov does not reference his sources here. We have to take on trust that the research he mentions exists. Why is this the case, especially when he has referenced other material elsewhere?

9

The actions Propp identified do not all have the same status. Some are optional, supplementary to the basic schema. For example, the little girl's absence at the time of the kidnapping may be motivated or not. Other actions are alternatives, of which at least one has to occur in the tale: these are concrete realizations of the action prescribed by the schema. For example, the little girl finds her brother thanks to the intervention of a helper; however, she might just as well have found him owing to her speedy legs, or her divinatory powers, and so forth. In his well-known book *La Logique du récit*, Claude Bremond has taken up the challenge of cataloging the possible alternatives available to any narrative whatsoever.[3]

10

But if the elementary actions are arranged hierarchically it is apparent that new relations prevail among them: sequence and consequence no longer suffice. The fifth element obviously echoes the first (the state of equilibrium), while the third is an inversion of the first. Moreover, the second and the fourth elements are symmetrically opposed: the little boy is taken away from home and is brought back home. Thus it is incorrect to maintain that the elements are related only by *succession*, we can say that they are also related by *transformation*. Here finally we have the two principles of narrative.

11

Can a narrative dispense with the second principle, transformation? In discussing the problems of definition and denomination, we need to be aware of a certain arbitrariness that invariably accompanies these gestures. We find ourselves confronting a continuum of facts and relationships; we then establish a limit somewhere, and call everything on one side of the limit "narrative," and everything on the other side "nonnarrative." But the words of the language we use have different nuances depending on who is speaking. A moment ago I contrasted narration and description by way of the two types of temporality they exhibit; however, others would call a book like Robbe-Grillet's *Dans le labyrinthe* a narrative, even though it suspends narrative time and posits variations in the characters' behavior as simultaneous. The same can be said regarding the presence or absence of relations of transformation between individual actions. A narrative lacking in such relations can be constructed artificially; real examples of the pure logic of succession may even be found in certain chronicles. But we shall have no trouble agreeing, I think, that neither these chronicles nor Robbe-Grillet's novels are typical representatives of narrative. We may take this argument even further: by bringing to light the difference between narration and description, or between the principle of succession and the principle of transformation, we have made it possible to understand why we perceive such narratives as marginal, in one sense of the term. Ordinarily, even the simplest, least elaborate narrative puts the two principles into action simultaneously. As (anecdotal) evidence, let us look at the French title of a recent spaghetti Western: *Je vais, je tire, je reviens* ("I go off, I shoot, I come back"): the apparently straightforward succession obscures a relation of transformation between "going off" and "coming back."

3. Claude Bremond, *La Logique du récit*, Collection Poétique (Editions du Seuil, 1973).

NOTES

9 ### Context

Is Bremond 'well-known', as Todorov says? Well known to whom?

10 ### Structure

This is an important summary of what has gone before; it is the conclusion of the evidence and analysis which has preceded it.

11 ### Content

Todorov makes an interesting concession here, for he notes that all theorising must encompass 'arbitrariness'. That is, while theory tries to make sense of the world, we can never fully pin it down because there are always exceptions and alternatives. In a sense, Todorov (and all theorists) are requesting you accept that what they are saying is convincing the majority of the time, and not to reject an idea just because of a few exceptions. Are you willing to go along with this request?

Context

Alain Robbe-Grillet was a French writer and film-maker, famous for attempting to dismantle traditional ways of constructing narratives, usually by refusing to adopt sequences of cause and effect, and playing about with the chronology of stories. Because we are used to reading stories in such a way, however, it is inevitable that most readers will attempt to construct a traditional story from his novels, because it is how we are used to making sense of things. Todorov acknowledges this, but notes we are aware of the difficulty of this process, and that Robbe-Grillet's novels do not feel 'typical'. See Stoltzfus (1964).

Writing Style

Why is this marked as 'anecdotal' evidence, unlike other evidence offered? Does this make it more valuable or less?

READING

12 What is the nature of such transformations? The one we have noted so far consists in changing some term into its opposite or its contrary; for simplicity's sake, we shall call it *negation*. Lévi-Strauss and Greimas have placed particular emphasis on this transformation. They have scrutinized its various manifestations to such an extent that one might conclude it is the only transformation possible. It is true that the transformation of negation enjoys a special status, no doubt owing to the privileged position occupied by negation in our system of thought. The passage from *A* to non-*A* is in a way the paradigm of all change. Still, this exceptional status must not be allowed to obscure the existence of other transformations – which are numerous, as we shall see. In the tale Propp analyzed, for instance, we can find a transformation of mode: the interdiction – in other words, a negative obligation – imposed upon the little girl by her parents (she was not to leave her brother's side for an instant). And there is a transformation of intention: the little girl decides to leave in search of her brother, then she actually leaves; the first action relates to the second as an intention to its realization.

13 Returning to our tale from the *Decameron*, we can see the same relationships there. Ricciardo is unhappy at the beginning, happy at the end: a transformation of negation. He wants to possess Catella, then he possesses her: a transformation of mode. But other relations seem to play an even more important role. A single action is presented three times: first of all, there is Ricciardo's plan for getting Catella into the bath house, then there is Catella's erroneous perception of that scene, when she thinks she is meeting her husband there; finally the true situation is revealed. The relation between the first and third propositions is that of a project to its realization; in the relation between the second and the third, an erroneous perception of an event is opposed to an accurate perception of that same event. This deception is obviously the key to Boccaccio's narrative. A qualitative difference separates the first type of transformations from the second. The first case involved a modification carried out on a basic predicate; the predicate was taken in its positive or negative form, modalized or unmodalized. Here the initial predicate turns out to be accompanied by a secondary predicate, such as "to plan" or "to learn." Paradoxically, this secondary predicate designates an autonomous action but at the same time can never appear all by itself: one always projects *toward* another action. The lineaments of an opposition between two types of narrative organization are beginning to take shape.

14 On the one hand we have narratives in which the logic of succession and transformations of the first type are combined; these will be the simpler narratives, as it were, and I should like to use the term *mythological* for this type of organization. On the other hand, we have the type of narrative in which the logic of succession is supported by the second sort of transformation, narratives in which the event itself is less important than our perception of it, and degree of knowledge we have of it: hence I propose the term *gnoseological* for this second type of narrative organization (it might also be called *epistemical*).

NOTES

12

Structure

Note how this paragraph begins with a question. This is a simple and useful way of telling a reader what it is they are about to encounter in the subsequent paragraph.

Writing Style

Do you think calling it 'negation' is 'for simplicity's sake'? Simple for whom, the reader or the writer? Also, note again the lack of references. It is to be presumed that Todorov is referring to Lévi-Strauss (1963 [1958]) and Greimas (1983 [1966]).

13

Content

You might find this whole paragraph difficult. The main reason for this is that it is actually saying something quite simple, but because it is something we are not used to analysing, and it is done in such detail, it seems to overcomplicate matters. Todorov is now less interested in specific events in the story, and more in the ways in which those events are related to one another, and rely on one another. If you find this section difficult, deal with it one sentence at a time. Do not be put off by thinking it is more complicated than it is.

14

Writing Style

Todorov here suggests that he is working through his ideas as he is writing them, something he does quite often in this reading. Most of the material you read probably does not do this, and instead presents an argument as fully worked through. There is a sense of *process* here, which makes sense considering he is discussing the linear interactions of narrative. Do you find these signposts useful?

READING

15

It goes without saying that an opposition of this sort is not intended to result in the distribution of all the world's narratives into two piles, with mythological stories on one side and gnoseological stories on the other. As in any typological study, I am seeking rather to bring to light the abstract categories that make it possible to account for real differences between one narrative and another. This does not mean, moreover, that a narrative must exhibit one type of transformation to the exclusion of the other. If we go back to "The Swan-Geese," we can find traces of gnoseological organization in it as well. For example, the brother's kidnapping took place in the little girl's absence; in principle, the girl does not know who is responsible, and there would be a place here for a quest for information. But the tale simply says: "The girl guessed that they had taken her brother away," without lingering over this process. On the other hand, Boccaccio's tale rests entirely upon ignorance followed by knowledge. If we want to attach narratives to a particular type of narrative organization, we have to look for the qualitative or quantitative predominance of certain transformations, not for their exclusive presence.

A glance at some other examples of gnoseological organization will be helpful. In a work like *La Quête du Graal*,[4] passages recounting actual events are often preceded by passages in which those same events are evoked in the form of a prediction. In this text, such transformations of supposition have a peculiar feature: they all come true, and are even perceived as moral imperatives by the characters. The outcome of the plot is related by Perceval's aunt at the very beginning of the section entitled "Aventures de Perceval": "For it is well known, in this country as elsewhere, that in the end three knights above all others will reap the glory of the Quest: two will be virgins and the third chaste. Of the two virgins, one will be the knight you are looking for, and you will be the other; the third will be Bohort de Gaunes. These three will succeed in the Quest" (118). And there is Perceval's sister, who predicts where her brother and Galahad will die: "For my honor, have me buried in the Spiritual Palace. Do you know why I request this? Because Perceval will be lying there, and you by his side" (272). In a general way, in the whole second part of the text the forthcoming events are first announced by Perceval's sister in the form of imperative predictions.

16

These suppositions prior to the event are matched by others recalled only after the event has taken place. The chance incidents of his journey lead Galahad to a monastery; the adventure of the shield begins; just as it ends, a heavenly knight appears and declares that everything has been foreseen in advance. "'So here is what you will do,' said Joseph. 'Put the shield where Nasciens is to be buried. To this place Galahad will come, five days after he receives the order of knighthood.' Everything happened as he had said, since on the fifth day you arrived at the abbey where Nasciens's body lies" (82). Gawain has the same experience; immediately after receiving a harsh blow from Galahad's sword, he remembers: "Now it has come true, what I heard the day of Pentecost about the sword I was reaching out for. It was announced to me that before long I would receive a terrible blow, and that is the very sword with which this knight has just struck me. It happened just as it was foretold to me" (230).

4. *La Quête du Graal*, ed. Albert Béguin and Yves Bonnefoy (Paris: Editions du Seuil, 1965) 118.

15 Content

As in Extract 11, Todorov notes the problems inherent in his theory, and acknowledges that the categorisations he is making do not fully work. If this is the case, what is the use in such theorising?

Structure

Todorov refers back to his earlier example here. This is intended to make his argument easier to understand. If you are finding it difficult, the sensible thing is to follow his advice, and go back and reread the story, and see if it helps demonstrate the ideas he is proposing. As structuralism is about texts, you can always draw on examples to help make sense of it, even if an author does not offer particular texts for you to draw on.

Context

The distinctions between qualitative and quantitative research are key; if you do not know what these words mean, and how they relate to research methods, find out.

16 Content

These two paragraphs might deal with an example you are probably unaware of; can you think of others that would work? There are lots of films, books, and other stories in which predictions come true, and the narrative relies on us knowing a certain future is predicted or warning is given. The whole of *The Lord of the Rings* (dir. Jackson, 2001–3) series works in this way; can you think of others?

READING

17 But even more characteristic of *La Quête du Graal* than the "announcement" is a transformation, not of supposition, but of knowledge; it consists in a reinterpretation of events that have already taken place. In general, *prud-hommes* and hermits give every earthly action an interpretation in the celestial order, often adding purely terrestrial revelations. Thus when we read the beginning of the story, we think everything is clear: we encounter the noble knights who decide to leave in search of the Holy Grail, and so forth. But little by little the narrative acquaints us with another meaning of these same scenes. Lancelot, whom we thought strong and perfect, is an incorrigible sinner, living in adultery with Queen Guinevere. Sir Gawain, who was the first to vow to undertake the quest, will never achieve it, for his heart is hard and he does not think enough about God. The knights we first admire are inveterate sinners who will be punished; they have not been to confession for years. When the opening events are alluded to later on, we are in possession of the truth and not deceived by appearances.

18 The reader's interest is not driven by the question What happens next?, which refers us to the logic of succession or to the mythological narrative. We know perfectly well from the start what will happen, who will reach the Grail, who will be punished and why. Our interest arises from a wholly different question which refers instead to the gnoseological organization: What is the Grail? The Grail narrative relates a quest; what is being sought, however, is not an object but a meaning, the meaning of the word Grail. And since the question has to do with being and not with doing, the exploration of the future is less important than that of the past. Throughout the narrative the reader has to wonder about the meaning of the Grail. The principal narrative is a narrative of knowledge; ideally, it would never end.

19 The search for knowledge also dominates another type of narrative that we might hesitate to compare to the quest for the Holy Grail: the mystery, or detective story. We know such narratives are constituted by the problematic relation of two stories: the story of the crime, which is missing, and the story of the investigation, which is present, and whose only justification is to acquaint us with the other story. Some element of that first story is indeed made available from the beginning: a crime is committed almost before our eyes; but we have been unable to determine its real agents or motives. The investigation consists in returning over and over to the events, verifying and correcting the smallest details, until the truth about the initial story finally comes out; this is a story of learning. But unlike the Grail story, what characterizes knowledge in detective fiction is that it has only two possible values, true or false. In a detective story, either we know who committed the murder or we do not, whereas the quest for meaning in the Grail story has an infinite number of intermediate degrees, and even in the end the quest's outcome is not certain.

NOTES

17 ## Writing Style

Notice again how Todorov assumes that 'we' all read the story in the same way; he doesn't acknowledge that different people might read the story in different ways. This is particularly striking considering he has repeatedly acknowledged that theory is incapable of explaining everything. One of the most common reasons that structuralism is criticised is because it assumes all readers make sense of stories in the same way.

18 ## Content

This is an interesting point. It might seem strange that Todorov argues that a story's interest doesn't lie in wondering what is going to happen next. But when you see most romantic comedies you know the couple will get together at the end, just as you know 007 will defeat the villain in any James Bond film. Such stories are interesting not because of *what* happens, but because of *how* it happens. What other examples of this can you think of?

19 ## Context

The mystery or detective story has been repeatedly of interest for structuralists, for the reasons Todorov outlines. They have a pretty rigid format, they work towards a definite end, and their chronological structure is quite fixed. We know the detective will solve the crime; what we are interested in is *how* the detective will solve it, and *how* and *why* the crime was committed. See Eco and Sebeok (1984), and Knight (1980).

READING

20

If we take as our third example one of Henry James's tales, we shall see that the gnoseological search can take other forms (Conrad's *Heart of Darkness* presents yet another variant, as we shall see). As in the detective story, James's search focuses on the truth about an actual event, not an abstract entity; but, as in *La Quête du Graal*, at the end of the story we are not sure we possess *the* truth; we have moved, rather, from primary ignorance to a lesser ignorance. *In the Cage*, for example, recounts the experience of a young woman telegraph operator. Her full attention is focused on two people she hardly knows, Captain Everard and Lady Bradeen. She reads the telegrams they send, hears fragments of sentences, but despite her skill at imagining the absent elements, she does not succeed in reconstituting a faithful portrait of the two strangers. Moreover, when she meets the Captain in person it does not help; she can see his physical build, observe his gestures, listen to his voice, but his "essence" remains just as intangible, if not more so, than when the glass cage separated them. The senses retain only appearances; truth is inaccessible.

Comprehension is made particularly difficult by the fact that the telegraph operator pretends to know much more than she really does, when under certain circumstances she has the chance to question intermediary third parties. Thus when she meets a friend, Mrs. Jordan, the friend asks: "'Why, don't you know the scandal? . . .' Our heroine thought, recollected; . . . 'Oh, there was nothing public . . .'"[5]

James always refuses to name "truth" or "essences" directly; these exist only in the form of multiple appearances. This position has a profound effect on the organization of his works and draws his attention to the techniques of "point of view," which he himself comes to call "that magnificent and masterly indirectness." *In the Cage* gives us the telegraph operator's perception as it bears upon Mrs. Jordan, who herself relates what she has gotten out of her fiancé, Mr. Drake, who in turn has only a remote acquaintance with Captain Everard and Lady Bradeen!

21

Once again, the process of acquiring information is *dominant* in James's tale, but its presence does not exclude all others. *In the Cage* is also subject to a principle of mythological organization. The original equilibrium of the telegraph operator is disturbed by her encounter with the Captain; at the end of the narrative, however, she returns to her initial project, which was to marry Mr. Mudge. On the other hand, alongside transformations of knowledge as such, there are others that possess the same formal properties without having to do with the same process (the *term gnoseological* no longer applies); this is particularly true of what one might call *subjectivation*, a personal reaction or response to an event. Proust's *A la Recherche du temps perdu* develops this latter transformation to the point of hypertrophy: the most trivial incident of the narrator's life, like the grain of sand around which a pearl grows, serves as a pretext for long descriptions on the way the event is experienced by one character or another.

5. Henry James, *In the Cave* (New York: Fox Duffield Company, 1906).

20 Structure

As Todorov notes, this is his third example; why so many? And how are these examples similar or different to one another?

21 Content

It is interesting that Todorov here explores how literature attempts to capture the variety of ways in which different (fictional) people react to events – what he calls 'subjectivation' – yet he doesn't assume that readers of those stories will themselves understand them in a variety of ways.

READING

22

Here we need to distinguish two ways of judging transformation: according to their *formative* power or to their *evocative* power. By formative power I mean the transformation's aptitude for forming a narrative sequence all by itself. It is difficult (although not impossible) to imagine a narrative that would include only transformations of subjectivization, a narrative that would be reduced, in other words, to the description of an event and various characters' reactions to it. Even Proust's novel includes elements of mythological narrative: the narrator's inability to write will be overcome; Swann's way and Guermantes' way, at first completely separate, will converge with Gilberte's marriage to Saint-Loup. Negation is clearly a transformation with great formative power; but the coupling of ignorance (or error) and knowledge also serves quite often to frame narratives. The other devices of the mythological narrative seem less apt (at least in our culture) to form sequences on their own. A narrative that included only modal sequences would resemble a didactic and moralizing text, with sequences like the following: "*X* must behave like a good Christian – *X* behaves like a good Christian." A narrative formed exclusively of transformations of intention would resemble certain passages in *Robinson Crusoe*: Robinson decides to build himself a house – he builds himself a house: Robinson decides to put a fence around his garden – he puts a fence around his garden; and so on.

23

But this formative (or syntactic) power of certain transformations must not be confused with what we particularly appreciate in a narrative, either what is richest in meaning or what makes it possible to distinguish one narrative from another. I recall that one of the most exciting scenes of a spy movie, *The Ipcress File*, consisted in showing us the main character in the process of fixing himself an omelet. Naturally, the narrative importance of that episode was nonexistent (he could just as well have eaten a ham sandwich); but this crucial scene became something like the emblem of the film as a whole. This is what I call the evocative power of an action; it seems to me that transformations of manner in particular serve to characterize a given fictional universe as opposed to some other, yet on their own they would have great difficulty producing an autonomous narrative sequence.

24

Now that we are beginning to become familiar with this opposition between the principle of succession and the principle of transformation (and with the variants of the transformation principle), we may wonder whether it is not identical to Jakobson's opposition between metonymy and metaphor. The association is possible, but I do not think it necessary. It is difficult to assimilate all transformations to relations of similarity, just as it is difficult to assimilate all similarity to metaphor. Nor does the principle of succession have anything to gain by being called metonymy, or contiguity, especially since the former is essentially temporal and the latter spatial. The association would be all the more problematic in that,

22   Context

It is noticeable that Todorov only fleetingly acknowledges the cultural specificity of his reading, when he notes that certain kinds of stories are more likely than others.

23   Content

How does Todorov know what we 'appreciate'? What does he assume here?

24   Structure

After presenting an argument, Todorov here shows how it relates to – and develops – the ideas of someone else. Placing your work within the context of others is important, and helps build up a body of knowledge. You will probably see in your reading that some do this more than others; it is worthwhile wondering why it is that some writers are more willing than others to relate their work to that of other people.

READING

according to Jakobson, "the principle of similarity underlies poetry," and that "prose, on the contrary, is forwarded essentially by contiguity,"[6] whereas from our viewpoint succession and transformation are equally necessary to narrative. If we had to contrast narrative and poetry (or epic and lyric), we might focus, in the first place, on the transitive or intransitive character of the sign (in this we are in agreement with Jakobson); in the second place, on the nature of the temporality represented: discontinuous in one instance, a perpetual presence in the other (which does not mean atemporality); in the third place, on the nature of the names that occupy the place of the semantic subject, or theme, in the one case and the other: narrative recognizes only individual names in the position of subject, whereas poetry allows both individual names and common nouns.

25

Philosophical discourse, for its part, is characterized both by the exclusion of individual names and by atemporality; in this view poetry is an intermediate form between narrative discourse and philosophical discourse.

26

But let us return to narrative and ask rather whether all relations between one action and others can be distributed between the mythological and the gnoseological types. The tale Propp analyzed included an episode that I skimmed over earlier. Having set out to find her brother, the little girl encountered some potential donors. First she met a stove whom she asked for information and who promised it to her if she would eat one of its rye-cakes; she insolently refused. Then she met an apple tree and a river: "similar proposals and similar arrogant replies."[7]

27

Precisely how are these three episodes related? We have seen that, in relations of transformation, two propositions turn out to be associated; the transformation involves a modification of the predicate. But at present, in the three actions Propp describes, the predicate specifically remains unchanged: in each instance, one character offers, the other insolently refuses. What changes are the agents (the subjects) of each proposition, or the circumstances. Rather than being transformations of each other, these propositions appear as *variants* of a single situation, or as parallel applications of the same rule.

One might then conceive of a third type of narrative organization, no longer mythological or gnoseological but, let us say, *ideological*, inasmuch as an abstract rule, an idea, produces the various peripeties.

6. Roman Jakobson, "Two Aspects of Language and Two Types of Aphasic Distrubance," in *Selected Writings II: Word and Language* (The Hague: Mouton, 1971) 258–9.
7. Propp, *Morphology of the Folktale*, 88.

25   Context

In his analysis of poetry, Todorov demonstrates how structuralism arose from linguistics, and therefore has its roots in examination of the written and spoken word. He has made some reference to film, but his main focus is literature. Much media theory has its roots in other subjects; it is often your job to take theory developed from analysis of one form and relate it to another.

26   Writing Style

It is good that Todorov notes he's 'skimmed over' parts of his analysis. Do all theorists similarly acknowledge what they've left out?

27   Writing Style

'Ideological' is used here in quite a different way from the ones you might come across in other readings. Again this demonstrates how you have constantly to bear in mind how particular authors use particular words. That said, if Todorov could have used any word he wanted, you might wonder why it is that he chose that one to convey the idea he wanted to express.

READING

28

The relation of the propositions among themselves is no longer direct; one no longer moves from a negative to a positive version, or from ignorance to knowledge. Instead, actions are linked through the intermediary of an abstract formula: in the case of "The Swan-Geese," that of the proffered assistance and the insolent refusal. Often, in order to find the relation between two actions that are completely independent of each other in material terms, we must look for a highly developed abstraction. I have attempted to describe the logical rules, the ideological imperatives that govern the events of the narrative universe of a number of different texts (this could also be done for each of the narratives we have referred to above).

Thus, in *Les Liaisons dangereuses*, all the characters' actions can be presented as the product of some very simple and abstract rules; these rules in turn refer to the organizing ideology of the work as a whole.

29

The same is true for Constant's *Adolphe*. The rules that govern the characters' behavior can be reduced to two. The first stems from the logic of desire as asserted by this text, which might be formulated as follows: one desires what one does not have, one flees what one has. Consequently, obstacles reinforce desire, and any help weakens it. A first blow strikes Adolphe's love when Ellénore leaves Count P . . . to come live with Adolphe. A second blow is struck when she devotes herself to caring for Adolphe after he is wounded. Each of Ellénore's sacrifices exasperates Adolphe: they leave him fewer and fewer things to desire. On the other hand, when Adolphe's father decides to bring about the separation of the couple, the opposite effect is achieved, and Adolphe states this explicitly: "Thinking you are separating me from her, you may well attach me to her for ever."[8] The tragic aspect of the situation stems from the fact that desire, in order to follow this particular logic, still does not stop being desire, that is, does not stop causing unhappiness in the one who is unable to satisfy it.

30

The second law of this universe, also a moral law, is formulated by Constant as follows: "The great question in life is the pain one causes and the most ingenious metaphysics cannot justify a man who has broken the heart which loves him" (169). One cannot govern one's life by the search for good, for one person's happiness is always another's misfortune. But one can organize one's life on the basis of the requirement that one should do as little harm as possible: this negative value turns out to be the only one to have the status of an absolute here. The commandments of this second law take precedence over those of the first when the two

8. Benjamin Constant, *Adolphe, and the Red Note-Book*, intro. Harold Nicolson, trans. Carl Wildman (Indianapolis: Bobbs-Merrill, 1959), 104.

NOTES

28   Content

Les Liaisons Dangereuses (2008 [1782]) is a novel by Pierre Choderlos de Laclos. It has been adapted as a television series and film many times, perhaps most famously as *Dangerous Liaisons* (dir. Frears, 1988). It is also the inspiration for *Cruel Intentions* (dir. Kumble, 1999). The fact that a novel from three centuries ago should remain popular today, and inspire successful mainstream films, shows how narratives remain stable over time, and that the core structures which structuralism finds are indeed consistent.

29   Content

This idea of wanting and fleeing can be seen in a host of narratives. Can you think of examples of such stories happening in soap operas? What about sitcoms?

30   Context

Note here how Todorov suggests that stories offer morals and rules for living our lives. That is, they're not completely abstract entertainments, but they help us make sense of the world around us and our own lives. This is why structuralists argue that their analysis is important; that it doesn't just tell us how stories work, but that such structures clearly have much more profound implications for morals, ethics and our understanding of society.

READING

30

(continued)

are in contradiction. This is why Adolphe has so much trouble telling Ellénore the "truth." "Whilst speaking thus, I saw her face suddenly bathed in tears. I stopped, I retraced my steps, I retracted and explained" (89). In chapter 6, Ellénore hears him out; she falls into a faint, and Adolphe can only assure her of his love. In chapter 8, he has a pretext for leaving her but fails to exploit it: "Could I punish her for an imprudence which I made her commit and, with cold hypocrisy, find a pretext in these imprudences to abandon her without pity?" (139). Pity takes precedence over desire.

31

Thus isolated and independent actions, often accomplished by different characters, reveal the same abstract logic, the same ideological organization.

32

Ideological organization seems to possess a weak formative power: narratives that do not frame the actions that result from this organization with another order, adding a second organization to the first, are hard to find. For one can illustrate a logic or an ideology ad infinitum; and there is no reason for one particular illustration to precede – or follow – any other. Thus in *Les Liaisons dangereuses* the actions described are presented within a framework based on ideological organization: the exceptional state constituted by the reign of the "roués," Valmont and Merteuil, will be replaced by a return to traditional morality.

33

The cases *of Adolphe* and Dostoevsky's *Notes from the Underground*, another text illustrative of ideological organization, are a little different, as we shall see in detail in a later chapter. Another order – which is not the simple absence of the preceding ones – is instituted. It consists of relations that might be called "spatial": repetitions, antitheses, and gradations. Thus in *Adolphe*, the sequence of chapters follows a precise route: there is a portrait of Adolphe in chapter one; we observe the development of his sentiments in chapters two and three, their slow disintegration in chapters four through ten. Each new manifestation of Adolphe's feelings has to be superior to the previous one in the rising section, inferior in the descending section. The end becomes possible owing to an event that seems to have an exceptional narrative status: death. In *Notes from the Underground*, the succession of events is determined both by gradation and by the law of contrast. The scene with the officer presents in summary form the two roles available to the narrator; next he is humiliated by Zverkov, and he humiliates

31 Content

An important point: that what may seem like quite different and various events in stories might actually, through structuralist analysis, turn out to be pretty much the same.

32 Content

Again, it does not really matter if you don't fully understand this example because you do not know the story being referred to; can you make out what is being argued, without this knowledge?

33 Structure

Todorov refers to a later chapter, which is not reproduced here. This is another useful signpost pointing to the argument's wider structure.

Content

It might seem odd to call 'death' nothing more than an 'exceptional narrative status'. But think of the number of narratives you have encountered which end with a death, often of the major character. Indeed, during some stories you might be expecting one of the characters to die: that is, you apply a structure to a story, and therefore predict its development. Endings are important to narratives, and have been explored by lots of people: see Frank Kermode's *The Sense of an Ending* (1967). You might also think about how this relates to stories which usually lack endings, such as soap operas.

READING

33

(continued)

Lisa in turn, even more seriously. The narrative is interrupted owing to the announcement of a different ideology, embodied by Lisa, which consists in rejecting the master-slave logic and in loving others for themselves.

Once again, it is clear that individual narratives exemplify more than one type of narrative organization (in fact, any one of them could have served to illustrate all of these organizational principles); but the analysis of a specific type is more helpful for the comprehension of a particular text.

34

One might make an analogous observation by radically changing levels and declaring that a narrative analysis will be more helpful for the study of certain types of texts than for others. For what I am examining here is not *text*, which has its own varieties, but *narrative*, which may play an important role or none at all in the structure of a text, and which appears in literary texts as well as in other symbolic systems. It is a given that the narratives that all society seems to need in order to live depend today, not on literature, but on cinema: filmmakers tell us stories, whereas writers play with words. The typological remarks I have just presented thus have to do in principle not only with literary narratives, such as the ones I used as examples, but with all types of narrative; they stem less from *poetics* than from a discipline that seems to me to have every right to exist and that should be called *narratology*.

34

Structure

Todorov once again helpfully summarises the argument he is presenting.

Context

Todorov notes how cinema is now the dominant narrative form, which has required literature to take on a different role. Do you think this still applies? What about television and the internet? Do you think different media alter because of what other media are doing? Also note that he says this 'is a given'; where's his evidence?

Content

The distinction between 'poetics' and 'narratology' is important. Todorov is generally considered to have initiated the term 'narratology', and it represents a significant shift in the study of stories. 'Poetics' had been the standard way of analysing texts for centuries, as it can be traced back to Aristotle (384–322 BC). While Aristotle analysed poetry – which is where poetics gets its name from – the principles he used are not confined to poetry. Aristotle discussed narrative, but was primarily interested in the differences between comedy and tragedy; this is clearly genre analysis, but it explores *what* happens in such stories rather than *how*. As can be observed, Todorov's interest is the *how*, and this can be seen as the methodological shift that 'narratology' brought in.

REFLECTING ON THE READING

As always, the first thing to do when reflecting on a reading is to summarise what you have understood, and try to make sense of what you found difficult. Perhaps the best way to do this is to return to Todorov's examples. Even though they're probably of texts that you don't have much knowledge of, his theorising and analysis should have helped make sense of them. If, as he argues, these narrative structures are inherent in most stories, it shouldn't matter that you do not know the exact story, because you should be able to guess most of it.

As has been suggested throughout the reading, thinking of your own examples is always a good way of applying theory, and making it relate to things that you know. It is worth-while keeping in mind the character types and events that Todorov notes, to see if you come across them when you consume media. Much structuralist analysis applies to fictional texts, but some have argued that they can be seen in factual ones. So, for example, in the news, you still have certain character 'types', and there are chains of cause and effect which are central to the usual ways in which stories are told. This is a good thing to do because it helps relate theory to your everyday life. As it can be tempting to think of theory as something to be worked on in class, but which has no relationship to the world around you, it is a good idea to always be on the lookout for places where theory can be applied.

Todorov refers to genres, and this is something that is easy to do work on, especially with reference to expectations. Think about what certain genres mean to you. In cinema, for example, what are your expectations for a science fiction film, or a romantic comedy, or a horror film? In television, what do you expect from the news, or a sitcom, or reality television? In magazines, how do news magazines look different to music ones, or 'lads mags'? This is not to say that each category is completely different: indeed, genres often have a lot in common with other genres. But it's likely that you respond to media using such categorisations. As has been noted, media is often advertised this way too, so expectations are set up beforehand. Go to http://trailers.apple.com and look at the posters for forthcoming films; which ones would you like to see and which ones would you not? Why is this? What kinds of audiences do you think they are intended for? Once you have done this, look at some of the trailers, and see if your expectations change or are confirmed. You can carry this task out next time you go to the cinema, and watch the trailers before the main film. Also, when new programmes are advertised on television, how do you decide which ones you might like to watch, and which ones you want to avoid? All of these tasks will, it is hoped, show how important expectations are to our understanding of media – and this idea is central to structuralism.

But you might also want to think about the problems structuralism has. One of the main ones is that it assumes that everyone reads media texts in roughly the same way, and that those structures that it finds are similarly meaningful for everyone. But you might want to think about whether this is always the case. Have there been times when you have disagreed with someone about what happened in a film or in a television programme, which shows you've not read it in the same way? What about television programmes like *Lost* (ABC: 2004–10), which invited you to guess what was going on during its run; didn't lots of different people have different theories about where the island was and what it was for (and even though the programme has now finished don't people *still* debate these questions)? To extend this idea further, think about what structuralism *doesn't* investigate or think about. You could relate this to other theories in this book, which might examine aspects of media which structuralism doesn't. No theory covers everything; but it is a good idea for you to know the limitations of every one you read.

Key terms to explore

equilibrium/disequilibrium; gnoseological organisation; ideological organisation; narrative function; morphology; mythological organisation; narrative; narratology; negation; qualitative; quantitative; subjectivation; succession/transformation; temporality; text.

Key writers who are mentioned

A.J. Greimas; Roman Jakobson; Claude Lévi-Strauss; Vladimir Propp; Alain Robbe-Grillet.

RECOMMENDED READING

Frow, J. (2006) *Genre*, London and New York: Routledge.

Helpful overview of theories of genre, covering a range of media and referring to literary theory.

Hawkes, T. (2003) *Structuralism and Semiotics*, 2nd edition, London and New York: Routledge.

Summary of structuralist theories, covering their origins in literature and anthropology; also critiques the value and novelty of these theories.

Propp, V. (1968 [1928]) *Morphology of the Folktale*, translated by Laurence Scott, Austin and London: University of Texas Press.

Classic structuralist study of fairytales, looking at narrative structure and character types; findings still applicable to contemporary media.

CHAPTER 16

Feminist media theory

van Zoonen, L. (1994) *Feminist Media Studies*, London: Sage, pp. 11–18, 21–8.

In 2006 the high-street newsagent chain WHSmith decided that 'lads mags' *Nuts* and *Zoo* should not be shelved with other lifestyle magazines as they previously had, but would instead sit on the top shelf, within the area commonly associated with more adult material, and out of the reach of children's hands. In doing so, WHSmith were responding to complaints from the public about the covers of these magazines which usually featured topless women. For those upset by this decision, it was evidence of the unnecessary encroachment of feminism into everyday life, in which the supposed harmless appreciation of the female body is a bit of a laugh, and quite different from pornography. Debates about the appropriacy of representations of women are quite common; many were outraged by the massive posters advertising Pulp's *This is Hardcore* (1998), which depicted a naked woman, especially as the album's title linked the picture to pornography. How do you respond to this; should *Nuts* and *Zoo* be classed as pornography, or are they the same as other magazines such as *FHM* or *Loaded*? Indeed, should *FHM* and *Loaded* also be put on the top shelf? Why is it that such representations enrage some people, while others see them as harmless?

The fact that WHSmith responded in this way shows how the debates central to feminist media theory have become common in contemporary society. This is not to suggest that all the changes that feminism often fights for have been achieved; but it is to note that issues about gender and representation are often debated, and not just within universities. Certainly concerns about women's role in the workplace, and the recurring problem of disparities between what men and women are paid for doing the same job, have been repeatedly maligned. For example government and international legislation has been introduced in order to combat such inequality (European Commission 2006; European

Commission 2010), and the United Nations has set as one of its 'Millennium Development Goals' the aim to 'Promote gender equality and empower women' (2010). Research shows repeatedly how this problem is common within the media industries, as Byerly (2004) illustrates in her analysis of the working practices of newsrooms. So while it can be argued that feminism has made significant inroads into questioning and changing sexist practices in society, it can also be seen that there is still lots of work to be done.

'Feminism' is a word you have probably come across before. It is likely to be a term that engenders quite strong responses when it is mentioned, and the ways in which people think about it has changed over time. For many people, it currently has quite negative connotations, and feminists are often stereotyped as short-haired, men-hating lesbians, as in *Viz* comic's 'Millie Tant'. Indeed, many women are now insistent on *not* being defined as feminists, for fear of being seen as overtly political, joyless, and full of anger and hatred about the world around us (Tasker and Negra 2007). The fact that feminism, and many of the women associated with it, have come to be thought of in this way, can be seen as indicative of the ways in which society consistently (and successfully) tries to marginalise feminism and feminists, highlighting only certain kinds of feminism and fixating on that and exaggerating it until it is seen as having little relevance to the ways in which the majority of people live their lives. Alternatively, it could also be seen as evidence of the ways in which many of the key ideas which feminism has fought for – in particular those associated with equality, such as the right for women to vote and have access to education, in accordance with the rights of men – are now accepted as unquestionable in many cultures. This is not to suggest that society is now equal; but it is to suggest that *some* of the sexist assumptions which feminism fought are now seen as outdated, in theory if not in practice. Indeed, if you are reading this and thinking you are not a feminist (whether you are female or male), ask yourself whether you think it is right that there are women in your class and that women should have the same access to university education as men; if your answer is 'yes', then you are in agreement with one of the key ideas of feminism.

What makes this more complicated is that there are lots of different kinds of feminism, so we should talk of 'feminisms' rather than 'feminism'. Some of these feminisms disagree with one another, and they often respond to particular local conditions; therefore, race and feminism has been much more central in America than in Britain (Reames 2007), for example, whereas recurring concerns over class issues in the United Kingdom has meant this has been much more central to feminist debates, as it has to media theory as a whole (Skeggs 2004). Analysis of colonialism has led to 'Third World feminism', even though there's a discussion about the appropriateness of this term (Walters 2005: 118). Over time feminist thought has developed too, so you may come across terms such as 'second wave feminism' and 'post-feminism'.

As a consequence of feminism questioning assumptions about gender norms, there has also recently been a growth in the analysis of masculinity, exploring the ways in which 'male-ness' is constructed and, often, presented as a social norm (Beynon 2002). In questioning the rigidity of femininity and masculinity, 'academic writers [show that] gender is a matter of power relations' (MacKinnon 2003: 4) and critique the idea that 'boys and girls are "naturally" and fundamentally different' (Carter and Steiner 2004: 12). Probably most famous in this argument is Judith Butler, whose *Gender Trouble* (1990) utterly rejects the duality of biological distinctions required in order for the categories of 'male' and 'female' to make sense, and instead sees gender merely as a socially required and defined 'performance' (see Salih 2002: 43–71 for a useful summary). Once again, we come across issues of power, which recur throughout media theory. Overall, then, feminism is a complex set of ideas, whose definitions are hotly debated over, and which incorporates a bewildering array of approaches and arguments. What might be most useful for you to think about is that feminism insists that debates about sex and gender *matter*, regardless of precisely how those debates are carried out, because gender is a key to the ways in which societies work.

For media studies, the idea that these discussions are important has predominantly been explored through the issue of representation: that is, how are men and women represented on television, on film, in adverts, and so on? Also, what kinds of representations are we invited to sympathise with and see as role models? This idea is important because it assumes that the ways in which we act in society are in some way affected by the kinds of gender representations which surround us (this is related to the material on media effects explored in Chapter 14). This is *not* to suggest that there is a simple, direct causal link between representation and action, nor to suggest that it is impossible to act in a manner contradictory to such representations; but it is to say that 'we "know" what a man or a woman is because we have representations that tell us what they are, and how they differ (however valid or invalid these "truths" may be)' (Webb 2009: 78–9). As Gauntlett notes, men wearing make-up have to endure ridicule and censure, when they are only engaging in an activity carried out by millions of women the world over every day (2002: 94). Much feminist media theory argues that the kinds of representations on offer for women are limited, and are commonly distinguished from those of men. For example, Mulvey famously discusses women's 'to-be-looked-at-ness' (2000 [1975]: 40) in cinema, arguing that film usually offers females as objects which men get pleasure from looking at. Lots of textual work has demonstrated how female representations are limited, and always marked as different from the more central and supposedly unarguable masculine view, which Gill calls the 'male as norm problem' (2007: 9).

What this means is that feminism is not just about analysing society, culture and media; it is about actively trying to critique and *change* it. While this is the case for much theory, it could be argued that the critique on offer by feminist media theory is more critical and political than may be the case for other approaches covered in this book. If you sometimes find media theory difficult to deal with because it feels detached from the real world around you, it is unlikely you will have this response to feminist thought. Indeed, the fact that gender debates are often some of the most heated and vocal in media theory demonstrates that, whether you agree with the arguments being proposed or not, it is clear that academics – as well as society as a whole – see discussions about women and men as something central to the kind of society we live in.

INTRODUCTION TO THE READING

This reading is an edited chapter from Liesbet van Zoonen's book, *Feminist Media Studies* (1994). As always, it is useful to know what the entirety of a book an extract comes from is about, although you should also get used to dealing with extracts without having read everything around it; indeed, in order to remain on top of a subject, it is vital to learn how to extract relevant material from larger texts. As already stated, this chapter is edited; this means you are not getting the *whole* chapter, and instead a three-page section has been removed where, at the end of Extract 23, you see the symbol [. . .]. This removed section deals with pornography in more detail, and it is felt that you can make sense of this reading without it. When you look at readers and edited collections and see that paragraphs or pages have been edited out of the versions you are being given, it might be worth wondering what has gone. It also shows that if you intend to do more detailed work on this area, you should go back to the original book, because here you are not getting the full work. In that sense, textbooks or readers are starting points, albeit very useful ones when you are dealing with a topic for the first time, or just need to get the basic, key information on a topic.

Van Zoonen's book is both a theoretical analysis of how feminist media studies can be carried out, and a set of analyses of texts, such as television programmes, romance novels, and adverts. This means it carries out empirical work in order to develop theory, and it is noticeable that the theoretical debates are outlined before the textual analyses, showing how such research can be used to test and develop theoretical models which have been outlined. The chapter this reading comes from is called 'New themes' and it is followed by one called 'A new paradigm?'; the focus on 'new' shows that van Zoonen is attempting to develop novel ways of thinking about the topic. While this is common in much media theory, it can also be seen as representing the desire of feminist media studies to present new ways of thinking, because it is argued that the 'traditional' ways of carrying out analysis are incapable of exploring the kinds of questions which are important to feminism. Carrying out feminist media studies is not just about looking at unexplored texts or presenting new arguments; it is also about developing whole news ways of thinking about the subject of media studies as a whole, and suggesting new methods and novel theoretical approaches must be worked through. Van Zoonen's first chapter covers Stuart Hall's 'Encoding/Decoding' model (1980c), which is explored in Chapter 11 in *this* book. While this demonstrates the interplay between different kinds of theory, it also places van Zoonen's work in a particular context, suggesting that she sees her writing as a development of Hall's. As always, theory never arises out of a vacuum; the fact that this was written in 1994 places it in a particular historical moment, and you might want to question how appropriate van Zoonen's work continues to be, and whether her model requires more work in order to bring it up to date.

Because feminism is, as noted above, a topic which is debated in the world outside of university, this is a reading that you are likely to bring assumptions to more than some of the others in this book. Before encountering this reading, then, it would be worth you thinking about what 'feminism' means to you. Do you see it as a positive or negative term? Would you describe yourself as a feminist? Do you think feminism has ever done any good? Do you think power inequalities based around gender still exist in society? Do you think feminism still has a role to play in modern society? Jot down your initial responses to these questions, and look back at them after finishing the reading; you might find some of your views changed, while others have instead been confirmed. As it is likely feminism already means something to you, you can compare what you read to your existing views. However, because feminism often causes such strong opinions, you should also ensure you are *open* to this reading, and willing to respond to arguments and evidence which undermines your views. Reading theory requires you to be open in this way, whether you agree or disagree with the content. It is only by being open to it that you can ever hope to *understand* it, which is not necessarily the same as *agreeing* with it: indeed, if you *disagree* with it you still need to understand it, in order to better argue why and how you disagree.

READING

1

Liesbet van Zoonen

Feminist media studies 'New' Themes

The media have always been at the centre of feminist critique. In the book that stimulated the revival of the American women's movement in the mid-1960s, the media and in particular women's magazines were scorned for their contribution to 'The Feminine Mystique' – as the book was called – the myth that women could find true fulfilment in being a housewife and a mother. Author Betty Friedan – a former women's magazine editor herself – accused the media and a range of allied experts such as doctors, psychiatrists and sociologists, of installing insecurity, fear and frustration in ordinary women who could not and would not live up to the ideal of the 'happy housewife heroine' (Friedan, 1963). In another feminist classic, *The Female Eunuch*, Germaine Greer (1971) raged against mass produced romantic fiction for conning women into believing in fairy tales of heterosexual romance and happiness.

2

Obviously, the media had to become important targets of the American women's movement. American communication legislation offered ample opportunity to challenge broadcasters' policies towards the portrayal and employment of women. In the 1970s and 1980s many local television stations saw their legal licence to broadcast challenged by women's groups because of their sexist representation of women and their neglect of women's issues. Media, and television in particular, were supposed to provide women with more positive and liberating role models instead. Although none of these legal complaints ('petitions to deny') was successful, they did raise the awareness of broadcasters to the depiction of women, and they triggered academic research to document and support the claims of the women's movement (Cantor, 1988).

3

In other countries the portrayal of women in the media has aroused similar impassioned feminist critique. For instance, in the mid-1980s, Clare Short, a British Labour Party Member of Parliament, became so infuriated by the display of topless pin-up girls in the tabloid press that she introduced a bill to ban these 'Page Three Girls'. Her campaign received enormous support from ordinary women throughout Britain who finally felt encouraged to express their frustration about what they saw as a daily insult that had to be endured in public places like subways and workplaces, as well as in the home from husbands or sons. Newspapers and MPs of both parties were extremely critical of Short's campaign and accused her of trying to

NOTES

1 Structure

This whole opening section of the chapter is about van Zoonen putting the analysis she is going to carry out within the context of feminist analysis more generally. In this way, she is demonstrating where her work comes from, and acknowledging the history – both theoretical and practical – that informs what she is doing.

Context

Betty Friedan and Germaine Greer are mentioned here. Their books are key texts in the development of feminist theory and analysis. Indeed, Friedan and Greer are people you might have come across outside of your studies; Greer, especially, appears on television a lot, and is a busy cultural commentator. That some feminist academics should be known outside of universities shows how feminism occupies a central position within social and political debates generally.

2 Context

There are two contexts being discussed here. In discussing America, van Zoonen is placing her work in a national context: by discussing the 1970s and 1980s she is exploring a historical context. Acknowledging context like this is a way of making explicit that things might vary at different times and in different places. Therefore, while feminism sometimes does make general, universalised statements about the relationship between women and media, it has also been keen to acknowledge the specifics of different places, times and individuals. This has important implications, for it insists on seeing people as *individuals*, whose histories, activities and motivations are as valid as each other. What consequences might thinking of people in this way have for some of the other theories you have come across in this book?

3 Writing Style

While van Zoonen is continuing to put her work in a specific context here, note the ways in which this is written. She offers a number of historical examples, and here, in her summary of Clare Short's campaign against 'Page Three Girls', is recounting a very specific case study. Choosing to write in this way demonstrates a desire to place feminist media theory in the everyday, and to show how it has practical implications for the media we consume; there is a definite desire, then, not to present purely abstract theorising. Does this make her writing easier to follow for you? And, in adopting such a style, what is being left out?

3

(continued)

introduce censorship. Other arguments brought against Short claimed that she represented a prudish morality, an anachronism in a modern, sexually liberated society. Parts of the gay movement and the women's movement feared that, once accepted, Short's bill would legitimize government measures against gay literature and other representations of gay sexuality. There were also feminists who suggested calling for equal treatment by publishing pictures of male pin-ups. Although Short's bill was not passed, the uproar it caused forced one tabloid to move (temporarily) its Page Three Girl to page seven, but more importantly it launched a wider national debate on the representation of women in the media (Short, 1991).

4

As these examples show, representation has always been an important battleground for contemporary feminism. The women's movement is not only engaged in a material struggle about equal rights and opportunities for women, but also in a symbolic conflict about definitions of femininity (and by omission masculinity). Such a double-edged politics is currently found in other new social movements as well. Alberto Melucci (1988) has characterized new social movements as new media that 'publicize' existing conflicts and produce a symbolic challenge to the dominant codes of society. The communication of that challenge exists within a symbolic excess of old and new, strange and familiar, common and exotic signs, and is reconstructed by other communicators, the mass media being definitely among the most powerful (cf. van Zoonen, 1994).

5

Since the early 1970s a considerable collection of feminist action and thought about the media has accumulated. The purpose of this chapter is to introduce the reader to some salient issues in feminist media theory and research of the past two decades which will lead up to the theoretical framework laid out in Chapter 3. There are several ways of structuring such an overview. A number of authors, myself among them (van Zoonen, 1991a, 1992a), have used typologies of feminist thought. Leslie Steeves (1987) for instance, distinguishes between radical feminism which has a strong interest in pornography, liberal feminism concerned among other things with stereotypes and gender socialization, and Marxist and socialist feminism focusing on the interaction between gender, class and ideology. In Steeves' classification psychoanalysis and cultural studies are discussed in the context of socialist feminism. I use similar distinctions in an article called 'Feminist perspectives on the media' (1991a) seeing cultural studies, however, as a body of thought in itself departing in some fundamental ways from socialist feminism.

NOTES

3

(continued)

Context

Considering this chapter began with summaries of the debates about *Nuts*, *Zoo*, *FHM*, and other men's magazines, are we in a different context now to the one Short was in twenty years ago? What does this tell you about the changes that debates about media and feminism have brought?

4

Content

The examples and histories outlined in the preceding paragraphs are put in a broader theoretical context here. Note how the language changes. There are ideas here that you need to have a good grasp of in order for the rest of the reading – and feminist debates about media more generally – to make sense. So, what 'new social movements' is van Zoonen referring to? And what is 'symbolic excess'? To think through these questions, you need to think about the relationships between media and society more generally, and the uses to which media are often put.

5

Structure

Here, van Zoonen tells us what the purpose of this chapter is. Why has she done so in the fifth paragraph of the reading, and not at the beginning? How does this strengthen her introduction and is this an effective way to set up her argument?

READING

6

The problems with such classifications are manifold. To begin with political and theoretical strands tend to be conjoined in a manner that obscures important differences between and within theories. Liberal feminism, for instance, is much more prominent in the United States than in Britain or continental Europe where the impression is that liberal feminism is a political strategy mainly that has not produced the same elaboration of theory as has arisen from socialist and radical traditions.[1] This is connected with a second point – that liberal, radical and socialist feminism have, over the past twenty years, undergone considerable change and encompass a range of theoretical developments and a huge diversity of positions. Distinctions that used to be meaningful, for instance between liberal and radical feminism, have now become blurred (Eisenstein, 1981) and certainly at odds with the current fragmentation of feminist thought. A diversity, moreover, which is not culturally consistent, in the sense that radical feminism in the Netherlands, for instance, is of a different nature from radical feminism in the United States or in Britain.

7

Presenting feminism in typologies tends to obscure this change and diversity, and also the ways in which feminist perspectives have developed through debate, critique and counter-critique. The existence and importance of black feminism – which is itself diverse and not a monolithic entity – has not been easily recognized in any of these typologies. The same goes for other typologies based on theoretical rather than political differences. Kaplan (1987), for instance, distinguishes between essentialist and non-essentialist feminism; Hermes (1993) differentiates modernist from postmodernist thought; others discern between thinking in terms of gender equality versus thinking in terms of gender difference (Hermsen and van Lenning, 1991). Apart from the explanatory and catalyst value of these juxtapositions, such dichotomies are also bound to elide the variety and intermingledness of feminist theory.

1. This point was brought to my attention by Stevi Jackson.

NOTES

6 Content

Note that van Zoonen states there are many ways in which feminist thought can be categorised and structured. That is, feminism encompasses a variety of approaches, and there are many different kinds of feminism; some of these overlap, some support one another, some have very different views and approaches. Therefore, there's a debate about what feminism is, what it was, what it should do, and how its aims can be best achieved. Here van Zoonen acknowledges that hers can never be a definitive summary of feminist thought; more importantly, it tells you that you should not aim to find one. In this sense, she is stating that *debate* over its meaning is one of the key characteristics of feminist thought; as has been noted in other chapters, such debate is central to theory as a whole.

7 Context

Here van Zoonen states how important 'debate, critique and countercritique' are and central to the development of a range of feminisms. Later she notes the 'variety and intermingledness of feminist theory'. What this suggests is that such theory is a *process*, which responds to things which are happening in the world, but which also develops in response to discussion and analysis. In this way, we can only ever talk about what particular kinds of feminism thought are/were at particular times in specific places, rather than thinking of it as some coherent, monolithic set of accepted ideas and approaches.

Content

Note the different kinds of feminist thought mentioned here: 'modernist', 'post-modernist', 'essentialist', 'non-essentialist', 'gender equality', and so on. While it is probably not necessary for you to grasp the intricate specifics of each of these approaches, it is worthwhile you exploring some different kinds of feminism so you can see the range of ideas and perspectives it can adopt. Also note how, in some cases, feminist thought is connected to other theories covered in this book, such as postmodernism. It's important, then, that while the theories are divided up into chapters in this book – and a similar approach is probably adopted when you are taught about them – you shold see that they are also often interconnected, and certainly often respond to one another.

READING

8

Another problem of many of the typologies mentioned, political and theoretical, is that they are construed out of general feminist thinking (for example, Jaggar, 1983; Tong, 1989) and then applied to feminist media studies imposing a more or less extraneous and not always relevant order on the field. An example of that can be seen in my own typology of liberal, radical and socialist feminist media theory (van Zoonen, 1991a). I suggested that research on stereotypes and socialization belongs typically to liberal feminist media research given its epistemological and political-philosophical premises, therewith overlooking the fact that many feminist communication scholars engaged in that area do not perceive themselves as 'liberal' at all and consider their work misrepresented (for example, Gallagher, 1992).

9

A typology therefore does not seem to be the most adequate instrument to provide the reader with an introduction to some issues in feminist media critique.[2] I will adopt a different angle, following Brunsdon's observation (1993) that in the past two decades feminist media critique has moved from outside to inside the academic disciplines of communication, media and cultural studies.

> While in 1976 the feminist critic writes a primary address to her movement sisters, in a tone quite hostile to the mass media, yet concerned to justify her attention to television, by the mid-1980s she inhabits a more academic position, tends to address other scholars and is beginning to be anthologized in books used on both Communication and Women's Studies courses.
>
> (1993: 309)

Useful questions for this chapter thus may be how and to what extent feminism has acquired a position in these fields, how its themes have been incorporated into the agenda and how it contributed to a paradigm shift. These particular questions are inspired by Sandra Harding's landmark study on gender and science, *The Science Question in Feminism* (1987).

2. Originally, this chapter was divided into three sections on liberal, radical and socialist feminism, the latter including psychoanalysis. Instructive and constructive criticism, in particular from Margaret Gallagher, Stevi Jackson, Irene Meijer and my students who did not feel very updated with this tripartition made me decide to use another angle.

8 ## Writing Style

Van Zoonen mentions more 'types' of feminist thought here, but note that at no point has she defined any of them in detail. Why might this be?

9 ## Writing Style

Note here how van Zoonen makes clear the structure of her work, helping the reader.

READING

10

Feminist critiques on communication studies[3]

Harding identifies several ways in which feminist scholars have criticized traditional science. To begin with feminists have drawn attention to the underrepresentation of women in higher education and as scientists. Formal and informal discrimination have prevented women from gaining access to the academic world. In communication and cultural studies, both in the United States and Europe,[4] the situation is not fundamentally different, with male faculty dominating, despite the high numbers of female students (Schamber, 1989).

11

Secondly, feminists have pointed to the sexist use of science and shown how disciplines such as biology and the social sciences have contributed to the needs of 'sexist, racist, homophobic and classist social projects' (Harding, 1987: 21). Helen Baehr (1980: 144) claims that the selection of an all-female sample in the by now classic communication study on media and personal influence 'the two-step flow' study of Katz and Lazarsfeld (1955), reflected 'the fact that American women represented an enormously profitable pool of consumers whom it was vital to "persuade" via advertising'. According to Baehr the study obscured the real interests of women in according them relevance as housewives and consumers only.

A third type of critique on traditional science concerns the themes, theories and methodologies which have been shown to be male-biased in the sense that women's problems have been ignored in many research agendas and that the particular experience of men has often been presented as having universal validity, overlooking the particular experiences of women. Apart from the neglect of specific themes, an issue to which I shall return later, communication studies has at least one exceptional case here in the 'two-step flow' study mentioned before. Although based on an all-female sample, it did acquire classic status as the way media *in general* influence people, thus accrediting universal value to the experiences of women, usually perceived as merely particular.

A fourth challenge feminists have presented to science, according to Harding, concerns the tenets of science itself. Feminists have claimed that objectivity, value-freeness and neutrality are offsprings of the hegemony of masculine modes of thinking that cherish dichotomies such as objectivity vs subjectivity, reason vs emotion, expert vs lay knowledge, abstract vs concrete, etc. It is argued that traditional science not only ignores women's themes and experiences, it also denies the validity of women's ways of knowing. Brenda Dervin (1987), discussing the potential contribution of feminist scholarship to the field of communication, argues that

3. I use the term 'communication studies' to refer to mass communication, journalism, media studies etc.
4. The observation on the United States is based on Schamber, 1989. The observation on Europe is based on personal communication with faculty of the more than twenty universities from ten countries involved in the Erasmus student and staff exchange network 'European Cultural and Media Studies'.

10   ## Structure

Harding's book is mentioned *before* the subheading, but only summarised *after* it. This means the paragraphs before and after the subheading only make sense in conjunction with one another, but they have a subheading sandwiched in between them. Why has van Zoonen structured her writing in this way, and how might you usefully use such a technique in your essay-writing?

11   ## Content

Much of the debate here is about science. This might seem a little strange in a reading about media studies. But van Zoonen does not so much discuss what science tells us as look at the approaches and methods it uses to make sense of the world. In that sense, science is as much a constructed discipline – with recurring characteristics and ways of thinking – as any other subject. The argument is that the research methods that are used by science, and the resulting data it unearths, rely on masculine ways of thinking, which are so ingrained in our society that they are not seen as masculine, but are instead perceived as 'normal'. This is a recurring theme in much feminist thought: that much of what we commonly perceive as 'ordinary' and 'normal' is, in fact, highly gendered and constructed, but because certain ways of thinking are so dominant, it is almost heresy to suggest that there could be other suitable approaches.

READING

11

(continued)

feminist scholars bring a 'female' viewpoint to the field, which is 'a new perspective, a new microscope for observation, that is not possible of somebody who is in the system. Women live outside the master's house[5] and therefore cannot use the master's tools for their own articulations' (1987: 113).

12

Finally, the feminist challenge to traditional science has produced a postmodernist understanding of science as socially constructed, as situated knowledge, grounded in the social experiences of its practitioners which are traversed by the contradictory claims of being a scientist, black, woman, feminist, socialist etc. A notable example in communication studies is Janice Winship's analysis (1987) of women's magazines in which she does not claim to speak for all women or from 'a female experience', but in which she uses her own individually, socially and culturally specific preferences as a starting point to understand the differential meanings of these magazines.

13

The multifaceted critique of feminist researchers does not seem to have resulted in an acknowledgement of the importance of gender issues in communication studies as a whole.[6] To mention some arbitrary examples: in Denis McQuail's bestselling *Introduction to Mass Communication Theory*, first published in 1983, there is no reference to 'woman', 'gender', 'sexuality' or other feminist concerns. In the revised second edition in 1987 one paragraph on feminist content analysis has been added. In special issues on communication research in western and eastern Europe published by the *European Journal of Communication* (1990) and *Media, Culture & Society* (1990) references to gender or feminism are all but absent. Moreover, there are still various areas in mass communication research that seem relatively untouched by feminist research, such as the study of new information technologies (van Zoonen, 1992a) and (tele)communication policy (Moyal, 1992) or research focusing on media and citizenship, such as political communication and news research (van Zoonen, 1991b, 1994). Although sometimes labelled a little derisorily as the 'add women and stir' approach (cf. Franklin et al., 1991: 2), in such areas it is still necessary to raise the simple question: how about women? In these areas Reinharz's description of the past still holds: 'At first, the very act of discovering sexism in scholarship was revolutionary. . . . it was radical simply to study women' (1992: 11).

---

5. Dervin (1987) includes the following note at this point: 'The term is from Lourde's *Sister Outsider*: 'For the master's tool will never dismantle the master's house.'

6. With the exception of some special issues of journals, such as *Communication* (1986), *Journal of Communication Inquiry* (1987). The tendency seems to be, however, to treat feminism as a separate area rather than incorporating its concepts into mainstream research.

12 Content

You might usually think that feminist thought suggests there is such a thing as a 'female experience', but van Zoonen here refers to Winship's work which resolutely rejects that idea. Some feminists dislike the idea of talking about women as if they're a coherent group, because this denies difference and individuality. But if research about people cannot be used to make broader statements about society as a whole, what is its use? If Winship examines her own preferences, but sees these are predominantly individual, what can we do with her findings? Some would suggest that our desire to extrapolate larger conclusions from small-scale studies is a part of the masculine ways in which research has traditionally been carried out. Are you convinced by this? And if so, what are the consequences for research as a whole?

13 Context

Here, van Zoonen places her thinking very squarely within the context of research and publishing on media and communications. Rather than exploring a *social* context, she is demonstrating an *academic* context, although that is not to say the two are unrelated. Why is it that such prestigious and international journals have not acknowledged women in the issues van Zoonen mentions? Have things changed since this chapter was written?

READING

14

In spite of the marginal position of feminist media studies in the discipline as a whole, there are at least two themes taken up and/or revitalized by feminist communication scholars which have gained a more habitual importance: stereotypes and gender socialization, and ideology, the latter of course erstwhile prominent in critical studies. Pornography, a third prominent issue in feminist media theory and research, has not gained similar interest and status within the academic sphere. The observant reader will notice that these are the three themes which some authors say 'belong' to particular currents of feminism, respectively liberal, radical and socialist feminism. However, as said earlier, debate on stereotypes, pornography and ideology has been engaged in by researchers from diverse feminist backgrounds, undermining theoretical or political 'monopolies' on any of these issues.

15

Feminist themes in communication studies

Stereotypes and socialization

Initially, the new themes that feminist media scholars added to the agenda of communication research were the stereotypical images of women in the media and the effects of these images on the audience. Rakow (1986) identifies two reasons for these particular themes: they were key elements of early feminist texts, such as Betty Friedan's *The Feminine Mystique* (1963), and they fitted well into the empirical research paradigm of communication studies. The latter is supported by an argument of Stacey and Thorne (1985) that a prerequisite for a successful intervention in any discipline is the existence of a tradition or subject matter related to feminist concerns.

16

The early review articles of images and effect research did not yet address the biases of communication research itself and seemed rather optimistic about the flexibility of the discipline. Busby (1975), for instance, claims that the latest feminist movement may have raised some consciousness within the academic community. Tuchman, however, is much more critical of the communication research community and argues that its scholars have not been very interested in the subject 'woman': 'And why should they? Before the advent of the women's movement these stereotypes seemed natural, "given". Few questioned how they developed, how they were reinforced, or how they were maintained. Certainly the media's role in this process was not questioned' (1978a: 5).

NOTES

14 Content

Why might pornography not have become a key topic within the academic sphere?

Writing Style

Why has van Zoonen acknowledged the 'observant reader'? What other kind of reader might there be?

Structure

Note the 'as said earlier' here; such writing helps link together different parts of the reading, aiding the reader's navigation through the chapter.

15 Writing Style

It is worth pointing out here how much van Zoonen refers to other writers. This is quite different from many of the other readings in this book. This may be because she has a desire for this reading to function as a summary, especially considering the position it occupies in the book it is taken from. However, it might also be related to the feminist approach which is being adopted which, as van Zoonen has noted, is quite different from the 'masculine' approaches used by much academic work. What is your response to this? Does referring to so many other writers give you a clearer overview of the topic? Or does it worry you because it implies there is lots of other stuff you need to read in order to understand the topic?

16 Structure

Note how two authors – Busby and Tuchman – are quickly summarised and contrasted here. It is this kind of writing which you are probably required to do in your coursework. Writing in this way shows you're acknowledging a range of views, and makes it clear that the issues are hotly debated by many people.

READING

17

Tuchman was among the first to produce research within a well-developed theoretical framework. In her introductory statement to a collection of articles about women and the media, she says:

> Our society, like any other society, must pass on its social heritage from one generation to the next. The societal need for continuity and transmission of dominant values may be particularly acute in times of rapid social change, such as our own. Then, individuals need some familiarity with the past, if the society is to survive, but they must also be prepared to meet changing conditions. Nowhere is that need as readily identifiable as in the area of sex roles.
>
> (1978a: 3)

18

Drawing from different research data, Tuchman shows that at present the media fail to live up to this function. While an impressive social transformation has taken place with over half of all American women in the labour force, television shows hardly anything of the kind. Television symbolically annihilates women, according to Tuchman, and tells society women are not very important by showing an overwhelming majority of men in almost all kinds of television output. Only in soap operas do women dominate the screen. Not only does television tell us that women don't matter very much except as housewives and mothers, but also it symbolically denigrates them by portraying them as incompetent, inferior and always subservient to men. The symbolic annihilation of women will endanger social development, according to Tuchman, for girls and mature women lack positive images on which to model their behaviour:

> Girls exposed to 'television women' may hope to be homemakers when they are adults, but not workers outside the home. Indeed, as adults these girls may resist work outside the home unless necessary for the economic well being of their families. Encouraging such an attitude in our nation's girls can present a problem in the future . . . the active participation of women in the labor force is vital to the maintenance of the American economy.
>
> (Tuchman, 1978a: 7)

17   Writing Style

This is quite a big quote. There's another significant quote in the next paragraph. It is worth considering why such large quotes have been used, especially as, in most of the rest of the reading, van Zoonen has been happy to succinctly summarise the work of others.

18   Content

What is meant by 'symbolically annihilate'? Why is such powerful language used to describe the process under discussion?

READING

19

Tuchman's analysis contains the basic elements of a functionalist feminist media theory: media reflect society's dominant social values and symbolically denigrate women, either by not showing them at all, or by depicting them in stereotypical roles. The models that media offer are restrictive and endanger the development of girls and women into complete human beings and socially valuable workers. Why the media function in such a counterproductive way is not explicitly answered by Tuchman, but other authors working in this paradigm have pointed to the dominance of male broadcasters and journalists whose gender socialization causes them to reproduce society's dominant values (Butler and Paisley, 1980).

20

An abundance of this type of research has been carried out all over the world, using primarily quantitative content analysis and social experimental methods. Gallagher (1980, 1985) summarized these projects and found depressing similarities between western industrialized, eastern communist and southern developing countries: women are underrepresented in the media, in production as well as in content. Moreover, the women that do appear in media content tend to be young and conventionally pretty, defined in relation to their husband, father, son, boss or another man, and portrayed as passive, indecisive, submissive, dependent etc. Social experimental studies trying to establish the impact of these sex role stereotypes on children in particular have shown contradictory results. Some studies support the socialization hypothesis, while others find too many intervening factors to justify a conclusion about media effects.

21

Recently, black researchers have raised the question of how black women are portrayed in western mass media. A study by Preethi Manuel (1985) of blacks in British television drama (referring to people from African, Indian, Pakistani and West Indian origin) showed that of the total number of actors involved in more than 600 drama programmes, only 2.25 per cent were black. Mostly they were cast as low-paid workers, students and law breakers, or as background figures. Black women hardly appeared at all. Most worrying to Manuel is the complete absence of black families from British TV drama. She concludes:

> In relegating blacks to the 'fringe' and giving them little to say, in portraying them as belonging to a subversive minority, it can only be said that negative attitudes of society towards blacks will be perpetuated. Black children are growing up without positive role models and consequently with a lowered self-image – the effect on white children is potentially as damaging. Inevitably, the pressing need for fair representation is inseparable from the pressing need for a harmonious existence in today's 'multi-cultural society'.

(Manuel, 1985: 41–3)

NOTES

19 Content

Note again how van Zoonen is careful to place the work she discusses within particular realms; she defines Tuchman's work as 'functionalist feminist media theory', and later refers to it as a 'paradigm'. In doing so, she is maintaining her awareness of the complexities of the topic, and her refusal to simplify matters. Such writing is difficult to do, but it is worth looking at how it is done here, because you are likely to be required to do such work in your studies.

20 Writing Style

Note the word 'depressing'; what does this tell you about van Zoonen's view of the data she refers to?

Content

So, different studies give different results; how are they useful then? What can we do with such information? And how can van Zoonen support her views on women and representation if such studies give contradictory data? What about the ways in which women are represented in the programmes you watch; what kind of results would they offer?

21 Writing Style

How recently is 'recently', and why does it matter?

READING

22 From Melbourne Cummings' (1988) discussion of the changing image of the black family on American television, it appears that television draws from widespread stereotypes about black women. One stereotype of the black woman that is particular to American history is the loud but lovable 'mammy to massa's three little children' (1988: 81). More widespread stereotypes mentioned by Cummings concern the image of the black matriarch, the overpowering black woman and the sexually insatiable black woman. The latter stereotype pervades the European colonial heritage as well. Rana Kabbani's (1986) work on European myths of the Orient shows how racist and sexist illusions of uninhibited black female sexuality abound in the work of British and French writers and painters.[7]

23 Theory and research on stereotypes has proved particularly valuable for its exhaustive documentation of stereotypes and prejudice which women in many countries have been able to use to raise the awareness of communicators and put pressure on their media to improve the images of women. However, on a theoretical as well as an empirical level this approach is not very satisfactory. I shall briefly mention some points that will be taken up in further detail in Chapter 3. Many analyses tend to generalize about the stereotypical nature of media content being insensitive to the specificities of genres, media and audience experiences. Further, the assumption that media content can be adequately characterized by a reference to the stereotypical *roles* of its population is rather incomplete. The mutual relationships of characters, their contribution to and involvement in the narrative, their visualization and their status in a particular genre, are all equally important. Finally, this type of research assumes an unequivocal meaning and effect of media content, with stereotypical images leading more or less unproblematically to stereotypical effects and traditional socialization patterns. The audience is thus implicitly conceptualized as a rather passive mass, merely consuming media messages.

[. . .]

24 *Ideology*

Theories of ideology are part of the 'critical' domain in communication studies and cultural studies. Critical communication scholars used to ignore gender just like mainstream communication scholars did, as the account of the Women's Studies Group of the Centre for Contemporary Cultural Studies (CCCS) at Birmingham confirms: 'We found it extremely

7. The representation of gender and ethnicity will be discussed further in Chapter 5.

NOTES

22   ## Writing Style

The word 'stereotype' is used here, without any discussion of what it means. Clearly van Zoonen assumes we understand the term. Yet there are many debates about what constitutes a stereotype, how they work, and what consequences they have (Pickering 2001). Considering the effort that has been put into acknowledging the variety of approaches relevant to her topic, why doesn't van Zoonen engage in the one about stereotypes?

23   ## Writing Style

What is the difference between the 'theoretical' and the 'empirical' here?

Content/Context

In questioning the ways in which media research views the audience, we can place this work within the debates about media reception explored in Chapter 23 in *this* book. By examining media content in order to critique stereotyping, much work has assumed straightforward social consequences. It might be worth noting here that, so far, van Zoonen has found problems with pretty much every approach she has discussed; does this render them all worthless, then? And if there are so many problems, why has she included them?

24   ## Writing Style

Why is 'critical' in inverted commas? It is important you have a good grasp of this word; see the discussion about it in the 'What is Theory?' Chapter 2 in this book.

Context

The work of the Birmingham Centre for Contemporary Cultural Studies (CCCS) is covered in Chapter 11 in *this* book. It is worthwhile noting that, while that Centre is often seen as promoting debate about the relationships between social structures and power, it is criticised here for not

READING

24

(continued)

difficult to participate in the CCCS groups and felt, without being able to articulate it, that it was a case of the masculine domination of both intellectual work and the environment in which it was being carried out' (*Women Take Issue*, 1978: 11). Feminist interventions in ideology theory have come from radical and Marxist, but in particular from socialist feminism. Because the cultural studies perspectives that will be discussed in the following chapter are in large part grounded in socialist feminist theory, ideology will be discussed more extensively than the previous themes of stereotypes and pornography.

25

Socialist feminists have shown a profound theoretical and political interest in connecting the capitalist mode of production to the oppression of women. Neo-Marxism, psychoanalysis and ideology theory provide the sources for this theoretical project.

26

From Marxism it takes not only the political economic analysis of capitalism, but also a conception of human nature as constituted in society: 'Specific historical conditions create distinctive human types' (Jaggar, 1983: 125). But whereas Marxists only recognize the capitalist and the worker as human types, socialist feminism acknowledges that human beings are defined by gender, race, ethnicity, age, sexuality and nationality as well. Its theoretical challenge has been to relate these differences, and gender difference in particular, to historical, social and economic conditions.

27

Among the different psychoanalytic theories adopted by socialist feminists the reinterpretation of Freud by the Frenchman Jacques Lacan and the work of the American Nancy Chodorow are of particular importance. Freud located the development of gendered subjectivity in the 'phallic stage' of infancy when children discover their genitals. This phase is characterized by the Oedipus and castration complexes that need to be negotiated in order to develop into 'normal' adults. Freud argued that at the same time a little boy becomes aware of his love for his mother, he recognizes her lack of a penis and becomes afraid that he might

NOTES

24

(continued)

doing so enough with reference to gender. Indeed, it could be argued that the Centre was much more successful in examining class than it was gender. This shows that approaches and theories are always up for discussion, and even those which are generally regarded as successful and positive are problematic for some thinkers.

Structure

Note how van Zoonen outlines the structure of the book from which this reading is taken, justifying her decision to focus on one topic more than others.

25 ### Writing Style

This is a dense paragraph, probably denser than anything in this reading up to this point. Van Zoonen clearly assumes the reader understands terms such as 'neo-Marxism' and 'psychoanalysis'. Also, what is a 'theoretical project'? Note that van Zoonen remarks on the relationship between the 'theoretical' and the 'political', which highlights the interplay between theory and debates about society, which is common in all theory, but which is given an extra impetus in much feminist thought because of criticism of gender inequality. See Chapter 12 on political economy and Chapter 17 on cultural theory in *this* book for more discussion of the relationship between the 'theoretical' and the 'political'.

26 ## Content

'Political economic analysis' is explored in Chapter 12 in *this* book; can you see how it relates to the feminist thought being presented here?

Writing Style

'Challenge' is an interesting word here; who is challenging socialist feminism to make the links mentioned here? Why is it presented as a 'challenge', rather than, for example, a 'goal' or 'intention'?

27 ## Content

This is a useful summary of the psychoanalytic theories of Freud. You may find Freud's suggestions of 'penis envy' and the 'superego' odd, and there is much debate over these ideas and, to an extent, the validity of the evidence Freud gave to support his theories (Thwaites 2007). What matters is not so much whether everyone passes through these phases in a complete and identical manner, but rather the social and cultural processes they might symbolise. In the next paragraph, van Zoonen refers to Lacan's (2006 [1953–64]) development of Freud's theories, which have been useful in feminist thinking, and which, to an extent, might feel a bit more 'believable' to you.

READING

27

(continued)

lose his penis too. He perceives his father as the powerful figure possessing his mother and capable of castrating the boy for his desire for the mother. To develop a 'normal' masculine subjectivity then, it is necessary that the boy denies his love for his mother, identifies with his father and internalizes his values. In the process he develops a 'superego'; the condensation of the patriarchal social conscience. Were the boy not to emerge from the Oedipal position and were he to remain immersed in maternal plenitude, his 'normal' masculinity would be endangered and indeed he would end up symbolically castrated. Thus, for a boy to become a man he has to separate from his mother and identify with his father. The little girl on the other hand passes these phases differently. As she becomes aware of her own lack of a penis, she develops penis envy and resents the mother for badly equipping her. To take revenge she turns to the father, competing for his love with her mother and desiring his penis. Only if the girl succeeds in substituting her phallic desire by the wish to have a baby – the ultimate penis substitute for women according to Freud – will she develop as an untroubled mature woman.

28

In Lacan's rewriting of Freud it is not so much the physical penis that is central, but the social and cultural power it represents, the phallus. Lacan argues that the child's separation from the mother takes place through the acquisition of language, or to put it differently, by the child's entry into the symbolic order. Without such a symbolic order which connects human beings to each other and makes sense of human experience, people cannot function and end up as psychotic. The Lacanian symbolic order is inevitably patriarchal, due to the structural position of the father as the intervening third party between mother and child: 'In the imagination, the father's position is the same as that occupied by language, in that language intervenes in the imaginary dyad [between mother and child] as the symbolic words that rupture the threads of phantasy that hold lack at bay and the illusion of union in place' (Brennan, 1989: 3). The patriarchal nature of the symbolic is thus a product of the equivalent structural position of language and the father as interveners in the mother–child bond. Submission to the patriarchal symbolic order – the Law of the father in Lacan's words – is a prerequisite for human autonomy and sanity. However, for boys the process implies access to social power, whereas for girls it involves entry into a patriarchal order in which 'the feminine' has no place and cannot be spoken.

28	## Content

'Patriarchy' is an important idea for feminist thought, and is a key topic in much media and cultural studies, whether that work is explicitly feminist or not. It assumes that masculine ways of being are normalised and dominant in our society, and here Lacan argues that, in order to make sense of the world as we are growing up, we have to accept this system. You might want to think about this in terms of the different ways in which boys and girls are often treated as they are growing up: for example, the kinds of toys they play with, the clothes they wear, and assumptions that are made about sports and hobbies that they would (and should) be interested in.

Writing Style

Note the very deliberate use of 'submission' here; does this suggest a positive view of the process being described or not?

READING

29

According to the materialist psychoanalysis of Nancy Chodorow, the acquisition of gender identity takes place before the Oedipal phase. In this early period in life the child is completely dependent on the parent, usually the mother and there is a strong mother–child symbiosis in which the child continually wonders whether he or she and the mother are one. This symbiosis is much stronger for mother and daughter since they are of the same sex: daughters develop a personal identification and a more continuous relationship with the mother. Boys have less opportunity for such direct identification because of the relative absence of the father. The boy develops a sense of being not feminine, and identifies with the position of the father rather than with his person. As a result, girls come to think of themselves in relation to others (the mother) while boys perceive themselves as unconnected individuals (the absent father). Penis envy in Chodorow's theory is not the female desire for the physical thing, but represents the desire to separate from the mother and become an autonomous person.

30

There is a crude resemblance to the developmental ideas of Freud and Lacan, but the major difference is that Chodorow's psychoanalysis is materialistic in that it explains gender difference from the social process of mothering. In Chodorow's theory femininity is not characterized by 'lack' or 'otherness' but by the capacity for meaningful triadic relationships.

31

Psychoanalysis has been instrumental to socialist feminist thought through locating the reproduction of gender and patriarchal relations at the level of ideology, as theorized in particular by neo-Marxists like Althusser and Gramsci. Within Marxist/socialist theory, ideology is the key concept to explain why it is that the conditions necessary for the capitalist mode of production are maintained and, for instance, workers do not revolt against their oppression. More formally ideology has been defined as:

> The means by which ruling economic classes generalize and extend their supremacy across the whole range of social activity, and naturalize it in the process, so that their rule is accepted and natural and inevitable, and therefore legitimate and binding.

> (O'Sullivan et al., 1989: 109)

While Althusser's and Gramsci's theories ignore the gender issue, the ideological mechanisms they analyse have been a source of inspiration for socialist feminists, who claim that gender is a crucial component of ideology.

NOTES

29 ## Content

What is 'materialist psychoanalysis', and how is it different to the approaches employed by Freud and Lacan?

30 ## Writing Style

Again, van Zoonen helpfully summarises and contrasts the ideas of multiple thinkers here, demonstrating the interconnectedness of theory, and the ways in which what one person thinks often responds to the analysis of another. This again demonstrates how theory is an ongoing *process*.

31 ## Content

You will have come across the concept of ideology throughout this book, and it is a key concern of much media studies. See Chapter 17, on cultural theory, for more exploration of this idea.

Writing Style

Again, note the deliberate language: 'revolt', 'oppression', 'supremacy'. What does this tell you about these authors' views on the topic?

READING

32

Althusser drew from the Lacanian notion of subjectivity as constituted in language for the development of his theory of ideology. According to Althusser people become subjects because of interpellation by ideology. This is to say that we are only able to make sense of ourselves and our social experiences within the limits and possibilities that language and the meaning systems available in a given society set for us. Language is not seen as a transparent medium conveying one's authentic experiences, or what really happened, but as constructing subjectivity and reality. According to the Lacanian dictum: 'we don't speak language, language speaks us'.

33

Althusser introduced the term ideological state apparatuses (ISAs) to refer to institutions such as religion, education, politics, the law, the family, media and culture. Although relatively autonomous from the state and capital and despite their variety and internal contradictions these institutions are said to function as agents of the state and the ruling class. Since ISAs cannot be directly controlled by the ruling class, they are ideological battlegrounds that betray the contradictions within dominant ideology. In the end, however, ISAs will function in favour of dominant ideology, although Althusser fails to explain exactly why and how this is achieved.

34

In Althusserian theories of ideology the individual is interpellated by dominant ideology; in other words, individuals are inexorably drawn into dominant ideology. Gramsci's notes on 'hegemony' provide an important addition to such a concept of ideology. Gramsci used 'hegemony' to refer to the *process* by which general consent is actively sought for the interpretations of the ruling class. Dominant ideology becomes invisible because it is translated into 'common sense', appearing as the natural, unpolitical state of things accepted by each and everyone. Like Althusser, Gramsci identifies ideological institutions and intermediaries like the priest and the intellectual, who translate the concepts of the ruling class into the ordinary language and experiences of the worker.

NOTES

32 | ## Structure

Van Zoonen acknowledges here that the theories of Althusser and Gramsci have been adopted and used by feminist theorists for purposes which were not the original authors' intentions, on a subject they didn't discuss. It is often said that influential theorists might be quite surprised – and, in some cases, outraged – by what subsequent thinkers have done with their theories. This shows how theories are often seen as a *starting point* for thinking, and while it is important we try to understand what original authors are trying to say, it is perfectly valid – indeed, necessary – for ideas to be developed, applied to new events and topics, and moved into areas for which they were not originally conceived. Because media studies is a relatively new subject it does this quite commonly, taking theory from other subjects and using it to its own ends. Do you think this is good practice?

33 | ## Context

Van Zoonen helpfully outlines the meanings of difficult ideas here, such as 'ideology', 'interpellation', and 'ideological state apparatuses'. As noted above, such ideas were not developed by thinkers whose aim was to examine gender *per se*, but have been adopted for these purposes by subsequent feminist thinkers. It is worth noting different contexts here, then; Althusser was writing at a specific place at a particular time, and his work was very grounded within that context. You might want to question how straightforward it is to apply it to the contexts van Zoonen, and other feminist thinkers, want to explore.

34 | ## Content

The Gramscian and Althusserian ideas of ideology and hegemony are ones which you'll come across throughout this book, in the readings on the public sphere (Chapter 13) and on cultural theory (Chapter 17), for example. Note that Althusser saw education as one of the 'ideological state apparatuses' that he criticised; you might want to bear that in mind as you continue your studies.

READING

35

Clearly, the media are the contemporary mediators of hegemony, the question being how, and to whose avail, particular ideological constructs of femininity are produced in media content. Much of the research done in this vein consists of ideological analyses of singular media texts using the instrumentarium offered by psychoanalysis, structuralism and semiotics (for example, Coward, 1984). The idiosyncratic nature of these analyses makes any comprehensive and meaningful review impracticable and therefore I shall discuss only one research project, which, although dating from the early 1980s, exemplifies the approach and issues concerned.

36

A typical ideological analysis of popular culture for women is Angela McRobbie's (1982) examination of the British teenage magazine *Jackie*, aimed at girls in the ten to fourteen age group. McRobbie sets out with a brief description of the publishing house responsible for *Jackie*, D.C. Thompson of Dundee, whose history is characterized by 'a vigorous antiunionism' and a 'strict code of censorship and content', according to McRobbie. Its annual profit margins rise as high as 20 per cent even in a time of crisis in the publishing industries. Having thus identified D.C. Thompson as a classic capitalist entrepreneur, McRobbie argues that these companies are not simply pursuing profits, but they are involved in 'an implicit attempt to win consent to the dominant order – in terms of femininity, leisure and consumption, i.e. at the level of culture' (p. 87). Publishing companies are part of the relatively autonomous apparatuses of the social formation that have their own particular operational modes and that cannot be seen as a unified whole. McRobbie acknowledges the internal contradictions of hegemony and argues that the working class, and especially the working class youth, has found ways to subvert hegemony by reappropriating cultural products and incorporating them into oppositional and subcultural styles of their own. However, the possibilities for that reappropriation are much more difficult for girls, says McRobbie, since the cultural forms available to girls are limited and their use – such as reading teenage magazines – is primarily confined to the personal sphere. Thus, while for working class male youth a cultural negotiation of the dominant social order is thought feasible, McRobbie finds resistance much harder to envisage in teenage girls' subcultural practices. In their leisure time, free of any direct coercion from work, school or the family, girls enjoy the illusion of freedom. But capital effectively controls leisure time as well, with magazines like *Jackie* as intermediaries. How does McRobbie think this control is achieved in *Jackie*?

NOTES

35   ## Writing Style

Considering how much depth and detail van Zoonen has given to a whole range of theoretical approaches, as well as many types of evidence she has offered, you might want to question why she is happy to make a significant statement about the media being 'the contemporary mediators of hegemony' with little evidence. She uses the word 'clearly': it seems she is not expecting any disagreement with her position.

36   ## Structure

We are now moving into the key argument of van Zoonen's chapter, and she uses evidence from Angela McRobbie's research (1982 [1978]). But note the problems here. We are meant to take this one study as exemplifying many others, and van Zoonen suggests it is okay to outline only one piece of research because the field is 'idiosyncratic'. Is this a valid justification? This whole paragraph is very important in the structure of the chapter as it is where we move from the theoretical to the practical analysis of those theories within feminist thought; you should note its brevity and its assumptions. Are you convinced?

Writing Style

'Typical' by what measure? How does this square with the assertion in the previous paragraph that such analyses are 'idiosyncratic'?

Context

Class is a recurring theme in media studies, but may be an idea you are not so comfortable talking about. Certainly, it's often argued that we now live in a 'classless society', particularly in comparison to previous ones (Adonis and Pollard 1997). However, media studies does not accept this, and sees class as very important to its analyses; this was a key idea in the work of the Centre for Contemporary Cultural Studies. Therefore, van Zoonen is comfortable discussing class, and inevitably connects it to issues of social power and hegemony.

Content

It is not stated as such, but it is quite clear that McRobbie – and therefore van Zoonen – sees the different opportunities for men and women that are outlined here as a bad thing. Indeed, you might want to notice how criticism is implied in the writing, without it explicitly being said. The vast majority of this kind of work adopts this position, and assumes that things need to be changed somehow. By not stating this viewpoint explicitly, van Zoonen is perhaps assuming her readers hold similar views.

READING

McRobbie uses semiology, the analysis of visual and verbal signs, to examine the 'connotative codes' present in *Jackie*. 'Connotation' here refers to implied or associative meanings of signs whereas 'denotation' refers to their literal meaning. For instance, in *Jackie*'s picture stories brunette girls do not only have brown hair and probably brown eyes, but the brunette is also usually involved in some vicious plot to get the man she wants, her best friend's boyfriend for instance. Brunettes thus mean trouble (connotation). McRobbie distinguishes four codes of connotation in *Jackie*: the code of romance; the code of personal/domestic life; the code of fashion and beauty; the code of pop music. Heterosexual romance is the core theme of *Jackie* and it comes to the reader in picture stories, on the problem page and in 'true life' stories. The picture stories usually feature two or three main characters, who are a little older than the average reader, their social backgrounds are unclear and their surroundings or use of language do not give them away either. The main characters come in easily recognizable stereotypes, according to McRobbie. Boys are irresistible charmers, tousled scatterbrains, sensitive artists or wild but sexy delinquents. Girls are blonde, quiet and timid, unreliable brunettes or plain ordinary. They are a fun loving group whose main occupation is to pursue each other. For girls the main task in life is to get and keep a man and in this respect other women cannot be trusted. 'The girl's life is defined through emotions – jealousy, possessiveness and devotion. Pervading the stories is a fundamental fear, fear of losing your boyfriend or of never getting one' (p. 107). And it is not simply the boy that the girls are after, what they want is romance, a publicly recognized relationship. Girls in *Jackie* see boys as romantic objects not as sexual objects, McRobbie claims. The code of romance in *Jackie* thus constructs hetereosexual romance as the all-pervasive concern of girls' adolescence and solidifies at the same time separate and distinct male and female roles.

In real life these themes are fraught with problems of course and these are indeed discussed on the problem page. Here, the ideological operations of *Jackie* show more openly, encouraging conventional individualism and conformist independence. 'That is: the girl is channelled both toward traditional female (passive) behaviour and to having a mind of her own. She is warned of the dangers of following others blindly and is discouraged from wasting time at work, playing truant from school or gossiping' (p. 115).

Fashion, cosmetics and beauty are signs of another central code in adolescent femininity. Clothing and cosmetics themselves are signs that girls are taught to operate to create a particular and recognizable image for themselves. While fashion and beauty are not central to the magazine, their message is that they are absolutely necessary components of a girl's life. It is taken for granted that the adolescent female body is in need of continuous maintenance and improvement, and *Jackie* provides step-by-step manuals to achieve self-improvement.

Finally, pop music is a central element of *Jackie*; however, it is not the music itself that matters but the star, with each week a single and double page devoted to a pop musician. In fact, the pictures of pop stars enable *Jackie* readers once again to fantasize about romance: 'Instead of being encouraged to develop an interest in this area, or to create their own music, the readers are presented, yet again, with another opportunity to indulge their emotions, but this time on the pop star figure rather than the boyfriend' (p. 126).

NOTES

37 Content

Semiology is discussed in Chapter 15 of *this* book.

Context

McRobbie's work is over thirty years old; are her arguments still valid today? You might want to think about concerns over size-0 models, debates about eating disorders, and the worries about the normalisation of pornography and lap-dancing clubs. Also, though, think about whether things have changed for men. How different is the context now from the context then?

READING

38

All in all, *Jackie* articulates the centrality of personal life for girls. It presents an all-embracing, suffocating totality of romance and emotion, stopping girls from doing or thinking about anything else. Although McRobbie cautions in her conclusion against the idea that readers will swallow the ideological axioms without question, she does consider the discourse of *Jackie* as immensely powerful, 'especially if we consider it being absorbed, in its codified form, each week for several years at a time' (p. 131).

39

McRobbie's analysis is a good example of an ideological analysis of popular culture. She focuses on the ideological operations of media texts produced within a capitalist context leaving the impression of an all pervasive hegemonic process from which there is no escape. McRobbie later conceded that her textual analysis 'created an image of *Jackie* as a massive ideological block in which readers were implicitly imprisoned' (1991, p. 141). While McRobbie's project allows for contradictions in the hegemonic process, in the actual analysis of *Jackie*, theoretical sophistication gives way to a rather straightforward interpretation of *Jackie* as a monolithic ideological construction of adolescent femininity. Later research among the readers of *Jackie* showed a multiplicity of interpretations and reactions not necessarily in line with hegemony (Frazer, 1987).

40

Aside from adding new themes to the research agenda or transforming old ones, a more fundamental issue concerns the question whether feminist media theory and research has offered new ways of approaching these themes. Did feminist communication scholars develop new frameworks, new designs and new methods, and did these innovations affect the guiding paradigms in the discipline at large?

41

In order to answer that question, it is necessary to take a closer look at the theories of communication behind the three themes discussed – stereotypes and socialization, pornography and ideology. Contrary to the first impression, the work done on these topics shares similar assumptions on the role of the media in the construction of gender. They are perceived as the main instruments in conveying stereotypical, patriarchal and hegemonic values about women and femininity. In research on all three themes media are conceptualized as agents of social control: in research on stereotypes it is said that media pass on society's heritage – which is deeply sexist – in order to secure continuity, integration and the incorporation of change

NOTES

38 **Writing Style**

Check you know what a 'discourse' is.

39 **Writing Style**

Why does van Zoonen see this work as a 'good example'? What other ones is it compared to?

Content

Here it is acknowledged that research on readers of *Jackie* came out with quite different results from the analysis of the text that McRobbie carries out. This shows the importance of examining reader responses; this is explored in Chapters 23 and 24 in *this* book.

40 **Writing Style**

Why does it matter if 'new ways' of thinking have been developed?

Structure

This is a concluding, summary section of the reading, and so the key topics and approaches are brought together here. The intention is to outline what has been covered, in preparation for what is to be explored in the subsequent chapters.

41 ## Content

See Chapter 7 in *this* book for more detail on Lasswell.

READING

41

(continued)

(Tuchman, 1978a); anti-pornography campaigners argue that media serve the needs of patriarchy by representing women as objects and by suppressing women's own experiences (Dworkin, 1981); and in theories of ideology media are viewed as hegemonic institutions that present the capitalist and patriarchal order as 'normal', obscuring its ideological nature and translating it into 'common sense' (*Women Take Issue*, 1978). In all three areas a structural functionalist media theory is employed, following the Lasswellian question: who, says what, to whom, and with what effect? Carey (1989: 15) has labelled this conceptualization as a transmission view of communication: 'The center of this idea is the transmission of signals and messages over distance for the purpose of control.' In feminist terminology media are thought to transmit sexist, patriarchal or capitalist values to contribute to the maintenance of social order. In such models meaning is located primarily in relatively consistent and uncontradictory media texts.

42

The transmission view of communication has become subject to strong criticism, from feminist and other communication scholars, to the extent that several authors now argue that the academic study of mass communication is in the middle of a paradigm shift involving a movement toward perspectives in which meaning is understood as constructed out of the historically and socially situated negotiation between institutional producers of meaning and audiences as producers of meaning.[8] As alluded to in Chapter 1, meaning is no longer conceptualized as a more or less consistent entity, but is seen as contradictory, divided and plural, in other words as polysemic (Morley, 1989). The ample acknowledgement of the importance of Ien Ang's (1985) and Janice Radway's (1984) work on the interpretative activities of audiences of soaps and romances respectively, shows that feminist media research has certainly played a part in this reconceptualization of meaning and communication. However, it would be hard to isolate the feminist impact and distinguish it from other influences, in particular those of cultural studies.

43

As said in the Introduction of this book, it is precisely at the junction of feminist and cultural studies that the most innovative and inspiring research is carried out. In the next chapter, I shall expand this discussion, laying out the flaws of feminist transmission models of communication in more detail and build from that a cultural studies framework for feminist media theory.

8. Other authors argue against the idea of a paradigm shift (Curran, 1990).

NOTES

42 ## Context

In acknowledging that media studies might be going through a 'paradigm shift', van Zoonen places her work in a specific context. Note that this is a context of *change*: that is, researchers are attempting to do work while the key ideas and methods informing that work are changing and being changed. Again, it is important to bear in mind the state of flux within which theory works; indeed, in putting forward new ideas, theory often contributes to, and constitutes, that flux.

Content

See the Ang reading in Chapter 23 of *this* book.

Writing Style

'Innovative' and 'inspiring' by what standards? Why might the innovative and inspirational aspects of theory be seen as important, considering theory is a *process*?

43 ## Structure

Van Zoonen ends by placing her writing within the context of her book as a whole. In that sense, she is noting that the content of this chapter constitutes a justification for the material that will follow it. What do you think the following chapter will contain?

REFLECTING ON THE READING

As was noted in the introduction to the reading, it is likely that you have a sense of what 'feminism' means to you before encountering van Zoonen's writing, so the first thing you should do is think to what extent this reading confirmed or undermined the assumptions you already had. Has this made you think about feminism in a different way, at all? This does not have to mean that your views on feminism have completely changed, but it might mean they've been modified a little. Also, remember that this is only one way of thinking about feminism and its relationship to media, and that there are many different kinds of feminisms. Any criticisms you have of van Zoonen's work might be answered by a different kind of feminism, and so it is important to be aware of those differences.

You might also want to refer to feminist thinking that you might have come across elsewhere, especially as certain thinkers and writers are now relatively famous, and appear on television quite often. For example, you may have come across people like Germaine Greer (mentioned in the article because of her seminal book *The Female Eunuch* (1970), and a sort of sequel, *The Whole Woman* (2000)) because she regularly writes for newspapers and magazines, and sometimes appears on television as a cultural commentator. You might want to think about why it is that some academics associated with feminism have managed to 'break through' into the public consciousness, especially as many of the writers you encounter in your studies remain predominantly unknown to the general public.

This chapter was written over a decade ago; do you think its arguments are still relevant today? For example, van Zoonen criticises much academic analysis of media because it often ignores issues concerning women and gender; has this been your experience of your studies? Think about the people who are teaching you; what is their gender split? How about your peers? Do you think van Zoonen could make exactly the same critique today, or have things changed? At one point she refers to McRobbie's analyses of *Jackie* magazine; could this analysis be applied to contemporary magazines? If you look at the ways in which magazines are divided up in most newsagents, into 'men's' and 'women's' sections, what does this tell us about gender assumptions? For many, we now live in a 'post-feminist' (Tasker and Negra 2007) age, exemplified by programmes such as *Sex and the City*, in which women can be both powerful, economically independent and sexually active, *and* interested in fashion, family and relationships (Akass and McCabe 2004). Yet research still shows women are paid less than men, do more housework than men, and suffer from prejudice at work and in the home. While it may be tempting (and true?) to say that things are 'better' than they once were, would you say that now both genders are treated equally, all the time? What value do you see feminist debates having *now*?

As can be seen below, van Zoonen refers to a lot of writers, far more than many of the other readings in this book. Why might this be? And how do you, as a reader, follow all these references up? It is impossible for you to read *all* of them, so how do you decide which are the most important, or most relevant to your studies? You always need to think of reading theory as an introduction to ideas and discussions presented by other writers, and van Zoonen clearly places her work in this context by referring to so many other people. But you need to work out how you follow this up. It is important to develop skills in sifting all the possible sources you could go and read so that you can select the ones which are most useful to you. That said, it is also good to remember that, quite often, the readings which have the most profound effect on you, and which open up new ways of thinking for you, can sometimes be those which *aren't* immediately connected to what you need to know right now. The possibility of stumbling across interesting reading is one of the excitements of study, and so you should never think any reading is wasted because it is not directly relevant to a piece of work you are carrying out.

One of the reasons van Zoonen refers to so many other writers is that she clearly places her work within a complex theoretical context. Because feminism encompasses a range of approaches, it often connects to other theoretical models. As noted in the introduction, the first chapter in van Zoonen's book is about Hall's 'Encoding/Decoding' model (1980c): the conclusion of this reading refers to cultural studies/cultural theory. Both of these are covered in *this* book (Chapters 11 and 17). It would be a good idea for you to look at those chapters, then, and to think through the ways in which these theoretical models intersect. While it is most likely that you come across theory via certain categories, it is important you try to see the links between different approaches. Rather than this making it seem as if theory is all one big, unfathomable mass, it should help you see that much of it comes from broadly similar origins; and if you grasp some key ideas, it is likely that these will help you make sense of a large amount of theory. Therefore, what have you read in this chapter which has reminded you of arguments, approaches and ideas that you've come across elsewhere? Are there recurring topics which seem to constitute media theory's key ideas?

Key terms to explore

cultural studies; discourse; hegemony; ideological state apparatuses; ideology; interpellation; Oedipal phase; patriarchy; penis envy; representation; stereotype; subculture; typologies.

Key writers who are mentioned

Helen Baehr; Charlotte Brunsdon; Denis McQuail; Betty Friedan; Germaine Greer; Sandra Harding; Jacques Lacan; Angela McRobbie; Preethi Manuel; Alberto Melucci; Clare Short; Leslie Steeves; Janice Winship.

RECOMMENDED READING

Gauntlett, D. (2002) *Media, Gender and Identity: An introduction*, London: Routledge.

Readable overview of issues of media and gender, with lots of examples.

Mulvey, L. (2000 [1975]) 'Visual pleasure and narrative cinema', in *Feminism and Film*, Kaplan, E.A. (ed.), Oxford: Oxford University Press, pp. 34–47.

Classic and seminal study of women in cinema, and central to many feminist analyses; that is not to say it is easy reading, though.

Walters, M. (2005) *Feminism: A very short introduction*, Oxford: Oxford University Press.

Short introduction to feminism, covering its history, its relationships to society and culture, and its development into a range of feminisms.

CHAPTER 17

Cultural theory

Williams, R. (1961) *The Long Revolution*, Orchard Park: Broadview Press, pp. 57–70.

INTRODUCTION TO CULTURAL THEORY

What does it mean to talk about 'culture'? When people worry about the ways in which 'British culture' is changing because of, for example, immigration, what are they worrying about losing? When someone is described as 'cultured', what's implied about them? When you go abroad on holiday and experience a different 'culture', what parts of that society make up that culture? BBC2 currently broadcasts *The Culture Show* (2004–); what kinds of topics are covered in that programme? What's the difference between 'culture' and 'art'? In addition, what are the differences between 'culture' and 'society'?

These are complex questions, with answers that are hotly debated. Their difficulty is at least partly a consequence of the problems involved in defining what 'culture' means. Let's think about it this way, though; what kinds of culture were you taught about at school? What kinds of books (literature, plays, poetry) were you required to study, and think about? What parts of history were you taught about, and which historical people did you learn about? What kind of music did you study? After answering those questions, think about what kinds of things you *didn't* study; what kinds of books and what kinds of music were not covered in the classroom? Also, if you studied abroad, do you think you would have covered the same kinds of material? In Britain, many school-children are required to study Shakespeare as part of English literature; do you think this would have been the case if you went to school in France? In America? In China? Why is it that different nations require their citizens to learn about particular cultural artefacts?

It is hoped that from this, we can see that culture – and the kinds of culture which we are most likely to encounter – is one of the ways in which our sense of self is constructed, especially in relation to national identity. While you may find Shakespeare difficult to understand and boring to read, it is likely that you are aware that he is British, and he is one of the ways in which 'Britishness' is understood by foreigners. This is shown by the way in which his hometown, Stratford-on-Avon, is full of shops and museums catering to the international tourist industry; it is one of the few places in the country where prices in shops are displayed in pounds, Euros, American dollars, and Japanese yen. When tourists visit the town, and perhaps see a Shakespeare play, they are getting a sense of British culture (or, more accurately, a particular kind of British culture) which, importantly, is likely to be different from the kinds of culture they experience at home.

Similarly, think about the BBC as producing culture; why do we have a *British* Broadcasting Corporation? Why is broadcasting defined by nation, especially in a globalised world where we can download television programmes from all over the world, thanks to the internet? The same is true for newspapers; more and more people get their news from the internet, yet we're used to the idea of *national* newspapers. If you look at British cinema, such as *Four Weddings and a Funeral* (dir. Newell 1994), *East is East* (dir. O'Donnell 1999), *Shaun of the Dead* (dir. Wright 2004), *An Education* (dir. Scherfig 2009) or *The King's Speech* (dir. Hooper 2010), how do you think these films are different from those made by, for example, Hollywood? What is British music, and how is it distinct from American music, or that produced in other European countries, or elsewhere around the globe? While these categories are never fully concrete, you can probably see that one of the ways in which we think of 'us' as a nation is through the kinds of culture our society produces and consumes; similarly, when you go abroad one of the things you do is experience a 'different' culture, by, for example, sampling local food, joining in with national ceremonies, seeing people in different clothing, and so on.

What's important here is that there is a link between culture (however we describe it) and the ways in which we think about ourselves (as part of a nation, or as part of a different kind of grouping, or even as an individual). Culture is important because it is connected to a sense of 'us'. It is therefore not 'just' entertainment, or a commercial product: it is a part of social processes, and results from those social processes. The reasons why you are taught about certain kinds of culture at school, but not others, is because culture has this significant social role. Cultural theory – and cultural studies, the subject it comes from – is interested in these ideas. As Barker notes, 'We should not ask what culture "is". Rather, we need to enquire about how the language of culture is used and for what purposes' (2008: 39).

Cultural studies is a very new discipline, only really coming into existence in the middle of the last century. It grew out of a particular set of historical circumstances in Britain, and took some time to establish itself. It has become important to media studies because the questions it asks about culture have helped inform debates about media, as the two are quite obviously related. However, it is important to remember they're *not* the same, even if there's a lot of overlap. This is shown by the ways in which cultural studies is taught; many universities do not have discrete cultural studies departments, and the subject is instead often a part of departments of media studies, English, or sociology; again, this has a national inflection, as discrete cultural studies departments are much more common in, say, Australia. While most regions of Britain offer an A level in media studies, and many schools now teach the subject as a part of GCSE provision, cultural studies as a named topic is much rarer. However, this is not to say you won't have come across the kinds of questions it asks before, because cultural theory has had significant influence on a whole range of subjects and, in its analysis of the kinds of culture which are taught in schools, it has affected the nature of education in Britain overall to a great degree.

Like many of the theories covered throughout this book, cultural theory is interested in ideas of *power*. That is, it sees culture – and the kinds of culture which are preserved and taught – as one of the ways in which power is expressed and maintained in society. For example, the fact that certain kinds of culture are taught in school, while others are not, helps suggest that some forms of culture are more important, and more worthy, than others. Cultural theory, however, has a 'suspicion of unthinking tendencies to privilege certain perspectives over others' (Gibson 2007: 15) and aims for 'the rehabilitation of popular mass culture as a legitimate object of scientific study' (Schrøder et al. 2003: 41). In that sense, cultural theory is important to media studies because it helps justify the study of populist forms such as television and video games in the first place, which has helped legitimise media studies as an important and worthy academic discipline.

INTRODUCTION TO THE READING

Raymond Williams is probably the key figure in the creation of cultural studies. His books and other writings constitute some of the core texts of the discipline, and his work has 'influenced many academic disciplines, including history, literature, cultural studies, mass communications, and education' (Dworkin and Roman 1993: 1). He was born into a working-class family in Wales in 1921, and went to Cambridge University in 1939. After serving in the Second World War, he worked in adult education from 1946 to 1961, and then became a lecturer in English at Cambridge, eventually becoming a professor (Pinkney 1991: 11). His work is deeply affected by this history, because not many people from his background ended up working in higher education, and he therefore felt he was an 'outsider' for much of his career; he has noted that 'It was not my Cambridge' (Williams 1989: 3). His work as an adult education tutor shows his sympathy for other such 'outsiders', as he attempted to bring education to those often excluded from the system. Also, the Welsh town he was born in – Pandy – was on the border with England, and thus fitted squarely into neither country, so he was a geographical outsider too. This constant feeling that he was not a fully accepted member of the parts of society he was involved in fuelled discussion of the social structures which he felt excluded from; its significance can be shown in the title of his first novel, *Border Country* (1960).

Because of this, Williams was interested in social and cultural structures, and saw contemporary society as a result of a set of historical processes. That is, how we think about now is affected by what we think about the past, which is in turn affected by the bits of the past contemporary societies decide to remember. These debates about the past and the present were very common at the time he was writing because of the Second World War. This global conflict led to nations the world over debating how such bloodshed could be avoided in the future, and how better, more equal, more progressive societies could be engineered. After the Second World War, Britain was a battered and bruised country; it was also optimistic and enthusiastic, and determined to construct a better future, deserving of the people who had fought. There was also a desire to make life better for 'ordinary', working-class people, considering the sacrifices the nation had made in order to win the war. It was in this spirit that, for example, the National Health Service was set up in 1948, so that *all* people had access to healthcare, rather than just those that could afford it.

Raymond Williams, then, comes out of a period of history in which the nature of British society itself was very much up for debate, and he fed off, and into, an energetic optimism for change.

What Williams saw were social structures which had historically downplayed the importance of working-class people and their culture. Importantly, he saw education as one of the most significant institutions which excluded the working-class, and in doing so upheld elitist distinctions between 'high' and 'low' culture (During 2005: 193–207). Again, debates about education were common after the Second World War, partly in response to equality, but also in response to the nation's economic needs. Williams was not alone in fighting for educational and societal equality: During notes 'the often-told epic story of heroic dissident British intellectuals (Richard Hoggart, Raymond Williams, Stuart Hall, the Birmingham school) battling for democratisation against elitism and hegemony in the sixties and seventies' (2005: 14; see Woodhams 2001 for a fuller account of this history); Stuart Hall and the Birmingham school are explored in Chapter 11 in *this* book. Notions such as equal access to education for all might seem obvious and commonplace now; however, at the time these arguments 'aroused an enormous amount of hostility' (O'Connor 1989: 105) because they so clearly questioned the ways in which society had been structured and run for centuries, and we should thank Williams and others for fighting this corner so consistently and persuasively. In that sense, we should always be aware of the radical and politically charged nature of this reading, even if what it says seems pretty obvious now; if it is obvious, this is only because Williams's arguments have been taken up by much academic thinking. Indeed, if you are now studying at university but you come from a background where, historically, many people didn't continue their education beyond that which was compulsory, you should thank Williams and others for demonstrating that you should have access to such opportunities.

This reading is taken from a chapter in *The Long Revolution* (1961) called 'The analysis of culture'. This book is a continuation of the ideas Williams outlined in *Culture and Society: 1780–1950* (1958), and these two books together work towards the larger debate about the role of culture in society that informs much of Williams's writing. Williams states *The Long Revolution*'s aims as 'questions in the theory of culture, historical analysis of certain cultural institutions and forms, and problems of meaning and action in our contemporary cultural situation' (1961: 9), which shows his interest in the interplay between culture, history, institutions and contemporary society. The book's title shows that Williams felt that society was changing, and that centuries-old social structures were falling apart in response to developments in work, industry, society and democracy. Indeed, he argues there have been three revolutions; a democratic one, an industrial one and a cultural one. It is the latter which forms the topic of this book, and Williams suggests in quite optimistic tones that he's living in a society where there is an 'aspiration to extend the active process of learning . . . to all people rather than to limited groups' (p. 11). Remember, though, that this was written in the 1960s; do you think this desire still holds true today?

As with all chapters taken from full-length studies, we need to think about what we are missing. However, in your studies you will often be presented with readings that have been taken out of their original context, and so it is important that you learn to make sense of them as stand-alone pieces. As it happens, Williams makes very few references in this reading to the rest of his book, and so it is unlikely to make you feel that you have missed out on something. What the reading does is think through some of the ways in which 'culture' can be thought about, and the social and political consequences of that word being defined in particular ways. Elsewhere, Williams has argued that 'culture is one of the two or three most complicated words in the English language' (1983 [1976]: 87). For example, Rojek defines 'culture' as having '*social* meanings having to do with urban-industrial forms of knowledge and power' (2007: 5), while During sees it as 'a set of trans-actions, processes, mutations, practices, technologies, institutions, out of which things and events . . . are produced' (2005: 6). Before starting the reading it is worth you thinking about the question; what does 'culture' mean to you?

1

Raymond Williams

The Long Revolution

There are three general categories in the definition of culture. There is, first, the 'ideal', in which culture is a state or process of human perfection, in terms of certain absolute or universal values. The analysis of culture, if such a definition is accepted, is essentially the discovery and description, in lives and works, of those values which can be seen to compose a timeless order, or to have permanent reference to the universal human condition.

2

Then, second, there is the 'documentary', in which culture is the body of intellectual and imaginative work, in which, in a detailed way, human thought and experience are variously recorded. The analysis of culture, from such a definition, is the activity of criticism, by which the nature of the thought and experience, the details of the language, form and convention in which these are active, are described and valued. Such criticism can range from a process very similar to the 'ideal' analysis, the discovery of 'the best that has been thought and written in the world', through a process which, while interested in tradition, takes as its primary emphasis the particular work being studied (its clarification and valuation being the principal end in view) to a kind of historical criticism which, after analysis of particular works, seeks to relate them to the particular traditions and societies in which they appeared.

NOTES

1   Content/writing style

This idea that there are three ways of thinking of 'culture' is key to Williams's analysis. What is significant is that it means culture has no fixed, absolute meaning, which means it becomes a context that can be discussed. This also means that how 'culture' is thought about at particular times and by certain groups of people, may tell us something about those people. Williams states there are three categories in a factual manner, as if it is not up for discussion; while he goes on to give evidence to support his statement, do you accept that these three are convincing? Are there ways of thinking about culture he has not acknowledged?

Structure

Williams offers no examples here; he outlines his theoretical position first (which is what encompasses this reading) and only goes on to look at examples much later. This may make his analysis difficult to follow. We can speculate as to why he has chosen such a structure. In offering examples later, Williams clearly accepts that theory needs to be tested and demonstrated. But by placing his theorising first, he is suggesting that theory is worthwhile in and of itself, and should be offered even if subsequent analysis finds it at fault. This is key to theory and theorising; but it may be difficult for you if you are used to working from evidence first.

2   Writing Style

'Documentary' is placed in inverted commas here, to show concern about its meaning. Indeed, Williams is probably using it in a way you are not used to. If you remember that the word comes from 'document', what he is saying is that culture 'documents' how we live; we can gain insights into other societies by looking at their culture and what it 'documents' about them.

Content

The notion of 'criticism' is a complicated one. First, it is commonly used in a negative sense, that we criticise when something is bad; however, in the academic sense it can be positive, negative or neutral, as it suggests the activities of analysing, questioning and debating, which may have a range of outcomes. As Williams notes below, how criticism is carried out can vary, from that which intends to demonstrate what is 'good' culture and what is 'bad' culture, to that which ignores such distinctions but is instead interested in how forms of culture 'work'. In your studies, you may carry out both of these kinds of criticism. Much contemporary media studies isn't interested in saying what's 'good' or 'bad', but *is* interested in examining *why* and *how* we categorise culture in this way. However, it's difficult to escape the idea that some forms of culture are 'better' than others, so we inevitably end up distinguishing between 'good' and 'bad' culture. Indeed, the kinds of films, television programmes and websites that you are required to study as part of your course might tell you something about what your teacher, or your university, sees as 'good' forms of culture that are appropriate to be taught.

READING

3

Finally, third, there is the 'social' definition of culture, in which culture is a description of a particular way of life, which expresses certain meanings and values not only in art and learning but also in institutions and ordinary behaviour. The analysis of culture, from such a definition, is the clarification of the meanings and values implicit and explicit in a particular way of life, a particular culture.

4

Such analysis will include the historical criticism already referred to, in which intellectual and imaginative works are analysed in relation to particular traditions and societies, but will also include analysis of elements in the way of life that to followers of the other definitions are not 'culture' at all: the organization of production, the structure of the family, the structure of institutions which express or govern social relationships, the characteristic forms through which members of the society communicate. Again, such analysis ranges from an 'ideal' emphasis, the discovery of certain absolute or universal, or at least higher and lower, meanings and values, through the 'documentary' emphasis, in which clarification of a particular way of life is the main end in view, to an emphasis which, from studying particular meanings and values, seeks not so much to compare these, as a way of establishing a scale, but by studying their modes of change to discover certain general 'laws' or 'trends', by which social and cultural development as a whole can be better understood.

3 Content

Here Williams introduces the 'social' aspect of his analysis. As has been noted, this approach to culture is important to cultural studies, and has its origins in Williams's work. The 'institutions' he mentions include things like the government, the legal system, education, the police, and so on. 'Ordinary behaviour' is that which we do every day; talking to people, eating, going out, and so on. In that sense, there isn't anything excluded from this definition of culture, which might make it difficult to grasp. Yet this is Williams's point, for he sees culture as something all-encompassing, intertwined with every aspect of our lives; this is also, therefore, why he sees it important to discuss what culture is.

Writing Style

You can see that Williams starts to struggle with language once he argues that culture is all-encompassing. By saying that 'the analysis of culture' is about looking at a 'particular culture', he seems to be repeating himself. Theory often has these struggles, because people are trying to discuss concepts and ideas which do not exist, and they either have to make words up to express them, or redefine existing ones. Indeed, this discussion over the meaning of culture is indicative of how such terms have various and changing meanings. Theory such as this may be hard, therefore, because it requires you, as a reader, to be flexible in your understanding of language, and willing to go along with the ways in which writers want to use particular words at particular times. Of course, this becomes *even more* difficult when *different* writers use the *same* word in *different* ways! Williams tries to make sense of all of this in his book *Keywords: A vocabulary of culture and society* (1983 [1976]), where he works through the various ways in which certain words – such as 'society', 'work', 'culture', and 'art' – are used. Rather than being like a dictionary, this analysis helps show how language responds to, and reflects, a society's concerns, and pre-empts a lot of media studies in its examination of the communication processes we often take for granted.

4 Context

Note that Williams has mentioned 'historical criticism' and 'traditions'. This places his thinking about the present within an understanding of the past, and he certainly sees contemporary life as a result of a series of historical developments. For Williams, 'now' can only be understood by reference to 'then', so the past is a constant context to his work.

Writing Style

Williams notes that his definition of 'culture' encompasses ideas which may not usually be incorporated into understandings of the word. In a subtle way, then, he is signalling what it is that is *new* about his argument, and how it *differs* from conventional thinking on the matter.

READING

5

It seems to me that there is value in each of these kinds of definition.

6

For it certainly seems necessary to look for meanings and values, the record of creative human activity, not only in art and intellectual work, but also in institutions and forms of behaviour. At the same time, the degree to which we depend, in our knowledge of many past societies and past stages of our own, on the body of intellectual and imaginative work which has retained its major communicative power, makes the description of culture in these terms, if not complete, at least reasonable. It can indeed be argued that since we have 'society' for the broader description, we can properly restrict 'culture' to this more limited reference. Yet there are elements in the 'ideal' definition which also seem to me valuable, and which encourage the retention of the broad reference.

7

I find it very difficult, after the many comparative studies now on record, to identify the process of human perfection with the discovery of 'absolute' values, as these have been ordinarily defined. I accept the criticism that these are normally an extension of the values of a particular tradition or society. Yet, if we call the process, not human perfection, which implies a known ideal towards which we can move, but human evolution, to mean a process of general growth of man as a kind, we are able to recognize areas of fact which the other definitions might exclude.

NOTES

5 Writing Style

Are you allowed to write 'It seems to me' in your essays? What does the use of such a phrase imply about Williams's understanding of his readers, and what he expects of them?

6 Content

It's important you have a working understanding of the distinction between 'culture' and 'society' Williams offers here. That is not to say this is easy; nor is it to say that Williams has no reservations about what he is proposing; but it is to note that the interplay between culture and society is at the heart of Williams's work, and key to many contemporary approaches in media studies.

Writing Style

Do you think it is okay for Williams to suggest that his argument should be accepted because it's 'reasonable', even if it has flaws? In writing in this way, Williams is inviting the reader to 'go along' with what he is saying for now, because the development of his argument rests on the distinction he is proposing. We could critique what he is doing at this stage in the reading; or, instead, we could agree to go along with it, and decide whether it is reasonable when we get to the end, as the insights his theorising is giving might be worth the problematic statement being made here.

7 Writing Style

Again, note how comfortable Williams is with using 'I' and 'me'. In doing so he makes his writing more personal, demonstrating that his approach is connected to who he is. In this way, there's no suggestion that his analysis is *the* correct one, or has no problems; he is instead offering his particular view of things. It is rare that you come across writing in this way in, for instance, the sciences. But it is quite common in the humanities, and has been even more common in analysis which takes a cultural approach, for that approach assumes that our understanding of the world is inevitably inflected through who we are, so it is pointless to pretend we're a detached, objective outsider looking in on our object of study.

Content

There is much discussion of 'process' here. The idea of processes and systems is central to much media studies, which attempts to look at how a variety of phenomena are interlinked and interdependent. For Williams – and for cultural studies – it is meaningless to look at media without exploring the process it is a part of, and its relationship to those processes. This idea of process is also related to the historical focus discussed in Note 4, because history is itself a process.

READING

8

For it seems to me to be true that meanings and values, discovered in particular societies and by particular individuals, and kept alive by social inheritance and by embodiment in particular kinds of work, have proved to be universal in the sense that when they are learned, in any particular situation, they can contribute radically to the growth of man's powers to enrich his life, to regulate his society, and to control his environment. We are most aware of these elements in the form of particular techniques, in medicine, production, and communications, but it is clear not only that these depend on more purely intellectual disciplines, which had to be wrought out in the creative handling of experience, but also that these disciplines in themselves, together with certain basic ethical assumptions and certain major art forms, have proved similarly capable of being gathered into a general tradition which seems to represent, through many variations and conflicts, a line of common growth. It seems reasonable to speak of this tradition as a general human culture, while adding that it can only become active within particular societies, being shaped, as it does so, by more local and temporary systems.

9

The variations of meaning and reference, in the use of culture as a term, must be seen, I am arguing, not simply as a disadvantage, which prevents any kind of neat and exclusive definition, but as a genuine complexity, corresponding to real elements in experience. There is a significant reference in each of the three main kinds of definition, and, if this is so, it is the relations between them that should claim our attention. It seems to me that any adequate theory of culture must include the three areas of fact to which the definitions point, and conversely that any particular definition, within any of the categories, which would exclude reference to the others, is inadequate. Thus an 'ideal' definition which attempts to abstract the process it describes from its detailed embodiment and shaping by particular societies – regarding man's ideal development as something separate from and even opposed to his 'animal nature' or the satisfaction of material needs – seems to me unacceptable. A 'documentary' definition which sees value only in the written and painted records, and marks this area off from the rest of man's life in society, is equally unacceptable. Again, a 'social' definition, which treats either the general process or the body of art and learning as a mere by-product, a passive reflection of the real interests of the society, seems to me equally wrong. However difficult it may be in practice, we have to try to see the process as a whole, and to relate our particular studies, if not explicitly at least by ultimate reference, to the actual and complex organization.

NOTES

8 Writing Style

What is Williams suggesting about the process he is discussing by saying they are 'kept alive'? How does this relate to the idea of 'process'?

Content

What 'ethical assumptions' and 'major art forms' is Williams referring to here?

Context

Again, note the historical context the analysis is being placed in. 'A line of common growth' suggests the onward march of history, in which many societies develop in broadly similar ways. However, Williams is also keen to note the specifics of individual cases, as he talks of 'particular societies', and factors which are 'local' and 'temporary'. In these ways he is suggesting that the analysis of culture is *complicated*, as it must take into account a vast array of factors. This is an important statement, especially as we often think of the development of our culture as pretty straightforward and inevitable. This complexity is explored in the next paragraph.

9 Content

So far Williams has been highlighting the distinctions between the three meanings of 'culture' he has been discussing; here he brings them together. Theoretical analysis often does this, exploring the relationships between material rather than attempting to 'prove' or 'disprove' the appropriateness of a set, unarguable idea. This is shown by 'ideal' being in inverted commas, suggesting that Williams believes coming to a perfect, unquestionable understanding of the word is not possible.

Context

Williams keeps referring to 'man', meaning 'mankind'. Such a use of the word is often critiqued by feminists today, as it ignores women. Williams wrote in a historical context in which it is unsurprising – which is not the same as saying acceptable – that he would use the word in this way. However, it is worth noting that this chapter was written before feminism had its major impacts on the debates about society and culture, and so you could think about whether questions of gender would give a different inflection to the theory outlined here; see Chapter 16 in *this* book.

READING

10

We can take one example, from analytic method, to illustrate this. If we take a particular work of art, say the *Antigone* of Sophocles, we can analyse it in ideal terms – the discovery of certain absolute values, or in documentary terms – the communication of certain values by certain artistic means. Much will be gained from either analysis, for the first will point to the absolute value of reverence for the dead; the second will point to the expression of certain basic human tensions through the particular dramatic form of chorus and double *kommos*, and the specific intensity of the verse. Yet it is clear that neither analysis is complete. The reverence, as an absolute value, is limited in the play by the terms of a particular kinship system and its conventional obligations – Antigone would do this for a brother but not for a husband. Similarly, the dramatic form, the metres of the verse, not only have an artistic tradition behind them, the work of many men, but can be seen to have been shaped, not only by the demands of the experience, but by the particular social forms through which the dramatic tradition developed. We can accept such extensions of our original analysis, but we cannot go on to accept that, because of the extensions, the value of reverence, or the dramatic form and the specific verse, have meaning only in the contexts to which we have assigned them. The learning of reverence, through such intense examples, passes beyond its context into the general growth of human consciousness.

11

The dramatic form passes beyond its context, and becomes an element in a major and general dramatic tradition, in quite different societies. The play itself, a specific communication, survives the society and the religion which helped to shape it, and can be re-created to speak directly to unimagined audiences. Thus, while we could not abstract the ideal value or the specific document, neither could we reduce these to explanation within the local terms of a particular culture.

NOTES

10

Structure

Williams *finally* gets on to an example, to outline his thinking. Yet note that in this (very long) paragraph he doesn't actually deal with his example in much detail, and instead takes it as a general example to make broad statements. You might also question the appropriacy of the choice of a classical Greek play as an example, and what this suggests about the audience Williams felt he was writing for. As he never outlines the play's content, or the significance of some aspects of it, such as the use of a chorus, he certainly assumes you know what *Antigone* (*c.* 442 BC) is, what its storyline is, and the conventions of Greek drama.

Writing Style

Who is this 'we' Williams is referring to here? How come he is now talking about 'we', when previously he was talking about 'I'?

Content

This is an important point about the significance of a historical context. Williams is arguing that while such a context clearly informed *Antigone* – and therefore all culture – when it was read by contemporaneous audiences, the fact that we, now, over 2,000 years later, can still make broad sense of such cultural texts, demonstrates how culture draws on, and reproduces, general understandings of society and culture that are relatively unchanged. People today enjoy music, art, literature, architecture, and other forms of culture that were produced hundreds, if not thousands, of years ago, and this could only be the case if they are similar in some ways to the culture produced now. This is not to deny differences; but it is to say that we should perhaps be surprised that we can so easily make sense of culture from the past, especially when we often think of ourselves and our society as so different to those from hundreds of years ago.

11

Content

Here the complexity of the terms 'society' and 'culture' is demonstrated. When thinking about culture, we often discuss it in terms of the society that produced it; in contemporary terms, we might argue, for example, that you can only properly understand anime if you place it in its Asian context. However, Williams argues that this suggests societies *produce* culture, when we should be thinking that society *is* culture. That is, the society that produces that culture is itself created by that culture, for we make sense of the world around us at least partly by looking at the culture which helps us understand it. This is important, because it means we shouldn't just look at culture as an abstract, desocialised phenomenon; it is, instead, a significant factor in how our society is constructed, justified and upheld. This, then, justifies the analysis of culture, for it's an integral part of society, politics and power.

READING

12

If we study real relations, in any actual analysis, we reach the point where we see that we are studying a general organization in a particular example, and in this general organization there is no element that we can abstract and separate from the rest. It was certainly an error to suppose that values or art-works could be adequately studied without reference to the particular society within which they were expressed, but it is equally an error to suppose that the social explanation is determining, or that the values and works are mere by-products. We have got into the habit, since we realized how deeply works or values could be determined by the whole situation in which they are expressed, of asking about these relationships in a standard form: 'what is the relation of this art to this society?' But 'society', in this question, is a specious whole. If the art is part of the society, there is no solid whole, outside it, to which, by the form of our question, we concede priority. The art is there, as an activity, with the production, the trading, the politics, the raising of families. To study the relations adequately we must study them actively, seeing all the activities as particular and contemporary forms of human energy. If we take any one of these activities, we can see how many of the others are reflected in it, in various ways according to the nature of the whole organization. It seems likely, also, that the very fact that we can distinguish any particular activity, as serving certain specific ends, suggests that without this activity the whole of the human organization at that place and time could not have been realized. Thus art, while clearly related to the other activities, can be seen as expressing certain elements in the organization which, within that organization's terms, could only have been expressed in this way.

13

It is then not a question of relating the art to the society, but of studying all the activities and their interrelations, without any concession of priority to any one of them we may choose to abstract. If we find, as often, that a particular activity came radically to change the whole organization, we can still not say that it is to this activity that all the others must be related; we can only study the varying ways in which, within the changing organization, the particular activities and their interrelations were affected. Further, since the particular activities will be serving varying and sometimes conflicting ends, the sort of change we must look for will rarely be of a simple kind: elements of persistence, adjustment, unconscious assimilation, active resistance, alternative effort, will all normally be present, in particular activities and in the whole organization.

12 ## Writing Style

Williams repeatedly refers to 'relations' and 'activities', much like his earlier analysis of 'processes'. Note how all these words are active, suggesting that culture isn't just there, but is an active part of the system in which we live.

What kinds of 'organization' is Williams referring to here?

Content

Here Williams notes the difficulty in demonstrating that any changes in any organisation can be attributed to a single factor, as the interrelationships between a range of factors in any system means causes can be traced to many origins. In a sense, he is arguing that things are *complicated*. You might bemoan the fact that theory often insists on complicating things; Williams would argue that's because you live in a social system which justifies itself, at least partly by suggesting it is *not* complicated, and it is that falsehood which is one of the main motivators for his thinking.

13 ## Content

Following on from his statements that systems are complicated, Williams here notes that how individuals may respond to that system is complicated too. This is important, because when we discuss such all-encompassing ideas as society and culture, it is often tempting to forget the individuals who exist within them, and instead treat people as a mass. However, while Williams notes the particularities of individual responses, it is important not to overstate this, and assume someone can do whatever they want with the society they live in. This debate about the amount of power an individual has to resist and reshape the society which surrounds them is a key one, and different thinkers have quite different views on how powerful individuals are.

READING

14

The analysis of culture, in the documentary sense, is of great importance because it can yield specific evidence about the whole organization within which it was expressed. We cannot say that we know a particular form or period of society, and that we will see how its art and theory relate to it, for until we know these, we cannot really claim to know the society.

15

This is a problem of method, and is mentioned here because a good deal of history has in fact been written on the assumption that the bases of the society, its political, economic, and 'social' arrangements, form the central core of facts, after which the art and theory can be adduced, for marginal illustration or 'correlation'. There has been a neat reversal of this procedure in the histories of literature, art, science, and philosophy, when these are described as developing by their own laws, and then something called the 'background' (what in general history was the central core) is sketched in. Obviously it is necessary, in exposition, to select certain activities for emphasis, and it is entirely reasonable to trace particular lines of development in temporary isolation. But the history of a culture, slowly built up from such particular work, can only be written when the active relations are restored, and the activities seen in a genuine parity. Cultural history must be more than the sum of the particular histories, for it is with the relations between them, the particular forms of the whole organization, that it is especially concerned.

I would then define the theory of culture as the study of relationships between elements in a whole way of life.

The analysis of culture is the attempt to discover the nature of the organization which is the complex of these relationships. Analysis of particular works or institutions is, in this context, analysis of their essential kind of organization, the relationships which works or institutions embody as parts of the organization as a whole. A key-word, in such analysis, is pattern: it is with the discovery of patterns of a characteristic kind that any useful cultural analysis begins, and it is with the relationships between these patterns, which sometimes reveal unexpected identities and correspondences in hitherto separately considered activities, sometimes again reveal discontinuities of an unexpected kind, that general cultural analysis is concerned.

14 ## Context

This sentence is, in essence, a justification for cultural studies, as Williams is stating why studying culture is important. Bear in mind that when this was written, cultural studies and media studies did not exist in any meaningful way, which means Williams is required to state *why* the work he is outlining should be carried out, and *why* it matters. Because cultural studies is now an accepted discipline, many writers nowadays do not give justifications for what they are doing; this means they assume you *already know* why it is important.

15 ## Content

In thinking about method, Williams demonstrates the often unexamined ways in which many subjects – his example here is history – carry out research. He notes that history usually sees certain topics – such as politics and economics – as more important than the cultural phenomena he is interested in, and this is problematic for Williams for two reasons. First, history rarely questions why it does this; secondly, in separating economics and politics from culture, history ignores or downplays how they are interconnected and interdependent. Debates about method are important, because methods reveal what a subject thinks is important. Cultural studies has commonly tried to develop new research methods, precisely because it argues that existing ones are incapable of exploring the research questions which it sees as necessary. Note that Williams does not suggest specific methods here: that is because theory must come *before* method, as method is a tool employed to think through theory that has been proposed.

Writing Style

In distinguishing between 'history' and 'cultural history', Williams is making an explicit statement about the differences he sees between the two approaches. Note that he goes on to define a 'theory of culture'; how useful do you think this definition is?

READING

16

It is only in our own time and place that we can expect to know, in any substantial way, the general organization. We can learn a great deal of the life of other places and times, but certain elements, it seems to me, will always be irrecoverable. Even those that can be recovered are recovered in abstraction, and this is of crucial importance. We learn each element as a precipitate, but in the living experience of the time every element was in solution, an inseparable part of a complex whole. The most difficult thing to get hold of, in studying any past period, is this felt sense of the quality of life at a particular place and time: a sense of the ways in which the particular activities combined into a way of thinking and living. We can go some way in restoring the outlines of a particular organization of life; we can even recover what Fromm calls the 'social character' or Benedict the 'pattern of culture'. The social character – a valued system of behaviour and attitudes – is taught formally and informally, it is both an ideal and a mode.

17

The 'pattern of culture' is a selection and configuration of interests and activities, and a particular valuation of them, producing a distinct organization, a 'way of life'. Yet even these, as we recover them, are usually abstract. Possibly, however, we can gain the sense of a further common element, which is neither the character nor the pattern, but as it were the actual experience through which these were lived. This is potentially of very great importance, and I think the fact is that we are most conscious of such contact in the arts of a period. It can happen that when we have measured these against the external characteristics of the period, and then allowed for individual variations, there is still some important common element that we cannot easily place. I think we can best understand this if we think of any similar analysis of a way of life that we ourselves share. For we find here a particular sense of life, a particular community of experience hardly needing expression, through which the characteristics of our way of life that external analysts could describe are in some way passed, giving them a particular and characteristic colour. We are usually most aware of this when we notice the contrasts between generations, who never talk quite 'the same language', or when we read an account of our lives by someone from outside the community, or watch the small differences in style, of speech or behaviour, in someone who has learned our ways yet was not bred in them. Almost any formal description would be too crude to express this nevertheless quite distinct sense of a particular and native style. And if this is so, in a way of life we know intimately, it will surely be so when we ourselves are in the position of the visitor, the learner, the guest from a different generation: the position, in fact, that we are all in, when we study any past period. Though it can be turned to trivial account, the fact of such a characteristic is neither trivial nor marginal; it feels quite central.

NOTES

16 Content

This may seem like an admission of failure, but Williams is here stating that, when looking at the past, there are some things *we can never know*. We can never recreate the 'felt sense of the quality of life' because the multitude of factors which make up society and culture are so inter-dependent that, in looking at them from now, we remove them from their full context. You may have experienced this at museums, which re-create the living or working conditions of a historical period as often as they can; but they can never be the same as *being there* and living in that society, because we bring our contemporary understandings to bear on them. No one can ever fully grasp someone else's 'way of thinking and living'; you might ask, then, what is the point in carrying out such work?

Writing Style

How is the 'valued system' Williams discusses 'taught'? Does he mean formally, in school? Or does he mean something else?

17 Writing Style

Note the kinds of terms Williams offers here: 'way of life', 'sense of life', 'community of experience'. These are all quite vague, but they are *deliberately* so. In arguing that the analytical tools we have are incapable of capturing and expressing certain aspects of society and culture, Williams shows that he does not have the language to definitively pinpoint his argument. This has important con-sequences, especially as cultural studies and structuralism (see Chapter 15) have repeatedly argued that language is a powerful social tool because it limits us to expressing ideas which there are words for. If historians have not come up with terms to express the kinds of history Williams says matters, this says something about what historians see as important; more importantly, it tells us what they see as irrelevant. Williams is arguing that history has repeatedly ignored lots of areas, and that the choices made about what should be studied and what shouldn't is itself expressive of power distinctions within society.

Content

Williams equates studying another period with being a 'visitor'. And just as visitors are interested in viewing particular parts of a culture they visit, so academics are interested in certain aspects of their subject. It is important to note, then, that in studying another culture we are always an outsider.

READING

18 The term I would suggest to describe it is *structure of feeling*: it is as firm and definite as 'structure' suggests, yet it operates in the most delicate and least tangible parts of our activity. In one sense, this structure of feeling is the culture of a period: it is the particular living result of all the elements in the general organization. And it is in this respect that the arts of a period, taking these to include characteristic approaches and tones in argument, are of major importance. For here, if anywhere, this characteristic is likely to be expressed; often not consciously, but by the fact that here, in the only examples we have of recorded communication that outlives its bearers, the actual living sense, the deep community that makes the communication possible, is naturally drawn upon. I do not mean that the structure of feeling, any more than the social character, is possessed in the same way by the many individuals in the community. But I think it is a very deep and very wide possession, in all actual communities, precisely because it is on it that communication depends.

19 And what is particularly interesting is that it does not seem to be, in any formal sense, learned. One generation may train its successor, with reasonable success, in the social character or the general cultural pattern, but the new generation will have its own structure of feeling, which will not appear to have come 'from' anywhere. For here, most distinctly, the changing organization is enacted in the organism: the new generation responds in its own ways to the unique world it is inheriting, taking up many continuities, that can be traced, and reproducing many aspects of the organization, which can be separately described, yet feeling its whole life in certain ways differently, and shaping its creative response into a new structure of feeling.

20 Once the carriers of such a structure die, the nearest we can get to this vital element is in the documentary culture, from poems to buildings and dress-fashions, and it is this relation that gives significance to the definition of culture in documentary terms. This in no way means that the documents are autonomous. It is simply that, as previously argued, the significance

NOTES

18 Content

'Structure of feeling' is a very famous, and oft-quoted, phrase of Williams'. Note how it brings together the idea of organisation and systems, with the more emotive, and probably personal, idea of 'feeling'. In this sense, Williams is keen for us to think through how living in a culture 'feels', which is often ignored by a variety of academic disciplines. Note that 'feeling' here is not a solely personal act, for there is a 'structure' which constructs and helps define it.

Context

This is an important idea, that the 'examples' we have of a past culture are limited and particular. One of the questions cultural studies has repeatedly asked is why societies decide to preserve certain aspects of itself, and isn't worried about others. Most cities in Britain have some kind of historical museum; yet what that museum contains is selective, and ignores a whole range of artefacts and experiences which made up the 'structure of feeling' of a society. Cultural studies has, therefore, often examined the museum: see Henning (2006) and Macdonald (2006). The important thing here is we can never 'know' the past, because we don't have access to *all* aspects of it.

19 Writing Style

The choice of the word 'learned' is significant. We may associate it with formal education, in schools, colleges and universities. Yet Williams is arguing that we 'learn' from a variety of sources, including our families, media, friends, and culture as a whole. The important point is that if it is 'learned', it is not natural or inevitable, and we can instead question why it is that particular ideas are passed on from generation to generation. This also means that, while cultural ideas may develop over time, and may differ between individuals, the amount of variation is limited by the kinds of material that are taught by one society to the members of another.

Content

Note here how the idea that society and culture develop, change and evolve is made explicit. This means they are difficult to pin down, and also difficult to categorise. This reinforces the idea that society and culture are *processes*, responding to relationships between the past and current times, rather than something set in stone.

20 Writing Style

Williams refers back to a previous argument here. He rarely includes such signposts in his writing. Do you think it would have helped if he had made his argument's structure more explicit throughout?

READING

20

(continued)

of an activity must be sought in terms of the whole organization, which is more than the sum of its separable parts. What we are looking for, always, is the actual life that the whole organization is there to express. The significance of documentary culture is that, more clearly than anything else, it expresses that life to us in direct terms, when the living witnesses are silent. At the same time, if we reflect on the nature of a structure of feeling, and see how it can fail to be fully understood even by living people in close contact with it, with ample material at their disposal, including the contemporary arts, we shall not suppose that we can ever do more than make an approach, an approximation, using any channels.

21

We need to distinguish three levels of culture, even in its most general definition. There is the lived culture of a particular time and place, only fully accessible to those living in that time and place. There is the recorded culture, of every kind, from art to the most everyday facts: the culture of a period. There is also, as the factor connecting lived culture and period cultures, the culture of the selective tradition.

22

When it is no longer being lived, but in a narrower way survives in its records, the culture of a period can be very carefully studied, until we feel that we have reasonably clear ideas of its cultural work, its social character, its general patterns of activity and value, and in part of its structure of feeling. Yet the survival is governed, not by the period itself, but by new periods, which gradually compose a tradition. Even most specialists in a period know only a part of even its records. One can say with confidence, for example, that nobody really knows the nineteenth-century novel; nobody has read, or could have read, all its examples, over the whole range from printed volumes to penny serials. The real specialist may know some hundreds; the ordinary specialist somewhat less; educated readers a decreasing number: though all will have clear ideas on the subject. A selective process, of a quite drastic kind, is at once evident, and this is true of every field of activity. Equally, of course, no nineteenth-century reader would have read all the novels; no individual in the society would have known more than a selection of its facts. But everyone living in the period would have had something which, I have argued, no later individual can wholly recover: that sense of the life within which the novels were written, and which we now approach through our selection. Theoretically, a period is recorded; in practice, this record is absorbed into a selective tradition; and both are different from the culture as lived.

20 ## Content

(continued)

The recurring critique of the ability of historians to understand the past is put into context here. That is, Williams argues that it is difficult for those living in a culture to make sense of it, precisely because the 'structure of feeling' is undefined, and often personal. In your studies you have probably been required to examine films and television programmes in a pretty abstract way, exploring what is contained 'within' the texts. It is less likely that you have thought about the 'structure of feeling' within which that text exists, partly because this is not the 'traditional' way of carrying out academic work, and partly because it is very difficult. Williams is here stating that we need to explore how we think about, and examine, our *own* culture, because our relationship to it is itself inflected through a range of contributory factors, just as is the case for historians.

21 ## Structure

Without stating he is doing so, Williams offers a summary here. This idea of 'three levels of culture' is what he has been discussing, but we may think about them differently now, as he has explored them in a variety of ways. This is a useful way of reflecting back on the reading, and seeing if the argument has altered how we make sense of what Williams is discussing.

22 ## Content

Here Williams notes that we can never fully grasp the past, because what we know of the past is affected by those who are put in charge of preserving it. You might think about this relative to what you studied in history in school, or when you visit a museum. What kinds of things have been kept and preserved, and are we told about, from the past, and what things are left out? Very often it is easy to see portraits of rich landowners from the past, but much more difficult to come across paintings of 'ordinary people', for example. Also, think about which aspects of culture from *now* are likely to be the kinds of things people in the future will be told about us; is it likely that future historians will know *everything* about how you lived your life, or is it more likely that certain kinds of things will be preserved while others won't? What will a museum of the early twenty-first century look like?

Writing Style

The 'sense of the life' is another important idea of Williams. Note again the kind of language he is using; this phrase is deliberately quite vague, in order to encompass the variety of ways in which people might feel about the culture they live in; this might be quite different from the kind of writing you have come across in other readings.

READING

23

It is very important to try to understand the operation of a selective tradition. To some extent, the selection begins within the period itself; from the whole body of activities, certain things are selected for value and emphasis. In general this selection will reflect the organization of the period as a whole, though this does not mean that the values and emphases will later be confirmed. We see this clearly enough in the case of past periods, but we never really believe it about our own. We can take an example from the novels of the last decade. Nobody has read all the English novels of the nineteen-fifties; the fastest reader, giving twenty hours a day to this activity alone, could not do it. Yet it is clear, in print and in education, not only that certain general characteristics of the novel in this period have been set down, but also that a reasonably agreed short list has been made, of what seem to be the best and most relevant works. If we take the list as containing perhaps thirty titles (already a very drastic selection indeed) we may suppose that in fifty years the specialist in the novel of the 1950s will know these thirty, and the general reader will know perhaps five or six.

24

Yet we can surely be quite certain that, once the 1950s have passed, another selective process will be begun. As well as reducing the number of works, this new process will also alter, in some cases drastically, the expressed valuations. It is true that when fifty years have passed it is likely that reasonably permanent valuations will have been arrived at, though these may continue to fluctuate. Yet to any of us who had lived this long process through, it would remain true that elements important to us had been neglected. We would say, in a vulnerable elderly way, 'I don't understand why these young people don't read X any more', but also, more firmly, 'No, that isn't really what it was like; it is your version'. Since any period includes at least three generations, we are always seeing examples of this, and one complicating factor is that none of us stay still, even in our most significant period: many of the adjustments we should not protest against, many of the omissions, distortions and reinterpretations we should accept or not even notice, because we had been part of the change which brought them about. But then, when living witnesses had gone, a further change would occur.

25

The lived culture would not only have been fined down to selected documents; it would be used, in its reduced form, partly as a contribution (inevitably quite small) to the general line of human growth; partly for historical reconstruction; partly, again, as a way of having done with us, of naming and placing a particular stage of the past. The selective tradition thus creates, at one level, a general human culture; at another level, the historical record of a particular society; at a third level, most difficult to accept and assess, a rejection of considerable areas of what was once a living culture.

NOTES

23 Writing Style

The word 'operation' is a carefully chosen one. It implies an organised process, with recurring and specific features. But Williams does not suggest that an individual is in charge of this operation; it is, instead, a result of the ways in which societies have thought about culture over time.

Context

Once again, Williams uses literature as his example. We can relate this to his career as a teacher of literature. But we can also relate this to the debates about literature and education which were going on more generally at the time this book was written. Debates about what the most important literature is – often called 'the canon' – continue, and these have a significant impact on education. For example, should all schoolchildren be required to read Shakespeare? Is it okay for schools to teach about rap lyrics rather than 'traditional' poetry? This discussion about the content of education, and how it commonly prioritises certain kinds of culture over others, has been a recurring debate in cultural studies.

24 Content

What's being made clear here are the *difficulties* involved in describing a culture, because different people within that culture will have different experiences of it. For example, you probably have different musical preferences to your parents, and the kinds of comedy people like are often related to their age. This means while it is hard to make sense of the past, we can have similar problems with the present.

25 Structure

Here Williams summarises his argument, and, in doing so, demonstrates why this line of thinking matters. Notably, his 'selective tradition' has to work from 'rejection' of certain kinds of culture: that there are lots of things from the past which are not preserved in museums, for example. This is a key idea in cultural studies, for it argues that those things which are not preserved are usually those made by, and consumed by, the poorer, working-class members of society. In this way, one of the ways in which poorer people are less powerful in society is because their culture is devalued by the 'selective tradition'. The loss of some kinds of culture is maligned not just because it is inaccurate history, then; it is, more importantly, seen as a problem because it is one of the processes which helps uphold class and power distinctions. Here you can clearly see links to Marxism. Williams moves on to discuss class in the next paragraph.

READING

26

Within a given society, selection will be governed by many kinds of special interest, including class interests. Just as the actual social situation will largely govern contemporary selection, so the development of the society, the process of historical change, will largely determine the selective tradition. The traditional culture of a society will always tend to correspond to its *contemporary* system of interests and values, for it is not an absolute body of work but a continual selection and interpretation. In theory, and to a limited extent in practice, those institutions which are formally concerned with keeping the tradition alive (in particular the institutions of education and scholarship) are committed to the tradition as a whole, and not to some selection from it according to contemporary interests. The importance of this commitment is very great, because we see again and again, in the workings of a selective tradition, reversals and re-discoveries, returns to work apparently abandoned as dead, and clearly this is only possible if there are institutions whose business it is to keep large areas of past culture, if not alive, at least available. It is natural and inevitable that the selective tradition should follow the lines of growth of a society, but because such growth is complex and continuous, the relevance of past work, in any future situation, is unforeseeable.

27

There is a natural pressure on academic institutions to follow the lines of growth of a society, but a wise society, while ensuring this kind of relevance, will encourage the institutions to give sufficient resources to the ordinary work of preservation, and to resist the criticism, which any particular period may make with great confidence, that much of this activity is irrelevant and useless. It is often an obstacle to the growth of a society that so many academic institutions are, to an important extent, self-perpetuating and resistant to change. The changes have to be made, in new institutions if necessary, but if we properly understand the process of the selective tradition, and look at it over a sufficiently long period to get a real sense of historical change and fluctuation, the corresponding value of such perpetuation will be appreciated.

NOTES

26 # Content

Here Williams notes that the canon can change, that what we preserve and discuss of the past is defined by our present interests. We often think of the past, and the kinds of culture which are seen as important from the past, as fixed, but this is not the case. Museums change their contents, just as educational institutions alter their teaching. Governments also vary what they require schools to teach about the past and about culture.

Context

Again, we can place the reference to educational institutions within Williams's own experiences as a teacher. It also relates to the debates about the nature and content of education which flourished in Britain in the 1950s and 1960s. The rest of this paragraph goes on to discuss the difficult position many educational establishments are in, considering the social roles they're required to play.

Writing Style

What is meant by the word 'business' here? Does it have a purely financial connotation? How does it relate to the idea of 'operation' in Note 23?

27 ## Context

Why are academic institutions so 'resistant to change'? Think about the social role they have, and the relationships they have with the public and governments. Also, bear in mind that Williams worked in such institutions; does this make his argument more convincing because he has witnessed this stability first hand, or might it mean he is generalising too much from his own, personal experiences?

Writing Style

Again note how Williams fails to use specific examples to help illustrate, and support, his arguments. This writing remains theoretical, and we have to take his arguments on trust; how appropriate is this, for you?

Content

In suggesting that what research can do is make clear the ways in which contemporary society defines the past, Williams is, in essence, making a *methodological* statement. He is saying that there are some kinds of research that are not being done, and should be. Much theory, in attempting to think about the world in new and different ways, has to make pleas for new methods, because it assumes that existing methods respond to particular ways of thinking. It is because of this that cultural studies has often experimented with research methods – such as audience research as shown by the Ian Ang reading in Chapter 23 in *this* book – and sees such experimentation as an important way of breaking from the research traditions of other subjects.

READING

28

In a society as a whole, and in all its particular activities, the cultural tradition can be seen as a continual selection and re-selection of ancestors. Particular lines will be drawn, often for as long as a century, and then suddenly with some new stage in growth these will be cancelled or weakened, and new lines drawn. In the analysis of contemporary culture, the existing state of the selective tradition is of vital importance, for it is often true that some change in this tradition – establishing new lines with the past, breaking or re-drawing existing lines – is a radical kind of *contemporary* change. We tend to underestimate the extent to which the cultural tradition is not only a selection but also an interpretation. We see most past work through our own experience, without even making the effort to see it in something like its original terms. What analysis can do is not so much to reverse this, returning a work to its period, as to make the interpretation conscious, by showing historical alternatives; to relate the interpretation to the particular contemporary values on which it rests; and, by exploring the real patterns of the work, confront us with the real nature of the choices we are making. We shall find, in some cases, that we are keeping the work alive because it is a genuine contribution to cultural growth. We shall find, in other cases, that we are using the work in a particular way for our own reasons, and it is better to know this than to surrender to the mysticism of the 'great valuer, Time'. To put on to Time, the abstraction, the responsibility for our own active choices is to suppress a central part of our experience. The more actively all cultural work can be related, either to the whole organization within which it was expressed, or to the contemporary organization within which it is used, the more clearly shall we see its true values.

29

Thus 'documentary' analysis will lead out to 'social' analysis, whether in a lived culture, a past period, or in the selective tradition which is itself a social organization. And the discovery of permanent contributions will lead to the same kind of general analysis, if we accept the process at this level, not as human perfection (a movement towards determined values), but as a part of man's general evolution, to which many individuals and groups contribute. Every element that we analyse will be in this sense active: that it will be seen in certain real relations, at many different levels. In describing these relations, the real cultural process will emerge.

NOTES

28 Writing Style

Considering Williams has repeatedly noted the ways in which culture is selected and structured, it seems odd that he sees some selections as 'genuine' here. What is meant by this word? Does this suggest some culture exists *outside* of the operations he has outlined? How convincing is this? Also note the reference to the 'real' and the 'true' throughout this paragraph. Williams is suggesting that by using appropriate methods, we can get access to the 'correct' answers. This might seem odd today in a postmodern world, which argues there's no such thing as 'truth' (see Chapter 19).

29 Content

It is important that the kind of analysis Williams promotes leads to discussion of the 'social', for it is society which is at the core of cultural studies. He is arguing that analysis of texts and culture leads us to thinking about society more broadly; indeed, for Williams it is a bit pointless to do the former unless it leads to the latter. This idea that culture can tell us about society might be a new idea for you, and forces you to think about culture in a much larger context. The relationships between the two are so central to Williams's thinking that one of his key books is called *Culture and Society* (1958).

Structure

This reading ends at a natural break in the chapter it is taken from; the next section is separate from it. Therefore, Williams sees his argument as, to an extent, complete here. As an ending, how satisfactory do you find it? What kinds of questions do you still have?

REFLECTING ON THE READING

The next sentence in *The Long Revolution* after this reading is 'Any theoretical account of the analysis of culture must be tested in the course of actual analysis' (1961: 70). Here, Williams, is making a clear statement about the need for theory to be tested against the 'real world'. He then goes on to do so by discussing, for example, Victorian literature, belying his roots as a teacher of English. We have noted throughout this reading that there is a lack of examples, which might have made it difficult to follow. You could go on to read the rest of the chapter, to see how Williams illustrates his argument. However, before doing that, it would be better if you thought through what kinds of examples *you* can think of that support the theory. For instance, are there times when you think the kinds of culture you are interested in are ignored by the educational establishments you have been in? Are the kinds of books, music, art, and media you find interesting a core component of the school curriculum? If not, why not? Do you think this lack has any social implications, as Williams suggests? Also, who gets to decide what is taught and preserved, and why might they have made such decisions? The fact that English schools have a national curriculum shows that the government feels there are key topics which *all* children must be taught; what social consequences might this have?

You should also think about *why* Williams has chosen to separate his theoretical analysis from its application to examples which follows it. As has been stated, this could be because it is viable to offer a theoretical model before going on to see whether it works when related to real-world examples. The fact that the model might *not* work does not invalidate it as a model, because it still might be useful for introducing us to new ways of thinking. Theorising about the world is a *different* process from testing such theory, even though you might (rightly?) see this as quite pointless. Although, think about the times you theorise about things; if you predict the outcome of a football match, say, you are theorising about sets of activities, drawing on your experiences of previous matches and the teams involved in order to present a 'model' of the forthcoming match. Your predictions might prove entirely wrong, but this does not fully invalidate your theorising; instead, the question becomes *why* the match did not pan out quite as was expected. Indeed, bookmakers make their living out of theorising about future events from their understanding of the past, and they employ a broad range of models in order to predict outcomes. Before criticising Williams for his lack of examples, then, it would be worthwhile you thinking about the number of times you theorise and predict in your everyday life, and how often such predictions are wrong.

Throughout the reading, Williams argues that culture is complicated, individual and specific. However, he also makes statements about the operations of culture and society more broadly, which are necessary in order for him to criticise, from his Marxist perspective, social structures. But isn't there a contradiction here? If culture is made up of individual and specific moments, how can we bring all of these together to make statements about culture as a whole? A lot of cultural studies fieldwork deals with small-scale studies, but uses such results to demonstrate arguments about much larger social systems. Do you think this is appropriate? And what is left out when general, social conclusions are extrapolated from small studies?

Following on from this, Williams argues that our understanding of the past is always affected by present concerns, and that different people will have different views of history depending on their priorities. If this is the case, how can we justify discussing the past at all? That is, if there is no such thing as a 'true', 'correct' version of the past, what is the value in thinking about the topic at all? Also, do you agree with Williams that the past is always viewed from the present in this way? Think about times you might have had disagreements with people older or younger than you about historical events; your grandparents might have different views on the Second World War from you, for example, and different generations often have conflicting views about the role of immigration in the history of Britain.

Overall, what we're discussing here are concerns about *methods*. Throughout his writing, Williams is, in essence, arguing that society has traditionally asked the wrong questions about culture, and instead what we should be researching and thinking about is quite different. It is this insistence that there are new, important topics of research that education is currently ignoring which led to the creation of cultural studies as a discipline, because its concerns did not 'fit' into any existing subjects. So, you should think about *how* we can go about exploring and critiquing the topics Williams outlines. Think about what you see as 'your' culture; how can this best be researched, do you think?

Finally, we need to place cultural studies within media studies; as was noted at the start of this chapter, it might seem odd that a book on media theory is discussing cultural theory. What value do you see in Williams's work for the study of media? What can it add to the discussions, debates and ideas which are covered by the subject? In that sense, how are 'media' and 'culture' related, and how are they different? An important part of cultural theory is the analysis of *society*, in particular power relationships within society; what has this to do with media?

Key terms to explore

structure of feeling; the sense of the life.

Key writers who are mentioned

Erich Fromm; Ruth Benedict.

RECOMMENDED READING

Lewis, J. (2008) *Cultural Studies: The basics*, 2nd edition, London: Sage.

Containing many contemporary case studies, this volume encompasses a range of relevant approaches with an international focus.

Longhurst, B., Smith, G., Bagnall, G., Crawford, G., Ogborn, M., Baldwin, E. and McCracken, S. (2008) *Introducing Cultural Studies*, 2nd edition, Harlow: Pearson.

Useful overview of a multitude of key debates and thinkers, with lots of examples.

Williams, R. (1983 [1976]) *Keywords: A vocabulary of culture and society*, London: Fontana.

Williams's attempt to define many words important to cultural studies, such as 'power', 'class', and 'society'; useful for showing the complexity lying behind seemingly 'commonsense' terms.

CHAPTER 18

New media

Jenkins, H. (2006) *Convergence Culture: Where old and new media collide*, New York and London: New York University Press, pp. 1–10.

INTRODUCTION TO NEW MEDIA

'New media' is one of those terms that you're likely to have come across outside of your studies. But what exactly is meant by it? Which media are 'new' and which are 'old'? What makes a medium 'new', and how is it different from those which are not thought of as 'new'? Are new media *completely* 'new', or do they have similarities to 'old' media? What about the relationships between 'new' and 'old' media? And what consequences do new media have for media theory; do we need to rewrite everything we've previously thought about media?

As Flew notes, 'the lines between "new" and "old" media are hard to draw' (2005: 4), not least because technologies like the internet that are often thought of as 'new' contain swathes of material that is often 'derived from already existing media content' (p. 4) such as books, television and music. In the introduction to his book Flew outlines multiple ways we can think of new media as representing some kind of development from older media. First, digitisation means that media content is stored in a very different way from previously (LPs, film, video tape) and can therefore be distributed over networks more quickly and more widely than used to be the case (pp. 8–9). This digitisation has, according to Flew, led to convergence, whereby the *differences* between various kinds of media have collapsed and so producers and consumers have access to media in very different ways (pp. 10–11); for example, whereas in the past you needed different machines to watch television, listen to music and see a film, these can now all be done on a single machine like a PC. Secondly, interactivity is now a norm in media consumption, but Flew is keen to note that 'different media forms possess different degrees of interactivity, and some forms of digitised and converged media are not in fact interactive at all' (p. 13).

Finally, new media is seen as relying on 'networks' – and this is such a key concept in the analysis of new media that it is discussed in more detail below. You can see that the three key tenets of new media analysis outlined here are about media forms and technology, but, as Flew notes (p. 2), all of this is only seen as interesting if you ask the question, 'what is new for society from the new media?' So, simply noting that technologies and industries have changed is assumed to not really get us anywhere: all of this matters because new media might lead to new forms of society, new ways of living our lives, and new power structures within societies. In that sense, there is a strong sociological strain to the analysis of new media, which mirrors the interests of the majority of media theory. So while new media may be new, the key questions and interests for the analysis of it remain the same.

As noted above, one of the key ideas in new media theory is the concept of the network; that is, that such technologies allow people who would previously have been unable to communicate with one another to come together and discuss, debate and act. This centrality is shown in the title of Castells' books *The Rise of the Network Society* (2010). Castells sees networks as 'set[s] of interconnected nodes through which communication flows occur, that are open, flexible, and adaptable forms able to expand without limits as long as communication codes are shared within the network' (Flew 2005: 16). These networks are assumed to have significant consequences for many aspects of society, not least the rise of a 'digital economy' (Malecki and Moriset 2008) whereby goods can be distributed to larger markets more quickly and cheaper via 'networks' capable of disseminating digital products. For the individual, these networks are argued to be extremely powerful because they undermine the traditional power hierarchies that exist in 'old' media. So, Castells argues that 'The Internet, the World Wide Web, and wireless communication are not media in the traditional sense. Rather, they are means of interactive communication' (2010: xxvi). Overall, then, new media forms – and the networks they rely on and reproduce – are seen via such analyses as revolutionary developments, questioning the majority of assumptions about social structures that have persisted for some time. It is for these reasons that van Dijk asserts that 'With little exaggeration, we may call the twenty-first century the age of networks' (2006: 2).

All of these developments are seen as important because it is argued that new media leads to 'a transformation of space and time in the human experience' (Castells 1996: xxxi). Castells argues that new technologies allowing people from all over the world to communicate mean that space feels smaller, and so how we think about geography has changed. Similarly, our sense of time has altered because everything is always available and we do not have to fit our lives around the scheduling of others so much; he calls this 'timeless time' (p. xlii). For theories like these, then, such technologies are important not simply because they are newer kinds of media, but because of how they impact upon the lives of those who use them. This means that exploring new media is not just about marvelling at the graphics of video games or being able to access swathes of information on Wikipedia; it is seen to matter because social structures are changing in response to these technologies, and this has implications for social power, how individuals live their lives, business and commerce, and the relationships citizens have with institutions such as governments.

It's also worth acknowledging here that one of the recurring debates about new media is precisely its 'new-ness', and many have been criticised for overstating the effects new media have had, or might have, on the way the world works. In *The New Media Book* (Harries 2002) there are chapters on 'Old Media as New Media' (Manovich 2002; Uricchio

2002) and 'New Media as Old Media' (Simons 2002; Boddy 2002) demonstrating the links between the two and cautioning against overstating how much things have changed. Furthermore, insisting new media represents a significant change assumes that media were static prior to it, when many people would argue that the history of media is one of constant change and innovation, and so new media are merely the next step in that process. Van Dijk, for example, asserts that 'In the history of the media, several communications revolutions have taken place' (2006: 4) and it is hard to think of a time when media companies were not developing new technologies or audiences were not experimenting with their own media consumption. So this requires you, as someone examining media, to be very precise about what is new and what is old and – perhaps more interestingly – to think about why it might be that while some things change, others seem to stay the same.

To that end, new media theory is an interesting context for you to place some of the other readings in this book, and other theories you will encounter. For example, the fact that new media gives individuals access to a wealth of information previously unobtainable means that it can be seen to have parallels with the 'information society', which is explored in *this* book in Chapter 20. Yet Castells sees a difference between the two, for while debates about the information society explore the *roles* information and data play in everyday life, new media theory is instead interested in the *technologies* and *networks* that allow that information to circulate in productive ways (2010: 21). Another example would be debates about the 'public sphere' (see Chapter 13). The fact that, on the face of it, the internet is a space where *anyone* can join in debates and discussions about any topic means that new media have been seen as having the potential of fulfilling the role of a public sphere; this means we can all become a 'cybercitizen' (Cavanagh 2007: 76). Yet as Cavanagh also shows, there are problems in such statements, for three reasons; first, access to new media is unequal, especially in global terms; secondly, much of what the internet is used for is not political activity but entertainment; thirdly, because there has been so little audience research on internet use we have very little idea what real people actually do with new media technologies (pp. 64–80).

Overall, then, there's still much work to be done for thinking about new media. Perhaps the most useful thing for you to bear in mind is that while it might be tempting to think of new media as overturning all aspects of society and therefore rendering older media theories as outdated and useless, the development of new media theory has instead been most fruitful when it has been used to think about those debates – such as the public sphere – which have defined the field for decades. After all, 'the new is surprisingly often just a line-extension of the old' (Caulkin 2004: xiii), and so the ways in which we have thought about the relationships between media, the individual and society remain prescient.

INTRODUCTION TO THE READING

This reading comes from Henry Jenkins's book, *Convergence Culture* (2006). As has been explored in the introduction above, issues of convergence are central to debates about new media, and Jenkins's book is a key work in these discussions. Note that the subtitle of the book – 'Where old and new media collide' – shows how Jenkins feels that new and old media have a relationship with one another rather than the former replacing the latter. Indeed, talking about media forms 'colliding' also suggests he doesn't necessarily see this as a smooth coming together of types of media, and 'collisions' also implies that some of the outcomes might have been unplanned, unexpected and therefore unpredictable. Throughout the book Jenkins discusses things which might usually be thought of as old media – such as films like *The Matrix* (dir. Andy Wachowski and Larry Wachowski 1999), television programmes such as *Survivor* (CBS 2000–), and books including the Harry Potter series – but is interested in how these 'traditional' forms employ newer forms of media, as well as how audiences use new media to interpret, reinvent and discuss media texts. You'll see in the reading that Jenkins suggests that media industries are still working this 'collision' out, with creative professionals continuing to debate what new media means for their work and the creative industries. In that sense, Jenkins is one of those thinkers who are very aware of overstating the revolutionary potential of new media, and instead offers a more nuanced discussion of what is happening in the real world, and what this tells us about media in society more generally.

Indeed, if Jenkins thinks new media has any kind of radical potential it seems that he places this in the hands of consumers rather than producers. Looking at the history and development of Jenkins's writing it is fair to say that his exploration of new media comes not out of an interest in those forms themselves, but what they contribute to topics he was writing about *before* new media. So, Jenkins is associated very strongly with work on audiences and, in particular, fans. His book *Textual Poachers* (1992) explores fans of science fiction, fantasy and cult television and film and rejects stereotypes of them as unthinking weirdos, and instead sees them as highly creative communities who 'poach' the programmes they like through fanzines, conventions and fan fiction (2009). It's easy to see how, for someone interested in topics such as these, moving on to analysing new media makes sense, because those fan communities have, in many ways, moved their communities online, and continue to 'poach' media through fansites, video mash-ups, fan fiction, and other productive activities (2002). Throughout his work Jenkins has foregrounded his own status as a fan, referring to himself on his website as an 'aca-fan'; that is, 'a hybrid creature which is part fan and part academic' (2011a). This personal aspect of media consumption is something rare in much media theory (though becoming increasingly common) and Jenkins has repeatedly returned to it; his book *The Wow Climax* (2007a), for example, looks at emotional responses to popular media, when it is very rare for analysis to explore emotions at all. That said, it's worth noting that writers such as McKee (2007) argue that all academics are, in fact, fans, but it's just that because what they are fans of – academic work and theory – is seen as 'legitimate' that they are categorised as 'experts' and 'authorities' rather than 'fans'; Jenkins himself has also questioned these categorisations (2007b). Presumably you are studying media theory because you find it interesting; are you, then, comfortable calling yourself a 'fan' of media theory?

You will therefore see when you explore this reading that it is written in a style markedly different from much of the material in the rest of this book. Jenkins includes anecdotes and personal experiences, and makes joking asides. His analysis rests on *his* experience of the world, tempered by a significantly broader understanding of the topic at hand. You will also see that Jenkins discusses attending media events and conferences which bring together academics, people from the media industries and other interested parties. That is, he talks to a wider range of people than we might expect many academics to do, and on his website he states that he takes it 'as a personal challenge to find a way to break cultural theory out of the academic bookstore ghetto and open up a larger space to talk about the media that matters to us from a consumer's point of view' (Jenkins 2011a). This is certainly a laudable aim, and congruent with many contemporary academic ambitions. But what does this do for the analysis he is proposing? Are things lost as well as gained? Indeed, does this read like theory to you *at all*?

READING

1

H. Jenkins

Introduction: "Worship at the Altar of Convergence"

A New Paradigm for Understanding Media Change

> Worship at the Altar of Convergence
> —slogan, the New Orleans Media Experience (2003)

The story circulated in the fall of 2001: Dino Ignacio, a Filipino-American high school student created a Photoshop collage of *Sesame Street*'s (1970) Bert interacting with terrorist leader Osama Bin Laden as part of a series of "Bert Is Evil" images he posted on his homepage. Others depicted Bert as a Klansman, cavorting with Adolf Hitler, dressed as the Unabomber, or having sex with Pamela Anderson. It was all in good fun.

2

In the wake of September 11, a Bangladesh-based publisher scanned the Web for Bin Laden images to print on anti-American signs, posters, and T-shirts. *Sesame Street* is available in Pakistan in a localized format; the Arab world, thus, had no exposure to Bert and Ernie. The publisher may not have recognized Bert, but he must have thought the image was a good likeness of the al-Qaeda leader. The image ended up in a collage of similar images that was printed on thousands of posters and distributed across the Middle East.

CNN reporters recorded the unlikely sight of a mob of angry protestors marching through the streets chanting anti-American slogans and waving signs depicting Bert and Bin Laden. Representatives from the Children's Television Workshop, creators of the *Sesame Street* series, spotted the CNN footage and threatened to take legal action: "We're outraged that our characters would be used in this unfortunate and distasteful manner. The people responsible for this should be ashamed of themselves. We are exploring all legal options to stop this abuse and any similar abuses in the future." It was not altogether clear who they planned to set their intellectual property attorneys on—the young man who had initially appropriated their images, or the terrorist supporters who deployed them. Coming full circle, amused fans produced a number of new sites, linking various *Sesame Street* characters with terrorists.

NOTES

1 ## Structure

This is how Jenkins opens his book – does this seem like an odd opening to you?

Content

Jenkins does not give references for this story – he merely says it 'circulated'. While he could be criticised for this, does it really matter if we do not know exactly where it came from. And because it 'circulated', does that not imply it can be found in many places; that is, that there is no one definitive source that sums the whole thing up?

2 ## Context

Note the international context to this story, as it depicts the global flow of images and ideas. Analyses of new media are often interested in these ideas of globalisation and the trans-national circulation of media, as this shows how national borders are becoming less important and people from all over the world can come together. Yet also note the legal implications of something like this, for it means that the Children's Television Workshop cannot control their own output. That is, there are problems with the collapse in national contexts, not least because the ways in which media products make money are dependent on legal systems which are upheld by national justice systems and governments. Do you think this matters? Should the Workshop be upset at how images of their characters are being used? To what extent should they be allowed to control this material? And how might laws be rewritten to take into account these globalised contexts?

Writing Style

It's clear that we're meant to find this story quite funny, for the juxtaposition of Bert and Bin Laden is so extreme as to be ridiculous. Why might Jenkins begin his book with a funny story? Are we meant to find it nothing but funny?

Structure

Jenkins clearly states what the book is about – and then goes on to define those terms. That is, his argument has an extremely clear and stated aim. And he mentions the glossary at the back of the book – would that be something useful in more readings?

READING

2

(continued)

From his bedroom, Ignacio sparked an international controversy. His images crisscrossed the world, sometimes on the backs of commercial media, sometimes via grassroots media. And, in the end, he inspired his own cult following. As the publicity grew, Ignacio became more concerned and ultimately decided to dismantle his site: "I feel this has gotten too close to reality. . . . "Bert Is Evil" and its following has always been contained and distanced from big media. This issue throws it out in the open." Welcome to convergence culture, where old and new media collide, where grassroots and corporate media intersect, where the power of the media producer and the power of the media consumer interact in unpredictable ways.

This book is about the relationship between three concepts—media convergence, participatory culture, and collective intelligence.

By convergence, I mean the flow of content across multiple media platforms, the cooperation between multiple media industries, and the migratory behavior of media audiences who will go almost anywhere in search of the kinds of entertainment experiences they want. Convergence is a word that manages to describe technological, industrial, cultural, and social changes depending on who's speaking and what they think they are talking about. (In this book I will be mixing and matching terms across these various frames of reference. I have added a glossary at the end of the book to help guide readers.)

3

In the world of media convergence, every important story gets told, every brand gets sold, and every consumer gets courted across multiple media platforms. Think about the circuits that the Bert Is Evil images traveled—from *Sesame Street* through Photoshop to the World Wide Web, from Ignacio's bedroom to a print shop in Bangladesh, from the posters held by anti-American protestors that are captured by CNN and into the living rooms of people around the world. Some of its circulation depended on corporate strategies, such as the localization of *Sesame Street* or the global coverage of CNN. Some of its circulation depended on tactics of grassroots appropriation, whether in North America or in the Middle East.

4

This circulation of media content—across different media systems, competing media economies, and national borders—depends heavily on consumers' active participation. I will argue here against the idea that convergence should be understood primarily as a technological process bringing together multiple media functions within the same devices. Instead, convergence represents a cultural shift as consumers are encouraged to seek out new information and make connections among dispersed media content. This book is about the work—and play—spectators perform in the new media system.

Content

(continued)

Are you convinced by the definition of 'convergence' Jenkins outlines here? Perhaps more importantly – and we'll keep coming back to this question – to what extent is such convergence that different from how media and culture have functioned in the past? If new media theory is insistent that such media offers opportunities unavailable before then it needs to demonstrate clearly that these differences exist, and that they are of a notable degree.

Context

In talking about 'content', 'industries' and 'audiences' Jenkins sees convergence as being relevant to all aspects of media analysis. That is, such an argument undermines the 'production, text, audiences' division which much media analysis relies on, and which can be seen in Chapters 21–23 in *this* book. Chapter 24 – on audiences as producers – similarly queries this division, and so a congruity can be seen between that reading and Jenkins's analysis here.

Writing Style

Note the 'I' here – that is, that Jenkins refers to himself. Have you come across this often in your reading? How do you respond to such self-referencing?

Context

In his use of the word 'circuits' Jenkins is drawing on an idea common to much new media analysis. As noted in *this* chapter's introduction, Manuel Castells refers to such configurations as 'networks' (2010), and this idea is important for how we think about how media is circulated and the relationships between producers and consumers. But why might Jenkins prefer 'circuits' to 'networks'? What does his word imply that Castells's does not? Which do you prefer?

Content

Does '*every* important story get told'?

Structure

In noting what he is going to 'argue . . . against' Jenkins makes clear the norms of media research and his analysis's contribution to such debates. In that sense he's acknowledging the wealth of material against him – much of which can be found in *this* book.

Content

In a number of readings in *this* book you will have come across debates about audiences and how they can best be understood; for example, Gauntlett (Chapter 14) rejects simplistic notions of

READING

(continued)

The term *participatory culture* contrasts with older notions of passive media spectatorship. Rather than talking about media producers and consumers as occupying separate roles, we might now see them as participants who interact with each other according to a new set of rules that none of us fully understands. Not all participants are created equal. Corporations—and even individuals within corporate media—still exert greater power than any individual consumer or even the aggregate of consumers. And some consumers have greater abilities to participate in this emerging culture than others.

5

Convergence does not occur through media appliances, however sophisticated they may become. Convergence occurs within the brains of individual consumers and through their social interactions with others. Each of us constructs our own personal mythology from bits and fragments of information extracted from the media flow and transformed into resources through which we make sense of our everyday lives. Because there is more information on any given topic than anyone can store in their head, there is an added incentive for us to talk among ourselves about the media we consume. This conversation creates buzz that is increasingly valued by the media industry. Consumption has become a collective process—and that's what this book means by collective intelligence, a term coined by French cybertheorist Pierre Lévy. None of us can know everything; each of us knows something; and we can put the pieces together if we pool our resources and combine our skills. Collective intelligence can be seen as an alternative source of media power. We are learning how to use that power through our day-to-day interactions within convergence culture. Right now, we are mostly using this collective power through our recreational life, but soon we will be deploying those skills for more "serious" purposes. In this book, I explore how collective meaning-making within popular culture is starting to change the ways religion, education, law, politics, advertising, and even the military operate.

NOTES

4

(continued)

media 'effects', while Ang (Chapter 23) queries the usefulness of the concept of 'the audience' at all, and explores why some people might want to insist on keeping it. Jenkins's notion of 'participatory culture', you will see, similarly relates to these debates. Jenkins uses the word 'participants', and applies it to both producers *and* consumers; in that sense, he rejects the word 'audience' *entirely*. Do you think this is a useful word? Is it appropriate to use the *same* word for these categories of people that have, in the past, been kept separate? And is the level and type of participation the same for all people in a media exchange?

Context

Jenkins refers to the 'circulation' of content, seeing those systems usually used to control such content ('national borders' and 'media systems') as irrelevant in the new media world. Again, such analysis rejects some of the key ideas you would have come across in your media theory readings. Indeed, some might argue that such control and borders are vital for progressive media; a public sphere (Chapter 13), for example, can only really work if borders exist, so it can be agreed who is and is not allowed to participate. In that sense, while the collapse of controls might be liberating, is there also an argument to be made that they can sometimes be more progressive and productive than unrestricted participation?

5

Context

Jenkins rejects the idea that technology creates convergence, and instead sees it resulting from the activities of individuals and communities. In doing so he is rejecting ideas of 'technological determinism' (Katz et al. 2003: 6, 154) often associated with the Toronto School (see Chapter 10). Indeed, by being interested in what people do Jenkins can be seen as being part of wider approaches to studying the media over the past few decades which have argued that individuals are far more empowered than previous analyses suggested. This debate about the 'passive' or 'active' nature of media audiences is one of the area's key debates, and work on new media can be seen as the next step in this ongoing discussion.

Jenkins mentions Lévy but doesn't mention his key book; it is *Cyberculture* (2001). In that book Lévy argues that new media are evidence of 'an authentic social movement' (p. 105) dependent on 'interconnectivity' (pp. 107–8). That is, if people can talk to one another, things can happen.

Content

Look at some of the language used here. What is meant by our own 'personal mythology' – is this different from 'personality', or 'personal experiences'? What are our 'everyday lives'?

Jenkins refers to 'the media flow'. 'Flow' is a term associated with Raymond Williams (see Chapter 17) who, in his book *Television: Technology and cultural form* (1974), describes an evening's viewing of television as a 'flow' in which the experience of the medium is one in which programmes, adverts, trailers and channels are all intertwined. This is contrasted with other forms of media – such as books or newspapers – which are discrete entities. 'Flow' can, of course, be applied to

READING

6

Convergence Talk

Another snapshot of convergence culture at work: In December 2004, a hotly anticipated Bollywood film, *Rok Sako To Rok Lo* (2004), was screened in its entirety to movie buffs in Delhi, Bangalore, Hyderabad, Mumbai, and other parts of India through EDGE-enabled mobile phones with live video streaming facility. This is believed to be the first time that a feature film had been fully accessible via mobile phones. It remains to be seen how this kind of distribution fits into people's lives. Will it substitute for going to the movies or will people simply use it to sample movies they may want to see at other venues? Who knows?

Over the past several years, many of us have watched as cell phones have become increasingly central to the release strategies of commercial motion pictures around the world, as amateur and professional cell phone movies have competed for prizes in international film festivals, as mobile users have been able to listen in to major concerts, as Japanese novelists serialize their work via instant messenger, and as game players have used mobile devices to compete in augmented and alternate reality games. Some functions will take root; others will fail.

7

Call me old-fashioned. The other week I wanted to buy a cell phone—you know, to make phone calls. I didn't want a video camera, a still camera, a Web access device, an MP3 player, or a game system. I also wasn't interested in something that could show me movie previews, would have customizable ring tones, or would allow me to read novels. I didn't want the electronic equivalent of a Swiss army knife. When the phone rings, I don't want to have to figure out which button to push. I just wanted a phone. The sales clerks sneered at me; they

NOTES

(continued)

newer forms of media or the use of multiple forms of media simultaneously; watching television while surfing the net, texting friends and listening to music can be seen as a 'flow' of media. The question that arises out of this is to what extent such 'flow' can be seen as empowering or not; we could see 'flow' as evidence of individuals' ability to rewrite media for their own uses, or we could see it as evidence of the dominance of media in our everyday lives. What do you think?

Writing Style

Why is 'serious' in inverted commas?

6   Structure

As Jenkins notes, here's another example. Or, as he calls it, a 'snapshot'. Is it useful to have these brief stories? Does it help develop the argument? Do we get all the information about these stories that we need?

Writing Style

Note here how Jenkins undercuts his own authority. It is not often that a writer says 'Who knows?', is it? Similarly, while he states at the end that some 'functions' will work and others will 'fail' he does not appear to predict which will be which or, indeed, be interested that much in that question. This might partly be because so many people who have made predictions have turned out to be wrong, and Jenkins does not want to be one of them. But perhaps it is also because trying to guess what will and will not succeed is not really what his analysis is interested in. Instead, the main concern is the fact that media changes, that success and failure always go together, and it is this constantly changing landscape which new media analysis is interested in. So, making definitive statements is always a problem; it is the specifics of particular media, or texts, or circumstances, that matter. However, if that is the case, how can theory work? What is new media theory if it never offers larger, over-arching ideas? Is it just made up of 'snapshots'?

7   Writing Style

This is a personal anecdote offered as evidence – is it helpful? Whether you think it gives us an insight into a larger truth or not, it is clear that Jenkins has no qualms about talking about himself and his own experiences, and he does not attempt to pretend that he is an objective observer. Indeed, the title of his blog – 'Confessions of an Aca-Fan' (2011b) – demonstrates this, as we are invited to see Jenkins's analysis of himself as 'confessions'. Indeed, on that blog Jenkins states 'I never can keep my personal life separated from my professional life', for his work is 'driven by an autobiographical impulse' and is therefore 'deeply personal' (2011a). This is likely to be extremely different to the writing style of much theory you have come across, especially that from some time ago. Jenkins comes out of a tradition which says the individual can never fully expunge themselves

READING

7

(continued)

laughed at me behind my back. I was told by company after mobile company that they don't make single-function phones anymore. Nobody wants them. This was a powerful demonstration of how central mobiles have become to the process of media convergence.

You've probably been hearing a lot about convergence lately. You are going to be hearing even more.

8

The media industries are undergoing another paradigm shift. It happens from time to time. In the 1990s, rhetoric about a coming digital revolution contained an implicit and often explicit assumption that new media was going to push aside old media, that the Internet was going to displace broadcasting, and that all of this would enable consumers to more easily access media content that was personally meaningful to them. A best-seller in 1990, Nicholas Negroponte's *Being Digital*, drew a sharp contrast between "passive old media" and "interactive new media," predicting the collapse of broadcast networks in favor of an era of narrowcasting and niche media on demand: "What will happen to broadcast television over the next five years is so phenomenal that it's difficult to comprehend." At one point, he suggests that no government regulation will be necessary to shatter the media conglomerates: "The monolithic empires of mass media are dissolving into an array of cottage industries . . . Media barons of today will be grasping to hold onto their centralized empires tomorrow. . . . The combined forces of technology and human nature will ultimately take a stronger hand in plurality than any laws Congress can invent." Sometimes, the new media companies spoke about convergence, but by this term, they seemed to mean that old media would be absorbed fully and completely into the orbit of the emerging technologies. George Gilder, another digital revolutionary, dismissed such claims: "The computer industry is converging with the television industry in the same sense that the automobile converged with the horse, the TV converged with the nickelodeon, the word-processing program converged with the typewriter, the CAD program converged with the drafting board, and digital desktop publishing converged with the linotype machine and the letterpress." For Gilder, the computer had come not to transform mass culture but to destroy it.

NOTES

7

(continued)

from their work and be objective, so you might as well acknowledge this problem and instead use and explore it. But think about your studies; to what extent are you encouraged to think about, and write about, yourself? And what does this add to the debate – and what does it make difficult?

Content

Do you think Jenkins is 'old-fashioned'?

8

Context

Jenkins places his analysis in a historical context. This is less so that what is happening *now* can be understood as a result of what happened in the past, but more to signal that we need to be careful about how we talk about new media because it is easy to get over-excited by it and insist that it changes everything. You will see more about this in the next paragraph of this reading.

Structure

The argument being constructed here is drawing on the work of two other writers: Nicholas Negroponte and George Gilder. As you will see, Jenkins disagrees with these two writers; or, at least, feels their arguments need to be somewhat modified. Yet by including them he is acknowledging the range of ways in which this topic has been talked about, and therefore places *his* analysis within an environment of discussion and debate. Note also that Jenkins outlines the other writers *before* presenting his own views; this demonstrates how seriously he takes those views, and suggests he wants the reader to see his own analysis within the context of others'.

Writing Style

Notice some of the words used here. Jenkins refers to the debates occurring in the 1990s as 'rhetoric'; do you think this word has positive or negative connotations? He also refers to 'paradigm shift[s]'. This is a term, now quite widely used, that was coined by Thomas Kuhn in his book *The Structure of Scientific Revolutions* (1962). In that book Kuhn argued that there are times in history where how we think about the world suddenly changes – Darwin's theory of evolution would be one such time, for example – with far-reaching consequences, and these changes he calls 'paradigm shifts'. However, Kuhn also argues that these shifts do not happen 'naturally', but are instead the consequence of how society is structured, and the desire for such change. In that sense Jenkins's use of the term 'paradigm shift' might have the same implication, suggesting that the widespread talk about media changes in the 1990s was as much a result of the *desire* of some people to see such a shift happen as it was based on evidence. It is, of course, in the interest of new media gurus to argue that everything we once knew has now changed; if they did not they would not really have a job, would they?

9

The popping of the dot-com bubble threw cold water on this talk of a digital revolution. Now, convergence has reemerged as an important reference point as old and new media companies try to imagine the future of the entertainment industry. If the digital revolution paradigm presumed that new media would displace old media, the emerging convergence paradigm assumes that old and new media will interact in ever more complex ways. The digital revolution paradigm claimed that new media was going to change everything. After the dot-com crash, the tendency was to imagine that new media had changed nothing. As with so many things about the current media environment, the truth lay somewhere in between. More and more, industry leaders are returning to convergence as a way of making sense of a moment of disorienting change. Convergence is, in that sense, an old concept taking on new meanings.

10

There was lots of convergence talk to be heard at the New Orleans Media Experience in October 2003. The New Orleans Media Experience was organized by HSI Productions, Inc., a New York–based company that produces music videos and commercials. HSI has committed to spend $100 million over the next five years, to make New Orleans the mecca for media convergence that Slamdance has become for independent cinema. The New Orleans Media Experience is more than a film festival; it is also a showcase for game releases, a venue for commercials and music videos, an array of concerts and theatrical performances, and a three-day series of panels and discussions with industry leaders.

Inside the auditorium, massive posters featuring images of eyes, ears, mouths, and hands urged attendees to "worship at the Altar of Convergence," but it was far from clear what kind of deity they were genuflecting before. Was it a New Testament God who promised them salvation? An Old Testament God threatening destruction unless they followed His rules? A multifaced deity that spoke like an oracle and demanded blood sacrifices? Perhaps, in keeping with the location, convergence was a voodoo goddess who would give them the power to inflict pain on their competitors?

NOTES

9 Context

The 'dot-com bubble' and 'crash' was the rapid growth in investment in internet companies and related industries, followed by a collapse in those companies and the stock market associated with them, that occurred in the middle and end of the 1990s. This failure of what had been assumed was going to be the next big thing troubled the media industries, threw international financial markets into chaos (Ofek and Richardson 2003) and led to increased suicide rates (Wong et al. 2008). A number of histories and analyses of this time have been written, such as Lowenstein's *Origins of the Crash* (2004) and Cassidy's *Dot.Con* (2002). How we think about new media *now* is often within the context of that time, for the 'bubble' undermined the faith many had that new media would change business and society forever. Indeed, it is worth noting that while there have, of course, been many online businesses since the 'bubble' which are thought of as successful – such as YouTube and Facebook – these took a very long time to make a profit, and their continued existence rests on the assumption that someone, in the future, will work out how to make money consistently from them. In that sense contemporary understandings of the business and economics of new media could be seen to be as optimistic and unrealistic as those that led to the 'bubble'. For more information on these debates see Budd and Harris (2004).

10 Context

The Media Experience Jenkins discusses is clearly a space where a wide range of communities come together, from many different media forms, and from both industry and academic backgrounds. But, from the sound of it, would it be the kind of place you would be interested in attending? Does the commercial aspect of the event prove that contemporary media are completely beholden to the 'culture industries' (see Chapter 6)? And this is an event taking place in America: would you expect similar events to occur in European countries that have a stronger tradition of funding culture with public money?

Writing Style

This is a writing style quite different from those in many other readings in this book. Jenkins is clearly attempting to be funny here, with a sarcastic tone. Indeed, this kind of writing might sound more suitable for journalism or reportage, rather than academic work. Yet many contemporary media writers – especially those interested in new media and/or debates about audiences and consumers – write in this way. Such a style can be seen to be an attempt to undercut the authoritative tone adopted by many academics, because such a tone is a display of expertise that does not give the reader much room to discuss, debate and disagree. This means a choice of tone in writing becomes an important act, signalling how you see your audience and the space you want to give them for discussion. You might want to bear this in mind in future when engaging with readings.

READING

11

Like me, the participants had come to New Orleans hoping to glimpse tomorrow before it was too late. Many were nonbelievers who had been burned in the dot-com meltdown and were there to scoff at any new vision. Others were freshly minted from America's top business schools and there to find ways to make their first million. Still others were there because their bosses had sent them, hoping for enlightenment, but willing to settle for one good night in the French Quarter.

The mood was tempered by a sober realization of the dangers of moving too quickly, as embodied by the ghost-town campuses in the Bay Area and the office furniture being sold at bulk prices on eBay; and the dangers of moving too slowly, as represented by the recording industry's desperate flailing as it tries to close the door on file-sharing after the cows have already come stampeding out of the barn. The participants had come to New Orleans in search of the "just right"—the right investments, predictions, and business models. No longer expecting to surf the waves of change, they would be content with staying afloat. The old paradigms were breaking down faster than the new ones were emerging, producing panic among those most invested in the status quo and curiosity in those who saw change as opportunity.

Advertising guys in pinstriped shirts mingled with recording industry flacks with backward baseball caps, Hollywood agents in Hawaiian shirts, pointy-bearded technologists, and shaggy-haired gamers. The only thing they all knew how to do was to exchange business cards.

As represented on the panels at the New Orleans Media Experience, convergence was a "come as you are" party, and some of the participants were less ready for what was planned than others. It was also a swap meet where each of the entertainment industries traded problems and solutions, finding through the interplay among media what they can't achieve working in isolation. In every discussion, there emerged different models of convergence followed by the acknowledgment that none of them knew for sure what the outcomes were going to be. Then, everyone adjourned for a quick round of Red Bulls (a conference sponsor) as if funky high-energy drinks were going to blast them over all of those hurdles.

10

(continued)

Structure

In a similar fashion to other parts of this reading, Jenkins acknowledges his own experiences here, as he discusses his attendance at the Media Experience. By thinking about himself, and the relationships between his everyday experiences and wider theoretical arguments, Jenkins is following in a tradition from cultural theory (see Chapter 17) which sees the personal, the ordinary and the mundane as not only worthy of analysis, but also indicative of much bigger social and cultural contexts.

11

Context

As noted in point 9 above, the bursting of the 'dot-com bubble' destabilised many different communities that had assumed that digital media represented the obvious next step. Jenkins refers here to business people – both those who have been 'burned' by the bubble as well as ones still interested in its potential – and graduates from business schools. This shows how these sets of debates have an economic and industrial inflection, and so the new media discussions are ones with consequences beyond media theory. That said, it is not as if hordes of business people spend their time reading academics like Jenkins. Why might this be? Might the industry work better if it did? And how can academics go about – as Jenkins says he wants to – engaging with other audiences such as those within industry? Why, conventionally, do these communities so rarely talk to one another?

Jenkins refers to the problems being encountered by the 'recording industry'. Indeed, perhaps one of the most visible consequences of new media and digitisation has been the requirement by the music industry to adapt. Websites such as MySpace have allowed musicians to reach audiences without going via 'intermediaries' (Flew 2005: 94) such as the traditional large recording and distribution companies. More importantly, though, the ease with which digital files can be shared has meant that controlling the sale and distribution of music has become extremely difficult, leading to debates about music piracy (Thomas 2002). Legal disputes continue concerning this, and this has been an even more difficult problem than usual because while legal systems are usually nation-based, file-sharing is, of course, global, and therefore deciding who has jurisdiction over what is complex (Bach 2004; Spinello and Tavani 2005). This debate is seen as so central to how we think about the relationships between culture and society that a political party – the Pirate Party – has been standing for election in many countries across the world with the aim of inaugurating a 'fair and balanced copyright law that is suitable for the 21st century' (Pirate Party UK 2011). It could be the case that, in the future, elections may be won and lost on these debates.

Content

Note that Jenkins makes plain here that even though everyone's agreed that convergence is the way forward, no one seems to know what that really means or how to put it into practice. There are 'different models of convergence'; there isn't one single idea of convergence. In a sense, this shows that 'convergence', at the moment, remains a theoretical concept rather than a way of working. There are, then, a set of theoretical debates going on here, and these debates are seen as important as they will influence future business decisions. This shows how theoretical analysis is a part of the way in which all communities work, and therefore its value as a process overall.

READING

12

Political economists and business gurus make convergence sound so easy; they look at the charts that show the concentration of media ownership as if they ensure that all of the parts will work together to pursue maximum profits. But from the ground, many of the big media giants look like great big dysfunctional families, whose members aren't speaking with each other and pursue their own short-term agendas even at the expense of other divisions of the same companies. In New Orleans, however, the representatives for different industries seemed tentatively ready to lower their guard and speak openly about common visions.

13

This event was billed as a chance for the general public to learn first-hand about the coming changes in news and entertainment. In accepting an invitation to be on panels, in displaying a willingness to "go public" with their doubts and anxieties, perhaps industry leaders were acknowledging the importance of the role that ordinary consumers can play not just in accepting convergence, but actually in *driving* the process. If the media industry in recent years has seemed at war with its consumers, in that it is trying to force consumers back into old relationships and into obedience to well-established norms, companies hoped to use this New Orleans event to justify their decisions to consumers and stockholders alike.

Unfortunately, although this was not a closed-door event, it might as well have been. Those few members of the public who did show up were ill-informed. After an intense panel discussion about the challenges of broadening the uses of game consoles, the first member of the audience to raise his hand wanted to know when *Grand Theft Auto III* was coming out on the Xbox. You can scarcely blame consumers for not knowing how to speak this new language or even what questions to ask when so little previous effort has been made to educate them about convergence thinking.

NOTES

12 Context

'Political economy' is explored in Chapter 12. Again, this shows how a media theory concept that might seem detached from 'the real world' – political economy – is, in fact, part of the everyday processes of, for example, business.

13 Context

It might sound like overstating things to say there has been a 'war' between producers and consumers, but this merely acknowledges the problems media producers have encountered because audiences have used technology to their own ends. In that sense, the 'traditional' model of the media industries worked from the idea that audiences would behave as they were told, and that regulation and technology would ensure that that was the case. Yet we need to explore some of the contradictions here. While the active and productive nature of audiences using new technologies can certainly be seen as having some kind of progressive outcome, would you see the complete collapse of large media industries as a good thing? It is unlikely that 'participatory culture' will lead to the kind of big budget media productions that, say, Hollywood routinely produces. Would an explosion of cheaper, independently produced fare make up for that? That is, is there something positive and productive about the 'traditional' media industries which might be worth preserving?

Writing style

In his analysis Jenkins uses the word 'perhaps', suggesting he is not certain if the argument he is offering is convincing or correct. This uncertainty is perhaps rare in academic writing. Do you find it useful, or would you rather Jenkins made more definitive claims?

Content

You might be surprised to read here that Jenkins refers to the activities of some members of the public as 'ill-informed', considering he is someone who has spent much of his career arguing that when audiences do things not expected of them this is interesting and shows they can 'poach' texts. Jenkins then goes on to suggest that such audience members require education to resolve this problem. What *is* evident here is the disparity between the interests of producers and (some) consumers. Furthermore, Jenkins states that a 'new language' is required for these debates, and yet no one seems quite sure what this is. In all, this story makes clear that all participants were part of an event where no one had quite worked out what the rules or expectations were. We can therefore place Jenkins within the camp of new media analysts who are very aware of the problems raised by newer media forms rather than simply celebrating their radical and progressive potential. Indeed, you might find all of this rather off-putting and depressing. If this is the case, why is Jenkins *starting* his book with such an account? Why might he want to raise these matters *right at the outset*?

READING

14

At a panel on game consoles, the big tension was between Sony (a hardware company) and Microsoft (a software company); both had ambitious plans but fundamentally different business models and visions. All agreed that the core challenge was to expand the potential uses of this cheap and readily accessible technology so that it became *the* "black box," the "Trojan horse" that smuggled convergence culture right into people's living rooms. What was mom going to do with the console when her kids were at school? What would get a family to give a game console to grandpa for Christmas? They had the technology to bring about convergence, but they hadn't figured out why anyone would want it.

Another panel focused on the relationship between video games and traditional media. Increasingly, movie moguls saw games not simply as a means of stamping the franchise logo on some ancillary product but as a means of expanding the storytelling experience. These filmmakers had come of age as gamers and had their own ideas about the creative intersections between the media; they knew who the most creative designers were, and they worked the collaboration into their contract. They wanted to use games to explore ideas that couldn't fit within two-hour films.

15

Such collaborations meant taking everyone out of their "comfort zones," as one movieland agent explained. These relationships were difficult to sustain, since all parties worried about losing creative control, and since the time spans for development and distribution in the media were radically different. Should the game company try to align its timing to the often unpredictable production cycle of a movie with the hopes of hitting Wal-Mart the same weekend the film opens? Should the movie producers wait for the often equally unpredictable

↓

NOTES

14 Content

There is lots of interesting language in this section, which reveals how the industry thinks of the consumers it makes its products for. The idea that convergence culture might be 'smuggled' into people's homes suggests the industry knows it is producing products that people do not *need*, and so they have to create what Adorno calls 'false needs' (see Chapter 6) via what Veblen refers to as 'conspicuous consumption' (1957 [1899]). Marcuse argues that 'products indoctrinate and manip-ulate' (2002 [1964]: 14) because we join in and support the economic system that produces them when we buy them, even though that system simultaneously renders us powerless and creates a wealthy elite. Indeed, much of the analysis of media and culture throughout this book works from the assumption that the ways in which large media industries now sell us culture is a problem. What is interesting here is that Jenkins finds that the media industries so expressly acknowledge this as their aim!

However, the second paragraph here suggests a more positive aspect of convergence. That is, Jenkins notes that for some creative people having multiple platforms to tell a story opens up the richness of the experience and means different kinds of stories can be told. As Structuralism (see Chapter 15) suggests that only certain kinds of stories can be told and this therefore places limits on the political possibilities of culture, we can see the desires Jenkins outlines here as positive, perhaps. It is worth thinking about this; what kinds of stories work best for which kind of media? What does the story of a computer game need, say, which would not work in a film? And what happens if you have a story which works across both? Is something added, or is it just more of the same?

Context

Jenkins's acknowledgement of the ways stories can now move across media highlights the context that media production now functions within. For example, the BBC has requested that people pitching programmes to them acknowledge the need for '360 degree multi-platform content crea-tion' (Thompson, quoted in BBC Press Office 2006) whereby the content for a proposed television programme would work on a website, or for a podcast, so that what the BBC produces works across a range of media. In that sense, thinking about each medium separately becomes pointless, and is not what the industry is interested in. If *you* want to work in the creative industries after your studies how might this affect how you go about doing your work?

15 Context

What Jenkins highlights here is that while one of the key reasons creative personnel are worried is that the future financial status of the industry is in question, there are also personal reasons why such people want their work to be protected. 'Creative control' becomes an important idea here, and research shows that one of the reasons why people work in the creative industries (and put up with the long hours, job instability, and poor pay compared to many other careers; see Deuze 2007: 1–44 and Ross 2009: 15–52) is that there is often more opportunity for control and flexibility over

READING

15

(continued)

game development cycle to run its course, sitting out the clock while some competitor steals their thunder? Will the game get released weeks or months later, after the buzz of the movie has dried up or, worse yet, after the movie has bombed? Should the game become part of the publicity buildup toward a major release, even though that means starting development before the film project has been "green lighted" by a studio? Working with a television production company is even more nerve wracking, since the turnaround time is much shorter and the risk much higher that the series will never reach the air.

If the game industry folks had the smirking belief that they controlled the future, the record industry types were sweating bullets; their days were numbered unless they figured out how to turn around current trends (such as dwindling audiences, declining sales, and expanding piracy). The panel on "monetizing music" was one of the most heavily attended. Everyone tried to speak at once, yet none of them were sure their "answers" would work. Will the future revenue come from rights management, from billing people for the music they down-load, or from creating a fee the servers had to pay out to the record industry as a whole? And what about cell phone rings—which some felt represented an unexplored market for new music as well as a grassroots promotional channel? Perhaps the money will lie in the intersection between the various media with new artists promoted via music videos that are paid for by advertisers who want to use their sounds and images for branding, with new artists tracked via the Web, which allows the public to register its preferences in hours rather than weeks.

16

And so it went, in panel after panel. The New Orleans Media Experience pressed us into the future. Every path forward had roadblocks, most of which felt insurmountable, but somehow, they would either have to be routed around or broken down in the coming decade.

The messages were plain:

1. Convergence is coming and you had better be ready.
2. Convergence is harder than it sounds.
3. Everyone will survive if everyone works together. (Unfortunately, that was the one thing nobody knew how to do.)

NOTES

15

(continued)

what you do and who you work with in comparison to lots of other jobs (Florida 2003: 152; Hesmondhalgh 2007: 199–201). Therefore, creative people are willing to give up some of the financial benefits other work would give them for the satisfaction derived from working on things they care about and having some control over their labour and their life. As noted earlier, Jenkins has explored how fans of culture often 'poach' texts, rewriting them to their own ends. While Jenkins celebrates this, you can see how it might be the case that, for many people working in the creative industries, such 'poaching' is instead quite threatening as things you have worked on and which may mean a lot to you get redrafted by other people. 'Poaching', then, is about *undermining* the creative control media professionals have (which is why some people, like Jenkins, see it as important). But what happens to the media professional if *everyone* can make videos and put them on YouTube, or write a song and distribute it via MySpace? Will we lose the idea of the professional altogether? Some of these questions are discussed in the Clay Shirky reading in Chapter 24.

Writing Style

Again, notice the uncertainty in the language here; 'perhaps' and 'should', and the paragraph is littered with question asked by those in the industry (and, by extension, by Jenkins himself). Do you think he is inviting you to try to answer those questions? Or are they there for some other purpose? Do you think Jenkins thinks it is *his* role, as an academic, to try to answer those questions? Or are there others he is more interested in?

16

Structure

This is the final paragraph in this section of Jenkins's book, and he moves on after this to discuss the history of debates about convergence. So, he ends this section with a summary of the key points. But, of course, these are not Jenkins's key points; they are those that arose from the Media Experience. So, while this is a useful summary of what we have read, it still does not really tell us much about what Jenkins thinks. This reading is, therefore, structured in a manner which means we have, so far, been given little understanding of what the author actually wants to argue. Is it helpful that he lets others speak so much first?

Writing Style

What do you think of the tone of this final section? Does Jenkins seem convinced by the arguments presented by others? From this tone, where do you think this book will go next, and can you infer what Jenkins's wider argument might be?

REFLECTING ON THE READING

One of the ways you could think about this reading is by placing it in the context of others in this book. The Hesmondhalgh reading in Chapter 21 is about production and the creative industries, and so gives a wider overview of the people and the institutions Jenkins explores here. The Shirky reading in Chapter 24 explores similar ideas of convergence and participatory culture; it is also worth comparing the tones and writing styles of Shirky and Jenkins, and wondering why it is that they write in a manner quite different from many others in this book. And related to the discussion Jenkins engages in about the relationships between commerce and culture and the roles culture plays in society for giving people a voice, you could look at the chapters on the culture industry (Chapter 6) and the public sphere (Chapter 13).

In his outlining of the confusion and indecision inherent in the media industries when discussing convergence, have you been heartened or depressed? As was noted in the introduction, many writers have been extremely positive about the potential of new media, seeing it as able to usher in a new dawn of civic engagement and social equality. Yet Jenkins does not appear to have the same attitude. At least, the people from the creative industries he discusses here might not give you much optimism. So how has this made you think about the media industries and those who work within them? Does this account make you think they know what they are doing? Does the industry seem like the kind of place you might want to work in? Is optimism justified?

Finally, it is worth thinking about what convergence has meant to your everyday life. How has it affected the kinds of media you consume, and how you consume them? While the media industries may be converging, is this true for the technology you use to access media? In thinking about this we have to be wary of what Jenkins calls the 'black box fallacy' (2006: 13). That is, 'Sooner or later, the argument goes, all media content is going to flow through a single black box into our living rooms (or, in the mobile scenario, through black boxes we carry around with us' (p. 14). But Jenkins sees this as a fallacy because, over time, he seems to have *more and more* black boxes, not fewer; 'my VCR, my digital cable box, my DVD player, my digital recorder' and so on, resulting in a 'perpetual tangle of cords that stands between me and my "home entertainment"' (p. 15). Are you like one of his students that he sees 'lugging around multiple black boxes – their laptops, their cells [mobile phones], their iPods, their Game Boys, their Blackberrys, you name it' (p. 15)? Do you feel like you're living in a new media world where convergence is key?

Key terms to explore

collective intelligence; convergence; grassroots; media flow; participatory culture; piracy.

Key writers who are mentioned

George Gilder; Pierre Lévy; Nicholas Negroponte.

RECOMMENDED READING

Flew, Terry (2005) *New Media: An introduction*, 2nd edition, Oxford: Oxford University Press.

Explores new media within a global context, in social, economic and politics terms.

Kyong, W.H., and Keenan, T. (eds) (2006) *New Media, Old Media: A history and theory reader*, New York and London: Routledge.

Useful collection of readings, especially as it makes links between all forms of media and offers a historical context.

van Dijk, J.A.G.M. (2006) *The Network Society: Social aspects of new media*, 2nd edition, London: Sage.

Foregrounds the idea of the network, exploring to what extent new media has consequences for wider society.

CHAPTER 19

Postmodernism

Baudrillard, J. (1994 [1981]) 'The implosion of meaning in the media', in *Simulacra and Simulation*, translated by Glaser, S.F., Ann Arbor: University of Michigan Press, pp. 79–86.

INTRODUCTION TO POSTMODERNISM

Madonna keeps changing how she looks in her videos. In *Like a Virgin* (1984) she is a sexy pop queen, dancing around the canals of Venice; in *Like a Prayer* (1989) she's a brunette, troubled, entering a church and kissing a black statue that may or may not be Jesus; in *Justify My Love* (1990) she has various sexual encounters in a stylised, monochrome world; in *Ray of Light* (1998) she dances hyperkinetically to a speedy dance song; in *Don't Tell Me* (2000) she adopts a traditional American look, wearing jeans and a check shirt and surrounded by cowboys; in *Hung Up* (2005) she returns to 1970s disco, performing in a leotard in a dance studio. For eight years she was married to the British film director Guy Ritchie, and spent that time living in England, taking on the role of mother and English gentry. In her continuing reign as the queen of international pop, Madonna's career has rested on her continuing image changes, some of which have outraged sections of the public, and others which have been seen as more acceptable. What is significant here is how a career can be built on *image*, and on images that can *change*; in a sense, Madonna's success is down to her ability to convince us that she can be a variety of things, and therefore, in the end, it becomes almost impossible to know the 'real' her. In this way, 'Madonna can be apprehended as a postmodern myth' (Guilbert 2002: 2).

So what do we mean by postmodernism? Unlike many of the theories or terms you come across in this book, postmodernism is one which can sometimes be heard outside of academic discussion. This is because rather than just being relevant to media, postmodernism has been used to describe virtually everything about how we live our lives now. It is used to discuss a variety of cultural forms, from television to cinema to art to advertising to music videos to architecture. Yet it is also used to describe the social conditions within which we currently live, and therefore has connections to politics, economics, history, and our sense of identity. In these ways, postmodernism is a big theory, and those who espouse it suggest we're living in a postmodern world *right now*.

Yet defining postmodernism has proved disconcertingly difficult. Different thinkers have different approaches and different definitions; indeed, it has been argued that the difficulty in saying what postmodernism is, is itself postmodernist. But if we take the Madonna example, we can see that there are recurring ideas which are common to most understandings of postmodernism.

First, the idea that Madonna is all about *image* is key. That is, that the ways in which we understand people, and the world around us, is through the surface appearance of things. It is argued that this has come about because of the media-saturated society in which we live, in which we are bombarded by images. These images are seen to have replaced the 'real' world; we feel like we have 'seen' polar bears in the wild because we have watched a natural history documentary of them, when in fact we never left our living rooms. In this way, experiencing the image of something comes to replace the thing itself. Baudrillard in *Simulacra and Simulation* calls this 'the loss of the real' (1994 [1981]), and he argues we now live lives with little similarity to those lived by people centuries ago in a pre-industrial, pre-modern, pre-technological society. It is this idea that is central to *The Matrix* (dir. Wachowski Brothers, 1999); Neo discovers that the world he thinks is 'real' is in fact a simulation, nothing but surface, and he fights to dismantle that image and gain access to the real world. *The Matrix* is a film all about postmodernism, and it is no accident that, early in the film, Neo's money and computer files are stored in a copy of Baudrillard's *Simulacra and Simulation*.

Indeed, *The Matrix* shows the contradictions of living in a postmodern world. First, the film prefers the real world to the imaginary one created by intelligent machines, as Cypher's choice to return to the fictional world because he likes the taste of steak is clearly presented as a villainous act. Yet the film is itself all about surface, and offers pleasures associated with the 'look' of cinema. The much-vaunted 'bullet-time' sequences, in which time is slowed down to an astonishing degree, along with the hyperkinetic action sequences, and the fetishisation of weaponry alongside the athletic bodies of its main stars, is itself postmodern because we are meant to enjoy a film with little connection to the everyday 'reality' we know and understand. What is enjoyable is how the film *looks*, not what it *says*, and this is a key idea of postmodernism. This is why MTV is seen as 'an example of postmodern corporate global media culture' (Bignell 2000: 174); that the music video presents performers as things to be looked at, with little interest in them below their surface, therefore constructs 'a seamless realm of simulations that hinder our acquisition of the *really real*' (Collins 1992: 332).

Jameson (1991) suggests that postmodernism is a consequence of the industrialised nature of much of society, and the fact that we live in a capitalist, consumerist world. That is, if the primary activity of the public is to buy things, then it is not surprising that the ways in which we make sense of the world – and attempt to define ourselves – is through appearances and objects. In this way we have become detached from the processes which produce things – we no longer make our own clothes or grow our own food, for example – and instead are only interested in the final product, which is pre-packaged for us, and whose suitability we decide upon based on image. This clearly applies to media; while some people do make their own films, or write their own music, the vast majority of media we encounter is made by others for us, and is usually distributed through capitalist global corporations.

In that way, and because of its name, postmodernism has often been understood in response to modernism; after all, it is *post*-modernism. Modernism is a social and cultural movement that affected much of the western world in the early twentieth century (Childs 2007; Lewis 2007); you may have come across it if you study literature or art. Yet the links between modernism and postmodernism are open to much debate: it is hard to see where the one ends and the other begins; it is debatable whether postmodernism grows out of, responds to, or rejects modernism; or maybe the two are utterly unconnected. Whatever, it is worth bearing in mind that the two concepts are often seen as having some kind of connection, and therefore postmodernism is commonly placed in a historical context, coming out of specific social, political and cultural dimensions.

INTRODUCTION TO THE READING

Jean Baudrillard is seen as one of the key thinkers in discussions about postmodernism; others include Jean-François Lyotard and Fredric Jameson. Baudrillard is French, and like many French academics and cultural theorists his work ranges across many disciplines. He is, therefore, a cultural theorist, philosopher, political commentator, and photographer. His work has repeatedly focused on the ways in which social events are communicated and mediated, and the changes to the 'truth' that occur because of this process. Perhaps his most famous – or infamous – work is *The Gulf War Did Not Take Place* (1995 [1991]). In this, Baudrillard takes to task the events which occurred during the first Gulf War (1991) which, he argues, were unlike anything that has traditionally been seen to define 'war'. That is, while he accepts that fighting took place and many people died, the images of events which were broadcast across the world showed that the ways in which the fighting was carried out were less about the conflict and more about demonstrating the might of each side to those watching it on television. The camera-mounted 'smart bombs', were perfect examples of this; they produced excellent images which hoped to prove America's dominance in warfare technology, and which were therefore more about the surface of the images they produced than their effectiveness on the battlefield. In these ways, Baudrillard has repeatedly placed his work within contemporary political contexts, and is therefore quite a controversial figure.

The reading here comes from *Simulacra and Simulation*, which outlines many of Baudrillard's key ideas and is a primary text in discussions about postmodernism. It may be worth bearing in mind that this is a translation from the French original, and therefore at least part of the meaning rests on the translator's felicity; it is quite common for various translations to be quite different (this is also true of the Barthes reading in Chapter 22 in *this* book). Also note that Baudrillard does not mention media specifically throughout; this is one of those cases where media studies has drawn on theories which are not completely about the media, but finds those theories of relevance to the media studies project. This therefore may make this a difficult read; it would be worthwhile for you to think about how it relates to media throughout, in order to ground the reading in your own experience.

READING

1

J. Baudrillard

The implosion of meaning in the media

We live in a world where there is more and more information, and less and less meaning.
Consider three hypotheses.

2

Either information produces meaning (a negentropic factor), but cannot make up for the brutal loss of signification in every domain. Despite efforts to reinject message and content, meaning is lost and devoured faster than it can be reinjected. In this case, one must appeal to a base productivity to replace failing media. This is the whole ideology of free speech, of media broken down into innumerable individual cells of transmission, that is, into "antimedia" (pirate radio, etc.).

Or information has nothing to do with signification. It is something else, an operational model of another order, outside meaning and of the circulation of meaning strictly speaking. This is Shannon's hypothesis: a sphere of information that is purely functional, a technical medium that does not imply any finality of meaning, and thus should also not be implicated in a value judgment. A kind of code, like the genetic code: it is what it is, it functions as it does, meaning is something else that in a sense comes after the fact, as it does for Monod in *Chance and Necessity*. In this case, there would simply be no significant relation between the inflation of information and the deflation of meaning.

Or, very much on the contrary, there is a rigorous and necessary correlation between the two, to the extent that information is directly destructive of meaning and signification, or that it neutralizes them. The loss of meaning is directly linked to the dissolving, dissuasive action of information, the media, and the mass media.

NOTES

1 Structure

In this short, opening paragraph, Baudrillard presents his argument as unarguable fact; the rest of the chapter goes on to demonstrate what he means. It could be argued that Baudrillard goes on to find evidence that supports his hypotheses, rather than doing some research and drawing hypotheses from what he finds. In this way, we can see that a polemical approach is being taken towards the subject, and the chapter's function is to demonstrate that Baudrillard is 'right'.

Content

Who is the 'we' Baudrillard mentions here? What does the word's use tell us about who he assumes his readership is?

2 Structure

In these three paragraphs, Baudrillard outlines three possible relationships between information and the methods that are used to communicate that information. The validity of his writing rests on his belief that one of those relationships is truer than the others; questioning which of these three hypotheses you find most convincing is a useful way into questioning the chapter as a whole. This also means it is worth spending time making sure you see the differences between these three ideas, as they are vital to an understanding of the chapter as a whole.

Content

Why does Baudrillard think his argument matters? Note he talks about 'failing media' and a 'loss of meaning'. How does this relate to key ideas in postmodernism overall?

READING

3

The third hypothesis is the most interesting but flies in the face of every commonly held opinion. Everywhere socialization is measured by the exposure to media messages. Whoever is underexposed to the media is desocialized or virtually asocial. Everywhere information is thought to produce an accelerated circulation of meaning, a plus value of meaning homologous to the economic one that results from the accelerated rotation of capital. Information is thought to create communication, and even if the waste is enormous, a general consensus would have it that nevertheless, as a whole, there be an excess of meaning, which is redistributed in all the interstices of the social—just as consensus would have it that material production, despite its dysfunctions and irrationalities, opens onto an excess of wealth and social purpose. We are all complicitous in this myth. It is the alpha and omega of our modernity, without which the credibility of our social organization would collapse. Well, *the fact is that it is collapsing*, and for this very reason: because where we think that information produces meaning, the opposite occurs.

4

Information devours its own content. It devours communication and the social. And for two reasons.

5

1. Rather than creating communication, *it exhausts itself in the act of staging communication*. Rather than producing meaning, it exhausts itself in the staging of meaning. A gigantic process of simulation that is very familiar. The nondirective interview, speech, listeners who call in, participation at every level, blackmail through speech: "You are concerned, you are the event, etc." More and more information is invaded by this kind of phantom content, this homeopathic grafting, this awakening dream of communication. A circular arrangement through which one stages the desire of the audience, the antitheater of communication, which, as one knows, is never anything but the recycling in the negative of the traditional institution, the integrated circuit of the negative. Immense energies are deployed to hold this simulacrum at bay, to avoid the brutal desimulation that would confront us in the face of the obvious reality of a radical loss of meaning.

NOTES

3 · Writing Style

Baudrillard mentions 'every commonly held opinion'; where is his evidence? Who is he talking about? Throughout his writing Baudrillard rarely refers to other writers, or offers supporting evidence; this is the kind of writing you would get criticised for if you did it in an essay.

Content

What does Baudrillard mean by 'an excess of meaning'? Do you think he is right? You may want to think about this by comparing contemporary society to older, pre-industrial societies.

4 · Writing Style

Note the concise writing style here, like that in the opening paragraph. Again, Baudrillard offers a hypothesis which is to be tested in his subsequent paragraphs.

5 · Content

For Baudrillard, the media's techniques in creating meaning replace the meaning which is offered. He argues that the way the media invite the audience to react to what it is presented with – to laugh, to cry, to get angry – has become more important than the information we might get from a text. This is very similar to contemporary debates about 'dumbing-down', that the news no longer offers us thoughtful, complex ideas and information, but instead gives us exciting images and personalised stories which we can emotionally react to and then forget about (Mosley 2000). This means that the complex debates Baudrillard outlines here can actually be seen in very everyday discussions of the ways in which the media does or does not affect society.

Writing Style

The writing style is quite poetic here; does that help Baudrillard express his argument, or not? Does it convince of its truth, or not? Why has he chosen to write in this way? What does 'immense energies' mean?

READING

6

It is useless to ask if it is the loss of communication that produces this escalation in the simulacrum, or whether it is the simulacrum that is there first for dissuasive ends, to short-circuit in advance any possibility of communication (precession of the model that calls an end to the real). Useless to ask which is the first term, there is none, it is a circular process—that of simulation, that of the hyperreal. The hyperreality of communication and of meaning. More real than the real, that is how the real is abolished.

7

Thus not only communication but the social functions in a closed circuit, as a *lure*—to which the force of *myth* is attached. Belief, faith in information attach themselves to this tautological proof that the system gives of itself by doubling the signs of an unlocatable reality.

8

But one can believe that this belief is as ambiguous as that which was attached to myths in ancient societies. *One both believes and doesn't.* One does not ask oneself, "I know very well, but still." A sort of inverse simulation in the masses, in each one of us, corresponds to this simulation of meaning and of communication in which this system encloses us. To this tautology of the system the masses respond with ambivalence, to deterrence they respond with disaffection, or with an always enigmatic belief. Myth exists, but one must guard against thinking that people believe in it: this is the trap of critical thinking that can only be exercised if it presupposes the naïveté and stupidity of the masses.

6　Content

If this is a 'circular process' how can we escape from it?

7　Content

The idea that we have 'faith in information' means that the kind of communication we count as information is defined as such because it is communicated to us by those who have the authority to do so: and they have the authority because they know that information. This is a circular logic. For example, your lecturers are allowed to teach you things because they know the kinds of things which the educational system says count as information, which is itself defined by those within it. By this argument, there is no such thing as information, just those things which a social system defines as such.

8　Content

Baudrillard offers a positive note here. While he spends much of the chapter showing how people are powerless, he states here that the masses know this is the case, and are aware of the system that entraps them. If the masses are aware of the system they are entrapped in, is that a good or a bad thing? Does it mean they can question and attack that system, or are the public resigned to powerless acquiescence? You might think about this relative to plummeting voting rates in many industrialised countries; what do these say about the public's view of the social forces which govern them?

READING

9

> 2. Behind this exacerbated mise-en-scène of communication, the mass media, the pressure of information pursues an irresistible destructuration of the social.
>
> Thus information dissolves meaning and dissolves the social, in a sort of nebulous state dedicated not to a surplus of innovation, but, on the contrary, to total entropy.[1]

10

> Thus the media are producers not of socialization, but of exactly the opposite, of the implosion of the social in the masses. And this is only the macroscopic extension of the *implosion of meaning* at the microscopic level of the sign. This implosion should be analyzed according to McLuhan's formula, *the medium is the message*, the consequences of which have yet to be exhausted.

1. Here we have not spoken of information except in the social register of communication. But it would be enthralling to consider this hypothesis even within the parameters of cybernetic information *theory*. There also, the fundamental thesis calls for this information to be synonymous with negentropy, with the resistance to entropy, with an excess of meaning and organization. But it would be useful to posit the opposite hypothesis: INFORMATION = ENTROPY. For example: *the information or knowledge that can be obtained about a system or an event is already a form of the neutralization and entropy of this system* (to be extended to science in general, and to the social sciences and humanities in particular). *Information in which an event is reflected or broadcast is already a degraded form of this event.* Do not hesitate to analyze the media's intervention in May 1968 in these terms. The extension of the student action permitted the general strike, but the latter was precisely a black box that neutralized the original virulence of the movement. Amplification was itself a mortal trap and not a positive extension. One should be wary of the universalization of struggles through information. One should be wary of solidarity campaigns at every level, of this simultaneously electronic and worldly solidarity. Every strategy of the universalization of differences is an entropic strategy of the system.

9 ## Content

What is a 'nebulous state'?

10 ## Content

The argument here is that in offering up a wealth of information that is poorly contextualised and in excess of what any individual can make sense of, modern societies start to break down the social structures which have traditionally been central to human existence. How are we, as individuals and societies, meant to know what to do when we are constantly trying to keep up with all the information we're bombarded with?

Context

How true do you think it is that the media destroy socialisation? Is this a convincing viewpoint when more and more 'ordinary' people appear on television, when the public are making their own programmes and distributing them on the internet, and we get to see images and voices from all over the world? Baudrillard would insist his argument is correct despite all of these innovations; how can that be?

Marshall McLuhan's theories of the media are some of the most famous in the world, and 'The medium is the message' is one of his key ideas. He argues that the content of media is less important than the medium itself, that television is less significant because of the individual programmes it broadcasts, and more because of the ceaseless nature of the medium which is quite different from other media. McLuhan's ideas go in and out of fashion quite a lot, but he is someone you should know about (see 1951b, 1962, 1964; also see Chapter 10 in *this* book). Here Baudrillard draws on McLuhan's ideas but also critiques and develops them; in a chapter noticeably devoid of references to other writers, it might be significant that Baudrillard spends so much time discussing McLuhan.

READING

11

That means that all contents of meaning are absorbed in the only dominant form of the medium. Only the medium can make an event—whatever the contents, whether they are conformist or subversive. A serious problem for all counterinformation, pirate radios, antimedia, etc. But there is something even more serious, which McLuhan himself did not see. Because beyond this neutralization of all content, one could still expect to manipulate the medium in its form and to transform the real by using the impact of the medium as form. If all the content is wiped out, there is perhaps still a subversive, revolutionary use value of the *medium as such*. That is—and this is where McLuhan's formula leads, pushed to its limit— there is not only an implosion of the message in the medium, there is, in the same movement, the implosion of the medium itself in the real, the implosion *of the medium and of the real* in a sort of hyperreal nebula, in which even the definition and distinct action of the medium can no longer be determined.

12

Even the 'traditional' status of the media themselves, characteristic of modernity, is put in question. McLuhan's formula, *the medium is the message*, which is the key formula of the era of simulation (the medium is the message—the sender is the receiver—the circularity of all poles—the end of panoptic and perspectival space—such is the alpha and omega of *our* modernity), this very formula must be imagined at its limit where, after all the contents and messages have been volatilized in the medium, it is the medium itself that is volatilized as such. Fundamentally, it is still the message that lends credibility to the medium, that gives the medium its determined, distinct status as the intermediary of communication. Without a message, the medium also falls into the indefinite state characteristic of all our great systems of judgment and value. A single *model*, whose efficacy is immediate, simultaneously generates the message, the medium, and the "real."

11 ## Context

How do the media 'make an event'? For example, think about the role of the media in things like the Olympics, 9/11, and the death of Princess Diana. Would these have been significant as events if the media hadn't covered them, and how do they change because they did?

Content

Note Baudrillard talks about the possibility of television being 'subversive' and 'revolutionary'; in this way, we can see that we can place him within the critical focus of media studies, which assumes that the media should in some way aid social progress and question social and power structures. The fact that there is no need for Baudrillard to state that this is his viewpoint shows how it is assumed that that is the subject's aim.

Writing Style

The 'hyperreal nebula' is the idea that the real world and the media that present it to us are one and the same thing, so it is impossible to make sense of the world without using media conventions. This means that all that exists is the version of the world the media presents to us, and we use those ideas when we think about the real world around us. We can see this, for example, in the ways in which eating disorders have been linked to images in advertising, so that people judge their body's social acceptability not by the world around them but by the version of that world presented in the media (Cole and Daniel 2005). For Baudrillard, the media version of the world has not merely replaced the real world: it is one and the same thing.

12 ## Content

Here Baudrillard continues his discussion of McLuhan, arguing that his prioritisation of the medium *over* the message ignores the symbiotic relationship *between* the medium and the message. Outlining, examining and developing the works of others is a key method employed in academic writing; indeed, one of the main ways in which academics are judged to be of significance or not is through how often they are mentioned by other writers. In referring to McLuhan, Baudrillard applies significance to his own argument by drawing on the significance of McLuhan's work. This shows the system within which academic work circulates, and it is one of the reasons it is sometimes criticised for being too self-obsessed.

READING

13 Finally, *the medium* is *the message* not only signifies the end of the message, but also the end of the medium. There are no more media in the literal sense of the word (I'm speaking particularly of electronic mass media)—that is, of a mediating power between one reality and another, between one state of the real and another. Neither in content, nor in form. Strictly, this is what implosion signifies. The absorption of one pole into another, the short-circuiting between poles of every differential system of meaning, the erasure of distinct terms and oppositions, including that of the medium and of the real—thus the impossibility of any mediation, of any dialectical intervention between the two or from one to the other. Circularity of all media effects. Hence the impossibility of meaning in the literal sense of a unilateral vector that goes from one pole to another. One must envisage this critical but original situation at its very limit: it is the only one left us. It is useless to dream of revolution through content, useless to dream of a revelation through form, because the medium and the real are now in a single nebula whose truth is indecipherable.

The fact of this implosion of contents, of the absorption, of meaning, of the evanescence of the medium itself, of the reabsorption of every dialectic of communication in a total circularity of the model, of the implosion of the social in the masses, may seem catastrophic and desperate. But this is only the case in light of the idealism that dominates our whole view of information. We all live by a passionate idealism of meaning and of communication, by an idealism of communication through meaning, and, from this perspective, it is truly *the catastrophe of meaning* that lies in wait for us.

14 But one must realize that 'catastrophe' has this 'catastrophic' meaning of end and annihilation only in relation to a linear vision of accumulation, of productive finality, imposed on us by the system. Etymologically, the term itself only signifies the curvature, the winding down to the bottom of a cycle that leads to what one could call the 'horizon of the event,' to an impassable horizon of meaning: beyond that nothing takes place *that has meaning for us*—but it suffices to get out of this ultimatum of meaning in order for the catastrophe itself to no longer seem like a final and nihilistic day of reckoning, such as it functions in our contemporary imaginary.

15 Beyond meaning, there is the fascination that results from the neutralization and the implosion of meaning. Beyond the horizon of the social, there are the masses, which result from the neutralization and the implosion of the social.

NOTES

13 Writing Style

Note how Baudrillard uses the word 'mediating' here, to define the ways in which certain technologies, such as television, are employed to mediate meaning from producers to consumers. We rarely explicitly think of the media in this way; it is worth constantly bearing in mind the origins of the word 'media', because this process is at the heart of what media studies often chooses to analyse.

Context

Here Baudrillard discusses 'revolution', while noting its impossibility. Note, though, that he does not state *why* there should be a revolution; perhaps this draws on Baudrillard's French national identity – in which the French Revolution often looms large – and the history of the Paris riots in 1968 (Quattrocchi and Nairn 1998). If revolution cannot be achieved through form *or* content, how can it be achieved? Or is Baudrillard trying to say something else here?

14 Content

Why are 'catastrophe' and 'catastrophic' in quotation marks here? What 'system' is Baudrillard referring to here?

15 Structure

Like Extract 1, this is a short and concise paragraph; however, unlike Extract 1 this paragraph summarises and draws on the previous content, rather than offering a hypothesis that is then explored.

READING

16 What is essential today is to evaluate this double challenge—the challenge of the masses to meaning and their silence (which is not at all a passive resistance)—the challenge to meaning that comes from the media and its fascination. All the marginal, alternative efforts to revive meaning are secondary in relation to that challenge.

17 Evidently, there is a paradox in this inextricable conjunction of the masses and the media: do the media neutralize meaning and produce unformed [*informe*] or informed [*informée*] masses, or is it the masses who victoriously resist the media by directing or absorbing all the messages that the media produce without responding to them? Sometime ago, in "Requiem for the Media," I analyzed and condemned the media as the institution of an irreversible model of communication *without a response*. But today? This absence of a response can no longer be understood at all as a strategy of power, but as a counterstrategy of the masses themselves when they encounter power. What then?

18 Are the mass media on the side of power in the manipulation of the masses, or are they on the side of the masses in the liquidation of meaning, in the violence perpetrated on meaning, and in fascination? Is it the media that induce fascination in the masses, or is it the masses who direct the media into the spectacle? Mogadishu-Stammheim: the media make themselves into the vehicle of the moral condemnation of terrorism and of the exploitation of fear for political ends, but simultaneously, in the most complete ambiguity, they propagate the brutal charm of the terrorist act, they are themselves terrorists, insofar as they themselves march to the tune of seduction (cf. Umberto Eco on this eternal moral dilemma: how can one not speak of terrorism, how can one find a *good use* of the media—*there is none*). The media carry meaning and countermeaning, they manipulate in all directions at once, nothing can control this process, they are the vehicle for the simulation internal to the system and the simulation that destroys the system, according to an absolutely Möbian and circular logic—and it is exactly like this. There is no alternative to this, no logical resolution. Only a logical *exacerbation* and a catastrophic resolution.

NOTES

16 ### Context

If 'silence' is not 'a passive resistance', what is it? According to Baudrillard and postmodernism, why are the masses silent?

Content

Like his talk of revolution above, here Baudrillard discusses the 'challenge'. That is, he is not analysing media merely to see what it does and how it works; he insists there is a 'challenge' which must be acknowledged and fought. And note that that challenge is discussed relative to the masses; again, this kind of language assumes particular things about what media studies should do and who it should do it for.

17 ## Content

Baudrillard questions here the relationship between media and the masses, offering two possible scenarios. How could you examine which of these two is more convincing? What kind of study could be done? And – perhaps more relevant to this chapter – why doesn't Baudrillard do it?

Context

Here Baudrillard refers to his own previous work. In doing so, he not only shows his recurring interest in the same set of ideas but also suggests that as his previous work has dealt with some of these ideas, there is no need for him to go over them again. Therefore, this chapter is a development of his existing publications. This shows how much academic work is always in progress, and writers often examine and critique their own writing in later work. Hence, we often have to read a range of work by an author in order to get an overview of the ways in which it has developed.

18 ### Writing Style

Finally, Baudrillard uses a specific example. However, it is noticeable that he goes into little detail. He states what the media did, but he neglects to state how he came to that conclusion, so we have to take his word that his reading is sound. How useful is this as an example, then?

Context

In what ways are the media 'terrorists'? Note that this chapter was written a long time before the 'War on Terror', when the term may have had quite a different meaning. Also, as a Frenchman, Baudrillard's relationship to terrorists and terrorism would be different to that of people from other countries.

19

With one caution. We are face to face with this system in a double situation and insoluble double bind—exactly like children faced with the demands of the adult world. Children are simultaneously required to constitute themselves as autonomous subjects, responsible, free and conscious, and to constitute themselves as submissive, inert, obedient, conforming objects. The child resists on all levels, and to a contradictory demand he responds with a double strategy. To the demand of being an object, he opposes all the practices of disobedience, of revolt, of emancipation; in short, a total claim to subjecthood. To the demand of being a subject he opposes, just as obstinately, and efficaciously, an object's resistance, that is to say, exactly the opposite: childishness, hyperconformism, total dependence, passivity, idiocy. Neither strategy has more objective value than the other. The subject-resistance is today unilaterally valorized and viewed as positive—just as in the political sphere only the practices of freedom, emancipation, expression, and the constitution of a political subject are seen as valuable and subversive. But this is to ignore the equal, and without a doubt superior, impact of all the object practices, of the renunciation of the subject position and of meaning— precisely the practices of the masses—that we bury under the derisory terms of alienation and passivity.

18

(continued)

Content

This is a very pessimistic and all-encompassing conclusion, that the media are themselves 'terrorists' for the ways in which they have undermined social processes and destroyed the power of the masses. Such pessimism is common in a lot of (though not all) postmodern thinking. It is noticeable, however, that Baudrillard acknowledges the other possible ways in which postmodernism can be read, and therefore insists on a complexity to his argument. While some of the writing style could be criticised for being polemical, it can be seen that Baudrillard at least engages with alternative readings of the world around him. You may or may not think that this is an essential thing for academic writing to do.

19

Content

Why refer to 'children' here? What assumptions about children is Baudrillard making? Where is his evidence that this is, indeed, how children behave? And what emotive consequences does using them as an example have?

Context

Baudrillard distinguishes between a person as a 'subject' and as an 'object'; this is a key idea in much recent work on individuals and identity. However, it is hotly debated – especially in relation to postmodernism (see Bukatman 1993; Doy 2004) – and yet it is noticeable that Baudrillard clearly sees the distinction as one that can be unproblematically assumed.

READING

20

The liberating practices respond to *one* of the aspects of the system, to the constant ultimatum we are given to constitute ourselves as pure objects, but they do not respond at all to the other demand, that of constituting ourselves as subjects, of liberating ourselves, expressing ourselves at whatever cost, of voting, producing, deciding, speaking, participating, playing the game—a form of blackmail and ultimatum just as serious as the other, even more serious today. To a system whose argument is oppression and repression, the strategic resistance is the liberating claim of subjecthood. But this strategy is more reflective of the earlier phase of the system, and even if we are still confronted with it, it is no longer the strategic terrain: the current argument of the system is to maximize speech, the maximum production of meaning. Thus the strategic resistance is that of the refusal of meaning and of the spoken word—or of the hyperconformist simulation of the very mechanisms of the system, which is a form of refusal and of non-reception. It is the strategy of the masses: it is equivalent to returning to the system its own logic by doubling it, to reflecting meaning, like a mirror, without absorbing it. This strategy (if one can still speak of strategy) prevails today, because it was ushered in by that phase of the system which prevails.

21

To choose the wrong strategy is a serious matter. All the movements that only play on liberation, emancipation, on the resurrection of a subject of history, of the group, of the word based on 'consciousness raising,' indeed a 'raising of the unconscious' of subjects and of the masses, do not see that they are going in the direction of the system, whose imperative today is precisely the overproduction and regeneration of meaning and of speech.

NOTES

20 ## Writing Style

This is a long and complicated final paragraph. It's made more difficult because Baudrillard moves away from focusing squarely on the media, and instead discusses how the individual can respond to, and undermine, the social system he outlines as being so repressive. He argues that the conventional ways of expressing rejection of the system – by voting, arguing and political participation – are merely 'playing the game', helping the system continue unabated because the notion of freedom of expression is itself constructed by the system. Instead he argues we can undermine the system by our apathetic disengagement, accepting the constraints which we live under and therefore explicitly demonstrating the inescapability of the system. Perhaps this can be seen in governments' desires to get more people voting; that the shrinking voter turnout, may, in the long term, do more to undermine the validity of the political process than voting particular parties in and out (Jefferys 2007).

Context

Baudrillard sees apathy and a refusal to liberate ourselves as the most powerful way of undermining the social system he maligns; how convincing is this? Can society really change because of so many people doing nothing? Can't totalitarian governments rule most effectively with a public that works in this way? Is this really what Baudrillard is saying?

21 ## Content

Note how Baudrillard insists this is a 'serious matter'. Also note how he discusses the actions of 'they'; that is, not himself.

Structure

How far from the subject of the media have we travelled? Look back at the title of this chapter: is this still relevant to Baudrillard's discussion? Therefore, what are the key aims behind this chapter?

REFLECTING ON THE READING

As was noted at the beginning of this chapter, this is not an easy reading. It would be worthwhile you ensuring you understand what Baudrillard means by the 'key words' listed below. You might also want to look up the other writers he mentions, to see how his work fits into, and responds to, theirs. It is always important to remember that most writers produce material as a response to what others have said, and so placing this article in the context of others' ideas and writings will help you situate it better.

The notes attached to the reading make it clear that, on the whole, Baudrillard does not discuss specific media matters in detail; instead, his is a theory which has a broader social analysis, and media studies thinkers have used his writings as a way of thinking about media. A good thing to do, then, is for you to think about how the writing relates to specific media examples you can think of. In the introduction to this chapter it was shown how some people think Madonna is representative of postmodernism; are there other singers or performers who are similarly postmodern? And are there other films – like *The Matrix* – which you see as examples of the ideas Baudrillard is talking about? It would be good to draw up a list of other forms of media – such as television programmes, radio programmes or magazines – which you would categorise as postmodern.

At the same time, you need to think about the limits of these ideas. Baudrillard suggests that postmodernism encapsulates *all* aspects of life; how convincing is this? Are there media texts which you would argue are not postmodern, as they lack the qualities which are most associated with the idea? In reflecting on the reading, it is always worthwhile thinking about what appears less convincing to you, so that you do not just read the material, but critique it and question it. By categorising media forms which you see as postmodern, and those which you do not, you can begin to question the appropriacy of Baudrillard's argument and this reading as a whole.

Key words to explore

negentropic; simulation; hyperreal; hyperreality; mise-en-scène.

Key writers who are mentioned

Claude Shannon; Jacques Monod; Marshall McLuhan; Umberto Eco.

RECOMMENDED READING

Bignell, J. (2000) *Postmodern Media Culture*, Edinburgh: Edinburgh University Press.

Explores producers, texts and consumers via a range of postmodern thinkers and theories, as well as examining a range of key terms, such as 'modernity'.

Butler, C. (2002) *Postmodernism: A very short introduction*, Oxford: Oxford University Press.

Straightforward introduction to the key debates, with a section on Baudrillard.

Guilbert, G. (2002) *Madonna as Postmodern Myth: How one star's self-construction rewrites sex, gender, Hollywood and the American dream*, Jefferson: McFarland.

Helpful application of postmodern ideas to an example known to many; explores Madonna's career and her reinventions, outlining what this implies about contemporary society.

CHAPTER 20

The information society

Webster, F. (2002) *Theories of the Information Society*, 2nd edition, London: Routledge, pp. 8–21.

INTRODUCTION TO THE INFORMATION SOCIETY

When you are set an essay as an assignment as part of your studies, how do you go about working on it? Presumably you think about the material you have covered in class, and see how any of that can be used in the essay. But then you might also use other resources to carry out research. Some of this research might involve working in the library, looking through books and journals which have been recommended to you or you have found yourself. But perhaps you also look for information on the internet, Googling the names of key writers or looking up key terms, finding a wealth of sites that give you short, succinct, helpful information, complete with links to other useful pages. Perhaps you use Wikipedia, even though, quite often, universities and academics warn against its inaccuracies and omissions. After all, Wikipedia is a useful starting point for research, which, if used correctly, can be a good source of information which points towards more thorough material produced by experts. What is noticeable about Wikipedia, and the internet more generally, is how *quick* and *easy* it is to access information, and that for very little work lots of material can be accumulated. The problem with this process is that it is hard to discern the quality of such material, and that the internet is not very good at pointing out what kinds of things *cannot* be found on it. In carrying out such research, whichever way you do it, you are engaged in a search for *information*, which you can then use for your assignment. Similarly, surfing websites for updates on sports reports, or using Facebook to find out what friends are doing, or accessing strange video clips from a faraway country via YouTube, is all about finding things out. Noticeably, such activities were much more difficult only a few decades ago, and often one of the ways in which the internet is lauded is its ability to give us access to so much more information quickly and easily.

What this demonstrates is how important *information* is to the way we live our lives, and how media technologies give us access to that information. It is often said that we now have more access to more information more easily than ever before, and that this therefore changes how society is structured. New technologies are seen to have made this possible; the internet is an obvious example, but other media, such as television and newspapers, also made information more easily accessible to a larger number of people than was the case centuries ago (Flew 2005: xv). Also, think about the kind of job you want to go into after your studies; is it likely to be a manual job, say working in a factory or on a farm, or more likely to be one in which your knowledge and thinking skills are more valuable than your physical ones? Education spends much of its time developing your thinking and critical skills, teaching you how to access, work with, and develop information. Therefore, education can be seen to be another way in which information plays a central role in society.

The assumption that the developments outlined above have occurred, and have significant implications for society as a whole, is summed up in the idea of the *information society*. This concept suggests that our society is structured around, and relies upon, the efficient gathering of, and use of, information. Importantly, the concept of the information society only matters if it is assumed that this was not always the case; that is, that this is a recent development, and is therefore a specifically contemporary phenomenon. It is argued that hundreds of years ago, when the majority of the population lived in rural areas and were involved in manual labour such as farming, information as a commodity was nowhere near as significant as it is now. Similarly, after the industrial revolution, when thousands of people ended up moving to the cities and working in factories, technology became important but, still, few workers spent much time manipulating information. The information society, then, is usually placed within this historical context, where links between technology and society are seen as significant. This is why the concept of the 'information society' is often equated with new media, but it is important to be aware that the two are not the same, and nor are they inevitably linked. New media are a set of *technologies* (usually thought of as the internet and digital technologies; see Chapter 18), although 'the lines between "new" and "old" are hard to draw' (Flew 2005: 4); the information society, on the other hand, depicts *social* change, in which globalisation and convergence are seen to have altered how societies function and interact. While many argue that the one is the consequence of the other, this is by no means proven, and, considering debates persist concerning both of these terms, offering evidence for their interdependence is difficult.

The information society is an idea which has its origins in economics and sociology, when various people tried to make sense of how society was changing in response to globalisation and capitalism. So, it is not a theory whose origins lie in media studies, but the media has been seen as a central part of the new age, as they are industries based around the collection and distribution of information. In these ways, the media turns information into products. Unfortunately, different people call the information society different things: it is linked to Daniel Bell's concept of the 'post-industrial society' (1973); Alvin Toffler calls what we are in now a 'Third Wave economy' (1980), after the First (agrarian) and Second (industrial) Waves; Manuel Castells calls it a 'network society' (1996), as does van Dijk (2006), which places focus on the networks which carry information as defining society, rather than the information itself; Anthony Giddens refers to a 'knowledge/service economy' (2007: xii) which places emphasis on the kinds of jobs most people do. What all this demonstrates is how these ideas are up for debate, and that while there may be disagreement over the exact nature of the society we currently live in, there is an assumption that there is *something* which defines it as different to those from the past.

Of course, there are some people who question the validity of this idea, and Frank Webster, the author of this reading, is one of them. Lash, for example, argues that all that has happened is that the knowledge of 'traditional' skills has merely been replaced by 'discursive knowledge' (2002: 141) which is abstract, simplified, and not really of much use in society. In that sense, we are now overwhelmed with information for information's sake, and, as individuals, we end up being disempowered because it is difficult to decide what is the most useful information for us, and we do not know what to do with the information we do have. For Zygmunt Bauman, this means we live in an 'individualized society' (2001). An ongoing question about the information society is the extent it can be seen to define the *whole* of society: that is, what about those people who lack access to information, or whose lives are relatively unchanged by it? It is an oversimplification to assume that *everyone* uses the internet regularly, when costs and technological limitations mean access is not equal, either globally or nationally. This 'digital divide' (van Dijk 2005: 9–26) not only questions how universal such changes are, but also suggests that lack of access to information might be a powerful way for social distinctions to be upheld. Such distinctions might apply in the fields of work, health, democracy and identity (see Ducatel et al. 2000 for chapters on these areas), amongst others, with the implication that the assumption that the information society exists ignores a whole range of everyday processes which the majority of people engage in. What this means is that while it is tempting to see the information society as a fact, especially if you regularly engage with all the informational technologies mentioned earlier in this introduction, it should instead be seen as a theory of media, technology and society, whose appropriateness is still contested. Indeed, it is precisely this question which is at the core of the Webster reading in this chapter.

INTRODUCTION TO THE READING

Frank Webster is one of the principal thinkers in debates about the information society. He is a professor of sociology, and the leading editor of *The Information Society Reader* (2004). This reading comes from *Theories of the Information Society*, which is probably the foremost book in the field, which many other authors refer to. It is so central to these debates that there have been three editions of the book: the first came out in 1995, the second (which this reading comes from) in 2002, and a third edition was published in 2006. These various editions have allowed Webster to update his thinking in response to what is going on in the world, as well as respond to articles and books written by other people. Again, this shows how theory is a process and a dialogue, which is being constantly developed in response to the ideas of others. You might want to compare the three editions of the book, to see how Webster's thinking has changed.

In this reading, Webster questions the methods used by many writers to demonstrate that the information society exists. He examines work by many authors, and finds that their evidence can be categorised in various ways. He then shows how there are problems with each of these approaches, which questions the validity of the assumption of the existence of the information society. In this way, Webster is examining the *methods* employed by various people, questioning *how* they collate and assess the evidence they offer for their argument. This interest in methods is evident in many readings in this book, and debates persist about how best to make sense of the world around us. In critiquing other authors Webster is keen to question the 'common sense' assumption that the information society exists; he insists that, rather than this being taken as a given, it must be shown to be so. Thus he places these ideas in their historical context, and questions whether the differences many authors cite are as significant as is often assumed.

It is important to bear in mind that while Webster questions the methods of these authors, that does not necessarily mean he thinks they are *wrong*. That is, in showing that it is hard to prove that the information society exists, Webster is not arguing that it, in fact, does not; instead, he is arguing that the methods used to reach this conclusion are flawed. In a sense, he is agreeing with their conclusions, but finding issue with how those conclusions were reached. This is an important idea because it shows that when authors critique or criticise others, they do not necessarily think they are wrong (although some do); instead, it might merely be a call for a more rigorous and convincing way of demonstrating conclusions. For Webster, working out how best to show that the information society exists is useful because it forces us to think about what we mean by the term, for we can only show something if we have an idea of what it is we are trying to show. Many people use the term 'information society' in different ways, which renders the concept fairly useless. In calling for a more concrete use of the idea, as well as convincing evidence to show its applicability, Webster is arguing for a more useful and worthwhile definition, which will then offer an excellent grounding for future researchers to work from.

READING

1

Frank Webster

The idea of an information society

Before we can adequately appreciate different approaches to understanding informational trends and issues nowadays, we need to pay attention to the definitions which are brought into play by participants in the debates. It is especially helpful to examine at the outset what those who refer to an information society mean when they evoke this term. The insistence of those who subscribe to this concept, and their assertion that our time is one marked by its novelty, cries out for analysis, more urgently perhaps than those scenarios which contend that the status quo remains. Hence the primary aim of this chapter is to ask: what do people mean when they refer to an information society? Later I comment on the different ways in which contributors perceive 'information' itself. As we shall see – here, in the very conception of the phenomenon which underlies all discussion – there are distinctions which echo the divide between information society theorists who announce the novelty of the present and informatisation thinkers who recognise the force of the past weighing on today's developments.

2

Definitions of the information society

What strikes one in reading the literature on the information society is that so many writers operate with undeveloped definitions of their subject. They write copiously about particular features of the information society, but are curiously vague about their operational criteria. Eager to make sense of changes in information, they rush to interpret these in terms of different forms of economic production, new forms of social interaction, innovative processes of production or whatever. As they do so, however, they often fail to establish in what ways and why information is becoming more central today, so critical indeed that it is ushering in a new type of society. Just what is it about information that makes so many scholars think that it is at the core of the modern age?

3

We may distinguish five definitions of an information society, each of which presents criteria for identifying the new. These are:

- technological
- economic
- occupational
- spatial
- cultural

NOTES

1 ## Structure

Webster begins by noting that certain kinds of analysis can only be carried out once other work is done. That is, theorising rests on prior theorising, which offers suitable tools for future work. Here Webster insists on defining terms; this is something you may have been required to do in class. It is certainly something you will be marked on in assignments. Ensuring that definitions of key terms are understood is vital, otherwise different people may be talking about quite different things.

Writing Style

See how Webster lays the structure of his writing bare, noting what is to come in his book, and offering an overall structure which (it is hoped) makes it easier for you to understand where he is going.

Content

Immediately, the fact that different people use the term 'information society' differently is noted. You might find this a frustrating aspect of theory; instead, you should see this as one of the main points of theory, because if definitive, straightforward answers could be found, there is not much point talking about things. It is also important to get a sense of the range of ways in which a term might be used so you can think through where *you* stand in such debates.

2 ## Content

The criticism Webster makes here is one you might have come across in assignment feedback. He notes that it is a problem that so many people insist that the information society is a key component in modern societies, not because they have gone out and found this to be the case, but because as lots of other people say it, 'it must be true'. Questioning what seem like common-sense statements such as these is central to theory. Note, however, that while Webster is questioning the assumptions others are making, he is not necessarily saying they are wrong; what he is saying is that their points might be valid, but how they *demonstrate* those points is questionable.

3 ## Content

The five-point bullet list is now one of the primary ways many people approach debates about the information society, and so is a seminal model. This is not to say that there is no debate about them, but to say that such debates almost always refer to Webster's list, because it is known that most people know it.

READING

4

These need not be mutually exclusive, though theorists emphasise one or other factors in presenting their particular scenarios. However, what these definitions share is the conviction that quantitative changes in information are bringing into being a qualitatively new sort of social system, the information society. In this way each definition reasons in much the same way: there is more information nowadays, therefore we have an information society. As we shall see, there are serious difficulties with this *ex post facto* reasoning.

5

There is a sixth definition of an information society which is distinctive in so far as its main claim is not that there is more information today (there obviously is), but rather that the character of information is such as to have transformed how we live. The suggestion here is that *theoretical knowledge/information* is at the core of how we conduct ourselves these days. This definition, one which is singularly qualitative in kind, is not much favoured by information society proponents, though it may be the most persuasive argument for the appropriateness of the information society label. Let us look more closely at these definitions in turn.

6

Technological

Technological conceptions centre on an array of innovations that have appeared since the late 1970s. New technologies are one of the most visible indicators of new times, and accordingly are frequently taken to signal the coming of an information society. These include cable and satellite television, computer to computer communications, personal computers (PCs), new office technologies, notably online information services and word processors, and CD.Rom facilities. The suggestion is, simply, that such a volume of technological innovations must lead to a reconstitution of the social world because its impact is so profound.

7

During the late 1970s and early 1980s commentators got excited about the 'mighty micro's' capacity to revolutionise our way of life (Evans, 1979; Martin, 1978), and none more so than the world's leading futurist, Alvin Toffler (1980). His suggestion, in·a memorable metaphor, is that, over time, the world has been decisively shaped by three waves of technological innovation, each as unstoppable as the mightiest tidal force. The first was the agricultural revolution and the second the industrial revolution. The third is the information revolution that is engulfing us now and which presages a new way of living (which, attests Toffler, will turn out fine if only we ride with the wave).

NOTES

4   **Writing Style**

You may note that this is not the first time that Webster mentions 'theorists' without saying exactly who he is talking about. Do you think this is a helpful approach?

Context

By repeatedly referring to other theorists, Webster is placing his work in a particular academic context, and therefore noting how his ideas draw on, and respond to, those of others.

5   ## Content

Webster has referred to qualitative approaches a couple of times here; you should ensure you understand the differences between quantitative and qualitative methods.

6   **Writing Style**

Why does Webster include the word 'simply' here? Is it to signal his intention to make things easily understandable for the reader? Or does it imply an oversimplification, which must therefore be examined and critiqued?

7   ## Context

Webster summarises Toffler's ideas very briefly here. Do you feel he gives enough context for you to follow the argument? What does he assume readers already know about Toffler? If you feel you need more context, you should investigate Toffler's work.

Writing Style

Note that, in this and subsequent paragraphs, Webster refers in detail to other writers and theorists, specifying which ones he is talking about. This is in contrast to his introductory paragraphs, where he dealt with the topic much more generally.

READING

8

More recently, futurism's enthusiasms have been boosted by computing's capacity to transform telecommunications, to in effect merge the two technologies (Toffler, 1990). It is this spread of computer communications technologies (e-mail, data and text communications, online information exchange, etc.) that currently inspires most speculation about a new society in the making (Negroponte, 1995; Gates, 1995; Dertouzos, 1997). The rapid growth of the Internet especially, with its capacities for simultaneously promoting economic success, education and the democratic process, has stimulated much commentary. Media regularly feature accounts of the arrival of an information 'superhighway' on which the populace must become adept at driving. Authoritative voices are raised to announce that 'a new order . . . is being forced upon an unsuspecting world by advances in telecommunications. The future is being born in the so-called *information superhighways* . . . [and] anyone bypassed by these highways faces ruin' (Angell, 1995, p. 10).

9

More soberly, the spread of national, international and genuinely global information exchanges between and within banks, corporations, governments, universities and voluntary bodies indicates a similar trend towards the establishment of a technological infrastructure that allows instant computer communications at any time of day in any place that is suitably equipped (Connors, 1993).

10

Most academic analysts, while avoiding the exaggerated language of futurists and politicians, have nonetheless adopted what is at root a similar approach (Feather, 1998; Hill, 1999). For instance, from Japan there have been attempts to measure the growth of Joho Shakai (Information Society) since the 1960s (Duff et al., 1996). The Japanese Ministry of Posts and Telecommunications (MPT) commenced a census in 1975 which endeavours to track changes in the volume (e.g. numbers of telephone messages) and vehicles (e.g. penetration of telecommunications equipment) of information using sophisticated techniques (Ito, 1991, 1994). In Britain, a much respected school of thought has devised a neo-Schumpeterian approach to change. Combining Schumpeter's argument that major technological innovations bring about 'creative destruction' with Kondratieffs theme of 'long waves' of economic development, these researchers contend that information and communications technologies represent the establishment of a new epoch (Freeman, 1987) which will be uncomfortable during its earlier phases, but over the longer term will be economically beneficial. This new 'techno-economic paradigm' constitutes the 'Information Age' which is set to mature early in the twenty-first century (Hall and Preston, 1988).

NOTES

8 ## Context

This assumption that the internet is changing society – especially democracy – for the better is a common one. However, we have to be cautious, and it is this caution which Webster notes. Global inequalities in new media certainly question to what extent such advances are helping *everyone*, and issues of ownership and control mean that the access and freedom which the internet is often seen to herald might be overstated. Note that Webster begins his next paragraph 'soberly': that is, he invites everyone to calm down a bit and not get overexcited about the effects of new media.

9 ## Writing Style

Note the 'genuinely' here; this clearly signals Webster's distinction between *actual* social changes and those that are just assumed.

10 ## Content

It is assumed here that you know who Schumpeter and Kondratieff are. While it is worthwhile finding this information out, it is also worthwhile seeing if you can make sense of the argument without this information. When reading, you will always encounter names you do not know; rather than fearing this, you should try to work out how essential they are to understanding the whole.

Structure

Note how many ideas and thinkers are crammed into this paragraph. Summarising a large amount of material in a short space, by seeing the links between various thinkers, is an efficient way of showing your understanding of a topic.

READING

11

It has to be conceded that, commonsensically, these definitions of the information society do seem appropriate. After all, if it is possible to see a 'series of inventions' (Landes, 1969) – steam power, the internal combustion engine, electricity, the flying shuttle – as the key characteristic of the 'industrial society', then why not accept the virtuoso developments in ICT as evidence of a new type of society? As John Naisbitt (1984) puts it: 'Computer technology is to the information age what mechanization was to the industrial revolution' (p. 28). And why not?

12

It may seem obvious that these technologies are valid as distinguishing features of a new society, but when one probes further one cannot but be struck also by the vagueness of technology in most of these comments. Asking for an empirical measure – in *this* society *now* how much ICT is there and how far does this take us towards qualifying for information society status? How much ICT is required in order to identify an information society? Asking simply for a usable measure, one quickly becomes aware that a good many of those who emphasise technology are not able to provide us with anything so mundanely real-worldly or testable. ICTs, it begins to appear, are everywhere – and nowhere too.

13

This problem of measurement, and the associated difficulty of stipulating the point on the technological scale at which a society is judged to have entered an information age, is surely central to any acceptable definition of a distinctively new type of society. It is ignored by popular futurists: the new technologies are announced and it is unproblematically presumed that this in itself heralds the information society. This issue is, surprisingly, also bypassed by other scholars who yet assert that ICT is the major index of an information society. They are content to describe in general terms technological innovations, somehow presuming that this is enough to distinguish the new society.

Another objection to technological definitions of the information society is very frequently made. Critics object to those who assert that, in a given era, technologies are first invented and then subsequently *impact* on the society, thereby impelling people to respond by adjusting to the new. Technology in these versions is privileged above all else, hence it comes to identify an entire social world: the Steam Age, the Age of the Automobile, the Atomic Age (Dickson, 1974).

14

The central objection here is not that this is unavoidably technologically determinist – in that technology is regarded as the prime social dynamic – and as such an oversimplification of processes of change. It most certainly is this, but more important is that it relegates into an entirely separate division social, economic and political dimensions of technological innovation. These follow from, and are subordinate to, the premier league of technology which appears to be self-perpetuating, though it leaves its impress on all aspects of society.

NOTES

11 Content

Webster acknowledges the allure of common-sense approaches here. In the introduction to this book, different kinds of theorising were outlined, including common-sense approaches. It is Webster's intention to show the attraction of such thinking, while also showing what flaws it has.

12 Content

What Webster is arguing here is that you can only define an information society if you have some measurement which a society must reach to enter that category; you must also, therefore, have an idea of what is *not* an information society. His criticisms are quantitative ones, for he desires a way to *measure* different societies. For you, what is it that might distinguish advanced societies from others? Can you give Webster the criteria he seeks?

13 Context

Throughout these paragraphs, Webster is attempting to relate technological change to social change. This relationship is a key one in media studies, which is often interested in how society is affected by, and inflected through, technological and cultural forms. He raises the valuable questions: what comes first, the technology or the change?

14 Content

Webster distinguishes between the social, the economic and the political here. This is not to say they are utterly unrelated, but it is to say that it is a problem to unthinkingly conflate them. You might want to think about the media theories you have come across, and see whether their focus is the social, the economic, or the political. In addition, how do these aspects relate to research methods?

15

But it is demonstratively the case that technology is not aloof from the social realm in this way. On the contrary, it is an integral part of the social. For instance, research and development decisions express priorities and from these value judgements particular types of technology are produced (e.g. military projects received substantially more funding than health work for much of the time in the twentieth century – not surprisingly a consequence is state-of-the-art weapon systems which dwarf the advances of treatment say of the common cold). Many studies have shown how technologies bear the impress of social values, whether it be in the architectural design of bridges in New York, where heights were set that would prevent public transit systems accessing certain areas; the manufacture of cars which testify to the values of private ownership, presumptions about family size (typically two adults, two children), attitudes towards the environment (profligate use of non-renewable energy alongside pollution), status symbols (the Porsche, the Beetle, the Skoda), and individual rather than public forms of transit; or the construction of houses which are not just places to live, but also expressions of ways of life, prestige and power relations, and preferences for a variety of lifestyles. This being so, how can it be acceptable to take what is regarded as an asocial phenomenon (technology) and assert that this then defines the social world? It is facile (one could as well take any elemental factor and ascribe society with its name – the Oxygen Society, the Water Society, the Potato Age) and it is false (technology is in truth an intrinsic part of society) and therefore ICT's separate and supreme role in social change is dubious.

16

Economic

This approach charts the growth in economic worth of informational activities. If one is able to plot an increase in the proportion of gross national product (GNP) accounted for by the information business, then logically there comes a point at which one may declare the achievement of an information economy. Once the greater part of economic activity is taken up by information activity rather than say subsistence agriculture or industrial manufacture, then it follows that we may speak of an information society (Jonscher, 1999).

In principle straightforward, but in practice an extraordinarily complex exercise, much of the pioneering work was done by Fritz Machlup (1902–83) of Princeton University (Machlup, 1962); His identification of information industries such as education, law, publishing, media and computer manufacture, and his attempt to estimate their changing economic worth, has been refined by Marc Porat (1977b).

15 ### Structure

This is one of Webster's few examples. Does it help you understand his argument?

Context

We often think of technology as arising naturally from scientific development and research. But, as Webster notes here, such development requires funding, and that funding is often given by bodies (such as governments) which have particular priorities and/or assumptions. How we view society, then, makes certain kind of technological developments more likely than others, and so we should not see science and technology as divorced from the vagaries of society and culture.

Writing Style

This writing is more argumentative and strident than much else in the chapter. Do you find it convincing and/or acceptable? In addition, why might it be at this point in the reading that Webster decides to write in this way?

16 ## Content

In these two paragraphs Webster makes a useful statement about the complexity of theory. That is, in the first paragraph he offers a *theoretical* way of defining an information society; in the second paragraph he states that this theory is extremely difficult to put into practice. This is not to invalidate the theory, but it is to note that it is often difficult to work out what are the best ways of testing whether theories can be applied to 'real world' situations.

READING

17

Porat distinguished the primary and secondary information sectors of the economy, the former being susceptible to ready economic valuation since it had an ascribable market price, the latter, harder to price but nonetheless essential to all modern-day organisation, involving informational activities within companies and state institutions (for example, the personnel wings of a company, the research and development (R&D) sections of a business). In this way Porat is able to distinguish the two informational sectors, then to consolidate them, separate out the non-informational elements of the economy, and, by reaggregating national economic statistics, is able to conclude that, with almost half the United States' GNP accounted for by these combined informational sectors, 'the United States is now an information-based economy'. As such it is an 'information society [where] the major arenas of economic activity are the information goods and service producers, and the public and private (secondary information sector) bureaucracies' (Porat, 1978, p. 32).

18

This quantification of the economic significance of information is an impressive achievement. It is not surprising that those convinced of the emergence of an information society have routinely turned to Machlup and especially Porat as authoritative demonstrations of a rising curve of information activity, one set to lead the way to a new age. However, there are difficulties too with the economics of information approach (Monk, 1989, pp. 39–63). A major one is that, behind the weighty statistical tables that are resonant of objective demonstration there is a great deal of hidden interpretation and value judgement as to how to construct categories and what to include and exclude from the information sector.

19

In this regard what is particularly striking is that, in spite of their differences, both Machlup and Porat create encompassing categories of the information sector which exaggerate its economic worth. There are reasons to query their validity. For example, Machlup includes in his 'knowledge industries' the 'construction of information buildings', the basis for which presumably is that building for, say, a university or library is different from that intended for the warehousing of tea and coffee. But how then is one to allocate the many buildings which, once constructed, change purpose (many university departments are located in erstwhile domestic houses, some even in former warehouses)?

Again, Porat is at some pains to identify the 'quasi-firm' embedded within a non-informational enterprise. But is it acceptable, from the correct assumption that R&D in a petrochemical company involves informational activity, to separate this from the manufacturing element for statistical purposes? It is surely likely that the activities are blurred, with the R&D section intimately tied to production wings, and any separation for mathematical reasons is unfaithful to its role. More generally, when Porat examines his 'secondary information sector' he in fact splits every industry into the informational and non-informational domains. But

17   Content

This is a statement about research method; Webster includes it so you can think about how Porat came to his conclusions, which you might not necessarily think is the best way of approaching the subject. Indeed, the next few paragraphs are all concerns about method.

18   Writing Style

Why does Webster include his praise that this work is an 'impressive achievement'? Is such a commendation similar in writing style to the rest of this reading?

Context

There is an ongoing debate about whether research can ever be objective, and it is clear here what Webster's position is on the subject. But note how this sentence is written: rather than a damning critique, the objection is presented much more subtly. Why is this?

19   Content

There is much to absorb in these sections. They involve detailed analysis of readings you are likely not to have come across. Sometimes references to other readings will encourage you to go and read them first-hand; Webster offers enough detail here that this is unnecessary. But note the complexities that are raised by these debates about method. Webster is not arguing that Machlup and Porat's distinctions between different informational realms are wrong; he is stating that such distinctions are always open to debate and are inevitably a consequence of the researcher's own priorities. Webster does not offer a better set of definitions, because his own would, too, be

READING

19

(continued)

such divisions between the 'thinking' and the 'doing' are extraordinarily hard to accept – where does one put operation of computer numerical control systems or the line management functions which are an integral element of production? The objection here is that Porat divides, arbitrarily, within industries to chart the 'secondary information sector' as opposed to the 'non-informational' realm. Such objections may not invalidate the findings of Machlup and Porat, but they are a reminder of the unavoidable intrusion of value judgements in the construction of their statistical tables. As such they support scepticism as regards the idea of an emergent information economy.

Another difficulty is that the aggregated data inevitably homogenise very disparate economic activities. In the round it may be possible to say that growth in the economic worth of advertising and television is indicative of an information society, but one is left with an urge to distinguish between informational activities on qualitative grounds. The enthusiasm of the information economists to put a price tag on everything has the unfortunate consequence of failing to let us know the really valuable dimensions of the information sector. This search to differentiate between quantitative and qualitative indices of an information society is not pursued by Machlup and Porat, though it is obvious that the multi-million sales of *The Sun* cannot be equated with – still less be regarded as more informational, though doubtless it is of more economic value – the four hundred thousand circulation of *The Financial Times*. It is a distinction to which I shall return, but one which suggests the possibility that we could have a society in which, as measured by GNP, informational activity is of great weight, but which in terms of the springs of economic, social and political life is of little consequence.

20

A nation of couch potatoes and Disney-style pleasure seekers consuming images night and day?

21

Occupational

This is the approach most favoured by sociologists. It is also one closely associated with the work of Daniel Bell (1973), who is the most important theorist of 'post-industrial society' (a term virtually synonymous with information society, and used as such in Bell's own writing). Here the occupational structure is examined over time and patterns of change observed. The suggestion is that we have achieved an information society when the preponderance of occupations is found in information work. The decline of manufacturing employment and the rise of service sector employment is interpreted as the loss of manual jobs and its

19
(continued)

personal in some way. This symbolises an important factor of looking at research, which is that there will always be debates about the best way to carry out research projects. It is unlikely that we will ever come to a conclusion that everyone is satisfied with. Instead, what matters is whether approaches and methods can be *justified*, and whether researchers acknowledge and *reflect* on the limitations and problems in their approaches. This shows the ongoing debate about how to carry out research and which theory is engaged in. It also shows that you should not be trying to find out the 'right' way that research is being carried out or for topics to be theorised; instead, you should be interested in whether such approaches are appropriate and reflected upon.

20 **Writing Style**

This is a very odd way to end this section. What is Webster trying to say, and why is this sentence a question?

21 **Context**

In referring to sociologists, Webster is noting that different academic disciplines have different approaches, assumptions and interests. This often causes conflict in a subject like media studies, which draws on ideas from a range of disciplines such as sociology, literary studies, politics and economics. There is always much discussion about interdisciplinary work, drawing together researchers and ideas from a range of subjects; in practice, this happens rarely, as the disciplines are defined by their differences. In reading media theory, then, you should be aware of which assumptions are underpinning a writer's work, and these can often be related to the discipline their background is in.

21
(continued)

replacement with white-collar work. Since the raw material of non-manual labour is information (as opposed to the brawn and dexterity plus machinery characteristic of manual labour), then substantial increases in such informational work can be said to announce the arrival of an information society.

There is prima facie evidence for this: in western Europe, Japan and North America over 70 per cent of the workforce is now found in the service sector of the economy, and white-collar occupations are now a majority. On these grounds alone it would seem plausible to argue that we inhabit an information society, since the 'predominant group [of occupations] consists of information workers' (Bell, 1979, p. 183).

22

An emphasis on occupational change as the marker of an information society has displaced once dominant concerns with technology in recent years. It should also be appreciated that this conception of the information society is quite different from that which suggests it is information and communications *technologies* which distinguish the new age. A focus on occupational change is one which stresses the transformative power of information itself rather than the influence of information technologies, information being what is drawn upon and generated in occupations or embodied in people through education and experiences. Charles Leadbeater (1999) titled his book to highlight the insight that it is information which is foundational in the present epoch. 'Living on thin air' was once a familiar admonition given by the worldly wise to those reluctant to earn a living by the sweat of their brows. But all such advice is now outdated, Leadbeater arguing that this is exactly how to make one's livelihood in the information age. *Living on Thin Air* (1999) proclaims that 'thinking smart', being 'inventive', and having the capacity to develop and exploit 'networks' is actually the key to the new 'weightless' economy (Coyne, 1997; Dertouzos, 1997), since wealth production comes, not from physical effort, but from 'ideas, knowledge, skills, talent and creativity' (Leadbeater, 1999, p. 18). His book highlights examples of such successes: designers, deal-makers, image-creators, musicians, biotechnologists, genetic engineers and niche-finders abound.

23

Leadbeater puts into popular parlance what more scholarly thinkers argue as a matter of course. A range of influential writers, from Robert Reich (1991), Peter Drucker (1993), to Manuel Castells (1996–8), suggest that the economy today is led and energised by people whose major characteristic is the capacity to manipulate information. Preferred terms vary, from 'symbolic analysts', 'knowledge experts', to 'informational labour', but one message is constant. Today's movers and shakers are those whose work involves creating and using information.

NOTES

22   ## Context

Webster is noting that definitions have changed: that is, what is seen as important in theory develops over time. Indeed, Webster's book was published a few years ago, and things may have changed again by now. For this reason, it is always important that you check when something was published to put it in context. This is not to say that anything more than a few years old should be disregarded, but it does help for you to know the context that the writing arises from.

Writing Style

What is implied by the term 'worldly wise'; do you think Webster attaches a positive or a negative connotation to it?

Content

Think about the career you want to go into; is it one of these areas of the 'weightless' economy that Webster refers to? Do you think more people have such jobs than those who 'earn a living by the sweat of their brows'? What do these differences tell us?

23   ### Writing Style

Think about the implications of various terms here. What is the difference between 'popular parlance' and the ways in which 'scholarly thinkers' write? Which do you think Webster prefers?

Content

This shows the difficulty that, quite often, different thinkers use different words to refer to the same idea.

READING

24

Intuitively it may seem right that a coal miner is to industrial as a tour guide is to information society, but in fact the allocation of occupations to these distinct categories is a judgement call that involves much discretion. The end product – a bald statistical figure giving a precise percentage of 'information workers' – hides the complex processes by which researchers construct their categories and allocate people to one or another. As Porat puts it: when 'we assert that certain occupations are primarily engaged in the manipulation of symbols. . . . It is a distinction of degree, not of kind' (Porat, 1977a, p. 3). For example, railway signal workers must have a stock of knowledge about tracks and timetables, about roles and routines. They need to communicate with other signal workers down the line, with station personnel and engine drivers, they are required to 'know the block' of their own and other cabins, must keep a precise and comprehensive ledger of all traffic which moves through their area, and have little need of physical strength to pull levers since the advent of modern equipment. Yet the railway signaller is, doubtless, a manual worker of the 'industrial age'. Conversely, people who come to repair the photocopier may know little about products other than the one for which they have been trained, may well have to work in hot, dirty and uncomfortable circumstances, and may need considerable strength to move heavy machinery and replace damaged parts. Yet they will undoubtedly be classified as 'information workers' since their work with new age machinery suits Porat's interpretations. The point here is simple: we need to be sceptical of conclusive figures which are the outcomes of researchers' perceptions of where occupations are to be most appropriately categorised.

25

A consequence of this categorisation is often a failure to identify the more strategically central information occupations. While the methodology may provide us with a picture of greater amounts of information work taking place, it does not offer any means of differentiating the most important dimensions of information work. The pursuit of a quantitative measure of information work disguises the possibility that the growth of certain types of information occupation may have particular consequences for social life. This distinction is especially pertinent as regards occupational measures since some commentators seek to characterise an information society in terms of the 'primacy of the professions' (Bell, 1973), some as the rise to prominence of an elite 'technostructure' which wields 'organised knowledge' (Galbraith, 1972), while still others focus on alternative sources of strategically central information occupations.

It has to be said that counting the number of 'information workers' in a society tells us nothing about the hierarchies – and associated variations in power and esteem – of these people. For example, it could be argued that the crucial issue has been the growth of computing and telecommunications engineers since these may exercise a decisive influence over the pace of technological innovation. A similar, perhaps even greater, rate of expansion in social workers to handle problems of an ageing population, increased family dislocation and juvenile delinquency may have little or nothing to do with an information society, though undoubtedly social workers would be classified with ICT engineers as 'information workers'.

24   Content

Again, the point is made here that categorisations which appear to be objective are, in fact, often questionable and depend on the assumptions of the person making them.

25   Content

Webster makes the link here between the theories and evidence put forward by various thinkers, and their consequences for society. That is, the ways in which this topic is theorised matters because it is seen to have implications for society. As has been noted for many readings in this book, the relationships between media and society are key to media studies; therefore, because theorising media may have implications for society, we need to be really careful about how we go about it.

READING

26

Perhaps we can better understand this need to qualitatively distinguish between groups of 'information workers' by reflecting on study by social historian Harold Perkin. In *The Rise of Professional Society* (1989) Perkin argues that the history of Britain since 1880 may be written largely as the rise to pre-eminence of 'professionals' who rule by virtue of 'human capital created by education and enhanced by . . . the exclusion of the unqualified' (p. 2). Perkin contends that certified expertise has been 'the organising principle of post-war society' (p. 406), the expert displacing once-dominant groups (working-class organisations, capitalist entrepreneurs and the landed aristocracy) and their outdated ideals (of co-operation and solidarity, of property and the market, and of the paternal gentleman) with the professional's ethos of service, certification and efficiency. To be sure, professionals within the private sector argue fiercely with those in the public, but Perkin insists that this is an internecine struggle, one within 'professional society', which decisively excludes the non-expert from serious participation and shares fundamental assumptions (notably the primacy of trained expertise and reward based on merit).

27

Alvin Gouldner's discussion of the 'new class' provides an interesting complement to Perkin's. Gouldner identifies a new type of employee that has expanded in the twentieth century, a 'new class' that is 'composed of intellectuals and technical intelligensia' (Gouldner, 1978, p. 153) which, while in part self-seeking and often subordinate to powerful groups, can also contest the control of established business and party leaders. Despite these potential powers; the 'new class' is itself divided in various ways. A key division is between those who are for the most part technocratic and conformist and the humanist intellectuals who are critical and emancipatory in orientation. To a large extent this difference is expressed in the conflicts identified by Harold Perkin between private and public sector professionals. For instance, we may find that accountants in the private sector are conservative while there is a propensity for humanistic intellectuals to be more radical.

28

My point here is that both Gouldner and Perkin are identifying particular changes within the realm of information work which have especially important consequences for society as a whole. To Gouldner the 'new class' can provide us with vocabularies to discuss and debate the direction of social change, while to Perkin the professionals create new ideals for organising social affairs. If one is searching for an index of the information society in these thinkers, one will be directed to the quality of the contribution of certain groups. Whether one agrees or not with either of these interpretations, the challenge to definitions of an information society on the basis of a count of raw numbers of 'information workers' should be clear. To thinkers such as Perkin and Gouldner, the quantitative change is not the main issue. Indeed, as a proportion of the population the groups they lay emphasis upon, while they have expanded, remain distinct minorities.

NOTES

26 ## Structure

Notice the structural marker here. Webster makes it clear that his intention in using Perkin as an example is to better understand the ideas outlined in the previous paragraph. This links these two parts of the reading together, and offers hope to any reader that might be a bit confused or unsure about some of the ideas.

Writing Style

Notice how Webster distances himself from the ideas he is summarising, by saying 'Perkin argues', 'Perkin contends', and 'Perkin insists'. That is, he is making it clear these are Perkin's ideas, and not his own. Whether Webster agrees with them or not is not known at the moment, but he is ensuring the reader knows that what he is doing is offering a summary of someone else's work.

27 ## Structure

There is a clear and helpful structure here, which Webster employs to lead you through the various discussions he is outlining. After the summary of Perkin we get Gouldner's ideas as an 'interesting complement'. That is, Gouldner's work adds more to Perkin's. If Perkin and Gouldner said pretty much the same thing they may as well be dealt with in the same paragraph; the fact that they are, initially at least, in different paragraphs shows that Webster feels they are of equal importance and so deserve a paragraph each. In the next paragraph Webster brings the two together, dealing with what they have in common. This structure is a useful way of dealing with a number of writers very succinctly, and could be one you adopt in literature reviews or surveys that you are required to write.

28 ## Writing Style

Webster's use of 'my point here' helps tell us that he is moving from merely summarising Perkin and Gouldner to his own analysis of it; this distinction between what others are saying and what he is saying is important, so we can be clear which ideas belong to which writer.

Content

In Note 5, the distinction between qualitative and quantitative methods was mentioned. Here the importance of quantitative approaches is downplayed: that is, counting does not help us answer the question, and we can say we are in an 'information society' even if only a minority of people are engaged in work that might be categorised as such. Are you convinced by this? Is society significantly different even if only a few people are actively engaged in those processes which are seen to symbolise that difference?

READING

29

Spatial

This conception of the information society, while it does draw on economics and sociology, has at its core the geographer's distinctive stress on space. Here the major emphasis is on information networks which connect locations and in consequence can have profound effects on the organisation of time and space. It has become an especially popular index of the information society in recent years as information networks have become prominent features of social organisation.

30

It is usual to stress the centrality of information networks that may link together different locations within and between an office, a town, a region, a continent, indeed the entire world. As the electricity grid runs through an entire country to be accessed at will by individuals with the appropriate connections, so too may we imagine now a 'wired society' operating at the national, international and global level to provide an 'information ring main' (Barron and Curnow, 1979) to each home, shop, university and office – and even to mobile individuals who have their laptop and modem in their briefcase.

31

Increasingly we are all connected to networks of one sort or another – and they themselves are expanding their reach and capabilities in an exponential manner (Urry, 2000). We come across them personally at many levels: in electronic point of sale terminals in shops and restaurants, in accessing data across continents, in e-mailing colleagues, or in exchanging information on the Internet. We may not personally have experienced this realm of 'cyberspace', but the information ring main functions still more frantically at the level of international banks, inter-governmental agencies and corporate relationships.

NOTES

29   Context

At the beginning of the previous section Webster referred to sociologists; here it is geographers. This shows the range of disciplines media theory draws from.

30   Writing Style

Note 'it is usual'. This suggests that this approach is so common Webster does not need to tell us who says it; it is helpful, however, that he does, later, go on to refer to specific writers. This generalised approach can be seen in a later paragraph, too, with a phrase such as 'a popular idea'. You might ask, 'popular amongst whom'?

31   Writing Style

There is no evidence offered for the assertion that we are all increasingly connected to networks. You may agree with this 'common-sense' statement; but is it okay for Webster to make it without anything other than anecdotal evidence?

READING

32

A popular idea here is that the electronic highways result in a new emphasis on the flow of information (Castells, 1996), something which leads to a radical revision of time/space relations. In a 'network society' constraints of the clock and of distance have been radically relieved, the corporations and even the individual being capable of managing their affairs effectively on a global scale. Academic researchers no longer need to travel from the university to consult the Library of Congress since they can interrogate it on the Internet; the business corporation no longer needs to fly out its managers to find out what is happening in their Far East outlets because computer communications enable routine and systematic surveillance from afar. The suggestion of many is that this heralds a major transformation of our social order (Mulgan, 1991), sufficient to mark even a revolutionary change.

No one could deny that information networks are an important feature of contemporary societies: satellites do allow instantaneous communications round the globe, databases can be accessed from Oxford to Los Angeles, Tokyo and Paris, facsimile machines and interconnected computer systems are a routine part of modern businesses. Yet we may still ask: why should the presence of networks lead analysts to categorise societies as information societies? And when we ask this we encounter once again the problem of the imprecision of definitions. For instance, when is a network a network?

33

Two people speaking to one another by telephone or computer systems transmitting vast data sets through a packet-switching exchange? When an office block is 'wired' or when terminals in the home can communicate with local banks and shops? The question of what actually constitutes a network is a serious one and it raises problems not only of how to distinguish between different levels of networking, but also of how we stipulate a point at which we have entered a 'network/information society'.

34

It also raises the issue of whether we are using a technological definition of the information society – i.e. are networks being defined as technological systems? – or whether a more appropriate focus would be on the flow of information which for some writers is what distinguishes the present age. If it is the former, then we could take the spread of ISDN (integrated services digital network) technologies as an index, but few scholars offer any guidance as to how to do this. And if it is the latter, then it may reasonably be asked how much and why more volume and velocity of information flow should mark a new society.

Finally, one could argue that information networks have been around for a very long time. From at least the early days of the postal service, through to telegram and telephone facilities, much economic, social and political life is unthinkable without the establishment of such information networks. Given this long-term dependency and incremental, if accelerated, development, why should it be that only now have commentators begun to talk in terms of information societies?

NOTES

32 Context

The notion that changes in technology result in changes in society is often called 'technological determinism'; it is worth you finding out about this concept (Smith and Marx 1994). (See Chapter 10 in *this* book.) Webster does not refer to it, probably because it is an idea which falls in and out of favour: that is, his work was not written in a context where many people refer to 'technological determinism'.

33 Content

Like previous sections, Webster shows that while he agrees with the broad ideas which thinkers use to demonstrate that there is an information society, the problem is in the detail. Note that he is asking questions here, questions he does not answer. You should think about your answers to those questions, because if you do not see the problems that Webster does, perhaps then you agree with the theorists he is critiquing.

34 Content

Key in both of these paragraphs is the idea of change. That is, even if the evidence which many people offer is true, is there evidence that things have not always been like this (or, at least, have been like this for longer than is often assumed)? To argue that we live in an information society *now* requires evidence that we did not live in one *previously*; while many people give evidence of the role of information in today's society, they do not show how this is a major change from the past. It is often easy to overstate change in society, and this therefore demonstrates the importance of placing the contemporary within a historical context.

READING

35

Cultural

The final conception of an information society is perhaps the most easily acknowledged, yet the least measured. Each of us is aware, from the pattern of our everyday lives, that there has been an extraordinary increase in the information in social circulation. There is simply a great deal more of it about than ever before. Television has been in extensive use since the mid-1950s in Britain, but now its programming is pretty well round-the-clock. It has expanded from a single channel to five broadcast channels and digitalisation promises very many more. Television has been enhanced to incorporate video technologies, cable and satellite channels, and even computerised information services. PCs, access to the Internet and the palm-held computer testify to unrelenting expansion here. There is very much more radio output available now than even a decade ago, at local, national and international level. And radios are no longer fixed in the front room, but spread through the home, in the car, the office and, with the Walkman, everywhere. Movies have long been an important part of people's information environment, but movies are today very much more prevalent than ever: available still at cinema outlets, broadcast on television, readily borrowed from video rental shops, cheaply purchased from the shelves of chain stores.

36

Walk along any street and it is almost impossible to miss the advertising hoardings, the billboards, the window displays in shops. Visit any railway or bus station and one cannot but be struck by the widespread availability of paperback books and inexpensive magazines. In addition, audiotape, compact disc and radio all offer more, and more readily available music, poetry, drama, humour and education to the public. Newspapers are extensively available and a good many new titles fall on our doorsteps as free sheets. Junk mail is delivered daily.

37

All such testifies to the fact that we inhabit a media-laden society, but the informational features of our world are more thoroughly penetrative than this list suggests. It implies that new media surround us, presenting us with messages to which we may or may not respond. But in truth the informational environment is a great deal more intimate, more constitutive of us, than this suggests. Consider, for example, the informational dimensions of the clothes we wear, the styling of our hair and faces, the very ways in which nowadays we work at our image. Reflection on the complexities of fashion, the intricacy of the ways in which we design ourselves for everyday presentation, makes one aware that social intercourse nowadays involves a greater degree of informational content than previously. There has long been adornment of the body, clothing and make-up being important ways of signalling status, power and affiliation. But it is obvious that the present age has dramatically heightened the symbolic import of dress and the body. When one considers the lack of range of meaning that characterised the peasant smock which was the apparel of the majority for centuries, and the uniformity of the clothing worn by the industrial working class in and out of work up to the 1950s, then the

35 Context

You might think about the context Webster is assuming here. While it is true that the changes he cites have indeed occurred, have they done so equally and in the same way in every place? The technologies he mentions might be very common in rich, western societies, but can the same be said for all nations of the world? Similarly, have all these technologies reached everyone in western societies in the same way? Surely, some people have access to more technology, both at home and at work, than others. What is significant here is that Webster does not acknowledge that he is only talking about certain global locations. The vast majority of media theory you come across comes from western societies, and this means ways of life in large parts of the globe are rarely theorised. While this is not necessarily to criticise this approach, it is important that you are aware of it.

36 Context

You might notice that Webster does not mention the internet here, which is often seen as the most obvious example of how we now have more access to a range of media than before. This is especially odd considering it *is* mentioned elsewhere in the reading. This is likely to be because when the first edition of the book was written – 1995 – the internet was not the global presence it is today. This shows how the examples which writers refer to are historically specific, and, when carrying out reading, you should be aware of when and where something was written.

37 Content

This might be a definition of 'information' which is different from how you would use the term. Do you agree that items such as clothing are ways in which we present information about ourselves? Putting this in a historical context, is there any difference between the ways in which we use clothes for these purposes now and how this was done in the past, as Webster argues?

READING

37

(continued)

explosion of meaning in terms of dress since is remarkable. The availability of cheap and fashionable clothing, the possibilities of affording it, and the accessibility of any amount of groups with similar – and different – lifestyles and cultures all make one appreciate the informational content even of our bodies.

38

Contemporary culture is manifestly more heavily information laden than any of its predecessors. We exist in a media-saturated environment which means that life is quintessentially about symbolisation, about exchanging and receiving – or trying to exchange and resisting reception – messages about ourselves and others. It is in acknowledgement of this explosion of signification that many writers conceive of our having entered an information society. They rarely attempt to gauge this development in quantitative terms, but rather start from the 'obviousness' of our living in a sea of signs, one fuller than at any earlier epoch.

39

Paradoxically, it is perhaps this very explosion of information which leads some writers to announce, as it were, the death of the sign. Blitzed by signs all around us, designing ourselves with signs, unable to escape signs wherever we may go, the result is, oddly, a collapse of meaning. As Jean Baudrillard puts it: 'there is more and more information, and less and less meaning' (1983a, p. 95). In this view signs once had a reference (clothes, for example, signified a given status, the political statement a distinct philosophy). However, in the post-modern era we are enmeshed in such a bewildering web of signs that they lose their salience. Signs come from so many directions, and are so diverse, fast-changing and contradictory, that their power to signify is dimmed. In addition, audiences are creative, self-aware and reflective, so much so that all signs are greeted with scepticism and a quizzical eye, hence easily inverted, reinterpreted and refracted from their intended meaning. As people's knowledge through direct experience declines, it becomes evident that signs are no longer straightforwardly representative of something or someone. The notion that signs represent some 'reality' apart from themselves loses its credibility. Rather signs are self-referential: they – simulations – are all there is; They are, again to use Baudrillard's terminology, the 'hyper-reality'.

People appreciate this situation readily enough: they deride the poseur who is dressing for effect, but acknowledge that it's all artifice anyway; they are sceptical of politicians who 'manage' the media and their image through adroit public relations (PR), but accept that the whole affair is a matter of information management and manipulation. Here it is conceded that people do not hunger for any true signs because they recognise that there are no longer any truths. In these terms we have entered an age of 'spectacle' in which people realise the artificiality of signs they may be sent ('it's only the Prime Minister at his latest photo opportunity', 'it's news manufacture', 'it's Jack playing the tough guy') and in which they also acknowledge the inauthenticity of the signs they use to construct themselves ('I'll just put on my face', 'there I was adopting the "worried parent" role').

NOTES

38　Context

It is noticeable that this 'symbolisation' process that Webster refers to is one which is often equated with postmodernism (see Chapter 19). This is even more noticeable as Webster goes on to refer to Baudrillard. Why might it be that Webster does not refer to post-modernism directly here, but does mention it later? By not feeling that he needs to mention it explicitly from the start what is he assuming about you as a reader?

39　Writing Style

Throughout these paragraphs, Webster gives lots of anecdotal examples. As always, you might question the validity of these, even if you agree with some of them, or have experienced them yourself.

40

As a result signs lose their meaning and people simply take what they like from those they encounter (usually very different meanings than may have been intended at the outset). And then, in putting together signs for their homes, work and selves, happily revel in their artificiality, 'playfully' mixing different images to present no distinct meaning, but instead to derive pleasure' in parody or pastiche. In this information society we have then 'a set of meanings [which] is communicated [but which] have no meaning' (Poster, 1990, p. 63).

Experientially this idea of an information society is easily enough recognised, but as a definition of a new society it is more wayward than any of the notions we have considered. Given the absence of criteria we might use to measure the growth of signification in recent years it is difficult to see how students of postmodernism such as Mark Poster (1990) can depict the present as one characterised by a novel 'mode of information'. How can we know this other than from our sense that there is more symbolic interplay going on? And on what basis can we distinguish this society from say, that of the 1920s, other than purely as a matter of degree of difference? As we shall see, those who reflect on the 'postmodern condition' have interesting things to say about the character of contemporary culture, but as regards establishing a clear definition of the information society they are woeful.

41

Quality and quantity

Reviewing these varying definitions of the information society, what becomes clear is that they are either or both underdeveloped or imprecise. Whether it is a technological, economic, occupational, spatial or cultural conception, we are left with highly problematical notions of what constitutes, and how to distinguish, an information society.

40

Content

As in the other sections of this reading, Webster raises the problem of using anecdotal experiences as evidence of larger phenomena. More importantly, he questions how such phenomena can be measured, and how differences between the present and the past can be demonstrated. Running throughout this reading, then, is a concern with *methods* and *evidence*, which raises significant questions about the ways in which we attempt to make sense of the world.

Writing Style

Here Webster refers to a forthcoming part of his book, noting that he is going to return to the issues he has raised here.

41

Content

The final paragraph we have included in this reading is, in fact, the first paragraph of a much longer section. Note how this paragraph acts as a summary of all the sections covered before, and draws out the recurring problems which have been encountered. The book continues by taking this summary and then offering ways in which they can be dealt with or approached. In that sense, these recurring criticisms become the impetus for theorising, and this shows how theory usually draws on, and responds to, existing theory and approaches. In that sense, theory is always an ongoing *process*.

REFLECTING ON THE READING

This is a reading which spends much of its time questioning the work of other authors, and so we never really get to the gist of Webster's argument. However, Webster's categorisation of the approaches towards debates about the information society has been taken up by many authors, and it constitutes the basis on which many debates about defining such a society have been constructed since. It shows how theory arises from, and depends upon, previous theories; in this case, it also shows how theory can arise from criticising and critiquing others' theories. Do you think it is appropriate that Webster spends so much time dismantling the ideas of others?

Central to Webster's critique is the question of *method*: that is, recurring debates about *how* we go about finding things out. Many of the theories you will come across will use different methods. This is because what they are interested in varies, and methods are chosen depending on what is being found out. For example, if you are interested in the history of media, looking in archives is a good way to find material; however, if you are interested in audience responses to media, then surveys, interviews, or focus groups might be a better way to go about this. Media studies employs lots of methods, partly because different researchers are interested in different things, and partly because the subject's origins lie in many other fields, such as sociology, literature studies, and politics, and so the methods used by those subjects have been brought across to media studies. What is noticeable in this reading is that Webster engages in such a prolonged debate about methods. Much theory does not always outline its methods; indeed, quite often theorists avoid method because they are offering a theoretical model, and so it is up to someone else to decide what method can best be employed to test that model. It is important for you to be aware, though, that all theory employs *assumptions* about the world, even if these are not always explicitly expressed. Webster offers a useful way of seeing how critiquing methods can be carried out, so you might want to think about the kinds of objections he raises, and points he makes, when you are reading any theory.

Note, however, that Webster does not utterly reject the arguments put forward by many of the people he references. It is clear that he agrees that there is such a thing as an information society, and he includes much anecdotal evidence to demonstrate this. Instead, what he has a problem with are the criteria other thinkers have used to define an information society, and to demonstrate that it exists now when it previously did not. In that sense, he is finding problems with the methodological criteria adopted by these other writers. So, he believes that this phenomenon exists in the real world, but he cannot work out how to prove it. This might seem strange; if we all agree that it is common sense that the information society exists, why worry about definitively proving it? Well, because much theory spends a lot of time questioning common sense assumptions, and other kinds of evidence are usually required in order for a model to be accepted. Therefore, he is trying to work out how we can show that what we *think* is true, is *actually* true. This might seem tortuous and unnecessary, but can you see why such an activity is seen as important and vital?

Webster continually questions the objectivity of various research methods and approaches, showing that they are instead a result of the particular subjectivities of the person carrying out the research. Do you agree with him? For example, in the 'occupational' section he critiques Leadbetter's distinction between previous, manual jobs, and contemporary ones which are instead dependent on information. Do you agree with him? Or do you think there is a difference between these kinds of jobs? Would you be able to categorise occupations in this way? Perhaps more importantly, do you think it *is* possible for researchers to come up with criteria which are objective and unarguable?

You should also think about the broader implications of Webster's assertions. In stating that there is a difficulty in demonstrating what we commonsensically know to be true, and that supposed objective research is inevitably affected by the interests of the researcher, he raises questions about how we can ever research, or know, anything. If everything is subjective, then what is the point of theory and research? If all we are talking about are the particular, subjective viewpoints of specific individuals, how can any of this material be useful to society more generally? These are questions researchers and theorists continually grapple with; how do you think they might be resolved?

Key terms to explore

criteria and evidence; definitions; electronic highway; futurism; information; information economy; information society; information workers; knowledge industries; networks; post-industrial society; postmodernism; qualitative/quantitative research; space; technological determinism; technology; theoretical knowledge/information.

Key writers who are mentioned

Jean Baudrillard; Daniel Bell; Manuel Castells; Peter Drucker; John Kenneth Galbraith; Alvin Gouldner; Nikolai Kondratieff; Charles Leadbetter; Fritz Machlup; Harold Perkin; Marc Porat; Robert Reich; Joseph Schumpeter; Alvin Toffler.

RECOMMENDED READING

Toffler, Alvin (1980) *The Third Wave*, New York: Bantam Books.

Classic and influential study, with much pertinence for the study of media, although its focus on business and economics requires some effort.

van Dijk, J.A.G.M. (2006) *The Network Society: Social aspects of new media*, 2nd edition, London: Sage.

Examination of new media developments, exploring social and cultural impacts of recent technological developments, and their impact on public and private life.

Webster, F., Blom, R., Karvonen, E., Melin, H., Nordenstreng, K. and Puoskari, E. (eds) (2004) *The Information Society Reader*, London: Routledge.

Thorough collection of readings from key figures, covering both supporters and critics of the idea of the information society, plus chapters on topics such as surveillance and democracy.

PART IV

Media theory in context

CHAPTER 21

Production

Hesmondhalgh, D. (2007) *The Cultural Industries*, 2nd edition, London: Sage, pp. 3–8.

INTRODUCTION TO MEDIA INDUSTRIES

What job do you want after you have finished your studies? Many people go into media studies because they want a future career in the media: many students want to be film directors, or scriptwriters, or they enjoy doing camerawork. People always worry about wanting to go into this kind of work because there is so much competition, and only a very few people can make it to the top of their profession. Working in the media industries is often very competitive, and the vast majority of people get into it through jobs at the 'bottom end' of the industry, such as being a runner or a researcher. You may have had difficulty convincing your parents that media studies is a worthwhile topic to study, precisely because of the fears they have for the difficulties you may face. In all, working in the media industries is seen as more fraught with difficulties, harder to get into, and less secure work than that associated with many other professions.

Research, however, suggests this may not be the case in the United Kingdom. In 2007 an independent think tank called the Work Foundation produced a report called *Staying Ahead: The economic performance of the UK's creative industries* for the UK government. The report's aim was to 'see what binds the creative industries together' (2007: 8), and, by extension, to show how these industries perhaps differ from others. It takes as its definition of the creative industries the following areas: advertising; architecture; arts and antiques; crafts; design; designer fashion; film; music; performing arts; publishing; software and computer services; television and radio; video and computer games. It finds that the creative industries are a 'national asset' because 'The UK has the largest creative sector in the EU, and relative to GDP probably the largest in the world' (p. 16). The implication is that the creative industries not only make a valuable contribution to employment and the economy, but that they also play a significant part in the ways in which UK society is structured, and the nation's sense of itself. By showing that the creative industries employ more people than the pharmaceutical and engineering industries, and are on a par with the financial sector (p. 6), the report suggests that many people's fears about what someone with a degree in media studies could do after they graduate are rather unfounded.

Of those cultural industries listed above, only some are likely to appear in most people's definitions of the 'media industries', namely, advertising; film; music; publishing; software and computer services; television and radio; video and computer games. In adopting a primarily economic approach to these industries, the Work Foundation report demonstrates the ways in which culture is often justified less through its creativity and social purpose, and more through the amounts of money it can make. Criticisms of broadcasting, music, and cinema often bemoan the globalised conglomerates – such as Time Warner, or News International – that are assumed to reduce culture to nothing more than products to be bought and sold. These worries are likely to be ones you come across in much media theory, and recur throughout the material covered in this book. The readings in this book on issues such as the public sphere (see Chapter 13) argue that the social roles of media and communication are too important to be left to the market, for they are central to democracy's success. Indeed, the notion of public service broadcasting – as in the case of the BBC in the United Kingdom – shows how a society deems it worthwhile for *everyone* to contribute, via the licence fee, to the upkeep of a media industry which is intended to have positive social benefits.

Therefore, in theory about the media industries, the question is often raised concerning what roles we want the media to play in society. That is, rather than thinking of the media industries as nothing more than economic institutions similar to those that produce, say, food and clothes, theorising about industry involves placing this debate into broader ones about society, culture and nations. You may want to think about why it is that certain media are constructed in a manner which suggests their public and social role is seen as vital, when others are not. For instance, why is it that we have public service broadcasters which offer radio, television, and, more recently, internet services, but we do not have public service newspapers, music, or cinema? These latter media are, on the whole, left to the market, and this might seem particularly strange in the case of newspapers, which are a key source of information for many people, and often constitute a record of events which future generations will use to find out about historical moments. How comfortable would you be paying a licence fee for a public service newspaper? If you would worry that such a product would be nothing more than an opportunity for the government to disseminate propaganda, why do such fears arise so rarely in discussions about the BBC?

Another aspect central to the theorising of media industries is the ways in which people who work in them are situated by the working practices they encounter. For example, lots of studies of journalists in a range of media show that in becoming a part of a significant institution, many journalists quickly adopt the assumptions and working practices of those already employed (McNair 1998; de Bruin and Ross 2004); indeed, it might be demonstrating your willingness and ability to do this is the thing that gets you the job in the first place. While we may think of many people who work in the media industries as members of the 'creative class' (Florida 2003, 2005), it is also the case that many employees carry out vital tasks which are similar to those in other industries (finance, law, management). In that sense, for the majority of people, is working in the media industries that much different from employment in other sectors (Ross 2009)? The ways in which we see employees can be seen to have important ideological consequences. For example, Ursell summarises four ways in which people have thought about employees: as an economic resource; as exploited workers; as professionals; as having occupational identities constructed in discourse (2006: 167). The first two see employees as little more than cogs within big industrial machines, the third argues for media workers' autonomy because of their authority, while the last shows how work activity is created by social factors which can be difficult to see. Each of these approaches assumes quite different things about the amount of power – within the industry, and within society more generally – media workers, as individuals and as groups, have. Thinking about work and workers in a variety of ways demonstrates that the media industries, and those within it, can be theorised, even if the majority of those who carry out such work rarely theorise their activities in the same way.

There is a lack of work on media industries. That is, there's quite a lot of theorising about media institutions, but very little work – either theoretical or empirical – about the activities of those who work within them. Much of the material you will come across about media industries either adopts the economic approach like the Work Foundation report cited above, or instead makes normative statements about what media industries *should* be like, rather than seeking to think through what they actually *are* like. One of the ways in which media industries are often discussed is through history, with film history, in particular, a well-established discipline (Bordwell and Thompson 2003; Sedgwick and Pokorny 2004). There is less work on television history (Jacobs 2000; Crisell 2002) and popular music history (Friedlander and Miller 2006; Cateforis 2007), though this is expanding. It is noticeable that analysis which has involved media workers is much more common in America than it is in the United Kingdom, with many studies, for example, exploring material gathered from interviews from television workers (Gitlin 1983; Kubey 2004). The majority of such work that has been undertaken in Britain has noticeably focused on journalistic practice and newsrooms (Cottle 1995a, 1995b, 2003; Matthews 2010). Therefore, you might want to think about why it is that media theory has so rarely concerned itself with the activities of those who work in the industries it examines, especially as it so often has considerable criticisms to make of them.

INTRODUCTION TO THE READING

As was noted above, we need to distinguish between 'cultural industries' and 'media industries': therefore, we should note that this reading is from a book called *The Cultural Industries*, and so has a wider remit than just media. That said, the *theoretical* concerns between the two are largely the same. So while Hesmondhalgh may discuss cultural texts which you might insist do not count as media, it is important that you think about *what* he is saying about them, and whether such statements are *relevant* to debates about media.

In the preface to the book, Hesmondhalgh states that its aim is to give 'an account of how and why cultural production has changed since the early 1980s' (2007: xiii). In doing so, he looks at issues of ownership, policy, working practices, new technologies, and globalisation. Much of what is offered has empirical support, and the book contains many tables and references to statistical data. This might make it appear that the book is not theoretical, and instead offers a purely empirical view of the cultural industries. Yet Hesmondhalgh does more than merely chart such changes, for he also engages in discussions about the consequences and causes of these developments, and these are themselves theoretical. In a sense, you might find this reading easier to digest than many others in this book, partly because it is written in a helpfully plain style, but also because it repeatedly refers to 'real world' phenomena which help ground the debates in things you probably already know about. This can be a problem, because it means the theoretical debates can become easy to miss. Perhaps one of the reasons that some writers of theory adopt a complex and difficult style is that it forces you to think, and to constantly check you have understood what is said; the simplicity of Hesmondhalgh's style could, therefore, tempt you into thinking what is being argued is pretty straightforward, when instead it draws on many ideas and arguments central to media studies. This means you need to consciously adopt a critical approach to this material, even if it appears at first glance fairly straightforward.

Central to Hesmondhalgh's argument is the analysis of 'change/continuity' (2007: 3), and the relationships between the two. While the book does indeed mark many changes, it also insists repeatedly that continuity is, in fact, the major factor in the cultural industries: that is, things may not have changed as much as we might think they have. This reading is from the second edition of Hesmondhalgh's book; the first came out in 2002. The changes between this edition and the previous one, then, are a response to the five intervening years. Even there, though, he emphasises continuity, and the epigraph for the book is a quote attributed to Dwight D. Eisenhower: 'Things are more like they are now than they've ever been before.' While it is easy (and pleasurable) to get excited about new bands, new films, and new technology, Hesmondhalgh argues that these are very minor changes when put in the context of the cultural industries overall. You might want to think about the implications of this. For example, if much of society is so convinced that much culture is new and different and exciting, where has that notion come from? Why might it be that the cultural industries are keen to maintain continuity, while suggesting they are interested in change? What are the factors which promote continuity and change: are these artistic, cultural, economic, or institutional? And – going back to the question at the beginning of this chapter – how might this affect the kind of employment *you* might get in the industry?

READING

1

D. Hesmondhalgh

The Cultural Industries

Why do the cultural industries matter?

THE CULTURAL INDUSTRIES MAKE AND CIRCULATE TEXTS

More than other types of production, the cultural industries are involved in the making and circulating of products – that is, texts – that have an influence on our understanding of the world. Debates about the nature and extent of this influence comprise, in the words of a valuable survey of the concept, 'the contested core of media research' (Corner, 2000: 376). The best contributions to such debates suggest the complex, negotiated, and often indirect, nature of media influence, but of one thing there can be no doubt: the media do have an influence. We are influenced by informational texts, such as newspapers, broadcast news programmes, documentaries and analytical books, but also by entertainment. Films, TV series, comics, music, video games and so on provide us with recurring representations of the world and thus act as a kind of reporting. Just as crucially, they draw on and help to constitute our inner, private lives and our public selves: our fantasies, emotions and identities. They contribute strongly to our sense of who we are, of what it means to be a woman or a man, an African or an Arab, a Canadian or a New Yorker, straight or gay. For these reasons alone, the products of the cultural industries are more than just a way of passing time – a mere diversion from other, more important things. All the same, the sheer amount of time that we spend experiencing texts, however distractedly we might do so, in itself makes the cultural industries a powerful factor in our lives.

2

So, studying the cultural industries might help us to understand how texts take the form they do and how these texts have come to play such a central role in contemporary societies. Importantly, most texts that we consume are circulated by powerful corporations. These corporations, like all businesses, have an interest in making profits. They want to support conditions in which businesses in general – especially their own – can make big profits. This raises a crucial issue: do the cultural industries ultimately serve the interests of their owners and their executives and those of their political and business allies?

NOTES

 ### Structure

Hesmondhalgh begins by asserting the importance of the cultural industries. This is so he can legitimately justify the significance of what he is writing about. Do you agree that the texts he refers to do indeed have more of an influence on us than products made by other industries? What is your evidence for your answer?

Content

You might often hear news reports bemoaning the amount of time people spend watching and consuming media, and Hesmondhalgh clearly works from this assumption too. Have you seen evidence for such a statement? See Chapter 14 on 'media effects' in *this* book for more discussion of how this topic is central to media studies as a whole.

Writing Style

Is it true that 'there can be no doubt'? Would you be allowed to write this way in any of your essays?

Context

The debate about the relationship between our public and private lives is one that has become central to media studies and cultural studies, in response to analysis, such as that by Goffman (1969 [1959]), on the ways in which we 'perform' in society. Others argue that we now live in a 'surveillance society' (Lyon 1994, 2001; Lace 2005), meaning that we are used to being watched when we are in public, and so what we consider private is very important. In relating his analysis to the relationship between the public and the private, Hesmondhalgh is therefore placing his work in a particular context which assumes certain things about the ways in which most people now live their lives.

Context

Note how Hesmondhalgh acknowledges he is looking at *contemporary* societies. An important point here is that the cultural industries are different now from how they once were; this is the aspect of 'continuity and change' which is central to his book. It would be worth knowing how 'contemporary' is defined; how far back in time does it stretch?

Writing Style

Note here how Hesmondhalgh sets up a question at the end of one paragraph, and then begins to answer it in the next. By splitting his question and answer across two paragraphs, he invites you to make an assumption at the end of the first. Arguing that media industries want to make money is quite simplistic, so Hesmondhalgh insists that we need to think about the issue in a much more rigorous and nuanced way.

READING

3

It is important that we avoid simplistic answers to this vital question. Throughout this book, I argue for a view of the cultural industries and the texts they produce as **complex, ambivalent and contested**. In societies where the cultural industries are big business, cultural industry companies tend to support conditions in which large companies and their political allies can make money: conditions where there is constant demand for new products, minimal regulation by the state outside of general competition law, relative political and economic stability, workforces that are willing to work hard and so on. Yet, in contemporary societies, many of the texts produced and disseminated by the cultural industries do not simply support such conditions. Very often (not just occasionally) they tend to orientate their audiences towards ways of thinking that do not coincide with the interests of capitalism or of structured domination by men over women or institutional racism.

4

If this is true, why does it happen? Partly, it is for the simple economic reason that cultural companies have to compete with each other, as well as maintain general conditions in which to do business, and so they attempt to outstrip each other to satisfy audience desires for the shocking, the profane and the rebellious. It is also because of social and cultural factors deeply embedded in many societies regarding what we expect of art and entertainment. This takes us to a second argument for the importance of the subject of this book and into a domain that has been neglected in academic and public debate in recent years.

5

THE CULTURAL INDUSTRIES MANAGE AND CIRCULATE CREATIVITY

3 Structure

Here Hesmondhalgh makes clear what the argument for the rest of his book is going to be. Clear writing often helps guide the reader in this way.

Context

There is a link made between media and politics here; this is a link you will come across many times in your studies, as it is a key topic of media studies.

Content

This is a crucial point, because it is the key argument in the book. Hesmondhalgh insists that there is a contradiction within the actions of the cultural industries, and it is one he is determined not to oversimplify.

4 Writing Style

It may seem odd that Hesmondhalgh acknowledges his thesis may not be true; presumably this is because he has yet to demonstrate it, but wants to outline its importance at this stage, and will go on to give the required evidence in forthcoming chapters.

5 Structure

This book is, as here, chopped up into lots of smaller sections. This makes it easier to navigate as a whole. But you may want to think about what such segmentation does for the complexity of the argument overall.

READING

6

The cultural industries are concerned, fundamentally, with the management and selling of a particular kind of work. Since the Renaissance – and especially since the Romantic movement of the nineteenth century – there has been a widespread tendency to think of 'art' as being one of the highest forms of human creativity. Sociologists and Marxists have argued in response that artistic work is not so different from other kinds of labour, in that both are orientated towards the production of objects or experiences (Wolff, 1993, Chapter 1, provides an excellent summary of these debates). This view is important in countering the idea that 'artists' are different from the rest of us, that they are involved in some mystically special form of creativity. Nevertheless, there is something distinctive about that area of human creativity often called 'art'. The invention and/or performance of stories, songs, images, poems, jokes and so on, in no matter what technological form, involves a particular type of creativity – the manipulation of symbols for the purposes of entertainment, information and perhaps even enlightenment. Instead of the term 'art', with all its connotations of individual genius and a higher calling, I want to use the more cumbersome term *symbolic creativity*[1] and, instead of the term 'artists', I prefer the phrase *symbol creators* for those who make up, interpret or rework stories, songs, images and so on.[2]

7

Symbol creators have been pretty much ignored in recent thinking about the cultural industries because of an understandable, but excessive, reaction against the fetishisation of their work as extraordinary. For many years, in media and cultural studies, this took the form of an emphasis on the creativity of audiences, of those who do not, in general, work professionally as symbol creators, but, in the 1990s, a number of writers in these fields began to put symbol creators back in the picture (Born, 1993a, 1993b; McRobbie, 1998; Toynbee, 2000). After all, symbol creators are the primary workers in the making of texts. Texts, by definition, would not exist without them, however much they rely on industrial systems for the reproduction, distribution and marketing of and remuneration for their work. This does not mean that we should romantically celebrate the work of all musicians, authors, film-makers and so on. Ultimately, my interest in symbol creators derives, like that of Born, McRobbie and Toynbee, from a sense that symbolic creativity *can* enrich people's lives, even though it often doesn't.

1. My use of this term is borrowed from Willis (1990), but I differ from him in focusing on industrialised symbolic creativity, whereas he is concerned with the creativity of young people as consumers.
2. In the sense in which I am using the term, journalists and others dealing in the more information-orientated parts of the cultural industries are also symbol creators. Studies of journalism have a long and noble history of focusing attention on key symbol creators – that is, journalists.

NOTES

6   Context

A historical context is offered here. It is important to realise that while we may think it is 'obvious' that certain kinds of work require more skill or talent than others, and should therefore be seen as 'artistic', this is a relatively recent invention within most societies. Indeed, distinguishing between the 'cultural industries' and other industries is only worthwhile if we assume there is something different about the work carried out by such 'artists'. You might want to think about why it is that we now see some kinds of labour as more important than others, and what the consequences of this hierarchy are.

Writing Style

If Hesmondhalgh acknowledges that the term 'symbolic creativity' is cumbersome (as is 'symbol creators'), why does he use it? What is wrong with writing about 'art' and 'artists'? Why is 'art' in inverted commas? In the footnote, Hesmondhalgh notes he has taken the term from Willis, but is using it differently: why do that? The insistence on using particular terms – which are often at odds with those used in everyday life – is quite common in theoretical writing: why is this? How do you respond to it? Are there times when *you* insist on particular words being used in particular contexts?

7   Context

As Hesmondhalgh notes, much media studies has often moved away from exploring media workers as artists. Some of this is a reaction against the 'auteur' theory which is central to film studies, and examines individuals – usually the director – as the 'author' of a film (Grant 2008). In addition, work such as Hall's 'Encoding/Decoding model' (1980c; see Chapter 11 in *this* book) argues that readers are as much creators of texts' meanings as the authors. The attempt to explore what people do, especially through ethnographic work (see Chapter 23 on audiences), has been one of the ways that media studies has attempted to dismantle the power hierarchies it sees as an inevitable consequence of the valorisation of the activities of what Hesmondhalgh calls 'symbol creators'. In all, this means the cultural industries have been woefully under-researched, especially in comparison to the detailed work carried out on the film industry by film studies. As Hesmondhalgh goes on to note, some people have begun to carry out research on those who work in the cultural industries, and he places this book within that context.

Content

Note that this statement utterly contradicts much of the media studies work on audiences. Do you think what Hesmondhalgh says is true?

Writing Style

Note Hesmondhalgh's fear of carrying out research 'romantically'. This is presumably a dig at film studies, which often lauds its subjects, using words like 'artist' which Hesmondhalgh finds problematic.

READING

8

Other traditions of study have focused on especially talented or fêted symbol creators, at times hardly referring to the means by which authors, musicians and so on have reached their audiences. Some such studies amount to a pious and complacent celebration of the achievements of Western civilisation (Clark, 1969). The work of Raymond Williams (1981) and Pierre Bourdieu (1996), among others, suggests better ways of historicising symbolic creativity, by showing how such creativity has been a more or less permanent presence in human history, but its management and circulation have taken radically different forms in different societies. In Europe, for example, systems of patronage gave way in the nineteenth century to the organisation of symbolic creativity around the market. It was at this point that the cultural industries began to emerge. From the early twentieth century, this market organisation began to take a new, complex form. Examining changes in the cultural industries allows us to think about how symbolic creativity has been organised and circulated in our own lifetimes and, crucially in this book, how this might be changing.

9

Again, I must emphasise here the fundamentally *ambivalent* nature of the cultural industries. The way the cultural industries organise and circulate symbolic creativity reflects the extreme inequalities and injustices (along class, gender, ethnic and other lines) apparent in contemporary capitalist societies. There are vast inequalities in access to the cultural industries. Those who do gain access are often treated shabbily and many people who want to create texts struggle to earn a living. Failure is far more common than success. There are great pressures to produce certain kinds of texts rather than others and it is hard to come across information about the existence of organisations and texts that attempt to do things differently.

10

Some types of text are made much more available than others. These are bleak features of the cultural industry landscape, yet, because original and distinctive symbolic creativity is at a premium, the cultural industries can never quite control it. Owners and executives make concessions to symbol creators by granting them far more **autonomy** (self-determination) than they would to workers of equivalent status in other industries and to most workers historically. Paradoxically, this freedom – which is, in the end, a limited and provisional one – can then act as a form of control by maintaining the desirability of often scarce and poorly-paid jobs. However, it may also help to explain the ambivalence in texts referred to above.

8   Content

You may have found much of your education functioned in this way. If you studied Shakespeare at school, it is likely that you did not go into detail about the industry within which he worked, and you instead explored his works and why they are 'good'. Most contemporary magazines on music, film, books, theatre and other cultural forms function in this way, working to distinguish between the 'good' and the 'bad', and rarely exploring the social, cultural and industrial factors within which most people work.

Context

Issues of organisation and circulation are important. Industries are nothing more than forms of organisation, which produce products that are to be circulated in particular ways. The fact that how they do this nowadays is not the same as it always has been is seen to be telling for debates about contemporary society as a whole.

Williams is explored in Chapter 17 of *this* book.

9   Structure

Note how Hesmondhalgh keeps repeating and reiterating his arguments. Do you find this useful, or just repetitive?

Content

This is an important point, for Hesmondhalgh makes a link between power structures within the cultural industries, and those within society more generally. The fact that the role of production has been taken away from the majority of the population, and only a tiny minority gets to have the ability to produce cultural forms that reach large numbers of people, can be seen as symbolic of the central ideas of capitalism. Notions of inequality are central to media studies, and you will come across them repeatedly. This movement towards cultural industries which reflect a minority is explored by Adorno and Horkheimer (1972 [1947]; see Chapter 6 in *this* book).

10   Context

Why might it be hard to get such information?

Content

'Autonomy' is important here. Do you agree that many workers have more autonomy than those in the past? Hesmondhalgh acknowledges that such freedom is limited: to what extent? Also, note how Hesmondhalgh argues freedom can become a form of control.

READING

11

Cultural industry companies face another difficulty, too. They have to find audiences for the texts that symbol creators produce. Usually, this is not a matter of finding the greatest possible mass audience for a product. Different groups of people tend to have different tastes, so much of the work of cultural industry companies attempts to match texts to audiences, to find appropriate ways of circulating texts to those audiences and to make audiences aware of the existence of texts. As we shall see, this is a risky business. Many texts fail, even those that companies expect to succeed. The upshot of these processes is that cultural industry companies keep a much tighter grip on the *circulation* of texts than they do on their production.

The importance of symbolic creativity helps to explain the fact that the main focus of this book is on patterns of change/continuity in the cultural industries, as opposed to, say, change/continuity in the texts produced by those industries or in how audiences understand texts. As I should have made clear by now, however, this does not mean that I am interested only in the cultural industries as systems of production. The underlying interest is really **systems of production in relation to texts**. But all writers, given their limited time and energy, must make decisions about where to concentrate their attention and, rather than focusing on the texts themselves and then working backwards from there to the industries, my primary interest in this book is in the cultural industries.

12

THE CULTURAL INDUSTRIES ARE AGENTS OF ECONOMIC, SOCIAL AND CULTURAL CHANGE

NOTES

11 Context

While we often assume that the cultural industries are always trying to get mass audiences, Hesmondhalgh suggests otherwise here. A broadcaster like Channel 4, for example, survives by targeting particular audiences rather than mass ones, which means it can tell advertisers what kinds of people are likely to see their commercials (Brown 2007). It is important that you accept the idea that while industries are about making profits, reaching mass audiences is not always the best way to achieve this.

Content

Earlier, Hesmondhalgh outlined the link between 'production' and 'circulation'; here he argues that the latter is the most important to the cultural industries. This might be contrary to what you assumed, especially as many cultural workers bemoan the restrictions placed on them. In what ways do the industries attempt to control circulation in this way, and why might this be the more important aspect of their activities?

Structure

Here Hesmondhalgh reiterates what he is interested in, but also what his work will *not* be doing: that is, he won't be looking at texts or audiences. The fact that the majority of media theory *has* focused on texts and audiences, to the detriment of research on industries, might tell you something about the assumptions that underpin the field.

Writing Style

How helpful is it that some of Hesmondhalgh's text is in bold or italics?

12 Writing Style

In much of your reading, you might come across theoretical writing whose titles and subtitles are complex, full of puns, and with sub-clauses. Hesmondhalgh's writing is much 'plainer': how do you respond to this?

READING

13

A third and final reason for the importance of examining change and continuity in the cultural industries is that they are increasingly significant sources of wealth and employment in many economies. Measuring this importance is difficult and there are controversies, occasionally useful but sometimes tedious, about how best to do so. Much depends on how we define the cultural industries, an issue discussed later in this Introduction. It seems fair to say, though, that the economic role of cultural production is growing, but not nearly as much or as quickly as some commentators and policymakers claim.

14

That the cultural industries might be providing more wealth and employment is, of course, significant in itself, but it also has implications for how we understand **the relationships between culture, society and economy.** Many of the most important debates about these relationships over the last 30 years have concerned what we might call theories of transition. Have we moved from industrial societies to post-industrial or information societies, based on a much greater emphasis than before on knowledge? This was a line of thought initiated in the 1960s and 1970s by the work of, among others, Daniel Bell (for example, 1974) and maintained by writers such as Manuel Castells (such as, 1989, 1996) in the 1980s and 1990s. Have we moved from societies best characterised as 'modern', because of their increasing ephemerality, fragmentedness and flux, to a situation better characterised as 'postmodern', where these features become so accentuated that rationality and meaning seem to break down (Harvey, 1989; Lyotard, 1984)? In one version of such debates, some analysts (notably Castells, 1996; and Lash and Urry, 1994) suggested that symbolic creativity and/or information were becoming increasingly central in social and economic life. An important implication of this, drawn out more fully by Lash and Urry than by Castells, was that the cultural industries therefore increasingly provided a model for understanding transformations in other industries. Others claimed that the cultural industries themselves are becoming more like other industries and losing their distinctiveness as an economic sector (Padioleau, 1987).

NOTES

13   Context

You may not come across references to wealth and economics very often in your reading. As Hesmondhalgh is exploring an industry, it makes sense for him to look at these aspects. However, economics *is* important to media studies more generally, because money is clearly related to power. Indeed, when many writers discuss power, it is economic power which is uppermost in their minds, even if they don't say so. Perhaps media studies rarely consciously looks at economics because it is, as Hesmondhalgh says, 'tedious'.

Structure

Why is Hesmondhalgh leaving it so late to define 'cultural industries' when he acknowledges it is a problem?

14   Context

The Work Foundation report (2007) mentioned in this chapter's introduction makes such a claim for the growth of the cultural industries. As Hesmondhalgh notes, pointing this out is uninteresting, unless it has broader implications for society, culture and power.

Content

Here we deal with the difficulties in defining the kind of society we live in now. This refers back to Hesmondhalgh's uses of the word 'contemporary', which he does not offer a definition of. Throughout this paragraph, he notes that most people accept that society has changed; but exactly *how* it has changed, *when* that change happened, and what changes are *still* happening, is very difficult to demonstrate. Indeed, societies have always been in flux, and it might be overstating the case to suggest such transitions are more marked now than they were in the past.

Writing Style

Note that Hesmondhalgh is referring to a lot of other writers here, when the rest of the reading has very few references. Also note how he merely uses them to indicate certain schools of thought; does he make explicit what *he* thinks, and how his work fits into these debates?

READING

15

In the late 1990s, the rise of the Internet and the World Wide Web fuelled these debates. Academic study was echoed by business and management analysts, who placed increasing emphasis on firms' non-tangible assets, especially, the value of these businesses' brand names (see Wolf, 1999 for a popularising version). Brands can only be made valuable as a result of massive amounts of work being put into product names and logos and how they are represented and circulated. Cultural industry companies such as Disney, because they were considered so experienced in developing brands (in a sense, every film, every star, every book is something like a brand) were often named alongside companies such as Nike and more traditional firms such as Coca-Cola as leaders in this field.

16

Brands, however, were only one part of a surge of hype about the increasing role of information, culture and knowledge in modern economies. There was a seemingly unstoppable flow of books about 'the weightless world' (Coyle, 1999), about how, in the future knowledge economy, we would be 'living on thin air' (Leadbeater, 2000) rather than on material goods and so on. Closely related to this, enormous attention was paid, in the USA in particular, to 'the new economy' (see Henwood, 2003, for a critique of this idea) in which the traditional business cycles of boom and slump would be replaced by continuous growth; communication technologies, branding, information and culture were all seen as central to this new configuration. In the early 2000s, such notions were increasingly joined by a new concept, which is also of direct relevance to this book: the so-called 'creative economy' (Howkins, 2001).[3]

---

3. Mosco (2004) has provided a particularly valuable analysis of various ways in which computers and cyberspace have contributed to such 'mythical' thinking about economic and social futures.

15 Context

Referring to the internet places Hesmondhalgh's work within a much more recent context than the majority of the theory you will encounter in your studies. Such 'web studies' (Gauntlett 2004) raise many questions for lots of the arguments in media studies, not least because of issues of access (although it is important not to overstate this). While it is important to be aware of the historical context that theory was produced in, this is not the same as saying it is automatically irrelevant or wrong simply because it is out of date.

Content

Again, brands are a contemporary concern, usually because they are seen as indicative of global capitalism (Klein 2000; Haig 2006). However, there is an argument that brands have always been in existence: wasn't Mozart a brand; wasn't Shakespeare a brand; wasn't Jesus a brand?

16 ## Content

The interplay between 'information, culture and knowledge' can be seen in debates about the 'information society'. (Webster 2006; see Chapter 20 in *this* book.)

17

It would be very wrong to think that, with the bursting of the so-called dot.com bubble in 2000–2001, such ideas disappeared. The language of the popularising books may not be quite as millennial now as it was at the turn of the century, but new formulations of the idea that we are now living in societies and economies founded on information, knowledge and culture have continued to appear in influential and widely read magazines such as *Wired* and *Newsweek*. The latter, for example, devoted the 2006 version of its annual special issue preview of the forthcoming year to 'The Knowledge Revolution', including much discussion of the new magical word 'creativity' (see also Florida, 2002, 2005). Academic commentators, meanwhile, argued that creativity 'will be the driver of social and economic change during the next century' (Hartley, 2005: 1). If the cultural industries are playing a central part in these supposed transitions – to the information or knowledge society, to economies based on brands, on signs and meanings, on creativity – it is surprising how rarely systematic, historically informed analysis of changes in these industries has been carried out by those involved in such debates. An analysis of this kind may help to cast light on these various notions and on whether they exaggerate change at the expense of continuity.

NOTES

17 Context

For more information on the crash of the 'dot.com bubble' see Malmsten (2001) and Cellan-Jones (2003).

Content

Note here that Hesmondhalgh sets up a conflict between journalists and academics. Many academics argue that journalists have overstated the significance of recent cultural changes, and fail to take into account the inequalities media studies insists are important. The distinction between journalism and the academy is important, and it is not that often that people move from one discipline to the other: why is this?

Structure

At this point, it becomes clear why Hesmondhalgh is outlining these debates, and how they relate to this book. In effect, he is arguing that his analysis helps answer some of the questions raised by the differing views of contemporary society he cites. You may also note how careful much of this writing is; it is probably less strident than much of that you have come across. Perhaps this is a consequence of Hesmondhalgh's career working for the Open University.

REFLECTING ON THE READING

This chapter began by asking if you were interested in working in the media industries after your studies. It might be worth reflecting now on whether this reading has altered your views on this at all. Does working in film or television or the music industry seem more, or less, attractive now? Were issues discussed in the reading that you had not thought of as applicable to the media industries? Have the distinctions between the media industries and other professions been lessened in any way?

You will probably have found this reading 'easier' than others in this book. What benefits and problems did such a writing style create? Was it easier to make sense of what Hesmondhalgh was trying to say than other authors in this book? Why might Hesmondhalgh have adopted such a style? Perhaps more importantly, if Hesmondhalgh can do it, why isn't all media theory written in this way? Do you think anything is lost by writing so simply? Thinking about these questions should be helpful when you make decisions about how to write essays and other work you must do for your studies.

One of the key topics of Hesmondhalgh's work is the relationships between continuity and change. He repeatedly argues that while contemporary societies are quite different to those in the pre-industrial past, more recent changes are actually less significant than is often assumed. While many people insist that the internet has democratised media, and multi-channel broadcasting means there's no such thing as the mass audience, and the falling costs of film technology means anyone can make a film, Hesmondhalgh is sceptical about such changes. Where do you see aspects of continuity and change in the media industries? What about the products they make: are they broadly similar or different to those from the past? How do you think things will pan out in the future? Any why does continuity and change matter (you might want to think about issues of power here).

In terms of power, how does this chapter relate to the others in this book? Debates about political economy (see Chapter 12) examine issues of ownership and control within media, which clearly have connections to Hesmondhalgh's examination of the economic factors which affect working within the creative industries. Similarly, the reading on the public sphere (see Chapter 13) is one which argues that media industries should offer certain kinds of public value, and therefore must be organised and regulated in particular ways. The two chapters which follow *this* one – on texts and audiences – can be read in conjunction with this one, as the three look at the different players within media communication. Indeed, one of the recurring debates within media studies is which of these three – production, text, audience – is the most significant, and how research should explore the interplay between them (though note that Chapter 24, on 'audiences as producers', queries the neat 'production, text, audience' division). While Hesmondhalgh's writing might seem less theoretical than much of the material in this book, it is clear that he places his work within the theoretical context of media studies, offering information which can be used as a useful intervention in such theorising. As ever, then, it is important that you try to see the *links* between different readings, in order to build up an understanding of the subject area as a whole.

Finally, you might want to think about other ways in which the media industries could be theorised. As was noted earlier, there is surprisingly little work on the industries themselves, though perhaps this is changing. If you were to study the media industries, how would you go about it? What are the important questions? Is it important to know what individuals do, or should you instead examine the macro-processes of the institutions? More importantly, how do questions about the industries relate to recurring concerns in media studies, and media theory more generally; how are they connected to debates about power, class, ideology, representation, and so on?

Key terms to explore

'art' and 'artists'; autonomy; brands; capitalism; contemporary society; creativity; dot.com bubble; information societies; labour; post-industrial societies; production and circulation; 'symbolic creativity' and 'symbol creators'; systems of production; texts.

Key writers who are mentioned

Daniel Bell; Pierre Bourdieu; Manuel Castells; Diane Coyle; Richard Florida; John Hartley; Doug Henwood; John Howkins; Scott Lash; Charles Leadbetter; Jean-François Lyotard; Jean G. Padioleau; John Urry; Raymond Williams; Paul Willis; Michael J. Wolf.

RECOMMENDED READING

Gitlin, T. (1983) *Inside Prime Time*, New York: Pantheon Books.

Key book, detailing the workings of the American television industry, drawing on extensive interviews with workers carried out by the author.

Hesmondhalgh, D. (ed.) (2006) *Media Production*, Maidenhead: Open University Press.

A collection of articles on media ownership, organisational structures, and media workers, related to issues of autonomy, power and the relationships between media and society.

Work Foundation, The (2007) *Staying Ahead: The economic performance of the UK's creative industries*, London: The Work Foundation.

A report on the role the creative industries play within the British economy, with a useful range of facts, tables and international comparisons; available online at www.theworkfoundation.com/research/publications/publicationdetail.aspx?oItemId=176

CHAPTER 22

Texts

Barthes, R. (1977 [1967]) 'The death of the author', in *Image Music Text*, translated by Heath, S., London: Fontana, pp. 142–8.

INTRODUCTION TO TEXTS

Who is the author of *Romeo and Juliet*? The obvious answer is 'William Shakespeare', and, while there are some who argue that some of Shakespeare's plays were written by other people (Hope and Holston 1992), the 'accepted' answer is 'Shakespeare'. But what does it mean to be the 'author' of a play? Shakespeare may have written the script, but is he still the author when you see *Romeo and Juliet* at the theatre? Who or what has the most input into the experience you have: Shakespeare; the director; the set designer; the actors; the building itself? All of these make significant contributions; if they did not it would be pointless restaging the play again and again because each version would be exactly the same. What about if you watch the film, *William Shakespeare's Romeo + Juliet* (1996)? Is the director (Baz Luhrmann) the author, especially as the film's setting is transposed to a time and place Shakespeare cannot have envisaged? What about the contributions of the two stars, Leonardo DiCaprio and Claire Danes? The film uses lots of music, so are the writers of those songs authors too? The credits list both Shakespeare *and* Craig Pearce and Baz Lurhmann as scriptwriters, so does this mean this is not a Shakespeare play?

And what about other filmic versions of the play, such as those directed by Goerge Cukor (1936) and Franco Zeffirelli (1968)? What about films that draw on *Romeo and Juliet* for inspiration, such as *West Side Story* (dir. Robert Wise and Jerome Robbins, 1961) and *High School Musical* (dir. Kenny Ortega, 2006)? And considering Shakespeare's play is an adaptation of Arthur Brooke's poem 'The tragical history of Romeus and Juliet' (1562), which is itself a translation and adaptation of the Italian story 'Guiletta e Romeo' (1554) by Matteo Bandello, which itself draws on similar tales of thwarted young love that can be traced back to antiquity, why do we think of Shakespeare as the 'original' author at all? These sorts of questions show how difficult it is to state who it is who 'writes' any media text, often because there are so many people involved in the production process, all of whom make some sort of contribution.

In all of this, there is somebody left out in terms of deciding who it is that constructs a text; *you*. A film, television programme, piece of music, or newspaper, exists as an object before you encounter it; but it only has any *meaning* once you bring to bear your interpretative faculties upon them. Before you *read* a newspaper, it is nothing more than some wood pulp with coloured markings on it; once you bring to it your knowledge of the language it is written in, and the stories it refers to, it starts to have meaning. Similarly, film is nothing more than lights playing on a screen, with accompanying sound, until a reader interprets those images and sounds using the skills they have developed from previous encounters with cinema. In thinking about how texts make *meaning*, then, it is important to examine what audiences *do* with them, and the tools they use to make sense of them. This way of thinking about texts posits the *relationship* between the text and the reader as an important and significant one, and, unlike the majority of textual analysis you have probably engaged in, it sees the notion of the 'author' as problematic and, more importantly, pretty irrelevant.

If this is the case, why is it that audiences are so rarely studied in cultural analysis? It is likely that when you studied literature at school, while your teacher would have been interested in the various responses different people had to any book or poem you read, this was a precursor to detailed analysis which aimed to find the 'true' or 'best' meaning. In a sense, what is often taught is *appreciation* of culture. In order to appreciate culture in an appropriate way, we are taught skills of interpretation and context which help us achieve certain kinds of reading. What this does, importantly, is suggest that the vast majority of people read things wrongly – or, at least, do not have the skills to appreciate them fully – and that there are a limited number of critics or experts who can teach us how to do it 'properly'.

Media studies is interested in this idea because of its implications for social power. That is, media studies argues that one of the ways in which social hierarchies are maintained is through culture, where experts control the 'correct' meaning of texts, and the vast majority of understandings of any painting, book, or film are 'wrong'. In that sense, 'the controller of language controls the world' (Klinkowitz 1988: 63). This goes hand in hand with the idea that the meaning of a text is 'put there' by the author, and it is the critic's job to unearth what was intended. This is why when we learn about a play or book we also learn about the author, just as film studies spends a lot of its time discussing directors as 'auteurs' (Grant 2008).

Therefore, when examining the nature of texts, media studies tries to interrogate the relationships between the text, the author and the reader. For this approach *context* is significant, because it is assumed that readers and writers both work within social and historical contexts which influence the ways they make sense of things. One of the reasons that media texts from some time ago – such as early cinema, or the books of Charles Dickens – might be hard to make sense of now is because we live in a different context, and therefore bring different expectations to any form of culture we encounter. Similarly, Swedish literature or cinema is likely to make no sense (or, very little sense) to you if you do not understand Swedish; learning a foreign language is a process of learning the codes and structures which allow you to decipher a text in a meaningful way, giving you the required context to make sense of something.

This idea of context does not, however, suggest that once you have a grasp of it, you will therefore get the 'right' reading. It is clear that different people read texts in different ways; your friends might like music or television programmes that you dislike, even though you come from a similar background. So while context is an important factor, it is clearly not the only one, and it is one of the tools we draw on in order to make sense of media, even if it cannot fully guarantee that everyone will come to the same meaning. In order to try to communicate effectively media producers draw on those conventions and expectations, and posters for films clearly show how the cinema industry attempts to signal how they want films to be classified; posters for horror films, say, are quite different to those for romantic comedies. There are, then, conventions and contexts which are vital to all media.

What this suggests is that 'all forms of communication are artificial, since all of them work because of structure' (Thody and Course 1999: 16). That is, language is not 'natural'; it has to be 'made' by a society. As we grow up we have to learn language, and this is seen as so vital that it is one of the first things parents try to teach their children. But language here means more than 'English', for it also means the language of cinema, the language of pictures, the language of sounds, and so on: all of the structures we learn in order to make sense of the media around us. Foreign cinema – which may use costume, or editing, or actors differently to what you are used to – shows that the cinematic language we are used to is not natural or inevitable, but arises out of our society. This attempt to examine society and culture by exploring the structures which underpin its forms of communication is called 'structuralism' (see Chapter 15). This approach assumes that societies are not natural or inevitable, and are instead held together by a series of structures which have to be learned, but which are so ingrained that they appear normal and natural. The examination of things like television programmes and films can be a way into unearthing those structures, and therefore shed light on the ways in which a society works. Structuralism, then, does not really care who 'wrote' *Romeo and Juliet*; it is instead interested in the ways in which the play makes 'sense', and the structures it draws on – and we as readers draw on – to interpret it. This approach has, then, been very useful to media studies, because it offers a way of thinking about the relationships between society and culture, and the implications this has for social power, which is a recurring theme in the subject.

INTRODUCTION TO THE READING

This reading is by Roland Barthes, who was 'the leading French intellectual' (Culler 1983: 1) of the twentieth century. He was a critic, philosopher and social theorist whose work, while not coming directly out of media studies, has been subsequently taken up by many who analyse the media. Barthes wrote about novels, photography, popular culture, cinema and television, but rather than the focus of his studies being important, it is the approaches he employed to interrogate them that is significant. This can perhaps be best seen in his book *Mythologies* (1973 [1957]), which is a collection of articles examining such things as wrestling, food, cars, washing powder and Greta Garbo's face. While these might seem unrelated, Barthes's intention was to examine 'the "naturalness" with which newspapers, art and common sense constantly dress up a reality which, even though it is the one we live in, is undoubtedly determined by history' (p. 11). By 'history' he does not mean only 'the past'; what he means is 'the specifics of the time and place in which we live'. That is, things are made to seem 'natural', but are instead highly artificial, and this artificiality rests on cultural contexts that make sense to us. Barthes called these 'common sense' ideas about the world 'myths', which is where the book gets its title from. While Barthes employed a range of approaches across his career, this determination to question the 'naturalness' of things can be seen as a recurring and defining aspect of his work.

While Barthes is often categorised as a structuralist, he can also be seen as a post-structuralist. Post-structuralism was a response to structuralism (hence its name) which suggested that while there are indeed underlying social structures which are central to the analysis of texts, the interesting and important thing to analyse is not the structures themselves, but the ways in which individuals use those structures, and make sense of texts in various, complex, and idiosyncratic ways. It argued that it is impossible to ever 'know' what those structures are, because everyone interprets them and uses them differently, even though there is likely to be a commonality amongst many readings. So even though Barthes's work arose out of structuralism, because he was interested in 'the pleasures of reading and the reader's right to read idiosyncratically' (Culler 1983: 2), he helped the movement towards post-structuralist thought. Indeed, this article can be said to be 'a transitional one, in that within it the movement from Structuralism to Post-Structuralism can be detected' (Allen 2003: 74).

When it was first published, 'The death of the author' was extremely controversial. This was because it undermined the methods which the vast majority of critics and academics had used for centuries, suggesting that all their work was pointless. Furthermore, it argued that in carrying out that work, those critics and academics were engaged in a process which systematically upheld power distinctions, for Barthes saw 'academic criticism as serving the interests of the university system by preserving its privileged position as the custodian of a body of knowledge' (Ribière 2002: 29). Barthes argued that by saying only certain people – 'experts' – had the right and authority to say anything about culture, the pleasures, skills and interpretations invoked by the vast majority of people were rendered worthless, and they were thus removed from any kind of debate. In questioning 'experts' Barthes queries the entire system upon which societies are built, and raises doubts about our ability to 'know' anything definitively. It is, then, 'an essentially iconoclastic work' (Burke 1998: 26).

'The death of the author' was originally published in the art and culture journal, *Aspen* in 1967. The version here – and the one most commonly used – comes from *Image Music Text* (1977), which is an anthology of Barthes's writings. This means that the chapters in the book were written separately, and only brought together afterwards. Like *Mythologies*, then, the book covers a rag-bag of topics, including photography, music, the Bible and narrative analysis. Such eclecticism is itself significant, because it refuses to acknowledge traditional subject distinctions, and supports the idea that some analytical approaches can be used to interrogate anything and everything.

It is important to be aware that what you are reading is a translation from French. Translations immediately raise problems because of the differences between languages. One person may interpret something one way, whereas another will do so a different way. Translators have to decide whether it is best to attempt to translate word for word, to capture the 'spirit' of a text, or to do a bit of both (Steiner 1992; Will 1993). For structuralists translation is itself an interesting process, as it involves someone attempting to move a text from one set of linguistic structures to another. You will probably find this reading quite difficult, as it refers to many authors you are unlikely to have vast experience of, and the writing style is quite oblique and poetic; it seems to encourage you to interpret it however you want. It must be borne in mind that French academic writing has different expectations and norms from much of that in Britain; that is, it has different structures. As the translator of *Image Music Text* notes, 'there is (as yet?) no real overlap in theoretical context between the two languages' (1977: 7). So, the kind of writing you find here is not a deliberate attempt to make things difficult; it is instead a consequence of the context Barthes was writing in, compounded by the problems thrown up by the process of translation.

This use of oblique language is demonstrated by the title, which sounds more like a newspaper headline than that for an academic article. It does not offer much help in preparing you for what is to come; which author is dead, and how? In fact, Barthes is not talking about the death of any one particular author. He is instead arguing for the death of the *concept* of the author, especially when it is used to suggest that the author is the controller of the 'real' and 'true' meaning of the text. It is, then, an argument he is proposing, for he is saying that the concept of the author should be killed off, rather than saying it already has been. It is worth noting that Barthes made this plea in 1967, and yet the primary way in which media and culture is taught, and thought about, remains in the relationship to the author. Barthes may have wanted the 'author' dead, but it seems he/she is still very much alive.

READING

1

R. Barthes

The Death of the Author

In his story *Sarrasine* Balzac, describing a castrato disguised as a woman, writes the following sentence 'This was woman herself, with her sudden fears, her irrational whims, her instinctive worries, her impetuous boldness, her fussings, and her delicious sensibility.' Who is speaking: thus? Is it the hero of the story bent on remaining ignorant of the castrato hidden beneath the woman? Is it Balzac the individual, furnished by his personal experience with a philosophy of Woman? Is it Balzac the author professing 'literary' ideas on femininity? Is it universal wisdom? Romantic psychology? We shall never know, for the good reason that writing is the destruction of every voice, of every point of origin. Writing is that neutral, composite, oblique space where our subject slips away, the negative where all identity is lost, starting with the very identity of the body writing.

2

No doubt it has always been that way. As soon as a fact is *narrated* no longer with a view to acting directly on reality but intransitively, that is to say, finally outside of any function other than that of the very practice of the symbol itself, this disconnection occurs, the voice loses its origin, the author enters into his own death, writing begins. The sense of this phenomenon, however, has varied; in ethnographic societies the responsibility for a narrative is never assumed by a person but by a mediator, shaman or relator whose 'performance' – the mastery of the narrative code – may possibly be admired but never his 'genius'. The author is a modern figure, a product of our society insofar as, emerging from the Middle Ages with English empiricism, French rationalism and the personal faith of the Reformation, it discovered the prestige of the individual, of, as it is more nobly put, the 'human person'.

NOTES

 Context

Barthes begins with analysis of a piece of text. This use of examples can be seen to ground his thought in the real world, offering the reader a way 'in' to his argument. However, what he is referring to is likely to be a novel you have never read, by an author you have never heard of. While it is always hard for authors to select examples that mean something to everyone (indeed, that is one of the points of this reading), you might want to think about what kind of audience Barthes assumes is reading this; why has he chosen *this* example, rather than countless others?

Writing Style

Barthes does not reference his quotation; would you be allowed to do this in your essays? Also, this is complex, lyrical writing, that can be hard to make sense of. You will find such passages throughout this reading. A good tactic to deal with such difficulties is to not worry about this sentence now, but instead carry on with the reading and come back to it later, as subsequent parts of the reading may help you make sense of this section.

Content

If you have studied literature you may have discussed the 'voices' that authors – and texts – may adopt. This is an area explored less by media studies, though it is a worthwhile question. When you are watching television, where are you positioned? Normally, you are given a viewpoint that matches none of the characters, so where exactly are you looking from? Note also how Barthes distinguishes between 'Balzac the individual' and 'Balzac the author'; what is the difference between the two?

2 Content

Here the distinction between the 'real world' and texts which capture or reflect it is made clear. Barthes's notion of '*narrated*' suggests that facts exist whether or not they are said or written down; but once they become part of a text they become static and unchanging, which is unlike life. So, once the activity of 'laughter', for example, becomes written down as that word – 'laughter' – it becomes concrete, but also detached from the real world. Similarly, when you show friends holiday photos you are not showing them the 'real world', but such photos soon come to replace the reality you remember. In discussing *narrating*, Barthes is showing that it is the *way* in which stories are told that matters.

Writing Style

You might wonder what time-frame Barthes's use of the word 'modern' means here.

READING

3

It is thus logical that in literature it should be this positivism, the epitome and culmination of capitalist ideology, which has attached the greatest importance to the 'person' of the author. The *author* still reigns in histories of literature, biographies of writers, interviews, magazines, as in the very consciousness of men of letters anxious to unite their person and their work through diaries and memoirs. The image of literature to be found in ordinary culture is tyrannically centred on the author, his person, his life, his tastes, his passions, while criticism still consists for the most part in saying that Baudelaire's work is the failure of Baudelaire the man, Van Gogh's his madness, Tchaikovsky's his vice. The *explanation* of a work is always sought in the man or woman who produced it, as if it were always in the end, through the more or less transparent allegory of the fiction, the voice of a single person, the *author* 'confiding' in us.

4

Though the sway of the Author remains powerful (the new criticism has often done no more than consolidate it), it goes without saying that certain writers have long since attempted to loosen it. In France, Mallarmé was doubtless the first to see and to foresee in its full extent the necessity to substitute language itself for the person who until then had been supposed to be its owner. For him, for us too, it is language which speaks, not the author; to write is, through a prerequisite impersonality (not at all to be confused with the castrating objectivity of the realist novelist), to reach that point where only language acts, 'performs', and not 'me'. Mallarmé's entire poetics consists in suppressing the author in the interests of writing (which is, as will be seen, to restore the place of the reader). Valéry, encumbered by a psychology of the Ego, considerably diluted Mallarmé's theory but, his taste for classicism leading him to turn to the lessons of rhetoric, he never stopped calling into question and deriding the Author; he stressed the linguistic and, as it were, 'hazardous' nature of his activity, and throughout his prose works he militated in favour of the essentially verbal condition of literature, in the face of which all recourse to the writer's interiority seemed to him pure superstition.

NOTES

3 Context

Note how the contemporary world is put into the context of the past here, especially in terms of European ways of thinking. Importantly, this says that the ways in which we tell stories, and how we think about stories in everyday life, are not neutral or normal and have not always existed; they are consequences of social history and ways of thinking, even if they seem 'obvious' to us now. As Barthes points out, this preoccupation with the author is not a global one, for plenty of societies do not think about authors – or even have a similar concept – as we do.

Writing Style

Barthes very specifically uses the word 'unite' here. He is arguing that the analytical tools he is criticising try to see connections between the author and the text, so that each explains the other. Similarly, we assume authors are trying to 'say' something in their texts. This is very often how books, films and television programmes are promoted, as extensions of the author's personality, history and psychology. Importantly, this relationship must be seen to *make sense*; that is, it 'unites' the text and the author.

Again, note the careful use of language – in this case, '*explanation*'. This word suggests that analysis often assumes there is a real, true meaning to a text, which can be 'explained' by knowledge of the author. Indeed, you may have come across this approach in your studies. You might want to think about why it is that 'explaining' things is seen as so important in our culture; why isn't 'enjoying' them, or 'making sense' of them, enough?

4 Context

New criticism is the name given to literary criticism in America and Britain from about 1920 to 1960. It involved close readings of texts, irrespective of author's intentions or, indeed, any knowledge about the author. It argued that texts had multiple meanings, and so could be seen as helpful to Barthes's argument. However, new criticism often ignored the role of the reader in the meaning-making process, thus implying that the important person in the process *was* the author. Critics associated with the movement include Cleanth Brooks, John Crowe Ransom, and Robert Penn Warren. See Jancovich (1993) and Young (1976).

Content

Mallarmé is likely to be an author unknown to you, as is Valéry later in the chapter. Mallarmé is famed for his poetry which uses sound as much as language, and therefore opens up a range of possible readings for the reader. Valéry was a poet, essayist and philosopher, whose work is often related to Mallarmé's. In referring to them, Barthes is placing his discussion in a particular philosophical and literature tradition. See Anderson (2000), Weinberg (1966) and Williams (2004).

5

Proust himself, despite the apparently psychological character of what are called his *analyses*, was visibly concerned with the task of inexorably blurring, by an extreme subtilization, the relation between the writer and his characters; by making of the narrator not he who has seen and felt nor even he who is writing, but he who *is going to write* (the young man in the novel – but, in fact, how old is he and who is he? – wants to write but cannot; the novel ends when writing at last becomes possible), Proust gave modern writing its epic. By a radical reversal, instead of putting his life into his novel, as is so often maintained, he made of his very life a work for which his own book was the model; so that it is clear to us that Charlus does not imitate Montesquiou but that Montesquiou – in his anecdotal, historical reality – is no more than a secondary fragment, derived from Charlus.

6

Lastly, to go no further than this prehistory of modernity, Surrealism, though unable to accord language a supreme place (language being system and the aim of the movement being, romantically, a direct subversion of codes – itself moreover illusory: a code cannot be destroyed, only 'played off'), contributed to the desacrilization of the image of the Author by ceaselessly recommending the abrupt disappointment of expectations of meaning (the famous surrealist 'jolt'), by entrusting the hand with the task of writing as quickly as possible what the head itself is unaware of (automatic writing), by accepting the principle and the experience of several people writing together.

4

(continued)

As Barthes notes, Mallarmé attempted in his writing to 'impersonalise' himself, forcing readers to engage with the language rather than the author. Much of television does this; it is unlikely in soap operas, for example, that you are aware who the author (however that is defined) is, and instead what you engage with is the programme itself, with little regard for who made it. It is noticeable that there is a cultural hierarchy at play here, for the majority of 'high' culture texts are seen to be 'authored', whereas one of the reasons why things like soaps are seen as 'low' culture is because they lack an easily identifiable author who 'explains' the text.

5 ## Content

More French literature! Marcel Proust is most famous for his novel *Remembrance of Things Past* (*À la recherché du temps perdu*, 1913–27). Again, we can wonder what kind of audience Barthes assumes he is writing for. Proust is significant because his novel is seen as one of the major works of the twentieth century, as it experiments with ideas of time, identity and memory. Charlus, whom Bathes mentions later in this paragraph, is commonly assumed to be based on the real-life Robert de Montesquiou, who was a French poet and novelist. In examining the relationship between Charlus and Montesquiou, Barthes suggests that we understand the latter as least partly through the former, so that 'fiction' comes to influence 'fact'. This would mean it is pointless wondering whether Charlus is a 'realistic' or 'true' depiction of Montesquiou, because both influence one another. This clearly has significant implications for things like biographies and autobiographies. While the examples Barthes uses might put you off making sense of what he is saying, it is important that you think about how his ideas can be transferred to examples that mean more to you; that is, just because Barthes is writing about French novelists, that does not mean his ideas are only relevant to such people. In using theory, your job is to see how well his ideas apply elsewhere.

6 ## Content

Surrealism is a cultural movement – usually associated with art – that spread across Europe in the 1920s or so. It is usually seen as a response to the First World War, with artists rejecting ideologies which they felt had led to the conflict. A central idea of surrealism was the attempt to capture the irrational and chaotic, and so artists developed creative methods which tried to cut out the rational working processes often associated with artistry. It attempted to be apolitical and amoral – in the sense that such opinions were human constructions that had led to the problems blighting society. In doing so, surrealism questioned much that was held dear in many societies, and it opened up revolutionary new ways of writing literature, making music, painting, and so on. It is one of the most influential artistic and cultural movements of the twentieth century. Because surrealism attempted to 'remove' the rationality of the artist from the creative process, it fits in well with Barthes's notion of the death of the author. Later in the paragraph Barthes mentions 'automatic

READING

7

Leaving aside literature itself (such distinctions really becoming invalid), linguistics has recently provided the destruction of the Author with a valuable analytical tool by showing that the whole of the enunciation is an empty process, functioning perfectly without there being any need for it to be filled with the person of the interlocutors. Linguistically, the author is never more than the instance writing, just as *I* is nothing other than the instance saying *I*: language knows a 'subject', not a 'person', and this subject, empty outside of the very enunciation which defines it, suffices to make language 'hold together', suffices, that is to say, to exhaust it.

8

The removal of the Author (one could talk here with Brecht of a veritable 'distancing', the Author diminishing like a figurine at the far end of the literary stage) is not merely an historical fact of an act of writing; it utterly transforms the modern text (or – which is the same thing – the text is henceforth made and read in such a way that at all its levels the author is absent). The temporality is different.

NOTES

6
(continued)

writing', where authors would not know what they had written until *after* they had done so. For such writing, it becomes absurd to ask about the author's intentions, or to insist on analysing the writing by thinking about the biography of the author. Ironically, of course, many surrealist artists (such as André Breton and Marcel Duchamp) *are* now lauded as visionary geniuses because of their importance in the movement; this is in direct contrast to their intentions, and shows how dominant the cult of the author is in our society. For more on surrealism see Hopkins (2003) and Richardson (2006).

7   ## Context

Note that Barthes sees distinctions between forms of culture as 'invalid'. You'll see throughout your reading that media theory is often adopted from analysis of other forms, and even though Barthes is repeatedly exploring literature, this is not to suggest that his arguments are only useful for the analysis of writing.

Content

The linguistic approaches Barthes is referring to – note he says they're 'recent' – are those structuralist ones which found a series of underlying principles in all communication, regardless of the author. Barthes argues that any writer (or director, or producer, or actor) is never more than simply another articulation of these underlying structures, and therefore these structures are more significant than anything new or different in any particular text. In that sense, it is the analysis of language (and remember that language has a broader definition here than we might usually ascribe it) which reveals meaning, and not analysis of the author.

8   ## Content

Bertolt Brecht was an important playwright and director who found the realism on offer in much theatre a problem because it offered audiences little chance to engage critically with the ideas any play might discuss. He felt much theatre presented arguments as if they were true, and required audiences to do little more than accept them. He developed what he called an 'epic theatre' which tried to engage audiences intellectually rather than emotionally. In order to do that, he broke down many of the theatre's conventions, creating plays which demonstrated their artifice, by, for example, getting actors to speak directly to the audience, or getting them to read out their stage directions. In attempting to encourage audiences to be critical and engaged, Barthes refused to let plays be 'works of art' which audiences should witness and marvel at; in that sense, he down-played the role of the author/creator, and instead hoped his theatre would be a place where audiences would create meaning, discuss and debate, and engage in the world around them. See Brecht (2001) and Styan (1981).

READING

9

The Author, when believed in, is always conceived of as the past of his own book: book and author stand automatically on a single line divided into a *before* and an *after*. The Author is thought to *nourish* the book, which is to say that he exists before it, thinks, suffers, lives for it, is in the same relation of antecedence to his work as a father to his child.

10

In complete contrast, the modern scriptor is born simultaneously with the text, is in no way equipped with a being preceding or exceeding the writing, is not the subject with the book as predicate; there is no other time than that of the enunciation and every text is eternally written *here and now*. The fact is (or, it follows) that *writing* can no longer designate an operation of recording, notation, representation, 'depiction' (as the Classics would say); rather, it designates exactly what linguists, referring to Oxford philosophy, call a performative, a rare verbal form (exclusively given in the first person and in the present tense) in which the enunciation has no other content (contains no other proposition) than the act by which it is uttered – something like the *I declare* of kings or the *I sing* of very ancient poets.

NOTES

9 Content

Here Barthes discusses the relationship between the author and the book. He argues that we normally think of the author as existing *before* the book, and the book is a result of the author's past. He says a book is a 'child' to the author, who is like a father figure. It is this notion that he is critiquing throughout this reading.

Writing Style

Note 'when believed in'. By using such a phrase Barthes is noting that the ways we carry out interpretation are affected by our beliefs. 'Beliefs' might be seen as the same as 'theories'; that is, each of the theories you come across are just the beliefs of the people who wrote it, and the ones you find most convincing or useful might say something about your beliefs more generally.

10 Structure

Compare the material here to that covered by Note 3, as Barthes is contrasting these two approaches. When he talks about the '*here and now*', he is referring to the moment of reading, for the meaning of any text only exists once someone reads it. When you're reading a book you are making sense of it, you are carrying out what Barthes calls 'enunciation'. At the same time, you are 'reading' the author, for you may be thinking that the text is typical of that author, or assuming something about them because of the text's contents. The '*here and now*' is important because it reflects the momentary nature of meaning. For example, when as an adult you see a film that you adored as a child, you might find it childish, or badly made, or worrying in its message. Because we change, and our lives change, and the world around us changes, every time we encounter a text we read it slightly differently, yet the text itself has not changed at all. It is likely that, as you progress through your studies, there are films or television programmes that you used to think of in one way, but now think of in another. The fact that, throughout our lives, we read texts in a variety of ways shows how there is no one, fixed, definitive meaning to them, and so all we can deal with are the readings we make '*here and now*'. Are you convinced by this?

Writing Style

Note how Barthes moves from talking about a 'fact' to merely stating 'it follows'. The latter shows how his statement is reliant on his previous argument, and is a useful way of constructing an argument that helps the reader follow the line of thought.

Content

Here Barthes argues that writing does not merely record or represent an event; it is instead an act (one he calls 'performative') of creating meaning by drawing on the linguistic structures and tools on offer. And just as authors draw on those structures and tools, so do readers (this is similar to Hall's 'Encoding/Decoding model' (1980c); see Chapter 11). How does this relate to media? It is often argued that photography *does* capture the 'real' world, because of the technological capabilities of

READING

11

Having buried the Author, the modern scriptor can thus no longer believe, as according to the pathetic view of his predecessors, that this hand is too slow for his thought or passion and that consequently, making a law of necessity, he must emphasize this delay and indefinitely 'polish' his form. For him, on the contrary, the hand, cut off from any voice, borne by a pure gesture of inscription (and not of expression), traces a field without origin – or which, at least, has no other origin than language itself, language which ceaselessly calls into question all origins.

12

We know now that a text is not a line of words releasing a single 'theological' meaning (the 'message' of the Author-God) but a multi-dimensional space in which a variety of writings, none of them original, blend and clash. The text is a tissue of quotations drawn from the innumerable centres of culture.

13

Similar to Bouvard and Pécuchet, those eternal copyists, at once sublime and comic and whose profound ridiculousness indicates precisely the truth of writing, the writer can only imitate a gesture that is always anterior, never original. His only power is to mix writings, to counter the ones with the others, in such a way as never to rest on any one of them.

NOTES

10
(continued)

the camera. But we still have to draw on structures to make sense of photographs. A picture of, say, a football team in the sports pages of a newspaper only makes 'sense' if we know what football is, if we know that the sports pages are at the back of the newspaper, and if we understand the game's rules enough to interpret the action being depicted. Because these structures are so commonplace we often think they are natural or normal; the argument here is that they are not, and by thinking through how they work we can learn a lot about our culture and society.

11 ## Writing Style

There is much careful use of language here. 'Pathetic' is likely to be meant in its earlier, literal sense: that is, to do with emotions. Note how, just as 'author' has been replaced with 'scriptor', so 'writing' has been replaced by 'inscription'. We also see how metaphorical language is used – just as the title of the reading does not suggest someone has actually died, so the author being 'buried' is not meant in a literal sense. It is this interplay of literal and figurative language that can sometimes make reading theory such as this difficult, especially for a British reader where this is a rarer writing style.

Context

This is an important idea: that language is a constructed system that we often use without thinking, but which draws on a range of social and cultural factors. In critiquing the transparency of language, Barthes notes that this calls into question the way in which we structure society as a whole. For example, different countries have different languages; why is this? Also, languages change over time; again, what does this tell us?

12 ## Structure

This is a useful summary of the argument so far.

13 ## Writing Style

More references to French literature. You might see that you do not need to know who Bouvard and Pécuchet are in order to make sense of the reading.

Content

Barthes argues that a writer can never be original, because they always have to use the language tools available to them. Do you agree? Is this the same for all media?

READING

14

Succeeding the Author, the scriptor no longer bears within him passions, humours, feelings, impressions, but rather this immense dictionary from which he draws a writing that can know no halt: life never does more than imitate the book, and the book itself is only a tissue of signs, an imitation that is lost, infinitely deferred.

15

Once the Author is removed, the claim to decipher a text becomes quite futile. To give a text an Author is to impose a limit on that text, to furnish it with a final signified, to close the writing. Such a conception suits criticism very well, the latter then allotting itself the important task of discovering the Author (or its hypostases: society, history, psyché, liberty) beneath the work: when the Author has been found, the text is 'explained' – victory to the critic. Hence there is no surprise in the fact that, historically, the reign of the Author has also been that of the Critic, nor again in the fact that criticism (be it new) is today undermined along with the Author. In the multiplicity of writing, everything is to be *disentangled*, nothing *deciphered*; the structure can be followed, 'run' (like the thread of a stocking) at every point and at every level, but there is nothing beneath: the space of writing is to be ranged over, not pierced; writing ceaselessly posits meaning ceaselessly to evaporate it, carrying out a systematic exemption of meaning. In precisely this way literature (it would be better from now on to say *writing*), by refusing to assign a 'secret', an ultimate meaning, to the text (and to the world as text), liberates what may be called an anti-theological activity, an activity that is truly revolutionary since to refuse to fix meaning is, in the end, to refuse God and his hypostases – reason, science, law.

14 · Content

Does life do nothing more than imitate a book? Also, what does Barthes mean by this? Does he mean it literally, or is there a more subtle intent? If you think about the ways in which we talk about, and memorialise our lives (in diaries, and blogs, and photos) you might be able to see what he is getting at.

15 · Content

It seems Barthes is determined the critic shall not have 'victory'. Indeed, the suggestion that texts have no definitive, true meaning renders criticism irrelevant, which might be why so many people argue against such an approach. If you agree with all of this, and think there is no true meaning, then what *is* the point of education?

Writing Style

Again, note the language here. What is the difference between '*disentangled*' and '*deciphered*'? Later on, why does Barthes say it is better to use the word '*writing*' than 'literature'? You can see here why precision in language is important, especially if you want to signal subtle but significant differences.

Structure

The sentence beginning 'In the multiplicity of writing . . .' is confusingly structured, with many commas, two semi-colons and a colon. Could Barthes have structured it more helpfully?

Context

This shows how there is a relationship between this kind of theory and broader social and cultural topics. If we accept that texts do not contain a definitive, unarguable meaning, then there is no 'truth' that we can all rely on. This means things like science and law are as open to interpretation as anything else. And this is certainly the case; judges and scholars debate how to apply laws in specific cases, often disagreeing over what is intended to be static, clear language. Similarly, theologians have debated the meanings of the Bible – along with other holy texts – for centuries. Yet the notion that there is no such thing as 'truth' is often threatening to many people, especially those in power, for their positions often rely on an assumption that they know more, and can tell us how the world works. Barthes says it is 'truly revolutionary'; so how come we have not had a revolution then?

READING

16

Let us come back to the Balzac sentence. No one, no 'person', says it: its source, its voice, is not the true place of the writing, which is reading. Another – very precise – example will help to make this clear:

17

recent research (J.-P. Vernant[1]) has demonstrated the constitutively ambiguous nature of Greek tragedy, its texts being woven from words with double meanings that each character understands unilaterally (this perpetual misunderstanding is exactly the 'tragic'); there is, however, someone who understands each word in its duplicity and who, in addition, hears the very deafness of the characters speaking in front of him – this someone being precisely the reader (or here, the listener).

18

Thus is revealed the total existence of writing: a text is made of multiple writings, drawn from many cultures and entering into mutual relations of dialogue, parody, contestation, but there is one place where this multiplicity is focused and that place is the reader, not, as was hitherto said, the author. The reader is the space on which all the quotations that make up a writing are inscribed without any of them being lost; a text's unity lies not in its origin but in its destination.

1. [Cf. Jean-Pierre Vernant (with Pierre Vidal-Naquet), *Mythe et tragédie en Grèce ancienne*, Paris 1972. esp. pp. 19–40, 99–131.]

16 Structure

Here Barthes returns to his opening example. This is a neat way to structure his argument, and signals to the reader that we're coming to the end of the reading.

17 Content

This is an important point about the ways in which audiences are positioned by texts. Barthes notes that often, in tragedies, the audience knows more about what is going on than any of the characters; the same is often true in soap operas, for example. This means we occupy a position impossible within the reality of the text, which shows how our relationship to the text is not comparable to any kind of truth, but purely a consequence of the ways in which texts are structured.

18 Content

This section helpfully summarises the key ideas. As you can see, Barthes argues that the reader carries out all of the activities usually ascribed to the author.

19

Yet this destination cannot any longer be personal: the reader is without history, biography, psychology; he is simply that *someone* who holds together in a single field all the traces by which the written text is constituted. Which is why it is derisory to condemn the new writing in the name of a humanism hypocritically turned champion of the reader's rights. Classic criticism has never paid any attention to the reader; for it, the writer is the only person in literature. We are now beginning to let ourselves be fooled no longer by the arrogant antiphrastical recriminations of good society in favour of the very thing it sets aside, ignores, smothers, or destroys; we know that to give writing its future, it is necessary to overthrow the myth: the birth of the reader must be at the cost of the death of the Author.

19 ## Content

What are the 'traces' Barthes refers to here?

Context

Think about this; how often in your studies have you come across analysis of readers? See Chapter 23 in *this* book, where Ien Ang (1991) argues that readers are only usually talked about as masses, when we are told how many people watched a programme, or the box office receipts for a film, for example. The activities of individual audience members are rarely discussed, and instead we are repeatedly told about the activities of individual authors. You might want to think about why it is that so many subject areas are repeatedly disinterested in the activities of the vast majority of 'ordinary' people.

Writing Style

This is clearly quite angry writing; calling a society 'arrogant' is not a neutral term. Also, 'overthrow' has interesting resonances of the 'revolution' Barthes mentioned earlier.

Structure

Barthes ends by envisioning a future, which is predicated on the changes he recommends. In this sense, this is critical analysis, which does not just examine how things are, but also suggests how they should be. He acknowledges there will be a 'cost'; a cost for whom, do you think?

REFLECTING ON THE READING

As noted at the start of this chapter, it is likely that you found this a difficult reading, more because of the use of language and the choice of examples than the actual content and argument. It is worth accepting that this is a difficult reading, and that making sense of it might take some rereading and thinking. Indeed, having a working knowledge of the article is what is necessary; that is, you do not need to get *everything* in a reading in order to grasp the main argument, and to be able to effectively summarise and apply it. Developing an awareness of how much of a reading you need to feel comfortable with is an important skill, as is being confident enough to skip past material that seems too hard, or irrelevant. Bear in mind this is not an excuse to avoid engaging with the reading thoroughly, though.

As with all readings, you should see whether you think the material is still relevant and applicable. Barthes was writing in a different country in a different century; do you see how his work might still be worthwhile? Think about the consequences of the academic industry he bemoans. You could do this by reflecting on how *you* have been taught; were you taught about culture mainly via the author, and to what extent were alternative readings of texts taken into account? Do you see your role as a scholar-to-be to learn how to 'better' read and understand media? Considering that power is such a key idea in media studies, how do you see these concerns as being related to power? Isn't the relationship between teacher and pupil one of power? And if we take what Barthes is arguing on board, and dismantle the hierarchical education structures he bemoans, what will it be replaced with? How can we have education if the author is dead?

Do you agree that texts do not contain meanings, but are instead merely artefacts which readers make sense of? If this is the case, that means we can never say a film is racist or sexist, because the film does not contain anything; we can only say that some people have read it in this way, and that they drew on certain social structures to do so. This has significant implications for things like the watershed on television, or the ratings system in cinema, which assume that texts do have a meaning which should be restricted to older people. Are you willing to accept the idea that, if you find something offensive, that is because of you rather than because of something 'contained' within the text?

Finally, there's an interesting irony for you to ponder. Barthes says we should not consider the author, yet he is himself an author. Indeed, the fact that there are books written about him, and which often trace a connection between him as a person and what he wrote, shows that Barthes has himself been positioned as an author in precisely the way he criticised. And it is not as if Barthes discouraged this – his books have his name on them. Similarly, while he criticised the hierarchical structures of education, he spent his life working at universities, ending up as a highly respected professor at the Collège de France, where he taught *his* theories. It could be argued that he was trying to bring the system down from the inside: it could be seen that he did not practise what he preached. Certainly the cult of the author has not died; *this* book is largely structured around authors. So, if you find Barthes's ideas convincing, how do you explain the fact that nothing has changed?

Key terms to explore

empiricism; new criticism; positivism; rationalism; surrealism.

Key writers who are mentioned

Bertolt Brecht; Marcel Proust; Jean-Pierre Vernant.

RECOMMENDED READING

Barthes, Roland (1973 [1957]) *Mythologies*, translated by Annette Lavers, London: Paladin.

One of Barthes's key works, in which he examines many everyday subjects – such as wrestling, advertising and soap – in order to show the complex communication conventions they rely on.

Burke, Seán (1998) *The Death and Return of the Author: Criticism and subjectivity in Barthes, Foucault, and Derrida*, 2nd edition, Edinburgh: Edinburgh University Press.

Complex debate responding to the idea of the author's 'death', placed within the context of literature as well as media and cultural theory.

Ribière, Mireille (2002) *Barthes: A beginner's guide*, London: Hodder & Stoughton.

Helpful overview of Barthes's thinking and writing, with examination of his key terms, and an exploration of the influence of his work on subsequent theory.

CHAPTER 23

Audiences

Ang, I. (1991) 'Audience-as-market and audience-as-public', in *Desperately Seeking the Audience*, London: Routledge, pp. 26–32.

INTRODUCTION TO AUDIENCES

Media producers are very keen to know how many people are watching, buying and enjoying their products. Every week the list of the top ten grossing films in the country is published in many newspapers and magazines; bookshops display the best-selling books, often divided up into various categories such as fiction and biography; BBC Radio 1 devotes much of Sunday afternoon to counting down the top forty. Being at 'number one' in any chart is a big accolade, not only because it means lots of people like your product, but also because the ensuing publicity is a way of keeping that product in the public eye. Measuring audiences in this way – by adding up the number of people who consumed a product – seems obvious and straightforward, and the simplest way of knowing how audiences behave.

Yet what exactly does such data really tell us? This approach to audiences is a *quantitative* one, which focuses on *quantities* and so relies on counting and figures to suggest something about how the world works and what people within it do. This information, though, is primarily of use to media producers, for it gives them an insight into what audiences like and dislike, which can then influence the future products they release. Such data are combined with that of focus groups, where small groups of people are shown a product and asked to give their opinions on it. But all of these approaches tell us very little about what audiences actually do.

For example, while a song may reach a high position in the music charts on Radio 1, we have no idea whether someone who bought it did so for themselves or as a present, whether the song has some special meaning for them, how often they play it, who they play it to and when, or anything else. The charts merely tell us who bought something, and while this is vital data for the media industries, there have been many questions raised by media theorists concerning the consequences of this approach to audiences, and whether there are better ways we can think of audience activity.

What this quantitative approach to audiences does is to see people as nothing more than consumers; that is, ratings, on the whole, only measure us when we buy something. For many people who criticise contemporary society for its consumerist and capitalist nature, this way of conceiving of audiences is a problem, as it suggests our only relationship with media and culture is one based around purchase. Furthermore, while we may know that 9 million people watched last night's episode of *Coronation Street* (ITV, 1960–), say, this is not an aspect of the experience of any individual watching that programme; that is, as a viewer, sitting at home, alone, we are utterly unaware of the masses of people across the nation also watching the programme, and, instead, being a viewer is a much more local, individual and domestic activity than raw ratings suggest. The term 'audience' insists on lumping together millions of individuals, carrying out millions of different and variable activities, as if they are all the same, reducing them to nothing more than a mass who consumed something; audiences are 'a figment of various imaginings' (Hartley 2002a: 60).

Media studies has, then, attempted to think about audiences in a variety of different ways. Its approach has often focused on trying to examine audience activity on a much smaller scale, exploring the variety of factors which go into consuming media and, therefore, 'produce a holistic description of a culture' (Seiter 1999: 10). For example, much new-audience research (Boyd-Barrett and Newbold 1995: 498–553) has adopted a broadly *ethnographic* approach, which means that researchers carry out long-term research on small groups of people in their normal environment, to try to place their media consumption within the everyday context. This could mean living with a family for months, as Morley (1980) did, to see what media means to individuals and how they place it within their everyday lives; significantly, this approach does not see the activity of buying as the only one worthy of interest. Such research examines what people do with media, and therefore suggests individual audience members are much more active, critical and distinctive than raw ratings might suggest. This kind of research is called *qualitative*, and is interested in contexts, events, processes and the complexity of people's everyday behaviour (for an outline account of the differences between qualitative and quantitative research methods see Schrøder et al. 2003: 26–43).

This also raises questions, importantly, about the relationship between media and people. As noted above, the reliance on ratings suggests audience activity is nothing more than a commercial one, which has consequences for the roles people are seen to play in society. Many media studies theorists dislike the idea of audiences being nothing more than consumers, and instead see the media as an important part of the ways in which democratic societies function; in doing so, they are drawing on aspects of the 'public sphere' (see Chapter 13 in this book). Examining audience activity in ways other than ratings, then, is not just about trying to find out the variety of things which people do; it is also an attempt to question the relationship between media and the public, and to argue that it can be seen as one which does not have to focus solely on the activities of buying and selling. Thinking about the best ways to research audiences is, then, an important part of thinking about the social roles the media play in our everyday lives as consumers, citizens, audiences and publics.

The discussion about how audiences can be defined is shown by the title of this reading: are audiences 'markets' or are they 'publics'? The reading is a chapter from Ien Ang's book *Desperately Seeking the Audience* (1991), whose title also suggests that working out what an audience is and what it does is something which a number of people – academics and industries – are 'desperate' to do. For Ang, the various ways in which different groups and institutions define the people who consume media tell us something about the systems in which they work, and the ways in which they are interested in audience activity. In this sense, measuring the audience is not a neutral act, because in doing so you have to decide what it is you are interested in and, therefore, what you are not interested in.

This chapter comes from a section in the book called 'Conquering the audience', and outlines Ang's argument that in foregrounding ratings as the prime measurement of audience activity, the audience is 'conquered' and reduced to nothing more than consumers; this can be seen as indicative of the media industries as a whole, who mainly want you to watch or buy things, and are relatively unconcerned about other things you do. Later in her book Ang discusses places where this may not be so stark, as she examines public service broadcasting in Europe which, to an extent, is interested in factors other than consumption, such as enjoyment, and the social role its broadcasting plays. However, it is still noticeable that these institutions are primarily interested in the public as a mass, and do little to explore the individuals who make up that mass.

It is because such institutions are interested in people as a mass that the term applied to that mass is a singular one – 'audience'. You might have noticed already that in this chapter the term has instead usually been in the plural; 'audiences'. This linguistic distinction is seen as important, and media studies often refers to 'audiences' rather than 'the audience'. The use of the plural insists on the plurality of audiences, and shows how researchers are often as interested in the *differences* between individual's consumption of media, as much as they are in the similarities. Using the plural therefore has implications for research methods, as it means you can ask questions that are still meaningful about specific individuals. However, the plural also has a political intent, because it is a term which refuses to lump together millions of people as an undistinguishable mass, and instead sees individual activity as indicative of audience power. You need to be careful when using the terms 'audience' and 'audiences' because they have different meanings, and they are often used in very specific ways in many readings you will come across.

This is shown in Ang's use of the plural when she outlines her book as one that 'aims to encourage the further development of an ethnographic understanding of television audiences' (1991: x). It was written at a time when media studies was developing a whole range of new approaches to audiences, and Ang was a significant part of that development. Indeed, Ang's most famous early work was *Watching Dallas: Soap opera and the melodramatic imagination* (1985), in which she interviewed a number of women about the ways in which they responded to the glossy American soap opera, *Dallas* (CBS, 1978–91). This work fits into the *ethnographic* tradition, which is a form of research with a 'focus on media uses as a part of people's everyday lives and applies the researcher's observation of an informal interaction with his and her informants as a major methodological tool' (Schrøder et al. 2003: 58). Ang's *theoretical* discussion of audiences can therefore be seen to be related to the *practical* research she has carried out. This helpfully demonstrates the interplay between theory and practice.

In preparing for the reading, you might first want to think about yourself as an audience. When you choose to see a film, or buy a CD, or watch a television programme, what factors lead to you making that decision? How does the media fit into your life, and what do you use it for? Is your media consumption primarily based around entertainment, or do you use it to inform yourself about the world around you? Who do you consume media with, and what pleasures do you get out of that social activity? Sometimes spotting media usage can be quite difficult, because it is such an ordinary, everyday activity; why not try keeping a media diary, then, noting each time you encounter all forms of media? When such studies have been carried out, people are often very surprised by the extent to which their lives intersect with media, showing how such activities are so 'ordinary' that we often cease to notice them.

It is hoped you will see that there is a variety of ways in which you interact with the media, and that you put it to a range of uses. If this is the case, how much do you think audience ratings – still the primary way in which audiences are measured – say about the things that you do and what the media means to you? Perhaps more importantly – especially as this is the motivation behind Ang's work – does it matter that ratings are the dominant method for measuring audience activity?

1

I. Ang

Audience-as-market and audience-as-public

So far, I have unproblematically described the operation of the television institution in commercial terms. But of course the institutional arrangement of television broadcasting is not always based upon commercial principles. While the United States is the home of the most full-fledged commercial system, the nation-states of Western Europe are the historical base of a range of public service broadcasting systems, embodied by state-regulated and collectively-financed organizations such as the British BBC, the Italian RAI, or the Dutch 'pillarized' system (see e.g. Kuhn 1985). The two systems are both formally built upon the communicative framework of broadcasting, but they differ fundamentally as regards assumptions about the cultural and political purpose of broadcasting, and this difference is inextricably linked to a marked distinction in how each system prefers to define the institution–audience relationship. In other words, although all broadcasting institutions must by definition imagine the audience as object to be conquered, the meaning, intent or import of the conquest is not construed in the same way in the two systems.

2

The pragmatic philosophy behind the commercial system is the easiest one to unravel, because its axioms are simple and straightforward. Commercial television can be characterized at several levels, but in its barest form it is based upon the intertwined double principle of the making of programmes for profit and the use of television channels for advertising. Thus, the driving force of the system is ultimately a purely economic matter: it is principally connected with the capitalist concern of making money. As Jay Blumler (1986: 1) has observed, 'individual broadcasters [in American commercial television] may be moved by aspirations of communication excellence, "love of television", social purpose or sheer creative autonomy. But in the end, all such aims must be subordinated to the overriding profit-maximising goal.'

NOTES

1

Structure

As the article begins with 'So far', it is clear that this is a chapter in a book and that some key arguments have already been outlined in the preceding chapter. This means that there might be references to previous material here. While this could suggest we must go back and read what's already been covered, it is often worthwhile reading material out of its natural context, in order to see what sense we can make of it; if you come across problems of understanding, you might decide to search out the preceding material.

Content

Here Ang makes distinctions between different kinds of broadcasting systems. As Chapter 21 in *this* book shows, there are various ways in which media systems could be organised, and these are usually responses to social and political factors. Ang mentions public service broadcasting; while this may be a term you are familiar with, it is worth investigating it in more detail, as it is a very complicated idea, with no fixed definition, and applied in different ways in different countries.

Context

Ang is making a link here between the structure of broadcasting institutions and the ways in which audiences are treated by them. However, she is also careful to note that we should not overstate the differences between public service broadcasting and commercial systems. Her argument here is clearly that in order to understand audiences, we need to examine the ways in which broadcasting institutions are structured.

Writing Style

Why does Ang call the audience an 'object to be conquered'? Conquered by whom, in what ways and to what ends? Do you think 'conquered' is the best word to describe the process she's outlining?

2

Context

Is commercial broadcasting 'simple and straightforward'? While we need to acknowledge the financial pressures which affect commercial broadcasting, are these the only factors which matter? And how is this so different from the pressures which affect non-commercial, public service broadcasting, which, after all, still needs money in order to make programming?

Writing Style

While outlining the 'bottom-line' economic pressures on commercial broadcasting, note that Ang is careful here not to condemn or criticise such a system.

READING

3

In principle, the workings of the system are relatively simple. Programmes are transmitted by commercial television networks and stations in order to carry commercials, which are usually inserted between programmes or sections of programmes. The advertisers whose products are offered for sale in the commercials pay large sums of money to the broadcasters in exchange for the air time they acquire to disseminate the messages. The system operates according to the laws of the capitalist market economy, so that advertising time in the most popular programmes is generally the most expensive. Thus, in the autumn of 1985, a thirty-second time spot in NBC's *The Cosby Show*, then the programme on American prime time television that was measured as drawing the largest audience, cost $270,000 (ibid.: 5).

4

It is for this precise economic reason that audience maximization has become so paramount a principle in commercial television, and concordantly, why the production of ratings through audience measurement has become an absolutely crucial subsidiary industry in the institutional framework of commercial television. The discourse of ratings, dry and technical as it is, provides knowledge about the television audience that is indispensable for the economic functioning of the system. Good ratings results are the agreed-upon signifier of effective communication between advertiser and audience, and the commercial networks must try to achieve those good ratings results – that is, to maximize their audience – through shrewd and attractive programming. As CBS executive Arnold Becker told Todd Gitlin (1983: 31): 'I'm not interested in culture. I'm not interested in pro-social values. I have only one interest. That's whether people watch the program. That's my definition of good, that's my definition of bad.'

5

The television programme then is the main instrument in commercial television's constant quest for the maximum audience. As Nick Browne (1984: 178) has noted, 'the network is basically a relay in a process of textualizing the interaction of audience and advertiser'. This process of textualizing – the process of translating the goal of maximum ratings results into concrete decisions about the programmes to be scheduled – is the core of the networks' task: the day-to-day activities of network managers ultimately revolve around constantly finding ways of regulating this difficult and complex process along orderly and manageable lines.

NOTES

3 Context

It might seem that Ang is stating the obvious here; presumably most of us know how commercials and advertising works. In that sense this paragraph is not about telling you something new; it is placing her argument in an agreed context that can be drawn on later.

4 Context

Is 'audience maximisation' the key factor in commercial television? What about niche audiences, where advertisers are paying not to reach a lot of people, but to reach the right kind of people? See Channel 4's remit, for example.

Writing Style

Note here that Ang is quoting Gitlin who is quoting Becker. We should think, then, about the selection process which has led to this quote; Ang has selected a particular part of Gitlin's book, and Gitlin has selected a particular part of his interview with Becker. We might want to question what has been left out.

Content

Do you think Arnold Becker really believes this? And how representative is he of others working in the industry?

5 Content

You need to ensure you have a good grasp of what Ang means by 'textualizing'. Key here is that Ang is talking about processes; the idea of processes working in particular ways and having particular outcomes is a key concept in media studies.

READING

6

Ratings play a central role in this process, but that role is a highly ambivalent one. On the one hand, it offers managers a sense of knowing how successful the textualizing has been (what is called 'feedback'), but on the other hand, it leaves them in profound ignorance, or at least in great doubt, about the precise ingredients of their success or failure. That is, although ratings produce some generalized information about who has watched which programmes, they do not give any clue about the more specific question of what made people watch the programmes, so that it is very difficult to use ratings to predict future success or failure (Pekurny 1982).

7

Nevertheless, in the political economy of commercial television audience measurement is an indispensable knowledge-producing instrument. In the commercial system, the imperative of conquering the audience ensues from the positioning of the audience as a market in which audience members are defined as potential consumers in a dual sense: not only of TV programmes, but also of the products being advertised through those programmes (McQuail 1987: 220–1). What is essential in this context is knowledge about the size of the market, and this is precisely what 'ratings' and 'shares' are purported to signify.

8

However, determining the size of the market is a difficult and problematic task, as is evidenced by the ever-increasing technological sophistication of the methods being used for measuring the audience, that took an accelarated pace in the 1980s and reached a temporary climax with the introduction of the so-called 'people meter', an advanced and expensive measurement device that provoked intense controversy in circles of the American television industry. This controversy, which shows how epistemological and political issues, issues of knowledge and power, are inextricably linked in commercial television's institutional point of view, will be described extensively in Part II.

NOTES

6 ## Content

In this paragraph Ang notes the drawbacks in ratings measurement techniques. Indeed, much of her writing has examined the limited data which ratings measurement can accumulate. What kinds of things can't ratings measurement find out? Why might those things it cannot find out be important? And how might the system be improved so that those things *can* be found out?

7 ## Context

See Chapter 12 in this book for more information on political economy.

Content

Here we get onto one of the key ideas of this chapter, which is reflected in its title. Ang – along with many others – argues that the commercial system is only interested in an audience as a 'market': that is, as a group of people to whom things can be sold. In these ways, our pleasures, or reasons for watching particular programmes do not matter, as long as we are there watching it. Ang argues this way of thinking of people is an inevitable consequence of the commercial system, and, later on, she contrasts this with other ways of thinking about audiences.

8 ## Content

A key point here is that in order to find out who is watching what, technology has to be used; the results are therefore only as good as the technology. Importantly, this technology changes, as Ang notes in her discussion of the 'people meter'. As networks pay the companies that measure audiences, those networks are obviously keen for the results to show that their audiences are as big as possible. Newer, better technologies, which might reveal that audiences are actually smaller than was previously thought are then dropped. Indeed, there are very many ways in which audiences can be measured, and they are all limited; as Ang notes at the end of this paragraph, then, the debate about which technology should be used has very important consequences, and broadcasters are understandably keen to only pay for information which serves them best.

Writing Style

Why does Ang call the people meter 'so-called'?

READING

9

In the philosophy of public service broadcasting, an altogether different place is reserved for the audience. Of course, the idea of 'public service' as such can be and has been interpreted and concretized in a variety of ways in diverse national contexts, manifested in historical particularities in institutional structure and socio-political and ideological grounding. However despite such idiosyncracies it can be said that in classic terms public service broadcasting institutions constitute what Williams (1976: 131) has called a 'paternal system'. A paternal system, Williams states, is 'an authoritarian system with a conscience: that is to say, with values and purposes beyond the maintenance of its own power'. In this philosophy, the institution–audience relationship is primarily defined in cultural and ideological terms: 'the paternal system transmits values, habits, and tastes, which are its own justification as a ruling minority, and which it wishes to extend to the people as a whole' (ibid.). 'Serving the public' then means, as Anthony Smith has put it, 'forcing [the audience] to confront the frontiers of its own taste' (in Kumar 1986: 59), although it should be noted that this ideal does not necessarily have to be linked to a conservative form of cultural elitism, as was the case in the early days of public service broadcasting. As we will see in more detail in Part III, contemporary public service broadcasting has over the years developed a much more eclectic conception of its task, emphasizing the duty to offer a broad range of high quality programmes (Blumler *et al.* 1986; Manschot 1988). Nevertheless, the relationship of public service institution to its audience remains essentially characterized, not by economic profit-seeking, but by a pervasive sense of cultural responsibility and social accountability, which is emphatically opposed to the easy-going commercial dictum of 'giving the audience what it wants'.

10

As a result, a different positioning of audience is at stake here. Not the audience-as-market, but the audience-as-public is the central object of concern within public service institutions (McQuail 1987: 219–220). The audience-as-public consists not of consumers, but of citizens who must be reformed, educated, informed as well as entertained – in short, 'served' – presumably to enable them to better perform their democratic rights and duties. Within this context, broadcasting has nothing to do with the consumerist hedonism of (American) commercial television – it is a very dignified, serious business. Typically, popular entertainment, so conspicuously and self-evidently the prevailing fare on American television, tends to be considered a less important programme category in European public service broadcasting, even though in practice entertainment programmes, both domestic and foreign, are an established part of the daily schedules of most public service channels (cf. Ang 1985a; 1985b).

NOTES

9 · Context

We now move from commercial broadcasting to its public service counterpart. Ang acknowledges the difficulties in defining what this term means, especially as different countries have interpreted it differently at various times. Note how, in order to deal with the difficulties in engaging with this convoluted and time-consuming debate, Ang draws on Williams to offer a definition. A key way in which many writers avoid having to cover all aspects of a debate is to refer to someone else who has already covered it. In drawing on Williams, who is a key figure in media studies (see Chapter 17), Ang also draws on his authority, assuming we will accept his statements as worthwhile. But are there problems in summarising public service broadcasting in Williams's terms? What does Ang mean by 'classic terms', and what does this leave out of the debate?

Content

If you're unsure how this 'paternal' system is different from the commercial one Ang described earlier, you should go back and check; it is key that the distinctions between them are understood.

Writing Style

Note the variety of words being used to describe people here – 'audience', 'public' – and how this is different from their earlier definition as 'consumers'. What are the differences between these terms and why might certain people choose to use each one?

Structure

As in section 1, Ang refers here to a part of her book not included in this reading. Again, it is worth seeing if you can make sense of her argument without worrying about going off to read Part III that she mentions.

10 · Structure

The two different definitions of audiences Ang mentions here are those in the chapter's title; clearly, then, this is a key part of her argument.

Writing Style

Why is 'served' in inverted commas? Why is 'American' in brackets?

Context

Here, there is a point made about different kinds of programming, and how they are viewed by different broadcasting systems. We can see, then, the link between the philosophy behind broadcasting systems and the kinds of programmes produced for audiences. This is one of the 'processes' which Ang was discussing earlier.

READING

11

The difference between the two paradigms of audience is impressive and can be clarified by placing them in two diverse theoretical models of mass communication. The audience-as-public idea is in fact the more classic one of the two and fits in the so-called transmission model of communication: here, communication is defined by such terms as sending or transmitting messages to others. Implied in this model is the conception of audiences as 'receivers' of those messages, and a more or less 'ordered transference of meaning' as the intended consequence of the process as a whole forms its basic rationale (McQuail 1987: 43–4; Carey 1989). In the audience-as-market idea, however, such purposive transfer of meaning is only of secondary importance. As McQuail (1987: 45) has remarked, 'the essence of any market is to bring goods and services to the attention of potential consumers, to arouse and keep their interest'. Thus, the essence of what McQuail calls the attention model of communication is comprised by the mere gaining or attracting of attention: communication is considered effective as soon as attention is actually given by audiences, no matter its quality or impact. This is the model of communication that undergirds the institutional arrangement of commercial broadcasting, but it is clearly insufficient and inadequate from the institutional perspective of public service broadcasting, for whom attention would only make sense when connected with some meaningful communicative purpose.

12

Audience-as-market and audience-as-public then are two alternative configurations of audience, each connected with one of the two major institutional arrangements – commercial and public service – of broadcast television. These two configurations provide the founding paradigms for the production of knowledge about the audience within specific institutions. Thus, institutional knowledge produced in the context of American commercial television generally displays a vocabulary and a set of preoccupations which articulate and ultimately fit into the idea that the audience is a market to be won, while the repertoire of institutional knowledge circulating within public service institutions in Europe and elsewhere needs to enhance and sustain the idea that the audience is a public to be served with enlightened responsibility.

11 Content

Note that Ang acknowledges the models of mass communication she explores are 'theoretical'; this implies there is a lack of empirical evidence to support their conclusions. While this could be read as invalidating their use, it is important to remember that theory is often seen as an end in itself, and its validity is not necessarily predicated on proof; indeed, some theories may be making claims whose proof is very difficult to obtain, but can still be extremely useful ways of thinking about the world.

Writing Style

What is meant by one model being 'more classic' than the other? 'Classic' defined by whom?

Context

Ang draws on McQuail's model of communication here. McQuail is a key thinker in this area (2002, 2005); however, it is worth noting that just because he is a key figure, that does not mean we do not explore the ideas he proposes critically.

12 Structure

This is a useful summary of Ang's argument so far. If you are still unclear of what has been argued previously in the reading, it would be worthwhile getting to grips with this summary and then going back to the bits you have found difficult. It is worth bearing in mind that, in many readings, the section that most clearly expresses the main argument may not be in the introduction or conclusion, and so it is often valuable to move around the piece in order to help your understanding.

Context

Again, Ang makes a distinction between American and European broadcasting; how convincing is this? What does it leave out? If the distinction is not as concrete as she suggests, why does she insist on making it?

READING

13 As we have seen, commercial television has equipped itself with a highly formalized procedure of knowledge production to buttress its audience-as-market paradigm, namely audience measurement. The audience-as-public paradigm however does not have such a readily-available and straightforward discursive instrument to assert itself. This is not surprising, for the desire to 'serve' the audience, the aim to transfer meaningful messages necessitates a much more intricate, multidimensional and qualitative discourse than one that capitalizes on numbers of people giving attention, as offered by audience measurement. Therefore, public service institutions tend to have more problems than their commercial counterparts in coming to a satisfying knowledge about their relationship to their audience: knowing the size of the audience alone is not sufficient to gauge the degree of success or failure of public service television's communicative efforts, not least because success and failure are a normative rather than a material issue here.

14 The recent changes in Western Europe's television landscape as a result of national and integrated European deregulation and privatization policies correlate closely with a crisis in the audience-as-public paradigm of public service broadcasting. With the proliferation of commercial television offerings in the European airwaves, the idea of audience-as-public comes more and more under pressure. Several observers have noted, generally in a tone not unaffected by a sense of nostalgia and regret, how European public service broadcasting is in practice gradually pervaded by a mass-marketing mentality to almost the same degree as in the United States (e.g. Gitlin 1983; Garnham 1983; Richeri 1985; Burgelman 1986). And indeed, the trend is unmistakable: more and more have public service organizations developed an explicit interest in ratings, 'audience maximization' and similar concerns that derive from the competitive commercial system. More and more have they implictly adopted, if not wholeheartedly and not completely, a limited attention model of communication to judge their own performance. More and more, in other words, is the audience-as-public transformed, at least apparently, into an audience-as-market.

NOTES

13 ## Context

Outlined here are the problems public service broadcasting has in making sense of its audience, precisely because it is not primarily interested in raw numbers; instead, these institutions want to know what audiences are doing with what they make, and the social and cultural consequences of their broadcasting. If you look at the reports the BBC produces on its audience (available at www. bbc.co.uk), what does that tell about how the Corporation sees its viewers?

Writing Style

What's the difference between 'normative' and 'material' here?

14 ## Context

Ang covers some recent broadcasting history in Europe here, and examines how it has affected the ways in which audiences are seen. She draws on the work of others as empirical evidence, though she also implies the regretful attitude they take towards what has happened. In a sense, we can see here why Ang feels that what she is writing about matters, because things are changing, and not for the better.

Writing Style

Is the trend really 'unmistakable', or is this an overstatement?

READING

15 But this process of paradigmatic transformation should not be seen as a mechanical one; on the contrary, as will become clear in Part III, it is accompanied by many tensions and difficulties within the public service broadcasting organizations themselves, tensions and difficulties having to do with the need for these organizations to develop a new, acceptable way of thinking about the specificity of their relationship toward the audience. In short, what they need to do is to somehow reconcile the two contrasting paradigms of audience. I will examine how this formidable work of discursive reconstruction has been accomplished, by delving into the histories of two particularly interesting European embodiments of the public service ideal: the British BBC and the Dutch VARA.

16 The BBC derives its relevance from its exceptional international influence and prestige when it comes to defending the value and superiority of public service broadcasting – something which is evidenced by the fact that British television has over the years won by far the greatest number of awards at television festivals such as Montreux and the Prix Italia (Blumler *et al.* 1986). VARA is a much less well-known institution internationally, but its case is equally interesting because of its unique democratic socialist roots (Ang 1987). While both organizations can pride themselves upon a long and strong tradition of 'serving the public' through broadcasting, then, the contrast between the two is also illuminating: while the ideological origins of the BBC, particularly as voiced by its first Director General, John Reith, represent an outstanding case of 'authoritarian paternalism', in which the audience is positioned as the public to be reformed 'from above', the history of VARA, based upon its founding philosophy of social democracy, is a peculiar case of what can be called 'populist paternalism', in which the desire for cultural uplift came 'from below', from (a segment of) the audience-as-public itself as it were.

15   ## Structure

Again, Ang refers to a part of her book not included here; again, it's worth seeing if you can make sense of her argument without it.

Content

'Acceptable' to whom?

Writing Style

Note the bold and clear statement of intention here. Not all writers tell you what they are going to do and why; but, here, this helps prepare you for the different turn this chapter is about to take. Note that this is a shift from primarily *theoretical* discussion to a more *empirical* analysis of specific examples. You might want to question why Ang feels it necessary to make this shift – why not remain at the level of the theoretical?

16   ## Structure

It is clear here that there are ways in which broadcasting institutions are perceived globally. You are probably aware that the BBC is a respected and well-known institution in many parts of the globe. By comparing it to VARA, Ang intends to demonstrate different ways in which public service broadcasting can function; such 'compare and contrast' approaches are common ways of making these kinds of arguments.

Content

What's the difference between 'authoritarian paternalism' and 'populist paternalism'? Why might the BBC and VARA – in many ways, two similar institutions – have adopted such different approaches to their duties?

READING

17

Despite this seemingly radical difference in origins, however, both organizations have evolved, in certain aspects at least, along remarkably similar lines. Briefly, both histories are marked by an increasing uncertainty about how a public service institution should establish and maintain its normatively-defined relationship to the television audience. This is expressed in a growing reliance within both organizations on the kind of knowledge about the audience that could be delivered by research, and by audience measurement in particular. In other words, the prevailing form of institutional knowledge employed within these organizations became less and less of a normative kind, and has taken more and more the form of factual information. However, this does not mean that the audience is now squarely conceived as a market; rather, as Part III will show, it is the intermingling of old public service commitments and market thinking that motivates the use of audience measurement and related forms of research in public service institutions. Ideally, the information delivered by audience research is assumed to aid public service institutions in their effort to better serve the audience in a time when their authority, so taken for granted in the past, has been eroded by the growth of commercial competition.

18

These developments point to the fact that while the philosophical assumptions of commercial and public service broadcasting are indeed radically different, there is also a fundamental commonality in the two institutional systems which tends to be obscured – a commonality which has everything to do with the fact that in practice both kinds of institutions inevitably foster an instrumental view of the audience as object to be conquered. Whether the primary intention is to transfer meaningful messages or to gain and attract attention, in both cases the audience is structurally placed at the reception end of a linear, one-way process. In other words, in both systems the audience is inevitably viewed either from 'above' or from 'outside': from an institutional point of view which sees 'television audience' as an objectified category of others to be controlled.

19

The paradigms of audience-as-public and audience-as-market are thus only relatively conflicting. As McQuail (1987: 221) has noted, 'We never conceive of ourselves as belonging to markets, rather we are placed in market categories or identified as part of a target group by others'. But in a similar vein we can state that when people watch television, they do not spontaneously conceive of themselves as members of an institutionally-defined public. To put it differently, if it is true that consumers must be made rather than found in order to create a market, so too are the citizens that form a public not naturally there, but must be produced and invented, made and made up, by the institution itself.

NOTES

17 Structure

Again, a 'compare and contrast' approach is taken here, but rather than contrasting the two broadcasting institutions, Ang compares their past and present approaches to their audiences. This is done in order to make a statement about change which, at the end of the paragraph, is put in the context of increasing commercial broadcasting.

Content

What is the difference between 'normative' approaches and 'factual' ones?

18 Structure

As Ang moves towards the end of the chapter, she starts to draw together all the examples and arguments which she has outlined so far. Her notion of 'commonality' is a way of signalling that there are recurring characteristics in the material she has explored. This summarising approach is common in conclusions; indeed, it may be one of the ways in which you have been advised to construct conclusions in your essays.

Content

Like earlier, Ang uses the word 'conquered' here. Has your understanding of her use of the term developed since her earlier use of it?

19 Structure

While Ang has, on the whole, contrasted the two versions of 'audience' she has examined, here she sees similarities in them; at least, she sees defining audiences as a necessary process for the broadcasting institutions, rather than required by the audiences themselves. Note the range of words used to describe audiences.

Content

What does it mean for consumers to 'be made rather than found'? And how is this the same for citizens?

READING

20

Both commercial and public service institutions then cannot, with their specific goals and interests in mind, stop struggling to conquer the audience, no matter whether audience members are identified as consumers or citizens. This brings me back to the more general discursive mechanisms of knowledge produced from the institutional point of view, based as it is upon the positing of a clearcut subject/object opposition and the construction of 'television audience' as a unitary, objectified category. We will now take a closer look at the assumptions and consequences, both epistemological and ontological, of this construction.

20 ## Structure

Ang ends by signalling what is to come in the next chapter. As she has referred to other parts of her book throughout this reading, this argument is clearly part of a much larger whole.

REFLECTING ON THE READING

Thinking about an audience as a theoretical construct might seem difficult at first, but it is hoped Ang's work has shown how it should be done and why. However, note the limited number of examples. She draws primarily on the BBC and VARA, and you might want to think how her work can be applied to other channels and broadcasters. Similarly, you could think about how her theories work in relation to other activities, such as film, advertising and radio.

Also, as this is a chapter from a book, you should think about what else might be covered in it, and whether there are other sections of it you feel you should read to fill in the gaps not explored in this reading. Yet it is also important to feel that you can get an initial grasp of the main arguments from this chapter alone; if you have been given a reading which is part of a larger volume, it is assumed that it works well enough on its own.

This reading clearly relates to other chapters in this book. For example, the reasons why media institutions construct audiences primarily as consumers can be discussed in terms of 'political economy' (Chapter 12); the rationale for the ethnographic approaches often employed by audience researchers arises out of arguments from 'cultural theory' (Chapter 17); audiences have been studied for decades, as demonstrated by the work carried out by Walter Lippmann; one of the key ways in which audiences have been explored is in terms of 'effects' (Chapter 14); and so on. Indeed, the audience lies at the heart of media theory, because unless it is assumed that there are social consequences which arise from media activities, the subject area is pretty redundant.

Therefore, you should be aware of activities when media audiences are talked about. For example, newspapers often carry reports detailing the ratings television programmes get, and whether they can be considered a 'hit' or a 'flop'. When you come across such reports, think about what version of the audience is being assumed here; is it a mass audience, an audience of individual people, a public, a group of citizens, or something else? Also note how, when people talk about audiences, they rarely define the term, and instead assume we 'know' what they mean because it is 'common sense'. Think about how *you* fit into that version of the audience, and whether you feel such definitions fully account for *your* activities. Thinking in this way may help you see why, for people such as Ang, discussing the audience is such an important activity.

Key terms to explore

public service broadcasting; textualising; political economy.

Key writers who are mentioned

Jay Blumler; Todd Gitlin; Denis McQuail; Raymond Williams.

RECOMMENDED READING

Gillespie, Marie (ed.) (2005) *Media Audiences*, Maidenhead: Open University Press.

Textbook of essays outlining theoretical debates about audiences, as well as extracts from many key studies referred to in this chapter.

Long, P. and Wall, T. (2009) *Media Studies: Text, production and context*, Harlow: Longman.

For a contextualising, detailed account of many of the issues raised in this chapter, this introduction is an excellent place to start.

Schrøder, K., Drotner, K., Kline, S. and Murray, C. (2003) *Researching Audiences*, London: Arnold.

Overview of a broad range of approaches to audiences, covering many methods as well as debates about how audiences should be researched.

CHAPTER 24

Audiences as producers

Shirky, C. (2008) *Here Comes Everybody: How change happens when people come together*, London: Penguin, pp. 55–66.

INTRODUCTION TO AUDIENCES AS PRODUCERS

Facebook has more than 400 million active users, who upload 3 billion photos every month, with the average user spending nearly an hour a day using the site (Website Monitoring 2010). 106 million people are registered with Twitter, sending 55 million tweets per day, and Twitter's search engine receives 600 million queries per day (Business Blogs Hub 2010). Eight years' worth of content is uploaded to YouTube every day (which means the site 'broadcasts' far more material than traditional television networks) and over 700 billion viewings occurred on the site in 2010 (YouTube 2011). Considering none of these sites existed ten years ago, their growth has been remarkable and, perhaps, can be seen as evidence of the shifting relationships people have with media, as we move from audiences being merely consumers of the media products produced for them, to being active makers and distributors of their own content. It is this idea that audiences are no longer passive recipients but are now the *producers* of media material which the reading in this chapter explores.

Indeed, this part of this book – 'media theory in context' – has, in its first three chapters, looked at production, texts and audiences. Very often media studies divides its analysis up into these three areas, and has developed different methodological approaches for exploring each of them. This has arisen because of the assumption that those who are involved in production are not really the same people as those involved in consuming media; that is, while millions of people watch films and read newspapers and listen to music, a significantly smaller number than that are involved in the actual making of these things. One of the key critiques media studies has repeatedly offered is that the 'culture industries' (Adorno 2006 [1991]; see Chapter 6 on the Frankfurt school) have turned the production of culture into nothing other than a commercial activity, and all we are required to do is spend money buying it. We are, by this argument, no longer producers, yet producing culture is an important activity because it is one of the ways we express ourselves, as an individual and as part of a community.

The internet, and the development of other forms of new media, has been seen by some as having the potential of overturning this producer–consumer relationship, enabling everyone to make and distribute forms of culture, thereby opening up the public sphere (see Chapter 13) to a wider range of voices and empowering everyone to be involved in the society they live in. This has been particularly associated with what has often been dubbed 'Web 2.0'; that is, 'a by now ubiquitous term that loosely refers to the proliferation of user-created content and websites specifically built as frameworks for the sharing of information and social networking, and platforms for self-expression such as the weblog, or using video and audio sharing' (Hands 2011: 79). As the statistics at the start of this chapter show, Web 2.0 sites are certainly popular, and enable forms of activity impossible prior to their development. The question becomes, then, to what extent this has actually made any sort of difference to how most people live their lives, and whether the radical potential often associated with these forms has come to fruition at all.

Evidence for this potential is found, for example, in the election of Barack Obama to the American presidency in 2008, which has been dubbed the first 'internet election' (Vaccari 2010), with Obama referred to as 'The first iPresident' (Simmons 2009). This is because Obama's campaign used social media to both disseminate its message and organise volunteers willing to help with all the work such a campaign requires. Similarly, the protests and campaigns across North Africa and the Middle East in 2011 known as the 'Arab Spring' have been seen to be reliant on social media such as Twitter, as these enable people not only to organise those protests, but also to spread information about the events to be reported by those involved rather than by 'traditional' media (Williamson 2011). Important for the Arab Spring is that it was an event in multiple regions and states, and this is seen as evidence of new media's ability to move across borders, not only bringing together people conventionally separate but also bypassing 'traditional' media which is often nation-based. Indeed, the idea of the importance of the crowd has recurred across such analyses, arguing that bringing people together is one of the most important things new media can do, for this has clear social, commercial and political implications (Botsman and Rogers 2011; Howe 2009; Papacharissi 2010; Surowiecki 2004).

However, some argue that it is too easy to get carried away with naïve celebration concerning the radical potential of new media, and the power it affords audiences as producers. For example, in *The Net Delusion* (2011) Morozov argues that the internet has been a far more useful tool for those *already* in power, for it allows businesses and governments to track the activities of citizens and disseminate propaganda, while the internet as a whole has become as commercialised and business-run as those systems it was supposed to subvert. Morozov therefore calls continued excitement about the liberating potential of the internet 'cyber-utopianism' (p. xiv). Similarly, concerns have been raised about the 'digital divide' (James 2003; Norris 2001; O'Hara and Stevens 2006); that is, that access to new media forms is not equal. While the internet is often referred to as 'free', it actually requires technologies (PCs, laptops, smartphones) which are not financially within the reach of everyone on the planet, meaning that it is often those from the most deprived areas who fail to have access to those forms of media it is argued will help them better their lives. It is also the case that the dominant language on the internet is English

(Internet World Stats 2010), disempowering those from others nations and, unfortunately, reinforcing those disparities the technology is assumed to problematise. In that sense, are new media not simply just the next phase of 'electronic colonialism' (McPhail 1981)?

So, how do *you* use new media? Do you have a Facebook page, or tweet on Twitter, or make videos and upload them to YouTube, or produce music and post it on MySpace? If so, what do you do these things for? Do you think they have any of the radical potential outlined above? Do you feel empowered by being able to do these things? And if you don't do them, why not? Are you concerned about issues of privacy, for example (Levmore and Nussbaum 2010)? It might be difficult to imagine a world without the internet: it's often difficult to remember what a new technology it is. Perhaps try this; go without the internet or other forms of social media for a week. What would be difficult, and in what ways might your life be better? And, bearing in mind the argument about the social and political possibilities of new media, would going without them for a week make you *more* or *less* engaged with the world around you?

INTRODUCTION TO THE READING

This reading is the opening section of the chapter 'Everyone is a media outlet' from Clay Shirky's book, *Here Comes Everybody: How change happens when people come together*. In the blurb on the frontispiece of the book, Shirky's aim is outlined as, 'to describe the intersection of social tools and social life, helping people both to understand what's happening around them, and how tools could be designed to better support social activity'. It's clear, then, that the book aims to place media and technology in a social context, seeing the ways in which people live their lives as intertwined with the media they use and consume. More than that, though, it appears that Shirky's aim is to think about how such technology could be used and designed *better*, enabling communities to function more productively, resulting in happier lives for all. In that sense, here is a book that could be seen as some kind of manifesto, so that it not only attempts to outline what's going on, but also to suggest how things could be improved. Like much media theory this book is therefore critical of how things are, and offers solutions or suggestions for how things could be better.

However, *Here Comes Everybody* is not really the same as the majority of the media theory you are likely to come across in this book or in your studies more generally. For a start, it's written for a much wider audience than much media theory. Its writing style is much more chatty, and Shirky draws on lots of personal anecdotes to support his argument (you'll see below that this chapter begins with Shirky writing about his uncle). Furthermore, while Shirky does offer some empirical evidence, with references, for some of his assertions, much of his analysis does not offer such data, and instead draws its weight from commonsense notions of media use, and from those anecdotes Shirky includes. It is likely that were you to write in such a style for your essays you would be told off: so why is it acceptable here? The reason is precisely because the audience for this reading is quite different; Shirky aims to reach business people, legislators and the general public, and so communicates in a manner appropriate to the multiple audiences he is aiming for. When you go through the reading you might want to reflect on the benefits and drawbacks to this approach; does it make the reading easier and, if so, is anything lost through the adoption of this writing style?

You can place the material in this reading in a wider context by looking at the other writing Shirky has done. His book *Cognitive Surplus: creativity and generosity in a connected age* (2010) argues that forms of technology in the last half of the twentieth century rendered most people passive, and therefore vast amounts of talent and skill were squandered. Newer technologies, such as the internet, instead not only allow people to be more creative, they also encourage collaborative work which brings people together and therefore instils forms of social cohesion. Shorter writing can be found at Shirky's website; www.shirky.com/writings/. These cover debates about technology, regulation, globalisation and economics. Running through them all is the activity of prediction; that is, Shirky functions as someone who, through analysis of the past and the present, offers governments, businesses, and communities predictions of how new technologies might offer radical potential for many aspects of everyday life. Again, this predictive aim is one you are not likely to encounter in the majority of media theory; nor is the positive tone that Shirky adopts. Indeed, you might wonder, considering Shirky and other authors show that there is a wide potential audience for debates about media and technology, why it is that the majority of media theory fails to engage the public. Do you think the writers you have encountered in this book could take some lessons from Shirky in how to engage wider audiences?

Finally, it's worth thinking about the title of the chapter this section comes from; 'Everyone is a media outlet'. This might seem like an odd claim; how am *I*, or *you*, a media outlet? It is likely we are used to thinking of media outlets as large corporations producing thousands of books, film, television programmes and adverts. It is precisely this assumption that Shirky wants to challenge. But also note his use of tense; it is not that everyone *can be* a media outlet, but that everyone *is* one. The suggestion is that we all already produce media, and via the reorganisation of certain social and technological structures we can all disseminate what we do in a much more productive manner. But how does it feel to *you* to be called a media outlet; do you think you are one, or would you like to be one?

By the way, do you know where the title of Shirky's book – *Here Comes Everybody* – comes from?

READING

1

C. Shirky

Everyone is a media outlet

Our social tools remove older obstacles to public expression, and thus remove the bottlenecks that characterized mass media. The result is the mass amateurization of efforts previously reserved for media professionals.

2

My uncle Howard was a small-town newspaperman, publishing the local paper for Richmond, Missouri (population 5,000). The paper, founded by my grandfather, was the family business, and ink ran in Howard's blood. I can still remember him fulminating about the rise of *USA Today*; he criticized it as "TV on paper" and held it up as further evidence of the dumbing down of American culture, but he also understood the challenge that *USA Today* presented, with its color printing and national distribution. The *Richmond Daily News* and *USA Today* were in the same business; even with the difference in scale and scope, Howard immediately got what *USA Today* was up to.

3

Despite my uncle's obsession, *USA Today* turned out to be nothing like the threat that old-time newspaper people feared. It took some market share from other papers, but the effect wasn't catastrophic. What was catastrophic was a less visible but more significant change, already gathering steam when *USA Today* launched. The principal threat to the *Richmond Daily News*, and indeed to all newspapers small and large, was not competition from other newspapers but radical changes in the overall ecosystem of information. The idea that some-one might build four-color presses that ran around the clock was easy to grasp. The idea that the transmission of news via paper might become a bad idea, that all those huge, noisy printing presses might be like steam engines in the age of internal combustion, was almost impossible to grasp. Howard could imagine someone doing what he did, but better. He couldn't imagine someone making what he did obsolete.

NOTES

1 ## Structure

Shirky begins his chapter with a summary of what it will contain. In essence, he outlines his argument beforehand, so you can be prepared for what you're going to read. How useful is this? Might it mean that you are primed to agree with what he has to say?

2 ## Writing Style

Shirky opens his analysis with a personal anecdote about his uncle Howard. You might find this writing style quite different to that in many of the other readings you encounter in your studies. How useful do you find this? Is it helpful to hear about Shirky's family? And how indicative should we find this story? Can we use it to think about the key arguments more generally, or might it be misrepresentative?

Context

This story aims to put debates about media change within a historical and social context. This story aims to make it clear that people have always debated media change, and have always been worried about how newer forms of media might affect existing ones. What contemporary examples of this phenomenon can you think of, and are these in any way different to the concerns Shirky's uncle Howard had?

Content

What does 'dumbing down' mean? Have you heard this term before? Do you think media are dumbing down? If so, does this apply to all forms of media, or is there also evidence of 'dumbing up'? And why does it matter if culture is dumbing down?

3 ## Content

Shirky notes here that while people may be right to worry about media changes, they are often wrong about which changes matter the most. In that sense, the things that affect us the most might be the ones we cannot predict, and the things we spend our time worrying about are instead of little threat at all. This might have implications for those who make a career out of predicting social, technological and cultural changes – often called futurologists – and our desire to plan in accordance with such predictions. It might be hard to imagine now how impossible it was in the past to conceive that news might be disseminated by any medium other than paper, but this simply shows how difficult it is to predict change. That said, has everything changed? Do newspapers not continue to use the 'huge, noisy printing presses' Shirky's uncle Howard was used to?

READING

4 Many people in the newspaper business, the same people who worried about the effects of competition like *USA Today*, missed the significance of the internet. For people with a professional outlook, it's hard to understand how something that isn't professionally produced could affect them—not only is the internet not a newspaper, it isn't a business, or even an institution. There was a kind of narcissistic bias in the profession; the only threats they tended to take seriously were from other professional media outlets, whether newspapers, TV, or radio stations. This bias had them defending against the wrong thing when the amateurs began producing material on their own. Even as web sites like eBay and Craigslist were siphoning off the ad revenues that keep newspapers viable—job listings, classified ads, real estate—and weblogs were letting people like gnarlykitty publish to the world for free, the executives of the world's newspapers were slow to understand the change, and even slower to react. How could this happen? How could the newspaper industry miss such an obvious and grave challenge to their business? The answer is the flip side of Howard's obsession with *USA Today* and has to do with the nature of professional self-definition (and occasional self-delusion).

5 A profession exists to solve a hard problem, one that requires some sort of specialization. Driving a race car requires special training—race car drivers are professionals. Driving an ordinary car, though, doesn't require the driver to belong to a particular profession, because it's easy enough that most adults can do it with a modicum of training. Most professions exist because there is a scarce resource that requires ongoing management: librarians are responsible for organizing books on the shelves, newspaper executives are responsible for deciding what goes on the front page. In these cases, the scarcity of the resource itself creates the need for a professional class—there are few libraries but many patrons, there are few channels but many viewers. In these cases professionals become gatekeepers, simultaneously providing and controlling access to information, entertainment, communication, or other ephemeral goods.

Content

Here Shirky introduces one of his key ideas; the concept of the 'professional'. Shirky goes on to debate what this term means and the cultural value attached to it. But before we get there, it might be worthwhile you thinking about this word and what it means to you. Which jobs do you consider as 'professions'? Does the word have positive or negative connotations? What else does the term mean to you? And how might the word's value be changing (if at all) due to recent media developments? Note that Shirky contrasts the word 'professional' with the word 'amateur'; again, what does this mean to you?

Writing Style

Shirky refers to 'many people', but note he does not say who, how many or give a reference for this assertion. Are you convinced by this statement? Does it matter if he does not offer specifics?

Structure

Shirky includes a number of key questions in this paragraph, questions he goes on to answer in the rest of the chapter. Note how these questions arise logically out of the case study he has offered. There is a clear line of thinking here, aiming to pique the reader's interest through a specific example (his uncle Howard), which then demonstrates a problem, which is then formulated as questions, which then justifies the analysis Shirky goes on to carry out. You could, perhaps, use such a format in any writing you have to do.

Structure

Here we get Shirky's definition of the 'professional'. Note that this definition does not draw on other writers, or give any other kind of evidential support for this use of the word. This is simply presented as an accepted, commonsense understanding of the term. Are you happy with this?

Context

Shirky places the idea of the 'professional' in lots of contexts. So while we may be interested in this work because of our media studies focus, Shirky instead sees the idea of the media professional as comparable to that in other fields, such as librarians and racing car drivers. In that sense, he places his ideas in a much bigger context than we might typically encounter in media studies, and therefore he implicitly rejects the idea that there is something specific or special about the media. Do you agree with this, or is there something about media professionals that is different to those in other fields? How useful is it for you to think about the relationships between media professionals and those in other fields?

6

To label something a profession means to define the ways in which it is more than just a job. In the case of newspapers, professional behavior is guided both by the commercial imperative and by an additional set of norms about what newspapers are, how they should be staffed and run, what constitutes good journalism, and so forth. These norms are enforced not by the customers but by other professionals in the same business. The key to any profession is the relations of its members to one another. In a profession, members are only partly guided by service to the public. As the UCLA sociologist James Q. Wilson put it in his magisterial *Bureaucracy*, "A professional is someone who receives important occupational rewards from a reference group whose membership is limited to people who have undergone specialized formal education and have accepted a group-defined code of proper conduct." That's a mouthful, but the two key ideas apply to newspaper publishers (as well as to journalists, lawyers, and accountants): a professional learns things in a way that differentiates her from most of the populace, and she pays as much or more attention to the judgment of her peers as to the judgment of her customers when figuring out how to do her job.

NOTES

5   Content

(continued)

Note that Shirky refers to a 'professional class', and he sees them as 'gatekeepers'. The idea that those working in media are gatekeepers is quite common; that is, in order for media to reach us it has to be let through by a number of people. So a film has to be okayed by many executives in a production studio and, once it is made, it only reaches cinemas if those who work in film distribution agree to it, while individual cinemas functions as gatekeepers too. One of the arguments extolling the virtues of the internet is that there are no, or fewer, gatekeepers, and now anyone can publish and distribute whatever they want. But how true is this? Are there really no gatekeepers in new media? Are there not laws that restrict media content? Do we not have to sign up to internet providers in order to use it? And are not many of the sites we might distribute material on owned and managed by others? How can we think about gatekeepers in the internet age?

6   Content

Shirky refers to sets of 'norms' in professions. The exploration of norms has been a key objective of media studies and cultural studies, because they argue that such norms are not natural or inevitable, but instead are indicative of, and uphold, regimes of power. So, the 'norms' of journalism mean that certain kinds of stories get reported while others get ignored, and only certain kinds of people get to be successful journalists. Note that Shirky states that these norms are upheld by other journalists; that is, it is journalism itself that is most invested in upholding these norms, and which therefore resists change. New media – and the amateurs Shirky's interested in exploring – can often be seen to ignore or reject these norms, and this is one of the reasons why, for example, the internet is seen as potentially revolutionary. But might there be some value in upholding such norms? Is journalism useful if it does not have such norms? Would you argue that these norms should be critiqued and rejected, or do you see any use in upholding them?

Context

Do you agree that professionals are more interested in impressing their peers than their audiences/customers? Do you think most professionals would agree with this statement? Is this how we normally think of professionals?

Writing Style

Note Shirky's use of 'her' to refer to a professional. Media studies has struggled for some time to deal with the sexist use of male language – such as 'he' and 'him' – to refer to people, as this ignores women. Some writers use 'him/her', but many find this an ugly compromise. Many, like Shirky, have simply replaced 'him' with 'her', arguing that while 'her' can be seen to ignore men, this is a small problem compared to the wealth of sexist language women encounter every day.

READING

7 A profession becomes, for its members, a way of understanding their world. Professionals see the world through a lens created by other members of their profession; for journalists, the rewards of a Pulitzer Prize are largely about recognition from other journalists.

8 Much of the time the internal consistency of professional judgment is a good thing—not only do we want high standards of education and competence, we want those standards created and enforced by other members of the same profession, a structure that is almost the definition of professionalism. Sometimes, though, the professional outlook can become a disadvantage, preventing the very people who have the most at stake—the professionals themselves—from understanding major changes to the structure of their profession. In particular, when a profession has been created as a result of some scarcity, as with librarians or television programmers, the professionals are often the last ones to see it when that scarcity goes away. It is easier to understand that you face competition than obsolescence.

9 In any profession, particularly one that has existed long enough that no one can remember a time when it didn't exist, members have a tendency to equate provisional solutions to particular problems with deep truths about the world. This is true of newspapers today and of the media generally. The media industries have suffered first and most from the recent collapse in communications costs. It used to be hard to move words, images, and sounds from creator to consumer, and most media businesses involve expensive and complex management of that pipeline problem, whether running a printing press or a record label. In return for helping overcome these problems, media businesses got to exert considerable control over the media and extract considerable revenues from the public. The commercial viability of most media businesses involves providing those solutions, so preservation of the original problems became an economic imperative. Now, though, the problems of production, reproduction, and distribution are much less serious. As a consequence, control over the media is less completely in the hands of the professionals.

7	Context

Like the Pulitzer Prize, the winners of many awards, in a range of industries, are decided by those in the same field. In that sense, awards function as peer recognition. Why might professions be interested in upholding this format? What happens when the public gets to choose winners? Are such awards as valued as those given by 'experts'?

8　Content

Shirky sees the notion of 'scarcity' as important to the ways in which industries and professionals work. That is, there are some products whose value is predicated on its scarcity, because not everyone has the skills or resources to make them. Shirky's examples of librarians and television programmers show this, but this could also apply to the film or music industry, where often large amounts of investment are required in order to produce a product, and talent is limited so not everyone has the ability to sing well or act convincingly. It is because there is scarcity that there is a market in these fields; famous Hollywood actors can demand massive salaries because their ability to attract audiences is a scarce commodity that the film industry is willing to pay for. But how true is this? Is there, in fact, far less scarcity than is assumed? Might it be that the closed world of the professional is a way of upholding scarcity, rather than ensuring limited resources can be utilised well? Might it be that newer forms of media show that the talents that were assumed to be scarce are, in fact, far more abundant than was supposed?

9　Context

Shirky foregrounds here the technological context that media industries work in, and sees it as the primary motivator for the business model that has sustained them. So, it used to be the case that music could only be disseminated on records, cassettes and CDs, and making those products was an expensive business that only few companies had the money and resources to do; it was pretty much impossible for an individual to press their own LPs and distribute them. But the digital distribution of music removes these costs, and now, with relatively little money, anyone can put their music online. This context is important because very often when we think about the media we focus on the texts, and examine what a film means, or the significance of the TV programme, for example. However, this analysis suggests that actually the key thing to examine when thinking about media is, in fact, *distribution*, for it is developments in how media can be distributed that has led to the changes worrying so many professionals in the media industries. Furthermore, if anyone can distribute what they make, then the 'gatekeepers' mentioned above become redundant. So, is exploring matters of distribution the most significant way for us to understand how media functions?

Writing Style

Note again that Shirky offers no evidence for his many assertions here. How does he know what media professionals do? Considering his argument, does it matter if we're given concrete evidence or not?

10 As new capabilities go, unlimited perfect copyability is a lulu, and that capability now exists in the hands of everyone who owns a computer. Digital means of distributing words and images have robbed newspapers of the coherence they formerly had, revealing the physical object of the newspaper as a merely provisional solution; now every article is its own section. The permanently important question is how society will be informed of the news of the day. The newspaper used to be a pretty good answer to that question, but like all such answers, it was dependent on what other solutions were available. Television and radio obviously changed the landscape in which the newspaper operated, but even then printed news had a monopoly on the written word—until the Web came along. The Web didn't introduce a new competitor into the old ecosystem, as *USA Today* had done. The Web created a new ecosystem.

11 We've long regarded the newspaper as a sensible object because it has been such a stable one, but there isn't any logical connection among its many elements: stories from Iraq, box scores from the baseball game, and ads for everything from shoes to real estate all exist side by side in an idiosyncratic bundle. What holds a newspaper together is primarily the cost of paper, ink, and distribution; a newspaper is whatever group of printed items a publisher can bundle together and deliver profitably. The corollary is also true: what doesn't go into a newspaper is whatever is too expensive to print and deliver. The old bargain of the newspaper—world news lumped in with horoscopes and ads from the pizza parlor—has now ended. The future presented by the internet is the mass amateurization of publishing and a switch from "Why publish this?" to "Why not?"

NOTES

9 Content

(continued)

Shirky rightly recognises that media industries respond to commercial pressures. But note that he assumes that all media is commercial, and that 'commercial viability' is a key motivator. But how do the arguments presented here apply to those media that are publically funded, such as the BBC? Are the concerns about obsolescence the same?

10 Content

Newspapers are referred to here as a 'physical object', with the implication that newer forms of distribution, such as those online, are not physical. These are arguments that are often presented, that newspapers and books require you to carry something, whereas online material simply exists on your computer in a virtual form. But are online materials any less physical? Is a laptop not a physical object? Which is easier to carry around or take on a bus – a newspaper or a laptop? While it is true that online material does not require the physical aspects of production, such as printing presses, it is surely not the case that we can access material without a physical object at all?

Context

One of Shirky's key questions here assumed that society should be 'informed of the news of the day'. Note that this is a common assumption about the social role of media, and the value of news to a democracy. Of course, some people might think that this is not an important use of media at all, and we should not worry if news simply disappears because it is no longer profitable. Would you see this as a problem?

11 Content

Shirky argues there's no 'logical connection' between the various elements in a newspaper. But what kinds of logical assumption is he assuming to be valuable here? Considering the social role it is often assumed newspapers should play, why might a reader be interested in accessing in one place the range of topics Shirky refers to here? Might there be a problem if all information is chopped up into 'logical' sections? Would such divisions help democracy and an informed citizenry?

Context

The switch of focus Shirky refers to in the last sentence clearly has massive implications for what gets disseminated. Rather than something having to prove its value to get published, here instead we assume everything should be published unless there is a reason not to. What kinds of reasons would you see as valid ones for arguing that something should *not* be published? What happens (to society, and to individuals) if everything is published?

Writing Style

Shirky offers a prediction here, as he supposes the 'future presented by the internet'. Considering he noted earlier how poor most people are at predicting the future, why should we believe him here? Are you convinced by this prediction?

12

The two basic organizational imperatives—acquire resources, and use them to pursue some goal or agenda—saddle every organization with the institutional dilemma, whether its goal is saving souls or selling soap. The question that mass amateurization poses to traditional media is "What happens when the costs of reproduction and distribution go away? What happens when there's nothing unique about publishing anymore, because users can do it for themselves?" We are now starting to see that question being answered.

13

Weblogs and Mass Amateurization

Shortly after his reelection in 2002 Trent Lott, the senior senator from Mississippi and then majority leader, gave a speech at Strom Thurmond's hundredth birthday party. Thurmond, a Republican senator from South Carolina, had recently retired after a long political career, which had included a 1948 run for president on an overtly segregationist platform. At Thurmond's hundredth birthday party Lott remembered and praised Thurmond's presidential campaign of fifty years earlier and recalled Mississippi's support for it: "I want to say this about my state: When Strom Thurmond ran for president, we voted for him. We're proud of it. And if the rest of the country had followed our lead, we wouldn't have had all these problems over all these years, either." Two weeks later, having been rebuked by President Bush and by politicians and the press on both the right and the left for his comment, Lott announced that he would not seek to remain majority leader in the new Congress.

14

This would have been a classic story of negative press coverage altering a political career—except that the press didn't actually cover the story, at least not at first. Indeed, the press almost completely missed the story. This isn't to say that they intentionally ignored it or even actively suppressed it; several reporters from national news media heard Lott speak, but his remark simply didn't fit the standard template of news. Because Thurmond's birthday was covered as a salutary event instead of as a political one, the actual contents of the evening were judged in advance to be relatively unimportant. A related assumption is that a story that is not important one day also isn't important the next, unless something has changed. Thurmond's birthday party happened on a Thursday night, and the press gave Lott's remarks very little coverage on Friday. Not having written about it on Friday in turn became a reason not to write about it on Saturday, because if there was no story on Friday, there was even less of one on Saturday.

12 ## Context

Again, Shirky sees the organisational contexts media industries work in as identical to those for other industries, such as those making soap. This context is, therefore, far wider than you might be used to encountering in media studies. Is it helpful for you to see these similarities? How do they affect your thinking about the media specifically?

Structure

Shirky raises a couple of questions towards the end of this section, and then ends with a statement that implies that the book's next section will answer them. Such a structure helpfully summarises the argument's key points, and then signals towards what will come next.

Writing Style

Who is the 'we' Shirky refers to in the last sentence? Does it include you?

13 ## Structure

Like the previous one, Shirky begins this section with an example. He does not state at the outset why it matters or how it is connected to his argument.

Writing Style

There are no references or sources for this story. Does this matter?

Context

Note that this case study is about politics. Is the implication that such debates matter more because they are about politics? What assumptions about the importance of events is Shirky drawing on here?

14 ## Content

What do you think Shirky means by 'the standard template of news'? Think about this in terms of the content of the story as well as the chronological context Shirky refers to. Where does this 'standard template' come from, and how might it be related to ideas of professionalism he has explored earlier? Do you think Shirky sees this 'template' as a good thing or not? Do you think it is a good thing?

15

William O'Keefe of *The Washington Post*, one of the few reporters to think Lott's comment, was important, explains the dilemma this way: "[T]here had to be a reaction" that the network could air alongside Lott's remarks, and "we had no on-camera reaction" available the evening of the party, when the news was still fresh. By the following night, he adds, "you're dealing with the news cycle: twenty-four hours later—that's old news." Like a delayed note to a friend, the initial lack of response would have meant, in any later version, having to apologize for not having written sooner.

16

Given this self-suppression—old stories are never revisited without a new angle—what kept the story alive was not the press but liberal and conservative bloggers, for whom fond memories of segregation were beyond the pale, birthday felicitations or no, and who had no operative sense of news cycles. The weekend after Lott's remarks, weblogs with millions of readers didn't just report his comments, they began to editorialize. The editorializers included some well-read conservatives such as Glenn Reynolds of the Instapundit blog, who wrote, "But to say, as Lott did, that the country would be better off if Thurmond had won in 1948 is, well, it's proof that Lott shouldn't be majority leader for the Republicans, to begin with. And that's just to begin with. It's a sentiment as evil and loony as wishing that Gus Hall [a perennial Communist candidate for president] had been elected."

NOTES

15   Writing Style

Why does Shirky note that O'Keefe works at the *Washington Post*? Is it simply because he works in the system Shirky is exploring? Would O'Keefe's comments have been as worthwhile to you as a reader, do you think, if Shirky had not acknowledged his position at the *Post*? Shirky seems to accept O'Keefe's version of events at face value; is this appropriate? Do you think Shirky would accept O'Keefe's comments in this way if O'Keefe had said something that disagreed with Shirky's argument? Is Shirky's use of evidence appropriate here?

Content

Have you come across the idea of the 'news cycle' before? It suggests there is a rhythm to the ways in which news stories rise up and down the agenda, and so stories require certain conditions and elements in order to become more prominent. Note here that it is assumed the story did not become big because of the lack of a 'reaction', suggesting that some kind of conflict is necessary for all news stories. The implication here is that this story's failure to be reported in the mainstream media was not because the event was not important, but because it did not quite have all the elements journalists look for in order to put a 'good' story together. What consequences might this have for the kinds of stories that do and do not make it onto the news?

16   Writing Style

What do you think Shirky means by 'self-suppression'? Is this an active or accidental piece of behaviour? Do you think Shirky sees it as a positive or negative act?

Content

Here a distinction is drawn between 'reporting' and 'editorialising'. This works from an assumption that reporting the news involves simply recounting what has occurred, whereas editorialising is the act of commenting on those events. A distinction between the two is often drawn which argues that the former is more objective, whereas the latter is highly subjective. Debates about the ways in which news is reported and editorialised persist in discussions about journalism and media regulation. Many British news broadcasters, for example, are bound by rules of impartiality, and are required to give equal weight to a range of views: in other countries, such as America, such regulations do not necessarily apply, and so news networks are permitted to follow and espouse a particular agenda. While there are concerns about the consequences of such subjective news, it is worth also acknowledging that some people would argue that *all* news is subjective, and arguing for objective reporting is pointless as it is an impossible goal. However, it remains the case that many people feel that reporting and editorialising are necessarily different acts, and should be signalled as such. What do you think? Should news reporting be objective and, if so, how would you ensure this takes place? Why does it matter if the news is subjective?

17

Even more damaging to Lott, others began to dig deeper. After the story broke, Ed Sebesta, who maintains a database of materials related to nostalgia for the U.S. Confederacy, contacted bloggers with information on Lott, including an interview from the early 1980s in *Southern Partisan*, a neo-Confederate magazine. The simple birthday party story began looking like part of a decades-long pattern of saying one thing to the general public and another thing to his supporters.

18

Like the story of Ivanna's lost phone (in Chapter 1), the story of Sebesta's database involves a link between individual effort and group attention. Just as Evan Guttman benefited from the expert knowledge of his readers, the bloggers posting about Lott benefited from Sebesta's deep knowledge of America's racist past, particularly of Lott's history of praise for same. Especially important, the bloggers didn't have to find Sebesta—he found them. Prior to our current generation of coordinating tools, a part-time politics junkie like Sebesta and amateur commentators like the bloggers would have had a hard time even discovering that they had mutual interests, much less being able to do anything with that information. Now, however, the cost of finding like-minded people has been lowered and, more important, deprofessionalized.

16

(continued)

Structure

For his argument, why does it matter to Shirky that Glenn Reynolds is 'well-read'? Considering Shirky is arguing that one of the interesting things about the amateurisation of media is that non-traditional voices can be expressed, why would he be interested in someone 'well-read'?

17

Content

Note here that while the thrust of Shirky's argument is the value of non-traditional media, the evidence used by Sebesta to support the criticisms of Lott is decidedly traditional, including a magazine. This suggests an interplay between old and new media, which means the latter is supplementing the former, rather than replacing it.

18

Structure

Shirky makes a link here between the examples he is exploring and those earlier in his book. In that way, a uniformity of argument is suggested, and the examples give consistent evidence for what is being said. This link also helps the reader make connections between a lengthy piece of work.

Writing Style

What is meant by a 'part-time politics junkie'? The term 'junkie' conventionally has negative connotations, but is that what's implied here? Also, what is meant by 'our current generation'? Who is included in 'our', and exactly what time period is meant by 'current'?

Content

At the end of this paragraph two important points are made. That is, that new technologies bring together people who would not have been able to communicate easily before, and that the activities such people carry out are similar to what we call 'professionals' even if those who do it are not typically recognised as such. You might think Shirky would see the first consequence as more important; that bringing people together is important for society and can clearly have significant social and political consequences as it allows people to work together towards a common goal. Yet Shirky sees the 'deprofessionalisation' as more important. Why might this be? Do you agree?

READING

19 Because the weblogs kept the story alive, especially among libertarian Republicans, Lott eventually decided to react. The fateful moment came five days after the speech, when he issued a halfhearted apology for his earlier remark, characterizing it as a "poor choice of words." The statement was clearly meant to put the matter behind him, but Lott had not reckoned with the changed dynamics of press coverage. Once Lott apologized, news outlets could cover the apology as the news, while quoting the original speech as background. Only three mainstream news outlets had covered the original comment, but a dozen covered the apology the day it happened, and twenty-one covered it the day after. The traditional news cycle simply didn't apply in this situation; the story had suddenly been transformed from "not worth covering" to "breaking news."

20 Until recently, "the news" has meant two different things—events that are newsworthy, and events covered by the press. In that environment what identified something as news was professional judgment. The position of the news outlets (the very phrase attests to the scarcity of institutions that were able to publish information) was like that of the apocryphal umpire who says, "Some pitches are balls and some are strikes, but they ain't nothin' till I call 'em." There has always been grumbling about this system, on the grounds that some of the things the press was covering were not newsworthy (politicians at ribbon cuttings) and that newsworthy stories weren't being covered or covered enough (insert your pet issue here). Despite the grumbling, however, the basic link between newsworthiness and publication held, because there did not seem to be an alternative. What the Lott story showed us was that the link is now broken. From now on news can break into public consciousness without the traditional press weighing in. Indeed, the news media can end up covering the story *because* something has broken into public consciousness via other means.

19 Writing Style

Without explicitly saying it, Shirky clearly sees as important that the traditional news media picked up a story that had only been kept alive by non-professional bloggers. In that sense, Shirky is presenting this outcome as evidence of the consequences of the bloggers', and it is a consequence he presumably sees as indicative of the power of new forms of media. However, note two things. First, that Shirky does not say this explicitly; we are required to make this assumption ourselves. Secondly, that in order to make that assumption we (and Shirky) must accept that the traditional news media remain the arbiter of what is and is not 'important' news. It could have been the case that the bloggers had covered this story in lots of detail and for a long time, but the evidence that this is significant is the traditional news media reporting the story. In that sense, how much of a change is this?

Content

Is it right that 'the traditional news cycle simply did not apply in this situation'? Is it not the case that, because of the bloggers' actions, the traditional news media had all the elements it required in order to report the story? So, what's new here?

20 Writing Style

This paragraph summarises the argument so far, showing how the case study outlined above demonstrates the differences Shirky sees as important. It therefore fulfils an important role in letting the reader know where we are, why it matters, and what the implications of this analysis are.

What role does Shirky's 'apocryphal umpire' play in the argument? Are you more convinced by its inclusion? Do you think this is the kind of writing that would be acceptable in one of your essays?

No specifics are given as to who has been 'grumbling'; who do you think has been grumbling, and why doesn't Shirky make this clear?

Shirky invites you to 'insert your pet issue here'; so what stories do you think are not reported enough? Why do you think this is? And can new media help change that, as Shirky suggests?

Content

Are you convinced that the 'link is broken'? Shirky argues that the traditional news media cover a story because new media have placed it in the public consciousness, but is there any evidence for this assertion? In terms of the Lott example, might it not be the traditional news media's eventual coverage of the story which was precisely what placed it in the public consciousness, even if this was motivated by the actions of the bloggers? Is the link simply different now, or has it broken?

READING

21

There are several reasons for this change. The professional structuring of worldview, as exemplified by the decisions to treat Lott's remarks as a birthday party story, did not extend to the loosely coordinated amateurs publishing on their own. The decision not to cover Trent Lott's praise for a racist political campaign demonstrates a potential uniformity in the press outlook. In a world where a dozen editors, all belonging to the same professional class, can decide whether to run or kill a national story, information that might be of interest to the general public may not be published, not because of a conspiracy but because the editors have a professional bias that is aligned by the similar challenges they face and by the similar tools they use to approach those challenges. The mass amateurization of publishing undoes the limitations inherent in having a small number of traditional press outlets.

22

As they surveyed the growing amount of self-published content on the internet, many media companies correctly understood that the trustworthiness of each outlet was lower than that of established outlets like *The New York Times*. But what they failed to understand was that the effortlessness of publishing means that there are many more outlets. The same idea, published in dozens or hundreds of places, can have an amplifying effect that outweighs the verdict from the smaller number of professional outlets. (This is not to say that mere repetition makes an idea correct; amateur publishing relies on corrective argument even more than traditional media do.) The change isn't a shift from one kind of news institution to another, but rather in the definition of news: from news as an institutional prerogative to news as part of a communications ecosystem, occupied by a mix of formal organizations, informal collectives, and individuals.

21 Context

Shirky notes that editors all belong to the same 'professional class' and this is an idea that has permeated discussion of the media – and especially news media – for some time. In Britain many editors and journalists come from an Oxbridge background, and there is a concern that this means they have a particular worldview that plays up certain kinds of stories and fails to understand how the majority of people live their lives. Furthermore, if those editors have been successful in the current social system it is unlikely that they would be willing to criticise it, because they probably will not have encountered the problems such a society causes so many people. You will have come across ideas of class many times in your study of media, and it is one of the field's key interests. But do you think this matters?

Content

What is the difference between a 'conspiracy' and 'professional bias'? Are the outcomes of these any different, or is the difference simply the causes? Is it convincing to say there has been a 'mass amateurisation of publishing'? How large is this kind of output?

22 Content

The end of this paragraph shows Shirky's key argument; that is is not that news has changed, but that the numbers and types of people involved in the production of news has changed, and this could have significant consequences for what kinds of news reach us and how. There is, then, a conversation between a range of news providers, rather than the 'gatekeeping' model of old. The word 'prerogative' is important here, for it shows that it was once assumed that only certain people had the right or the ability to decide what was and was not news, but now this prerogative has dissipated. If we can all decide what counts as news, then surely this is more productive for democracy? This means that, as Shirky notes, the 'definition of news' has changed; indeed, is it sensible in this kind of ecosystem to think of news as a discrete category at all?

Writing Style

How useful is the term 'ecosystem' here? What kind of analogy is being attempted here, bearing in mind that a word like 'ecosystem' is usually related to nature?

Context

Bear in mind that all of the examples Shirky has cited are American. As the introduction in this book to the reading showed, the democratic possibilities of new media have been argued by some to have been more effective in the United States than in many other countries. So how applicable do you think this analysis is to other regions or communities? Can this theory be applied to other contexts?

READING

23

It's tempting to regard the bloggers writing about Trent Lott or the people taking pictures of the Indian Ocean tsunami as a new crop of journalists. The label has an obvious conceptual appeal. The problem, however, is that mass professionalization is an oxymoron, since a professional class implies a specialized function, minimum tests for competence, and a minority of members. None of those conditions exist with political weblogs, photo sharing, or a host of other self-publishing tools. The individual weblogs are not merely alternate sites of publishing; they are alternatives to publishing itself, in the sense of publishers as a minority and professional class. In the same way you do not have to be a professional driver to drive, you no longer have to be a professional publisher to publish. Mass amateurization is a result of the radical spread of expressive capabilities, and the most obvious precedent is the one that gave birth to the modern world: the spread of the printing press five centuries ago.

23 Content

Shirky is clearly keen here to reject the argument that new media users are merely replacing or replicating those jobs carried out by traditional media professionals. Instead he wants to argue that what is going on here is something new and different, that does not fit into established definitions. This argument rests on the assumption that professionals can only be a minority, and once a majority is involved in an activity it cannot be defined a profession. How convinced are you by this? Cannot majorities be professionals? Indeed, are there not accepted standards of discourse and conduct on blogs, and are bloggers not assessed and validated by their peers in the same way that professionals are? So, how different is this?

Writing Style

What is meant by 'expressive capabilities', and how 'radical' is their spread?

Structure

This section ends pointing towards how these debates about new media have precedents half a millennium ago. In the next section Shirky outlines this history, going to show how new media debates arise out of ones which have been around for centuries. You can imagine that someone else writing this analysis might start off with the history, and then go on to explore the present day context; why does Shirky instead do the opposite? In terms of the structure of his argument, why might he want to talk about now before he talks about the past? Using this structure, what role does history play in his argument, which it might not have done if he had outlined it first?

REFLECTING ON THE READING

As has been noted throughout, this reading contains very few references or sources, and instead draws on anecdotal evidence. Indeed, unlike most of the chapters in this book, this one contains only one person in the 'key writers who are mentioned' section below. So, first it might be worth thinking about your own responses to this lack of specifics and referencing; to what extent does it affect how convincing Shirky's argument is to you? While it is easy to demand sources, would lots of footnotes and a massive bibliography have added anything to Shirky's case? Indeed, is there something that is added by the lack of such material? In some ways, does it not feel as if the writing is more liberated, and able to express possibilities and predictions, which are unavailable to theorising reliant on sources and references? What can this kind of writing do that others cannot, and vice versa? And are there places where this style might suit what you want to express too?

You might also want to reflect on the specific contexts Shirky writes about, and whether his arguments work as well in other places. It is clear the focus in the book is the United States, and the examples throughout repeatedly refer to this context. But to what extent is that context useful for thinking about how new media might work in others? For a start, the history of the media in the US is one in which private ownership, and profit-making, has repeatedly been seen as the norm. This is neither to state that there is no publically funded media in the United States, nor that other countries do not have private, commercial media. But how do Shirky's arguments work in non-commercial contexts, for example? The challenge Shirky sees facing newspapers, for example, is a failure to work out how to make a profit in the new media age. But what if profit is not a primary or even necessary motivation? If public broadcasters, for example, are meant to function as a coming-together of the citizens of nation-states, is not the collaborative work Shirky sees new media as facilitating already happening? In a British context, for instance, how do new media affect an institution such as the BBC?

One of the key claims made by Shirky is that new media allow for the explosion of amateurisation, and that the access wider society now has to public arenas is necessarily a progressive move. But do you think this amateurisation has taken place? Indeed, have not the professional and experts of old media simply been replaced by newer ones? For example, Frederick Levy's book *15 Minutes of Fame* (2008) gives advice on how to make and upload videos to YouTube, drawing on interviews with people who have done just that. Is not then Levy some kind of expert? Are not those people making and uploading videos in some way developing a sense of professionalism? If not, why would Levy bother interviewing them? It is certainly the case that many people who would be highly unlikely to achieve a professional role in old media structures have been able to succeed within new media, but this suggests that all that has changed is the *people* not the *system*. Indeed, if the rejection of professionalism is a good thing, what are we to make of Shirky's position; is he a professional? Of course, acknowledging the similarities between old and new media systems does not necessarily refute the developments new media have brought; but it is worth thinking carefully about the extent to which this has happened, and querying the mass amateurisation Shirky describes.

Perhaps one of the simplest ways to reflect on this reading is to think about how you feel new media affects your own life. If you are on Facebook, and post videos to YouTube, or blog, or contribute to wikis, does this make you feel a part of a community in the ways Shirky espouses? What are your motivations for this behaviour? And if you do not carry out such activities, why not? Are there reasons why you (and others) might not be interested in being part of a community, bearing in mind, for example, debates about privacy or copyright? Perhaps more importantly though, Shirky (and other writers such as those referred to in the introduction to this chapter) sees a value in the community-building aspects of new media because it allows for different formulations of communication and society, and therefore has the potential for changing the ways we live our lives every day. But does it feel like this to you? Is posting on someone's wall on Facebook a socio-political act? Has your online behaviour changed what you think, or how you behave, or how you see the world around you? Are new media political?

Key terms to explore

professional; amateur; gatekeeper; lulu; news cycle; blogger; professional class.

Key writers who are mentioned

James Q. Wilson.

RECOMMENDED READING

Berners-Lee, T. (1999) *Weaving the Web: The past, present and future of the world wide web by its inventor*, London: Orion Business.

The inventor of the web outlines his vision for his creation, insisting it's a tool for social inclusion, collaboration and, perhaps most importantly, should be free and open.

Castells, M. (2001) *The Internet Galaxy: Reflections on the internet, business, and society*, Oxford: Oxford University Press.

Examines how the internet has altered business, society, politics and culture, using a global perspective and lots of empirical data.

Gauntlett, D. (2011) *Making is Connecting: The social meaning of creativity, from DIY and knitting to YouTube and Web 2.0*, Cambridge: Polity.

Exploration of creativity as a whole, arguing that new media is ushering in a new age of people making things; useful historical contexts that draws parallels between contemporary debates and centuries old ones.

Bibliography

A

Abercrombie, N. and Longhurst, B. (2007) *The Penguin Dictionary of Media Studies*, London: Penguin.

Adonis, A. and Pollard, S. (1997) *A Class Act: The myth of Britain's classless society*, London: Hamish Hamilton.

Adorno, T. (2006 [1991]) *The Culture Industry: Selected essays on mass culture*, London: Routledge.

Adorno, T. and Horkheimer, M. (1972 [1947]) *Dialectic of Enlightenment*, New York: Herder & Herder.

Akass, K. and McCabe, J. (eds) (2004) *Reading Sex and the City*, London: IB Tauris.

Allan, S. (1999) *News Culture*, Buckingham: Open University Press.

Allen, G. (2003) *Roland Barthes*, London: Routledge.

Anderson, K. (2000) *Paul Valéry and the Voice of Desire*, Oxford: Legenda.

Ang, I. (1985) *Watching 'Dallas': Soap opera and the melodramatic imagination*, London: Methuen.

Ang, I. (1991) *Desperately Seeking the Audience*, London: Routledge.

Ang, I. (1996) *Living Room Wars: Rethinking media audiences for a postmodern world*, London: Routledge.

Arendt, H. (1958) *The Human Condition*, Chicago: University of Chicago Press.

Aristotle (1996 [*c.*335 BC]) *Poetics*, translated by Heath, M., London: Penguin.

Armstrong, R. (2005) *Understanding Realism*, London: British Film Institute.

Arnold, M. (1869) *Culture and Anarchy: An essay in political and social criticism*, London: Smith & Elder.

Asgill, J. (1712) *An Essay for the Press*, London: A. Baldwin.

B

Bach, D. (2004) 'The double punch of law and technology: Fighting music piracy or remaking copyright in a digital age?', *Business and Politics* 6 (2): 1–12.

Bagdikian, B.H. (1992) *The Media Monopoly*, 4th edition, Boston: Beacon Press.

Bakir, V. and Barlow, D.M. (2007) *Communication in the Age of Suspicion: Trust and the media*, Basingstoke: Palgrave Macmillan.

Barker, C. (2008) *Cultural Studies: Theory and practice*, 3rd edition, London: Sage.

Barker, M. and Petley, J. (eds) (1997) *Ill Effects: The media/violence debate*, London: Routledge.

Barry, P. (2002) *Beginning Theory: An introduction to literary and cultural theory*, 2nd edition, Manchester: Manchester University Press.

Barry, P. (2009) *Beginning Theory: An introduction to literary and cultural theory*, 3rd edition, Manchester: Manchester University Press.

Barthes, R. (1973 [1957]) *Mythologies*, translated by Lavers, A., London: Paladin.

Barthes, R. (1977 [1967]) *Image Music Text*, translated by Heath, S., London: Fontana.

Barthes, R. (2006 [1967]) *The Language of Fashion*, translated by Stafford, A., Oxford: Berg.

Baudrillard, J. (1994 [1981]) *Simulacra and Simulation*, translated by Glaser, S.F., Ann Arbor: University of Michigan Press.

Baudrillard, J. (1995 [1991]) *The Gulf War Did Not Take Place*, translated by Patton, P., Sydney: Power.

Bauman, Z. (2001) *The Individualized Society*, Cambridge: Polity Press.

BBC Press Office (2006) 'BBC reorganises for an on-demand creative future', *BBC*, http://www.bbc.co.uk/pressoffice/pressreleases/stories/2006/07_july/19/future.shtml.

Bell, D. (1973) *The Coming of Post-Industrial Society*, Harmondsworth: Penguin.

Benjamin, W. (1970) *Illuminations*, translated by Zohn, H., London: Cape.

Bennett, T. (1995) 'Popular Culture and "the Turn to Gramsci"' in *Approaches to Media: A reader*, Boyd-Barrett, O. and Newbold, C. (eds), London: Arnold.

Bentham, J. (1820–21) *On the Liberty of the Press and Public Discussion*, W. Hone: London.

Berelson, B., Lazarsfeld, P.F. and McPhee, W.N. (1954) *Voting: A study of opinion formation in a presidential campaign*, Chicago: University of Chicago Press.

Berners-Lee, T. (1999) *Weaving the Web: The past, present and future of the world wide web by its inventor*, London: Orion Business.

Beynon, W.J. (2002) *Masculinities and Culture*, Maidenhead: Open University Press.

Bignell, J. (2000) *Postmodern Media Culture*, Edinburgh: Edinburgh University Press.

Blondheim, M. (2003) 'Harold Adams Innis and his bias of communication', in *Canonic Texts in Media Research*, Katz, E., Peters, J.D., Liebes, T. and Orloff, A. (eds), Cambridge: Polity Press.

Boddy, W. (2002) 'New media as old media: Television', in *The New Media Book*, Harries, D. (ed), London: British Film Institute.

Bordwell, D. and Thompson, K. (2003) *Film History: An introduction*, 2nd edition, New York: McGraw-Hill.

Botsman, R. and Rogers, R. (2011) *What's Mine is Yours: How collaborative consumption is changing the way we live*, Hammersmith: HarperCollins.

Bottomore, T. (1984) *The Frankfurt School*, Chichester: Ellis Horwood Limited; London: Tavistock Publications.

Boyd-Barrett, O. (1995a) 'Conceptualising the "public sphere"', in *Approaches to Media: A reader*, Boyd-Barrett, O. and Newbold, C. (eds), London: Arnold.

Boyd-Barrett, O. (1995b) 'Early theories in media research', in *Approaches to Media: A reader*, Boyd-Barrett, O. and Newbold, C. (eds), London: Arnold.

Boyd-Barrett, O. (1995c) 'The political economy approach', in *Approaches to Media: A reader*, Boyd-Barrett, O. and Newbold, C. (eds), London: Arnold.

Boyd-Barrett, O. (1995d) 'The analysis of media occupations and professions', in *Approaches to Media: A reader*, Boyd-Barrett, O. and Newbold, C. (eds), London: Arnold.

Boyd-Barrett, O. and Newbold, C. (eds) (1995) *Approaches to Media: A reader*, London: Arnold.

Braham, P. and Janes, L. (2002) *Social Differences and Divisions*, Oxford: Blackwell.

Brecht, B. (2001) *Brecht on Theatre: The development of an aesthetic*, translated by Willett, J., London: Methuen.

Briggs, A. and Burke, P. (2002) *A Social History of the Media: From Gutenberg to the internet*, Cambridge: Polity Press.

Bromley, M. and O'Malley, T. (eds) (1997) *A Journalism Reader*, London: Routledge.

Brown, M. (2007) *A Licence to be Different: The story of Channel 4*, London: British Film Institute.

Brunsdon, C. and Morley, D. (1978) *Everyday Television: Nationwide*, London: British Film Institute.

Bryant, J. and Oliver, M.B. (eds) (2009) *Media Effects: Advances in theory and research*, 3rd edition, New York and London: Routledge.

Bryson, L. (ed.) (1948) *The Communication of Ideas*, New York: Harper & Brothers.

Buckingham, D. (1993) *Children Talking Television: The making of television literacy*, London: Falmer Press.

Buckingham, D. (2007) *Beyond Technology: Children's learning in the age of digital culture*, Cambridge: Polity Press.

Budd, L. and Harris, L. (eds) (2004) *E-Economy: Rhetoric or business reality?*, London: Routledge.

Bukatman, S. (1993) *Terminal Identity: The virtual subject in postmodern science fiction*, London: Duke University Press.

Bullock, A. and Stallybrass, O. (1977) *The Fontana Dictionary of Modern Thought*, London: Fontana.

Burke, S. (1998) *The Death and Return of the Author: Criticism and subjectivity in Barthes, Foucault, and Derrida*, 2nd edition, Edinburgh: Edinburgh University Press.

Burton, G. (2005) *Media and Society: Critical perspectives*, Maidenhead: Open University Press.

Busher, L. (1846 [1614]) 'Religious peace: or, a plea for liberty of conscience', in *Tracts on Liberty of Conscience and Persecution, 1614–1661*, Underhill, E.B. (ed.), London: J. Haddon.

Business Blogs Hub (2010) 'Twitter facts and timeline including 2010', *Business Blogs*, http://www.businessblogshub.com/2010/10/twitter-facts-and-timeline-including-2010/.

Butler, C. (2002) *Postmodernism: A very short introduction*, Oxford: Oxford University Press.

Butler, J. (1990) *Gender Trouble: Feminism and the subversion of identity*, London: Routledge.

Byerly, C.M. (2004) 'Feminist intervention in newsrooms', in *Women and Media: International perspectives*, Ross, K. and Byerly, C.M. (eds), Oxford: Blackwell.

Cantril, H., Gaudet, H. and Herzog, H. (1940) *The Invasion from Mars*, Princeton: Princeton University Press.

Carey, J. (1975) 'Canadian communication theory: extensions and interpretations of Harold Innis', in *Studies in Canadian Communications*, Robinson, G.J. and Theall, D.F. (eds), Montreal: McGill University.

Carey, J.W. (1989) *Communication as Culture*, Boston: Unwin Hyman.

Carey, J.W. (1996) 'The Chicago school and mass communication research', in *American Communication Research: The remembered history*, Dennis, E.E. and Wartella, E. (eds), New Jersey: Lawrence Erlbaum.

Carter, C. and Steiner, L. (eds) (2004) *Critical Readings: Media and gender*, Maidenhead: Open University Press.

Cassidy, J. (2002) *Dot.Con: The greatest story ever sold*, London: Allen Lane.

Castells, M. (1996) *The Rise of the Network Society*, Oxford: Blackwell.

Castells, M. (2001) *The Internet Galaxy: Reflections on the internet, business, and society*, Oxford: Oxford University Press.

Castells, M. (2010) *The Rise of the Network Society*, 2nd edition, Oxford: Blackwell.

Cateforis, T. (ed.) (2007) *The Rock History Reader*, New York: Routledge.

Caulkin, S. (2004) 'Foreword', in *E-Economy: Rhetoric or business reality?*, Budd, L. and Harris, L. (eds), London and New York: Routledge.

Cavanagh, A. (2007) *Sociology in the Age of the Internet*, Maidenhead: Open University Press.

Cellan-Jones, R. (2003) *Dot.Bomb: The Strange Death of Dot.Com Britain*, London: Aurum.

Chambers, E. and Northedge, A. (1997) *The Arts Good Study Guide*, Milton Keynes: Open University Press.

Chandler, D. and Munday, R. (2011) *A Dictionary of Media and Communication*, Oxford: Oxford University Press.

Childs, P. (2007) *Modernism*, 2nd edition, London: Routledge.

Choderlos de Laclos, P. (2008 [1782]) *Les Liaisons Dangereuses*, translated and edited by Parmé, D., Oxford and New York: Oxford University Press.

Chomsky, N. (1982) *Towards a New Cold War*, New York: Pantheon.

Chomsky, N. (1987) *The Chomsky Reader*, New York: Pantheon.

Chomsky, N. (1991) *Deterring Democracy*, London: Verso.

Chomsky, N. (2002) *On Nature and Language*, Cambridge: Cambridge University Press.

Cole, E. and Daniel, J.H. (eds) (2005) *Featuring Females: Feminist analyses of media*, Washington: American Psychological Association.

Collins, J. (1992) 'Television and postmodernism', in *Channels of Discourse, Reassembled: Television and contemporary criticism*, Allen, R.C. (ed.), London: Routledge.

Cottle, S. (1995a) 'Producer-driven television', *Media, Culture and Society* 17 (1): 159–66.

Cottle, S. (1995b) 'The production of news formats: determinants of mediated public contestation', *Media, Culture and Society* 17 (2): 275–91.

Cottle, S. (ed.) (2003) *Media Organization and Production*, London: Sage.

Crisell, A. (2002) *An Introductory History of British Broadcasting*, 2nd edition, London: Routledge.

Critcher, C. (1979) 'Sociology, cultural studies and the post-war working class', in *Working Class Culture*, Clarke, J., Critcher, C. and Johnson, R. (eds), London: Hutchinson.

Culler, J. (1983) *Barthes: A very short introduction*, Oxford: Oxford University Press.

Curran, J. (1996) 'Mass media and democracy revisited', in *Mass Media and Society*, 2nd edition, Curran, J. and Gurevitch, M. (eds), London: Arnold.

Curran, J. (1997a) 'Politics of the media', in *Power and Responsibility: The press and broadcasting in Britain*, 5th edition, Curran, J. and Seaton, J. (eds), London: Routledge.

Curran, J. (1997b) 'Press history', in *Power and Responsibility: The press and broadcasting in Britain*, 5th edition, Curran, J. and Seaton, J. (eds), London: Routledge.

Curran, J. (1997c) 'Theories of the media', in *Power and Responsibility: The press and broadcasting in Britain*, 5th edition, Curran, J. and Seaton, J. (eds), London: Routledge.

Curran, J. (2000) 'Rethinking media and democracy', in *Mass Media and Society*, 3rd edition, Curran, J. and Gurevitch, M. (eds), London: Arnold.

Curran, J. (2005) 'Mediations of democracy', in *Mass Media and Society*, 4th edition, Curran, J. and Gurevitch, M. (eds), London: Arnold.

Curran, J. and Park, M. (2000) *De-Westernizing Media Studies*, London: Routledge.

Curran, J. and Seaton, J. (eds) (1997) *Power and Responsibility: The press and broadcasting in Britain*, 5th edition, London: Routledge.

Curran, J. and Seaton, J. (eds) (2009) *Power and Responsibility: The press and broadcasting in Britain*, 7th edition, London: Routledge.

Curran, J., Gurevitch, M. and Woollacott, J. (1977) *Mass Communication and Society*, London: Arnold.

Curran, J., Gurevitch, M. and Woollacott, J. (1995) 'The study of the media: theoretical approaches', in *Approaches to Media: A reader*, Boyd-Barrett, O. and Newbold, C. (eds), London: Arnold.

D

Dahlgren, P. (ed.) (1991) *Communication and Citizenship: Journalism and the public sphere in the new media age*, London: Routledge.

de Bruin, Marjan and Ross, K. (eds) (2004) *Gender and Newsroom Cultures: Identities at work*, Cresskill: Hampton.

de Tocqueville, Alexis (2000 [1835–40]) *Democracy in America*, translated by Mansfield, H. and Winthrop, D., Chicago: University of Chicago Press.

Dennis, E.E. and Wartella, E. (eds) (1996) *American Communication Research: The remembered history*. New Jersey: Lawrence Erlbaum.

Deuze, M. (2007) *Media Work*, Cambridge and Malden: Polity.

Devereux, E. (2007) *Understanding the Media*, 2nd edition, London: Sage.

Docherty, D., Morrison, D. and Tracey, M. (1993) 'Scholarship as silence', in *Defining Media Studies*, Levy, M. and Gurevitch, M. (eds), Oxford: Oxford University Press.

Downing, J. (1995) 'Alternative media and the Boston Tea Party', in *Questioning the Media*, 2nd edition, Downing, J., Mohammadi, A. and Sreberny-Mohammadi, A. (eds), London: Sage.

Doy, G. (2004) *Picturing the Self: Changing views of the subject in visual culture*, London: IB Tauris.

Ducatel, K., Webster, J. and Herrmann, W. (eds) (2000) *The Information Society in Europe: Work and life in an age of globalization*, Lanham: Rowman & Littlefield.

Duff, D. (ed.) (2000) *Modern Genre Theory*, Harlow: Pearson.

Duke, C. and Layer, G. (eds) (2005) *Widening Participation: Which way forward for English higher education?*, Leicester: National Institute of Adult Continuing Education.

During, S. (2005) *Cultural Studies: A critical introduction*, London: Routledge.

Dworkin, D.L. (1993) 'Cultural studies and the crisis in British radical thought', in *Views Beyond the Border Country: Raymond Williams and cultural politics*, Dworkin, D.L. and Roman, L.G. (eds), New York: Routledge.

Dworkin, D.L. and Roman L.G. (eds) (1993) *Views Beyond the Border Country: Raymond Williams and cultural politics*, New York: Routledge.

E

Eco, U. and Sebeok, T.A. (eds) (1984) *The Sign of Three: Dupin, Holmes, Pierce*, Bloomington: Indiana University Press.

Eldridge, J. (1983) *C. Wright Mills*, Chichester: Ellis Horwood Limited; London: Tavistock Publications.

European Commission (2006) *'Making Work Pay' – Debates from a Gender Perspective: A comparative review of some recent policy reforms in thirty European countries*, Luxembourg: Office for the Official Publications of the European Communities.

European Commission (2010) *The Gender Pay Gap from a Legal Perspective*, Luxembourg: Publications Office of the European Union.

F

Fairbairn, G.J. and Fairbairn, S.A. (2001) *Reading at University: A guide for students*, Buckingham and Philadelphia: Open University Press.

Fiske, J. (1989a) *Understanding Popular Culture*, London: Unwin Hyman.

Fiske, J. (1989b) *Reading the Popular*, London: Unwin Hyman.

Flew, T. (2005) *New Media: An introduction*, 2nd edition, Oxford: Oxford University Press.

Florida, R. (2003) *The Rise of the Creative Class*, New York: Basic Books.

Florida, R. (2005) *Critics and the Creative Class*, New York: Routledge.

Franklin, B. (2004) *Packaging Politics: Political communications in Britain's media democracy*, 2nd edition, London: Arnold.

Fraser, N. (1992) 'Rethinking the public sphere: a contribution to the critique of actually existing democracy', in *Habermas and the Public Sphere*, Calhoun, C. (ed.) Cambridge: MIT Press.

Friedan, B. (1963) *The Feminine Mystique*, Harmondsworth: Penguin.

Friedlander, P. with Miller, P. (2006) *Rock and Roll: A social history*, Boulder, CO: Westview Press.

Frow, J. (2006) *Genre*, London: Routledge.

G

Garnham, N. (1979) 'Editorial', *Media Culture and Society* 1(2): 119–21.

Garnham, N. (1986) 'The media and the public sphere', *Intermedia* 14(1): 28–33.

Garnham, N. (1990) *Capitalism and Communication: Global culture and the economics of information*, London: Sage.

Gauntlett, D. (2002) *Media, Gender and Identity: An introduction*, London: Routledge.

Gauntlett, D. (ed.) (2004) *Web Studies*, 2nd edition, London: Arnold.

Gauntlett, D. (2005) 'Ten things wrong with the media "effects" model', *Theory.org.uk: the Media Theory Site*, www.theory.org.uk/tenthings.htm.

Gauntlett, D. (2011) *Making is Connecting: The social meaning of creativity, from DIY and knitting to YouTube and Web 2.0*, Cambridge: Polity.

Gibson, M. (2007) *Culture and Power: A history of cultural studies*, Oxford: Berg.

Giddens, A. (1990) *The Consequences of Modernity*, Cambridge: Polity Press.

Giddens, A. (2007) *Europe in the Global Age*, Cambridge: Polity Press.

Gilbert, S.M. and Gubar, S. (1979) *The Madwoman in the Attic: The woman writer and the nineteenth-century literary imagination*, London: Yale University Press.

Gilder, G. (1994) *Life After Television*, New York and London: Norton.

Gill, R. (2007) *Gender and the Media*, Cambridge: Polity Press.

Gillespie, M. (ed.) (2005) *Media Audiences*, Maidenhead: Open University Press.

Gitlin, T. (1983) *Inside Prime Time*, New York: Pantheon Books.

Gitlin, T. (1995) 'Media sociology: the dominant paradigm', in *Approaches to Media: A reader*, Boyd-Barrett, O. and Newbold, C. (eds), London: Arnold.

Gitlin, T. (2002) 'Media sociology: the dominant paradigm', in *McQuail's Reader in Mass Communication Theory*, McQuail, D. (ed.), London: Sage.

Godfrey, D. (1986) 'Foreword', in *Empire and Communications*, Innis H.A. (ed.) Victoria: Press Porcepic.

Goffman, E. (1969 [1959]) *The Presentation of Self in Everyday Life*, London: Allen Lane.

Golding, P. and Murdock, G. (2000) 'Culture, communications and political economy', in *Mass Media and Society*, 3rd edition, Curran, J. and Gurevitch, M. (eds), London: Arnold.

Goodwin, W. (1976 [1798]) *Enquiry Concerning Political Justice*, Harmondsworth: Penguin.

Grant, B.K. (ed.) (2008) *Auteurs and Authorship: A film reader*, Oxford: Blackwell.

Greer, G. (1970) *The Female Eunuch*, London: MacGibbon & Kee.

Greer, G. (2000) *The Whole Woman*, London: Transworld.

Greimas, A.J. (1983 [1966]) *Structural Semantics*, translated by McDowell, D., Schleifer, R. and Velie, A., Lincoln: Nebraska University Press.

Guilbert, G. (2002) *Madonna as Postmodern Myth: How one star's self-construction rewrites sex, gender, Hollywood and the American dream*, Jefferson: McFarland.

Guy, A., Green, E. and Banim, M. (eds) (2001) *Through the Wardrobe: Women's relationships with their clothes*, Oxford: Berg.

H

Habermas, J. (1989 [1962]) *The Structural Transformation of the Public Sphere: An inquiry into a category of bourgeois society*, Cambridge: Polity Press.

Habermas, J. (1974 [1964]) 'The public sphere: an encyclopedia article', *New German Critique* 3(1): 49–55.

Haig, M. (2006) *Brand Royalty: How the world's top 100 brands thrive and survive*, London: Kogan Page.

Hall, S. (1980a) 'Cultural studies: two paradigms', *Media, Culture and Society* 2(1): 57–72.

Hall, S. (1980b) 'Cultural studies and the centre: some problematics and problems', in *Culture, Media, Language: Working papers in cultural studies, 1972–9*, Hall, S., Hobson, D., Lowe, A. and Willis, P. (eds), London: Hutchinson.

Hall, S. (1980c) 'Encoding/Decoding', in *Culture, Media, Language: Working papers in cultural studies, 1972–9*, Hall, S., Hobson, D., Lowe, A. and Willis, P. (eds), London: Hutchinson.

Hall, S. (1984) *The Idea of the Modern State*, Milton Keynes: Open University Press.

Hall, S. (ed.) (1997) *Representation: Cultural representations and signifying practices*, London: Sage.

Hall, S. and du Gay, P. (eds) (1996) *Questions of Cultural Identity*, London: Sage.

Hall, S., Hobson, D., Lowe, A. and Willis, P. (eds) (1980) *Culture, Media, Language: Working papers in cultural studies, 1972–9*, London: Hutchinson.

Halloran, J.D. (1995) 'The context of mass communications research', in *Approaches to Media: A reader*, Boyd-Barrett, O. and Newbold, C. (eds), London: Arnold.

Hamelink, C.J. (1995) 'Information imbalance across the globe', in *Questioning the Media: A critical introduction*, 2nd edition, Downing, J., Mohammadi, A. and Sreberny-Mohammadi, A. (eds), London: Sage.

Handelman, D. (2003) 'Towards the virtual encounter: Horton's and Wohl's "mass communication and para-social interaction"', in *Canonic Texts in Media Research*, Katz, E., Peters, J.D., Liebes, T. and Orloff, A. (eds), Cambridge: Polity Press.

Hands, J. (2011) *@ is for Activism: Dissent, resistance and rebellion in a digital culture*, London: Pluto Press.

Hardt, H. (1995) 'On ignoring history: mass communication research and the critique of history', in *Approaches to Media: A reader*, Boyd-Barrett, O. and Newbold, C. (eds), London: Arnold.

Harries, D. (ed) (2002) *The New Media Book*, London: British Film Institute.

Hartley, J. (2002a) 'The constructed viewer', in *Television Studies*, Miller, T. (ed.), London: British Film Institute.

Hartley, J. (2002b) *Communication, Cultural and Media Studies: The key concepts*, 3rd edition, London: Routledge.

Hartley, J. (2005) *Creative Industries*, London: Blackwell.

Harvey, D. (1986) *The Condition of Postmodernity*, Oxford: Blackwell.

Harvey, L. (1987) *Myths of the Chicago School of Sociology*, Aldershot: Avebury.

Hawkes, T. (2003) *Structuralism and Semiotics*, 2nd edition, London and New York: Routledge.

Hebdige, D. (1979) *Subculture: The meaning of style*, London: Methuen.

Hebdige, D. (1982) 'Towards a cartography of taste 1935–1962', in *Popular Culture: Past and present*, Waites, B., Bennett, T. and Martin G. (eds), London: Routledge.

Held, D. (1980) *Introduction to Critical Theory: Horkheimer to Habermas*, Cambridge: Polity Press.

Henning, M. (2006) *Museums, Media and Cultural Theory*, Maidenhead: Open University Press.

Herman, E.S. (1981) *Corporate Control, Corporate Power*, London: Macmillan.

Herman, E.S. (1982) *The Real Terror Network: Terrorism in fact and propaganda*, Boston: South End Press.

Herman, E.S. (1995a) 'Media in the US political economy', in *Questioning the Media: A critical introduction*, 2nd edition, Downing, J., Mohammadi, A. and Sreberny-Mohammadi, A. (eds), London: Sage.

Herman, E.S. (1995b) *Triumph of the Market: Essays on politics, economics and the media*, Boston: South End Press.

Herman, E.S. (2002) 'The propaganda model: a retrospective', in *McQuail's Reader in Mass Communication Theory*, McQuail, D. (ed.), London: Sage.

Herman, E.S. and Chomsky, N. (1994 [1988]) *Manufacturing Consent: The political economy of the mass media*. London: Vintage Books.

Hesmondhalgh, D. (2002) *The Cultural Industries*, London: Sage.

Hesmondhalgh, D. (2005) 'The production of media entertainment', in *Mass Media and Society*, 4th edition, Curran, J. and Gurevitch, M. (eds), London: Hodder Arnold.

Hesmondhalgh, D. (ed.) (2006) *Media Production*, Maidenhead: Open University Press.

Hesmondhalgh, D. (2007) *The Cultural Industries*, 2nd edition, London: Sage.

Higgins, J. (ed.) (2001) *The Raymond Williams Reader*, London: Blackwell.

Hjarvard, S. (1993) 'Pan-European television news: towards a European political public sphere', in *National Identify and Europe*, Drummond, P., Paterson, R. and Willis, J. (eds), London: British Film Institute.

Hobson, D. (1982) *Crossroads: The drama of a soap opera*, London: Methuen.

Hobson, D. (2010) 'Television', in *The Media: An introduction*, 3rd edition, Albertazzi, D. and Cobley, P. (eds), Harlow: Pearson.

Hoggart, R. (1958) *The Uses of Literacy: Aspects of working class life*, London: Pelican.

Hope, W. and Holston, K. (1992) *The Shakespeare Controversy: An analysis of the claimants to authorship, and their champions and detractors*, Jefferson: McFarland.

Hopkins, D. (2003) *Dada and Surrealism: A very short introduction*, Oxford: Oxford University Press.

Horkheimer, M. and Adorno, T.W. (2002 [1944]) *Dialectic of Enlightenment: Philosophical fragments*, translated by Jephcott, E., Stanford: Stanford University Press.

Howe, J. (2009) *Crowdsourcing: How the power of the crowd is driving the future of business*, London: Random House.

Huxley, A. (1958) *Brave New World Revisited*, London: Chatto & Windus.

I

Innis, H.A. (1946) *Political Economy in the Modern State*, Toronto: Ryerson Press.

Innis, H.A. (1951) *The Bias of Communication*, Toronto: University of Toronto Press.

Innis, H.A. (1971 [1923]) *A History of the Canadian Pacific Railway*, Toronto: University of Toronto Press.

Innis, H.A. (1972 [1950]) *Empire and Communications*, Toronto: University of Toronto Press.

Innis, H.A. (1978 [1940]) *The Cod Fisheries: The history of an international economy*, Toronto: University of Toronto Press.

Innis, H.A. (1984 [1930]) *The Fur Trade in Canada: An introduction to Canadian economic history*, Toronto: University of Toronto Press.

Internet World Stats (2010) 'Internet world users by language', *Internet World Stats*, http://www.internetworldstats.com/stats7.htm.

J

Jacobs, J. (2000) *The Intimate Screen: Early British television drama*, Oxford: Oxford University Press.

James, J. (2003) *Bridging the Global Digital Divide*, Cheltenham: Edward Elgar.

Jameson, F. (1991) *Postmodernism, or, the Cultural Logic of Late Capitalism*, London: Verso.

Jancovich, M. (1993) *The Cultural Politics of the New Criticism*, Cambridge: Cambridge University Press.

Jankowski, N. and Prehn, O. (2002) *Community Media in the Information Age: Perspectives and practice*. Cresskill: Hampton Press.

Jefferys, K. (2007) *Politics and the People: A history of British democracy since 1918*, London: Atlantic.

Jenkins, H. (1992) *Textual Poachers: Television fans and participatory culture*, London: Routledge.

Jenkins, H. (2002) 'Interactive audiences?', in *The New Media Book*, Harries, D. (ed.), London: British Film Institute.

Jenkins, H. (2006) *Convergence Culture: Where old and new media collide*, New York and London: New York University Press.

Jenkins, H. (2007a) *The Wow Climax: Tracing the emotional impact of popular culture*, New York: New York University Press.

Jenkins, H. (2007b) 'Afterword: The future of fandom', in *Fandom: Identities and communities in a mediated world*, Gray, J. Sandvoss, C. and Harrington, C.L. (eds), New York and London: New York University Press.

Jenkins, H. (2009) 'What happened before YouTube', in *YouTube*, Burgess, J. and Green, J. (eds), Cambridge: Polity Press.

Jenkins, H. (2011a) 'About me', *Confessions of an aca-fan: The official weblog of Henry Jenkins*, www.henryjenkins.org/aboutme.html.

Jenkins, H. (2011b) 'Latest posts', *Confessions of an aca-fan: The official weblog of Henry Jenkins*, www.henryjenkins.org/index.html.

Johnson, S. (2005) *Everything Bad is Good for You: How today's popular culture is actually making us smarter*, New York: Riverhead.

Jones, P. (2004) *Raymond Williams's Sociology of Culture: A critical reconstruction*, Basingstoke: Palgrave.

K

Katz, E. (1996) 'Diffusion research at Columbia', in *American Communication Research Remembered*, Dennis, E.E. and Wartella, E. (eds), New Jersey: Lawrence Erlbaum.

Katz, E. and Dayan, D. (2003) 'The audience is a crowd, the crowd is a public: latter-day thoughts on Lang and Lang's "McArthur Day in Chicago"', in *Canonic Texts in Media Research*, Katz, E., Peter, J.D., Liebes, T. and Orloff, A. (eds), Cambridge: Polity Press.

Katz, E., Peters, J.D., Liebes, T. and Orloff, A. (eds) (2003) *Canonic Texts in Media Research*, Cambridge: Polity Press.

Keane, J. (1991) *The Media and Democracy*, Cambridge: Polity Press.

Keane, J. (1995) 'Democracy and media: without foundation', in *Approaches to Media: A reader*, Boyd-Barrett, O. and Newbold, C. (eds), London: Arnold.

Kermode, F. (1967) *The Sense of an Ending: Studies in the theory of fiction*, Oxford: Oxford University Press.

King, G. (2005) *The Spectacle of the Real: From Hollywood to reality TV and beyond*, Bristol: Intellect.

Klapper, J. (1960) *The Effects of Mass Communication*, Glencoe: Free Press.

Klein, N. (2000) *No Logo: No space, no choice, no jobs*, London: Flamingo.

Klinkowitz, J. (1988) *Rosenberg/Barthes/Hassan: The postmodern habit of thought*, Athens: University of Georgia Press.

Knight, S. (1980) *Form and Ideology in Crime Fiction*, London: Macmillan.

Kroeber, A.L. (1944) *Configurations of Cultural Growth*, Berkeley: University of California Press.

Kroker, A. (1984) *Technology and the Canadian Mind: Innis/McLuhan/Grant*, New York: St. Martin's Press.

Kubey, R. (2004) *Creating Television: Conversations with the people behind 50 years of American TV*, Mahwah and London: Lawrence Erlbaum.

Kuhn, T. (1962) *The Structure of Scientific Revolutions*, Chicago and London: Chicago University Press.

Kyong, W.H. and Keenan, T. (eds) (2006) *New Media, Old Media: A history and theory reader*, New York and London: Routledge.

L

Lacan, J. (2006 [1953–64]) *Écrits*, translated by Fink, B., London: W.W. Norton.

Lace, S. (2005) *The Glass Consumer: Life in a surveillance society*, Bristol: Policy.

Lash, S. (2002) *Critique of Information*, London: Sage.

Lasswell, H.D. (1927) *Propaganda Techniques in the World War*, New York: Peter Smith.

Lasswell, H.D. (1930) *Psychopathology and Politics*, Chicago: University of Chicago Press.

Lasswell, H.D. (1948) 'The structure and function of communication in society', in *The Communication of Ideas*, Bryson, L. (ed.), New York: Institute for Religious and Social Studies.

Laughey, D. (2007) *Key Themes in Media Theory*, Maidenhead: Open University Press.

Lazarsfeld, P.F. and Katz, E. (1955) *Personal Influence: The part played by people in the flow of mass communication*, Glencoe: Free Press.

Lazarsfeld, P.F. and Merton, R.K. (1948) 'Mass communication, popular taste and organized social action', in *The Communication of Ideas*, Bryson, L. (ed.), New York: Harper & Brothers.

Lazarsfeld, P.F., Berelson, B. and Gaudet, H. (1944) *The People's Choice: How the voter makes up his mind in a presidential campaign*, New York: Columbia University Press.

Leavis, F.R. (1930) *Mass Civilisation and Minority Culture*, Cambridge: Minority Press.

Leavis, F.R. (1932a) *How to Teach Reading: A primer for Ezra Pound*, Cambridge: Minority Press.

Leavis, F.R. (1932b) *New Bearings in English Poetry: A study of the contemporary situation*, London: Chatto & Windus.

Leavis, F.R. (1933) *For Continuity*, Cambridge: Minority Press.

Leavis, F.R. (1948) *The Great Tradition: George Eliot, Henry James, Joseph Conrad*, London: Chatto & Windus.

Leavis, F.R. (1975) *The Living Principle: 'English' as a discipline of thought*, London: Chatto & Windus.

Leavis, F.R. and Thompson, D. (1933) *Culture and Environment: The training of critical awareness*, London: Chatto & Windus.

Lebowitz, M.A. (1992) *Beyond Capital: Marx's political economy of the working class*, London: Macmillan.

Lechte, J. (1994) *Fifty Key Contemporary Thinkers*, London: Routledge.

Lévi-Strauss, C. (1963 [1958]) *Structural Anthropology*, translated by Jacobson, C. and Schoepf, B.G., New York: Basic Books.

Levine, M.P. and Harrison, K. (2009) 'Effects of media on eating disorders and body image', in *Media Effects: Advances in theory and research*, 3rd edition, Bryant, J. and Oliver, M.B. (eds), New York and London: Routledge.

Levmore, S. and Nussbaum, M.C. (eds) (2010) *The Offensive Internet: Speech, privacy and regulation*, Cambridge: Harvard University Press.

Levy, F. (2008) *15 Minutes of Fame: Becoming a star in the YouTube revolution*, New York: Alpha.

Lévy, P. (2001) *Cyberculture*, translated by Bononno, R., Minneapolis and London: University of Minnesota Press.

Lewis, G. and Slade, C. (1994) *Critical Communication*, Sydney: Prentice Hall.

Lewis, J. (2008) *Cultural Studies: The basics*, 2nd edition, London: Sage.

Lewis, P. (2007) *The Cambridge Introduction to Modernism*, Cambridge: Cambridge University Press.

Lichtenberg, J. (2002) 'Foundations and limits of freedom of the press', in *McQuail's Reader in Mass Communication Theory*, McQuail, D. (ed.), London: Sage.

Liebes, T. (2003) 'Herzog's "On borrowed experience": its place in the debate over the active audience', in *Canonic Texts in Media Research*, Katz, E., Peter, J.D., Liebes, T. and Orloff, A. (eds), Cambridge: Polity Press.

Lippmann, W. (1913) *A Preface to Politics*, New York: Mitchell Kennerley.

Lippmann, W. (1914) *Drift and Mastery*, New York: Mitchell Kennerley.

Lippmann, W. (1925) *The Phantom Public*, New York: Harcourt.

Lippmann, W. (1929) *A Preface to Morals*, New York: Macmillan.

Lippmann, W. (1937) *The Good Society*, Boston: Little, Brown.

Lippmann, W. (1943) *U.S. Foreign Policy: Shield of the republic*, Boston: Little, Brown.

Lippmann, W. (1947) *The Cold War*, London: Hamish Hamilton.

Lippmann, W. (1955) *Essays in the Public Philosophy*, Boston: Little, Brown.

Lippmann, W. (1965 [1922]) *Public Opinion*, Glencoe, NY: Free Press.

Lippmann, W. and Merz, C. (1920) 'A test of the news', *The New Republic*, 4 August.

Livingstone, S. (2002) *Young People and New Media: Childhood and the changing media environment*, London: Sage.

Locke, J. (2006 [1689]) *Epistola de Tolerantia ad Clarissimum Virum*, Oxford: Clarendon.

Löhr, P. and Meyer, M. (eds) (1999) *Children, Television and the New Media*, Luton: University of Luton Press.

Long, P. and Wall, T. (2009) *Media Studies: Text, production and context*, Harlow: Longman.

Longhurst, B., Smith, G., Bagnall, G., Crawford, G., Ogborn, M., Baldwin, E. and McCracken, S. (2008) *Introducing Cultural Studies*, 2nd edition, Harlow: Pearson.

Lowenstine, R. (2004) *Origins of the Crash: The great bubble and its undoing*, London: Penguin.

Lynd, R.S. and Lynd, H.M. (1929) *Middletown: A study in American culture*, London: Constable.

Lyon, D. (1994) *The Electronic Eye: The rise of the surveillance society*, Cambridge: Polity Press.

Lyon, D. (2001) *Surveillance Society: Monitoring everyday life*, Buckingham: Open University Press.

Lyotard, J. (1979) *The Postmodern Condition: A report on knowledge*, Manchester: Manchester University Press.

M

McCullagh, C. (2002) *Media Power: A sociological introduction*. Basingstoke: Palgrave.

Macdonald, S. (2006) *A Companion to Museum Studies*, Oxford: Blackwell.

McGuigan, J. (1996) *Culture and the Public Sphere*, London: Routledge.

McKee, A. (2007) 'The fans of cultural theory', in *Fandom: Identities and communities in a mediated world*, Gray, J., Sandvoss, C. and Harrington, C.L. (eds), New York and London: New York University Press.

McKillop, I. (1995) *F.R. Leavis: A life in criticism*, London: Penguin.

MacKinnon, K. (2003) *Representing Men: Maleness and masculinity in the media*, London: Arnold.

McLuhan, M. (1951a) 'Introduction', in *The Bias of Communication*, Innis, H.A. (ed.), Toronto: University of Toronto Press.

McLuhan, M. (1951b) *The Mechanical Bride: Folklore of industrial man*, New York: Vanguard Press.

McLuhan, M. (1962) *The Gutenberg Galaxy: The making of typographic man*, Toronto: University of Toronto Press.

McLuhan, M. (1964) *Understanding Media: The extensions of man*, New York: McGraw-Hill.

McLuhan, M. (1970a) *Culture is Our Business*, New York: McGraw-Hill.

McLuhan, M. (1970b) *From Cliché to Archetype*, New York: Viking Press.

McLuhan, M. and Fiore, Q. (1967) *The Medium is the Massage: An inventory of effects*, New York: Bantam Books.

McNair, B. (1998) *The Sociology of Journalism*, London: Arnold.

McPhail, T. (1981) *Electronic Colonialism: The future of international broadcasting and communication*, Newbury Park: Sage.

McQuail, D. (1977) 'The influence and effects of mass media', in *Mass Communication and Society*, Curran, J., Gurevitch, M. and Woollocott, J. (eds), London: Arnold.

McQuail, D. (ed.) (2002) *McQuail's Reader in Mass Communication Theory*, London: Sage.

McQuail, D. (2005) *McQuail's Mass Communication Theory*, 5th edition, London: Sage.

McRobbie, A. (1982 [1978]) *'Jackie': An ideology of adolescent femininity*, Birmingham: Centre for Contemporary Cultural Studies.

Maker, J. and Lenier, M. (1996) *Academic Reading with Active Critical Thinking*, Belmont: Wadsworth.

Malecki, E.J. and Moriset, B. (2008) *The Digital Economy: Business organization, production processes and regional developments*, London and New York: Routledge.

Malmsten, E. (2001) *Boo Hoo: A dot.com story from concept to catastrophe*, London: Random House.

Manoff, R. and Schudson, M. (1986) *Reading the News*, New York: Pantheon.

Manovich, L. (2002) 'Old media as new media: Cinema', in *The New Media Book*, Harries, D. (ed.), London: British Film Institute.

Marcuse, H. (2002 [1964]) *One-Dimensional Man: Studies in the ideology of advanced industrial society*, 2nd edition, London and New York: Routledge.

Marsh, D., Richards, D. and Smith, M.J. (2001) *Changing Patterns of Governance in the United Kingdom: Reinventing Whitehall?*, Basingstoke: Palgrave.

Marshall, G. (1998) *Oxford Dictionary of Sociology*, 2nd edition, Oxford: Oxford University Press.

Matthews, J. (2010) *Producing Serious News for Citizen Children: A study of the BBC's Children's Programme 'Newsround'*, New York: Edwin Mellen Press.

Melody, W.H. (1981) 'Introduction', in *Culture, Communication, and Dependency: The tradition of H.A. Innis*, Melody, W.H., Salter, L. and Heyer, P. (eds) New Jersey: Ablex.

Merton, R. (1946) *Mass Persuasion: The social psychology of a war bond drive*, New York: Harper & Brothers.

Merton, R. (1949a) 'Patterns of influence: a study of interpersonal influence and communications behaviour in a local community', in *Communications Research*, Lazarsfeld, P.F. and Stanton, F. (eds), New York: Harper and Brothers.

Merton, R. (1949b) *Social Theory and Social Structure*, Glencoe: Free Press.

Merton, R. and Lazarsfeld, P.F. (1943) 'Studies in radio and film propaganda', *Transactions of the New York Academy of Sciences* 6(1): 58–78.

Messenger Davies, M. (1997) *Fake, Fact and Fantasy: Children's interpretations of television reality*, Mahwah: Lawrence Erlbaum.

Meyrowitz, J. (1985) *No Sense of Place: The impact of electronic media on social behaviour*, Oxford: Oxford University Press.

Meyrowitz, J. (2002) 'Media and behaviour: a missing link', in *McQuail's Reader in Mass Communication Theory*, McQuail, D. (ed.), London: Sage.

Meyrowitz, J. (2003) 'Canonic anti-text: Marshall McLuhan's *Understanding Media*', in *Canonic Texts in Media Research*, Katz, E., Peters, J.D., Liebes, T. and Orloff, A. (eds), Cambridge: Polity Press.

Miah, A. and Rich, E. (2010) 'The body, health and illness', in Albertazzi, D. and Cobley, P. (eds) *The Media: An introduction*, 3rd edition, Harlow: Pearson.

Miege, B. (1979) 'The cultural commodity', *Media, Culture and Society* 1(3): 297–311.

Miege, B. (1987) 'The logics at work in the new cultural industries', *Media, Culture and Society* 9(3): 273–89.

Miege, B. (1989) *The Capitalization of Cultural Production*, New York: International General.

Mill, J. (1967 [1811]) 'Liberty of the press', in *Essays on Government, Jurisprudence, Liberty of the Press and Law of Nations*, New York: Kelley.

Mill, J.S. (1848) *The Principles of Political Economy: With some of their applications to social philosophy*, London: Longmans.

Mill, J.S. (1859) *On Liberty*, London: Longmans.

Mill, J.S. (1863) *Utilitarianism*, London: Longmans.

Mill, J.S. (1869) *The Subjection of Women*, London: Longmans.

Mill, J.S. (1873) *Autobiography of John Stuart Mill*, London: Longmans.

Mill, J.S. (1874) *Three Essays on Religion*, London: Longmans.

Mill, J.S. (1997 [1859]) 'Of the liberty of thought and discussion', in *A Journalism Reader*, Bromley, M. and O'Malley, T. (eds), London: Routledge.

Mills, C.W. (1951) *White Collar: The American middle classes*, New York: Oxford University Press.

Mills, C.W. (1956) *The Power Elite*, London: Oxford University Press.

Mills, C.W. (1959) *The Sociological Imagination*, London: Oxford University Press.

Mills, C.W. (1967) *Sociology and Pragmatism: The higher learning in America*, New York: Oxford University Press.

Milton, J. (1644) *Areopagitica: A speech for the liberty of unlicensed printing to the Parliament of England*, London: s.n.

Morley, D. (1980) *The 'Nationwide' Audience: Structure and decoding*, London: British Film Institute.

Morozov, E. (2011) *The Net Delusion: How not to liberate the world*, London: Allen Lane.

Mosco, V. (1996) *The Political Economy of Communication*, London: Sage.

Mosley, I. (ed.) (2000) *Dumbing Down: Culture, politics and the mass media*, Thorverton: Imprint Academic.

Mulhern, F. (1981) *The Moment of 'Scrutiny'*, London: Verso.

Mulvey, L. (2000 [1975]) 'Visual pleasure and narrative cinema', in *Feminism and Film*, Kaplan, E.A. (ed.), Oxford: Oxford University Press.

Munt, S. (ed.) (2000) *Cultural Studies and the Working Class: Subject to change*, London: Cassell.

Murdock, G. and Golding, P. (1973) 'For a political economy of mass communications', in *The Socialist Register*, Miliband, R. and Saville, J. (eds), London: The Merlin Press.

Murdock, G. and Golding, P. (2005) 'Culture, communications and political economy', in *Mass Media and Society*, 4th edition, Curran, J. and Gurevitch, M. (eds), London: Hodder Arnold.

N

Naylor, R., Smith, J. and McKnight, A. (2002) *Sheer Class? The extent and sources of variation in the UK graduate earnings premium*, London: Centre for Analysis for Social Exclusion.

Neale, S. (1980) *Genre*, London: British Film Institute.

Negroponte, N. (1996) *Being Digital*, London: Coronet.

Newbold, C. (1995a) 'Approaches to cultural hegemony within cultural studies', in *Approaches to Media: A reader*, Boyd-Barrett, O. and Newbold, C. (eds), London: Arnold.

Newbold, C. (1995b) 'The media effects tradition', in *Approaches to Media: A reader*, Boyd-Barrett, O. and Newbold, C. (eds), London: Arnold.

Newman, M. (2002) *Ralph Miliband and the Politics of the New Left*, London: Merlin Press.

Noerr, G.S. (2002) 'Editor's afterword', in *Dialectic of Enlightenment: Philosophical fragments*, Horkheimer, M. and Adorno, T.W. (eds), Stanford: Stanford University Press.

Norris, P. (2001) *Digital Divide: Civic engagement, information poverty and the internet*, Cambridge: Cambridge University Press.

O

O'Connor, A. (1989) *Raymond Williams: Writing, culture, politics*, Oxford: Basil Blackwell.

O'Hara, K. and Stevens, D. (2006) *Inequality.com: Power, poverty and the digital divide*, Oxford: Oneworld.

Ofek, E. and Richardson, M. (2003) 'DotCom mania: The rise and fall of internet stock prices', *The Journal of Finance* 58(3): 1113–1137.

O'Sullivan, T., Hartley, J., Saunders, D. and Fiske, J. (1989) *Key Concepts in Communication*, London: Methuen.

P

Packard, V. (1957) *The Hidden Persuaders*, London: Longman Green.

Paine, T. (1791–2) *Rights of Man*, London: J.S. Jordan.

Papacharissi, Z. (2010) *A Private Sphere: Democracy in a digital age*, Cambridge: Polity.

Peirce, C.S. (1982) *The Writings of Charles S. Peirce: A chronological edition*, Bloomington: Indiana University Press.

Peters, J.D. (1993) 'Distrust of representation: Habermas on the public sphere', *Media, Culture and Society* 15(4): 541–71.

Peters, J.D. (2003) 'The subtlety of Horkheimer and Adorno: reading "The culture industry"', in *Canonic Texts in Media Research*, Katz, E., Peter, J.D., Liebes, T. and Orloff, A. (eds), Cambridge: Polity Press.

Pickering, M. (2001) *Stereotyping: The politics of representation*, Basingstoke: Palgrave.

Pinkney, T. (1991) *Raymond Williams*, Bridgend: Seren.

Pirate Party UK (2011) 'Manifesto: copyrights and patents', *Pirate Party UK*, www.pirateparty.org.uk/policies/uk-2011/copyrights-patents/.

Poole, R. (1989) 'Public spheres', in *Australian Communications and the Public Sphere*, Wilson, H. (ed.), Melbourne: Macmillan.

Postman, N. (1985) *Amusing Ourselves to Death: Public discourse in the age of show business*, New York: Penguin.

Presdee, M. (2000) *Cultural Criminology and the Carnival of Crime*, London: Routledge.

Priestly, J. (1768) *An Essay on the First Principles of Government; and on the Nature of Political, Civil and Religious Liberty*, London: J. Dodsley.

Proctor, J. (2004) *Stuart Hall*, London: Routledge.

Propp, Vladimir (1968 [1928]) *Morphology of the Folktale*, translated by Scott, L., Austin: University of Texas Press.

Q

Quattrocchi, A. and Nairn, T. (1998) *The Beginning of the End: France, May 1968, what happened, why it happened*, London: Verso.

R

Reames, K.L. (2007) *Women and Race in Contemporary US Writing: From Faulkner to Morrison*, New York: Palgrave.

Redley, M. (2007) 'Some origins of the problem of trust: propaganda in the First World War', in *Communicating in the Age of Suspicion: Trust and the media*, Bakir, V. and Barlow, D.M. (eds), Basingstoke: Palgrave Macmillan.

Reid, I. (1998) *Class in Britain*, Cambridge: Polity.

Ribière, M. (2002) *Barthes: A beginner's guide*, London: Hodder & Stoughton.

Richards, I.A. (1924) *Principles of Literary Criticism*, London: Kegan Paul.

Richards, I.A. (1926) *Science and Poetry*, London: Kegan Paul.

Richardson, M. (2006) *Surrealism and Cinema*, Oxford: Berg.

Robinson, G.J. (1996) 'Constructing a historiography for North Amercan communication studies', in *American Communication Research: The remembered history*, Dennis, E.E. and Wartella, E. (eds), New Jersey: Lawrence Erlbaum.

Rojek, C. (2003) *Stuart Hall*, Cambridge: Polity Press.

Rojek, C. (2007) *Cultural Studies*, Cambridge: Polity Press.

Rosenberg, S.W. (2002) *The Not So Common Sense: Differences in how people judge social and political life*, London: Yale University Press.

Ross, A. (2009) *Nice Work if You Can Get It: Life and labor in precarious times*, New York: New York University Press.

Rothenbuhler, E.W. (2003) 'Community and pluralism in Wirth's "Consensus and mass communication"', in *Canonic Texts in Media Research*, Katz, E., Peter, J.D., Liebes, T. and Orloff, A. (eds), Cambridge: Polity Press.

Ryan, A. (1969) 'John Stuart Mill', in *The Founding Fathers of Social Science*, Raison, T. (ed.), Harmondsworth: Pelican Press.

S

Salih, S. (2002) *Judith Butler*, London: Routledge.

Scannell, P. (2003) 'Benjamin contextualized: On "The work of art in the age of mechanical production"', in *Canonic Texts in Media Research*, Katz, E., Peter, J.D., Liebes, T. and Orloff, A. (eds), Cambridge: Polity Press.

Scannell, P. (2007) *Media and Communication*, London: Sage.

Schiller, H.L. (1998) 'Striving for communications dominance: a half-century review', in *Electronic Empires: Global media and local resistance*, Thussu, D. (ed.), London: Arnold.

Schramm, W. (ed.) (1949) *Mass Communications*, Urbana: University of Illinois Press.

Schrøder, K., Drotner, K., Kline, S. and Murray, C. (2003) *Researching Audiences*, London: Arnold.

Seaton, J. (1997) 'The sociology of the mass media', in *Power without Responsibility: The press and broadcasting in Britain*, 5th edition, Curran, J. and Seaton, J. (eds), London: Routledge.

Sedgwick, J. and Pokorny, M. (2004) *An Economic History of Film*, London: Routledge.

Seiter, E. (1999) *Television and New Media Audiences*, Oxford: Oxford University Press.

Shirky, C. (2008) *Here Comes Everybody: How change happens when people come together*, London: Penguin.

Shirky, C. (2010) *Cognitive Surplus: Creativity and generosity in a connected age*, London: Allen Lane.

Sills, D.L. (1996) 'Stanton, Lazarsfeld, and Merton: pioneers in communication research', in *American Communication Research Remembered*, Dennis, E.E. and Wartella, E. (eds), New Jersey: Lawrence Erlbaum.

Simmons, E. (2009) 'The first iPresident', *Dialog: A Journal of Theology* 48(2): 118–20.

Simons, J. (2002) 'New media as old media: Cinema', in *The New Media Book*, Harries, D. (ed.), London: British Film Institute.

Simonson, P. and Weimann, G. (2003) 'Critical research at Columbia: Lazarsfeld's and Merton's "Mass communication, popular taste, and organized social action"', in *Canonic Texts in Media Research*, Katz, E., Peter, J.D., Liebes, T. and Orloff, A. (eds), Cambridge: Polity Press.

Skeggs, B. (2004) *Class, Self, Culture*, London: Routledge.

Smith, B.L., Lasswell, H.D. and Casey, R.D. (1935) *Propaganda and Promotional Activities: An annotated bibliography*, Princeton: University Press.

Smith, B.L., Lasswell, H.D. and Casey, R.D. (1946) *Propaganda, Communication, and Public Opinion: A comprehensive reference guide*, Princeton: Princeton: University Press.

Smith, C. (1998) *Creative Britain*, London: Faber & Faber.

Smith, M.R. and Marx, L. (1994) *Does Technology Drive History? The dilemma of technological determinism*, London: MIT Press.

Sparks, C. (2001) 'The internet and the global public sphere', in *Mediated Politics: Communication in the future of democracy*, Bennett, W.L. and Entman, R.M. (eds), Cambridge: Cambridge University Press.

Spinello, R.A. and Tavani, H.T. (2005) *Intellectual Property Rights in a Networked World: Theory and practice*, London: Information Science.

Stamps, J. (1995) *Unthinking Modernity: Innis, McLuhan, and the Frankfurt School*, Montreal: McGill-Queen's University Press.

Steiner, G. (1992) *After Babel: Aspects of language and translation*, 2nd edition, Oxford: Oxford University Press.

Stevenson, N. (2002) *Understanding Media Cultures*, 2nd edition, London: Sage.

Stoltzfus, B. (1964) *Robbe-Grillet and the New French Novel*, Carbondale: Southern Illinois University Press.

Storey, J. (2006) *Cultural Theory and Popular Culture: A reader*, 3rd edition, Harlow: Pearson.

Stratton, J. and Ang, I. (1996) 'On the impossibility of a global cultural studies: "British" cultural studies in an "international" frame', in *Stuart Hall: Critical dialogues in cultural studies*, Morley, D. and Chen, K. (eds), London: Routledge.

Styan, J.L. (1981) *Modern Drama in Theory and Practice, Volume 3: Expressionism and epic theatre*, Cambridge: Cambridge University Press.

Surowiecki, J. (2004) *The Wisdom of Crowds: Why the many are smarter than the few and how collective wisdom shapes business, economics, societies, and nations*, New York and London: Doubleday.

T

Tasker, Y. and Negra, D. (2007) *Interrogating Postfeminism: Gender and the politics of popular culture*, London: Duke University Press.

Theall, D.F. (1975) 'Communication theory and the national culture: the socio-aesthetic dimensions of communication study', in *Studies in Canadian Communications*, Robinson, G.J. and Theall, D.F. (eds), Montreal: McGill University.

Thody, P. and Course, A. (1999) *Introducing Barthes*, Cambridge: Icon.

Thomas, D. (2002) 'Innovation, piracy and the ethos of new media', in *The New Media Book*, Harries, D. (ed.), London: British Film Institute.

Thomas, W.I. (1918–20) *The Polish Peasant in Europe and America*, Chicago: University of Chicago Press.

Thompson, J.B. (1994) 'Social theory and the media', in *Communication Theory Today*, Cowley, D. and Mitchell, D. (eds), Cambridge: Polity Press.

Thornham, S. (2007) *Women, Feminism and Media*, Edinburgh: Edinburgh University Press.

Thussu, D. (2006) *International Communication: Continuity and change*, 2nd edition, London: Arnold.

Thwaites, T. (2007) *Reading Freud: Psychoanalysis and cultural theory*, London: Sage.

Tindal, M. (1704) *Reasons Against Restraining the Press*, London: *s.n.*

Todorov, T. (1977 [1971]) *The Poetics of Prose*, translated by Howard, R., Oxford: Blackwell.

Todorov, T. (1990 [1978]) *Genres in Discourse*, translated by Porter, C., Cambridge: Cambridge University Press.

Todorov, T. (1999 [1984]) *The Conquest of America: The question of the other*, translated by Howard, R., Norma: University of Oklahoma Press.

Todorov, T. (2003 [2000]) *Hope and Memory: Lessons from the twentieth century*, translated by Bellos, D., London: Atlantic Books.

Toffler, A. (1980) *The Third Wave*, New York: Bantam Books.

Toynbee, A. (1934–61) *A Study of History*, 12 volumes, Oxford and New York: Oxford University Press.

Turner, G. (1996) *British Cultural Studies: An introduction*, 2nd edition, London: Routledge.

Turner, G. (2003) *British Cultural Studies: An introduction*, 3rd edition, London and New York: Routledge.

U

United Nations (2010) 'Promote gender equality and empower women', *United Nations Millennium Goals*, www.un.org/millenniumgoals/pdf/MDG_FS_3_EN.pdf.

Uricchio, W. (2002) 'Old media as new media: Television', in *The New Media Book*, Harries, D. (ed.), London: British Film Institute.

Ursell, G. (2006) 'Working in the media', in *Media Production*, Hesmondhalgh, D. (ed.), Maidenhead: Open University Press.

V

Vaccari, Cristian (2010) '"Technology is a commodity": The internet in the 2008 United States Presidential Election', *Journal of Information Technology and Cultural Politics* 7(4): 318–39.

van Dijk, J.A.G.M. (2005) *The Deepening Divide: Inequality in the information society*, Thousand Oaks: Sage.

van Dijk, J.A.G.M. (2006) *The Network Society: Social aspects of new media*, 2nd edition, London: Sage.

van Evra, J. (2004) *Television and Child Development*, 3rd edition, Mahwah: Lawrence Erlbaum.

van Zoonen, L. (1994) *Feminist Media Studies*, London: Sage.

Veblen, T. (1957 [1899]) *The Theory of the Leisure Class: An economic study of institutions*, London: Allen and Unwin.

Verstraeten, H. (1996) 'The media and the transformation of the public sphere', *European Journal of Communication* 11(3): 347–70.

W

Walsh-Childers, K. and Brown, J.D. (2008) 'Effects of media on personal and public health', in *Media Effects: Advances in theory and research*, 3rd edition, Bryant, J. and Oliver, M.B. (eds), New York and London: Routledge.

Walters, M. (2005) *Feminism: A very short introduction*, Oxford: Oxford University Press.

Walwyn, W. (1644) *The Compassionate Samaritane*, London: *s.n.*

Watson, J. and Hill, A. (2000) *A Dictionary of Communication and Media Studies*, London: Arnold.

Wayne, M. (2003) *Marxism and Media Studies: Key concepts and contemporary trends*, London: Pluto Press.

Webb, J. (2009) *Understanding Representation*, London: Sage.

Website Monitoring (2010) 'Facebook facts and figures (history and statistics)', *Website Monitoring Blog*, www.website-monitoring.com/blog/2010/03/17/facebook-facts-and-figures-history-statistics/.

Webster, F. (1995) *Theories of the Information Society*, 1st edition, London: Routledge.

Webster, F. (2002) *Theories of the Information Society*, 2nd edition, London: Routledge.

Webster, F. (2006) *Theories of the Information Society*, 3rd edition, London: Routledge.

Webster, F., Blom, R., Karvonen, E., Melin, H., Nordenstreng, K. and Puoskari, E. (eds) (2004) *The Information Society Reader*, London: Routledge.

Weinberg, B. (1966) *Limits of Symbolism: Studies of five modern French poets*, Chicago: University of Chicago Press.

Wertham, Frederic (1954) *Seduction of the Innocent: The influence of comic books on today's youth*, New York: Reinhart.

Westwood, S. (2002) *Power and the Social*, London: Routledge.

Wiggershaus, R. (1994) *The Frankfurt School: Its history, theories and political significance*, Cambridge: Polity Press.

Will, F. (1993) *Translation Theory and Practice: Reassembling the tower*, Lampeter: Edwin Mellen Press.

Williams, H. (2004) *Mallarmé's Ideas in Language*, Oxford: Lang.

Williams, K. (1998) *Get Me A Murder A Day!: A history of mass communication in Britain*, London: Arnold.

Williams, K. (2003) *Understanding Media Theory*, London: Arnold.

Williams, R. (1958) *Culture and Society 1780–1950*, London: Chatto & Windus.

Williams, R. (1960) *Border Country: A novel*, London: Chatto and Windus.

Williams, R. (1961) *The Long Revolution*, Orchard Park: Broadview Press.

Williams, R. (1974) *Television: Technology and cultural form*, London: Fontana.

Williams, R. (1983 [1976]) *Keywords: A vocabulary of culture and society*, London: Fontana.

Williams, R. (1989) *What I Came to Say*, London: Hutchinson Radius.

Williams, R. (2001) 'Culture is Ordinary' in Higgins, J. (ed.) *The Raymond Williams Reader*, Oxford: Blackwell.

Williamson, A. (2011) 'Social media and the New Arab Spring', *Hansard Society*, www.hansardsociety.org.uk/blogs/edemocracy/archive/2011/04/19/social-media-and-the-new-arab-spring.aspx.

Willis, P. (1977) *Learning to Labour: How working class kids get working class jobs*, Farnborough: Saxon House.

Wilson, J.Q. (1989) *Bureaucracy: What government agencies do and why they do it*, New York: Basic Books.

Winn, M. (1985) *The Plug-In Drug: Television, children, and the family*, revised edition, New York: Penguin.

Winston, B. (1995) 'How are the media born and developed?', in *Questioning the Media*, 2nd edition, Downing, J., Mohammadi, A. and Sreberny-Mohammadi, A. (eds), London: Sage.

Wollstonecraft, M. (1792) *Vindication of the Rights of Woman*, London: Johnson.

Wong, P., Chan, W., Chen, E., Chan, S., Law, Y. and Yip, P. (2008) 'Suicide among adults aged 30–49: A psychological autopsy study in Hong Kong', *BMC Public Health* 8(1): 147.

Woodhams, S. (2001) *History in the Making: Raymond Williams, Edward Thompson and radical intellectuals, 1936–1956*, London: Merlin.

Wordsworth, W. and Coleridge, S.T. (1798) *Lyrical Ballads*, London: J. & A. Arch.

Work Foundation, The (2007) *Staying Ahead: The economic performance of the UK's creative industries*, London: The Work Foundation.

Wyatt, J. (1990) *Commitment to Higher Education*, Buckingham: Society for Research into Higher Education and Open University Press.

Y

Young, T.D. (ed.) (1976) *The New Criticism and After*, Charlottesville: University Press of New Virginia.

YouTube (2011) 'YouTube: statistics', *YouTube*, www.youtube.com/t/press_statistics.

Index

ABC (Australia) 99, 274, 278
abstract empiricism 175
'aca-fan' 463
academic language, and reading 32–5
academic theory 9
Accuracy in Media (AIM) 284
Active Critical Thinking (ACT) process 28–9
Adaptation (Journal) 79
administrative research and critical research 135
Adorno, Theodor 13, 82, 84–5, 87, 153, 481, 483, 563, 624
  background 88
  Dialectic of Enlightenment 88–102
Advertisement Writing 76–7
advertising/advertisers,
  audiences and 606
  canalizing of pre-existing attitudes 164
  flak and 282, 284
  newspapers and 276, 278
  status conferral function 146, 147
  television and 278, 606
  use of connotations of object for its appeal 244, 245
Aeschylus 210
agenda-setting research 170
alphabet 210
Althusser, Louis 412, 414, 415
Alton, David 322
amateurs 630, 631
American Enterprise Institute 282
American Legal Foundation 284
American Revolution 40
Americanisation 70, 83

Ang, Ien 455, 471
  'audience-as-market' and 'audience-as-public' 602–622
  Desperately Seeking the Audience 602
  Watching Dallas 602
Angell, Norman 72–3, 520
'anomie' 172, 197
anti-communism 272, 284, 285, 287
anti-establishment 295
anti-nuclear 288
anti-semitism 85
Antigone 440, 441
antisocial behaviour 342, 344, 346
'antisocial' and 'prosocial' 337
apologists 295
Approaches to Audiences (Dickenson *et al*) 326
'Arab Spring' 625
Arendt, Hannah *The Human Condition* 196
Aristotle 323, 381
Arnold, Mathew 60, 62
  Culture and Anarchy 61, 64–6
'art' 561, 576
  mass 160
Asgill, John 42
Aspen 577
Assyrians 206, 208, 209
attention structure 125
Athens 210, 210–214, 211, 212, 213, 214
attention 108
attention aggregates and publics 124–5
attention frames 110, 122–3, 130
attention model of communication 612
audience 12
audience analysis 106, 130
audience research 228
audience/s 183, 564, 575, 595, 600–622

Ang's audience-as-market and audience-as-public 612–22
  concept 471
  consumers 611
  creativity of 560
  mass 272, 344, 565
  mass media and 142
  maximization 606, 607
  measurement of 608, 609, 614, 618
  new media and 469, 477, 481
  niche 607
  positioning 610
  ratings 603, 606, 622
  technology and 609
  texts and 565, 595
  use of new media 463
audiences 264, 572
audiences as producers 624–51
'auteur' theory 258, 561
author 574–5
  death of 577–99
automatic writing 584, 596
automobile 142–5

Babylonia 208
Baehr, Helen 396
Bagdikian, Ben *The Media Monopoly* 265, 272
Baghdad 214, 215
Baldwin, Faith 144
ballads 110
Balzac, Honoré de 581, 594
  Sarrasine 580
Bandura's 'bobo' doll experiments 338, 339
Barker, C. 427
Barthes, Roland 31, 244, 247, 490
  background 576–7
  Death of the Author 227, 577–98

Image Music Text 227, 577, 578
Mythologies 245, 576–7
Baudelaire, Jean 68, 489
    background 489
    Gulf War Did Not Take Place, The 490
    'implosion of Meaning in the Media'
        492–510
    Simulacra and Simulation 489, 490
Bauman, Zygmunt 514
BBC 99, 155, 427, 483, 552, 604, 615,
    616–17, 622, 650
Beaverbrook, Lord 73
Beavis and Butt Head 336, 337
Becker, Arnold (CBS executive) 606
Bell, Daniel 513, 528, 530, 532, 566
Benedict, Ruth 446
Benjamin, Walter 13, 87, 95
Bentham, Jeremy *On the Liberty of the
    Press and Public Discussion* 42–3
Berelson, B. 133
bias 186, 187, 199, 202, 204, 269
    of the newspaper 221
'Bias of communication' (Innes) 200–224
biological analogy 113, 115, 121, 129
    analysis of communication 105–128
'biological equivalences' 109
Bureau of Applied Social Research 136
Birmingham Centre for Contemporary
    Cultural Studies *see* CCCS
'black box fallacy' 486
black feminism 392
black women 404
    portrayal and stereotyping of in mass
        media 404, 405
Blair, Tony 102
bloggers 640, 642, 645
Blondheim, M. 201–2, 205, 222–3
Blumler, Jay 604, 610
Boddy, W. 'New Media as Old Media' 462
Bono 296, 297, 301
books 217, 223
Bourdieu, Pierre 562
bourgeois 304, 305, 307, 308, 309, 311,
    314, 320
bourgeois media 315
bourgeois public sphere 304, 305, 306, 307,
    308, 309, 310, 314
bourgeoisie 309, 314, 315, 320
Boyd-Barrett, O. 105, 109, 134–5, 174, 197,
    264–5, 298, 601
brands 568
Branson, Richard 263
Brecht, Bertolt 587
Bremond, Claude *Logique du Récit* 362
Breton, André 587
Briggs, A. and Burke, P. 40, 43, 87, 104,
    130, 217
Brissot, Jacques-Pierre *Memoire on the
    Need to Free the Press* 40
British Board of Film Classification 343
British cultural studies 426, 427
Bromley, M. and O'Malley, T. 42–3
Brooks, Cleanth 583
Browne, Nick 340, 606
Brunsdon, Charlotte 13, 394
Brunsdon, Charlotte and Morley, David
    Everday Television 226
Bryce, James 149, 158
Bryson, Lyman *The Communication of
    Ideas* 104–5, 136, 145
BSkyB 263
Bücher, Karl 310
Bulger, James 322
'bullet model' 103, 134
Bullock, A. and Stallybrass, O. 60
bureacratisation 171
Bureau of Applied Social Research 133
bureaucracy 172
Burke, Kenneth, *Attitudes Towards History*
    164
Burroughs, Edgar Rice 74
Busby 400
Busher, Leonard 42
Burton, G. 198
Busby 400
Bush, George 287, 638
business,
    as media source
    resentment towards media's criticism of
Butler, Judith *Gender Trouble* 385
Byerly, C.M. 385

Calvert, Lord 146
campaign for press and Broadcasting
    Freedom
Canadian communication theory 198
'Canadian social theory' 198
canalisation 136, 163–4, 170, 171
canon 88, 455
Capital Legal Foundation 284
capitalism 87, 196, 294, 307, 308, 315, 408,
    513, 604
capitalist ideology 582
Carey, James 105, 130, 134, 199, 203, 219,
    222–3
Carphone Warehouse 263
Casey, Ralph D. 103
Castells, M. 469, 513, 530, 538, 566
    The Rise of the Network Society 461
Caulkin, S. 462
Causation, correlation and 340, 341
Cavanagh, A. 462
Caxton, William 216
CBS 133, 143–4, 274, 284
CCCS 13, 59, 61, 130, 198, 225–59, 406–8
    background 225–7
closure of 227
focus on class 226
Hall's Encoding/Decoding 228–59
Women's Studies Group 406
Celebrity Big Brother 263, 285
cell phone rings 483
cell phones 472
censorship 293, 390
Center for Media and Public Affairs 284
centralisation 221
Centre for Media and Cultural Studies
certified knowledge 171
Chance and Necessity 492
change/continuity cultural industries 554,
    564, 566
Chartist movement 315, 320
Chénier, Marie-Joseph, *Denunciation of
    the Inquisitors of Thought* 40
Chicago school 104, 222
children,
    concern over use of internet 322
    need to protect from effects of media
        324
    treating as inadequate 332–4
Children's Television Workshop 466, 447
China 214, 215
Chodorow, Nancy 408, 412
Chomsky, Noam 266
church 306, 307
cinema 381
    rating system 598
    representation of women 386
    see also films
circulating libraries 218, 219
circulation 171, 468
circulation circuit model 330, 331
class 409, 417, 573, 647
class interest 256, 339
classical liberal theory 57
classical political economy 264
'classless society' 226, 417
clothing 418, 540, 541–2
CNN 468
Coffee houses
Cold War 135, 288
collective intelligence 470
collisions 376, 463, 468
Columbia Broadcasting System *see* CBS
Columbia School 132–71, 170
    background 132–5
    Lazarsfeld and Merton's Mass
        communication, popular taste and
        organized social action 136–71
Columbine High School (shootings) 322,
    323
Comics Code Authority 323
commercial broadcasting 605, 611
'commercial cities' 215, 217

commercial revolution 216
commercial television 604, 606, 607, 614
commercialism 221
communication process 234
common sense 9, 41, 186–7, 332, 333, 515, 517, 537, 576, 622
  notions of media use 626
communication,
  artificial 576
  channels controlled 126, 130
  collapse in costs 634
  hypodermic needle model 103, 134
  limitations of 214
  mass media of 126–7
  media 228, 572
  problems with 139
  process 105, 234–5, 238
  research on 122
  social class and 121
  social conflicts and 118
  theory of 105
  three social functions 107–8
communication studies 88, 104
communications ecosystem 646
communism 284, 285, 286, 287, 292, 294
computers 159, 520, 522
conductance 108–110, 113, 122–3, 130
Confucianism 214
connotation/denotation 242, 243, 244, 246
Conrad, Joseph *Heart of Darkness* 370
'consciousness raising' 508
conservatism 335, 339
'conspicious' consumption 483
Constant, Benjamin *Adolphe* 376, 378
Constantinople 212
consumer culture 297, 310, 313, 320, 481
consumption 470
content analysis 106, 130
context 575, 576
  theory and 12, 13, 16
continuity,
  problem of time 208
  problems of 207
continuity and time 213
  problems of 220
control analysis 106, 130
Cooley, Charles 180–81
convergence, 478, 479, 482, 485, 513
  culture of 462
  media and 468, 474
  definition 469
  function of societies and 513
  within brains of individual consumers 470
copyability, a lulu 636
copyright law 479
correlation 107, 128
correlation causation and 341

Cosby Show, The 606
cottage industries 474
Coughlan, Father 164–5
'creative control' 483
'creative economy' 568
creative industries 101–2, 486, 551–2
Criminal Justice Act (1994) 322
criminologists 330, 331
critical political economy 263
critical reading 24
critical research and administrative research 135
critical theory 10, 16, 85, 87
criticism 592
cultural determinism 95
cultural elitism 610
cultural hierarchy 585
cultural industries 553, 556, 561
  as agents of economic, social and cultural change 564–70
  ambivalent nature of 562
  audiences 565
  brands and 568
  change/continuity 554, 564, 572
  inequalities in access to 562, 563
  managing and circulating og creativity 558–64
  matching text to audiences 564, 565
  serving interests of owners issue 556, 564
  sources of wealth and employment 564
cultural production 566
cultural studies 427, 445, 458, 459, 557
cultural theory 415, 426–58, 622
  background 426–8
  out of bookstore ghetto 464
  Williams *The Long Revolution* 429–58
'cultural tradition' 265, 456
cultural workers 565
culturalism 265
culture 426, 430, 443, 458
  appreciation of 575
  definitions 432, 433, 434, 435, 436, 439
  difficulties in describing 452, 453
  'documentary' definition 430, 432, 434, 436, 444, 450
  historical context 440, 441
  'ideal' definition 432, 434, 440
  information society and 540–44
  Leavis on mass civilization and minority 59–83
  lived 450, 452
  loss of some kinds 453
  maintaining of hierarchies through 575
  patterns of 444, 445
  recorded 450
  selective tradition 450, 452, 453, 454, 456

society and 441, 443
structure of feeling and 448, 449, 450, 451
three levels of 450, 451
culture industry 92–4
  consumer and 94, 96, 97
  relationship with other industrial sectors 92–4, 95, 97
  technology and 92–4
  trends 97
Culture Show, The 426
Cummings, Melbourne 406
Curran, J. 40, 56, 87–8, 135, 315, 319, 320
'cybercitizen' 462
Cyberculture 471
'cyberspace' 536

Dahlgren, P. 315, 317, 320
Daily Herald 72
Daily Mail 72
Dallas 602
Davies, Nick (*Guardian*) 39
de Saussure, Ferdinand 353
'death of the author' (Barthes) 227, 577–98
democracy 181, 220, 521
democratic theory 127
denotation/connotation 242, 243, 244, 246
denotation/connotation 242–3
deprofessionalisation 642–3
deregulation 264, 614
Dervin, Brenda 396, 398
detective story 368
developmental psychology 332
deviant case analysis 134
dialectic 192–3
Dickinson, Roger 326
dictionaries 31
diffusion research 133
digital divide 514
digital revolution 476
digital technologies 513
digital television 95
discourse 231–2, 236, 248, 258, 303, 421
Disney 568
dissident voices 282, 295
diversity of opinion 51
dominant cultural order 246, 248
dominant hegemonic 252, 254, 255
dominant ideology 295, 414
'dominant paradigm' 134, 170
Dostoevsky, Fyodor Mikhailovich *Notes from Underground* 378
dot.com.bubble 476–7, 479, 570
Downing, John 265, 282
drama 210
dress 540
Drucker, Peter 530

dualism 151
Duchamp, Marcel 587
'dumbing down' 62, 73, 196, 237, 279, 495, 628–9
During, S. 529
Durkheim, Emile 105, 111, 172

e-mail, efficiency and 121
eBay 478, 630
Eco, Umberto 240, 242, 369, 504
economic(s) 223, 567, 568
    communication and 223
    information society and 524–8
'ecosystem' 647
EDGE enabled mobile phones 472
educated elites 215
education 314, 453, 454, 481, 513, 563
    equal access to 429
    spread of popular 156
    universal compulsory 181
'effect' 237
effect analysis 106, 130
efficient communication 121, 130
    limiting factors 120
Egyptian Empire
Egyptians ancient 208, 206, 207
Eisenhower, Dwight D. 554
'electronic colonialism' 626
elites 190, 191
Elliott, P. 43, 234
empiricism 134–5, 228, 252
employees 552–3
Empson, William 138, 141
encoding/decoding (Hall) 10, 228, 230, 233, 236–8, 250, 561
England 218
English Civil War 40
English Language 14
enlightenment 125, 127, 131, 478
    as deception 90, 102
    equivalent 126–7, 131
entertainment 268, 293, 303, 347, 468, 478
entropy 498
'epic theatre' 587
Epstein, Edward J. 368
equivalence circuits of communication 113
equivalences 112, 1130
esthetic tastes 158, 160
ethnographic societies 580
ethnographical approaches 561, 601, 622
Euripides 210
European Journal of Communication 398
'evidence' 189
experts,
    co-opting 282, 283
    questioning of by Barthes

Facebook 477, 512, 624, 650–51
'Fairness Doctrine' 274
'false analogy' 111
fansites 463
fascism 87, 91, 173
Federal Communications Commission (FCC) 273, 278, 279
feminism 225, 385, 424
    language and 33
    liberal 390, 392
    negative connotations 385
    science and 396, 397, 398
feminist media theory 13, 159, 384–425
    ideology 406–417
    marginal position of studies 385, 398, 400, 406–7
    representation of women 388, 390
    stereotypes and socialization 400–402, 420
    typologies of and problems with 392–4
    van Zoonen's Feminist Studies 386–418
feminists structuralism and 353
feudal 304, 305, 306, 307, 320
fiction 79, 136
fifth estate 41
film history 553
film industry 98, 99
film trailers 382
films 76, 77, 92, 94, 99, 142, 540, 575
    violence and 336, 337
Fiore, Quentin 199
First Amendment of the American Constitution 40, 219
First World War 84, 103, 173, 220–21, 585
flak 282, 283, 284, 285, 294
Flew, Terry 460, 479, 513
Florida, C. 485, 552, 570
flow 471
focus groups 227, 545, 600
Ford, Henry 79
'Fourth Estate' 41
Frankfurt School 10, 16, 84–102, 153, 174, 296, 309, 624
    Columbia school and 132, 135
    creation 85
    critical theory and 87
    Dialectic of Enlightenment and 88–102
    research undertaken in America 86
Franklin, B. 56, 97, 281
Fraser, N. 303, 311
free market 2, 276
'free market democracy 91
free press 221
free trade 223
free-market capitalism 197
'freedom of speech' 41, 57

French Revolution 40, 314
Friedan, Betty 388, 389
    The Feminine Mystique 400
Fromm, Eric 85, 446
functionalism,
    communications and 105, 130
    and feminism 404
    major interests of 109
futurologists 629

Gallagher, 404
Gans, Herbert 268
Garnham, Nicholas 101, 298, 307, 315, 320
gatekeeper(s) 268, 269, 270, 271, 288, 289, 292, 293, 295
    professionals and 630, 633, 635
Gauntlett, David 10, 286, 469, 569
    'Ten things wrong with the media effects model' 324–50
Geldof, Bob 297
gemeinschaft (community) 173
gender 384, 385, 387, 409, 415, 439
gender identity 412
General Electric (GE) 274, 276
General Line, The (film) 78
genre 354
geography 461
Georgetown Center for Strategic and International Studies 282
Gerbner, George 238, 286, 334, 344, 345
Germany 85
gesellschaft (association) 173
ghost town campuses 478
Gibson, M. 17, 226
Giddens, Anthony 223, 513
Gilder, George 474
Gill, R. 386
Gitlin, Todd 132, 134–5, 553
'global village' 200
globalisation 79, 111, 113, 223, 467, 513, 553, 627
gnoseological 364–8, 370, 374
Godfrey, D. 200
Golding, P. and Murdock, G. 189, 264, 294, 320
Goodwin, William Enquiry Concerning Political Justice 42
Gouldner, Alvin 534
government,
    as news source 270, 280
    relationship with media companies 276
Gramsci, Antonio 412, 414, 415
Grant, George 200, 258
grassroots 468, 484
Greater London Council (GLC) 101
Greece, ancient 210, 211, 212

Greek *polis* 56
Greer, Germaine, *The Female Eunuch* 388, 389, 424
Gresham Law 72–4, 83
Griffin, Christine 334
Grossman, Henryk 85
Grunberg, Carl 86
Guatamala 284
Guest, Edgar 144
Guilbert, G. 488
Gulf War (1991) 490
Gurland, Arkadji 85

Habermas, Jürgen 13, 85, 87, 125, 151, 237, 250, 296
    Structural Transformation of the Public Sphere 196, 298–319
Hagell and Newburn 330
Hall, S. 10, 13, 15, 225
    background 227–8
    'Encoding/Decoding 10, 226, 228–58, 425, 487, 589
Halloran, J.D. 135
Hands, D.J. 625
Harding, Sandra,
    The Science Question in Feminism 394, 396, 397
Hardt, H. 104, 132–3, 1335
Harindranath, Ramaswani 326
Harper's Weekly 150, 174
Harries, D. *The New Media Book* 461
Harris, Eric 322
Harry Potter series 463
Hartley, J. 60, 83, 87, 119, 570, 601
Harvey, David 223
Harvey, L. 222
Havelock, Eric 198
Hebdige, Dick, *Subculture* 226, 227
Hegel, G.W.F. 87
hegemony 171, 248, 414, 415, 416, 417, 420
Held, D. 84–7
Herd, Harold 76
'here and now' 589
Heritage Foundation 282
Herman, Edward 265–6
    media in the US economy 268–94
Herman, Edward and Chomsky, Noam 165, 191
    Manufacturing Consent 266, 294
    'propaganda model' 141
Hermes, 392
Hesmondhalgh, D. 89
    The Culture Industries 553–73
hieroglyphics 206, 207
high culture and low culture 141, 143, 157, 429, 585
historians in context 451

historical context 440, 441
history 444, 445, 447, 451, 458, 508, 577
Hitler, Adolf 100, 140
Hjarvard, S. 298, 309
Hobson, Dorothy, *Crossroads* 226, 263
Hoggart, Richard 13, 59
    The Uses of Literacy 226
Hohendahl, Peter 298, 303, 313
Hollywood 76, 89, 93
homogeneity 83?
Hoover, J. Edgar 286
horizontal integration 274, 275
Horkheimer, Max 13, 82, 84, 85, 86, 87, 153
    background 88
    Dialectic of Enlightenment 88–102
Huesmann, Eron 340
Huxley, Aldous *Brave New World Revisited* 196
hykos, the 206
hyper-reality 496
hyperreal nebula 500, 501
hypodermic needle model 103, 134

iconic sign 240–42
identity 324, 412
    providing of by the media 188, 189
ideological 375
ideological apparatuses (ISAs) 414, 415
ideological loyalties 184, 185, 197
ideological mobilisation 295
ideological state apparatuses (ISAs) 414
ideology 420, 422, 423
    Althusser 412, 414, 415
    definition 412
    feminist media theory and 406–417
    Gramsci and 412, 414
Ignacio, Dino 466, 467
image postmodernism and 488, 489
immigration 459
indoctrination 171
industrialism 196, 221
industrialization 315
inequality 563
information society 222, 264, 462, 512–47, 569
    cultural definition 540–44
    economic definition 524–7
    occupational definition 528–32
    origins of idea 513
    spatial definition 536
    technical definition 518–22
    Webster's *Theories of Information Society* 514–47
Information superhighways 520
'information workers' 530, 532, 534
Innis, Harold Adams 198–224
    The Bias of Communication 199–222
    The Fur Trade in Canada 199, 201

Institute for Religious and Social Studies 136
Institute of Social Research 85–6
institutions 116, 176, 181, 224
    resistance to change by academic 454
integrated services digital network (ISDN) 538
intelligence work 118
interactivity 460, 470
internet, the 12, 62, 294, 297, 301, 324
    concerns over children's use of 323
    English as dominant language 625
    entertainment and 462
    the future and 637
    violence and 322
    World Wide Web and 568
Ionic alphabet 210
Ipress File, The 372
Iraq 286, 287, 293, 296, 636
Ivanna's lost phone 642

Jackie 226, 416, 418, 420–21
Jacobsen, Roman 372, 374
James, Henry, *In the Cage* 370
Jameson, Frederic 489, 490
Japan 520
Japanese Ministry of Posts and Telecommunications (MPT) 520
je vais, je tire, je reviens (film) 362
Jenkins, Henry 10
    Convergence Culture 462–86
    Textual Poachers 463
John Paul II, Pope 288
Journal of Adaptation in Film and Performance 79
Journal of Applied Psychology 133
journalism/journalists 312, 313, 477, 522, 641
'junkie' 643

Kabinni, Rana 406
Kaplan, 392
Katz, E. 85, 87, 100, 132–3, 135, 170, 173, 471
Keane, John 40, 42, 56, 58, 189, 319
Kipling, Rudyard 78
Kircheimer, Otto 85
Klapper, Joseph *The Effects of Mass Communication* 135
Klebold, Dylan 322
knowledge economy 570
Kroeber, Professor A.L. 205
    Configurations of Cultural Growth 204
Kroker, A.I. 200
Kruger, Stephen 326
Kuhn, Thomas *The Structure of Scientific Revolutions* 475

Lacan, Jacques 408, 409, 410, 411, 412, 413
language 33–4, 341, 353, 410, 413, 414, 578
  cinematic 576
  of media 14
  new media 471
  subject and 586
  use of 583
laptops 486
Lash, S. 514, 566
Lasswell, Harold D. 103–131, 136, 421
  background 103–4
  structure and function of communication in society 104–131
Lazarsfeld, Paul F. and Merton, K.
  Mass communication, popular taste and organized social action 136–7, 138, 141, 143, 145, 149, 153, 157, 159, 163
Lazarsfeld, Paul 104, 132–3, 136
Lazarsfeld Stanton Program Analyser 134
Leadbetter, Charles *Living on Thin Air* 530, 546, 568
Leavis, F.R. 59, 174
  background 59–61
  Mass Civilization and Minority Culture 60–83
Leavis, Queenie 60–61, 67, 79
Lechte, J. 85, 88
legitimising 171
Lennox, Sara and Frank 298
Lévi-Strauss, Claude 364, 365
Levmore, S. and Nussbaum, M.C. 626
Lévy, Pierre 470
Lewis, G. and Slade, C. 105
Liaisons dangereuses, Les 376, 377, 378
liberal feminism 392
liberal press theory 39–58, 219
  arguments for press freedom 41–2
  concepts underpinning 41
  criticisms of 41
  idea of truth and 56
  limitations of truth and 56–7
  Mill's 'On liberty of thought and discussion 42–58
  relevance of today 57
liberal theorists 176, 197
liberal theory 320
liberty of thought 48–52
Licensing Act (1694) 218
Licensing Act (1695) 41
'limited effects' paradigm' 133
linguistic theory 242
linguistics 375
Linn, Olga 326
Lippmann, Walter 183, 186–7, 266, 622
literacy 315

literary journalism 310, 311, 312
literature 210, 218, 453
  and education 451, 452
Locke, John 42
Lott, Trent 639–40, 642–4, 646
Lowell, Lawrence 150
Lowenstein, R. *Origins of the Crash* 477
Löwenthal, Leo 85
Lukacs, Georg 87
Lyotard, Jean-François 566
  Lyrical Ballads 323
lyrical writing 581

McCarthy, Joseph 288
McCarthyism 282, 295
McGuigan, J. 101–2, 305
machine, the 70, 72, 73, 82
Machlup, Fritz 526, 527, 528
McKee, A. 463
McKillop, I. 61
McLuhan, Marshall 198–9, 202–3, 221, 498, 499, 500, 501
  The Mechanical Bride 61
  'the medium is the message' 200, 498, 499, 500
McQuail, Denis 130, 173–4, 196, 608, 612–13, 618
  Introduction to Mass Communication Theory 398
McRobbie, Angela 13, 417, 424, 560
Madonna 488, 510
magazines 96, 146, 154, 223, 277, 300, 311, 416
Maker, J. and Lenier, M. 28–9
Malinowski, Bronislaw 148
Mallarmé, Stéphane 582, 585
manipulation 134, 173, 181, 195
manipulators 192–3
Manoff, R. and Schudson, M. 130
Manson, Marilyn 322
Manuel, Preethi 404
manuscripts 216
Marcuse, Herbert 13, 85, 87
Marshall, G. 85, 87, 111, 127, 175
Marx, Karl 230–31, 245
  Capital 230, 234
Marxism 86–7, 134, 155, 408, 453, 458, 560
  ideology 412
  theory 155
masculinity 385, 401
mass amateurism 628, 636, 638, 646–8, 650
mass circulation 313
mass communication 112, 120, 133, 152, 173, 612
mass culture 60, 62, 78, 82, 87, 101, 173–4
mass deception 89, 100

mass entertainment 173
mass markets 173
mass media 62, 112, 126, 139–40, 154, 168, 173, 312, 346
  big business and 154
  commercialized 158
  mass audiences 323
  neo-conservative 269
  propaganda and 292
  social functions of 144, 146
  social norms and 151
mass persuasion 137, 166, 171, 179, 192, 195, 197
mass politics 173
mass production 92, 173
mass professionalization 648
mass society/mass society theory 134, 172–97
  background 172–3
  distinguishing from public 176, 178, 179, 194, 195
  features of 176, 178
  importance of mass persuasion in transition to 178, 179
  influence of 196
  Mills on 174–197
  Pessimism in 173–4
materialist psychoanalysis 413
Match of the Day 7
Matrix, The (film) 463, 489, 510
Mead, Margaret 105
media 282
  amateurisation of 643
  commercialized 154
  history of 462
  'ideological agencies' 134
  messages 273
  power of 140
  producers of 624
  radical 278, 279
  social 625
  traditional 481
  violent content 343, 344
media barons 57
Media, Culture & Society 398
media effects model 175, 322–50, 557
  artificiality within studies 338, 339
  assumption of superiority to the masses 40
  conservative ideology 334–6
  Gauntlett's Ten things wrong with media 'effects' model 326–50
  inadequacy of defining own subject of study 336–8
  lack of understanding of meanings of media 344–6
  misapplied methodology of studies of 340–41

media effects model (*continued*)
   not grounded in theory 346, 347, 348
   protecting of children debate 323
   selective in criticisms of violence
     depiction 342, 343
   tackling social problems backwards
     328–32
   treating children as inadequate 332–4
Media Experience 479
'media imperialism' 223
media industries 463, 552
   lack of work in 553
Media Institute 284
media studies 1, 546, 551, 557, 561, 572–3,
   611
   professional 633
Media Studies, The Essential Resource 326
media theory 552, 572
   in context 624
medium is the message 200, 498, 499, 500,
   502
Medved, Michael *Hollywood vs. America*
   336
Melchett, Lord 70
Melody, W.H. 222–3
Melucci, Alberto 390
Mercer, Johnny 144
Merton, Robert 133, 145, 151
'message' 344
'message form' 232
message handlers 114
methods/methodology 325, 340, 345, 374,
   459, 545, 546
   approaches 624
Meyrowitz, Joshua 200, 223
Microsoft 489
Middletown 61–2, 68–9
Miege, B. 101
military 307
Mill, James *Liberty of the Press* 42
Mill, J.S. 69
   background 43
   'On the liberty of thought and
     discussion' 42–58
   The Subjection of Women 47
Mills, C. Wright 82, 134, 165, 285
   background 174–5
   'the mass society' 174–97
   The Power Elite 174, 196
   The Sociological Imagination 174
Milton, John, *Areopagitica* 40–41
mise-en-scéne 498
modernism 13
   postmodernism 4
modernization theory 265
Mohammadi, Ali 265
Mohammedanism 214, 216
monopolies of religion 208, 224

monopolisation 136, 163, 170, 171, 187
monopolization of mass media 136, 162,
   163, 164, 165, 186, 187
monopoly 306
   over time and continuity 221
monopoly of bureaucracy 212
monopoly capitalism 315, 320
monopoly of knowledge 201, 206–7, 211,
   213–17, 219–21, 223, 224
Montesquiou, Robert de 585
moral philosophy 264
Morley, David 13, 601
   The 'Nationwide' Audience 227
Morley, Henry 422
Morozo, E. *The Net Delusion* 625
motor industry 98, 99
MTV 336, 489
Mulhern, F. 60–65, 67, 82
Mulvey, Laura 386
   'Visual pleasure and narrative cinema'
     13
Murdoch, Rupert 274, 275
Murdock, G. and Golding, P. 73
museums 449
MySpace 275, 479
myth 31, 117, 207, 494, 496
mythological organization and narrative
   364

Naisbitt, John 522
narcotizing dysfunctional 150, 152–3, 160,
   171
narrative 356–83, 580–81
   cinema and 378, 379?
   endings 378, 379
   gnoseological organization 366–70
   ideological organization 374, 376, 388
   linkage of discontinuous units 358
   mythological organization 364, 368,
     372, 374
   Propp's analysis of Russian fairy tales
     358, 359, 360–62
   reliance on cause and effect 358, 359
   transformation and 362, 364–74
narratology 380, 381
Nast, Thomas 150
National Health Service 428
naturalizing process 240, 241
Nazi Germany 84, 88, 139, 163, 164, 173
Nazism 87, 89, 166
NBC 274
negation 364
negotiated code 254–5
Negroponte, N. 520
   Being Digital 474
neo-conservatism 268, 269, 271, 289, 295
Neo-Marxism 408
networks 461

new class 534
new criticism 583
new economy 568
'new journalism' 221
New Labour 102
New Media 460–80, 625, 645, 649
   amteurisation and 650
   radical potential of 625
   transformation of space and time 461
New Orleans Media Experience 466, 476,
   478, 484
new social movements 390
New York Times, The 150, 270, 290, 646
Newbold, C. 134–5, 135, 601
news,
   definition of 646
   sourcing mass material 280–82, 294
   standard template of 639
News Corporation 147, 263, 264, 275
'news cycle' 641
News International 39, 552
news organizations 270
newsletters 218
newspapers 72, 142, 272, 310, 575
   advertising and 277
   bourgeois public sphere and 304, 305,
     306, 307, 309, 313
   displacement of journalism of
     conviction by journalism of
     commerce 312, 313
   imposition of taxes 218, 219
   Northcliffe 72, 73
   political 310
   public opinion and 310
   Worthy and unworthy victims 290, 291
Newsweek 290, 570
Nicaragua 284
Nicaraguan Contras 280
Nietzsche, F. 210, 211
Noerr, G.S. 89
'normative' approaches 615, 619
normative theory 10–11
'norms' 247, 339
   in professions 633
Northcliffe, Lord 72–3
Northern Rock Bank 39
novels 452
nuclear power 276

Obama, Barack 625
occupational change and information
   society 528–35
Oedipus complex 410, 412
Ofcom 264, 273, 275, 279, 323
Ofek, E. 477
Office of Radio Research 133
O'Keefe, William 640–41
On Liberty (Mill) 42–58

opinion-makers 187, 192, 195
oppositional code 257
oral tradition 202, 210–211, 213–15, 218
organizations 318
'other' 333
ownership mass media and 140, 152–3, 155, 160, 168, 272, 294, 572

Packard, Vance *The Hidden Persuaders* 193
'Page Three Girls' campaign' 388, 390
Paine, Tom *Rights of Man* 42
pamphlets 216, 217, 218
Panama 286
paper cost of 636
paper manufacturing 214, 215, 216
papyrus 210, 211, 212, 213
paradigm shift 474, 475
parchment 212–13, 215–16
Park, Robert E. 13
participatory culture 470–71
patriarchy 410, 411, 420, 422
'pattern of culture' 444, 446
patterns of the work 456
Pécuchet 590
Peirce, Charles S. 240, 241
'people meter' 608, 609
performative rules 248
Perkin, Harold 535
    The Rise of Professional Society 534
Persians 209, 210, 298
person as subject and object debate 506, 507
'personal influence' paradigm 133
persuasion 173, 195
Peters, J.D. 88, 89, 100, 174–5, 196, 305
philosophical discourse 374
phone movies 472
phoney public sphere 319
photography 589
Piaget, Jean 332
pictographs 214–15
Pirate Party 47
pluralism 101, 187, 246–7, 474
'poach' texts 481
'poaching' 485
poetics 380, 381
poetry 374, 375, 453
political economic analysis 409
political economy 263–95
    distinction between critical and classical 264–5
    Herman's Media in the U.S. political economy and 265–94
    key features of approach 264
    liberal press theory and 41
'political newspaper' 313
political organisation 224
Pollock, Frederich 85, 88

polysemy 246, 247
Poole, R. 315
Popieluszko, Father 290
popular culture 60, 174
popular taste impact of mass media on 156–64
Porat, Marc 524, 526, 527, 528, 532
pornography 387, 390, 400, 420
positivism 582
post-structuralism 13, 225, 577
Poster, Mark 544
Postman, Neil 323
postmodernism 13, 393, 488–510
    Baudrillard's 'The implosion of meaning in the media' 492–510
    definitions 488–9
    image and 488, 489
    Madonna and 488
    modernism and 490
    The Matrix and 489
poststructuralism 13, 57
power 17, 91, 92, 93–5, 97, 117, 122, 124, 126, 151, 178
    amount of 553
    of an individual 443
    and connotations 246, 247
    critical political economy 264
    cultural theory and 428
    debates about 573
    economic 567
    elites and 190
    of mass media 138, 189
    people in 593
    relationship with media 190, 191
    relationships 459
power elites 174, 191, 197
power structures 227
practice and theory 47
'preferred readings' 246, 247
prereading 28
press barons 73
press freedom 39–40
press, the 148, 219, 279, 311, 313, 414
    intellectual 312
    popular 315
priestly class 206
Priestly, Joseph 42
priestly organization 224
primary publics 179, 180, 182, 194–5, 197
Princess Diana 501
printing 216, 217, 218
privacy intrusion of 190, 191
private and public 148, 149, 151, 556, 557
privatisation 264, 265, 308, 614
process 436, 437
    theory as 8, 13, 15, 228, 393
Production 234, 551–73, 625
production/circulation 230, 234

professional bias 646–7
professional class 646, 647–8
professional code 252, 254
professionalism 634, 644
professions 630–32, 633–5
propaganda
    First World War 103, 173
    Herman and Chomsky model 266, 270, 271, 282, 289
    mass media for 163, 166, 293
    power of 138
    the press and 314
    for social objectives 162–6, 168
'propaganda phobia' 192
Propp, Vladimir 358, 374
    Morphology of the Folktale 359
Proust, Marcel 584
    A la Recherche du Temps perdu 370, 585
pseudo-world 189, 197
psychic management 181, 182
psychoanalysis 408, 412, 416
psychological exploitation 138
psychological illiteracy 182–3, 187, 189, 191, 197
'psychological monopoly' 166, 168
psychologists 334, 335, 348
psychology of childhood 332
'public' 127
public consciousness 644–5
public exposure 148
public opinion 297, 303, 304, 311, 312, 313, 320
    formation of 301
    informal control and 302
    leaders of 310
    'mere opinion' and 305
public and private 151
'public relations' 138, 192, 195, 280, 281
public service broadcasting 602, 604, 605, 611, 614, 616–17
public sphere 125, 296–318, 552, 574, 601
    bourgeois 304, 305, 306, 307, 308, 309, 313, 319, 320
    concept of 300–304
    Habermas and 298–320
    history 304, 306
    liberal model 308, 309, 312
    new media and 462, 471, 486, 625
    political and *literary* 302, 303
    querying existence of 312, 313
    refeudalisation of 317
    in the social welfare state mass democracy 314–18
    ways of invoking 296–7
public voice 279
publicity 148, 149, 309, 316, 317, 318, 320
public(s) 124, 125, 176
publishing 636–8, 646

publishing companies 416
    publishing of theory 11–12
Pulitzer Prize 634–5

qualitative approach 601
quantitative 518, 523, 528, 532, 534, 535,
    542, 600
*Questioning the Media; A critical
    introduction* 265
Quete du Graal, La 366, 368, 370
Quiller-Couch, Arthur *The Art of Writing*
    76

radical feminism 392
radio 93, 94, 142, 152, 220, 221
    centralisation and 220
    female listeners 173
    Lazarsfeld research into psychological
        effects 133
    notion of active and passive listeners 94,
        95
    Second World War 162
Radway, Janice 422
RAI 604
Rakow 400
Ransom, John Crowe 583
ratings 600–601, 602, 606, 608, 609, 614
'rational public opinion' 127, 131
Rayner, Philip 326
Richards, I.A. 66–7
reading 22–35
    academic language and 32–4
    active critical process and 27–9
    critically 24
    problems with and solutions to 29–32
    purpose of at university 24–5
    purpose of 23
    as reflective process 27
    the self and 26–9
    strategies of 25, 26–7, 30
Reagan, President 280, 286, 298
realism 240, 241
Red Hunters 284
'Red scares' 286, 288, 295
refeudalization 316, 317
regulation loosening of 273
Reich, Robert 530
Reith, John 616
'relay function' 122, 123
relay points 107, 108, 113
religions 206–7
religious monopolies of knowledge 209,
    217
religious organization 208, 212
representation 386
revolution 312
Richards, I.A. 66, 67, 69, 78
Richardson, M. 477

Richmond Daily News 628
ritual view of communication 170
roadblocks 484
Robbe-Grillet, Alan 363, 383
Robinson, G.J. 135, 200
Rockefeller Communications Group 104
Rockefeller Foundation 104, 136
Rojek, C. 225
Rok Sako To Rok Lo (Bollywood film) 472
Roman Empire 212, 213, 214
Romeo and Juliet (Shakespeare) 574, 576
Rothermere, Lord 73
Roussel, Raymond 358
Russell, Gilbert 76
Russell, Thomas 78
Russia 78, 152, 155
Russian fairy tales 358, 359, 360–62
Russian Revolution 84

Scannell, P. 61, 82, 199, 202, 209
scarcity 644
scatter studies 152
Schramm, Wilbur, *Mass Communications*
    104, 136
Schumpeter, P.A. 521
science feminism and 397, 398, 399
'scoop' 120, 281
Scrutiny (journal) 61
Seaton, J. 62, 82
Sebesta, Ed 642–3
Second World War 84, 135, 163, 170, 173,
    428, 429
selective tradition 453, 454
self-censorship 270, 271, 295
self-publishing 648
Selling of the Pentagon, The (documentary)
    284
semiology 418
semiotics 243, 247, 248
'sense of the life' 451
sentiment groups and publics 124–5, 131
sentinels 108
service sector employment 528, 530
Sesame Street 466, 468
Sex and the City 7, 424
Shakespeare, William 68, 218, 425, 426,
    569
    Romeo and Juliet 574
Shannon's hypothesis 492
Shirky, Clay 486, 626–50
    *Cognitive Surplus: Creativity in a
        connected age* 627
    Here Comes Everyone 626
Short, Clare 388, 389, 390, 391
Sigal, Leon 268, 270
sign death of 542, 544
Sills, D.L. 133–4
Simmons, E. 625

Simons, J. 462
Simonson, P. and Weimann, G. 104, 132,
    135–7, 170
Smith, Chris 102
Smith, Kate 162
Snowball sampling 134
soap operas 156, 159, 303, 337, 352, 353,
    422, 595
social change 513
    technical change and 522, 523
social conflict and communication 118,
    119
social conformism and mass media 154,
    155, 156
social feminism/feminists 390, 392,
    408, 412
social norms enforcement of by mass
    media 148–50, 170
social welfare state 316, 318
socialization 400, 404, 406, 420, 494, 498,
    499
society and culture 436, 437, 440, 441
sociology 61
Sophocles 210, 440
sourcing mass media news 280, 282, 392
Southern Partisan 642
Soviet Union 163, 173, 285, 294
space-biased media 202
space-biased or space-binding 213
Sparks, C. 320
'specialised agencies' 119
specialization 108, 112, 222
Spengler, Oswald 68–9, 80
Spinello, R.A. and Tavani, H.I. 479
Sreberny-Mohammadi, Annabelle 265
Stacey and Thorne 400
Stalinisation 84
stamp tax (1712) 218
Stamps, J. 61, 85, 198, 200, 202–3
standardisation 72, 79, 92
Stanton, Frank 133
status conferral 147, 171
status conferral function 146, 147, 166,
    168
Steeves, Leslie 390
stereotypes 182, 185, 187, 197, 220
Stevenson, N. 87, 198, 200, 320
Storey, J. 13
structural relationships 295
structural shift 182, 185
structuralism 13, 33, 352–83, 483
    criticism of 354
    definition 353
    history 100?
    problems of 382
    Todorov's *Genres in Discourse* 354–83
    translation 577–8
structure of feeling 448, 449, 451

subcultures 226
subjecthood 506, 508
subjectivation 371, 372
supplementation 136, 164, 170, 171
surrealism 584, 585
surveillance 105, 107, 128
survival 484
'Swan-Geese, The' 360, 362, 366, 372, 375
symbol creators 560, 561, 562, 563, 5631281
symbolic creativity 560, 561, 562, 564
symbolisation 542, 543

'taxes on knowledge' 41, 57, 219, 224
'technological determinism' 95, 198, 199, 201, 205, 539
technological developments 95
technology 513
    cultural industry and 92, 94
    and information society 518, 524
telegraph 219–20, 224
television 173, 540, 585
    and advertising 278, 606
    annihilation of women 402
    commercial 155, 604, 608, 612, 614, 618
    influence on children 323
    viewed as playing a useful role 12
    violence and 238, 330, 334
'television audience' 173
testimonials 146
text/s 59–60, 574–98
    Barthes, 'The Death of the Author' 577–98
    creation of 130
    definition by Barthes 590
    distinction between 'real' world and 513, 580
    making sense of by audiences 227, 228
    relationship between reader and 575, 594
textual analysis 60
textualizing 608
Thatcher, Margaret 298
theatre 587
theory 228, 235, 347, 348
    complexity of 525
    and context 12–13, 16
    of culture 444
    defining 7–9
    as a process 8, 13, 15, 228
    publishing of 12
    purpose of 9–11
    questioning of everything 14–15
    reasons for teaching 18–20
    requirement of hypothetical thinking 16, 18

responding to other theory 15
schools and fields of 13–14
taking active approach to 20
transferable skills 20
types of 9
usefulness of 349
why viewed as difficult 14–18
'Third World' 265, 276
'Third World feminism' 385
Thomas, D. 479
Thompson, D.C. 416
Thompson, J.B. 320
Thompson, Robert 322
Time 290
time and continuity problems of 209
'time space divide' 201–2, 211, 215, 221
Time Warner 552
Times, The 146
Tindate, Mathew 41
Tocqueville, Alexis de *Democracy in America* 172
Todorov, Tsvetan,
    background 354
    Genres in Discourse 354–83
Toffler, Alvin 513, 518, 519
Tönnies, Ferdinand 173
Top Gun 336
Toronto School 198–224, 471
    background 198–200
    Innis and *The Bias of Communication* 202–222
totalitarianism 173
Toynbee, Arnold 204, 205, 560
'traditional' media 481
tragedy 210, 594, 595
transition theories 566
translation 577–8
'transmission belt' theory 134
transmission model of communication 105, 106, 107, 108, 109, 128, 422
transport and communication 219
Trobriand Islanders 148
truth 48, 56, 125, 457
Tuchman, Gaye 268, 400, 401, 402, 405, 422
Turner, G. 59–60, 174, 228
TV murders 337
Tweed Ring 150
Twitter 624–5
two-step model 133

'uncanny' 354
United States 173–4, 218, 265
    history of press freedom 40
    relationship with Britain 73
universal suffrage 178–9, 197
urbanisation 173

Ursell, G. 553
USA today 628, 630
'uses and gratifications' 133
utilitarianism 42

Vaccari, Cristian 625
Valéry 582
values 117
van Dijk, J.A.G.M. 461, 462
Van Evra, J. 340
van Zoonen, Liesbet feminist media studies 386–425
VARA 616–17, 622
Veblen, T. 483
Venables, Jon 322
vernacular 216, 224
Vernant, Jean Pierre 594
Verstraeten, H. 313
video games 461, 489
'video nasties' 322
Vietnam War 292, 293
violence, 286, 297, 328
    anti-labor claims about 286
    cartoons and 337
    competitions which assume the form of 316
    comics and 323
    media content and social 339
    media depictions of 342
    messages about 238
    recorded act of 338
    screen 336
Virgin Media 263
voting 509

Wall, Peter 326
Walwyn, William *The Compassionate Samaritane* 40
'war on terror' 291, 294
Warner Brothers 98, 99
Warren, Robert Penn 583
Washington Post, The 270, 640
Web 2.0 sites 625
Weber, Max 173
weblog 625, 630, 644, 648
Webster, Frank *Theories of the Information Society* 514–47
Weil, Felix 86
Wells, H.G., *The Autocracy of Mr. Parham* 68
Wertham, Frederic, *Seduction of the Innocent* 323
Westinghouse 274, 276
Whitehouse, Amy 39
WHSmith 384
Wiggershaus, R. 84–6, 88
Wikipedia 461, 512
Williams 610, 611

Williams, K. 103–5, 130, 133–5, 172–4, 265, 331
Williams, Raymond 59–62, 67, 73, 82–3, 471, 562–3, 611
 background 428–9
 Culture is Ordinary 73
 Culture and Society 59, 429
 flow 471
 Long Revolution, The 59, 429–58, 458
Williamson, A. 625
Willis, Paul *Learning to Labour* 226, 227
Wilson, James Q. *Bureaucracy* 632
Winn, Marie 323
Winship, Janice 398, 399

wireless communication 451
Wollstoncraft, Mary 47
 Vindication of the Rights of Women 42
women 226, 346
 annihilation of in television 402
 debates about representations of 384
 freedom from Salic law 218
 male language and 633
 portrayal of black women in mass media 404, 406
 underrepresentation of in higher education and as scientists 396
 underrepresentation of in the media 404, *see also* feminist media theory

women's movement 400
Women's Studies Group 406
Work Foundation *Staying Ahead* report 551–3, 567
working class 416, 453
working-class media 278, 279
'world public' 125
'Worship at the Altar of Convergence' 466, 476
'worthy' and 'unworthy' victims 295
writing 210–214, 223, 580

York, Thom 296, 297, 301
YouTube 477, 512, 624, 650